ADO.NET Programmer's Reference

Jeffrey Hasan

John McTainsh

Adil Rehan

Fabio Claudio Ferracchiati

Naveen Kohli

Dushan Bilbaji

Paul Dickinson

Jon Reid

Matthew Milner

Jan Narkiewicz

Wrox Press Ltd. ®

ADO.NET Programmer's Reference

Published by Wrox Press Ltd,
Arden House, 1102 Warwick Road, Acocks Green,
Birmingham, B27 6BH, UK
Printed in the United States
ISBN 1-861005-58-X

Trademark Acknowledgements

Credits

Authors
Dushan Bilbaji
Paul Dickinson
Fabio Claudio Ferracchiati
Jeffrey Hasan
Naveen Kohli
John McTainsh
Matthew Milner
Jan Narkiewicz
Adil Rehan
Jon Reid

Technical Reviewers
Kapil Apshankar
Martin Beaulieu
Paul Churchill
Chris Crane
Dan Green
Mark Horner
Jody Kerr
Wendy Lanning
Don Lee
John McTanish
Arun Nair

Technical Editors
David Barnes
Victoria Blackburn
Garard Maquire

Category Manager
Kirsty Reade
Steve Farncombe

Technical Architect
Alastair Ewins

Author Agents
Avril Corbin
Chandima Nethisinghe

Project Administrator
Chandima Nethisinghe
Claire Robinson

Production Manager
Simon Hardware

Production Project Coordinator
Abbie Forletta

Additional Layout
Emma Eato

Index
Adrian Axinte

Proof Reading
Miriam Robinson

Figures
Abbie Forletta
Natalie O'Donnell

Cover
Dawn Chellingworth

About the Authors

Dushan Bilbija

Dushan Bilbija works as a consultant with clients in areas from academia, to software development, to wireless communications. He has been a part of the development community for 11 years, specializing in Visual Basic, Enterprise Applications, Application Integration, Database Development and System Architecture. He can be reached at dbilbija@pantheoncorp.com.

Dedication

I would like to thank my wife Robin (and baby on the way!) for tolerating the bizarre work hours it took to finish my contributions to this book. Thanks also go to the editors and reviewers at Wrox for their hard work and undaunted perseverance in putting this book together, and for giving me an opportunity to contribute to it.

Paul Dickinson

Paul was born very early on in life and has continued to age at a reasonable pace. He first discovered his computing prowess with the advent of the Atari ST and Kick Off 2. People came from far and wide only to be humiliated with his crushing one-twos and deadly banana shots. In order to better himself he went off to UMIST to study Computation. He graduated and spent several years cutting his software development teeth writing software to control mass spectrometers. His most recent resting place involves developing information management systems for laboratories. On the frequent occasions that Paul isn't in front of a computer he can be found hurtling round country roads in hired sports cars or searching for the perfect donner kebab.

Paul can be reached at www.pauldickinson.com.

Dedication

I would like to thank my beautiful wife Sue for giving me the will to sit in darkened rooms working all hours ;-)

Fabio Claudio Ferracchiati

Fabio Claudio Ferracchiati is a software developer and technical writer. In the early years of his ten-year career he worked with classical languages and old Microsoft tools like Visual Basic and Visual C++. After five years he decided to dedicate his attention to the Internet and all the related technologies. In 1998 he started a parallel career writing technical articles for Italian and international magazines. He works in Rome for CPI Progetti Spa (http://www.cpiprogetti.it) where he develops Internet/Intranet solutions using Microsoft technologies.

Dedication

I would like to thank Wrox people and in particular Alastair and Avril for their kindness. Every chapter I wrote in this book is dedicated to the person that fills every piece of his heart: Danila.

Jeffrey Hassan

Jeffrey Hasan is a technical architect specializing in Microsoft technology at LiveMarket, Inc., an e-business solutions provider in Orange County, California. He has extensive experience developing N-Tier applications with Visual Studio, SQL Server, Internet Information Server, Commerce Server and BizTalk Server. He has written numerous articles on application development, and is a contributing author to several Wrox books. He holds an M.S. degree from Duke University and is a Microsoft Certified Professional Developer. Jeff is a chronic traveler and an avid music fan, although he has yet to figure out how to combine the two. His passport has most recently been stamped in Costa Rica, Mexico, Pakistan, Sweden, the UK and a smattering of places in between. Email Jeff at: JHasan85@hotmail.com.

Naveen Kohli

Naveen Kohli is an independent software developer residing in scenic New Hampshire with his wife and son. He has been developing applications in very diverse areas ranging from Chemical Reactor Optimization to N-tier web applications. He started his professional career using FORTRAN and then moved on to BASIC and then to C/C++, Visual Basic and Java. He has been actively involved in the .NET movement right from its inception. He has a vast experience in writing middle tier components for extracting data from data sources like SQL Server, Oracle, Exchange Server and Access database.

Dedication

This book is dedicated to my parents for their ever-supportive love and guidance.

John McTainsh

John started coding in 1982, at high school, on the Apple II and ZX81. In the early days he worked mostly with the Motorola chipset in Assembler, making simple but fast games and programming microcontrollers. He completed his engineering degree in 1988 and moved to Asia to work in the offshore oil and gas exploration industry. Starting as a commercial diver he soon got back into coding, developing control systems for underwater robots in C and C++. Since then he has written many control systems and various other application and drivers, mostly for PC hardware. He currently lives in Australia and works as a team leader developing public safety software for computer aided dispatch systems used by Police, Fire and Ambulance vehicles.

Dedication

I would like to thank my parents for a great upbringing and wife and daughter for putting up with my tap tap coding late into the night. Thanks Claudia, Rebecca, Dorothy and Albert.

Matt Milner

Matt Milner works as a Technical Architect for BORN in Minneapolis where he designs and builds Microsoft solutions for clients in a variety of industries. Matt's primary focus has been using Windows DNA architecture and he is excited about the move to .Net and all the powerful new features. When Matt is not working at the computer, he spends his time in his woodshop, reading, or enjoying the many great natural resources of Minnesota.

Jan Narkiewicz

Jan D. Narkiewicz is Chief Technical Officer at Software Pronto, Inc (jann@softwarepronto.com).

Jan began his career as a Microsoft developer thanks to basketball star, Michael Jordan. In the early 90s Jan noticed that no matter what happened during a game, Michael Jordan's team won. Similarly, no matter what happened in technology Microsoft always won (then again this strategy is ten years old and may need some revamping). Clearly there was a bandwagon to be jumped upon.

Over the years Jan managed to work on an email system that resided on 17 million desktops, helped automate factories that make blue jeans you have in your closet (trust me, you own this brand) and developed defence systems. All this was achieved using technology such as COM/DCOM, COM+, C++, VB, C#, ADO, SQL Server, Oracle, DB2, ASP.Net, ADO.Net, Java, Linux and XML. In his spare time Jan is Academic Coordinator for the Windows curriculum at U.C. Berkeley Extension, he teaches at U.C. Santa Cruz Extension, writes for ASP Today and occasionally plays some football (a.k.a. soccer).

Adil Rehan

Adil Rehan works as an independent consultant for a Fortune 500 company. He has been involved in several books in different roles. He has been actively involved in design and implementation of enterprise Internet enabled solutions for different clients. He holds a Bachelor of Engineering degree in Electrical Engineering from NED University. When he is not working on computers, he likes watching movies, and traveling to far and distant places to explore the wonders of nature. He can be reached at adilrehan@yahoo.com

Thanks to my parents for bringing up right and giving me the inspiration to move forward, and to my wife and son for supporting me, when I needed it the most.

Jon Reid

Jon is the Chief Technology Officer for Micro Data Base Systems, Inc. (www.mdbs.com), maker of the TITANIUM™ Database Engine and GURU® Expert System tool. His primary current activity is developing database tools for the Microsoft.NET environment. He was editor for the C++ and Object Query Language (OQL) components of the Object Data Management Group (ODMG) standard, and has co-authored other Wrox titles including *Beginning C#* and *Professional SQL Server 2000 XML*. When not working, writing, or bicycling, he enjoys spending time with his wife and two young sons.

Dedication

I would like to thank my family and the team at Wrox (especially Alastair, Chandy, and Gerard) for their support and encouragement.

2002VBAProgrammersReferenceExce
VBAProgrammersReference
ProgrammersReferenceExcel

Table of Contents

Table of Contents

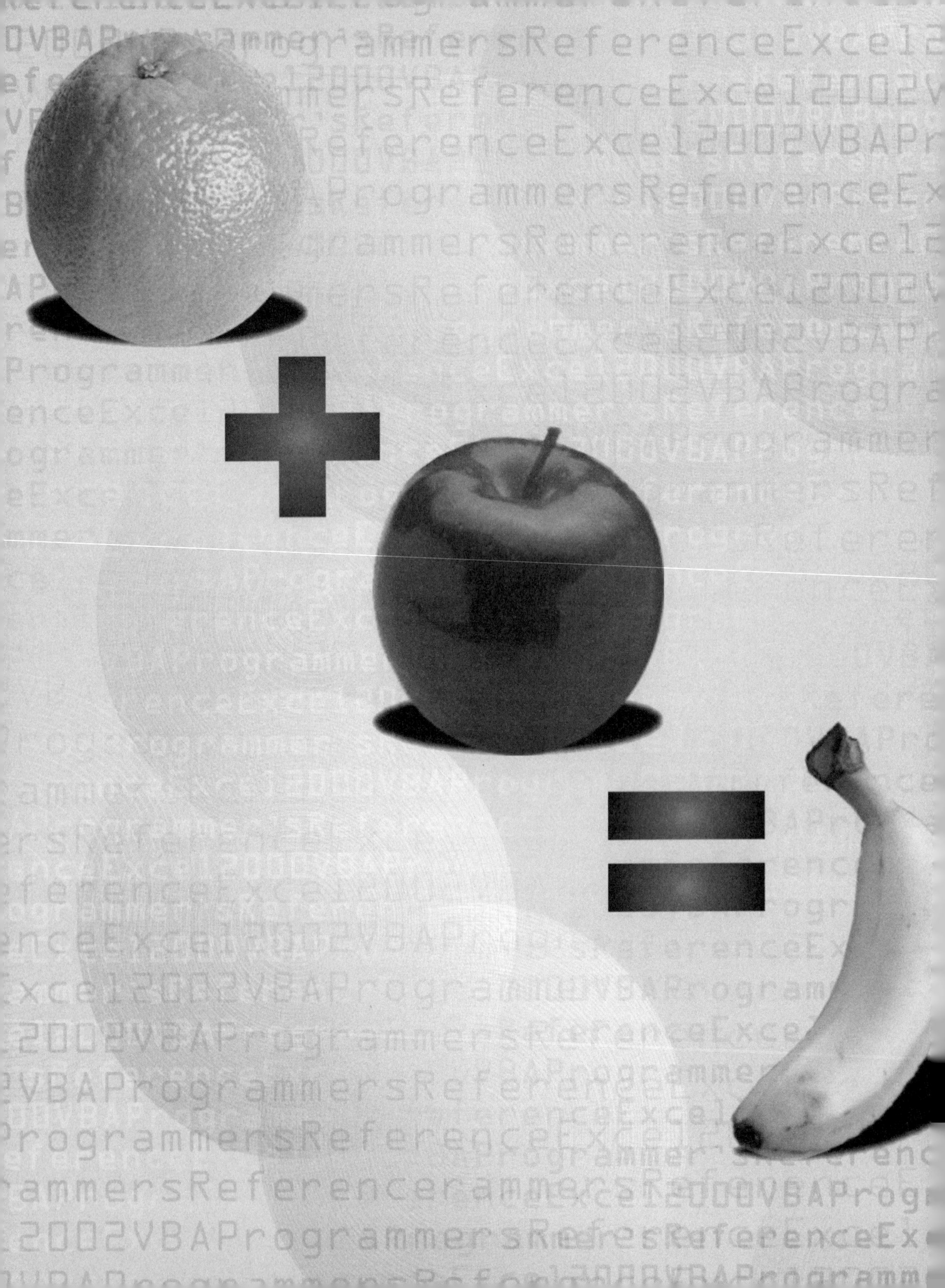

Introduction

There has been an enormous amount of interest in the .NET framework over the last year, even though the final release has not yet been launched. There is a simple explanation of why there has been such phenomenal interest: the .NET framework will provide an entirely new platform on which we, as developers, will build the next generation of application, and will open up the world of Web Services.

ASP.NET is far more than an upgrade of an existing technology. It represents an entirely new way in which large and complex Internet applications may be developed. Likewise, ADO.NET is far more than simply an upgrade of ADO. ADO.NET is a large set of .NET classes which enable us to interact with data sources, manipulate data, and communicate with other applications and Web Services in entirely new ways.

ADO.NET is a core part of the .NET Framework. As such, like the rest of the framework, it is built on the Common Language Runtime. This rich and flexible architecture will provide the base for the development of entirely new types of applications.

What Is ADO.NET?

ADO.NET is Microsoft's latest data access technology. It is a central part of the .NET framework and far more than an update to recent versions of ADO. Many of the concepts and components found in ADO.NET are completely new.

More than ADO, ADO.NET separates access to databases from manipulating data. We can create data structures in memory, disconnected from any data source, that include multiple tables, relationships, and constraints. We can write data changes back to the database when it is convenient – we do not need to maintain a persistent connection.

.NET OLE DB and ODBC drivers provide access to all the data sources accessible in ADO. There is also a .NET provider for SQL Server 2000, which provides better performance and additional SQL-Server specific features. It is likely that many database vendors will soon release high performance .NET providers for their databases.

Support for XML is an important aspect of the .NET framework. ADO.NET can persist entire data structures to standard XML for transmission over the Internet and to communicate with any XML supporting application.

The rise of the Internet has driven the development of .NET. Even internal applications are often now designed using similar tools and techniques to those employed on dynamic web sites. ADO.NET provides methods for scalable remote data access using a web browser to display server generated HTML, or through custom applications that process data without being connected to the data source

What does this book cover?

This book provides a reference to the features of ADO.NET. We describe the features and how to use them, as well as providing advice and explanation that will enable you to use ADO.NET to maximum effect. The code examples are concise and demonstrate how to use a specific techniques rather than how to build entire applications.

We have covered three .NET data providers – the SQL Server 2000 provider, the OLE DB provider, and the ODBC provider. All three are very similar, and using other .NET data providers is unlikely to be significantly different.

We have split the book into the following sections:

❑ Introduction to ADO.NET – what it is, how it's different to classic ADO, and an overview of its object models and namespaces

❑ Connecting to data stores with the `Connection` object

❑ The `Command` object and techniques for executing queries against a data store

❑ Using the `DataSet` object to manipulate complete in-memory data caches while disconnected from the data source

❑ The `DataReader` object – a lightweight object designed for fast, simple access to data sources

❑ Using the `DataAdapter` object to provide a link between the data-source independent DataSet and the data source

❑ The `DataTable`, `DataRelation`, `DataView`, and `Mapping` objects, and how to use them within `DataSets`

❑ Working with transactions in ADO.NET

❑ Using the `XmlDataDocument` object to provide further ADO.NET XML support

❑ Exceptions and error handling

❑ Working with database permissions in ADO.NET

❑ Using Interop to incorporate classic ADO components in .NET applications

We also provide appendixes containing:

❑ Examples of common ADO.NET techniques

❑ Additional references for the more obscure ADO.NET classes

Who Is This Book For?

This book is aimed at experienced developers, who have some experience of ASP or general development with Microsoft technologies, or experience of programming within the ,NET framework. It is not aimed at beginners and does not cover general programming techniques or the basics of programming languages.

Primarily, it is intended as a reference for .NET developers who have to integrate ADO.NET into their applications.

What you Need to Use this Book

To run the samples in this book you need to have the following:

- ❑ Windows 2000 or Windows XP.

- ❑ The .NET Framework SDK. The code in this book will not work with .NET Beta 1.

The complete source code for the samples is available for download from our web site at
http://www.wrox.com/Books/Book_Details.asp?isbn=186100588X.

Conventions

We've used a number of different styles of text and layout in this book to help differentiate between the different kinds of information. Here are examples of the styles we used and an explanation of what they mean.

Code has several fonts. If it's a word that we're talking about in the text – for example, when discussing a For...Next loop, it's in this font. If it's a block of code that can be typed as a program and run, then it's also in a gray box:

```
<?xml version 1.0?>
```

Sometimes we'll see code in a mixture of styles, like this:

```
<?xml version 1.0?>
<Invoice>
    <part>
        <name>Widget</name>
        <price>$10.00</price>
    </part>
</invoice>
```

In cases like this, the code with a white background is code we are already familiar with; the line highlighted in gray is a new addition to the code since we last looked at it.

Advice, hints, and background information comes in this type of font.

> **Important pieces of information come in boxes like this.**

Bullets appear indented, with each new bullet marked as follows:

- ❑ **Important Words** are in a bold type font.

- ❑ Words that appear on the screen, or in menus like the File or Window, are in a similar font to the one you would see on a Windows desktop.

- ❑ Keys that you press on the keyboard like *Ctrl* and *Enter*, are in italics.

Customer Support

We've tried to make this book as accurate and enjoyable as possible, but what really matters is what the book actually does for you. Please let us know your views, either by returning the reply card in the back of the book, or by contacting us via email at feedback@wrox.com.

Source Code and Updates

As we work through the examples in this book, you may decide that you prefer to type in all the code by hand. Many readers prefer this because it's a good way to get familiar with the coding techniques that are being used.

Whether you want to type the code in or not, we have made all the source code for this book available at our web site at the following address:

http://www.wrox.com/

If you like to type in the code, you can use our files to check the results you should be getting - they should be your first stop if you think you might have typed in an error. If you don't like typing, then downloading the source code from our web site is a must!

Either way, it'll help you with updates and debugging.

Errata

We've made every effort to make sure that there are no errors in the text or the code. However, to err is human, and as such, we recognize the need to keep you informed of any mistakes as they're spotted and corrected. Errata sheets are available for all our books at http://www.wrox.com. If you find an error that hasn't already been reported, please let us know. For more information on this, see Appendix D at the end of the book.

Our web site acts as a focus for other information and support, including the code from all Wrox books, sample chapters, previews of forthcoming titles, and articles and opinions on related topics.

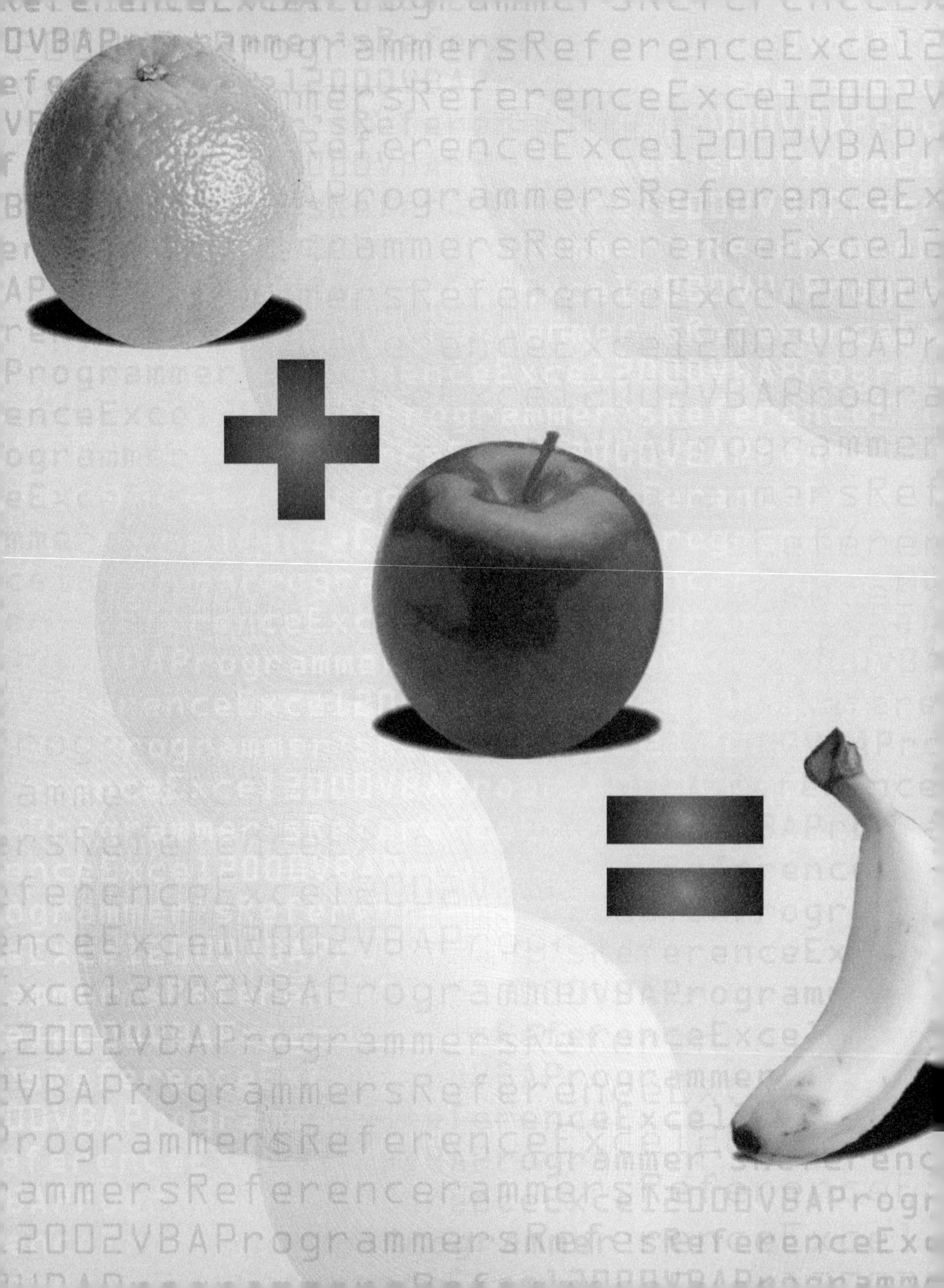

1

What Is ADO.NET?

ADO.NET. is a set of data access classes which form an integral part of the .NET Framework. As part of the .NET framework, they share the features of the .NET classes in general, such as type-safe standard data types, specialized network classes, and XML integration. ADO.NET is designed to provide highly efficient data access, especially for disconnected, n-Tier application architectures. XML plays a pivotal role in this new data access technology, as XML is *the* data representation language for the .NET framework. ADO.NET classes are tightly integrated with the XML framework classes, which provide seamless access to a host of XML-related services, including easy transfer of data between data sources and XML documents.

Before looking at ADO.NET in detail, we will take a general look at the .NET Framework.

The .NET Framework

The.NET Framework provides system-level services, classes, and data types, which significantly change the way we go about developing distributed applications. It encapsulates all system-level functionality into a framework of classes. Many of the low-level plumbing details that are required for components to work together, such as memory management, are handled automatically, and it introduces a high level of thread safety so that errant components cannot easily crash an application. In short, it allows us to concentrate on developing functionality, instead of worrying about management details.

Microsoft has positioned .NET as *the* platform for building Web Services, although Web Services are just one aspect of the .NET strategy. Web Services are components that communicate over HTTP using the **Simple Object Access Protocol** (**SOAP**), which is a protocol for sending packets of XML. They are designed to provide specific types of functionality in components that are accessible over the Internet to any XML-aware client.

An important part of the .NET framework, for the development of Internet applications and Web Services, is ASP.NET. This is tightly integrated with XML and standard Web protocols, including SOAP, thereby making it easy to build Web services.

> **For more information on ASP.NET, see** *Professional ASP.NET* **by Wrox Press. ISBN 1-861004-88-5.**

As we've seen, ADO.NET provides a set of specialized classes and types that are designed for data access. These classes are extended from the .NET Base Class Library, meaning that they are built directly on top of System-level classes.

The various components of the .NET Framework are shown in the figure below. We've highlighted those parts which are most important to the data access functionality in the .NET Framework, and which we will be looking at in this book:

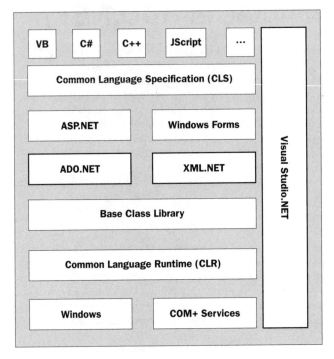

Let's take a look at some of these aspects of the .NET Framework in some more detail:

- ❑ **Common Language Runtime**: This is a rich runtime environment that handles important runtime tasks for the developer, including memory management and garbage collection. The Common Language Runtime is built around the Common Type System, which defines a common type system for all .NET compliant languages. Code that runs under control of the CLR is called **managed code**.

- ❑ **Base Class Library**: This is a rich set of functional base classes that encapsulate system functionality.

- **Extended Class Libraries**: These contain abstracted classes that focus on particular aspects of development: ASP.NET (for Web Services and Internet applications), ADO.NET (for data access), XML (to parse and manipulate XML documents), and Windows Forms (for developing Windows user interfaces).

- **Common Language Specification**: This defines the rules and requirements for .NET compliant languages.

- **Multiple Programming Languages**: VB.NET, C++, and C#, are just some of the languages that may be used for development within the .NET Framework. In the near future, the number of .NET compliant languages will increase enormously, as, in principle, any language can be integrated to work with the .NET framework. The .NET Framework provides one platform for many languages.

- **Visual Studio.NET**: Although not strictly part of the .NET Framework, this is integrated development environment for developing applications within the .NET Framework.

In brief, the most important aspects of the .NET Framework may be summed up in the following way:

- It is built on a common set of Framework classes

- It provides a Common Type System, which serves to provide support for all languages, via the CLS

- It provides a Common Language Runtime, which provides runtime services for individual components and entire applications

- It provides abstracted class sets for ASP.NET, ADO.NET, XML.NET, and Windows Forms

> **A definitive guide of the .NET famework may be found in** *Professional .NET Framework*, **Wrox Press, ISBN: 1-861005-56-3**

A History of ADO

We have become accustomed to Microsoft data access technologies evolving at breakneck speeds. The rapid evolution of data access technologies reflects the growth of the Internet, and the seemingly insatiable demand for faster, more scalable web applications.

Web applications need to access data quickly, regardless of how many active users may be logged on at any one time. Traditional ADO never quite gave us the lightweight data access objects that we might have wanted to meet the demands of scalable, highly available web applications. This was primarily because ADO's data exchange mechanism was better integrated with marshaled object calls, rather than with lightweight XML. The Internet space demands a data access technology that is tailored to delivering information to large numbers of individual clients who are accessing data remotely.

ADO 2.6 was designed for the tightly coupled application environments often found in traditional client/server applications. Such applications use n-Tier architectures with well-defined user services, business services, and data services layers. The middle-tier business layer typically manages all database access, and usually delivers data as recordsets, which are dependent on a persistent connection to the back-end database. ADO as a technology is well suited to this architecture, because it excels at providing rich recordsets with a flexible choice of cursors for accessing the data.

Web application architecture is based on the same n-Tier application architecture, but the relationships between the service layers are very different. Web applications have loosely coupled architectures, where the user interface and business tiers communicate over HTTP, and where state is not persisted between calls without explicit coding. The user services layer, in particular, is very loosely coupled to the business services layer.

Traditional client/server applications were designed to hold open a connection for the duration of a data access task, and close the connection only once the task is complete. Ideally, a Web application wouldn't dominate resources by maintaining such a connection. Web applications service a large number of users, and cannot effectively provide persistent connections to the database for every user on the system. Whereas, client/server applications might support several thousand users with several hundred concurrent users, Web applications, on the other hand, might need to support thousands to millions of concurrent users. ADO is simply not designed to support these kinds of loads.

The following diagrams compare the general structure a .NET application, showing the role of ADO.NET (on the right), with the general structure of a pre .NET application, built around ADO (on the left). Note, in particular, how, within the .NET model, XML is used as the transport between the User Services and the Business Services:

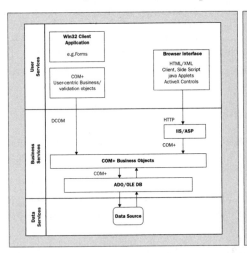
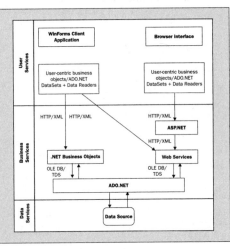

Client-side data access presents a significant challenge. It is a key aspect of any application that supports a large numbers of concurrent users, including web applications. The growth of the Internet, in particular, has created an upsurge in demand for fast, flexible, client-side data access technology. The recent evolution of ADO, up through version 2.6, has largely been driven by the quest to handle disconnected data access more effectively. With this in mind, in the following section, we will look at the recent development of traditional ADO.

Recent Developments in ADO

ActiveX Data Objects (ADO) was integrated with **OLE DB Providers** to provide a flexible data access technology that was also intuitive to use. ADO provides an easy-to-use interface for OLE DB, and a consistent programming model for use across all supported OLE DB Providers. Using specialized data providers in OLE DB, data access was made easy for widely different data sources: for non-relational as well as relational data sources. The following figure shows this ADO architecture:

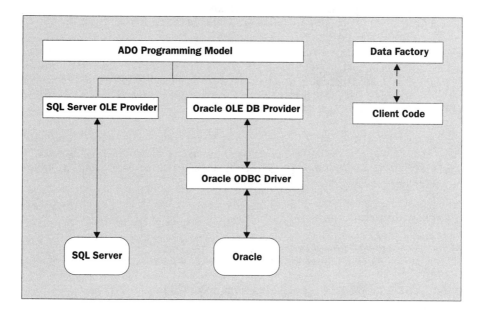

Unfortunately, ADO does not handle two things particularly well, namely disconnected recordsets and XML. As the Internet evolved, Microsoft attempted to develop the data access technology quickly to keep up. The **Microsoft Data Access Component (MDAC)** services were an integral part of this effort. This set of services included **Remote Data Services (RDS)**, which is based on the ADO programming model, and provides disconnected recordsets for the web client.

RDS recordsets are marshaled from the middle-tier to the client, and they provide cursor-based, flexible data access. They can be synchronized with the parent data source for updates and to refresh data views. RDS includes HTTP support, so that client-side scripts can communicate with the database and handle the results as recordsets. The advantage of RDS was that it was based on ADO recordsets, so that developers could utilize their existing knowledge of ADO to more easily bring data access to the client. Unfortunately, RDS was not only difficult to configure, but its reliance on the Recordset model meant that client-side data access was still not as lightweight as it could be.

The second area where ADO struggled was with XML. XML has been a powerful innovation in web technology. Developers were quick to realize the benefits of exchanging lightweight, text-based XML documents in place of expensive, marshaled object calls. Also, and this is a crucial point, XML may be passed over HTTP connections, meaning that communication between servers will be unimpeded by firewalls. It also has benefits over marshaled object calls, because XML does not make assumptions about how the data will be handled on the receiving end. Technologies such as RDS, which marshal recordsets, require specialized class factories for regenerating recordsets on the receiving side. The data is essentially unreadable, and therefore unusable, until this happens. XML does not have this same requirement, because XML provides clear text-based data that may be parsed in several ways on the receiving end.

Unfortunately, existing data access technologies were slow to integrate with XML. Developers welcomed the addition of XML to ADO when it was added in version 2.5, although it proved to be an imperfect solution. ADO has the ability to serialize to XML: for example, loading data from an XML document into a recordset. The XML schema is ADO-centric however, and does not conform to industry standards.

A major limitation with ADO's XML support is that ADO cannot open just any XML schema. Specifically, ADO (version 2.5 and up) supports an XML schema that parallels its **Advanced Data Tablegram (ADTG)** format, which is proprietary to Microsoft. ADO represents data as XML in accordance with the following XML schema:

```
xmlns:rs="urn:schemas-microsoft-com:rowset"
```

This XML namespace provides what is essentially a text-representation of the ADTG data storage format. This namespace defines the schema that ADO uses for persisting Recordset data as XML.

The Recordset object is the primary ADO object for manipulating data. ADO and OLE DB support different kinds of data sources, but the ADO programming model is still oriented towards relational data. For example, the RecordSet object is the original and oldest data container in ADO. It is squarely aimed at relational data sources, and is the most intuitive to use. Non-relational data sources must be manipulated using the newer Stream and Record objects. It is certainly easier to use ADO for relational database access over other kinds of data sources.

As XML has pervaded the Web, developers' data access needs have changed. XML data is hierarchical, not relational. On the Microsoft platform, most developers use MSXML 3.0 for programmatic access to the **Document Object Model (DOM)**, which allows us to traverse an XML document. Again, this is not the perfect, lightweight solution that developers require for the web. MSXML loads entire XML documents in memory, which is resource expensive, and certainly not an optimal data access technology for client-side scripting.

Developers, then, have been faced with two different data access technologies. On the one hand, they have ADO for relational database access. On the other hand, they have MSXML 3.0 for accessing XML documents.

ADO.NET addresses these limitations of ADO, and provides developers with a powerful data access technology that is optimized for disconnected, loosely coupled application architectures. This includes traditional, Windows DNA Web applications and also **Web Services**, which are components that expose their functionality on the Web. Web Services are disconnected, loosely coupled components that collaborate remotely to provide a business service. They are the driving business force behind Microsoft's .NET initiative.

ADO.NET may be a newer and very different data access technology, but it does not seek to make ADO entirely redundant. MDAC 2.7 (of which ADO is a subset) was released in June 2001, and provides support for 64-bit platforms. MDAC 3.0 is scheduled for release sometime next year, and is expected to improve on ADO's support of complex data structures. If you are heavily invested in an ADO code base, then, obviously, migrating an entire application to .NET may not be in your interests. A little later, we will discuss migration strategies and considerations for moving your ADO code to ADO.NET.

Overview of ADO.NET

ADO.NET presents a whole new data access architecture. In this section we will discuss the principal benefits of ADO.NET, and take a look at the important concepts behind the ADO.NET data architecture.

As mentioned above, ADO.NET is the .NET Framework's data access technology. It is designed with the goal of better serving the data access needs of web applications. As such, ADO.NET is designed to be data-centric, not database-centric; focused on handling disconnected data sets; and tightly integrated with XML, enabling better data sharing capabilities between components and tiers in an application.

We may understand the general strategy behind the development of ADO.NET, if we consider its design goals. These may be summed up in the following way:

- ❑ To provide data access classes that are integrated into the .NET Framework
- ❑ To provide deep integration with XML
- ❑ To provide better support for disconnected data
- ❑ To retain the feel of the ADO programming model
- ❑ To simplify the object model compared to ADO
- ❑ To make the object model less specific to relational databases
- ❑ To provide a common programming model for heterogeneous data sources

Let's look in a little more detail at the general architecture of ADO.NET.

ADO.NET Architecture

The ADO.NET object model is split into two layers. One layer is the **.NET Data Provider**, or connected layer, which contains Managed Providers for connecting to a data source and executing commands against it. The second layer is centered on the `DataSet` object. This is the disconnected layer: it handles data manipulation, and provides data serialization to XML. A rough object model of ADO.NET is shown in the figure below:

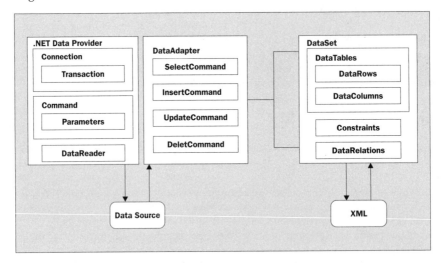

The .NET Data Provider object group contains objects for accessing SQL Server and OLE DB data sources, and includes `Connection` and `Command` objects that are similar to their ADO counterparts. The .NET Data Provider will handle standard data access and manipulation tasks for relational databases, including running stored procedures.

Numerous other .NET data providers are currently being developed, and these will emerge over the coming months and years. At the time of writing, an ODBC managed data provider was made available by Microsoft. This can be downloaded from:

`http://www.microsoft.com/downloads/release.asp?ReleaseID=31125.`

> **MDAC 2.6 is a requirement to run the .NET Framework SDK and Visual Studio.NET. MDAC contains a number of important data access components, including OLE DB data providers, which are still required in .NET for accessing data sources other than SQL Server 7.0 or later. MDAC 2.7, which features support for 64-bit processors, is highly recommended. This is necessary because every OLE DB data source still requires its own OLE DB Provider. The ADO.NET Managed Provider works with the OLE DB data providers that MDAC provides.**

The second group is centered on the `DataSet` object. This group provides a collection of objects for sophisticated data manipulation of any data source, relational or otherwise. The `DataSet` objects are removed from the actual connection. They are focused solely on data manipulation, and have no direct knowledge of the connection details for the data source. The link between the DataSet objects and the connection to the data source is provided by the `DataAdapter` object. The `DataAdapter` object is responsible for linking the `DataSet` objects to the .NET Data Provider.

This distinction between data objects and connection is a welcome improvement over the architecture provided by ADO. In ADO, objects like the `Recordset` object handle both data source access and data manipulation. By separating these, we achieve a higher degree of flexibility. For instance, we can choose to use different `Connection` objects to access data sources.

In Chapter 2, the Data Provider and DataSet objects will be discussed in greater detail.

Benefits of ADO.NET

ADO.NET has a number of advantages over ADO. The key advantages are:

❑　Disconnected data access

❑　XML Serialization

❑　Performance and Scalability

Let's take a look at these in turn.

Disconnected Data Access

ADO.NET is designed around providing disconnected data access. There are two key objects that may be utilized when accessing data: the `DataReader` object, and the `DataSet` object.

The `DataReader` object provides a read-only, forward-only stream of data that is lightweight and very suitable for lookups where the consumer does not need to edit the data. It is designed with web applications in mind, where users typically perform more data retrieval operations than data update operations.

The `DataSet` object, provides a disconnected, in-memory cache for data. The user can update this cache as needed, and then synchronize the actual data source once they are ready for the updates to be applied. The `DataSet` object is a huge improvement over ADO's `Recordset` object. Amongst other benefits, it enables us to represent numerous tables, and the relations and constraints between them, in a disconnected object. Also, as we've seen, it enables us to serialize to XML.

Traditional client/server applications typically use persistent database connections that stay open for the duration of a task, such as recordset updates. Web applications cannot afford to have persistent database connections open for every user. These connections are resource expensive because the database server must devote extra resources to keeping the connection open, and resolving concurrency issues. Database servers typically support only a limited number of concurrent open connections, and web applications typically support large numbers of users. The problem is alleviated somewhat by database connection pooling, which is supported by some newer OLE DB Providers, including the one for SQL Server 7.0 or later. However, connection pooling will only be effective for so long before user demand overwhelms the database server and causes problems. For this reason, ADO.NET is designed to support a disconnected architecture. Database connections are kept open only as long as it takes to retrieve relevant data.

ADO.NET disconnected data access is also integral to Web Services. Web Services are disconnected components that are accessible via SOAP calls over the Internet (or any network supporting HTTP). Web Services use XML for exchanging data, so that they benefit from an XML-centric data access technology such as ADO.NET. Web Services are very flexible: for instance, if necessary, they can collaborate in order to service a client request. They may be deployed across network boundaries, so it is essential that they are able to receive resultsets across the wire without holding on to a persistent database connection. With its disconnected architecture and tight integration with XML, ADO.NET gives Web Services that capability.

The decoupled nature of the DataSet object makes it natural that the DataSet should hold multiple resultsets from multiple data sources, which includes databases, spreadsheets and XML documents. The DataSet is not tied to any one data source. In fact, it couldn't care less where the data even comes from. That's the job of the Managed Provider.

DataSets and Recordsets

As we've seen, within ADO.NET, the new DataSet object replaces the old ADO RecordSet object. It extends far beyond the capabilities of the RecordSet object, which was essentially just an in-memory representation of a table or set of joined tables. In many cases, a RecordSet holds the result of a query that joins several tables. In some cases however we want to represent the data as several distinct tables. In ADO, we would need to load several recordsets, one per table, to do this. The DataSet object can represent data from multiple tables as distinct resultsets within the same DataSet object. This is useful because a single DataSet object may simultaneously hold several resultsets that originated from separate data sources.

The DataSet object is more than just a snapshot of resultsets. It is a working copy of the data that is disconnected from the original data sources. It is stored as a collection of DataTable and DataRow objects. A DataTable holds schema information, including field names and data types. A DataRow holds the actual data. If necessary, a DataSet will even enforce the constraints and describe the relationships that apply to the data in their parent tables. The DataRelation and DataConstraint objects manage these relationships and constraints on behalf of the DataSet object. The DataSet is a stand-alone, self-contained working set of data that is physically isolated from the parent data source and as such does not update a data source directly. Instead, it works with a separate object called the DataAdapter object to update any changes to the parent data source.

The DataSet may take the place of the ADO Recordset in this new framework, but we shouldn't approach it as just another upgrade to the familiar Recordset object. The DataSet is an entirely new data access container that is central to caching and manipulating data in ADO.NET.

XML Serialization

The DataSet object can load from XML or save to XML, including both data and the schema information. It may interact closely with the XmlDataDocument object , which holds relational data as XML. The XmlDataDocument is an XML view of the DataSet, which enables us to manipulate data using the Document Object Model (DOM). Changes made to the data via the XmlDataDocument are automatically synchronized with the view provided by the DataSet object.

What are the benefits of XML integration? The `DataSet` object can exchange XML data with any other XML compliant component, residing on any server. So XML makes ADO.NET highly interoperable with other systems. .NET Web Services may exchange data, and respond to requests, from any client that communicates with XML over HTTP. This would include clients that run on non-Windows platforms. ADO.NET also has benefits for data exchange within a single Web application whose individual tiers are deployed across several disconnected servers. XML is lightweight and text-based, so it transports easily over HTTP and passes through firewalls. It is therefore a good format for exchanging data etween the business services tier and the user interface tier within an application.

Marshaled object calls across firewalls are difficult to implement without configuring ports to allow binary content through. This adds an extra burden in configuring the firewall and the port socket – a burden that can be avoided by passing through text-based XML.

ADO.NET is tightly integrated with the XML Framework Classes, which provide a comprehensive set of classes for manipulating XML documents. It is not absolutely necessary that we have much knowledge of XML to use ADO.NET: all of the XML integration details are handled automatically. Having said this, it is very important for a .NET application developer to have a good understanding of XML, because it plays an important role in several areas of .NET. There will be times when we need to poke under the hood, for example, when manipulating an XSD schema with the XML Data Designer. We will be limited in what we can do without having a good understanding of XML: how it is structured, and how it is used in .NET.

ADO.NET also uses XML to describe the structure of the data that it holds. The `DataSet` object, for example, will generate an **XML Schema Document (XSD)**, to describe the structure of its data. The XSD is used to generate what's called a **typed dataset**, which is basically data that conforms to strict formatting rules and constraints. Typed datasets are compiled along with the XSD information, so they promote high integrity in our data. Typed datasets can be referenced using a hierarchical dot syntax notation rather than the index-based, collection-oriented notation that ADO programmers are used to. Typed datasets are an important feature of ADO.NET, which is not available in ADO.

Typed datasets may be created at design time using Visual Studio.NET's Component Wizard (described later in this chapter). They are a special subclasses of the `DataSet` object, which are compiled with their data and schema information. A typed dataset can be loaded into the XML Data Designer, which provides a graphical view of the schema that is available for editing.

Untyped datasets are not compiled with schema information, and cannot be viewed in the XML Data Designer. They do not hold any data at compile time, either. Schema information may be generated programmatically during runtime, once the untyped dataset is populated with data.

The Microsoft .NET Framework continues to implement the XML DOM for accessing XML. MSXML 3.0 has been replaced in the .NET Framework by classes in the `System.Xml` namespace, which unifies the DOM with ADO.NET's data access services. The `System.Xml` namespace provides support for both relational and regular XML documents.

Performance and Scalability

ADO.NET offers a distinct performance advantage over ADO for disconnected data access. The ADO.NET `DataSet` object exchanges data as XML. In ADO, disconnected `Recordsets` marshal data from one COM+ object to another using COM marshalling. This technology is resource-intensive, slower, and ultimately not scalable to the massive user load that an enterprise-level web application may experience. ADO.NET exchanges data between application tiers much more efficiently than ADO does.

ADO.NET is a more scalable data access technology than ADO, because it does not rely on persistent database connections or expensive database locks. These tie up database server resources and create concurrency problems when the number of application users is high. ADO.NET improves scalability because it provides truly disconnected `DataSet` objects, and easy serialization with industry-standard XML document formats. ADO.NET uses a dedicated `DataAdapter` object to synchronize changes between the disconnected `DataSet` and the parent data source. Every synchronization operation is prone to error, so the `DataSet` object provides a number of methods that enable us to scrutinize changes to data, and to trap errors that arise during the update operation.

ADO 2.6 and ADO.NET

The best way to learn about ADO.NET is to approach it as a new programming model. It is better not to transfer pre-conceived notions about "the way it was done in ADO" to the new programming model of ADO.NET. Having said that, many of us need a discussion of the comparisons, in order to make the conceptual leap to ADO.NET. For this reason, the following diagram compares ADO to ADO.NET:

Feature	ADO	ADO.NET
In-memory Data Container	Uses the `Recordset` object, which binds to one or more joined tables, and mimics a single table.	Uses the `DataSet` object, which binds to one or more separate tables, using a collection of `DataTable` objects.
Data Reads	Scans `dataRows` in the `Recordset` object in sequence.	Scans data sequentially or non-sequentially by following a path dictated by data relationships.
Linking Multiple Tables	Data is assembled from multiple tables using queries with the SQL `JOIN` keyword.	Associates data in one `DataTable` object with rows in another using the `DataRelation` object.
Data Source Access	The `Connection` object communicates to a data source using its OLE DB provider. The `Recordset` typically uses a `Connection` object to access the data source.	Uses a Managed Provider to communicate with the data source. The Managed Provider objects communicate directly with the SQL Server 2000 APIs. For other data sources, the Managed Provider objects communicate with its OLE DB Provider.

Feature	ADO	ADO.NET
Disconnected Data	Data access is typically connected, where the database connection is persisted for the duration of the task. The `Recordset` object provides limited disconnected data access, which is more effective for read-only datasets than for updateable data sets.	Provides strong support for disconnected data using the intermediate `DataAdapter` object, which manages all communication between the data source and the dataset. The updateable data set is held in the `DataSet` object, which is an in-memory data cache. The `DataAdapter` synchronizes the `DataSet` to the data source as needed.
Exchanging Disconnected Data	Uses COM marshalling to pass data between application tiers. COM marshalling only works with a limited set of data types, and it requires that data be marshaled from one object to another. COM marshalling does not work across firewalls without a lot of complicated configuration.	The `DataSet` object writes to an XML file format that stores the data and preserves the relational information. XML files are easy to exchange between application tiers. The receiving `DataSet` object easily loads the XML file. XML files are not limited to a restricted set of data types, and they are easy to transmit across the wire (over HTTP). They are not restricted by firewalls, because XML files are text-based.
Scalability	Limited, because database connections and locks are typically kept persistent for the length of a data operation. Connections are limited and expensive to keep open. Scalability and performance inevitably suffer when the application has large numbers of users.	Disconnected database access requires less database resources, because the database server does not need to maintain and open database connections for long periods of time. Limited database resources go further with disconnected access.

Migration and Interop

When it comes to migration, there is both good news and bad news. The bad news is that a significant development effort is required to migrate ADO code over to ADO.NET. In fact, migrating old code would probably involve rewriting just about every aspect of an application.

The good news is that you can still use ADO from within the .NET Framework, using **COM InterOp Services**. This enables us to utilize our existing code base, while moving over to the new .NET development platform.

COM InterOp Services provides an interface that allows any unmanaged components to be called from the managed .NET environment. The .NET Framework SDK ships with a utility called the **Type Library Importer**, TLBIMP.exe, which generates a .NET assembly from a COM+ type library. So the .NET application makes calls to the assembly, and COM InterOp services in turn marshals the call out to the actual COM+ component. Alternatively, we can import a COM object automatically using Visual Studio.NET.

Eventual migration to ADO.NET probably is a good idea, especially if your application depends on the use of disconnected data. ADO.NET offers superior functionality for managing disconnected data, and it may offer significant performance advantages for your application. If your application exchanges data remotely, then you should consider the programming, and the performance benefits that ADO.NET may offer you, not to mention the plethora of other advantages associated with .NET.

However, such a migration is likely to involve a significant amount of work, and a large investment of time, so you will want to do a careful cost-benefit analysis. To help you to do this, it may be useful to work on a pilot migration on a small section of your code base. This will give you a sense of what your migration effort may be like.

The Visual Studio.NET Component Designer

The **Component Designer** (also known as the **Data Designer**) is a developer productivity tool that provides a design-time interface for setting up common data access tasks. Visual Studio 6.0 provided a similar tool, except that its version provided special design-time controls that wrapped the actual ADO runtime classes. The .NET Component Designer gives us direct access to the ADO.NET runtime classes, directly from the Designer interface.

The Visual Studio.NET Component Designer enables us to set up several data access tasks at design time, including:

- ❏ Design Data Forms
- ❏ Browse data sources using the Server Explorer
- ❏ Configure the `Connection` and `DataAdapter` objects using a wizard
- ❏ Graphically create database queries
- ❏ Create typed `DataSet` from a data source
- ❏ Create XSD schemas from a data source

Let's take a look at how we could use the Component Designer.

Using the Component Designer

Visual Studio.NET's Component Designer is a graphical tool for configuring database connections and `DataAdapter` objects. Like previous tools, it is easy to use and makes for a good starting point for generating code. The Component Designer contains a built in **Query Builder** that enables us to set up complex queries using a drag-and-drop interface.

Let's look at an example of using the Component Designer to create a simple WinForms application that pulls sales data back from the Northwind database.

We start by creating a new Visual Basic Windows Application project named `TestADOApp1`. We then add a new Component Class to the project, using the **Project | Add Component** menu option. Select **Component Class** from the list of available templates, and name the new class `SalesData.vb`.

Select the toolbox and click on the **Data** tab. Drag and drop a `SqlDataAdapter` on to the design surface of the `SalesData` component.

A splash screen will fire up saying, Welcome to the DataAdapter Configuration Wizard. Click Next, then press the New Connection button. Enter the server name, database name (Northwind), and login information as shown below (except that your server name will be different).

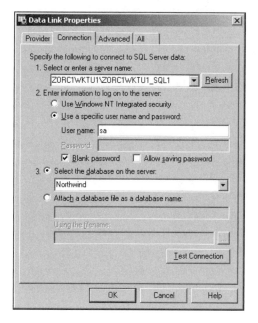

Click the Test Connection to verify that the settings are correct, and then click the OK button. Press the Next button, which brings you to the Choose A Query Type screen. Select Use existing stored procedures, as shown below:

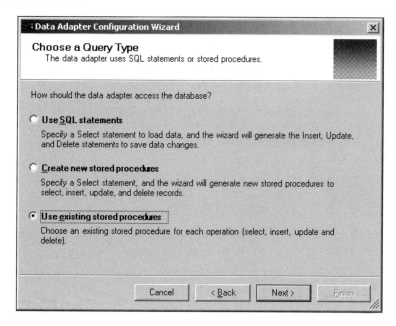

Choose the **Employee Sales by Country** stored procedure from the **Select** drop-down, as shown opposite:

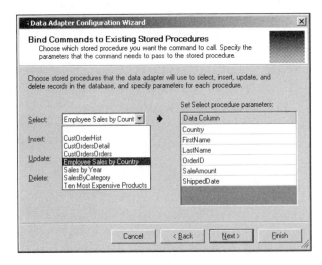

Click **Next** to take you to the last screen of the wizard, called **Complete the Data Adapter Configuration Wizard**. Click **Finish**, and you will return to the `SalesData.vb` design surface. You should see two components on the surface: `SqlConnection1` and `SqlDataAdapter1`.

Now, we will preview the data that the `DataAdapter` is binding to. Right-click on the `SqlDataAdapter1` component and select **Preview Data…** from the pop-up menu. You will now see the **Data Adapter Preview** screen. Enter a date range in the parameter list in the upper right: use a begin date of 06/30/1996 and an end date of 09/30/1996, as shown below:

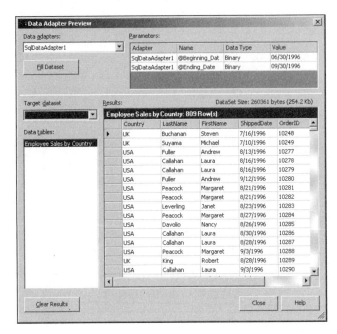

Click **Close** once you are satisfied with the data preview.

We need to add code in two places. First, we need to add code to the `SalesData` component class to return a `DataSet`. Second, we need to add a `DataGrid` to the form to display the data.

Switch over to the `SalesData.vb` tab, or right-click on the `SalesData.vb` design surface and select **View Code** from the pop-up menu. Add a new method called `FillSales`, so that the overall code listing looks like this:

```
Public Class SalesData
    Inherits System.ComponentModel.Component

    Public Function FillSales() As DataSet

        ' Declare a new DataSet object
        Dim dsSales As New DataSet()

        ' Use the DataAdapter to populate the new DataSet object
        Try
            ' Open the connection
            SqlConnection1.Open()
            ' Fill dsSales with data retrieved from SqlDataAdapter1
            SqlDataAdapter1.Fill(dsSales)
        Catch eFillError As System.Exception
            MsgBox(eFillError.ToString)
        Finally
            SqlConnection1.Close()
        End Try

        ' Return the populated DataSet
        Return (dsSales)

    End Function

End Class
```

Notice that this code listing references the `Connection` and `DataAdapter` objects that we created earlier with the Wizard. This listing creates a new `DataSet`, and populates it with data from the stored procedure resultset, using the `DataAdapter` object's `Fill` method.

Next, switch over to the **Form1** design surface, which you can identify by the tab that says **Form1.vb [Design]**. Select the toolbox and click on the **Windows Forms** tab. Drag and drop a **Button** control and a `DataGrid` control. Double-click on the button, which switches you into the code view, inside the button's `Click` event procedure.

We need to do two things here. First, add two `Imports` statements, so that we reference the namespaces that we need. Second, write code behind the button to populate the `DataGrid` with sales data (using the `SalesData.FillSales` method that we just created).

The final code listing should look like this:

```
Imports System.Data
Imports System.Data.SqlClient

Public Class Form1
  Inherits System.Windows.Forms.Form


  Private Sub Button1_Click(ByVal sender As System.Object, ByVal e As _
      System.EventArgs) Handles Button1.Click

    Dim objSales As New SalesData()
    Dim dsSales As New DataSet()

    dsSales = objSales.FillSales

    DataGrid1.DataSource = dsSales

  End Sub
End Class
```

Finally, press *F5* to compile the project. When the form opens, click the button to populate the
DataGrid. You should see something like this:

	Country	LastName	FirstName	ShippedDate	OrderID	SaleAmount	EmployeeID
▶	UK	Buchanan	Steven	7/16/1996	10248	440	5
	UK	Suyama	Michael	7/10/1996	10249	1863.4	6
	USA	Peacock	Margaret	7/12/1996	10250	1552.6	4
	USA	Leverling	Janet	7/15/1996	10251	654.06	3
	USA	Peacock	Margaret	7/11/1996	10252	3597.9	4
	USA	Leverling	Janet	7/16/1996	10253	1444.8	3
	UK	Buchanan	Steven	7/23/1996	10254	556.62	5
	UK	Dodsworth	Anne	7/15/1996	10255	2490.5	9
	USA	Leverling	Janet	7/17/1996	10256	517.8	3
	USA	Peacock	Margaret	7/22/1996	10257	1119.9	4
	USA	Davolio	Nancy	7/23/1996	10258	1614.88	1

A Second way of using the Component Designer

To illustrate how flexible the Component designer is, let's redo this project, except this time we'll use the
Query Builder to create the SQL code that currently resides in the Employee Sales by Country
stored procedure. Many of the steps are the same as before, so I will omit several of the descriptions,
screen shots and code listings that you saw above.

Switch to the design surface of SalesData.vb. Right-click on the SqlDataAdapter1 component
and select **Configure Data Adapter** from the pop-up menu. You will launch into the familiar
DataAdapter Configuration Wizard. Click **Next** past the connection information.

On the **Choose A Query Type** screen, select **Use SQL Statements**. Next, click the **Query Builder** button. You will see a pop-up menu of table names. Press the Control key, and select the `Employees` and `Orders` tables, then click **OK**. You will see the following:

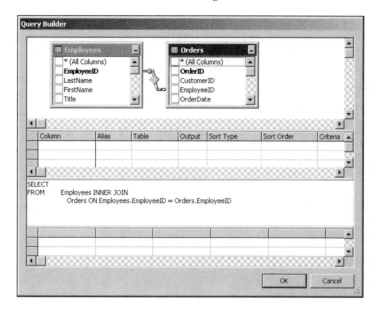

To build the query, click on the `Employees` table at the top of the Query Builder window and put checks in the boxes next to `LastName`, `FirstName`, and `Country`. Next, click on the `Orders` table and put checks in the boxes next to `OrderID` and `ShippedDate`. Now the screen should look as follows:

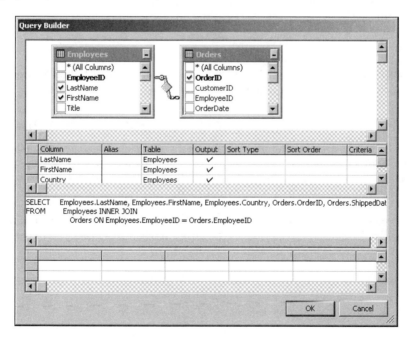

The SQL Query so far is not equivalent to the `Employee Sales by Country` stored procedure. To get it there, we will need to add some SQL statements manually to the SQL edit screen in the lower half of the **Query Builder** screen. Add the SQL code that you see in the screenshot below, and your screen should match:

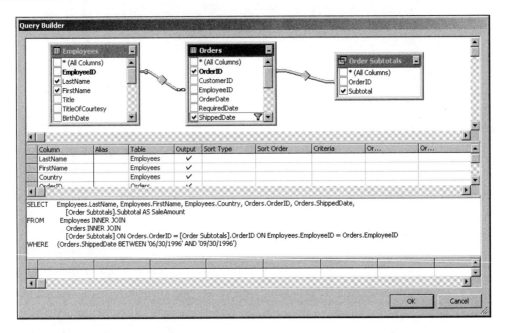

The third joined table, **Order Subtotals**, will appear automatically as soon as you've completed adding the rest of the SQL code. Notice that I've hard coded the date range in the WHERE clause to match the one we used previously.

Click **OK**, then **Finish** to complete the wizard.

Finally, click *F5* to compile the project. When the form pops up, click the button to populate the `DataGrid`. You should see the same data populated in the `DataGrid` as before.

Creating Typed DataSets in the Component Designer

Typed datasets are easy to create and provide your code with a lot of benefits. A typed dataset has intrinsic knowledge of its data's schema, which it leverages by exposing the fields as strong types in the IDE. So when you are accessing tables in a `DataSet` object, you will not need to remember what fields are present. Instead, they will pop up for you in the IDE.

Let's create a typed dataset for the `SalesData.FillSales` method that we created above. Switch to the design surface for `SalesData.vb`, and right-click anywhere in a blank part of the surface. Select **Generate DataSet...** from the pop-up menu.

You will see the **Generate Dataset** screen. Complete it as shown in the screen shot below:

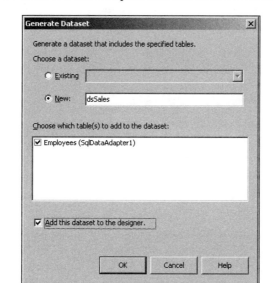

This will create a new typed dataset called `dsSales` for `SqlDataAdapter1`. Click OK, and you will return to the design surface where you should now see the `dsSales1` component (the typed dataset generator automatically appends a "1" to the end of the name that you choose).

Now let's use our new typed dataset. Switch over to the code listing for `SalesData.vb`, and add a second function that writes out all of the first names in the dataset:

```
Public Sub WriteFirstNames()
   Dim rowEmployee As dsSales.EmployeesRow

      For Each rowEmployee In DsSales1.Employees.Rows
         Console.WriteLine(rowEmployee.FirstName)
   Next
End Sub
```

As you type, you will see a pop-up menu of options for row **Employee** that will include each of the columns that are stored in the `SqlDataAdapter1` object, including `FirstName`.

Once the typed `DataSet` object has been generated, you can modify the earlier code listing for the `FillSales` method to reference the typed `DataSet`, `dsSales1`, instead of the untyped `DataSet`, `dsSales`. To do this, I have created an alternate version of the `FillSales` method called `FillSales2`, shown below:

```
Public Function FillSales2() As DataSet
   ' This function is equivalent to FillSales(), but it references
   ' the typed DataSet, dsSales1

   ' Use the DataAdapter to populate the new DataSet object
   Try
      SqlConnection1.Open()
      SqlDataAdapter1.Fill(DsSales1)
```

```
    Catch eFillError As System.Exception
        Console.WriteLine(eFillError.ToString)
    Finally
        SqlConnection1.Close()
    End Try

    ' Return the populated DataSet
    Return (DsSales1)

End Function
```

Using the XML Data Designer to view XSD schemas

Visual Studio makes it easy for you to view a `DataSet`'s XSD schema file. Once again, switch over to the `SalesData.vb` design surface in our sample project. Right-click on the `dsSales1` component and select **View Schema...** from the pop-up menu. This creates a new tab called `dsSales.xsd`. You are now inside the XML Data Designer. There are two views of the schema. The first one that you see is the `DataSet` view, as shown below:

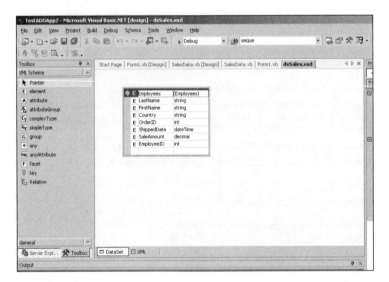

Now that we are in the XML Data Designer, the terminology used to describe things changes. The view that you see above is the `DataSet` view. It shows the `Employees` complex type, which is contained within the parent type `dsSales`.

Click on the small **XML** button at the bottom of the screen, and this will show you the actual XSD schema file. This is what it looks like for the `Employees` type:

```
<xsd:schema id="dsSales" targetNamespace=http://www.tempuri.org/dsSales.xsd
    xmlns=http://www.tempuri.org/dsSales.xsd
    xmlns:xsd=http://www.w3.org/2001/XMLSchema
    xmlns:msdata="urn:schemas-microsoft-com:xml-msdata"
    elementFormDefault="qualified">
 <xsd:element name="dsSales" msdata:IsDataSet="true">
  <xsd:complexType>
   <xsd:choice maxOccurs="unbounded">
```

```
    <xsd:element name="Employees">
      <xsd:complexType>
        <xsd:sequence>
          <xsd:element name="Country" type="xsd:string" minOccurs="0" />
          <xsd:element name="LastName" type="xsd:string" />
          <xsd:element name="FirstName" type="xsd:string" />
          <xsd:element name="ShippedDate" type="xsd:dateTime" minOccurs="0" />
          <xsd:element name="OrderID" msdata:ReadOnly="true"
                msdata:AutoIncrement="true" type="xsd:int" />
          <xsd:element name="SaleAmount" type="xsd:decimal" minOccurs="0" />
          <xsd:element name="EmployeeID" msdata:ReadOnly="true"
                msdata:AutoIncrement="true" type="xsd:int" />
        </xsd:sequence>
      </xsd:complexType>
    </xsd:element>
   </xsd:choice>
  </xsd:complexType>
 </xsd:element>
</xsd:schema>
```

This is a very simple XSD file, but they get more complex – especially when they are storing data relation information. The XML Data Designer provides tools that allow you to modify complex types and set up new relations. The changes will be automatically checked for obvious errors, in order to preserve the integrity of the schema. The XML Data Designer is discussed in more detail later on in the book.

Summary

In this chapter, we've taken a general look at ADO.NET data access. We have discussed the design goals behind ADO.NET, and its architecture. Specifically, we've looked at:

❑   The .NET framework and how ADO.NET fits into this application

❑   ADO.NET as a new data access technology that was designed in large part to better serve the needs of disconnected web applications

❑   How the ADO.NET object model divides into two groups: .NET Managed Data Providers, and the DataSet object and its collections

❑   Typed datasets, and how they provide more intuitive access to data, and reduce coding errors.

❑   The Visual Studio.NET Component Designer, and the wizards for setting up data connections, commands and adapters

❑   How the Visual Studio.NET XML Data Designer allows you to view and edit XML data schemas, both graphically and as XML

❑   Migration issues, and specifically, how migrating from ADO to ADO.NET is usually not easy

In the next chapter, we will look at the ADO.NET object model in more detail, including the role of namespaces. We will also focus attention on the significant role of XML in ADO.NET

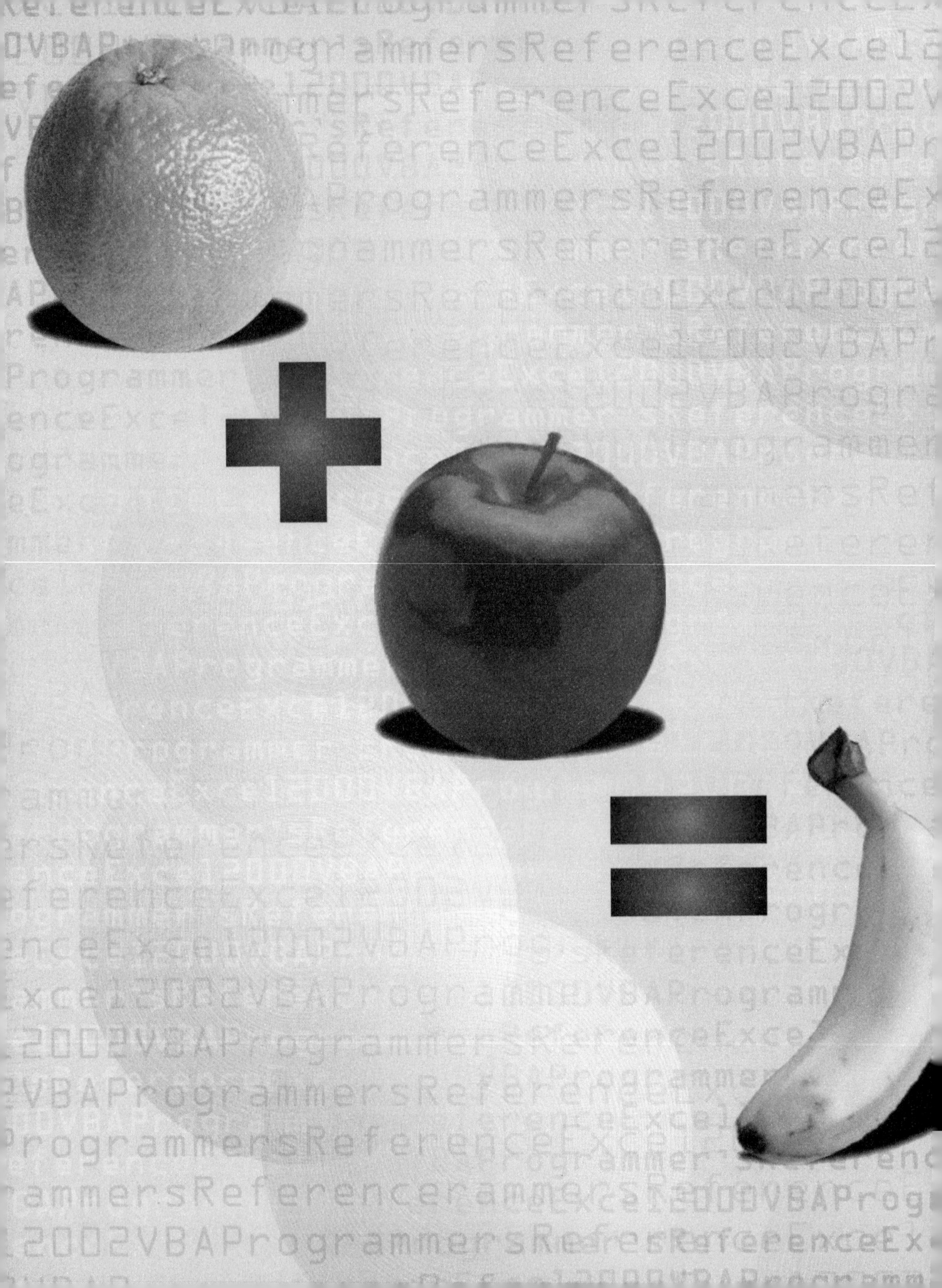

2

The ADO.NET Object Model

ADO 2.6, and former releases of ADO, struggled to meet the performance demands of distributed, multi-tier enterprise-level applications that support thousands of concurrent users. This class of applications includes both Web and client/server applications.

In principle, data should be accessed using disconnected recordsets whenever possible, so that the application does not need to maintain a persistent connection to a data source for any longer than necessary. Database resources are expensive to maintain, and ultimately reduce system resources, and thereby, application scalability. ADO provides a lot of support for disconnected recordsets, which enable the retrieval and manipulation of data without having a persistent database connection. ADO suffers however from two major flaws that limit its effectiveness for disconnected data access. First, ADO uses expensive object marshaling to move data sets between the user and business application tiers. Second, it lacks any objects that are optimized for manipulating disconnected data.

On the other hand, ADO.NET uses lightweight, text-based XML to move data between tiers, and provides a `DataSet` object that is optimized for handling disconnected data sets, thus overcoming these limitations.

In Chapter 1, we discussed what ADO.NET is, and provided a brief review of the ADO.NET classes and general concepts. In this chapter, we will drill into the object model further, and look at a number of ways of utilizing the ADO.NET objects.

This chapter begins with a review of the data-oriented classes in the .NET Framework. Next, we will look at the ADO.NET object model, and provide a number of examples to illustrate how to use specific objects. Finally, we will review the integration between ADO.NET and XML, which is one of the most exciting aspects of this new data access technology.

The .NET Class Framework

The .NET Framework provides access to the Windows system functionality using a set of object-oriented classes. The Framework provides base classes that can be used as they are, or easily extended and abstracted into custom classes. The System level classes provide the lowest level functionality. The Extended class libraries, such as ASP.NET, are simply an abstracted set of classes that are designed for a specific kind of application. ASP.NET, for example, is essentially just a set of classes that have been abstracted in a way that is useful for Web developers. You don't have to use ASP.NET for web development, if you are comfortable working directly with the set of base classes that sit below ASP.NET, in the Base Class Library.

As such, .NET presents us with a whole new range of functionality, and many of us are not yet familiar with how the classes are laid out. In this section, namespaces and how they relate to the class framework are going to be examined followed by details regarding data access within .NET.

Namespaces

The .NET Framework introduces the concept of namespaces, which are functionally related groups of classes, interfaces, and structures. Namespaces are organized in a hierarchy within the .NET Framework, and may contain:

- ❑ Classes

- ❑ Interfaces

- ❑ Types (Reference and Value)

- ❑ Enumerations

- ❑ Delegates

- ❑ Other namespaces

For example, the `System` namspace is the root namespace for the .NET framework. It contains classes such as `Console` and `Math`, types such as `Object` and `String`, and second-level namespaces such as 10 and security.

All system functionality within the .NET Framework is contained within an organized set of classes and structures, logically grouped into hierarchical namespaces. The .NET Framework's Base Class Library exposes the same set of namespaces to all .NET-supported languages. Namespaces reduce the ambiguity in code listings by providing what amounts to a pathway that leads to the class that you intend to use.

Namespaces are not automatically exposed to a .NET code project. They must be declared for use in the project, much like setting a dynamic link library reference in a Visual Studio 6.0 project. Namespaces are included in the header of a code module as follows:

In VB:

```
Imports System.Data.SqlClient
```

In C#:

```
using System.Data.SqlClient;
```

When we include a namespace in a project, all of the namespace classes are automatically included in that project. However, child namespaces are not automatically included, and must be imported separately. For example, the `System.Data.SqlClient()` namespace is a child of the `System.Data` namespace, but the following code listing will fail:

```
Imports System.Data
Dim sqlAdapt As SqlDataAdapter ' Member of the System.Data.SqlClient namespace
```

This listing will generate a compile-time exception saying that the `SqlDataAdapter` type is not defined. In addition, you will not see any IntelliSense for selecting child classes in the `System.Data.SqlClient` namespace. This exception goes away if you import the `System.Data.SqlClient` namespace directly, as in:

```
Imports System.Data
Imports System.Data.SqlClient
Dim sqlAdapt As SqlDataAdapter
```

As we will discuss later, the `DataSet` class is contained in the `System.Data` namespace. In your code you should reference the class as:

```
Imports System.Data
Imports System.Data.SqlClient

Public Class MyData

Public Function GetMyData() As DataSet
Dim objDataSet1 = New System.Data.DataSet()
' More code here
End Function

End Class
```

The table below summarizes all of the namespaces that play a role in data access. Some namespaces are directly involved in data access, for example, `System.Data.SqlClient`, which supports the SQL Server Managed Provider. Other namespaces play a support role, such as the family of XML namespaces, including `System.Xml.Schema`, which supports processing of XML Schema Documents (XSD):

.NET Framework Namespace	Description
System.Data	Contains base classes for the ADO.NET Architecture. ADO.NET enables you to build components that manage data from multiple data sources.
System.Data.Common	Contains shared classes for the .NET Managed Data Providers. The .NET Data Provider is a collection of classes for accessing a data source, and linking it to a `DataSet` object (via the managed provider's `DataAdapter` object).
System.Data.SqlClient	Contains classes that support the SQL Server .NET Data Provider. These provide managed access for SQL Server 7.0 or later.
System.Data.OleDb	Contains classes that support the OLE DB .NET Data Provider. These provide managed access for any supported OLE DB Provider, including Oracle, Jet, and SQL Server 6.5 or earlier.
System.Data.SqlTypes	Provides classes that represent SQL Server's native data types. These classes provide a type-safe way to reference SQL Server data types.
System.Xml	Contains classes that support XML processing.
System.Xml.Schema	Contains classes that support processing of XML Schema Definition Language (XSD).

.NET Framework Namespace	Description
System.Xml.Serialization	Contains classes that are used to serialize objects into XML data documents, or XML streams.
System.Xml.Xpath	Contains classes for the XPath parser and evaluation engine.
System.Xml.Xsl	Contains classes that support XSL/T transformations.

As can be seen, the fully qualified class names can often be very long, so to reduce the amount of typing you should set up an alias for the namespace. For example, here is how you would set an alias for the System.Xml.Schema namespace:

```
Imports xsd = System.Xml.Schema
```

Finally, .NET allows you to set up your own custom namespaces using the Namespace keyword. This ensures that your custom classes are properly qualified. For example, in Visual Basic:

```
Namespace MyNamespace
    Class MyClass
    End Class
End Namespace
```

The .NET Framework and Data Access

The .NET Framework diagram presented in Chapter 1 highlighted the three parts of the Framework that are integral to providing data access. These are:

❑ **ADO.NET** – Provides classes and types for data access.

❑ **XML** – Provides classes and types to access XML functionality, including: the Document Object Model (DOM), and read and write capability to W3C compliant XML documents.

❑ **Visual Studio.NET** – The integrated development environment for .NET. Provides several tools for data access, including:

❑ Design-time data controls for graphically configuring database connections and commands

❑ Bound data controls, such as the DataGrid, for displaying DataSets

❑ Design-time data configuration wizards, for setting up database connections, commands and DataAdapters

❑ Query Builder, for graphically setting up queries (similar to the tool provided in Access 2000)

❑ Component Designer, including an XML Data Designer for editing data schemas

We will discuss each of these in turn in detail later in the following sections of the chapter.

The .NET Framework is the first major building block of .NET. The second building block is .NET Enterprise Servers, which will also be discussed later in this chapter.

The ADO.NET Object Model

As we saw in Chapter 1, the ADO.NET objects are divided into two groups:

❑ **Managed Providers** (`Connection`, `Command`, `DataReader` and `DataAdapter` objects)

❑ **The DataSet Object**, and its collections

Managed Providers are the interface to a data source, and play a role that is analogous to that of OLE DB Providers in ADO. Managed providers take care of the following:

❑ Set a connection to a data source (using the `Connection` object)

❑ Get a stream of read-only data from the data source (using the `DataReader` object)

❑ Get a stream of data from the data source, and passes it to a `DataSet` object for viewing and updating (via the `DataAdapter` object)

❑ Synchronize changes in a `DataSet` with the original data source (via the `DataAdapter` object)

❑ Raise errors during data synchronization

The `DataSet` object is an in-memory, server-side data store that holds a working copy of data. The `DataSet` object is disconnected from the original data source, but it provides the same level of information as does the original data source. This enables you to modify a data set without being connected to the actual data source. The `DataSet` object provides the following:

❑ Holds an in-memory cache of data

❑ Provides views of both data and schema information

❑ Allows updating of data and schema information

❑ Acts as a disconnected data store, with no knowledge of the underlying data source (this is handled by the Managed Provider)

❑ Serializes to XML data documents, which hold both data and schema information

❑ Provides array-like indexing and strong typing

The .NET Data Provider Objects

ADO.NET provides what is called **Managed Data Access**. The .NET Framework uses the term **managed** to describe a class or a language that conforms to the standards laid out by the .NET Framework. These standards include conforming to a type-safe model, and utilizing primitive types and base classes provided by the .NET Framework. Managed code is executed under the strict control of the .NET Common Language Runtime, which provides a number of important services including memory management and garbage collection.

In ADO.NET, a **Managed Provider** is a set of objects that provides communication between a data source and a `DataSet` object. The figure below shows an overview of the Managed Data system. These systems use one set of objects for managing connections to the data source, and another set of objects for manipulating the data.

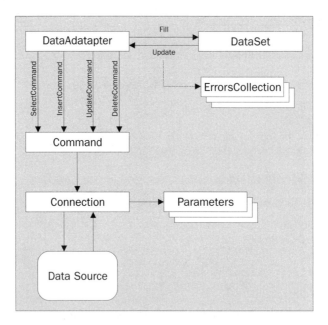

As we saw earlier, the **.NET Data Provider objects** are used for connecting to a data source, executing commands (stored procedures and SQL statements), and retrieving data. The .NET Data Provider can handle basic data manipulation, such as updates and inserts. Also, it handles basic data processing, and is sufficient for basic data manipulation in an environment where the connection stays persistent until the data manipulation work is done. But its primary focus is to retrieve data from a data source and pass it on to the DataSet object, where it can be manipulated and serialized to XML. The .NET Data Provider is designed to be a lightweight layer between the data source and the DataSet object. It provides high performance and functionality and, above all, simplicity.

Which .NET Managed Data Provider Do I Use?

ADO.NET ships with two kinds of Managed Data Provider, the **SQL Server .NET Data Provider** and the **OLE DB .NET Data Provider**. You will want to choose the provider that gives you the best performance for accessing your data source.

The **SQL Server .NET Data Provider** is used for accessing databases in SQL Server 7.0 or later. You can also use it for accessing Microsoft Data Engine (MSDE), which is the data format used by SQL Server Desktop Edition. For version 6.5 or earlier, you must use the OLE DB .NET Data Provider, with the OLE DB Provider for SQL Server. The SQL Server .NET Data Provider provides excellent performance, because it accesses SQL Server directly, instead of going through an intermediate OLE DB provider. This dedicated managed provider actually uses the Tabular Data Stream (TDS), which is SQL Server's native communication protocol.

SQL Server .NET Data Providers are located in the System.Data.SqlClient namespace. In order to use the provider you will need to include this namespace in your application.

VB:

```
Imports System.Data.SqlClient
```

C#:

```
using System.Data.SqlClient;
```

> A namespace is simply a logical grouping of related classes, interfaces and structures. The .NET Framework Class Library is organized in a system of hierarchical namespaces, beginning with the root **System** namespace. For example, the **System.Data** namespace contains classes for accessing data sources using ADO.NET. Namespaces are discussed in more detail in Chapter 2.

The **OLE DB .NET Data Provider** is used for accessing databases in SQL Server 6.5 or earlier, Oracle, and Microsoft Access. You have the choice of using this provider to access SQL Server 7.0 or later, but you will lose the performance benefits that are provided by the SQL Server .NET Data Provider.

OLE DB .NET Data Providers are located in the `System.Data.OleDb` namespace. Again, you will need to include this namespace in your application, in order to use the provider.

VB:

```
Imports System.Data.OleDb
```

C#:

```
using System.Data.OleDb;
```

ADO.NET continues to work with OLE DB Providers for all data sources. Currently, the OLE DB .NET Data Providers in ADO.NET are compatible with 3 OLE DB providers as shown in the table below:

Driver	Provider
SQLOLEDB	Microsoft OLE DB Provider for SQL Server
MSDAORA	Microsoft OLE DB Provider for Oracle
Microsoft.Jet.OLEDB.4.0	OLE DB Provider for Jet

ADO.NET will certainly be supporting more OLE DB Providers in the future. Microsoft has also released an ODBC .NET Data Provider that works with all compliant ODBC drivers. This is currently restricted to the SQL, Jet and Oracle ODBC drivers. Microsoft will continue in their tradition of encouraging third-party ISVs to develop extensions to their out-of-box data access technology.

.NET Managed Provider Objects

There are four objects that make up a .NET Data Provider:

- ❏ **Connection** – Establishes a connection to a data source
- ❏ **Command** – Executes commands on a data source
- ❏ **DataReader** – Used for data retrieval
- ❏ **DataAdapter** – Used to populate a **DataSet** object, and manage updates to a data source.

In the following sections, we will briefly discuss each of these.

The Connection Object

The .NET Data Provider `Connection` object is used to set a connection to a data source. It is analogous to the traditional ADO `Connection` object. Each .NET Provider has its own `Connection` object. For example, the SQL Server .NET Provider includes a `SqlConnection` object, while the OLE DB .NET Provider includes an `OleDbConnection` object. These are simply different flavors of the same kind of object. The .NET Framework lays out rules that valid .NET Providers must conform to. If you decide to create your own .NET Provider then it must provide the standard set of .NET Provider objects, which includes the `Connection`, `Command`, `DataReader` and `DataAdapter` objects. Each object in the provider must provide the expected interface, as laid out by the .NET Framework.

The ADO.NET `Connection` object provides a `ConnectionString` property for assigning the data source connection details. For the `OleDbConnection` object, this connection string format is identical to a typical OLE DB Provider string, as in:

```
Imports System.Data.OleDb

Dim sConn As String
sConn = "Provider=SQLOLEDB;Data Source=ZORC1WKTU1\ZORC1WKTU1_SQL1;" & _
        "Initial Catalog=Northwind;User ID=sa;"

Dim OleDbConn As OleDbConnection = New OleDbConnection(sConn)
```

For the `SqlConnection` object this string is like a typical OLE DB Provider string, except that you omit the `Provider` parameter. It is not needed, because the SQL Server Data Provider does not use an OLE DB Provider:

```
Imports System.Data.SqlClient

Dim sConn As String
sConn = "Data Source=ZORC1WKTU1\ZORC1WKTU1_SQL1; _
        Initial Catalog=Northwind;User ID=sa;"

Dim sqlConn As SqlConnection = New SqlConnection(sConn)
```

This code listing initializes a data source connection, but does not actually open it. The `Connection` object also includes `Open` and `Close` methods for setting the state of the connection.

The Command Object

Once you have established a connection to a data source, you can execute commands and return results using the `Command` object. The ADO.NET `Command` object is analogous to the traditional ADO `Command` object. Again, each .NET Data Provider includes its own version of the `Command` object. The SQL Server Managed Provider includes the `SqlCommand` object, while the OLE DB Managed Provider includes the `OleDbCommand` object. Each one behaves in the same way.

The `Command` object is very versatile. It will execute both stored procedures and Transact-SQL statements against a data source. It will return the resulting data stream as a `DataReader` object (described below). You can also use the Command object to execute action queries that return no results.

Finally, the `Command` object may be created as a stand-alone object that dynamically references a stand-alone `Connection` object for connecting to a data source. Alternatively, you can create the `Command` object directly using the `Connection` object's `CreateCommand` method.

The DataReader Object

The `DataReader` object is squarely aimed at web developers. It provides a fast, read-only, forward-only data stream that is designed to provide quick access to data. This is very useful for disconnected web clients. The `DataReader` object is easy to use, and an excellent option for quick access to a dataset. Unlike the ADO `Recordset`, the `DataReader` does not assume that you want to start displaying data from the first record, so it is unlike a cursor in this sense. The syntax for accessing records from a `DataReader` is shown below:

```
' Initialize the DataReader object
Dim drReader As SqlDataReader

' Call Connection and Command code (not shown)
' ...

' Execute the command and retrieve the data stream in the DataReader
drReader = sqlCmd.ExecuteReader(CommandBehavior.SequentialAccess)

' Loop through the DataReader's resultset
Do While drReader.Read()
    Console.WriteLine drReader("EmployeeID")
Loop

drReader.Close()
```

The `DataReader` object is more versatile than this simple code listing would suggest. It will retrieve multiple resultsets, such as data from two separate tables in the database. It will also return schema information for the underlying data source. Finally, the `DataReader` is an excellent choice for large datasets, because it provides a data stream instead of storing the data in memory.

The DataAdapter Object

The `DataAdapter` object is a very important member of the Managed Provider because it provides the link for exchanging data between a data source and a data set. ADO.NET provides the `DataSet` object for caching and manipulating data. The `DataSet` object is independent of the data source, and must be synchronized as updates are made. The `DataSet` object has no direct knowledge of the data source, so it communicates its data changes to the `DataAdapter`, which in turn communicates with the data source.

Data adapters can move any kind of data between a data source and a `DataSet` object as long as it is supported by a .NET Data Provider. For example, you could use one data adapter to move Oracle data into a `DataSet` object, and then use another to move SQL Server data into the same `DataSet`. The `DataAdapter` object provides a `Fill` method for populating a `DataSet` object with data. The `SqlDataAdapter` object is optimized for moving SQL Server 7.0 or later data between a data source and a `DataSet` object. The `OleDbDataAdapter` object is suitable for all OLE DB data sources, as well as older versions of SQL Server.

Also, adapters are very versatile. They can hold up to four open connections at a time, one for each operation that it can perform: select, update, insert, and delete. The `DataAdapter` object works with an ADO.NET `Command` object to execute each of these operations.

Finally, the `DataAdapter` object works with a centralized errors collection that holds exceptions that are raised during exchanges between the data source and the `DataSet`. For example, the SQL Server Managed Provider includes the `SqlExceptions` collection that holds all exceptions that are raised by the SQL Server database as data is retrieved or updated.

Overview of the System.Data.SqlClient namespace

Our code examples will use the NorthWind database that ships with SQL Server, and so we will focus on the SQL Server 7.0+ Data Provider, which is included in the `System.Data.SqlClient` namespace.

The important members of this namespace are shown in the table below:

Member (* Class, ** Enumeration)	Description
* `SqlConnection`	Represents an open connection to a SQL Server database.
* `SqlCommand`	Represents a Transact-SQL statement or stored procedure to execute at a SQL Server data source.
* `SqlDataReader`	Provides a means of reading a forward-only stream of rows from a SQL Server database.
* `SqlDataAdapter`	Represents a set of data commands and a database connection, which are used to fill the `DataSet` and update a SQL Server database.
* `SqlParameter`	Represents a parameter to a `SqlCommand`, and optionally, its mapping to DataSet columns.
* `SqlParameterCollection`	Collects all parameters relevant to a `SqlCommand` and their respective mappings to `DataSet` columns.
* `SqlError`	Collects information relevant to a warning or error returned by SQL Server.
* `SqlErrorCollection`	Collects all errors thrown by the `SqlDataAdapter`.
* `SqlException`	The exception that is thrown when SQL Server returns a warning, an error or an exception message.
* `SqlTransaction`	Represents a Transact-SQL transaction to be made in a SQL Server database.
** `SqlDbType`	Specifies SQL Server data types.

There are a number of other members in this namespace, but they are not important for this chapter. For a full listing of the namespace members you can consult the Visual Studio.NET Online Help, which contains a comprehensive set of online help files, reference information, and example code. The main limitation of the help files is that many of the code samples are overly simplistic. However, the coverage of the Framework classes in general, and the WinForms controls, in particular, is very helpful.

Using the System.Data.SqlClient namespace

SQL Server .NET Data Providers are located in the `System.Data.SqlClient` namespace. You will need to include this namespace in your application, in order to use the provider.

In VB:

```
Imports System.Data.SqlClient
```

In C#:

```
using System.Data.SqlClient;
```

> The code examples in this chapter are all included in the sample application that accompanies this chapter. You can download the sample application from the Wrox Press website, at http://www.wrox.com.

The SqlConnection Class

The `SqlConnection` object is analogous to the traditional ADO connection object, in that it manages a connection to a data source.

Here is an example of how the `SqlConnection` object connects to the Northwind database:

```
Imports System.Data.SqlClient

Dim sqlConn As System.Data.SqlClient.SqlConnection
Dim strConn As String

strConn = "Data Source=SVR1\SVR1_SQL1;Initial Catalog=Northwind;User ID=sa;"
sqlConn = New SqlConnection(strConn)

sqlConn.Open()
```

This listing specifies the fully qualified namespace for the `SqlConnection` namespace, but you don't actually need it. Instead, it is sufficient to just specify the class name.

An alternative way to initialize a connection object is to dimension and initialize it in a single line of code, as in:

```
Imports System.Data.SqlClient

Dim strConn As String
strConn = "Data Source=SVR1\SVR1_SQL1;Initial Catalog=Northwind;User ID=sa;"

Dim sqlConn As SqlConnection = New SqlConnection(strConn)

sqlConn.Open()
```

The `SqlConnection` class also initiates transactions, using its `BeginTransaction()` function. This function returns a `SqlTransaction` object, which represents the transaction, and allows you to complete, or cancel the transaction.

The SqlCommand Class

The `SqlCommand` object executes stored procedures and Transact-SQL statements against a data source. It is analogous to the ADO `Command` object. The `SqlCommand` object works in cooperation with the `SqlConnection` object to execute statements. It is very versatile, and will execute a number of different kinds of statements using dedicated methods including:

❑   `ExecuteReader` – Execute a query and build the results as a `DataReader` object

❑   `ExecuteNonQuery` – Execute a Transact-SQL statement and return the number of affected rows

❑   `ExecuteScalar` – Execute a query and return only the first column of the first row of the first resultset

❑   `ExecuteXmlReader` - Execute a query and build the results as an `XmlReader` object

The `SqlCommand`'s `New()` constructor creates and initializes an instance of a `SqlCommand` object. The `SqlCommand` constructor is said to be **overloaded**, meaning that it provides several versions of the same `New()` method. This concept will be very familiar to most object-oriented programmers, but less familiar to Visual Basic programmers.

There are four ways to construct and initialize a `SqlCommand` object:

❑   `New()` - Initializes a new instance of the `SqlCommand` class.

❑   `New(cmdText As String)` - The `cmdText` is the SQL Query.

❑   `New(cmdText As String, connection as System.Data.SqlClient.SqlConnection)`

❑   `New(cmdText As String, connection as System.Data.SqlClient.SqlConnection, transaction as System.Data.SqlClient.SqlTransaction)`

This enables you to choose the constructor that best suits the parameters that you want to use for initializing the `SqlCommand` object.

How is it possible to use different syntaxes for the same method? The `SqlCommand` class implements the `ISqlCommand` interface, which defines a set of members that the `SqlCommand` class provides. Object-oriented programming supports constructor overloading, as long as at least one interface member differs. That is, you can have several versions of the same method that are named the same, as long as at least one interface member is different. You don't have to worry about remembering the different versions, because Visual Studio.NET provides Intellisense guidance that describes how to construct the object. For example, Intellisense will provide you the four constructs for `SqlCommand` that are in the bullet list above.

An example of how to initialize a `SqlCommand` object that queries the Product table in the Northwind database can be written as:

```
Imports System.Data.SqlClient

Const strConn = "Data Source=SVR1\SVR1_SQL1;Initial Catalog=Northwind;" & _
                "User ID=sa;"
Const SQL_PRODUCTS = "SELECT * FROM Products"
```

```
Dim sqlConn As SqlConnection = New SqlConnection(strConn)
Dim sqlCmdProducts As SqlCommand = New SqlCommand(SQL_PRODUCTS, sqlConn)

' Open the connection
sqlConn.Open()
```

Alternatively, you can use the following, longer code listing to accomplish the same thing:

```
Imports System.Data.SqlClient

Const strConn = "Data Source=SVR1\SVR1_SQL1;Initial Catalog=Northwind;" & _
                "User ID=sa;"
Const SQL_PRODUCTS = "SELECT * FROM Products"

Dim sqlCmdProducts As SqlCommand

' Create and initialize a new connection object
Dim sqlConn As SqlConnection = New SqlConnection(strConn)

' Create a new command object
sqlCmd = New SqlCommand()

' Initialize the command object
With sqlCmd
    .Connection = sqlConn
    .CommandType = CommandType.Text
    .CommandText = SQL_PRODUCTS
End With

' Open the connection
sqlConn.Open()
```

It can get confusing if you are trying to find the "right" way to create a new instance of a `SqlCommand` object. The "right" method is the one that works best for your application, although I follow the rule of thumb that less code is always better.

Once you have initialized the `SqlCommand` object and are ready to execute a statement, you have a choice of approaches. These were outlined at the beginning of this section. They are: `ExecuteReader`, `ExecuteNonQuery`, `ExecuteScalar`, and `ExecuteXmlReader`.

For queries that return resultsets, you can populate a `DataReader` object:

```
Dim drResults As DataReader
drResults = sqlCmd.ExecuteReader()
```

Optionally, you can specify an enumerated `CommandBehavior` as an argument of the `ExecuteReader()` method. The `CommandBehavior` determines how the query is executed, which in turn impacts the effect of executing the query on the database. For example, `CommandBehavior.SequentialAccess` returns detailed sequential records, which may noticeably affect the database. `CommandBehavior.SchemaOnly` returns column information only, and does not affect the database. The `DataReader` object is discussed in further detail in the next section.

You can also run a query and build the resultset as an `XmlReader` object, which is the XML equivalent of a `DataReader` object. It provides fast, non-cached, forward-only access to an XML data stream. The `XMLReader` object may be used in place of the `DataReader` object if you need your data returned as an XML stream instead of as a recordset:

```
Dim xrReader As Xml.XmlReader
xrReader = sqlCmd.ExecuteXmlReader()
```

If you need to execute a Transact-SQL statement that does not return a resultset, then you can use the `ExecuteNonQuery()` method, as follows:

```
Dim intRowAffected As Integer
intRowAffected = sqlCmd.ExecuteNonQuery()
```

Finally, if you need to generate a set of records for editing, then you will need to load the resultset into a `DataSet` object. We discuss this later in the chapter, in the section on the `DataSet` object.

The SqlDataReader Class

The `SqlDataReader` object is an excellent option for quick access to a SQL Server data set. It provides a fast, forward-only, read-only data stream. Because the `SqlDataReader` is a stream, it will only provide data as long as the connection to the database remains open. This is an important aspect about using the `SqlDataReader` object that is not conveyed by many code examples. The `SqlDataReader` object is populated by the `SqlCommand` object's `ExecuteReader()` method.

The code listing below is taken from a WinForms application that retrieves a listing of countries from the Suppliers table in the Northwind database. This sample application is also available for download from the Wrox Press website. If you wish to start constructing this application as you read, then start by opening Visual Studio.NET and creating a new Visual Basic Windows Application, as shown in the figure below:

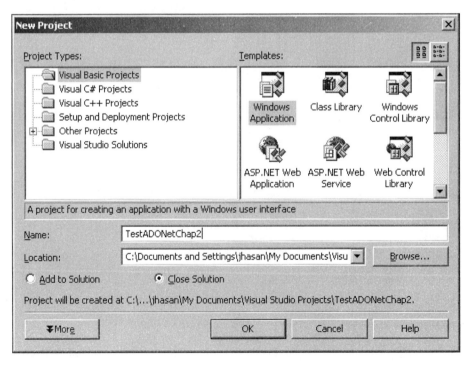

As we add windows controls and code to this application, the design view will develop into what you see in the figure below:

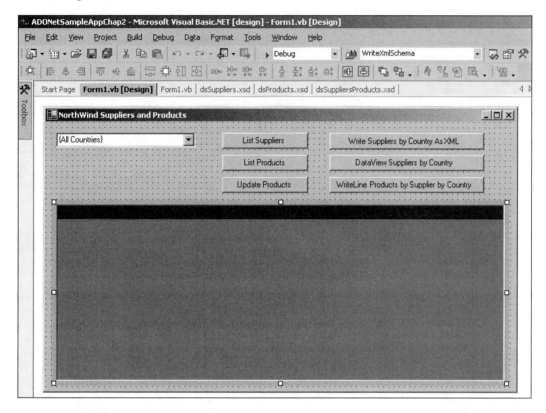

The initial sequence of the application is as follows:

1. The Windows Form loads, and the `Form_Load()` event calls the `FillComboBoxFromDataReader()` function, to populate a combo box on the form with a list of countries from the Suppliers table in the database.

2. This function, in turn, calls a helper function called `ListCountriesInDataReader()` that executes the `SqlCommand`, and builds the results into a `SqlDataReader`.

3. The list of countries is populated into the combo box on the form.

The code listing below shows the `FillComboBoxFromDataReader()` and `ListCountriesInDataReader()` functions:

```
Const SQL_CONNECTION = "Data Source=SQL1;Initial Catalog=Northwind;User ID=sa;"
Const SQL_COUNTRIES = "SELECT DISTINCT Suppliers.Country FROM Suppliers"

Private Function FillComboBoxFromDataReader()

    ' Purpose:  Populate the combo box with countries list, from a DataReader

    Dim sqlConn As SqlConnection        ' Form-level connection object
    Dim drCountries As SqlDataReader    ' Form-level DataReader object
```

```
        ' Create a new connection object
        sqlConn = New SqlConnection(SQL_CONNECTION)

        ' Load list of countries into the combo box, from the DataReader
        Call ListCountriesInDataReader(sqlConn, drCountries)

        ' Populate the combo box, cboCountries, with the DataReader output
        Do While drCountries.Read()
            ' Do something with the row
            cboCountries.Items.Add(drCountries.Item("Country").ToString())
        Loop

        ' Close DataReader and Connection objects
        drCountries.Close()

        ' Close the connection
        sqlConn.Close()

    End Function


    Public Function ListCountriesInDataReader(ByVal vSqlConn As _
        SqlClient.SqlConnection, _
            ByRef drResults As SqlClient.SqlDataReader)

        ' Purpose:  Return the Supplier Countries, in a DataReader

        Dim sqlCmd As SqlCommand
        Dim rowReader As SqlDataReader

        Try
            ' Create a new command object
            sqlCmd = New SqlCommand(SQL_COUNTRIES, vSqlConn)

            ' Open the connection, if required
            If vSqlConn.State = ConnectionState.Closed Then vSqlConn.Open()

            ' Execute the command and retrieve the records in the DataReader
            drResults = sqlCmd.ExecuteReader(CommandBehavior.SingleResult)

        Catch e As SqlException
            MsgBox("Error " & e.Number & ": " & e.Message & " [" & e.Source & "]")
        Finally
        ' You will get a DataReader error, if you close the connection
        'vSqlConn.Close() ' This line will break the function, if uncommented!
        End Try

    End Function
```

Notice the comment in the `Finally` block of the `ListCountriesInDataReader()` function: I've
added a line that closes the `SqlConnection` object that is passed into the function. This line is
commented out, because it would break the data stream and result in a null `SqlDataReader` being
passed back. This line is shown here as an example of what not to do.

The SqlDataAdapter Class

The `SqlDataAdapter` object provides a bridge between a SQL Server data source and a `DataSet`
object. The `DataSet` object has no knowledge of its underlying data source, so it relies on the
`SqlDataAdapter` object to synchronize `DataSet` changes back to the original data source.

An example of how to create a `SqlDataAdapter` object, and use it to populate a `DataSet` object, is shown in the code below:

```
Const SQL_ CONNECTION = "Data Source=SQL1;Initial Catalog=Northwind;User ID=sa;"
Const SQL_PRODUCTS = "SELECT * FROM Suppliers"

Public Function ListSuppliers() As DataSet

    ' Purpose:  Return list of Products, in a DataSet object

    Dim sqlConn As SqlConnection
    Dim sqlCmd As SqlCommand
    Dim sqlAdapt As SqlDataAdapter
    Dim rowDataSet As New DataSet()

    Try
        ' Create a new connection object
        sqlConn = New SqlConnection(SQL_CONNECTION)

        ' Create a new command object
        sqlCmd = New SqlCommand(SQL_SUPPLIERS, sqlConn)

        ' Open the connection
        sqlConn.Open()

        ' Open a DataAdapter object, using the command object
        sqlAdapt = New SqlDataAdapter(sqlCmd)

        ' Populate the DataSet from the DataAdapter
        Call sqlAdapt.Fill(rowDataSet, "Suppliers")

    Catch e As SqlException
        MsgBox("Error " & e.Number & ": " & e.Message & " [" & e.Source & "]")
    Finally
        sqlConn.Close()
    End Try

    Return (rowDataSet)

End Function
```

This code listing populates a list of suppliers from the Northwind database into a `DataSet`. Note that we close the `SqlConnection` object in the `Finally` block of the function. We can do this with a `DataSet`, but not with a `DataReader`, because, as said previously, it would interrupt the stream of data. The `DataSet` object, however, is disconnected from the underlying data source, and does not require a persistent database connection.

You may wonder why the class name for a `DataSet` object in this listing is not preceded by a "Sql" prefix, as are the other objects. This is because the `DataSet` class is a member of the `System.Data` namespace, not a member of the `System.Data.SqlClient` (Managed Provider) namespace. The `DataSet` class can be used with any managed provider.

The SqlException Class

The .NET Framework provides structured error handling that captures information about unexpected situations during execution. The `SqlException` class is created whenever the SQL Server .NET Data Provider encounters an unexpected data access issue. The `SqlException` class contains a collection of `SqlError` objects, one for each exception that can be encountered. The .NET Exception classes provide a wealth of useful information about errors and how they originate. You can even use the `Exception` class to access the call stack leading up to the exception.

In situations where you may expect to see errors, you should structure your code within `Try... Catch... Finally` code blocks, as shown here:

```
Dim sqlConn As New SqlConnection(strConnectionString)

Try
    SqlConn.Open()
Catch e As SqlException
    Dim colErrors As SqlErrorCollection = e.Errors
    Dim i As Integer
    For i = 0 To colErrors.Count
        Console.WriteLine("Error #" & e.Number & "[" & e.Source & "] " & _
                e.Message & ControlChars.CrLf & "Raised from stack trace: " & _
        e.StackTrace)
    Next
Finally
    SqlConn = Nothing
End Try
```

Here is the error that I raised from `ListSuppliers()`, after intentionally setting the table source name to `SUPPLIERS2`, which does not exist:

```
Error #208[SQL Server Managed Provider] Invalid object name 'SUPPLIERS2'.
Raised from stack trace:
at System.Data.SqlClient.SqlCommand.ExecuteReader(CommandBehavior cmdBehavior,
    RunBehavior runBehavior, Boolean returnStream)
at System.Data.SqlClient.SqlCommand.System.Data.IDbCommand.ExecuteReader(
    CommandBehavior behavior)
at System.Data.Common.DbDataAdapter.Fill(Object data, Int32 startRecord,
    Int32 maxRecords, String srcTable, IDbCommand command, CommandBehavior
    behavior)
at System.Data.Common.DbDataAdapter.Fill(DataSet dataSet, Int32 startRecord,
    Int32 maxRecords, String srcTable, IDbCommand command, CommandBehavior
    behavior)
at System.Data.Common.DbDataAdapter.Fill(DataSet dataSet, String srcTable)
at TestADONetChap2.Form1.ListSuppliers() in C:\Documents and Settings\jhasan\
    My Documents\Visual Studio Projects\TestADONetChap2\Form1.vb:line 456
```

In summary, you should always use structured error handling in your database access code, because database access is inherently error-prone, and it's important to capture errors in a meaningful way.

The DataSet Object

The `DataSet` object has already been discussed previously in Chapter 1. It is the important second layer of the ADO.NET object model and the one where most of the actual data manipulation takes place. As we discussed earlier, the `DataSet` object is populated using a `DataAdapter` object in the managed provider. The `DataSet` can be modified, then the changes committed to the original data source via the `DataAdapter` object's `Update` method.

The `DataSet` object contains a collection of:

❑ **Tables** – Stored as a collection of `DataTable` objects, which in turn each hold collections of `DataColumn` and `DataRow` objects. The `DataColumn` objects allow you to view and edit data schema information. The actual data is stored in the `DataRow` objects, which can be added to, edited and filtered.

❑ **Relationships** – Stored as a collection of `DataRelation` objects that describe the relationships between tables, much like a SQL JOIN statement does. The `DataRelation` object tracks the columns that relate the tables. The difference between a `DataRelation` object and a SQL JOIN statement is that the `DataTable` objects remain distinct, whereas a JOIN statement blends tables together in a view.

❑ **Constraints** – Includes the `UniqueConstraint` and `ForeignKeyConstraint` objects, which track the information that ensures data integrity.

The `DataSet` object provides several collections of object that provide access to data and schema information. These are shown in the figure below:

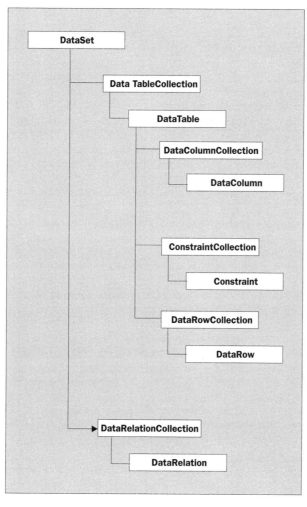

The `DataSet` object represents a significant advance in data access technology, because it is a virtual cache of a database, including not only data, but also schemas, relations, and constraints. The `DataSet` object is disconnected from the parent data source, so you effectively have full access to the data without needing a persistent connection to the data source. In fact, the `DataSet` object by design cannot have any knowledge of its underlying data source. The .NET Managed Provider objects manage the connection details for the `DataSet`.

Inevitably, you may be tempted to compare the ADO.NET DataSet object to the ADO Recordset. There are similarities in that both objects are data containers. But below the hood the similarities break down, because the DataSet object is structured very differently and provides richer functionality. The ADO Recordset is tightly bound to the underlying database, and in a sense it looks very much like the data entity that it represents. For example, an ADO Recordset is typically bound to one or more joined tables, and the fields in the Recordset appear just as they would in the underlying tables. The DataSet object, however, is disconnected from the underlying data source. The DataSet object provides database-like storage of the data, where the integrity of the underlying data is strictly enforced. It will support flexible data views, but it will not actually store the data in a blended set of columns. The DataSet object preserves the integrity and schema of the underlying data while providing flexible views of the data. It even includes a collection of dedicated DataView objects for storing multiple views of the same data set.

The DataSet object is structured very efficiently. A DataSet object may hold several resultsets at once. For example, you could query the Supplier table *and* the Products table, and hold both resultsets in the same DataSet at the same time. A separate DataTable object in the Tables collection would represent each table. The Columns collection represents the data schema, while the Rows collection represents the actual data. Each DataColumn in the Columns collection represents a different field in the data schema. And each DataRow in the Rows collection represents a different record of data. This is a departure from what ADO developers are familiar with. In ADO, the Recordset object provides a collection of Field objects that hold both the schema information and the actual data values. In ADO.NET, the schema information has been broken out from the data values, and is represented by different collections of objects.

A typical usage scenario for the DataSet object would include the following:

1. Open a connection to a data source using the .NET Managed Provider.

2. Create a new DataSet, then populate it with a set of records using the Fill() method of the DataAdapter object. A single DataSet may hold data from several database tables.

3. Manipulate data and schema information in the DataSet. For example, editing values, and adding additional table columns, and additional relations between tables.

4. Examine the DataSet for errors due to data changes. For example, if a field is set to a value that is not consistent with the field's data type, then the DataSet object's HasErrors property will equal true. In this case, you need to examine each DataTable object's HasErrors property, and then drill down to the RowError property of each row, to determine the specific error.

5. Persist the data changes back to the parent data source by calling the Update() method on the DataAdapter object. Updates may only be persisted once the DataSet object's HasErrors property is false.

One of the most exciting features of the DataSet object is its ability to serialize to XML data documents. The DataSet object provides ReadXML and WriteXML methods for serializing to XML data documents. These methods transfer both data and schema information. You can also call the WriteXmlSchema method, if schema information is all that you are interested in.

Finally, as discussed in Chapter 1, ADO.NET supports the **typed dataset**. This is a great new feature that will spare us the ambiguity of index-based recordset retrieval that exists in ADO. Typed datasets are generated by the Visual Studio .NET Data Designer, via the XSD.exe tool that is provided with the .NET Framework SDK. Typed datasets are subclassed DataSet objects that have a specific database schema coded directly into the class. This prevents any ambiguity in referencing data sets, because the object has an intrinsic knowledge of the dataset's schema. Typed datasets provide cleaner, more readable code, and enable type checking at compile time. They also prevent avoidable errors caused by misspelling field names.

To illustrate, here is how you might access a field using an untyped ADO.NET DataSet:

```
myID = ds.Tables("Employees").Rows(0)("EmployeeID")
```

With typed datasets, they syntax changes to:

```
myID = ds.Employees(0).EmployeeID
```

In summary, the DataSet object represents a new kind of data container, one that is a disconnected, virtual cache of a data store. The DataSet object has certain similarities with the ADO Recordset object, but overall it is a very different kind of object. Newcomers to .NET are initially perplexed that the Recordset object, as we know it, no longer exists in ADO.NET. The DataSet object is not the next version of the ADO Recordset; instead, it is a replacement.

Overview of the System.Data Namespace

The DataSet class and all of its collection classes are members of the System.Data namespace. The important class members of this namespace are shown in the table below:

Class Member	Description
Constraint	Represents a constraint that can be enforced on one or more DataColumn objects.
ConstraintCollection	Represents a collection of constraints for a DataTable.
DataColumn	Represents one column of data in a DataTable.
DataColumnCollection	Represents a collection of DataColumn objects for a DataTable.
DataException	Represents the exception that is thrown when errors are generated using ADO.NET components.
DataRelation	Represents a parent/child relationship between two tables.

Table continued on following page

Class Member	Description
DataRelationCollection	Represents the collection of relations, each of which allows navigation between related parent/child tables.
DataRow	Represents a row of data in a DataTable.
DataRowCollection	Represents a collection of rows for a DataTable.
DataSet	Represents an in-memory cache of data.
DataTable	Represents one table of in-memory data.
DataTableCollection	Represents the collection of tables for the DataSet.
DataView	Represents a data-bindable, customized view of a DataTable for sorting, filtering, searching, editing, and navigation.

Again, there are many other class members in this namespace, but this table only highlights the most important class members for this chapter. In addition, the namespace supports an extensive number of interfaces and enumerations. We have already encountered the CommandBehavior enumeration, which is used by the SqlCommand class for specifying how to retrieve data directly.

ADO.NET Integration with XML

ADO.NET provides extended support for XML using the classes in the .NET Framework's System.Xml namespace. ADO.NET will generate industry-standard XML that is suitable for any client or consumer capable of working with XML. The .NET Framework implements the XML DOM, to provide access to data in XML documents, as well as classes for reading, writing and navigating XML documents. The System.Xml namespace contains classes that combine the XML DOM with ADO.NET data access services. This includes a special class called the XmlDataDocument, which is a subset of the XML DOM that holds relational data. The XmlDataDocument allows the ADO.NET DataSet object to map relational data out to XML, and vice versa. ADO.NET can also map out schema information only, using the XML Schema Definition language (XSD).

The XmlDataDocument is suitable for storing relational data, but this is not the only kind of data that a DataSet object can hold. The DataSet object will also serialize to a standard XML document. The System.XML namespace provides several classes for processing XML documents and streams. The XmlTextReader class, for example, is the XML equivalent to the ADO.NET DataReader object. It provides a fast, non-cached stream of XML data. The DataSet object will serialize to an XML document, or output stream, which can in turn be picked up by the XMLTextReader class, and streamed out to the consumer.

We will look at some specific examples of how ADO.NET serializes to XML later in this chapter. Before we get to examples, it's important to cover more details about the .NET Framework's XML capabilities.

Overview of the System.Xml Namespace

The System.Xml classes provide object-oriented access to the XML Document Object Model (DOM). This namespace provides classes to support every aspect of an XML document, from the header, to the elements and attributes, to the values. The XML classes support a number of XML industry standards, including:

❑ XML 1.0 - http://www.w3.org/TR/1998/REC-xml-19980210 - including DTD support (XmlTextReader)

❑ XML Namespaces - http://www.w3.org/TR/REC-xml-names/ - both stream level and DOM.

❑ XML Schemas - http://www.w3.org/TR/xmlschema-1/ - supported for schema mapping, and serialization, but not yet for validation (see also XmlSchemaCollection which currently provides XDR schema validation)

❑ XPath expressions - http://www.w3.org/TR/xpath (XmlNavigator)

❑ XSL/T transformations - http://www.w3.org/TR/xslt (XslTransform)

❑ DOM Level 2 Core - http://www.w3.org/TR/DOM-Level-2/ - for (XmlDocument)

❑ SOAP 1.1 - http://msdn.microsoft.com/xml/general/soapspec.asp (including the Soap Contract Language and Soap Discovery) used in XML object serialization.

The important class members of the System.Xml namespace are listed shown below:

Class Member	Description
XmlDataDocument	Allows structured data to be stored, retrieved, and manipulated through a relational DataSet.
XmlDocument	Represents an XML document.
XmlDeclaration	Represents the XML declaration node: `<?xml version='1.0' ...?>`.
XmlAttribute	Represents an XML attribute.
XmlElement	Represents an XML element.
XmlNode	Represents a single node in the document. This class is abstract and is inherited by other classes that work with nodes.
XmlReader	Represents a reader that provides fast, non-cached forward only access to XML data. This class is abstract, and is inherited by other XML reader classes.
XmlTextReader	Represents a reader that provides fast, non-cached forward only access to XML data.

Table continued on following page

53

Class Member	Description
XmlNodeReader	Represents a reader that provides fast, non-cached forward only access to XML data in an XmlNode.
XmlWriter	Represents a writer that provides fast non-cached forward-only way of generating streams or files containing XML data that conform to the W3C Extensible Markup Language (XML) 1.0 specification and the Namespaces in XML specification. This class is abstract, and is inherited by the XmlTextWriter class.
XmlTextWriter	Represents a writer that provides fast non-cached forward-only way of generating streams or files containing XML data that conform to the W3C Extensible Markup Language (XML) 1.0 specification and the Namespaces in XML specification.

The System.Xml namespace contains many more classes than are shown here with this table only highlighting the classes that are most relevant to the current discussion.

XML Schema Reference (XSD)

The XML Schema Definition language (XSD) describes data schemas in XML. An XSD schema defines elements, attributes, and data types that make up the schema. The data types are used to describe the values and ranges (if applicable) for the elements and attributes in the schema. XSD supports built-in types such as integers and strings, but it also lets you define custom types. Basically, there are two different types:

- ❑ **Simple types** – A single text value for an element or attribute. It cannot contain other elements or attributes.

- ❑ **Complex types** – A compound type definition for an element or attribute that contains other elements or attributes.

We saw an example of a complex type in Chapter 1. Recall that we loaded a set of joined tables from the Northwind database into a DataSet object, and then used the XML Data Designer to generate an XSD schema. The joined tables were Employees, Orders, and Order Subtotals. The purpose was to display all orders by sales employee. The fields in the joined tables combine to make up the Employees complex type. So any element that conforms to the Employees complex type must contain values for EmployeeID, LastName, FirstName, Country, OrderID, SaleAmount, and ShippedDate.

Now let's look at some specific examples of how ADO.NET serializes to XML.

How ADO.NET Serializes to XML

The `XmlDataDocument` class allows structured, relational data to be stored, retrieved, and manipulated through a `DataSet` class. The `DataSet` class maps to the `XmlDataDocument` class, and vice versa. The example below shows how to map a `DataSet` out to an `XmlDataDocument`:

```
' Open a DataAdapter object, using the command object
sqlAdapt = New SqlDataAdapter(sqlCmd)

' Populate the DataSet from the DataAdapter
Call sqlAdapt.Fill(rowDataSet, "Suppliers")

'Load the document with the DataSet.
Dim doc As XmlDataDocument = New XmlDataDocument(rowDataSet)
```

The `XmlDataDocument` constructor accepts a `DataSet` object, which in this case contains a list of suppliers from the `Northwind` database. Once you have loaded up the document you can either read it, or write it out to a specified format.

The `XmlDataDocument` class provides an overloaded `Save()` method to persist XML as:

❑   `Save(filename As String)` – The location of the file where you want to save the document

❑   `Save(outStream As System.IO.Stream)` – The output stream to which you want to save

❑   `Save(writer As System.IO.TextWriter)` – The `TextWriter` to which you want to save

❑   `Save(writer As System.Xml.XmlWriter)` – The `XmlWriter` to which you want to save

For example, to stream the `XmlDataDocument` out to the console window:

```
'Load the document with the DataSet.
Dim doc As XmlDataDocument = New XmlDataDocument(rowDataSet)

'Display the XmlDataDocument.
doc.Save(Console.Out)
```

A portion of the output will look like this:

```
<NewDataSet>
  <Suppliers>
    <SupplierID>7</SupplierID>
    <CompanyName>Pavlova, Ltd.</CompanyName>
    <ContactName>Ian Devling</ContactName>
    <ContactTitle>Marketing Manager</ContactTitle>
    <Address>74 Rose St. Moonie Ponds</Address>
    <City>Melbourne</City>
    <Region>Victoria</Region>
    <PostalCode>3058</PostalCode>
    <Country>Australia</Country>
    <Phone>(03) 444-2343</Phone>
    <Fax>(03) 444-6588</Fax>
  </Suppliers>
  <Suppliers>
    <SupplierID>8</SupplierID>
    <CompanyName>Specialty Biscuits, Ltd.</CompanyName>
    <ContactName>Peter Wilson</ContactName>
```

```
    <ContactTitle>Sales Representative</ContactTitle>
    <Address>29 King's Way</Address>
    <City>Manchester</City>
    <PostalCode>M14 GSD</PostalCode>
    <Country>UK</Country>
    <Phone>(161) 555-4448</Phone>
  </Suppliers>
</NewDataSet>
```

You can get the same result by calling the `DataSet` object's `WriteXml()` method, as in:

```
' Write out an XML data file
rowDataSet.WriteXml("c:\Suppliers.xml")
```

You can also write out the `DataSet` object's schema information only, as an XSD file, using the `DataSet` object's `WriteXmlSchema()` method, as in:

```
' Write out an XML Schema Definition file
rowDataSet.WriteXmlSchema("c:\Suppliers.xsd")
```

With output like:

```
<?xml version="1.0" standalone="yes"?>
<xsd:schema id="NewDataSet" targetNamespace="" xmlns=""
xmlns:xsd="http://www.w3.org/2001/XMLSchema" xmlns:msdata="urn:schemas-microsoft-
com:xml-msdata">
  <xsd:element name="NewDataSet" msdata:IsDataSet="true">
    <xsd:complexType>
      <xsd:choice maxOccurs="unbounded">
      <xsd:element name="Suppliers">
        <xsd:complexType>
          <xsd:sequence>
            <xsd:element name="SupplierID" type="xsd:int" minOccurs="0" />
            <xsd:element name="CompanyName" type="xsd:string" minOccurs="0" />
            <xsd:element name="ContactName" type="xsd:string" minOccurs="0" />
            <xsd:element name="ContactTitle" type="xsd:string" minOccurs="0" />
            <xsd:element name="Address" type="xsd:string" minOccurs="0" />
            <xsd:element name="City" type="xsd:string" minOccurs="0" />
            <xsd:element name="Region" type="xsd:string" minOccurs="0" />
            <xsd:element name="PostalCode" type="xsd:string" minOccurs="0" />
            <xsd:element name="Country" type="xsd:string" minOccurs="0" />
            <xsd:element name="Phone" type="xsd:string" minOccurs="0" />
            <xsd:element name="Fax" type="xsd:string" minOccurs="0" />
            <xsd:element name="HomePage" type="xsd:string" minOccurs="0" />
          </xsd:sequence>
        </xsd:complexType>
      </xsd:element>
      </xsd:choice>
    </xsd:complexType>
  </xsd:element>
</xsd:schema>
```

A significant limitation in the generated XSD file with Visual Studio.NET Beta 2 was data that relations were not written out to the XSD file. This would include, for example, the relation between the `Suppliers` and `Products` tables, based on the `SupplierID` field. This issue should be resolved in the release version of Visual Studio.NET. The XML Data Designer allows you to customize the XSD file as needed, like the following outline of an XSD schema that could define the relationship between the `Suppliers` and `Products` tables:

```
              <xsd:element name="Suppliers">
                <xsd:complexType content="elementOnly">
                <xsd:all>
              ' Element names go here
                </xsd:all>
                </xsd:complexType>
              </xsd:element>
              <xsd:element name="Products">
                <xsd:complexType content="elementOnly">
                <xsd:all>
              ' Element names go here
                </xsd:all>
                </xsd:complexType>
              </xsd:element>
              <xsd:keyref name="SuppliersProducts" refer="Constraint1">
                <xsd:selector>.</xsd:selector>
                <xsd:field>SupplierID</xsd:field>
              </xsd:keyref>
```

The primary advantage of persisting data as XML is that you can pass XML files very easily between disconnected components, such as Web Services, or between different tiers in a web application. We've discussed how a DataSet object serializes out to XML, but how about in? As you would expect, it is very easy to load up an XML document into a DataSet object with the primary methods being:

❑   ReadXml – Reads an XML file into a DataSet

❑   ReadXmlSchema – Reads an XSD file into a DataSet

Let's look at an example of how to read an XSD schema into a new DataSet object:

```
' Read the XML Schema Definition back in to a DataSet

' Create a new dataset
Dim dsSuppliersProducts As New DataSet("SuppliersProducts")

' Open a new filestream object, to open the XML file
Dim fsReadXml As New System.IO.FileStream("c:\SuppliersProducts.xsd", _
    IO.FileMode.Open)

' Create an XMLTextReader object, to read the XML
Dim fsXmlReader As New System.Xml.XmlTextReader(fsReadXml)

' Read the XSD document into the DataSet
dsSuppliersProducts.ReadXml(fsXmlReader)

' Close the XML Text Reader
fsXmlReader.Close()

' Write the XSD to the console window
Console.WriteLine(dsSuppliersProducts.GetXmlSchema())
```

Conversely, the DataSet class provides two methods that automatically output its data and schema as string representations of the XML and XSD, which are:

❑   GetXml – Returns the XML representation of the data stored in the DataSet

❑   GetXmlSchema - Returns the XSD schema for the XML representation of the data stored in the DataSet

The last line of the above code listing uses the `GetXmlSchema()` method to output the XSD schema to the console window.

This concludes our discussion of how ADO.NET integrates with XML. For more information on how to work with XML and XSD, you can consult the Visual Studio.NET Online Help for the `System.XML` namespace. Also, Chapters 13 and 14 in this book delve further into XML and XSD.

COM Interoperability

We saw in Chapter 1 that we can access Com objects from .NET. Let's take a brief look at how to import the ADO type library.

Open up a new project in Visual Studio.NET, select the **Project | Add Reference** menu option, then switch to the **COM** tab and select the ADO type library from the list of available COM+ objects, as shown in the figure below:

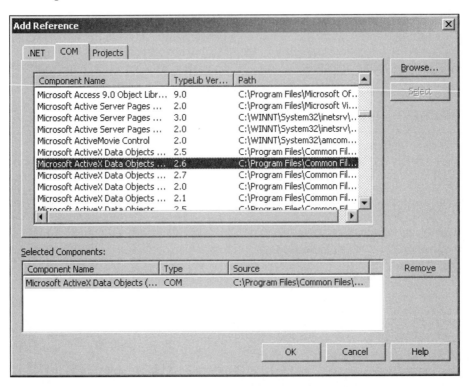

Next, Visual Studio will notify us with a message box that it could not locate the wrapper for this COM+ object, and will ask if we want to generate one. Click **OK** and the wrapper will be generated. From this point on, the ADO classes are available to us, just like native ADO.NET classes. For example, the following code illustrates how we would create and populate an ADO recordset object in Visual Basic.NET:

```
Private Sub LegacyADOExample()

    ' This example is provided for illustrative purposes only.
    ' You will need to generate an ADO .NET wrapper for this code to be valid.
```

```
      Dim adoConn As New ADODB.Connection()
      Dim adoCmd As New ADODB.Command()
      Dim adoRS As New ADODB.Recordset()

      adoConn.ConnectionString = "Data Source=ZORC1\ZORC1_SQL1; " & _
          "Initial Catalog=Northwind;User ID=sa;"
      adoCmd.ActiveConnection = adoConn
      adoCmd.CommandText = "SELECT * FROM Suppliers"
      adoCmd.CommandType = ADODB.CommandTypeEnum.adCmdText

      adoRS.Open(adoCmd, adoConn, ADODB.CursorTypeEnum.adOpenForwardOnly, _
          ADODB.LockTypeEnum.adLockReadOnly)

      Do While Not adoRS.EOF
          ' Work with recordset here
      Loop
  End Sub
```

The Visual Studio.NET Server Explorer

The Server Explorer is an amazing new graphical interface for accessing and manipulating system resources on any accessible server on your network. It looks similar to the tree-view of Microsoft Management Console (MMC) snap-ins. The Server Explorer is very versatile, especially for data access. It provides functionality that is similar to the SQL Server 2000 Enterprise Manager, such as the ability to browse databases, and to execute stored-procedures from a graphical interface. The Server Explorer enable automatic code generation for a number of resources, including database and messaging resources. You can drag and drop resources from the Server Explorer onto your code designer, and the IDE will automatically generate components and/or code for that resource.

The Server Explorer allows you to do the following:

- ❑ Open data connections to SQL Servers and other databases and explore their contents

- ❑ Execute stored procedures

- ❑ Log on to servers and display their databases and system resources, including:

    - ❑ Event Logs

    - ❑ Loaded Modules

    - ❑ Message Queues

    - ❑ Performance Counters

    - ❑ Processes

    - ❑ Services

    - ❑ SQL Servers

    - ❑ Web Services

- ❑ View information about available Web Services, including their interfaces

- ❑ Drag resources from Server Explorer into a Visual Studio.NET project. This enables the project to reference the resource and add programming code around it

The figure below shows an example of the Server Explorer, with selected nodes expanded:

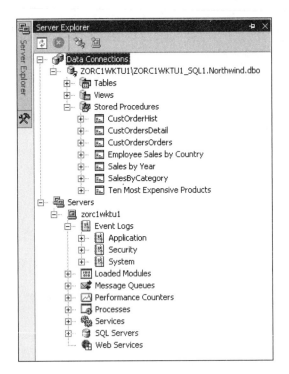

The resources in the Server Explorer are referred to as nodes. The top-level nodes are SQL Servers and Enterprise Servers. Each top-level node has child nodes. The top-level SQL Server node, for example, has child nodes that show tables, views, and stored procedures for the selected SQL Server.

Using the Server Explorer for Data Access

The Server Explorer provides a number of useful features for data access.

Running Stored Procedures

You can run stored procedures directly from the Server Explorer in order to preview the resultset. Essentially, you are seeing a preview of the data that the stored procedure provides. Visual Studio.NET provides an Output window in the IDE that is similar to the Immediate window, except that it is dedicated entirely to output parameters.

For example, switch over to the Server Explorer and expand the Data Connections top-level node. Expand the Northwind database node, and then expand its Stored Procedures child node. Next, right-click on the "Ten Most Expensive Products" stored procedure and select "Run Stored Procedure" from the pop-up menu. Finally, switch over to the Output window in Visual Studio.NET's IDE, and you should see the results of the stored procedure, as:

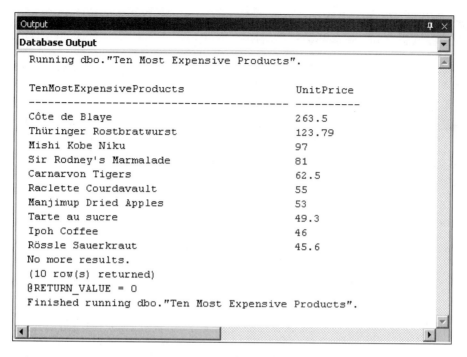

You can also run parameterized stored procedures from the Server Explorer. For example, right-click click on the "Sales by Year" stored procedure, and select "Run Stored Procedure". You will get a pop-up window for entering in the parameters, like the one below:

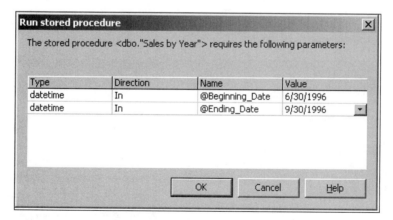

Click OK, and the results will show in the IDE's Output window.

Adding Items from Server Explorer to the Visual Studio.NET IDE

You can drag and drop selected items from the Server Explorer to Visual Studio.NET designers, then program against them. For example, you can drag a SQL Server data connection from the Server Explorer to a Form designer in Visual Studio.NET. The IDE will automatically create a new SQL connection called SqlConnection1 (if this is the first data connection in the project). You can then select the newly created SQL connection and view its Property sheet, to verify that the settings have been configured correctly:

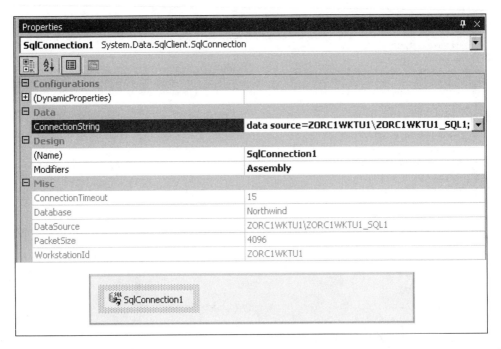

Similarly, you can drag and drop a stored procedure from the Server Explorer into the designer. This will create a new `SqlConnection` object for the connection, and a new `SqlCommand` object for the stored procedure. There is no actual code generated, but these objects are immediately available to program around, which will save you time.

The figure below shows the results of dropping the "Sales by Year" parameterized stored procedure from the Server Explorer onto the designer:

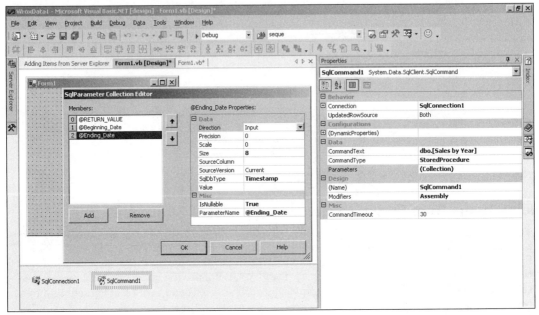

The parameters may be set at runtime, or, you can set them at design time by clicking on **Parameters |
Collection...** in the `SqlCommand1` property sheet. This brings up the floating window that you see in the
figure above.

Summary

To summarize the important points about ADO.NET:

❑ ADO.NET is the .NET Framework's new data access technology.

❑ ADO.NET leverages many benefits of the .NET Framework, including type safety, memory
management, exception handling, and a rich set of extensible base classes.

❑ ADO.NET is optimized for disconnected data access. It provides a disconnected `DataSet`
object for in-memory caching and editing of data. It provides a fast, lightweight `DataReader`
object to stream data.

❑ ADO.NET is tightly integrated with XML.

❑ Visual Studio.NET provides excellent RAD support for distributed architecture, disconnected
data access and XML.

ADO.NET is a flexible, functional, efficient data access technology. The Internet has changed the data
access needs that applications have. Distributed architecture is replacing client/server architecture, and
applications must increasingly integrate data from heterogeneous sources. XML has emerged as the
universal data format for data exchange, and applications must increasingly be able to collaborate and
exchange data quickly and seamlessly. ADO.NET helps meet the challenge of providing data access for the
next generation of applications.

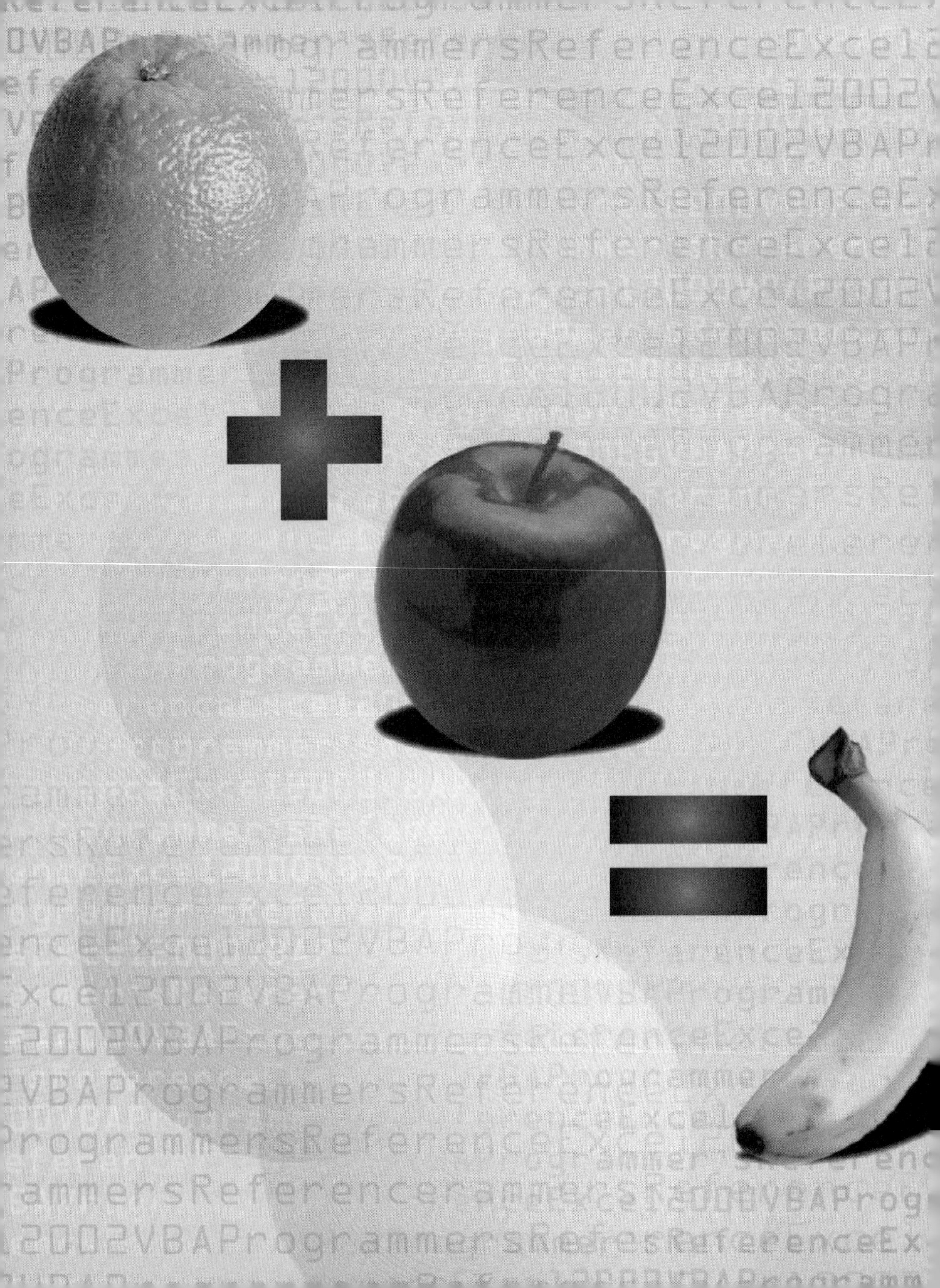

3

The Connection Object

Introduction

The ADO.NET `Connection` object links the data consumer to the data provider. The `Connection` represents a unique session on the provider's database. Other objects, such as the `Command objects`, use the `Connection` object to perform operations on the database. There are three types of `Connection` object: `SqlConnection` for accessing Microsoft SQL Server 7.0 and higher; `OdbcConnection` for using ODBC data sources; and `OleDbConnection` for connecting to all other OLE DB database sources.

Generally the connection is constructed, used and released in the following way:

- ❏ The object is instantiated using its constructor or implicitly using `Command` or `DataAdapter` objects
- ❏ Instructions for establishing the connection are provided as the `ConnectionString`
- ❏ The `Open` method establishes the connection defined by `ConnectionString`
- ❏ Operations are performed with the data
- ❏ The connection is closed using the `Close` method
- ❏ If required, a new connection is established by providing a new `ConnectionString` and calling the `Open` method again
- ❏ `Close` or `Dispose` is called before the object is discarded

The `ConnectionString` provides instructions for *establishing* the connection, it cannot be changed after the connection has been established.

The `Connection` object can be constructed explicitly using `new`, or implicitly through an object that uses a connection, such as the `OleDbCommand`/`SqlCommand` objects. Even if created implicitly the `Connection` object still behaves in the same manner, requiring the same connection string and exception handling. This chapter will show how to create and use the connection object to connect to a variety of data sources.

IDbConnection

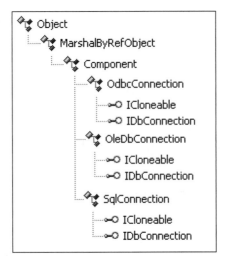

OdbcConnection, OleDbConnection, and SqlConnection implement the IDbConnection interface. This interface defines a contract of methods and properties necessary to implement a connection to a data service provider, and is implemented by .NET data providers that access relational databases. By implementing IDbConnection, database vendors could provide their own implementation of a Connection specific to their products' requirements. Vendors can also provide ODBC or OLE DB drivers however to enable data access using ADO.NET objects.

Required Namespaces

To use a particular Connection object, it is necessary to add the namespaces as follows:

```
VB:
Imports System.Data.SqlClient ' When using SqlConnection
Imports System.Data.OleDb     ' When using OleDbConnection
Imports System.Data.Odbc      ' When using OdbcConnection


C#:
using System.Data.SqlClient;  // When using SqlConnection
using System.Data.OleDb;      // When using OleDbConnection
using System.Data.Odbc;       // When using OdbcConnection
```

When working with console applications or projects where the connection object has not been added to the project from the form designer's toolbar, you may also need to add the System.Data or System.Data.Odbc Reference to the project. To do this, select Project | Add Reference. Select System.Data.dll or System.Data.Odbc.dll, then Select and OK. Of course, if you are only using Sql, then only import SqlClient, and vice versa.

Construction

Creates and initializes a new instance of the `Connection` object. If a string is provided it is parsed and assigned to the `ConnectionString`.

```
VB:
Public Sub New()
Public Sub New(ByVal connectionString As String)


C#:
public OleDbConnection();
public OleDbConnection(string connectionString);
public SqlConnection();
public SqlConnection(string connectionString);
```

Parameter	Type	Description
connectionString	String	The connection string to use when Open is called. This string defines how and where the connection is made. It is defined in more detail in the following sections.

It is not necessary to provide a connection string during construction. However, the connection string must be provided before `Open` is called. If a connection string is provided it does not automatically open the connection. Although the constructor does not connect to the data source, it can still raise an `ArgumentException` if the connection string given could not be parsed correctly or had invalid parameters.

In the following sections references to `ConnectionString` apply to either the object's `ConnectionString` property, or the string provided at instantiation.

Visual Construction

You can also use the form designer to create the connection object. In this example we will add a `SqlConnection` called `m_sqlConn` to our form:

- ❑ In the form designer view, open the **Toolbox**.
- ❑ Select the **Data** tab.
- ❑ Select and drag the `SqlConnection` icon to the form:

❑ The object will be placed in an area below the form and named `sqlConnection1`.

❑ Right click on this object and select properties:

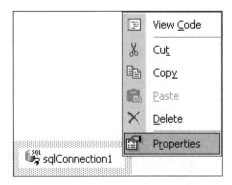

❑ As this is a class member change the (Name) to m_sqlConn.

❑ Highlight the `ConnectionString` cell and select **<New Connection...>** from the drop list.

❑ First specify the server name and choose a security authentication method.

❑ If security is set correctly you will be able to select the database on the server. If you have trouble, see Chapter 16 – Permissions for setting the correct access modes.

❑ Test the connection with the **Test Connection** button then choose **OK** to finish:

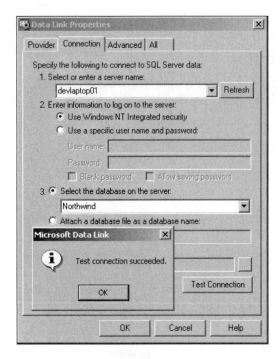

This will automatically add the code to the form. A private class attribute should have been added as:

```
VB:
Me.m_sqlConn = New System.Data.SqlClient.SqlConnection()
```

```
C#:
private System.Data.SqlClient.SqlConnection m_sqlConn;
```

The new attribute is initialized in `InitializeComponent` as:

```
VB:
'
'm_sqlConn
'
Me.m_sqlConn.ConnectionString = "data source=devlaptop01;" & _
        "initial catalog=Northwind;" & _
        "integrated security=SSPI;persist security info=False;" & _
        "workstation id=PPRO200DOTNET;packet size=4096"
```

```
C#:
//
// m_sqlConn
//
this.m_sqlConn.ConnectionString = "data source=devlaptop01; "+
        "initial catalog=Northwind;"+
        "integrated security=SSPI;persist security info=False; "+
        "user id=devlaptop01\\devadmin;workstation id=PPRO200DOTNET; "+
        "packet size=4096";
```

To use the `m_sqlConn` object simply call the `Open` method to connect to the database. Note that visual creation of the `Connection` object is only possible when the connection is associated with a form. Console applications do not have a form and so must add the member manually. Also note that when the object is added to the form its scope is throughout the class or module. If access is restricted to a single method then define the connection object manually within the method.

Instance Properties

The ConnectionString Property

Contains the details used to create a connection to a data source. It consists of a series of semi-colon delimitated parameters in the form `parameter name='parameter value';`.

```
VB:
Public Property ConnectionString As String
```

```
C#:
public string ConnectionString {get; set;}
```

The `ConnectionString` is parsed and placed in other properties such as `Provider` and `Database`. Limited verification is performed on the data when it is written to the string. Text placed in the constructor is also written into the `ConnectionString`. Connection values that have a default, such as `PacketSize` and `ConnectionTimeout`, are not shown in the connection string unless a value is written to the connection string to override the default.

Many of the `Connection` object's properties are read-only and provide information extracted from the connection string. These properties are set using `ConnectionString` prior to opening a connection. The following table details some of the more common connection string parameters with the name of their associated read-only `connection` object property:

Parameter	Description	Object Property
Provider	The name of the OLE DB provider. See the `Provider` property for more information and examples. This is not used for `SqlConnection` objects.	Provider
Data Source or DSN	The name of the data source. Usually this is a file or machine name. See the `DataSource` property for more information.	DataSource
User ID	User name to be used when accessing the data.	
Password	Password to be used with the User ID. Once `Open` is called the Password cannot be read back from the `ConnectionString` property.	
Mode	Does not apply to SQL Server connections. 1 = Read only 2 = Write 3 = Read / Write 4 = No others can open to Read 8 = No others can open to Write 12 = No others can open to Read or Write 16 = Access is not denied to others	
Connection Timeout	The amount of time in seconds to wait for `Open` to return a connection. See `ConnectionTimeout` property below for more details.	ConnectionTimeout
Initial Catalog or DBQ	The database or file opened to work with. See the `Database` property that follows for more details.	Database

Parameter	Description	Object Property
Packet Size	The number of bytes in the network packets sent and received from SQL Server. See `PacketSize` property for more details.	PacketSize
Workstation ID or WSID	Workstation name of the client machine. See `WorkstationId` property for details.	WorkstationId

The type of OLE DB provider used for the connection will determine what parameters should be used. In some cases these will include vendor specific parameters, for example the JET specific locking mode is represented by `"Jet OLEDB:Database Locking Mode=1;"`. At the very minimum a `Provider` must be given for `OleDbConnections` or a `Data Source` must be given for an `SqlConnection`.

If we need to change connection parameters it is necessary to close the connection (if open), change the connection string and reopen the connection to have the changes take effect.

> Note: The **ConnectionString** can only be written to when the connection is closed.

Most examples in this chapter show connection strings in the constructors, the following shows a simple read-only connection to a Microsoft Excel spreadsheet. Note that it is opened in read-only mode and extended properties are used to define the file format:

```vb
VB:
Dim oledbConn As OleDbConnection = New OleDbConnection()
oledbConn.ConnectionString = "Provider=Microsoft.Jet.OLEDB.4.0;" & _
                             "Data Source=C:\Data\TimeSheet.xls;Mode=1;" & _
                             "Extended Properties='Excel 8.0;';"
oledbConn.Open()
```

```csharp
C#:
OleDbConnection oledbConn = new OleDbConnection();
oledbConn.ConnectionString = "Provider=Microsoft.Jet.OLEDB.4.0;" +
                             "Data Source=C:\\Data\\TimeSheet.xls;Mode=1;" +
                             "Extended Properties='Excel 8.0;';";
oledbConn.Open();
```

The ConnectionTimeout Property

The length of time, in seconds, that the `Open` method will wait to complete before aborting the attempt and throwing an exception.

```vb
VB:
Public ReadOnly Property ConnectionTimeout As Integer
```

```csharp
C#:
public int ConnectionTimeout {get;}
```

71

The property is read-only and reflects either the `Connect Timeout` parameter given in the `ConnectionString`, or the default value of 15 seconds.

To set the `Connect Timeout` to 60 seconds, for example, insert the following into the `ConnectionString` property:

```
Connect Timeout=60;
```

This will make the `Open` method wait until the connection is opened or for 60 seconds, whichever is shortest. A `Connect Timeout` value of zero will cause `Open` to return only when it has connected, which may be never.

A higher `Connect Timeout` may be required when connecting over a slow or busy network to compensate for network latency.

The following example sets the `Connect Timeout` to 60 seconds and verifies it by writing it to the console:

```
VB:
Dim sqlConn As SqlConnection = New SqlConnection( _
        "data source=DevLaptop01;initial catalog=Northwind;" & _
        "integrated security=SSPI;Connect Timeout=60;")
Console.WriteLine("Timeout = " & sqlConn.ConnectionTimeout)
sqlConn.Open()          'Allow 60s for connection
```

```
C#:
SqlConnection sqlConn = new SqlConnection(
        "data source=DevLaptop01;initial catalog=Northwind;"+
        "integrated security=SSPI;Connect Timeout=60;" );
Console.WriteLine( "Timeout = {0}", sqlConn.ConnectionTimeout );
sqlConn.Open();         //Allow 60s for connection
```

The Database Property

Read-only property returning a string containing the database name used once the connection is open:

```
VB:
Public ReadOnly Property Database As String
```

```
C#:
public string Database {get;}
```

The default value is an empty string. A value isn't always needed to successfully read from a database. The value can be set in one of three ways:

❑ By providing a connection string in the Constructor using the keyword of `Initial catalog`. This will take effect only if `Open` is called successfully

❑ By populating the `ConnectionString` property with the keyword of `Initial catalog` and calling `Open`

❑ By calling `ChangeDatabase` with the new required database. It is not necessary to call `Open` after this. See the `ChangeDatabase` method for more information

Note: this property is not necessary in all connections. For example, if connecting to a Microsoft Excel spreadsheet or an Access database the Database property will be blank because `Data Source` alone defines the exact database.

The `ChangeDatabase` method example (later in this chapter) demonstrates opening the Northwind database and then changing to the BookStore database. The database is first set in the constructor, then changed in the `ChangeDatabase` method.

The Driver Property – Odbc only

Returns the name of the DLL used to provide the ODBC connection.

```
VB:
Public ReadOnly Property Driver As String
```

```
C#:
public string Driver {get;}
```

The `Driver` property is only set once `Open` has been successfully called. Prior to this it is empty. Some `OdbcConnection` strings and driver values follow:

Database	ConnectionString	Driver
SQL Server 2000	DSN=MySqlSystemDSN; DATABASE=Northwind;	SQLSRV32.DLL
Microsoft Access 2000	DSN=MS Access Database; DBQ=D:\Data\Northwind.mdb;	odbcjt32.dll
Microsoft Excel 2000	DSN=Excel Files; DBQ=C:\Managers.xls;	odbcjt32.dll
DBase files	DSN=dBase Files; DBQE=D:\\CS\\UNSTATUS.DBF;	odbcjt32.dll
FoxPro files	DSN=FoxPro Files - Word; DBQ=D:\\CS\\UNSTATUS.DBF;	VFPODBC.DLL

The DataSource Property

With `OleDbConnection`, sets the fully qualified machine name or path and file name pointing to the location of the data. With `SqlConnection`, sets the name of the SQL Server or SQL Server and Instance to which the connection is made.

```
VB:
Public ReadOnly Property DataSource As String
```

```
C#:
public string DataSource {get;}
```

By default this value is empty and must be defined to enable the connection to be opened. The read-only property is provided to extract the data source from the connection string where it is defined.

Below are some samples showing how the `Data Source` property can be defined in the connection string.

`OleDbConnection` to a Microsoft Access database:

```
"Provider=Microsoft.Jet.OLEDB.4.0;Data Source=C:\Data\NorthWind.MDB;"
```

`OleDbConnection` to a SQL Server database on the same machine:

```
Provider=SQLOLEDB;Data Source=localhost;Initial Catalog=Northwind;";
```

`SqlConnection` to a SQL Server 7 or higher database located on the `DevServ06` machine:

```
"data source=DevServ06;initial catalog=Northwind"
```

`SqlConnection` to a SQL Server 7 or higher database located on the `DevServ06` machine with a named instance or `CdLibrary`:

```
"data source=DevServ06\CdLibrary;initial catalog=Northwind"
```

The Provider Property – OleDb Only

The OLE DB data `Provider` is read through this property. The `Provider` string is actually the `ProgID` of the COM object that is instantiated to access the data. `SqlConnection` does not use this property as it implements its own direct interface to the database server.

```
VB:
Public ReadOnly Property Provider As String

C#:
public string Provider {get;}
```

`Provider` has no default value so a provider must be defined before a connection can be created. One major feature of OLE DB comes from its ability to read from various data source types using the same set of methods, which is accomplished through the `Provider` property. The `Provider` is read-only and the value can only be set in the `ConnectionString` or the constructor.

There are as many OLE DB data providers as there are database vendors. The following is a list of some of the more popular ones with example connection strings:

Database	ConnectionString
AS/400	Provider=IBMDA400; Data source=theAS400; User Id=theUsername; Password=thePassword;
Active Directory Service	Provider=ADSDSOObject; User Id=theUsername; Password=thePassword;
DB2	Provider=DB2OLEDB; Network Address=theDB2Server; Network Transport Library=TCPIP; Package Collection=thePackage; Initial Catalog=theDB; User Id=theUsername; Password=thePassword;

Database	ConnectionString
Foxpro	`Provider=vfpoledb.1;` `Data Source=C:\Data\TimeSheets.dbc"`
Index Server	`Provider=msidxs;` `Data source=CatalogName;`

Internet Publishing	`Provider=MSDAIPP.DSO;`
	`Data Source=http://www.mctainsh.com/theData;`
	`User Id=theUsername; Password=thePassword;`

Microsoft Jet (Access97 and 2000)	`Provider=Microsoft.Jet.OLEDB.4.0;`
	`Data Source=C:\Data\Northwind.mdb;`
	`Jet OLEDB:Database Password="Frodo#3";`

Microsoft Jet (Excel)	`Provider=Microsoft.Jet.OLEDB.4.0;`
	`Data Source=C:\Data\TimeSheet.xls;`
	`Extended Properties=Excel 8.0;`

Microsoft SQL Server 2000, 7.0 or earlier.	`Provider=sqloledb;`
	`Data Source=theSqlServerName;`
	`Initial Catalog=Northwind;`
	`User Id=theUsername; Password=thePassword;`

Oracle (Microsoft)	`Provider=MSDAORA;`
	`Data Source=SomeOracleDB;`
	`User Id=theUsername; Password=thePassword;`

Simple Provider	`Provider=MSDAOSP;` `Data Source=SomeServerName;`

> **NOTE: MSDASLQ, OLE DB for ODBC is not supported by the .NET Data Provider. To access an ODBC data source use the OdbcConnection object directly.**

The PacketSize Property – Sql Only

This is the number of bytes used in the network packets sent between the SQL server and the client. This property is not available to the `OleDbConnection` or `OdbcConnection`.

```
VB:
Public ReadOnly Property PacketSize As Integer

C#:
public int PacketSize {get;}
```

Once the `Connection` object is constructed, the `PacketSize` property is set to a default value of 8192, which is satisfactory in most cases. The packet size can be set in the connection string using the `Packet Size` parameter. Communication performance can be improved by changing this value to suit the size of data packets being transferred between the client and server. The acceptable range is between 512 and 32767 bytes. If most communications involve small amounts of text and data then a value nearer 512 will increase data throughout. However using a smaller value with data containing very long string or large data blocks such as images can result in worse performance. In this case a larger packet size will improve performance.

As the packet size is set in the connection string, it is fixed once `Open` is called. To change the packet size after open is called, we need to close the connection, change the connection string, and open the connection. The following example sets the `PacketSize` in the connection string and displays the result.

VB:

```
Dim sqlConn As SqlConnection = New SqlConnection()
Console.WriteLine("1) Packet size = " & sqlConn.PacketSize)
sqlConn.ConnectionString = "data source=Dev01;initial catalog=Northwind;" & _
                           "Packet Size=1024;"
sqlConn.Open()
Console.WriteLine("2) Packet size = " & sqlConn.PacketSize)
```

C#:

```
SqlConnection sqlConn = new SqlConnection();
Console.WriteLine( "1) Packet size = " + sqlConn.PacketSize );
sqlConn.ConnectionString = "data source=Dev01;initial catalog=Northwind;" +
                           "Packet Size=1024;";
sqlConn.Open();
Console.WriteLine( "2) Packet size = " + sqlConn.PacketSize );
```

The above code will first display the default size when the object is constructed and the new size as follows:

1) Packet size = 8192
2) Packet size = 1024

The ServerVersion Property

Returns a string containing the version information of the database server the connection goes to.

VB:
```
Public ReadOnly Property ServerVersion As String
```

C#:
```
public string ServerVersion {get;}
```

This information is only available after the connection has been successfully opened. Reading before the connection is successfully opened will throw an InvalidOperationException. It is often useful to include this data in error logs or use it to verify that the database has the appropriate capabilities. For SQL Server 2000 the value may be "08.00.0194", and for Microsoft Access 2000 it may be "04.00.0000".

The following code displays the version information of the connection to the console. Note that this connection string can be used to connect to any Microsoft SQL Server database but if it is SQL Server 2000 it would be more efficient to use SqlConnection rather than OleDbConnection. Therefore we could parse the ServerVersion string and use the more appropriate connection if greater than 8.0.0.0.

VB:
```
Dim oledbConn As OleDbConnection = New OleDbConnection( _
        "Provider=SQLOLEDB;" & _
        "Data Source=DevLaptop01;" & _
        "Initial Catalog=Northwind;" & _
        "Integrated Security=SSPI;")
oledbConn.Open()
Console.WriteLine("Server Version = " & oledbConn.ServerVersion)
```

```
oledbConn.Close()
```

```
C#:
OleDbConnection oledbConn = new OleDbConnection(
        "Provider=SQLOLEDB;"+
        "Data Source=DevLaptop01;"+
        "Initial Catalog=Northwind;"+
        "Integrated Security=SSPI;" );
oledbConn.Open();
Console.WriteLine("Server Version = {0}", oledbConn.ServerVersion );
```

Output:

Server Version = 08.00.0194

The State Property

A read-only property indicating the current state of the connection.

```
VB:
Public ReadOnly Property State As ConnectionState
```

```
C#:
public ConnectionState State {get;}
```

Possible connection states in order of appearance are:

ConnectionState	Description
Closed	This is the state the object is in once it is created and after it is closed.
Connecting	Once Open is called and before it returns, the object is in the Connecting state.
Open	Open state is set only if the Open method returned successfully,
Executing	The object is executing a command.
Fetching	Data is being retrieved.
Broken	The object is broken. This can occur only after the connection has been opened. A connection in this state may be closed and then re-opened.

> Note, for version 1 of Managed Providers only the Closed and Open states will be returned.

As several methods and properties of the Connection object can only be called if the object is in the appropriate state, this property allows run time verification that the method call can be made. This could include checking the connection is open before checking the ServerVersion or ensuring the connection is closed before calling Open.

The following example uses the State to check if the connection is closed before opening it. This can be useful when the Connection object is declared as a class member and shared across several methods. Also note the connection is only opened if it has not been opened already. In this way the method may be called many times and will only incur the additional overhead of opening a new connection during the first call.

```vb
VB:
' Declare as a member of the module
Dim m_sqlConn As SqlConnection = Nothing

' ... Use in some module method ...
' Ensure the object exists
If m_sqlConn Is Nothing Then
    m_sqlConn = New SqlConnection()
End If
' Open the connection if necessary
If m_sqlConn.State = ConnectionState.Closed Then
    m_sqlConn.ConnectionString = "data source=localhost;" & _
                                 "initial catalog=Northwind;"
    m_sqlConn.Open()
End If
```

```csharp
C#:
// Declare as a member of the class
private SqlConnection m_sqlConn = null;

// ... Use in some class method ...
// Ensure the object exists
if( m_sqlConn == null )
    m_sqlConn = new SqlConnection();
// Open the connection if necessary
if( m_sqlConn.State == ConnectionState.Closed )
{
    m_sqlConn.ConnectionString = "data source=localhost;"+
                                 "initial catalog=Northwind;";
    m_sqlConn.Open();
}
```

The WorkstationId Property – Sql Only

This read-only property returns the network name of the client machine connecting to the database. This property is not available to the OleDbConnection.

```vb
VB:
Public ReadOnly Property WorkstationId As String
```

```csharp
C#:
public string WorkstationId {get;}
```

Once the Connection object is instantiated, the WorkstationId property is set to the network name of the machine where the Connection object was created. If a connection is passed off to another machine in a web service or other remoting method this property is useful in determining where the connection to the database originated. The following example sets the WorkstationId in the connection string and displays the result.

```
VB:
Dim sqlConn As SqlConnection = New SqlConnection()
Console.WriteLine("1) WorkstationId = " & sqlConn.WorkstationId)
sqlConn.ConnectionString = "data source=Dev01;initial catalog=Northwind;" & _
                 "Workstation ID=BilboBaggins;"
Console.WriteLine("2) WorkstationId = " & sqlConn.WorkstationId)
```

```
C#:
SqlConnection sqlConn = new SqlConnection();
Console.WriteLine( "1) WorkstationId = " + sqlConn.WorkstationId );
sqlConn.ConnectionString = "data source=Dev01;initial catalog=Northwind;" +
                 "Workstation ID=BilboBaggins;";
Console.WriteLine( "2) WorkstationId = " + sqlConn.WorkstationId );
```

The above code will first display the machine name where the object is constructed and then the changed name as follows:

1) WorkstationId = PPRO800DOTNET
2) WorkstationId = BilboBaggins

Methods

With the exception of GetOleDbSchemaTable, the Connection object methods are generally the same for SqlConnection, OleDbConnection, and OdbcConnection. However, there are subtle differences in their application.

The ReleaseObjectPool Method – OleDb and Odbc Only

Once called, the connection object pool will be cleared when the last connection is closed.

```
VB:
Public Shared Sub ReleaseObjectPool()
```

```
C#:
public static void ReleaseObjectPool();
```

See Connection Pooling later in this chapter for the advantages of pooling. It is not necessary to call this method, but connection resources will be freed sooner when ReleaseObjectPool is called. Do not call this method if the connection will be used in the near future. In most cases, ReleaseObjectPool is used when a connection will not be required for a period of time longer than the provider would keep the connection alive.

The Open Method

Opens the database defined earlier in the constructor or connection string.

```
VB:
NotOverridable Public Sub Open()
```

```
C#:
public void Open();
```

Before calling the Open method, ensure that the necessary parameters are set for the required connection. At the very minimum this includes Data Source for SqlConnection or Provider for OleDbConnection. Failure to do so, will result in an InvalidOperationException.

Unlike ADO, all connection requests are synchronous: they lock the calling thread while they attempt to connect. The thread is locked until the call returns successfully or it times out and throws an exception (see the ConnectionTimeout property for information about adjusting the waiting-time). To avoid blocking, perform the database operations in a separate thread. This is explained at the end of this chapter.

If the Open method fails it will throw an exception. This may be due to a programming error, configuration error, or hardware fault. For this reason, it should be performed using a try catch block. An InvalidOperationException is raised if the connection is already open and an OdbcException, OleDbException or SqlException is raised if connection-level error occurred while opening the connection.

An example of how to use the Open method appears in the next section, the CreateCommand method, and many of the examples in this chapter.

The CreateCommand Method

Is used to create a SqlCommand or OleDbCommand object that is associated with the connection object.

```
VB:
Public Function CreateCommand() As SqlCommand
```
or
```
Public Function CreateCommand() As OleDbCommand
```

```
C#:
public SqlCommand CreateCommand();
```
or
```
public OleDbCommand CreateCommand();
```

The following code opens a SqlConnection to the Northwind database located on DevLaptop01. A Command object is created and assigned a command string to extract all employees from the Northwind database. The command is then executed, returning the data to the DataReader. The DataReader is iterated through displaying the employees' titles. The connection is then closed:

```
VB:
Dim sqlConn As SqlConnection = New SqlConnection( _
        "data source=DevLaptop01;" & _
        "initial catalog=Northwind;" & _
        "integrated security=SSPI;")
sqlConn.Open()
Dim sqlCmd As SqlCommand = sqlConn.CreateCommand()
sqlCmd.CommandText = "SELECT * FROM EMPLOYEES"
Dim dataReader As SqlDataReader = sqlCmd.ExecuteReader()
While (dataReader.Read())
    Console.WriteLine(dataReader("Title"))
End While
sqlConn.Close()
```

```
C#:
SqlConnection sqlConn = new SqlConnection(
        "data source=DevLaptop01;"+
        "initial catalog=Northwind;"+
        "integrated security=SSPI;" );
sqlConn.Open();
SqlCommand sqlCmd = sqlConn.CreateCommand();
sqlCmd.CommandText = "SELECT * FROM EMPLOYEES";
SqlDataReader dataReader = sqlCmd.ExecuteReader();
while( dataReader.Read() )
        Console.WriteLine( dataReader["Title"] );
sqlConn.Close();
```

It is not necessary to call the CreateCommand method directly. An alternative is shown in the Close example. Here the Command object is created and passed the Connection object in the constructor. The second method is also able to provide the command string in the constructor. For further details on Command objects, see chapter 4.

The Close Method

Closes the connection to release associated resources.

```
VB:
NotOverridable Public Sub Close()
```

```
C#:
public void Close();
```

Calling Close will allow the release of resources associated with the connection. It is possible to let the Connection object go out of scope without calling Close explicitly. If this happens then any connections will remain until the Connection object is garbage collected. This may be a problem if more connections are requested than there are resources to support. It is good practice to call Close whenever you are finished using the connection.

The following example shows calling close from within the finally section of an exception wrapper. This means the resource will be released whether or not an error occurs during the Command or DataReader operations. An OdbcConnection object is instantiated, then it is used to instantiate an OdbcCommand object to select all data from the employees table. The OdbcCommand is used to create a DataReader that is used to iterate through the table, extracting and displaying column 3.

```vb
VB:
Dim odbcConn As OdbcConnection = New OdbcConnection( _
    "DSN=MS Access Database;DBQ=D:\\CS\\Northwind.mdb;")
Try
    odbcConn.Open()
    Dim odbcCmd As OdbcCommand = New OdbcCommand( _
      "SELECT * FROM EMPLOYEES", odbcConn)
    Dim dataReader As OdbcDataReader = odbcCmd.ExecuteReader()
    While (dataReader.Read())
        Console.WriteLine(dataReader(3))
    End While
Catch ex As Exception
    Console.WriteLine(ex.Message)
Finally
    odbcConn.Close()
End Try
```

```csharp
C#:
OdbcConnection odbcConn = new OdbcConnection(
    "DSN=MS Access Database;DBQ=D:\\CS\\Northwind.mdb;" );
try
{
    odbcConn.Open();
    OdbcCommand odbcCmd = new OdbcCommand(
        "SELECT * FROM EMPLOYEES", odbcConn);
    OdbcDataReader dataReader = odbcCmd.ExecuteReader();
    while( dataReader.Read() )
        Console.WriteLine( dataReader[3] );
}
catch( Exception ex )
{
    Console.WriteLine(ex.Message);
}
finally
{
    odbcConn.Close();
}
```

The ChangeDatabase Method

Efficiently changes from the currently open database to the one requested. Note that when reading from a Microsoft Access database, this method doesn't do anything. When working with a SQL Server, this method allows changing from one database to another on the same server instance.

```vb
VB:
NotOverridable Public Sub ChangeDatabase( ByVal value As String )
```

```csharp
C#:
public void ChangeDatabase( string value );
```

The parameter is as follows:

Parameter	Type	Description
Value	string	Name of the new database to connect to.

It is necessary to open the connection before calling this method. To set the Database before Open has been called, simply use the Database parameter in the connection string.

In the following sample code the OleDbConnection is initially connected to the Northwind database. At a later time the database is changed to the BookStore database. Closing the connection and reopening it with a new connection string would also achieve this, but ChangeDatabase is more efficient.

Also note in the example that we are connecting to a SQL Server database using OLE DB:

```vb
VB:
Dim oledbConn As OleDbConnection = New OleDbConnection( _
    "Provider=SQLOLEDB;" & _
    "Data Source=DevLaptop01;" & _
    "Initial Catalog=Northwind;" & _
    "Integrated Security=SSPI;")
oledbConn.Open()
' … Read some data from the Northwind database …
oledbConn.ChangeDatabase("BookStore")
' … Read some data from the BookStore database …
```

```csharp
C#:
OleDbConnection oledbConn = new OleDbConnection(
"Provider=SQLOLEDB;"+
    "Data Source=DevLaptop01;"+
    "Initial Catalog=Northwind;"+
    "Integrated Security=SSPI;" );
oledbConn.Open();
// … Read some data from the Northwind database …
oledbConn.ChangeDatabase( "BookStore" );
// … Read some data from the BookStore database …
```

The BeginTransaction Method

Creates an object representing a SQL transaction to be made at a data source.

```vb
VB:
Overloads Public Function BeginTransaction() As SqlTransaction
Overloads Public Function BeginTransaction( _
    ByVal isolationLevel As IsolationLevel ) As SqlTransaction
```

or

```vb
Overloads Public Function BeginTransaction() As SqlTransaction
Overloads Public Function BeginTransaction( _
    ByVal isolationLevel As IsolationLevel ) As SqlTransaction
```

```csharp
C#:
```

```
public SqlTransaction BeginTransaction();
public SqlTransaction BeginTransaction( IsolationLevel isolationLevel );
```

or

```
public SqlTransaction BeginTransaction();
public SqlTransaction BeginTransaction( IsolationLevel isolationLevel );
```

The parameter is as follows:

Parameter	Type	Description
IsolationLevel	IsolationLevel	Sets the transaction locking behavior for the connection. The levels are detailed in the following table.

Details of the different available isolation levels:

Parameter	Description
Chaos	Changes that have not been committed from a higher isolated transaction cannot be overwritten.
ReadCommitted	This is the default isolation level. Data that has not been committed cannot be read so dirty reads are not possible.
ReadUncommitted	It is possible to read uncommitted data. Reads can return data that may later be rolled back so dirty reads are possible.
RepeatableRead	Other users are prevented from updating the data in the query.
Serializable	This locks the entire query dataset. Other users are unable to update or insert into the query while the transaction is open.

Note that this method may throw an exception if the requested type of transaction is not supported, which may be due to database limitations or currently processing transactions. Transactions are described in detail in Chapter 12, Transactions. The following example shows the basic transaction layout. The connection is opened prior to calling this code segment. A transaction is commenced and a Command object created. Some database updates or inserts occur before calling the Commit method to close the transaction. Note, if an exception is thrown the transaction is rolled back to prevent half completed data entering the databases:

```
VB:
Dim trans As OleDbTransaction = Nothing
Try
    trans = oledbConn.BeginTransaction()
    Dim oledbCmd As OleDbCommand = oledbConn.CreateCommand()
    ' … Perform some database operations here …
    trans.Commit()
Catch ex As Exception
    If Not (trans Is Nothing) Then trans.Rollback()
End Try
```

```C#
C#:
OleDbTransaction trans = null;
try
{
    trans = oledbConn.BeginTransaction();
    OleDbCommand oledbCmd = oledbConn.CreateCommand();
    // … Perform some database operations here …
    trans.Commit();
}
catch( Exception ex )
{
    if( trans != null )
        trans.Rollback();
}
```

The GetOleDbSchemaTable Method – OleDb Only

Extracts the requested schema information using the restrictions, into a returned `DataTable` object.

```VB
VB:
Public Function GetOleDbSchemaTable( ByVal schema As Guid, _
    ByVal restrictions() As Object ) As DataTable
```

```C#
C#:
public DataTable GetOleDbSchemaTable( Guid schema, object[] restrictions );
```

Parameters are as follows:

Parameter	Type	Description
schema	Guid	Indicates the actual schema that is to be returned. For example `OleDbSchemaGuid.Indexes` will return the indexes defined in the catalog that are owned by a given user.
Restrictions	object[]	An array of `DataColumn` objects that define the filter on the returned `DataTable`.

This method only applies to `OleDbConnection`. `SqlConnection` provides schema data through stored procedures and informational views. The information returned in the `DataTable` can be used to verify all attributes of the Database including Catalogs, Columns, Foreign Keys, Procedures, Statistics, and others. Not all OLE DB providers are able to supply information for every `OleDbSchemaGuid`. If the information is not available a `NotSupportedException` is thrown. Possible schemas are shown below along with whether they are supported when using the following connection string:

Microsoft Access 2000

```
Provider=Microsoft.Jet.OLEDB.4.0;Data Source=D:\Data\NorthWind.MDB;
```

Microsoft SQL Server 2000

```
Provider=SQLOLEDB;Data Source=DevLaptop01;
Initial Catalog=Northwind;Integrated Security=SSPI;
```

The following table explains values for the schema parameter that return data about the features of the data provider:

Schema	Description	Access 2000	SQL 2000
DbInfoLiterals	List of provider-specific literals used in text commands. For example the literal with the name Like_Underscore has a value of _.	✓	✓
Provider_Types	The base data types supported by the .NET data provider. This includes data such as name, type, literal prefix and best match.	✓	✓
Sql_Languages	The conformance levels, options, and dialects supported by the SQL-implementation used by the provider.	✗	✗
Table_Statistics	Describes the available set of statistics on tables in the provider. For example, Statistic name and Last updated.	✗	✓
Trustee	Identifies the trustee users defined in the data source.	requires system .mdb	✗

The following OleDbSchemaGuid values return data based on information defined in the current catalog and owned by the current user – that is the authenticated database user set with userid or Integrated security:

Schema	Description	Access 2000	SQL 2000
Assertions	Returns the assertions owned by the user and defined in the catalog	✗	✗
Catalogs	Returns physical attributes for all catalogs available from the data source	✗	✓

Schema	Description	Access 2000	SQL 2000
Character_Sets	Returns the defined character sets that the user can access in the catalog .	✗	✗
Check_Constraints	Returns the constraints in the current catalog that are owned by the user.	✓	✓
Check_Constraints_By_Table	As above with associated table .	✗	✓
Collations	Returns the different methods that the catalog has available for sorting strings.	✗	✗
Columns	Returns information on the columns in all accessible tables and views in the catalog.	✓	✓
Column_Domain_Usage	Returns information on the columns in the catalog that are dependent on a domain (that is a restricted set of possible values).	✗	✗
Column_Privileges	Privileges on columns of tables that the user has available has granted to others.	✗	✓
Constraint_Column_Usage	Returns the columns used by referential constraints, unique constraints, check constraints, and assertions.	✓	✗
Constraint_Table_Usage	Returns the tables that are used by referential constraints, unique constraints, check constraints, and assertions.	✗	✗
Foreign_Keys	Returns details regarding the foreign keys including name and table association.	✓	✓
Indexes	Returns details of the indexes including names, uniqueness, table name and index names	✓	✓
Key_Column_Usage	Returns the columns defined in the catalog that are constrained as keys by a given user.	✓	✗
Primary_Keys	Returns details of the columns that are primary keys.	✓	✓

Table continued on following page

Schema	Description	Access 2000	SQL 2000
Procedures	Returns information about stored procedures such as name and creation date. Further information is available with Procedure_Columns and Procedure_Parameters.	✓	✓
Procedure_Columns	Information about the columns of rowsets returned by procedures.	✗	✗
Procedure_Parameters	The parameters and return codes of procedures including name and type information.	✗	✓
Referential_Constraints	Returns the relationships between tables with their update and delete rules.	✓	✗
Schemata	Returns schemata information such as default character set name and schema owner.	✗	✓
Statistics	Returns table names and cardinality.	✓	✓
Tables	Returns tables and views.	✓	✓
Tables_Info	As above with additional information such as Table version.	✓	✓
Table_Constraints	Compilation of Tables_Info and Check_Constraints.	✓	✓
Table_Privileges	Returns details on table privileges that the user has available or has granted to others.	✗	✓
Translations	Returns character translations available to the current user .	✗	✗
Usage_Privileges	Returns usage privileges on non-tabular objects, such as domains and translations, that the user has available or has granted to others.	✗	✗
Views	Returns details of the views or queries that are accessible.	✓	✗
View_Column_Usage	Returns the columns on which viewed tables, owned by the user, are dependent.	✗	✗
View_Table_Usage	Returns the tables on which viewed tables, owned by the user, are dependent.	✗	✗

The following code extracts index information for the Northwind access database and places it in a `DataGrid` object defined on the form as m_dataGrid:

```vb
VB:
' Open database and read schema
Dim oledbConn As OleDbConnection = New OleDbConnection( _
     "Provider=Microsoft.Jet.OLEDB.4.0;" & _
     "Data Source=C:\Data\NorthWind.MDB;")
oledbConn.Open()
Dim dt As DataTable
dt = oledbConn.GetOleDbSchemaTable(OleDbSchemaGuid.Indexes, Nothing)

' Attach table to Grid
Dim ds As DataSet = New DataSet()
ds.Tables.Add(dt)
m_dataGrid.DataSource = ds
oledbConn.Close()
```

```csharp
C#:
// Open database and read schema
OleDbConnection oledbConn = new OleDbConnection(
     "Provider=Microsoft.Jet.OLEDB.4.0;"+
     "Data Source=C:\\Data\\NorthWind.MDB;" );
oledbConn.Open();
DataTable dt = oledbConn.GetOleDbSchemaTable( OleDbSchemaGuid.Indexes, null );

// Attach table to Grid
DataSet ds = new DataSet();
ds.Tables.Add( dt );
m_dataGrid.DataSource = ds;
oledbConn.Close();
```

The populated `DataGrid` is shown below. Note that the column widths have been changed to show more information:

	TABLE_NAME	INDEX_NAM	PRIM	COLUMN_NAM	CARDINALIT	PA
▶	MSysAccessObjects	AOIndex	☑	ID	5	1
	Categories	CategoryNam	☐	CategoryName	8	1
	Categories	PrimaryKey	☑	CategoryID	8	1
	Customers	PrimaryKey	☑	CustomerID	91	1
	Employees	PrimaryKey	☑	EmployeeID	9	1
	MSysIMEXColumns	PrimaryKey	☑	SpecID	0	1
	MSysIMEXSpecs	PrimaryKey	☑	SpecName	0	1
	Products	PrimaryKey	☑	ProductID	77	1
	Shippers	PrimaryKey	☑	ShipperID	3	1
	Suppliers	PrimaryKey	☑	SupplierID	29	1

NewDataSet — Form1

Events

The Connection object's events provide a mechanism for notifying the application of changes in the status of the connection. The events are triggered by the Connection object and execute the delegates that the application defines to handle the event. The delegates execute in the thread context of the call that triggered the event.

Care must be taken when handling events generated by threads other than the user interface thread to ensure user interface objects are not called by the worker threads execution of the event handler. For example, if a Connection object was created in the user interface thread and passed off to another thread to call the open method, then the StateChange event would be executed in the context of the worker thread. It would be improper to use this handler to enable an **Open** button. To overcome this, Invoke should be used.

The InfoMessage Event

Occurs when the data server generates a warning or information message. The provider wraps this as an InfoMessage event to pass the message back to the application:

```
VB:
Public Delegate Sub OdbcInfoMessageEventHandler(ByVal sender As Object, _
            ByVal infoArgs As OdbcInfoMessageEventArgs)
Public Delegate Sub OleDbInfoMessageEventHandler(ByVal sender As Object, _
            ByVal infoArgs As OleDbInfoMessageEventArgs)
Public Delegate Sub SqlInfoMessageEventHandler(ByVal sender As Object, _
            ByVal infoArgs As SqlInfoMessageEventArgs)

Public Event InfoMessage As OdbcInfoMessageEventHandler
Public Event InfoMessage As OleDbInfoMessageEventHandler
Public Event InfoMessage As SqlInfoMessageEventHandler


C#:
public delegate void OdbcInfoMessageEventHandler(object sender,
    OdbcInfoMessageEventArgs infoArgs);
public delegate void OleDbInfoMessageEventHandler(object sender,
    OleDbInfoMessageEventArgs infoArgs);
public delegate void SqlInfoMessageEventHandler(object sender,
    SqlInfoMessageEventArgs infoArgs);

public event OdbcInfoMessageEventHandler InfoMessage;
public event OleDbInfoMessageEventHandler InfoMessage;
public event SqlInfoMessageEventHandler InfoMessage;
```

Parameter	Type	Description
sender	Object	References the object that fired the event. This is useful when the event handler is shared by more than one object instance.
infoArgs	OdbcInfoMessageEventArg OleDbInfoMessageEventArgs SqlInfoMessageEventArgs	Provides a collection of SqlError, OdbcError or OleDbError, objects containing information about the condition that triggered the event.

By monitoring this event delegate, it is possible to notify the user of special information and warnings related to the database connection.

This example will use the Form designer to create an `InfoMessage` event handler on the m_sqlConn object:

❑ Open the form designer.

❑ Drag and drop a `SqlConnection` object from the **Data** section of the toolbox onto the Form. The new object will appear in an area below the form.

❑ Select **properties** for the new `Connection` object and change its (name) to m_sqlConn.

❑ Press the **Events** (lightning bolt) button at the top of the connections property window. If the events button is not available, double click on the `Connection` object in the form designer.

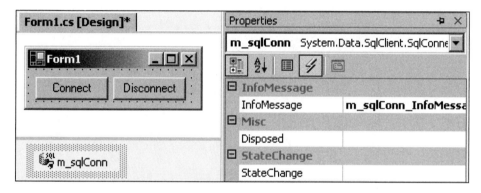

❑ Double click on the **InfoMessage** tag. This will add the event handler shown below into your code and attach it to the m_sqlConn object.

❑ Add the `foreach` loop (below). This code iterates through the `SqlInfoMessageEventArgs` object, extracting each `sqlErr` in turn and displaying it in a `MessageBox`.

❑ Note that the event will only fire when the connection is open so call `Open` to get started:

```
VB:
Private Sub m_sqlConn_InfoMessage(ByVal sender As System.Object, _
      ByVal e As SqlInfoMessageEventArgs) Handles m_sqlConn.InfoMessage
   Dim sqlErr As SqlError
   For Each sqlErr In e.Errors
      MessageBox.Show(sqlErr.Message, sqlErr.Server)
   Next
End Sub
```

```
C#:
private void m_sqlConn_InfoMessage(object sender, SqlInfoMessageEventArgs e)
{
    foreach( SqlError error in e.Errors )
         MessageBox.Show( error.Message,  error.Server );
}
```

The StateChange Event

Is fired when a change in the connection state occurs:

```
VB:
Public Delegate Sub StateChangeEventHandler( ByVal sender As Object, _
    ByVal sceArgs As StateChangeEventArgs )

Public Event StateChange As StateChangeEventHandler


C#:
public delegate void StateChangeEventHandler( object sender,
    StateChangeEventArgs sceArgs);

public event StateChangeEventHandler StateChange;
```

Parameter	Type	Description
sender	Object	References the object that fired the event. This is useful when the event handler is shared by more than one object instance.
sceArgs	StateChangeEventArgs	Provides information about the state change. Most importantly it includes Original and Current state.

> The **StateChange** event is only fired when a change actually occurs. Therefore if the connection is already closed and **Close** is called, no change occurs so no event is fired. Also note that if the **Open** fails no event occurs.

Calling methods that affect the connection, but are not Connection methods can also trigger this event. For example, if the DataReader throws an exception because it is unable to reach the database during a network outage, then the connection will be closed and the event fired.

This example uses a form with a **Connect** and a **Disconnect** button on it to control the connection. The StateChange event is used to control the enabled state of the two buttons. In Form1_Load the event is attached to the OnStateChangeEvent method.

At startup only the **Connect** button will be enabled. Once pressed both buttons will be disabled until the StateChange event fires indicating we are connected. This event will display a message and enable the disconnect button. The reverse occurs for the disconnect button. Note if the **Open** fails the button is re-enabled to allow another attempt:

```
VB:
Dim m_sqlConn As SqlConnection

' Setup the initial button states and event handlers
Private Sub Form1_Load(ByVal sender As System.Object, _
    ByVal e As System.EventArgs) Handles MyBase.Load
    m_sqlConn = New SqlConnection("data source=devlaptop01;" & _
```

```
                                        "initial catalog=Northwind;" & _
                                        "integrated security=SSPI;")
        AddHandler m_sqlConn.StateChange, AddressOf OnStateChangeEvent
        m_btnDisconnect.Enabled = False
    End Sub


    ' The Connect button should disable and call Open() request
    Private Sub m_btnConnect_Click(ByVal sender As System.Object, _
        ByVal e As System.EventArgs) Handles m_btnConnect.Click
        m_btnConnect.Enabled = False
        Try
            m_sqlConn.Open()
        Catch
            m_btnConnect.Enabled = True
        End Try
    End Sub


    ' The Disconnect button should disable and call Close()
    Private Sub m_btnDisconnect_Click(ByVal sender As System.Object, _
        ByVal e As System.EventArgs) Handles m_btnDisconnect.Click
        m_btnDisconnect.Enabled = False
        m_sqlConn.Close()
    End Sub

    ' Event handler to receive notification of change in connection state
    Public Sub OnStateChangeEvent(ByVal sender As Object, _
        ByVal e As StateChangeEventArgs)
        MessageBox.Show(e.CurrentState.ToString())
        If e.CurrentState = ConnectionState.Closed Then
            m_btnConnect.Enabled = True
        End If
        If e.CurrentState = ConnectionState.Open Then
            m_btnDisconnect.Enabled = True
        End If
    End Sub
End Sub
```

```
C#:
private SqlConnection m_sqlConn;

// Setup the initial button states and event handlers
private void Form1_Load(object sender, System.EventArgs e)
{
    m_sqlConn = new SqlConnection(    "data source=devlaptop01;"+
                                      "initial catalog=Northwind;"+
                                      "integrated security=SSPI;" );
    m_sqlConn.StateChange += new StateChangeEventHandler(OnStateChangeEvent);
    m_btnDisconnect.Enabled = false;
}

// The Connect button should disable and call Open() request
private void m_btnConnect_Click(object sender, System.EventArgs e)
{
    m_btnConnect.Enabled = false;
    try
```

```
        {
                m_sqlConn.Open();
        }
        catch(Exception ex )
        {
                m_btnConnect.Enabled = true;
        }
}

// The Disconnect button should disable and call Close()
private void m_btnDisconnect_Click(object sender, System.EventArgs e)
{
        m_btnDisconnect.Enabled = false;
        m_sqlConn.Close();
}

// Event handler to receive notification of change in connection state
private void OnStateChangeEvent( object sender, StateChangeEventArgs e )
{
        MessageBox.Show(e.CurrentState.ToString());
        if( e.CurrentState == ConnectionState.Closed )
                m_btnConnect.Enabled = true;
        if( e.CurrentState == ConnectionState.Open )
                m_btnDisconnect.Enabled = true;
}
```

You may also note that the first attempt at a connection takes much longer than the subsequent attempts. The first connection will be slowed down due to delays caused by locating or starting the server, authentication, etc. The subsequent fast connections are due to the magic of connection pooling, which is discussed next.

Connection Pooling

Connection pooling involves creating and maintaining a group (pool) of connections that can be handed out to applications requesting a connection. The process is as follows:

- ❑ An application calls Open to connect to the provider

- ❑ If no suitable connections are available a new connection is established with the provider. This often takes significant time

- ❑ The application uses the connection and then closes the connection when ready

- ❑ In the background the connection is not closed, but kept in a pool for later use

- ❑ At some later time, this or another application tries to open a connection to the same provider and with the same parameters

- ❑ If the matching connection is still in the pool it is immediately returned and the connection is ready to use again

Opening a connection to a remote or even local provider can be time consuming. The operation can take from milliseconds to tens of seconds and this is where connection pooling becomes useful. Taking a connection from a pool will be almost instantaneous compared to a five second delay of establishing a new connection over the network.

Some points to keep in mind about connection pooling:

❑ Connections are not shared. Only when the previous connection owner has called `Close` will the connection be given out to another requester.

❑ Only connections with exact matching connection details with those being requested are given from the pool. Your connection security setting will not be given out to another requester unless they have provided the exact details.

❑ Connection pooling may differ slightly for different providers.

❑ Pooled connections may be removed from the pool if not used for more than the timeout period.

❑ Connection pooling can be disabled.

You will probably never want to disable connection pooling. If you do wish to, include the following in the `ConnectionString`:

For `OleDbConnection` the parameter is:

```
OLE DB Services=-4;
```

For `SqlConnection` the parameter is as follows:

```
Pooling='false';
```

Asynchronous Connections

The ADO.NET `Connection` object does not directly support asynchronous connections, as ADO did. This means that waiting for a connection to open will hold up the execution of your code. To overcome this the `Connection` object and other database operations can be placed in another thread to decouple delays caused by the data transfer and connection establishment. The following example provides such a mechanism.

Care must be taken to ensure other threads do not call methods of user interface objects except via `Invoke`. The following example uses a worker thread to open the connection and then notify the user interface of the success or failure using `BeginInvoke`. The `SyncLock` (VB) or `lock` (C#) keyword is used to ensure both threads do not attempt to access the `m_sqlConn` at the same time. The form consists of an **Open** and **Close** button. When **Open** is pressed the thread is started and works on opening the connection. Because the connection takes place in another thread, it does not block the user from dragging the form around and interacting with it.

The four methods have the following purpose:

m_btnOpen_Click

The **Open** button has been clicked.

- ❏ An event handler delegate is created and assigned to `m_NotifyParent`. This delegate identifies the method to be called or invoked once the threaded `Connection.Open` method is complete.

- ❏ The connection thread is created and started at `OnThreadStart`.

- ❏ The **Open** button is disabled to prevent repeated presses during the connection attempt.

m_btnClose_Click

The **Close** button has been clicked.

- ❏ Using a synchronizing lock, `close` is called

- ❏ The **Open** button is enabled and the **Close** button is disabled

OnNotifyConnection

This is called when the worker thread is done processing the `Open` request. A message is displayed indicating the success or failure of the `Open` method and buttons are enabled as appropriate.

OnThreadStart

The framework calls `OnThreadStart` when the new thread is started.

- ❏ The synchronization lock is used to prevent both threads calling `Open` and `Close` together when the connection is attempted.

- ❏ If successful, "Connected" is the return message. Otherwise the error message is returned.

- ❏ If `OnThreadStart` is running in the same context as the form, `m_NotifyParent` is called directly; otherwise it is invoked for safety.

```
VB:
' Event delegate and Connection object definition
Dim m_sqlConn As SqlConnection = New SqlConnection()
Delegate Sub NotifyConnectionEventHandler(ByVal sMessage As String)
Dim m_NotifyParent As NotifyConnectionEventHandler = Nothing

Private Sub m_btnOpen_Click(ByVal sender As System.Object, _
    ByVal e As System.EventArgs) Handles m_btnOpen.Click
    ' Here we call open an another thread freeing the UI.
    m_NotifyParent = New NotifyConnectionEventHandler( _
        AddressOf OnNotifyConnection)
    Dim connectThread As Thread = New Thread( _
        New ThreadStart(AddressOf OnThreadStart))
    connectThread.Start()
    m_btnOpen.Enabled = False
End Sub
```

```vb
Private Sub m_btnClose_Click(ByVal sender As System.Object, _
    ByVal e As System.EventArgs) Handles m_btnClose.Click
    ' Safely call close (Not really necessary)
    SyncLock m_sqlConn
        m_sqlConn.Close()
    End SyncLock
    m_btnOpen.Enabled = True
    m_btnClose.Enabled = False
End Sub

' Notifications from thread arrives here
Private Sub OnNotifyConnection(ByVal sMessage As String)
    MessageBox.Show(sMessage, "OnNotifyConnection")
    If (m_sqlConn.State = ConnectionState.Open) Then
        m_btnClose.Enabled = True
        Return
    End If
    If (m_sqlConn.State = ConnectionState.Closed) Then
        m_btnOpen.Enabled = True
        Return
    End If
    MessageBox.Show("ERROR: Unexpected connection state!")
End Sub

' This may be executed in the IU thread or by another thread
Public Sub OnThreadStart()
    Dim sResult As String
    Try
        ' Setup connection and open safely
        SyncLock m_sqlConn
            m_sqlConn.ConnectionString = "data source=devlaptop01;" & _
                                         "initial catalog=Northwind;" & _
                                         "integrated security=SSPI;"
            m_sqlConn.Open()
        End SyncLock
        sResult = "Connected"
    Catch ex As Exception
        sResult = ex.Message
    End Try
    ' Return result
    If (InvokeRequired) Then
        BeginInvoke(m_NotifyParent, New String() {sResult})
    Else
        m_NotifyParent(sResult)
    End If
End Sub
```

```csharp
C#:
// Event delegate and Connection object definition
SqlConnection m_sqlConn = new SqlConnection();
delegate void NotifyConnectionEventHandler( string sMessage );
private NotifyConnectionEventHandler m_NotifyParent = null;

// Open pressed so start connection attempt.
```

```csharp
private void m_btnOpen_Click(object sender, System.EventArgs e)
{
     // Here we call open an another thread freeing the UI.
     m_NotifyParent = new NotifyConnectionEventHandler( OnNotifyConnection );
     Thread connectThread = new Thread( new ThreadStart( OnThreadStart ) );
     connectThread.Start();
     m_btnOpen.Enabled = false;
}


// Close the connection
private void m_btnClose_Click(object sender, System.EventArgs e)
{
     // Safely call close (Not really necessary)
     lock( m_sqlConn )
     {
          m_sqlConn.Close();
     }
     m_btnOpen.Enabled = true;
     m_btnClose.Enabled = false;
}


// Notifications from thread arrives here
private void OnNotifyConnection( string sMessage )
{
     MessageBox.Show( sMessage, "OnNotifyConnection" );
     switch( m_sqlConn.State )
     {
          case ConnectionState.Open :
               m_btnClose.Enabled = true;
               break;
          case ConnectionState.Closed :
               m_btnOpen.Enabled = true;
               break;
          default:
               MessageBox.Show( "ERROR: Unexpected connection state!" );
               break;
     }
}


// This may be executed in the IU thread or by another thread
public void OnThreadStart()
{
     string sResult;
     try
     {
          // Setup connection and open safely
          lock( m_sqlConn )
          {
               m_sqlConn.ConnectionString ="data source=devlaptop01;"+
                    "initial catalog=Northwind;"+
                    "integrated security=SSPI;";
               m_sqlConn.Open();
          }
          sResult = "Connected";
```

```
        }
        catch( Exception ex )
        {
                sResult = ex.Message;
        }
        // Return result
        if( InvokeRequired )
                BeginInvoke( m_NotifyParent, new string[]{ sResult }  );
        else
                m_NotifyParent( sResult );
}
```

Summary

We have discussed the Connection object and how it functions. The Connection object, whether explicitly or implicitly created, forms the basis of any ADO.NET database operation. Once the connection is established we need to execute a command against the database to perform read and write operations. The next chapter will discuss Commands further.

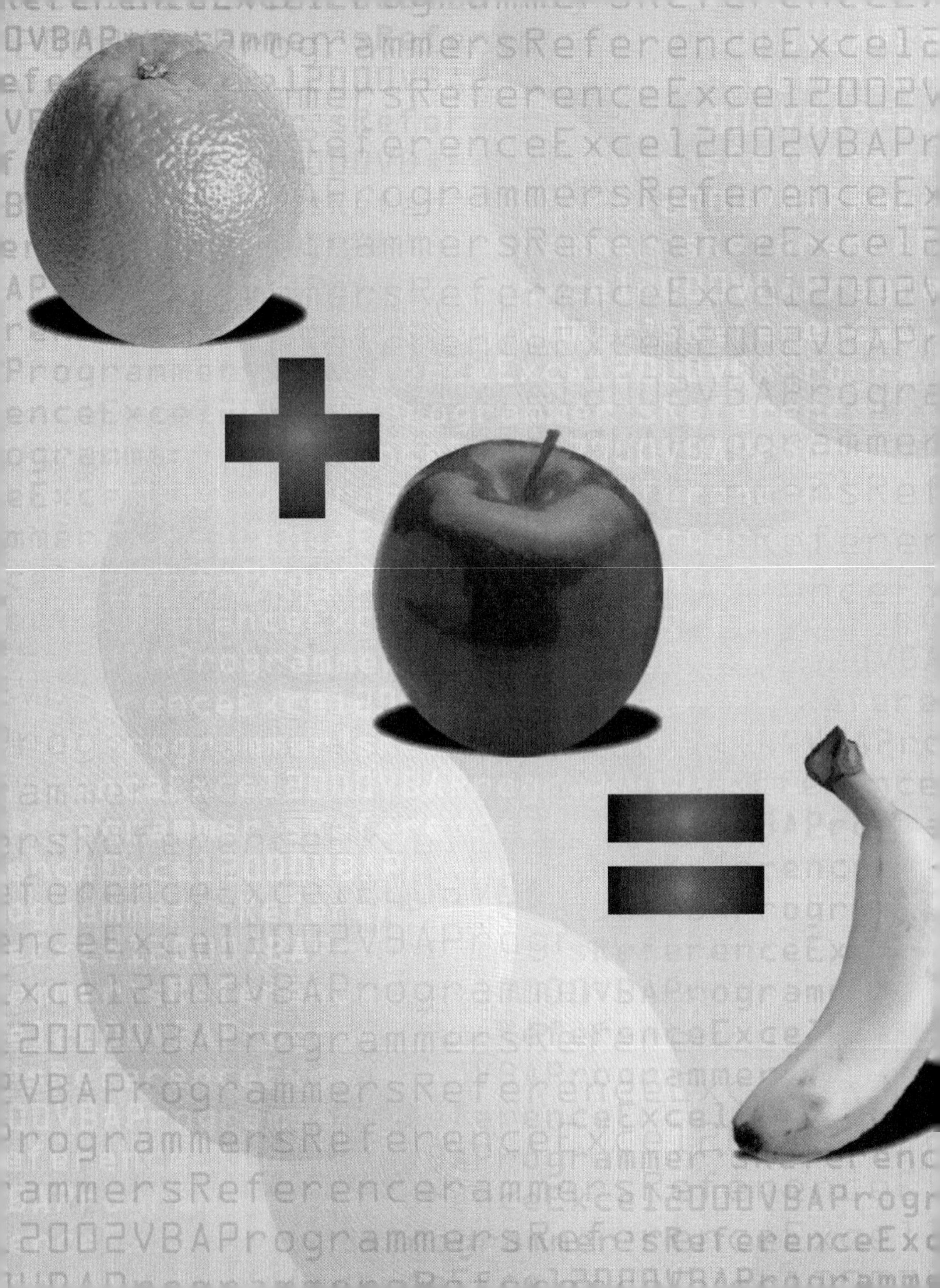

OleDbCommand / SqlCommand Objects

The OleDbCommand and SqlCommand objects let you encapsulate a command that could be executed against a data provider. OleDbCommand operates on OLE DB managed providers, such as Oracle, Jet, and many others and could be used for virtually all data providers that have corresponding OLE DB providers. SqlCommand operates on the SQL Server .NET managed provider and can execute a command on SQL Server version 7 and up.

Besides the OleDbCommand and SqlCommand objects, .NET contains a generic interface, IDbCommand, which is implemented by both SqlCommand and OleDbCommand. This IDbCommand interface sets the minimum requirements if you have to write a command object from your own managed data provider.

Recently, an Odbc .NET data provider has also become available but is not a part of Visual Studio.NET at the time of writing this book. This third .NET Provider is available as an add-on and you can download it from Microsoft's web site:

http://www.microsoft.com/downloads/release.asp?ReleaseID=31125

The Odbc .NET provider is simply a .NET wrapper around standard ODBC APIs and lets you take the benefits of ODBC connectivity directly. The classes related to this provider are contained in the System.Data.Odbc namespace. This namespace contains a set of classes that provide more or less the same functionality as that of ODBC API itself.

These classes provide a wide range of flexibility and functionality, especially when we have to execute stored procedures on a data provider. This makes it an important part of ADO.NET.

SqlCommand Class

SqlCommand is used to execute a T-SQL or stored procedure against SQL Server using the SQL Server .NET managed provider. It encapsulates a T-SQL command or a stored procedure. You can execute both queries, ones that return data as well as the ones that do not return data. You can also execute parameterized queries.

Here is the definition of the SqlCommand class:

VB.NET:

```
NotInheritable Public Class SqlCommand
    Inherits Component
    Implements IDbCommand, ICloneable
```

C#:

```
public sealed class SqlCommand : Component, IDbCommand, ICloneable
```

As you can see from the definition, you cannot inherit from this class. It implements IDbCommand and ICloneable. Implementation of the ICloneable interface enables us to clone any object created from this class.

The IDbCommand interface defines the minimum requirements that must be present when implemented by any managed data provider for a relational database system. It contains a list of properties, collections, and methods that have to be implemented by the implementing class.

As stated earlier, .NET comes with two sets of standard classes that implement this interface, SqlCommand and OleDbCommand classes. Lately, Microsoft has also released, as an add-on, a third set of classes, which implement this interface, the OdbcCommand class.

SqlCommand is a highly optimized implementation of the IDbCommand interface for Microsoft SQL Server 7.0 and up. These are very efficient because they use native SQL Server APIs to directly communicate with SQL Server and hence as a result they perform better and faster.

The OleDbCommand implements IDbCommand to provide a managed data provider over the OLE DB data provider. This saves you from calling native OLE DB methods manually using Interop.

The OdbcCommand implements this interface to provide a managed data provider over ODBC APIs.

We will cover OleDbCommand and OdbcCommand later in this chapter but we will start with the use of SqlCommand.

SqlCommand Constructors

SqlCommand has an overloaded constructor allowing you create a new instance of the SqlCommand class.

VB.NET:

```
public Sub New();
public Sub New( ByVal cmdText As String );
public Sub New( ByVal cmdText As String,
        ByVal connection As SqlConnection );
public Sub New( ByVal cmdText As String,
        ByVal connection As SqlConnection,
        ByVal transaction As SqlTransaction );
```

C#:

```
public SqlCommand();
public SqlCommand( string cmdText );
public SqlCommand( string cmdText, SqlConnection connection );
public SqlCommand( string cmdText, SqlConnection connection,
                SqlTransaction transaction );
```

The following table lists the arguments that could be provided to the constructor:

Argument	Type	Description
cmdText	string/ String	T-SQL statement or stored procedure name to be executed against SQL Server. By default it is set to an empty string. If you don't provide a command text at the time of creating the instance, you can use the CommandText (described in the next section) property later to assign a T-SQL statement or a stored procedure name.
connection	SqlConnection	SqlConnection object
transaction	SqlTransaction	SqlTransaction object

All of the above arguments of the constructors directly map to the corresponding properties.

An instance of a SqlCommand is created as below:

```
SqlCommand Cmd = new SqlCommand("Select * from Authors");
```

SqlCommand Properties

The CommandText Property

Sets or retrieves a T-SQL statement or stored procedure name to be executed against SQL Server.

VB.NET:
```
Property CommandText As String
```

C#:
```
string CommandText { get; set; }
```

You can also pass a value in the cmdText argument of the constructor to populate the value of the CommandText property. When you create an instance of SqlCommand, without providing a command text in its constructor, this property is set as an empty string.

For example you can pass a T-SQL statement in constructor to populate the value of CommandText property like this:

```
SqlCommand CmdSelect = new SqlCommand("Select * from Authors");
Console.WriteLine("CommandText: {0}", CmdSelect.CommandText );
```

Or you can explicitly set its value after creating the instance:

```
SqlCommand CmdSelect = new SqlCommand();
CmdSelect.CommandText = "Select * from Authors";
```

When you assign a stored procedure name to this property, you must set the `CommandType` property `CommandType.StoredProcedure`. When you assign a valid T-SQL statement to `CommandText`, you should also set the `CommandType` property to `Text`. However, as the default value of `CommandType` property is `CommandType.Text`, you don't have to do anything in this case:

```
SqlCommand Cmd = new SqlCommand();
Cmd.CommandType = CommandType.StoredProcedure
Cmd.CommandText = "sp_Get_Names"          // some stored procedure
```

You can also assign a parameterized query in the command text to execute against the data provider. SQL Server .NET managed provider does not support '?' placeholders in parameterized queries. You have to provide a named parameter like @name to execute. For example:

```
SqlCommand Cmd = new SqlCommand();
Cmd.CommandText = "Select au_fname from Author where au_lname=@lname";
Cmd.Parameters.Add("@lname", "white" );
Console.WriteLine("First Name: {0}", Cmd.ExecuteScalar());
```

The implementation of this property is required by the `IDbCommand` interface. No matter how you pass this command to the underlying data provider, all that is required is that it should be of string type.

Unlike the Oledb managed provider, the SQL managed provider does not support table names in its `CommandText` property. Doing so will result in an `InvalidOperationException` being thrown.

The CommandType Property

Sets or retrieves a flag to indicate to `SqlCommand` how to interpret the value contained in the `CommandText` property. It helps `SqlCommand` object to parse the value in the `CommandText` property.

VB.NET:
```
Public Property CommandType As CommandType
```

C#:
```
public CommandType CommandType { get; set; }
```

This property accepts a value of `CommandType` enum as shown in the table below:

Value	Description
Text	Instructs the `SqlCommand` object to interpret a T SQL statement. This is also the default value of `CommandType` property.
StoredProcedure	Indicates that the value in the `CommandText` is a stored procedure.
TableDirect	Not Supported for the SQL Server .NET managed provider

You can use the following code to call a stored procedure named `sp_Get_Authors`:

```
SqlCommand Cmd = new SqlCommand("sp_Get_Authors");
Cmd.CommandType = CommandType.StoredProcedure
```

If you assign an invalid value to this property, it will throw an `ArgumentException`.

Implementing a `CommandType` property is necessary for any class that implements the `IDbCommand` interface. However, it is not necessary for this implementation to use all of the command types. For example the `TableDirect` command type is not available for a `SqlCommand` implementation of this interface, but it is available for the `OleDbCommand` class.

The Connection Property

Sets or retrieves the `SqlConnection` object, used to execute commands.

VB.NET:

```
Public Property Connection As SqlConnection
```

C#:

```
public SqlConnection Connection { get; set; }
```

The `Command` property is also required to implement the `IDbCommand` interface.

VB.NET:

```
Property Connection As IDbConnection
```

C#:

```
IDbConnection Connection { get; set; }
```

According to the definition of this property with use with the `IDbCommand` interface, this property should be able to get or set an object that implements the `IDbConnection` interface. `SqlCommand` implements this property by allowing you to set or get a `SqlConnection` object, which in turn implements the `IDbConnection` interface. While, in a similar fashion, the `OleDbCommand` and `OdbcCommand` allow you to get or set the `OleDbConnection` and `OdbcConnection` respectively. Both of these connection objects also implement the `IDbConnection` interface. These connection objects provide the communication functionality needed to send the command to the data source.

`SqlCommand` is simply a wrapper around your T SQL statement or stored procedure; you need a `SqlConnection` object in order to execute it against the server. You can pass this `SqlConnection` object at the time of creating a `SqlCommand` object or you can explicitly assign a `SqlConnection` by using this property. You can assign a `SqlConnection` object at the time of creating instance of `SqlCommand` like this:

C#:

```
SqlConnection Cn = new

    SqlConnection("Server=MyServer;Database=MyDB;UID=user;PWD=pass;");
SqlCommand Cmd = new Command("Select * from MyTable", Cn );
```

Or you can explicitly assign a `SqlConnection` property to the `Connection` property like below:

C#:

```
SqlConnection Cn = new
        SqlConnection("Server=MyServer;Database=MyDB;UID=user;PWD=pass;");
SqlCommand Cmd = new Command("Select * from MyTable");
Cmd.Connection = Cn;
```

If the connection is already involved in a transaction and the `Transaction` property of the connection does not contain a null (`Nothing` in VB.NET), an exception of `InvalidOperationException` type will be thrown, when this connection object is assigned to a command object. No exception is thrown if the `Transaction` property is not null and the transaction has already been completed (either committed or roll backed).

For example, the following code will fail because the connection is involved in an incomplete transaction before being assigned to a command object:

```
SqlConnection Cn = new
        SqlConnection("Server=SAIMA;Database=pubs;UID=sa;PWD=;");
Cn.Open();
SqlTransaction tr =  Cn.BeginTransaction("MyTransaction");

// This is pending transaction
SqlCommand Cmd = new SqlCommand(null, Cn );
Cmd.CommandText = "select au_fname from authors where au_lname='white'";
string s = (string) Cmd.ExecuteScalar();  // This line will throw excptn
Console.WriteLine("First Name: {0}", s );
```

On the other hand, the following will execute without throwing an exception:

```
SqlConnection Cn = new
        SqlConnection("Server=SAIMA;Database=pubs;UID=sa;PWD=;");
Cn.Open();
SqlTransaction tr =  Cn.BeginTransaction("MyTransaction");
...
Tr.Commit();                       // This is completed transaction
SqlCommand Cmd = new SqlCommand(null, Cn );
Cmd.CommandText = "select au_fname from authors where au_lname='white'";
string s = (string) Cmd.ExecuteScalar();
Console.WriteLine("First Name: {0}", s );
```

The CommandTimeout Property

Specifies how long (in seconds) to wait while executing a command before terminating it and returning an error.

VB.NET:

```
Property CommandTimeout As Integer
```

C#:

```
int CommandTimeout { get; set; }
```

This property is also required to implement the `IDbCommand` interface.

You can set the value of this property to zero to force it to wait indefinitely while the command is executing. However, it is usually not a good practice, as it will hold the resources on the server for an indefinite time.

```
SqlCommand Cmd = new SqlCommand();
Cmd.Timeout = 10;
```

When the command is aborted because the timeout limit is reached, a `SqlException` is thrown. By default, this property is set to 30 seconds.

The Transaction Property

Sets or gets a transaction object for the command. This property accepts a `SqlTransaction` object.

VB.NET:
```
Public Property Transaction As SqlTransaction
```

C#:
```
public SqlTransaction Transaction { get; set; }
```

Most of the relational database systems support the notion of transactions and atomicity of operations. `IDbCommand` interface requires all of the managed data providers to encapsulate the transaction mechanism in a class that implements `IDbTransaction`.

VB.NET:
```
Property Transaction As IDbTransaction
```

C#:
```
IDbTransaction Transaction { get; set; }
```

If the data provider does not support transactions, even then it should provide a dummy method to implement the `IDbCommand` interface.

Transaction guarantees the atomicity of a series of operations on a database. All of the operations performed under a transaction are cached until the transaction is closed. A transaction can be closed in two ways: `Commit` or `Rollback`. When you commit the transaction all of the cached changes performed on the data are permanently written to the database. If you rollback a transaction, the cached changes are ignored and data remains unchanged.

There are a lot of situations when we have to perform more than one database operation to perform a transaction. The failure in any of the operations requires us to cancel all of the operations too. Consider the case fund transfer from one account to another. In this case you have to withdraw $100 from one account and deposit it into another account. Failing to do either of the operations requires us to cancel both operations. Otherwise the balance will not match in both accounts. Transactions are perfectly suited for these situations. The following code shows you how to perform the above operation using C#:

```
SqlConnection Cn = new
    SqlConnection("Server=SAIMA;Database=TestDB;UID=sa;PWD=;");
Cn.Open();
SqlTransaction trans = Cn.BeginTransaction();

SqlCommand Withdraw = new SqlCommand(null, Cn, trans );
Withdraw.CommandType = CommandType.StoredProcedure;
Withdraw.CommandText = "sp_Withdraw_Amount";
Withdraw.Parameters.Add("@act", SqlDbType.Int ).Value = 123456;
Withdraw.Parameters.Add("@amt", SqlDbType.Int ).Value = 100;
Withdraw.Parameters.Add("ret_val", SqlDbType.Int).Direction =
            ParameterDirection.ReturnValue;

SqlCommand Deposit = new SqlCommand(null, Cn, trans );
Deposit.CommandType = CommandType.StoredProcedure;
Deposit.CommandText = "sp_Deposit_Amount";
Deposit.Parameters.Add("@act", SqlDbType.Int ).Value = 654321;
Deposit.Parameters.Add("@amt", SqlDbType.Int ).Value = 100;
Deposit.Parameters.Add("ret_val", SqlDbType.Int).Direction =
            ParameterDirection.ReturnValue;
Withdraw.ExecuteNonQuery();
Deposit.ExecuteNonQuery();

if( Withdraw.Parameters["ret_val"].Value.Equals(0) &&
        Deposit.Parameters["ret_val"].Value.Equals(0) )
{
    trans.Commit();
    Console.WriteLine("Transaction Committed");
}
else
{
    trans.Rollback();
    Console.WriteLine("Transaction Rollbacked");
}
Cn.Close();
```

In the above code, after opening a connection, we started a transaction by calling the BeginTransaction method on a connection object with a SqlTransaction object returned. Then we created two SqlCommand objects, Withdraw and Deposit, and passed the SqlTransaction object in their constructors. This indicated that these commands will be part of the same transaction and they both have to succeed, for the transaction to be committed. After executing the ExecuteNoQuery method, we check the return value of both commands. If both succeed, then we explicitly called the Commit method on SqlTransaction object to tell the connection object to commit all of the changes made by both commands into the database. If either of the commands failed, we called the Rollback method of the transaction object to tell the command object to discard all the changes made by both commands.

To better use a transaction in a real-life application, consider using the Serviced component, which gives you transaction control at object level. They are the counterparts of COM+ components for managed code. For more information on Serviced Components, please see the ServicesComponent class in System.EnterpriseServices namespace.

The SqlTransaction Object

The SqlTransaction object represents a database transaction. You can either commit it or roll it back. It has several properties and methods which control the behavior of the transaction.

The IsolationLevel Property

It tells the transaction how it has to behave with more than one transaction running at the same time. `IsolationLevel` can contain any of the values from `IsolationLevel` enum shown in the table below:

Value	Description
ReadCommitted	ReadCommitted puts a shared lock on the data to avoid dirty reads. Other transactions will only be able to read the committed data from the transaction.
ReadUncommitted	It does not put any lock on the data and dirty reads are possible.
RepeatableRead	Puts a lock on all of the data used in a query. This stops other transactions modifying the data.
Serializable	Puts a range lock on data. This prevents others from modifying the data involved in the current transaction
Chaos	This insures that no other transaction overrides the data committed by the current transaction.
Unspecifed	Unknown isolation level

You can pass the isolation level at the time of creating the instance of the transaction object, by providing it in the argument of the `BeginTransaction` method of the `SqlConnection` object. For example:

```
SqlTransaction trans = Cn.BeginTransaction( IsolationLevel.Serializable );
```

You can change the `IsolationLevel` behavior anytime by setting the property. For example:

```
trans.IsolationLevel = IsolationLevel.Chaos;
```

The default `IsolationLevel` is ReadCommited.

The Commit Method

Makes all of the pending changes in a transaction permanent on the database. Calling a `Commit` method completes a transaction:

```
trans.Commit();
```

The Rollback Method

Discards all of the pending operations in a transaction:

```
trans.Rollback();
```

You can also provide the name of the transaction or a save point as an argument. Doing so will discard all of the changes made to data after the save point. This is useful in most of the cases where your transaction has more than one section. For example, in most batch applications, we write header information to the database and then process that batch data. You can put a save point after the header information is written to the database so in case of failure, you can rollback to the point where the header information was saved. For example the following code rollbacks a transaction to a save point named `myTrans`:

```
trans.Rollback("myTrans");
```

The Save Method

Creates a checkpoint in a transaction. A checkpoint is a marker which could be used to partially rollback a transaction. Although partial rollback is a nice feature, one has to be extra cautious when using it, because it may result in an invalid data state. Lets consider the example of the previous bank transaction. Physically it is a two step process. In the first step, the amount of money is withdrawn from one account and in the second step the same amount of money is deposited in the other account. If you use a save point in between the two steps and issued a rollback to this save point (in case of failure to deposit the money) the data will become invalid as the money was already withdrawn from the account. As you can see, to avoid this kind of situation you must be cautious of the use of this feature:

```
Trans = Cn.BeginTransaction ();
Cmd1.ExecuteNonQuery();
trans.Save("MyCheckPoint");
Cmd2.ExecuteNonQuery();
trans.Rollback("MyCheckPoint ");
trans.Commit();
```

In the above code fragment, command 1 will be committed but command 2 will be rolled back.

The UpdatedRowSource Property

Indicates how the results from the command will be used to modify a `DataRow` in a `DataSet`, when the `Update` method is called on `SqlDataAdapter`.

VB.NET:
```
Public Property UpdatedRowSource As UpdateRowSource
```

C#:
```
public UpdateRowSource UpdatedRowSource { get; set; }
```

This property is also required by the `IDbCommand` interface.

The `UpdateRowSource` property can be assigned to one of the following values of the `UpdateRowSource` enum:

❑ **FirstReturnedRecord:** Only first returned row from the command object will be mapped to the changed `DataRow` in the `DataSet` object. Any output parameter is ignored.

❑ **OutputParameters:** Only output parameters from the command object will be mapped to the changed `DataRow` in the `DataSet` object. Returned rows are ignored.

❑ **Both:** Both first returned record and output parameters are mapped to the changed DataRow in a DataSet object.

❑ **None:** None of the values is mapped.

When the SqlCommand object is used in UpdateCommand, InsertCommand, DeleteCommand, or SelectCommand properties of the SqlDataAdapter object, the value of the UpdatedRowSource property tells the data adapter object how to interpret the results from the command. Also, this property advises on how to apply the changes on the DataRow object contained in the DataSet object. The following example uses C# to show how to use this property. Here we have created a DataSet, ds, from the Authors table of the pubs database. After creating this data set, we changed au_lname for the fourth row in the DataSet. Finally, we used the Update method of SqlDataAdapter to send the changes to the data provider and synchronize the data set object with the database:

```
SqlDataAdapter da = new
    SqlDataAdapter("select au_id, au_lname from Authors", Cn);
//Cn - SqlConnection object from above code snippets'

SqlCommand Cmd = new
    SqlCommand("Update Authors SET au_lname = @au_lname "
    + "WHERE au_id = @au_id" , Cn);
Cmd.Parameters.Add("@au_lname", SqlDbType.VarChar, 20, "au_lname" );
SqlParameter prm = Cmd.Parameters.Add("@au_id", SqlDbType.VarChar, 20 );
prm.SourceColumn = "au_id";
prm.SourceVersion = DataRowVersion.Original;
Cmd.UpdatedRowSource = None;

da.UpdateCommand = Cmd;

Cn.Open();
DataSet ds = new DataSet();
da.Fill(ds, "Authors");


DataRow dr = ds.Tables["Authors"].Rows[3];
dr["au_lname"] = "Adil";


DataRow[] dr_modified = ds.Tables["Authors"].Select(null, null,
        DataViewRowState.ModifiedCurrent);
da.Update(dr_modified);
Cn.Close();
```

The DesignTimeVisible Property

Indicates if the command object should be visible on the Windows Forms Designer Control.

VB.NET:
```
Public Property DesignTimeVisible as Boolean
```

C#:
```
public bool DesignTimeVisible { get; set; }
```

The following code sets the value to `true` using C#:

```
SqlCommand Cmd = new SqlCommand();
Cmd.DesignTimeVisible = true;
```

Here is its equivalent in VB.NET:

```
Dim Cmd As SqlCommand
SqlCommand = New SqlCommand();
Cmd.DesignTimeVisible = True;
```

The default value for this property is `False`.

SqlCommand Methods

The ExecuteReader Method

Executes the command in `CommandText` against the assigned `SqlConnection` to return a `SqlDataReader` object. `SqlDataReader` is a read only, forward only cursor on the set of rows. You can also control the behavior of the returned `SqlDataReader` object by providing a `CommandBehavior` flag.

This method is overloaded:

VB.NET:
```
Overloads Public Function ExecuteReader() As SqlDataReader
Overloads Public Function ExecuteReader(
    ByVal behavior As CommandBehavior ) As SqlDataReader
```

C#:
```
public SqlDataReader ExecuteReader();
public SqlDataReader ExecuteReader( CommandBehavior behavior );
```

Both of the overloaded methods are required to implement the `IDbCommand` interface.

VB.NET:
```
Function ExecuteReader() As IDataReader
Function ExecuteReader( ByVal behavior As CommandBehavior ) As IDataReader
```

C#:
```
IDataReader ExecuteReader();
IDataReader ExecuteReader( Command Behavior behavior );
```

As per the definition of these methods in the `IDbCommand` interface, they should return an object that implements the `IDataReader` interface. The `IDataReader` interface sets the minimum requirements for an object to implement a forward only and read only cursor on a set of data (returned by a select query). The `ExecuteReader` method for the `SqlCommand` object returns a `SqlDataReader` object, which implements the `IDataReader` interface. This method is useful when you query a set of rows and you only need a forward only cursor to browse through the data rows.

Using the behavior argument, you can also control the behavior of the `SqlDataReader` object generated from this method. The argument behavior can be set to one of the values of the `CommandBehavior` enum:

- ❑ **CloseConnection**: as soon as you close the `SqlDataReader` object, the `SqlConnection` object associated with it will also be closed.

- ❑ **SchemaOnly**: does not return rows, only returns column information. It is just like putting SET FMTONLY ON before your query.

- ❑ **KeyInfo**: no matter which column you select in your query, the primary key is also returned in the data.

- ❑ **SingleResult**: returns a single result.

- ❑ **SingleRow**: returns only the first row of the result set.

The following example demonstrates the use of the `SingleRow` behavior:

```
//C#
SqlConnection Cn = new
        SqlConnection("Server=SAIMA;Database=pubs;UID=sa;PWD=;");
Cn.Open();
SqlCommand Cmd = new SqlCommand(null, Cn );
Cmd.CommandText = "select au_fname, au_lname from authors";

SqlDataReader dr = Cmd.ExecuteReader( CommandBehavior.SingleRow );
while( dr.Read() )
{
    for( int i=0; i<dr.FieldCount; i++ )
    {
        Console.Write( dr[i].ToString() );
        if( i == (dr.FieldCount-1) )
            Console.WriteLine("");
        else
            Console.Write(", ");
    }
}
Cn.Close();
```

Although the query in the `CommandText` property should return all rows from the Authors table, because of the `SingleRow` behavior only the first row will be returned. Here is the output of the above code segment:

Abraham, Bennet

The following C# code fragment uses the `KeyInfo` behavior to get the values from two columns in a table that are not the primary key in the table. However as the behavior of the `ExecuteReader` is set to `KeyInfo`, the values of the primary key for each row is also returned with the data. Using this behavior you don't have to include the column names of table's primary key in the `select` statement of the command object. This works for both simple primary keys where your primary key is composed of only one column, and also for composite primary key where it is composed of more than one column of the table:

```
SqlConnection Cn = new
        SqlConnection("Server=SAIMA;Database=pubs;UID=sa;PWD=;");
```

```
Cn.Open();
SqlCommand Cmd = new SqlCommand(null, Cn );
Cmd.CommandText = "select au_lname + ', ' + au_fname from authors";

SqlDataReader dr = Cmd.ExecuteReader( CommandBehavior.KeyInfo );
while( dr.Read() )
{
   for( int i=0; i<dr.FieldCount; i++ )
   {
      Console.Write( dr[i].ToString() );
      if( i == (dr.FieldCount-1) )
         Console.WriteLine("");
      else
         Console.Write(", ");
   }
}
Cn.Close();
```

Below is the output produced by this code snippet:

```
Bennet, Abraham, 409-56-7008
Blotchet-Halls, Reginald, 648-92-1872
Carson, Cheryl, 238-95-7766
...
White, Johnson, 172-32-1176
Yokomoto, Akiko, 672-71-3249
```

As you can see, the primary key is also returned for each row along with the first and last name.

The ExecuteNonQuery Method

Issues DDL commands or commands that do not return records, instead only returns number of rows affected, for example INSERT, UPDATE, or DELETE statements.

VB.NET:
```
NotOverridable Public Function ExecuteNonQuery() As Integer
```

C#:
```
public int ExecuteNonQuery();
```

In case of a DDL or a select statement, it returns -1.

This method is also required to implement the IDbCommand interface.

The following example uses C# to create a table, insert some rows and then try to select rows from the table:

```
int res;
SqlConnection Cn = new
   SqlConnection("Server=SAIMA;Database=TestDB;UID=sa;PWD=;");
Cn.Open();

SqlCommand CmdCreate = new SqlCommand(null, Cn );
```

```
CmdCreate.CommandText = "Create Table TestTable( col01 int )";
res = CmdCreate.ExecuteNonQuery();
Console.WriteLine("Table Created .... (Output: {0})", res );

SqlCommand CmdInsert = new SqlCommand(null, Cn );
CmdInsert.CommandText =
        "insert into TestTable Values(1); insert into TestTable Values(2)";
res = CmdInsert.ExecuteNonQuery();
Console.WriteLine("{0} Row(s) inserted", res );

// Select can't return rows nor give correct # of rows, it returns -1
SqlCommand CmdSelect = new SqlCommand(null, Cn );
CmdSelect.CommandText = "select * from TestTable";
res = CmdSelect.ExecuteNonQuery();
Console.WriteLine("Select stmt does not return correct # of rows .. {0}",
                            res );
Cn.Close();
```

The output for the code fragment is:

Table Created .... (Output: -1)
2 Row(s) inserted
Select stmt does not return correct # of rows .. -1

The ExecuteXMLReader Method

Sends the command to the data provider through a `SqlConnection` object and returns the data through an `XmlReader` object.

VB.NET:

```
NotOverridable Public Function ExecuteXMLReader() As XmlReader
```

C#:

```
public XmlReader ExecuteXMLReader();
```

This method is just like `ExecuteReader` except that it returns an XML reader instead of a `SqlDataReader`. SQL Server can return a formatted XML stream of data when you append a `FOR XML AUTO` clause at the end of the query. `ExecuteXMLReader` uses the same mechanism as previous to generate an XML stream from the database server and pass it back to the calling procedure in the form of XML. You can use an `XmlReader` object to process the XML data.

The following C# example sends the command to the data provider and saves the returned XML onto a disk file:

```
SqlConnection Cn = new
        SqlConnection("Server=SAIMA;Database=pubs;UID=sa;PWD=;");
Cn.Open();
SqlCommand Cmd = new SqlCommand(null, Cn );
Cmd.CommandText = "select * from authors for xml auto";
XmlReader xr = Cmd.ExecuteXmlReader();

DataSet ds = new DataSet();
ds.ReadXml( xr );
ds.WriteXml("c:\\authors.xml");
Cn.Close();
```

Keep in mind that, in order to use this method, your command should generate an XML document from the data provider. Otherwise an `InvalidOperationException` will be thrown.

The ExecuteScalar Method

Returns the value of the first column of the first row.

VB.NET:

```
NotOverridable Public Function ExecuteScalar() As Object
```

C#:

```
public object ExecuteScalar();
```

This property is also required by the `IDbCommand` Interface and is usually very helpful when you want only one data value to be returned. For example, if you have `au_id` (primary key on authors table) and you only want to get the first name of the author, you can use `ExecuteScalar` method using C# as below:

```
SqlConnection Cn = new
        SqlConnection("Server=SAIMA;Database=pubs;UID=sa;PWD=;");
Cn.Open();
SqlCommand Cmd = new SqlCommand(null, Cn );
Cmd.CommandText = "select au_fname from authors where au_id=@auid";
Cmd.Parameters.Add("@auid", "172-32-1176");

string s = (string) Cmd.ExecuteScalar();
Console.WriteLine("First Name is {0}", s );
Cn.Close();
```

You can also use this method for queries that have aggregate functions and return only one summarized value. The following C# code demonstrates how to do this:

```
SqlConnection Cn = new
        SqlConnection("Server=SAIMA;Database=pubs;UID=sa;PWD=;");
Cn.Open();
SqlCommand Cmd = new SqlCommand(null, Cn );
Cmd.CommandText = "select count(*) from authors ";

Console.WriteLine("Total number of Autors: {0}", Cmd.ExecuteScalar() );
Cn.Close();
```

The ResetCommandTimeout Method

Resets the value of the `CommandTimeout` property to its default value, 30 seconds.

VB.NET:

```
Public Sub ResetCommandTimeout()
```

C#:

```
public void ResetCommandTimeout();
```

The following code snippet demonstrates how to use this method:

```
SqlCommand cmd = SqlCommand();
cmd.CommandTimeout = 20;    // Sets CommandTimeout to 20 seconds
cmd.ResetCommandTimeout();   // Resets CommandTimeout to 30 seconds
```

The CreateParameter Method

Creates a new instance of a `SqlParameter` object. It is used when we have a parameterized query or a stored procedure in a `CommandText` property.

VB.NET:

```
Public Function CreateParameter() As SqlParameter
```

C#:

```
public SqlParameter CreateParameter();
```

This method is required to implement the `IDbCommand` interface.

VB.NET:

```
Function CreateParameter() As IDataParameter
```

C#:

```
IDataParameter CreateParameter();
```

The `IDbCommand` requires this method to return an object that implements the `IDataParameter` interface. The `IDataParameter` interface defines the specification for an object that can represent a parameter passed to a stored procedure or a parameterized query. If the data provider does not support parameterized queries or stored procedures that accept parameters, a dummy `IDataParameter` must be implemented by the provider. The `CreateParameter` method of the command object should create and return the instance of this dummy object. For `SqlCommand`, the corresponding `IDataParameter` object is the `SqlParameter` object.

A `SqlParameter` object is needed to pass parameters in stored procedures as well as in parameterized queries. These parameters can be input or output parameters. You can also use the same object to get the return code of the stored procedures. To create a `SqlParameter` object from the `CreateParameter` method, you can use the following C# code:

```
SqlParamater param = Cmd.CreateParameter();
param.ParameterName = "@FirstName";
param.SqlDbSize = SqlDbSize.VarChar;
param.Size = 30;
param.Value = "SomeValue"
Cmd.Parameters.Add( param );
```

After getting a reference to the `SqlParameter` object, you can set its name, data type, size, value, and so on. From the above code you can see that using the `CreateParameter` method does not append the parameter object onto the `Parameters` collections of the command object. You have to explicitly do it later on.

You can also create a parameter object explicitly without using `CreateParameter` method, such as:

```
SqlParameter param = new SqlParameter();
```

You can also use the `Add` method of the `Parameter` collection to create a parameter. It takes the parameter name with its data type and size as arguments. The following C# code snippet uses the `Add` method to create a `SqlParameter` object. It passes `"@amount"` as the parameter name with `SqlDbType.Int` as the data type of the parameter and indicates that the maximum size of this parameter will be 1000:

```
SqlParameter param = Cmd.Parameters.Add("@amount", SqlDbtype.Int );
param.Value = 1000;
```

If you use this method of creating a `SqlParameter` object, you don't have to add it to `Parameters` collection, as it has already been added.

The SqlParameter Class

As shown in the last section, you can explicitly create a new instance of the `SqlParameter` object using one of its constructors. For example you can use the following code to create a parameter of the type of varchar(30):

```
SqlParameter param = new SqlParameter("@fname", SqlDbType.VarChar, 30 );
```

The `SqlParameter` class has a number of constructors, as shown in the following list:

VB.NET:
```
Public Sub New()
Public Sub New( _
    ByVal parameterName As String, _
    ByVal value As Object )
Public Sub New( _
    ByVal parameterName As String, _
    ByVal dbType As SqlDbType )
Public Sub New( _
    ByVal parameterName As String, _
    ByVal dbType As SqlDbType, _
    ByVal size As Integer )
Public Sub New( _
    ByVal parameterName As String, _
    ByVal dbType As SqlDbType, _
    ByVal size As Integer, _
    ByVal sourceColumn As String )
Public Sub New( _
    ByVal parameterName As String, _
    ByVal dbType As SqlDbType, _
    ByVal size As Integer, _
    ByVal direction As ParameterDirection, _
    ByVal isNullable As Boolean, _
    ByVal precision As Byte, _
    ByVal scale As Byte, _
    ByVal sourceColumn As String, _
    ByVal sourceVersion As DataRowVersion, _
    ByVal value As Object )
```

C#:

```
public SqlParameter();
public SqlParameter(
    string parameterName,
        object value );
public SqlParameter(
        string parameterName,
        SqlDbType dbType );
public SqlParameter(
        string parameterName,
        SqlDbType dbType,
        int size );
public SqlParameter(
        string parameterName,
        SqlDbType dbType,
        int size,
        string sourceColumn );
public SqlParameter(
        string parameterName,
        SqlDbType dbType,
        int size,
        ParameterDirection direction,
        bool isNullable,
        byte precision,
        byte scale,
        string sourceColumn,
        DataRowVersion sourceVersion,
        object value );
```

All of the arguments in the constructors are mapped to the corresponding properties listed in the table below:

Property	Description
ParameterName	Name of the parameter
DbType	Generic data type of the parameter. Could be one of the values from the System.Data.DbType enum.
OleDbType	Data type of the parameter specific to the .NET data provider. OleDbType and DbType are internally linked changing the value of DbType also changes the value of OleDbType to corresponding data type. For a list of Data Type comparisons see next table.
Value	Value of the parameter
Direction	Indicates if it is an input parameter, output parameter or return value.

Table continued on following page

Property	Description
IsNullable	Indicates if the value of this parameter can be null or if not accepts a Boolean value.
Size	Indicates the maximum size of the data in the parameter in bytes.
Precision	Maximum number of digits to represent the value of the parameter, if it is numeric.
Scale	Maximum number of decimal places to be used to represent the value of the parameter.
SourceColumn	Contains the name of the DataColumn in a DataRow where the value of the parameter will be retrieved. For details see chapter 7 on the DataAdapter.
SourceVersion	Used in conjunction with SourceColumn by the DataAdapter to find which version of the DataRow is to be used to retrieve a parameter value. This could be one of the values from the DataRowVersion enum. For details see Chapter 7.

SqlDbType lists all of the supported data types by the SQL Server .NET managed provider. Below is the mapping between different data types. We will talk about OleDbType later in this chapter:

Framework Type	DbType	SqlDbType	OleDbType
bool	Boolean	Bit	Boolean
byte	Byte	TinyInt	UnsignedTinyInt
byte[]	Binary	VarBinary	VarBinary
char		N/S	Char
DateTime	DateTime	DateTime	DBTimeStamp
Decimal	Decimal	Decimal	Decimal
double	Double	Float	Double
float	Single	Real	Single
Guid	Guid	UniqueIdentifier	Guid
int		Int	Integer
Int16	Int16	SmallInt	SmallInt
Int32	Int32	Int	Int
Int64	Int64	BigInt	BigInt
long		BigInt	BigInt
object	Object	Variant	Variant

Framework Type	DbType	SqlDbType	OleDbType
short		SmallInt	SmallInt
string	String	NVarChar	VarWChar
UInt16	UInt16	N/S	Unsigned Small Int
UInt32	UInt32	N/S	UnsignedInt
UInt64	UInt64	N/S	UnsignedBogInt
	AnsiStrubg	VarChar	VarChar
	Currency	Money	Currency
	Date	DateTime	DBDate
	SByte	TinyInt	TinyInt
	Time	DateTime	DBTime
	VarNumeric	N/S	VarNumeric

The Prepare Method

Caches the commands on SQL Server resulting in faster execution of the command if called more than once.

VB.NET:

```
NotOverridable Public Sub Prepare()
```

C#:

```
public void Prepare();
```

This method is also required to implement the IDbCommand. If the data provider does not support compilation of commands, the managed provider should provide a dummy implementation for this method.

Consider the following example to better understand the use of the Prepare method. In this example, we are creating a prepared and an unprepared command and executing it against a SQL Server 30000 times. Both of the commands are executing the same stored procedure:

```
//C#
class ADONET_SQLCOMMAND
{
static void Main(string[] args)
    {
    DateTime StartTime;
    SqlConnection Cn = new
    SqlConnection("Server=FMC;Database=TestDB;UID=sa;PWD=pass;");
    SqlDataReader dr;

    Cn.Open();

    // Prepared Command Statement
```

```
SqlCommand Preparedcmd = new SqlCommand("Select * from Students",
                            Cn);
Preparedcmd.Prepare();
StartTime = DateTime.Now;
for( int i=0; i < 30000; i++ )
{
    dr = Preparedcmd.ExecuteReader();
    dr.Close();
}
Console.WriteLine("Prepared Command: {0}",
            DateTime.Now - StartTime );
// Unprepared Command Statement
SqlCommand cmd = new SqlCommand("Select * from Students", Cn);        StartTime =
DateTime.Now;
for( int i=0; i < 30000; i++ )
{
    dr = cmd.ExecuteReader();
    dr.Close();
}
Console.WriteLine("Normal Command  : {0}",
            DateTime.Now - StartTime );
Console.Read();
    }
}
Cn.Close();
```

From the output, you can see the prepared version ran faster:

```
Prepared Command: 00:00:19.9486848
Normal Command  : 00:00:22.4923424
```

It internally uses the `sp_prepexec` stored procedure on SQL Server to compile and cache commands on SQL Server. The next time the same command is executed, it calls the `sp_execute` stored procedure and provides the reference of the last compiled command. This compilation and caching is specific to the connection. As soon as you close the connection, it automatically destroys the execution plan from SQL Server by using the `sp_unprepare` stored procedure.

The Cancel Method

Cancels asynchronous executions of `SqlCommand`.

VB.NET:
```
Sub Cancel();
```

C#:
```
void Cancel();
```

This method is also required to implement the `IDbCommand` interface and gives a good opportunity to cancel long running queries without freezing the users screen.

SqlCommand Collections

The Parameters Collection

The Parameters collection is an instance of SqlParameterCollection and can contain a list of SqlParameter objects.

VB.NET:

```
Public ReadOnly Property Parameters As SqlParameterCollection
```

C#:

```
public SqlParameterCollection Parameters {get;}
```

This collection is necessary to implement the IDbCommand interface. According to the definition of this collection for the IDbCommand interface, this collection object must implement the IDataParameterCollection interface.

VB.NET:

```
ReadOnly Property Parameters As IDataParameterCollection
```

C#:

```
IDataParameterCollection Parameters { gets; }
```

The IDataParameterCollection interface sets the requirement for a collection of objects that implement the IDataParameter interface. For SQL managed providers, this collection is implemented by the ISqlParameterCollection which contains a list of the SqlParameter objects.

These SqlParameters objects are a list of parameters for stored procedures or parameterized queries contained in the CommandText property of the SqlCommand object. Parameters are passed to the data provider based on the name not on the basis of position in the Parameters collection, which is a read only collection. To add a SqlParameter object to this collection you can use the Add method. For example, the following code adds a parameter named "param1" of type SqlDbType.Int:

```
Cmd.Parameters.Add ("param1", SqlDbType.Int);
```

You can access this SqlParameter object later on, using the follow code:

```
Cmd.Parameters["param1"].Value = 123;
```

The SqlParameterCollection Collection

Contains the list of SqlParameter objects. It is a strongly typed collection. In the following sections, we will look at properties and methods of the SqlParameterCollection.

The Count Property

Indicates the number of SqlParameter objects contained in the collection. The following code lists the name of all of the parameters in the collection:

```
for( int i = 0; i < Cmd.Parameters.Count; i++ )
{
 Console.WriteLine("Parameter {0}: {1}", i,
            Cmd.Parameters[i].ParameterName );
}
```

As `SqlParameterCollection` implements the `IEnumerable` interface, you can also use it for each statement like this:

```
foreach( SqlParameter p in Cmd.Parameters )
{
    Console.WriteLine( p.ParameterName );
}
```

The Item Property

Accesses individual items in the collection, for example, to access a parameter name `"param1"`, you will use:

```
SqlParameter param = Cmd.Parameters.Item("param1");
```

You can also access the items using their index. For example to access the first item in the collection:

```
SqlParameter param = Cmd.Parameters.Item(0);
```

Finally, you can also use index as shown below:

```
SqlParameter param1 = Cmd.Parameters["param"]
SqlParameter param2 = Cmd.Parameters[0]
```

The Add Method

Adds a new item of `SqlParameter` in the collection.

VB.NET:
```
Overloads Public Function Add( _
    ByVal value As ISqlParameter ) As SqlParameter
NotOverridable Overloads Public Function Add( _
    ByVal value As Object ) As Integer
Overloads Public Function Add( _
    ByVal name As String, _
    ByVal value As Object ) As SqlParameter
Overloads Public Function Add( _
    ByVal name As String, _
    ByVal dbType As SqlDbType ) As SqlParameter
Overloads Public Function Add( _
    ByVal name As String, _
    ByVal dbType As SqlDbType, _
    ByVal size As Integer ) As SqlParameter
Overloads Public Function Add( _
    ByVal name As String, _
    ByVal dbType As SqlDbType, _
    ByVal size As Integer, _
    ByVal sourceColumn As String ) As SqlParameter
```

C#:

```
    public SqlParameter Add(
        ISqlParameter value );
    public int Add(
        object value );
    public SqlParameter Add(
        string name,
        object value );
    public SqlParameter Add(
        string name,
        SqlDbType dbType );
    public SqlParameter Add(
        string name,
        SqlDbType dbType,
        int size );
    public SqlParameter Add(
        string name,
        SqlDbType dbType,
        int size,
        string sourceColumn );
```

Here each argument of the Add method maps to a property in the SqlParameter object. For example to add a parameter name "param1" of varchar(20), you can use the following code:

```
    Cmd.Parameters.Add( "param1", SqlDbType.VarChar, 20 );
```

For more information see the CreateParameter section.

The Insert, Remove, RemoveAt and Clear Methods

Insert method inserts a new SqlParameter object at a specified location in the collection. Remove method removes an object from the collection, while RemoveAt removes an object from a specified location in the collection. Clear method removes all of the objects from the collection.

The following example use these methods:

```
    Cmd.Parameters.Add("param1", SqlDbType.Int );
    Cmd.Parameters.Add("param2", SqlDbType.Int );
    Cmd.Parameters.Inserts(1, new Sqlparameter("param1a", SqlDbType.Int) );
            // Inserts an object between 1st and 2nd object
    Cmd.Parameters.RemoveAt(0);
            // Removes first object
    Cmd.Parameters.Clear();
            // Removes all objects
```

The Contains and CopyTo Method

The Contains method checks if the object is already present in the collection or not. While the CopyTo method copies the list of parameters to an array of a SqlParameter object.

OleDbCommand and OdbcCommand Classes

`OleDbCommand` and its associated classes are contained in the `System.Data.Oledb` namespace and allows you to interact with the OLE DB .NET Data Provider. The OLE DB .NET Data Provider is one of the two managed data providers that ships with the .NET Framework. At the core, it is simply a .NET managed wrapper around traditional OLE DB providers. This gives you the flexibility to interact with any Unmanaged OLE DB Provider in your managed code, without having to worry about `Interop` and other technologies. Internally these classes perform all of the `Interop` calls for you, so that you can stay focused on your managed code.

`OleDbCommand` is one of the most useful classes in its namespace. Just like the `SqlCommand` class, this also encapsulates a command that could be submitted against a database, but through an OLE DB provider. As these sets of classes go through the OLE layer, their use of SQL Server is discouraged, as we have a managed provider for SQL Server, which directly connects to a SQL Server database using internal APIs.

OleDbCommand and OdbcCommand Constructors

`OleDbCommand` constructors are used to create new instances of the command object. The constructor for `OleDbCommand` is overloaded.

VB.NET:

```
Public Sub New()
Public Sub New( ByVal cmdText As String )
Public Sub New( ByVal cmdText As String,
        ByVal connection As OleDbConnection )
Public Sub New( ByVal cmdText As String,
        ByVal connection As OleDbConnection,
        ByVal transaction As OleDbTransaction )
```

C#:

```
public OleDbCommand();
public OleDbCommand( string cmdText );
public OleDbCommand( string cmdText, OleDbConnection connection );
public OleDbCommand( string cmdText, OleDbConnection connection,
            OleDbTransaction transaction );
```

Here is the list of constructors for the `OdbcCommand`:

VB.NET:

```
Public Sub New()
Public Sub New( ByVal cmdText As String )
Public Sub New( ByVal cmdText As String,
     ByVal connection As OdbcConnection )
Public Sub New( ByVal cmdText As String,
        ByVal connection As OdbcConnection,
        ByVal transaction As OdbcTransaction )
```

C#:
```
public OdbcCommand();
public OdbcCommand( string commandText );
public OdbcCommand( string commandText,
      OdbcConnection connection );
public OdbcCommand( string commandText,
      OdbcConnection connection,
      OdbcTransaction transaction );
```

The following table lists the arguments used in the constructors for both the `OleDbCommand` and `OdbcCommand` objects:

Argument	Type	Description
cmdText	string/ String	SQL statement or stored procedure name to be executed against OLE DB and ODBC data providers. By default it is set to an empty string. This argument is used to populate the `CommandText` property.
connection	OleDbConnection /OdbcConnection	`OleDbConnection` object or `OdbcConnection` object.
transaction	OleDbTransaction /OdbcTransaction	`OleDbTransaction` object or `OdbcConnection` object.

All of the above arguments of the constructors directly map to the corresponding properties.

To create an instance of the `OleDbCommand`:

```
OleDbConnection Cn = new OleDbConnection("some conn string")
OleDbCommand Cmd = new OleDbCommand("Select * from Puducts", Cn );
```

To create an instance of the `OdbcCommand`, you can use the following code with a data source name (DSN) of `myDSN` specified:

```
OdbcConnection Cn = new
          OdbcConnection("DSN=myDSN;UID=sa;PWD=sa");
OdbcCommand Cmd = new
          OdbcCommand("select * from authors", Cn );
```

OleDbCommand Properties

The CommandText Property

Contains the command encapsulated by the `OleDbCommand` object. This is the text that is passed to the underlying OLE DB data provider.

VB.NET:
```
Overridable Public Property CommandText As String
```

C#:

```
public string CommandText { get; set }
```

You can set the property to any valid command that your data provider supports, such as the name of a table, query, or a stored procedure. This represents the command that will be sent to the data provider. For example, to get all of the values from a table you can set this property to a table name. You will also have to set `CommandType` to `CommandType.TableDirect` to inform the command object that the text contained in the `CommandText` property is a name of the table:

```
OleDbCommand Cmd = new OlebCommand();
Cmd.CommandText = "Authors":
Cmd.CommandType = CommandType.TableDirect;
```

You can also set a query in the object to execute, for example:

```
OleDbCommand Cmd = new OlebCommand();
Cmd.CommandText = "select * from Authors":
Cmd.CommandType = CommandType.Text;
```

But in this case you will have to set the `CommandType` property to `Text`.

`CommandText` is also supported by the `OdbcCommand` but there are some things you have to keep in mind when using it. First of all, the `CommandText` for `OdbcCommand` supports "?" as the place holder for parameters. Secondly, when you set the `CommandType` for a stored procedure, you must use the full syntax of your ODBC driver. There are many ODBC drivers present in the market and each of them do special handling for several different commands and escape sequences.

The CommandType Property

Indicates the type of the command object. The value of this property also qualifies the value contained in the `CommandText` property. You can set the value of this property to one of the values of the `CommandType` enum, as follows:

❑ **Text:** Indicates that the value contained in the `CommandText` property is a `Text` command.

❑ **StoredProcedure:** Indicates that the `CommandText` property contains the name of a stored procedure.

❑ **TableDirect:** Indicates that the `CommandText` contains a name of a table on the data provider and the command has to connect to the table to get the data.

VB.NET:

```
Overridable Public Property CommandType As CommandType
```

C#:

```
public CommandType CommandType { get; set; }
```

This property is available for both `OleDbCommand` and `OdbcCommand` objects. However, there are some restrictions for this property with `OdbcCommand`. First, for an `OdbcCommand` you cannot set the value of this property to `CommandType.TableDirect` as it is not supported by the Odbc data provider. Second, when the value of this property is set to `CommandType.StoredProcedure`, you should set the `CommandText` property to a full ODBC call syntax. Failing to do so may result in an exception for some stored procedures.

Consider the following C# code that executes a stored procedure on SQL Server using the `OleDbCommand`:

```
OleDbCommand Cmd = OleDbCommand("sp_Get_Authors", Cn );
Cmd.CommandType = CommandType.StoredProcedure;
OleDbDataReader dr = Cmd.ExecuteReader();
```

Note, here we have used the full syntax of ODBC to call a procedure at the data provider.

```
OdbcCommand Cmd = new
    OdbcCommand("{call sp_Get_Authors}", Cn );
Cmd.CommandType = CommandType.StoredProcedure;
OdbcDataReader dr = Cmd.ExecuteReader();
```

The Connection Property

Indicates the `OleDbConnection/OdbcConnection` object associated with the `OleDbCommand/OdbcCommand` object. This connection object is the channel for the command object to get to the data source.

The definition of this property for `OleDbCommand` is:

VB.NET:
```
Public Property Connection As OleDbConnection
```

C#:
```
public OleDbConnection Connection { get; set; }
```

For `OdbcCommand`:

VB.NET:
```
Public Property Connection As OdbcConnection
```

C#:
```
public OdbcConnection Connection {get; set;}
```

You can set the connection property to an `OleDbConnection/OdbcConnection` object like this:

```
Cmd.Connection = Cn;
```

You can also set this property to a connection object at the time of creating the instance using a constructor, for example:

```
OleDbCommand Cmd = new OleDbCommand( null, Cn1 );

OdbcCommand Cmd = new OdbcCommand( null, Cn2 );
```

Where `Cn1` is a valid `OleDbConnection` object and `Cn2` is a valid `OdbcCommand` object.

When you assign a connection object to a command object, make sure that the connection is not involved in an active transaction, otherwise it will throw an exception. Disposing of a command object does not destroy the connection object. The connection object remains in the same state where it was before disposing of the command object.

The CommandTimeout Property

Indicates the time in seconds for a command object to wait before it terminates the execution of the query and generates an error. The default value of this property is 30 seconds.

VB.NET:
```
Overridable Public Property CommandTimeout As Integer
```

C#:
```
public int CommandTimeout { get; set; }
```

This property is available for both the `OleDbCommand` and `OdbcCommand` objects.

You can change the value of the property depending on how long your query normally takes to execute. Allowing a query to run for a longer time will result in holding up the resources for longer time. You can reset the default value of this property by using `ResetCommandTimeout` method. Consider the following code which uses this property:

```
//C#
OleDbCommand Cmd = new OleDbCommand();
...
Cmd.CommandTimeout = 120; // Sets the Command Timeout to 2 minutes
int res = (int) Cmd.ExecuteScalar();    // Executes a long running query
Cmd.ResetCommandTimeout();    // Sets back the Command Timeout to 30 secs.
...
```

Here is the equivalent code for an `OdbcCommand`, that uses the `CommandTimeout` property:

```
OdbcCommand Cmd = new OdbcCommand();
...
Cmd.CommandTimeout = 120;
int res = (int) Cmd.ExecuteScalar();
Cmd.ResetCommandTimeout();
```

The Transaction Property

Contains a reference to an `OleDbTransaction`/`OdbcTransaction` object, if the command is involved in a transaction. Otherwise this property will contain a null value.

VB.NET:

```
Public Property Transaction As OleDbTransaction
```

C#:

```
public OleDbTransaction Transaction {get; set;}
```

This property is also valid for `OdbcCommand` as it contains the reference to `OdbcTransaction`, which implements the `IDbTransaction`. For `OleDbCommand`, you can get a reference to an `OleDbTransaction` object by calling the `BeginTransaction` method on an `OleDbConnection` object, like this:

```
OleDbTransaction trans = Cn.BeginTransaction();
```

You can populate this property with a valid transaction object at the time of creating the instance using the appropriate constructor:

```
OleDbCommand Cmd = new OleDbCommand("sp_GetRate", Cn, trans );
```

You can also explicitly assign a transaction object to this property later on, for example:

```
OleDbCommand Cmd = new OleDbCommand();
Cmd.Connection = Cn;
Cmd.Transaction = trans;
```

The same methodology can also be use for the `OdbcTransaction` object. For example, the following C# code gets a reference to an `OdbcTransaction` object by calling the `BeginTransaction` method on the `OdbcConnection` object. It then uses this same transaction object to set the `Transaction` property of the `OdbcCommand` object:

```
OdbcTransaction trans = Cn.BeginTransaction();
OdbcCommand Cmd = new OdbcCommand();
Cmd.Connection = Cn;
Cmd.Transaction = trans;
```

Just like the `SqlCommand` object, the `OleDbCommand` and `OdbcCommand` objects also require that the transaction should be a valid object and must belong to the same connection object, being used by the command object. Failing to do this will throw an exception.

The UpdatedRowSource Property

Indicates how the result of the query will be applied to the `DataRow` object when the `Update` method of the `OleDbDataDriver` is executed.

VB.NET:
```
Overridable Public Property UpdatedRowSource As UpdateRowSource
```

C#:
```
public UpdateRowSource UpdatedRowSource {get; set;}
```

As it is clear from the definition of the property, it accepts a value from the `UpdateRowSource` enum. For a list of the possible values, see the `UpdatedRowSource` section of the `SqlCommand` class.

Both `OleDbCommand` and `OdbcCommand` implement this property. The following code sets the `OleDbCommand`/`OdbcCommand` objects to use the first returned record to update the `DataRow` object:

```
Cmd.UpdatedRowSource = UpdateRowSource.FirstReturnedRecord;
```

The DesignTimeVisible Property

Indicates if the object should be visible in design mode in a customized Windows Forms Designer Control. The default value is false.

VB.NET:
```
Public Property DesignTimeVisible As Boolean
```

C#:
```
public bool DesignTimeVisible( get; set; }
```

This property is available for both the `OleDbCommand`, as well as the `OdbcCommand` objects.

You can use this property as below:

```
Cmd.DesignTimeVisible = true;
```

OleDbCommand Methods

The ExecuteNonQuery Method

Executes a command against the data provider that does not return a data set. These statements could be: insert, delete, update, or DDL commands.

VB.NET:
```
NotOverridable Public Function ExecuteNonQuery() As Integer
```

C#:
```
public int ExecuteNonQuery();
```

This method returns the number of rows affected. However executing DDL statement or select statement using this method returns -1.

It is supported by both `OleDbCommand` and `OdbcCommand` objects.

For example, to insert a record in the `Products` table of an Access (`Northwind.mdb`) database, you can use the following C# code:

```
//C#
OleDbConnection Cn = new
    OleDbConnection("Provider=Microsoft.Jet.OLEDB.4.0;"
    + "Data Source=C:\\Access\\nwind.mdb;");
Cn.Open();
OleDbCommand Cmd = new OleDbCommand();
Cmd.CommandText = "Insert into Production( ProductName, SupplierID,"
    + "CategoryID, UnitPrice )"
    + "Values( 'Churs', 'Khan Chemicals', 'Produce', 99.99 )"
Cmd.Connection = Cn;
int res = Cmd.ExecuteNonQuery();
Console.WriteLine("Record inserted successfully");

Cn.Close();
```

The ExecuteReader Method

Executes the command against a data provider to get an `OleDbDataReader`/`OdbcDataReader` object.

The definition for this method for an `OleDbCommand` is:

VB.NET:
```
Overloads Public Function ExecuteReader() As OleDbDataReader
Overloads Public Function ExecuteReader( _
  ByVal behavior As CommandBehavior ) As OleDbDataReader
```

C#:
```
public OleDbDataReader ExecuteReader();
public OleDbDataReader ExecuteReader(
  CommandBehavior behavior );
```

For an `OdbcCommand` object:

VB.NET:
```
Overloads Public Function ExecuteReader() As OdbcDataReader
Overloads Public Function ExecuteReader( _
  ByVal behavior As CommandBehavior ) As OdbcDataReader
```

C#:
```
public OdbcDataReader ExecuteReader();
public OdbcDataReader ExecuteReader(
  CommandBehavior behavior );
```

133

You can also control how the `OleDbDataReader` object is created by providing a command behavior in one of its overloaded methods. For details of command behavior, see the `ExecuteReader` method for `SqlCommand`.

This method can be used to create a read only cursor on the data provider. For example, consider the following code, which uses an OLE DB provider for Microsoft Excel and gets all of the values from the first column (`CompanyName`) of the first sheet (`Sheet1$`) of the `Customer.XLS` file:

```C#
//C#
OleDbConnection Cn = new
    OleDbConnection("Provider=Microsoft.Jet.OLEDB.4.0;"
    + "Data Source=C:\\Customers.xls;"
    + "Extended Properties=Excel 8.0;");
Cn.Open();
OleDbCommand Cmd = new OleDbCommand("Sheet1$", Cn, null );
Cmd.CommandType = CommandType.TableDirect;
OleDbDataReader dr = Cmd.ExecuteReader();
while( dr.Read() )
{
    Console.WriteLine( dr["CompanyName"] );
}
dr.Close();
Cmd.Dispose();
Cn.Close();
```

Here is the same C# code, but using an Odbc data provider:

```C#
//C#
OdbcConnection Cn = new OdbcConnection("myXLDSN" );
Cn.Open();
OdbcCommand Cmd = new OdbcCommand("Sheet1$", Cn, null );
Cmd.CommandType = CommandType.TableDirect;
OdbcDataReader dr = Cmd.ExecuteReader();
while( dr.Read() )
{
    Console.WriteLine( dr["CompanyName"] );
}
dr.Close();
Cmd.Dispose();
Cn.Close();
```

The ExecuteScalar Method

Executes the command and returns the vale of the first column of the first row.

VB.NET:
```
NotOverridable Public Function ExecuteScalar() As Object
```

C#:
```
public object ExecuteScalar();
```

This method is supported by both `OleDbCommand` and `OdbcCommand` objects.

The `ExecuteScalar` method returns a single value from the data provider, when executed against the data provider. It is useful in cases when we have to lookup a description of a key from a data provider or get some summarized value (for example sum, count and so on) from the data provider.If more than one row, or more than one column, is retrieved after the execution against the data provider, then the first column of the first row is returned from this method.

Consider the following code fragment, which connects from a Microsoft Access database (`nwind.mdb`) and gets the company name of the customer with CustomerID equal to `'WILMK'`:

```
//C#
OleDbConnection Cn = new
       OleDbConnection("Provider=Microsoft.Jet.OLEDB.4.0;"
       + "Data Source=C:\\Access\\nwind.mdb;");
Cn.Open();
OleDbCommand Cmd = new OleDbCommand();
Cmd.CommandText =
    "Select CompanyName from Customers where CustomerID='WILMK'";
Cmd.Connection = Cn;
string CompanyName = (string) Cmd.ExecuteScalar();
Console.WriteLine( CompanyName );
Cmd.Dispose();
Cn.Close();
```

Here is what a typical call to this method using an `OdbcCommand` object would be:

```
//C#
OdbcConnection Cn = new OdbcConnection("myAccessDSN");
Cn.Open();
OdbcCommand Cmd = new OdbcCommand();
Cmd.CommandText =
    "Select CompanyName from Customers where CustomerID='WILMK'";
Cmd.Connection = Cn;
string CompanyName = (string) Cmd.ExecuteScalar();
Console.WriteLine( CompanyName );
Cn.Close();
```

The Cancel Method

Stops the execution of asynchronously invoked commands.

VB.NET:
```
NotOverridable Public Sub Cancel()
```

C#:
```
public void Cancel();
```

Invoking a long running query through a user interface can freeze the screen for a while and give users an unpleasant experience. To avoid this behavior of your user interface, you can invoke long running queries asynchronously and allow the user to cancel the query at anytime. The `Cancel` method can be used in these scenarios.

You can call the following code to cancel the execution of an asynchronous command:

```
Cmd.Cancel();
```

Currently, in Beta 1 version of the Odbc .NET data provider, the `Cancel` *method for the* `OdbcCommand` *object is not supported. Calling a* `Cancel` *method on an* `OdbcCommand` *object will result in a* `NotSupportedException` *being thrown.*

The CreateParameter Method

Creates a new instance of the `OleDbParameter`/`OdbcParameter` object.

Definition for the `OleDbCommand`:

VB.NET:

```
Public Function CreateParameter() As OleDbParameter
```

C#:

```
public OleDbParameter  CreateParameter();
```

Definition for the `OdbcCommand`:

VB.NET:

```
Public Function CreateParameter() As OdbcParameter
```

C#:

```
public OdbcParameter CreateParameter();
```

`OleDbParameter`/`OdbcParameter` objects are used to pass parameters to stored procedures and parameterized queries. For example, the following code creates a parameter named "`@emp_id`" and sets its data type to `Integer`:

```
OleDbCommand Cmd = OleDbCommand("sp_EmployeeInfo", Cn );
Cmd.CommandType = CommandType.StoredProcedure;
OleDbParameter param = Cmd.CreateParameter();
param.ParameterName = "@emp_id"
param.OleDbDbType = OleDbType.Integer;
param.Value = 1234;
Cmd.Parameters.Add( param );
OleDbDataReader dr = Cmd.ExecuteReader();
```

For a list of supported data types (OleDbType), see the `CreateParameter` method of the `SqlCommand` object.

It is worth noting that for the `OdbcCommand`, when the `CommandType` is set to a stored procedure, you cannot use named parameters, rather you have to use the full Odbc Syntax for the procedure. You can set the command text to something like `{call mySP( ?, ?)}`, where ? are the placeholders for the parameters. You have to add these parameters to the parameter collection in the same order as they should appear in the command text.

The Prepare Method

Compiles and reserves on the data source, the command encapsulated by OleDbCommand, so that it can execute faster when called more than one time.

VB.NET:

```
NotOverridable Public Sub Prepare();
```

C#:

```
public void Prepare();
```

This method is not supported by the OdbcCommand object in the current version.

The Prepare method only works when the value of the CommandType property is set to **StoredProcedure** or **Text**. It does nothing if the CommandType is set to **TableDirect**. In order to use this method, you must assign an open connection object to the command object or else it will throw an **InvalidOperationException**.

An example of how to use it is as follows:

```
//C#
try
{
    OleDbCommand Cmd = new OleDbCommand("some_sp", Cn );
    Cmd.Prepare();
    Cmd.ExecuteNonQuery();
}
catch( InvalidOperationException e )
{
    Console.WriteLine("Error: {0}", e.Message );
}
```

The Dispose Method

Disposes the resources held by the OleDbCommand object, so that they can be used by other objects. You can use this method to free both managed and unmanaged resources. Keep in mind that the OleDbCommand object uses Interop to connect to the OLE DB provider. This makes it able to reserve both managed and unmanaged resources. Because it is not recommended to call the Finalize method (as it is protected) of an object, the object should provide a mechanism for manually freeing up the resources held by the object.

The Dispose method has exactly the same method for OleDbCommand and OdbcCommand objects. Failing to call the Dispose method will leave the resources held until the .NET framework runtime disposes of it. When the runtime will garbage collect is indeterminate, so you must ensure you call this method or else the resources will be left reserved by the object for a longer time.

This method is inherited from the Component object with the following definition:

VB.NET:

```
Overrides Overloads Protected Sub Dispose()
Overrides Overloads Protected Sub Dispose( ByVal disposing As Boolean )
```

137

C#:

```
public void Dispose()
protected override void Dispose( bool disposing )
```

In this case, *disposing* is a boolean. Pass *True* to release both managed and unmanaged resources and *False* to release only unmanaged resources. Calling this method without any arguments will result in disposing of all resources.

In the following code only unmanaged resources are freed up by OleDbCommand:

```
OleDbCommand Cmd = new OleDbCommand();
...
Cmd.Dispose(false);    // Disposes only unmanaged resources held by Cmd
```

The ResetCommandTimeout Method

Resets the CommandTimeout property value to its default value (30 seconds). This is helpful when you have changed the CommandTimeout property to some higher value and now want to switch back to the old value. Using this method, you do not have to save the previous value of the CommandTimeout property.

The definition of the ResetCommandTimeout method is:

VBNET:

```
Public Sub ResetCommandTimeout()
```

C#:

```
public void ResetCommandTimeout();
```

This method is supported by both the OleDbCommand and OdbcCommand objects. The following C# code snippet shows the use of this method for the OleDbCommand object:

```
OleDbCommand Cmd = new OleDbCommand(...);
Cmd.CommandTimeout = 90;
// Run some long running queries
Cmd.ResetCommandTimeout();
```

Here is its equivalent for the OdbcCommand object:

```
OdbcCommand Cmd = new OdbcCommand(...);
Cmd.CommandTimeout = 90;
// Run some long running queries
Cmd.ResetCommandTimeout();
```

OleDbCommand Collections

The Parameters Collection

The `Parameters` collection is an instance of the `OleDbParameterCollection` class for `OleDbCommand` and an instance of the `OdbcParameterCollection` for the `OdbcCommand` object. It contains the list of the `OleDbParameter`/`OdbcParameter` objects.

The definition using `OleDbCommand` is:

VB.NET:

```
Public ReadOnly Property Parameters As OleDbParameterCollection
```

C#:

```
public OleDbParameterCollection Parameters {get;}
```

Using `OdbcCommand`:

VB.NET:

```
Public ReadOnly Property Parameters As OdbcParameterCollection
```

C#:

```
public OdbcParameterCollection Parameters {get;}
```

The `OleDbParameter` object encapsulates a parameter passed in a query or a stored procedure. You can create an `OleDbParameter` object in a number of ways. You can call the `CreateParameter` method of the `OleDbCommand` object to create an `OleDbParameter` object:

```
OleDbParameter prm = CreateParameter("EndingDate", OleDbType.Date );
```

Or it can be created using its constructor:

```
OleDbParameter prm = OleDbParameter("BeginingDate", OleDbType.Date );
```

Another way to create the `OleDbParameter` object is to use the `Parameters` collection itself:

```
OleDbParameter prm = Cmd.Parameters.Add("BeginingDate", OleDbType.Date );
```

When you create an `OleDbParameter` object using the `Parameters` collection, you do not have to add this parameter object to the collection, as it's already added. But when you create the object using the prior two methods, you will have to add it to the `Parameters` collection in order to pass to the data provider along with the command. You can add an `OleDbParameter` to the `Parameters` collection using the Add method:

```
Cmd.Parameters.Add( prm );
```

The `OdbcParameter` works in the same way as the `OleDbParameter` except that it uses an Odbc data provider. You can use the same methodology to create an `OdbcParameter` object as was done previously.

The C# code below demonstrates the use of the `Parameters` collection for an `OleDbCommand` object. Here we are calling a Query (`"Sales By Year"`) stored in a Microsoft Access database (`Northwind.mdb`). The query `"Sales By Year"` requires two parameter of date type, `BeginingDate` and `EndingDate`. In this example we are adding two `OleDbParameter` objects and setting their values to `"6/1/1996"` and `"6/30/1996"`:

139

```
//C#
OleDbConnection Cn = new
    OleDbConnection("Provider=Microsoft.Jet.OLEDB.4.0;"
    + "Data Source=C:\\Access\\nwind.mdb;");
Cn.Open();
OleDbCommand Cmd = new OleDbCommand();
Cmd.CommandText = "[Sales By Year]";
Cmd.CommandType = CommandType.StoredProcedure;
Cmd.Parameters.Add("BeginingDate", OleDbType.Date ).Value = "6/1/1996";
Cmd.Parameters.Add("EndingDate", OleDbType.Date ).Value = "6/30/1996";
Cmd.Connection = Cn;
OleDbDataReader dr = Cmd.ExecuteReader();

Console.WriteLine("Shipped Date          OrderID SubTotal");
Console.WriteLine("===================== ======= ========");
while( dr.Read() )
{
    Console.WriteLine( "{0} {1}    {2}", dr["ShippedDate"],
        dr["OrderID"], dr["SubTotal"] );
}
dr.Close();
Cmd.Dispose();
Cn.Close();
```

The following C# code performs the same function but it uses the `OdbcCommand` object. It is assumed that the DSN, `myAccessDSN`, is already present on the system and this DSN connects to an Access file `nwind.mdb` at C:\Access:

```
//C#
OdbcConnection Cn = new OdbcConnection("MyAcessDSN");
Cn.Open();
OdbcCommand Cmd = new OdbcCommand();
Cmd.CommandText = "{call [Sales By Year]( ?, ? }";
Cmd.CommandType = CommandType.StoredProcedure;
Cmd.Parameters.Add("BeginingDate", OdbcType.Date ).Value = "6/1/1996";
Cmd.Parameters.Add("EndingDate", OdbcType.Date ).Value = "6/30/1996";
Cmd.Connection = Cn;
OdbcDataReader dr = Cmd.ExecuteReader();

Console.WriteLine("Shipped Date          OrderID SubTotal");
Console.WriteLine("===================== ======= ========");
while( dr.Read() )
{
    Console.WriteLine( "{0} {1}    {2}", dr["ShippedDate"],
        dr["OrderID"], dr["SubTotal"] );
}
dr.Close();
Cmd.Dispose();
Cn.Close();
```

The output for the above code is:

```
Shipped Date          OrderID SubTotal
===================== ======= ========
6/3/1996 12:00:00 AM 11022   1402
6/3/1996 12:00:00 AM 11049   273.6

...

6/5/1996 12:00:00 AM 11069   360
```

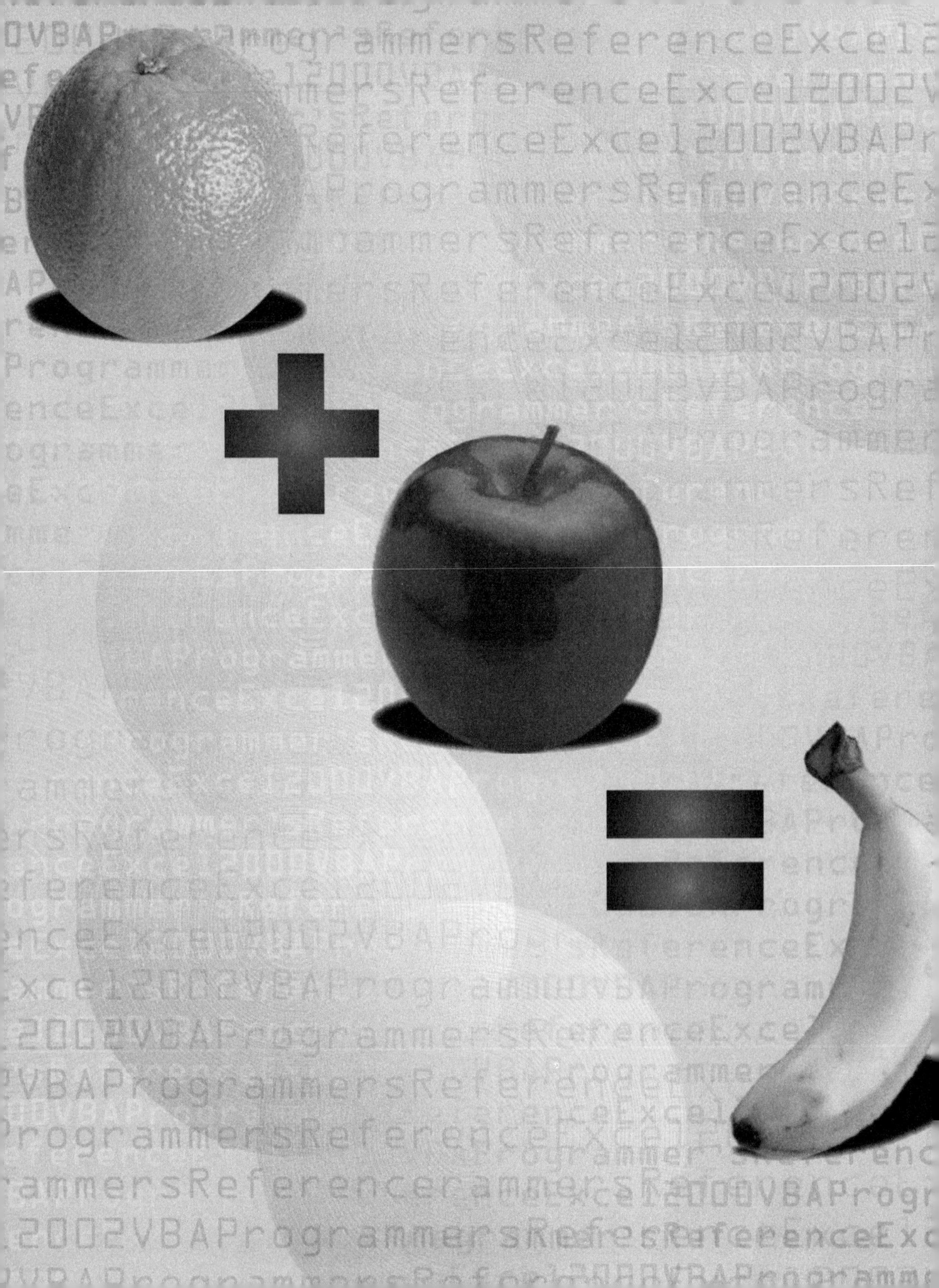

The DataSet Object

In this chapter, we'll detail one of the most important innovations introduced with ADO.NET, and, indeed, the entire .NET framework: the DataSet (part of the System.Data namespace). This object is an in-memory representation of one or more tables with records, constraints on columns, and relations among tables. We can use this object in three general ways:

❏   By programmatically creating a table structure with column definitions, constraints, and relations; and filling it by operating directly on the rows contained in the object

❏   By using the Fill() method, exposed by the DataAdapter object

❏   By using an XML schema, and an XML document, to fill and persist the data inside the object

It's possible to mix these methods to retrieve data in a DataSet. For example, we could retrieve an XML document, requiring some goods from a warehouse. We could load the DataSet with the data inside the XML document, and query the database for the goods availability always using the same object.

The first thing to understand is that the DataSet is an in-memory representation of the data contained physically in the database. So if we query data from the authors table of the pub database, we'll have a portion of memory formatted just like the authors table with columns having the same name and data type and with the resulting records queried from it. When we make any operation on the DataSet, such as adding a new row or modifying a column value, we are performing an operation on the in-memory data, and not the database.

The DataSet provides some methods to guarantee the data concurrency between it and the database. Using the same example, if we add a new row to the DataSet, we can call the Update() method, exposed by the DataAdapter object, to copy the new records contained in the DataSet into the database. This method uses a DataRow object characteristic: DataRowState enumeration value. After the DataSet creation and fill operation, all the data contained in the dataset is marked with the Unchanged state value: this indicates that it hasn't been manipulated since being retrieved from the data source. When we add the new record, the corresponding row inside the DataSet will get a new state value: Added. When calling the Update() method, all the rows not equal to Unchanged will be inserted or deleted in the database, in such a way that any changes made to the DataSet are implemented in the data source.

We now have a `DataSet` which is not fully aligned with the data source. In fact, although a new row may have been inserted in the database, the result is yet to be added to the `DataSet` object. We would achieve this with the `DataSet`'s `AcceptChanges()`.

After a committed database operation, we have to call this method in order to virtually commit even the data inside the `DataSet`, setting every row to the `Unchanged` state value. What happens if something goes wrong during update operation to the database? `DataSet` offers a `RejectChanges()` method in order to reject every row not marked with the `Unchanged` state value giving back a `DataSet` object like the original one.

Holding this concept fixed and clear in memory we can start to analyze each of the three methods to fill a `DataSet`.

Creating a DataSet

The `DataSet` contains two objects' collections useful to manage tables and relations among them. The `DataTableCollection` and `DataRelationCollection` objects allow tables and columns with data type definition adding and relation managing, respectively, and are accessible from the `Tables` and `Relations` property. In the following example a simple table is added to the `DataSet` object.

VB.NET:

```
' Create a table
Dim dt As New DataTable("tabAuthors")

' Create the ID column, no null allowed and must be unique
Dim dcID As New DataColumn("AuthorID", GetType(Int32))
dcID.Unique = True
dcID.AllowDBNull = False
dt.Columns.Add(dcID)

' Create the FirstName column, no null allowed
Dim dcAuthorFirstName As New DataColumn("Author_FirstName", GetType(String))
dcAuthorFirstName.MaxLength = 50
dcAuthorFirstName.AllowDBNull = False
dt.Columns.Add(dcAuthorFirstName)

' Create the LastName column, no null allowed
Dim dcAuthorLastName As New DataColumn("Author_LastName", GetType(String))
dcAuthorLastName.MaxLength = 50
dcAuthorLastName.AllowDBNull = False
dt.Columns.Add(dcAuthorLastName)

' Add the table to the DataSet
Dim dsWrox As New DataSet("WroxAuthors")
dsWrox.Tables.Add(dt)
```

C#:

```
// Create a table
DataTable dt = new DataTable("tabAuthors");

// Create the ID column, no null allowed and must be unique
DataColumn dcID = new DataColumn("AuthorID", typeof(Int32));
```

```
dcID.Unique = true;
dcID.AllowDBNull = false;
dt.Columns.Add(dcID);

// Create the FirstName column, no null allowed
DataColumn dcAuthorFirstName = new DataColumn("Author_FirstName",typeof(String));
dcAuthorFirstName.MaxLength = 50;
dcAuthorFirstName.AllowDBNull = false;
dt.Columns.Add(dcAuthorFirstName);

// Create the LastName column, no null allowed
DataColumn dcAuthorLastName = new DataColumn("Author_LastName",typeof(String));
dcAuthorLastName.MaxLength = 50;
dcAuthorLastName.AllowDBNull = false;
dt.Columns.Add(dcAuthorLastName);

// Add the table to the DataSet
DataSet dsWrox = new DataSet("WroxAuthors");
dsWrox.Tables.Add(dt);
```

As you can see, you have all the functionalities to specify an in-memory table with columns and data type, along with generic characteristics like max length and allow-null values. We have generated a complete table without opening a connection to the database. Now we go to the next step, adding some rows to the table:

VB.NET:

```
. . .

' Add a couple of rows
Dim r As DataRow =dsWrox.Tables(0).NewRow()
r("AuthorID") = 1
r("Author_FirstName") = "Fabio Claudio"
r("Author_LastName") = "Ferracchiati"
dsWrox.Tables(0).Rows.Add(r)

r =dsWrox.Tables(0).NewRow()
r("AuthorID") = 2
r("Author_FirstName") = "Alex"
r("Author_LastName") = "Homer"
dsWrox.Tables(0).Rows.Add(r)
```

C#:

```
. . .

// Add a couple of rows
DataRow r =dsWrox.Tables[0].NewRow();
r["AuthorID"] = 1;
r["Author_FirstName"] = "Fabio Claudio";
r["Author_LastName"] = "Ferracchiati";
dsWrox.Tables[0].Rows.Add(r);

r =dsWrox.Tables[0].NewRow();
r["AuthorID"] = 2;
```

```
r["Author_FirstName"] = "Alex";
r["Author_LastName"] = "Homer";
dsWrox.Tables[0].Rows.Add(r);
```

The columns are accessible directly using their names inside the `DataRow` object contained in the table. Now we can add a new table to demonstrate the power of the `DataRelation` object. Imagine that we have another table containing the payments made to the authors. These two tables are joined together by the `AuthorID` column:

VB.NET:

```
. . .

' Add another table
Dim dtPayment As New DataTable("tabPayments")

' Create the ID column, no null allowed and must be unique
Dim dcIDFK As New DataColumn("AuthorID", GetType(Int32))
dcIDFK.Unique = True
dcIDFK.AllowDBNull = False
dtPayment.Columns.Add(dcIDFK)

' Create the PaymentID column, no null allowed and must be unique
Dim dcPaymentID As New DataColumn("PaymentID", GetType(Int32))
dcPaymentID.Unique = True
dcPaymentID.AllowDBNull = False
dcPaymentID.AutoIncrement = True
dcPaymentID.AutoIncrementSeed = 1
dcPaymentID.AutoIncrementStep = 1
dtPayment.Columns.Add(dcPaymentID)

' Create the Payment column, no null allowed
Dim dcPayment As New DataColumn("Payment", GetType(System.Data.SqlTypes.SqlMoney))
dcPayment.AllowDBNull = False
dtPayment.Columns.Add(dcPayment)

dsWrox.Tables.Add(dtPayment)

' Add a couple of rows
' Since PaymentID is an auto-increment column we don't
' need to specify the value.
r = dsWrox.Tables("tabPayments").NewRow()
r("AuthorID") = 1
r("Payment") = 20
dsWrox.Tables("tabPayments").Rows.Add(r)

r = dsWrox.Tables("tabPayments").NewRow()
r("AuthorID") = 2
r("Payment") = 30
dsWrox.Tables("tabPayments").Rows.Add(r)

' Insert a Relation among the tables
Dim dr As New DataRelation("AuthorsToPaymentRel", dcID, dcIDFK, True)

dsWrox.Relations.Add(dr)
```

C#:

```
. . .

// Add another table
DataTable dtPayment = new DataTable("tabPayments");

// Create the ID column, no null allowed and must be unique
DataColumn dcIDFK = new DataColumn("AuthorID", typeof(Int32));
dcIDFK.Unique = true;
dcIDFK.AllowDBNull = false;
dtPayment.Columns.Add(dcIDFK);

// Create the PaymentID column, no null allowed and must be unique
DataColumn dcPaymentID = new DataColumn("PaymentID", typeof(Int32));
dcPaymentID.Unique = true;
dcPaymentID.AllowDBNull = false;
dcPaymentID.AutoIncrement = true;
dcPaymentID.AutoIncrementSeed = 1;
dcPaymentID.AutoIncrementStep = 1;
dtPayment.Columns.Add(dcPaymentID);

// Create the Payment column, no null allowed
DataColumn dcPayment = new DataColumn("Payment", typeof(SqlMoney));
dcPayment.AllowDBNull = false;
dtPayment.Columns.Add(dcPayment);

dsWrox.Tables.Add(dtPayment);

// Add a couple of rows
// Since PaymentID is an auto-increment column we don't
// need to specify the value.
r = dsWrox.Tables ["tabPayments"].NewRow();
r["AuthorID"] = 1;
r["Payment"] = 20;
dsWrox.Tables["tabPayments"].Rows.Add(r);

r = dsWrox.Tables["tabPayments"].NewRow();
r["AuthorID"] = 2;
r["Payment"] = 30;
dsWrox.Tables["tabPayments"].Rows.Add(r);

// Insert a Relation among the tables
DataRelation dr = new DataRelation("AuthorsToPaymentRel",dcID,dcIDFK,true);

dsWrox.Relations.Add(dr);
```

In the snippet of code above there are a couple of features to highlight. Whenever the data types in the column in the code is not similar to the related one in the database, you can use the namespace called System.Data.SqlTypes. In the example above, to define a column containing the money, the SqlMoney data type has been used as it is the best choice when you need to manage currency data type in your code. Moreover, as you can see from the snippet of code above, the DataColumn containing the AuthorID column has been redefined for the Payment table although an equal DataColumn was created previously in the code. The reason behind this, is that when you use the Add() method of a collection, you add a reference to the object and don't copy it inside the collection. So if you try to reuse the object an exception will be raised because the object has been already assigned to another table.

Now that we have two related tables we can navigate through their data using the `DataRow` object and its `GetChildRow()` method. Using the `Tables` property we can access every table within the `DataSet` using either an index array position or the table name. See the conclusion of the example:

VB.NET:

```
. . .

' Print to video
Dim d As DataRow
Dim childRow As DataRow

For Each d In dsWrox.Tables("tabAuthors").Rows
        Console.WriteLine("Author: {0} {1}", d("Author_FirstName"),
d("Author_LastName"))
        For Each childRow In d.GetChildRows(dr)
                Console.WriteLine("Payment: {0}$", childRow("Payment"))
        Next
Next
```

C#:

```
. . .


. . .

// Print to video
foreach (DataRow d in dsWrox.Tables["tabAuthors"].Rows)
{
        Console.WriteLine("Author: {0}
{1}",d["Author_FirstName"],d["Author_LastName"]);
        foreach (DataRow childRow in d.GetChildRows(dr))
                Console.WriteLine("Payment: {0}$",childRow["Payment"]);
}
```

Starting from a row contained in the `tabAuthors` table, you can go through each row in the `tabPayment` table joined to it calling the `GetChildRow()` method. In the following figure you can see the output of the example:

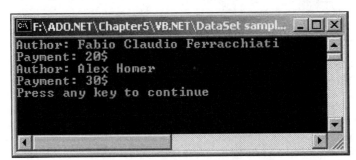

Filling a DataSet with a DataAdapter

I was born lazy, but I believe the 99% of readers have been asking the same thing: Do I write all that code manually in order to fill a `DataSet` with data and structures? The answer is, absolutely not. ADO.NET give us another great object called `DataAdapter` that provides table structure creation and data filling in a `DataSet`, automatically. The following figure describes a typical scenario:

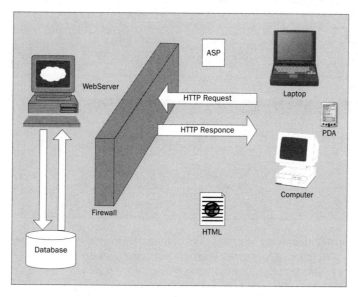

One or more clients send a request for information to a Web server using the HTTP protocol, the Web server queries the data to a database and returns an HTML page containing the result of the client request. Actually if the Web server is Internet Information Services then the ASP pages will use the ADO to retrieve the data through an OLE DB Data provider. If the programmer doesn't implement a disconnected recordset in the ASP pages, the more the requests increase, the more the global performance decreases. A disconnected implementation in this scenario is fundamental because an opened connection between a Web server and a database tie up the resources:

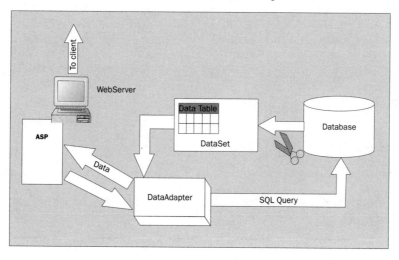

In the figure above, the Web server and the database side have been zoomed in to. In the ADO.NET technology the `DataSet` **is always disconnected** from the database. As you can see from the figure above, a `DataAdapter` is created from an ASPX page in order to retrieve the information from the database. The resulting data will be inserted in the `DataSet` and the corresponding tables, columns, relations, and constraint rules will be created by the `DataAdapter`, automatically. The scissors indicates that the connection will be cut as soon as the data are retrieved, leaving free the resources for other requests. Let's see, practically, an example of this scenario:

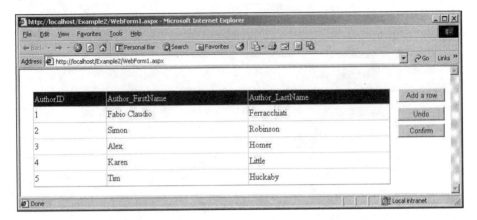

The `DataGrid` represented in the figure above retrieves five records contained in the `tabAuthors` table of the `WroxDB` database. During the `Page_Load()` event of the ASPX page we'll retrieve these records putting them into a `DataSet` used from the `DataGrid` to show the records.

VB.NET:

```
' Create a connection object
Dim dbConn As New
SqlClient.SqlConnection("server=localhost;uid=sa;pwd=;database=WroxDB")

' Create a data adapter specifying the query to execute
Dim da As New SqlClient.SqlDataAdapter("SELECT AuthorID, Author_FirstName,
Author_LastName FROM tabAuthors", dbConn)

' Create a dataset and fill it
Dim ds As New DataSet("dsAuthors")
da.Fill(ds)

' Associate the filled dataset to a datagrid
dgAuthors.DataSource = ds
dgAuthors.DataBind()
```

C#:

```
// Create a connection object
SqlConnection dbConn = new
SqlConnection("server=localhost;uid=sa;pwd=;database=WroxDB");

// Create a data adapter specifying the query to execute
SqlDataAdapter da = new SqlDataAdapter("SELECT AuthorID, Author_FirstName,
Author_LastName FROM tabAuthors",dbConn);
```

```
// Create a dataset and fill it
DataSet ds = new DataSet("dsAuthors");
da.Fill(ds);

// Associate the filled dataset to a datagrid
dgAuthors.DataSource = ds;
dgAuthors.DataBind();
```

In the ASPX page there is a `DataGrid` web component called `dgAuthors` that shows every record within the `DataSet`. As you can see from the snippet of code above, there is no code about column and table creation.

> The `Fill()` method will create the table schema analyzing the SQL Command provided during the `DataAdapter` object creation and will fill the `DataSet` with the records retrieved from the table in the database.

Certainly you have noted that no connection has been created, opened, and closed inside our code. In fact, `DataAdapter` will open the connection using the parameters specified during its creation and as soon as the data are retrieved, it closes the connection.

> Note: If you pass a connection object already opened, `DataAdapter` will use it but after having retrieved the data, the connection will remain opened.

At this point we can manipulate our data without requiring new resources from the database. I have added three buttons on the web forms. The first adds a new row, the second rolls back the changes and the last commits every change to the database. Let's look at the code behind the first button:

VB.NET:

```
Private Sub btnAddRow_Click(ByVal sender As System.Object, ByVal e As
System.EventArgs) Handles btnAddRow.Click
    ' Add a row to the dataset
    Dim ds As DataSet = CType(Session("ds"), DataSet)

    ' Check if the record I'm being to insert already exists
    Dim dv As New DataView(ds.Tables(0))
    dv.RowFilter = "AuthorID = 6"

    If dv.Count = 0 Then       Dim r As DataRow
        r = ds.Tables(0).NewRow()
        r("AuthorID") = 6
        r("Author_FirstName") = "Lee"
        r("Author_LastName") = "Witney"
        ds.Tables(0).Rows.Add(r)

        ' Show in the DataGrid the new content
        dgAuthors.DataBind()
    End If

End Sub
```

C#:

```csharp
private void btnAddRow_Click(object sender, System.EventArgs e)
{
    // Add a row to the dataset
    DataSet ds = (DataSet)Session["ds"];

    // Check if the record I'm going to insert already exists
    DataView dv = new DataView(ds.Tables[0]);
    dv.RowFilter = "AuthorID = 6";

    if (dv.Count == 0)
    {
        DataRow r;
        r = ds.Tables[0].NewRow();
        r["AuthorID"] = 6;
        r["Author_FirstName"] = "Lee";
        r["Author_LastName"] = "Witney";
        ds.Tables[0].Rows.Add(r);

        // Show in the DataGrid the new content
        dgAuthors.DataBind();
    }
}
```

The only thing to highlight in this simple snippet of code is that neither the `AcceptChanges()` or `Update()` methods are called after the row is added. That's because we allow the rollback of the changes by pressing the Undo button:

VB.NET:

```vbnet
Private Sub btnUndo_Click(ByVal sender As System.Object, ByVal e As
System.EventArgs) Handles btnUndo.Click
    ' Retrieve the dataset
    Dim ds As DataSet = CType(Session("ds"), DataSet)

    If ds.HasChanges(DataRowState.Added) Then
        ' Reject its changes
        ds.RejectChanges()

        ' Update the DataGrid
        dgAuthors.DataBind()
    End IfEnd Sub
```

C#:

```csharp
private void btnUndo_Click(object sender, System.EventArgs e)
{
    // Retrieve the dataset
    DataSet ds = (DataSet)Session["ds"];

    if (ds.HasChanges(DataRowState.Added))
    {
        // Reject its changes
        ds.RejectChanges();

        // Update the DataGrid
        dgAuthors.DataBind();
    }}
```

Finally, when we press the **Confirm** button, the code retrieves a new `DataSet` containing all the changes made on the original, if any:

VB.NET:

```
Private Sub btnConfirm_Click(ByVal sender As System.Object, ByVal e As
System.EventArgs) Handles btnConfirm.Click
    ' Retrieve the dataset
    Dim ds As DataSet = CType(Session("ds"), DataSet)
    ' Retrieve the data adapter
    Dim da As SqlClient.SqlDataAdapter = CType(Session("da"),
SqlClient.SqlDataAdapter)

    ' Retrieve the changes
    Dim dsTemp As DataSet = ds.GetChanges()

    If dsTemp Is Nothing Then
        Response.Write("No new records found!")
    Else
        ' Update the database
        da.Update(ds)

        ' Commit the records in the DataSet
        ds.AcceptChanges()

        ' Print to video
        Response.Write("Added records to the database")
    End If
End Sub
```

C#:

```
private void btnConfirm_Click(object sender, System.EventArgs e)
{
    // Retrieve the dataset
    DataSet ds = (DataSet)Session["ds"];
    // Retrieve the data adapter
    SqlDataAdapter da = (SqlDataAdapter)Session["da"];

    // Retrieve the changes
    DataSet dsTemp = ds.GetChanges();

    if(dsTemp != null)
    {
        // Update the database
        da.Update(ds);

        // Commit the records in the DataSet
        ds.AcceptChanges();

        // Print to video
        Response.Write("Added records to the database");
    }
    else
    {
        Response.Write("No new records found!");
    }
}
```

In the code above, `Update()` and `AcceptChanges()` are called to insert the new record in the database. As you'll learn in the Chapter 7, `DataAdapter` needs for an `InsertCommand`, `UpdateCommand`, and `DeleteCommand` SQL command to call when the `Update()` method is executed. Whenever you have a simple database structure with only a table to manage, you can use the `SqlCommandBuilder` object that creates these commands automatically. This object analyzes the `DataAdapter` provided as input parameter and creates the corresponding SQL commands automatically.

`DataSet` brings some innovations even in both classic client/server and desktop application scenarios providing a strict integration with the other .NET Framework classes. With a few instructions, it is possible to implement features as never was possible before. In the following example you can see how to use the `DataSet` in order to retrieve a BLOB (Binary Large Objects, useful when you need to perform database operations with large segments of data) column containing a JPEG image and show it in a picture box:

VB.NET:

```
' Create a connection object
Dim dbConn As New
SqlClient.SqlConnection("server=localhost;uid=sa;pwd=;database=WroxDB")

' Create the DataAdapter and fill the DataSet
Dim da As New SqlClient.SqlDataAdapter("SELECT Photo FROM tabAuthors where
AuthorId=1", dbConn)
Dim ds As New DataSet("PhotoDS")
da.Fill(ds)

' Retrieve the photo
Dim buff As Byte() = ds.Tables(0).Rows(0)("Photo")

' Show the photo in the PictureBox
If buff.Length > 0 Then
    Dim ms As New IO.MemoryStream(buff)
    ms.Position = 0
    pbPhoto.Image = System.Drawing.Image.FromStream(ms)
End If
```

C#:

```
// Create a connection object
SqlConnection dbConn = new
SqlConnection("server=localhost;uid=sa;pwd=;database=WroxDB");

// Create the DataAdapter and fill the DataSet
SqlDataAdapter da = new SqlDataAdapter("SELECT Photo FROM tabAuthors where
AuthorId=1",dbConn);
DataSet ds = new DataSet("PhotoDS");
da.Fill(ds);

// Retrieve the photo
byte[] buff = ds.Tables[0].Rows[0]["Photo"] as byte[];

// Show the photo in the PictureBox
if (buff != null)
{
    MemoryStream ms = new MemoryStream(buff);
    ms.Position=0;
    pbPhoto.Image = System.Drawing.Image.FromStream(ms);
}
```

After the call to the `Fill()` method, the `DataSet` will contain the binary representation of the image that we can associate to a `byte` array. The array is passed to the `MemoryStream` object in order to create a stream that will be provided to the `FromStream()` method of the `Image` class to be shown. The `MemoryStream` class represents a stream of data stored in memory instead of a file or a network connection.

Using XML to Fill the DataSet Object

A text file is the most easy way to exchange information between different operating systems but, usually, it contains information in desparate ways like comma-separated mode, tab spaced mode, and so on. Moreover, usually the text file contains untyped information and there isn't a standard way to describe the content of the file. In converse, XML is a W3C standard text file improved in these years with XSD, XSLT, and other language extensions. The XML schema (XSD) is a standard way to define the data type contained in the XML document with the possibility to include other characteristics like the maximum length of a string, mandatory fields, and so on. Actually XML is the best way to share information between different operating systems and, recently, it has been adopted by the SOAP protocol to realize remote procedure calls. In this scenario, ADO.NET couldn't ignore the importance of the XML standard and, in fact, it provides a full set of methods and properties inside the `DataSet` object.

The most useful methods are `ReadXml()` and `WriteXml()` which are useful to read from an XML document with or without a correlated schema and to write all the data contained in the object in to an XML document, respectively.

VB.NET:

```
' Fill the DataSet using the Diffgram
ds.ReadXml("Diffgram.xml", XmlReadMode.DiffGram)

' Write a XML with the schema
ds.WriteXml("WriteXmlStringWithSchema.xml", XmlWriteMode.WriteSchema)
```

C#:

```
// Fill the DataSet using the Diffgram
ds.ReadXml("Diffgram. xml", XmlReadMode.DiffGram);

// Write a XML with the schema
ds.WriteXml("WriteXmlStringWithSchema.xml", XmlWriteMode.WriteSchema);
```

Also, these methods read and write particular XML documents called `DiffGrams` (see the ReadXml() and WriteXml() section for more details). By using `DiffGrams`, ADO.NET provides a way to persist `DataSet` information including, in the XML document, the new, modified and deleted rows with their related row states. The following XML document shows a diffgram generated by a query on the **WroxDB** database where a row has been modified:

```
<?xml version="1.0" standalone="yes"?>
<diffgr:diffgram xmlns:msdata="urn:schemas-microsoft-com:xml-msdata"
xmlns:diffgr="urn:schemas-microsoft-com:xml-diffgram-v1">
  <DS>
    <Table diffgr:id="Table1" msdata:rowOrder="0">
      <AuthorID>1</AuthorID>
      <Author_FirstName>Fabio Claudio</Author_FirstName>
```

```
        <Author_LastName>Ferracchiati</Author_LastName>
      </Table>
      <Table diffgr:id="Table2" msdata:rowOrder="1" diffgr:hasChanges="modified">
        <AuthorID>2</AuthorID>
        <Author_FirstName>S.</Author_FirstName>
        <Author_LastName>Robinson</Author_LastName>
      </Table>
    <diffgr:before>
      <Table diffgr:id="Table2" msdata:rowOrder="1">
        <AuthorID>2</AuthorID>
        <Author_FirstName>Simon</Author_FirstName>
        <Author_LastName>Robinson</Author_LastName>
      </Table>
    </diffgr:before>
  </diffgr:diffgram>
```

Every change is signed with a specific diffgram tag like the `<diffgr:before>`, which indicates the values before the row change.

`DataSet` exposes another two useful methods: `ReadXmlSchema()` and `WriteXmlSchema()`. The former reads from the XML schema and creates the `DataSet` internal schema with relations, tables, and constraints also. The latter writes an XSD schema representing the internal structure of the `DataSet`. Usually the `ReadXmlSchema()` method is used before calling the `ReadXml()` in order to format the `DataSet` properly. Instead, `WriteXmlSchema()` is used to generate an XSD schema containing tables, data types and every other things describing your `DataSet` object.

VB.NET:

```
' Read an XML schema using the string parameter
ds.ReadXmlSchema("AuthorsSchema.xml")

' Write a XML using the string parameter
ds.WriteXmlSchema("WriteXmlSchema.xml")
```

C#:

```
// Read an XML schema using the string parameter
ds.ReadXmlSchema("AuthorsSchema.xml");

// Write a XML using the string parameter
ds.WriteXmlSchema("WriteXmlSchema.xml");
```

In the following figure, you can see a typical use of the XML and `DataSet` pair:

This figures shows how two different companies could exchange information using an XML document. For example, company A requires office furniture from company B, sending a complete XML document using company B's standard. Running on company B's servers is an application that uses `DataSet` methods and properties to read from the XML document and to interrogate the database in order to accomplish the order. The application then sends back an XML document containing the order acceptance or a message error.

`DataSet` offers a way to operate synchronously with an `XmlDataDocument` object that allows the reading of the XML document hierarchically. When you synchronize the two objects, every modification made to the data will be replicated in both objects allowing them to operate on the same set of data. You can join `DataSet` functionalities with the `XmlDataDocument` ones and access the entire suite of services. In that way you can query the data using the XML Path Language (XPath) or format the output with the Exstansible Stylesheet Language (XSL) and with XML Transformation. There are three different ways to synchronize a `DataSet` with the `XmlDataDocument`:

1. Create an `XmlDataDocument` object and use its `DataSet` property to set the schema and navigate through the data using the `DataSet`.

2. Create a `DataSet` with schema and data and then synchronize with the `XmlDataDocument` passing the `DataSet` as the parameter in the `XmlDataDocument`'s constructor.

3. Create a `DataSet`, populating only with the schema and then create the `XmlDataDocument` using its constructor with the `DataSet` parameter. You can load the `XmlDataDocument` from the Xml document adding a relational view over the existing hierarchical data.

In the following snippet of code you can see how to realize the synchronization methods described above:

VB.NET:

```
' First
Dim doc As New XmlDataDocument()
doc.Load("Document.xml")
Dim dsDoc As DataSet = doc.DataSet

' Second
Dim dsDoc As New DataSet()
DataAdapter.Fill(dsDoc) ' DataAdapter has been created before…
Dim doc As New XmlDataDocument(dsDoc)

' Third
Dim dsDoc As New DataSet()
DataAdapter.FillSchema(dsDoc, SchemaType.Source) ' DataAdapter has been created
before…
Dim doc As New XmlDataDocument(dsDoc)
doc.Load("Document.xml")
```

C#:

```
// First
XmlDataDocument doc = new XmlDataDocument();
doc.Load("Document.xml");
DataSet dsDoc = doc.DataSet;

// Second
DataSet dsDoc = new DataSet();
DataAdapter.Fill(dsDoc); // DataAdapter has been created before…
XmlDataDocument doc = new XmlDataDocument(dsDoc);

// Third
DataSet dsDoc = new DataSet();
DataAdapter.FillSchema(dsDoc, SchemaType.Source); // DataAdapter has been created
before…
XmlDataDocument doc = new XmlDataDocument(dsDoc);
doc.Load("Document.xml");
```

In the first and third case, the Xml tags must be identical to the DataSet tables and columns names otherwise a System.Xml.XmlException exception will be raised.

If you still don't see the need to synchronize the two objects, let me show you a scenario. Internally, Wrox exchange XML documents between office sections to produce books successfully. Inside the XML documents there is a lot of information like authors, book title, ISBN, and so on. When the document arrives at the financial office it is full of irrelevant information for the employee that has to pay the author. You can fill a DataSet object with a schema containing just the information needed to the employee, and allow them to be modified without changing the rest of the document. Imagine this is the XML document:

```xml
<?xml version="1.0" standalone="yes"?>
<WroxAuthors>
  <Author>
    <AuthorID>1</AuthorID>
    <Author_FirstName>Fabio Claudio</Author_FirstName>
    <Author_LastName>Ferracchiati</Author_LastName>
    <Payment>
      <AuthorID>1</AuthorID>
      <PaymentID>1</PaymentID>
      <Payment>20</Payment>
      <Paid>false</Paid>
    </Payment>
    <Book>
      <AuthorID>1</AuthorID>
      <Title>Professional Commerce Server 2000 Programming</Title>
      <ISBN>1861004648</ISBN>
      <Price>$59.99</Price>
    </Book>
  </Author>

...

</WroxAuthors>
```

The paid tag contains a Boolean value indicating whether the author has been paid (`true`) or not (`false`). The employee needs just a few pieces of information in this file. So an ad-hoc XML schema is created in order to retrieve and manage just the necessary tags:

```xml
<?xml version="1.0" standalone="yes"?>
<xsd:schema id="WroxAuthors" targetNamespace="" xmlns=""
xmlns:xsd="http://www.w3.org/2001/XMLSchema" xmlns:msdata="urn:schemas-microsoft-
com:xml-msdata">
  <xsd:element name="WroxAuthors" msdata:IsDataSet="true">
    <xsd:complexType>
      <xsd:choice maxOccurs="unbounded">
        <xsd:element name="Author">
          <xsd:complexType>
            <xsd:sequence>
              <xsd:element name="AuthorID" type="xsd:int" minOccurs="0" />
              <xsd:element name="Author_FirstName" type="xsd:string" minOccurs="0"
/>
              <xsd:element name="Author_LastName" type="xsd:string" minOccurs="0"
/>
            </xsd:sequence>
          </xsd:complexType>
        </xsd:element>
        <xsd:element name="Payment">
          <xsd:complexType>
            <xsd:sequence>
              <xsd:element name="AuthorID" type="xsd:int" minOccurs="0" />
              <xsd:element name="PaymentID" type="xsd:int" minOccurs="0" />
              <xsd:element name="Payment" type="xsd:decimal" minOccurs="0" />
              <xsd:element name="Paid" type="xsd:boolean" minOccurs="0" />
```

159

```
            </xsd:sequence>
          </xsd:complexType>
        </xsd:element>
      </xsd:choice>
    </xsd:complexType>
    <xsd:unique name="Constraint1">
      <xsd:selector xpath=".//Author" />
      <xsd:field xpath="AuthorID" />
    </xsd:unique>
    <xsd:keyref name="AuthorToPaymentRel" refer="Constraint1">
      <xsd:selector xpath=".//Payment" />
      <xsd:field xpath="AuthorID" />
    </xsd:keyref>
  </xsd:element>
</xsd:schema>
```

Now the employee can read the money amount to pay to the authors and store the new information into the same XML document without changing any other information.

Until now we have just seen the untyped `DataSet`. This is the way to retrieve the information within the object using row and columns collections, table indexing and so on. In the example above we encounter the typed `DataSet` that is a derived `DataSet` object where we can use the column and table names as properties and `DataSet` name as the class.

Creating a typed `DataSet` is really easy thanks to the **XSD.EXE** application. This program takes an XSD schema with the tag descriptions of your XML document and generates a source file that can be compiled in order to create the related assembly. Then you add the new namespace to your application and you can access the `DataSet` calling columns and tables with their name directly. In the following figure you can see the command options to generate the source file:

In order to create the `Wrox.Payments` namespace with C# language you can use the following syntax:

```
xsd.exe /d Schema.xsd /n:Wrox.Payments
```

To create the VB source code you can use this:

```
xsd.exe /d /l:VB Schema.xsd /n:Wrox.Payments
```

The resulting C# or VB file has to be compiled in order to generate an assembly file (a DLL file) that has to be referenced in our code and utilized with the following syntax:

VB.NET:

```
Imports Wrox.Payments

    . . .
```

C#:

```
using Wrox.Payments;

    . . .
```

At this point we can use the typed `DataSet` to retrieve the necessary information. From the following code you can note how it's easier to access the column values and names using a typed `DataSet`:

VB.NET:

```
' Create a typed DataSet
Dim wrox As New WroxAuthors()

' Create an XmlDataDocument and synchronize to the dataset
Dim doc As New Xml.XmlDataDocument(wrox)

' Load the XML document
doc.Load("Payment.xml")

' pay the authors
Dim paid As WroxAuthors.PaymentRow
For Each paid In wrox.Payment
     paid.Paid = True
Next

' save the new document
doc.Save("Payment_Done.xml")
```

C#:

```
// Create a typed DataSet
WroxAuthors wrox = new WroxAuthors();

// Create an XmlDataDocument and synchronize to the dataset
XmlDataDocument doc = new XmlDataDocument(wrox);

// Load the XML document
```

```
doc.Load("Payment.xml");

// pay the authors
foreach (WroxAuthors.PaymentRow paid in wrox.Payment)
{
    paid.Paid = true;
}

// save the new document
doc.Save("Payment_Done.xml");
```

Finally, the application launching has generated the following XML document:

```
<?xml version="1.0" standalone="yes"?>
<WroxAuthors>
  <Author>
    <AuthorID>1</AuthorID>
    <Author_FirstName>Fabio Claudio</Author_FirstName>
    <Author_LastName>Ferracchiati</Author_LastName>
    <Payment>
      <AuthorID>1</AuthorID>
      <PaymentID>1</PaymentID>
      <Payment>20</Payment>
      <Paid>true</Paid>
    </Payment>
    <Book>
      <AuthorID>1</AuthorID>
      <Title>Professional Commerce Server 2000 Programming</Title>
      <ISBN>1861004648</ISBN>
      <Price>$59.99</Price>
    </Book>
  </Author>

  ...

</WroxAuthors>
```

The DataSet Object

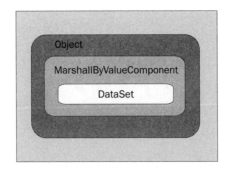

The `DataSet` object inherits from the `MarshalByValueComponent` and `Object` class part of its functionalities. Every class inside the .NET Framework is derived from the `Object` class that exposes the standard functionalities like the `ToString()` method and the `Equals()`. Instead, the `MarshalByValueComponent` implements the `IComponent` interface for the `DataSet` adding the base implementation for the marshalling mechanism that allows remote components exchanging.

Other than inheriting from the base classes, the `DataSet` object implements three interfaces: `IListSource`, `ISupportInitialize`, and `ISerializable`. The first interface implements a mechanism to retrieve a list that can be bound to a data source. The second, instead, adds functionality to the object that allows batch initialization. Finally, the third interface allows the `DataSet` to manage its own serialization and deserialization functionalities.

Let's start covering the `DataSet` object with its own constructor.

DataSet Constructors

VB.NET:

```
Public Sub New()

Public Sub New( _
    ByVal dataSetName As String _
)

Protected Sub New( _
    ByVal info As SerializationInfo, _
    ByVal context As StreamingContext _
)
```

C#:

```
public DataSet();

public DataSet(
    string dataSetName
);

protected DataSet(
    SerializationInfo info,
    StreamingContext context
);
```

As can be seen, the constructor comes in three different versions. The default constructor doesn't accept input parameters and creates just an empty `DataSet` object setting its internal variables to the default values.

VB.NET:

```
Dim ds As New DataSet()
```

C#:

```
DataSet ds = new DataSet();
```

The second constructor version accepts a string name to identify the new `DataSet` object.

VB.NET:

```
Dim ds As New DataSet("dsAuthors")
```

C#:

```
DataSet ds = new DataSet("dsAuthors");
```

This name will be inserted in the XML document associated to the `DataSet` at the root level:

```
<?xml version="1.0" standalone="yes"?>
<dsAuthors>
    <Table>
        <AuthorID>6</AuthorID>
        <Author_FirstName>Fabio Claudio</Author_FirstName>
        <Author_LastName>Ferracchiati</Author_LastName>
    </Table>
</dsAuthors>
```

The third and last version of the constructor accepts two parameters: a reference to a `SerializationInfo` object and a reference to a `StreamingContext`. The former allows object serialization and deserialization processes while the latter represents the source and the destination of a given serialized stream. However, this constructor has been created to operate expressly with an `ISerializable` interface.

DataSet Properties

The `DataSet` object exposes twelve proprietary properties and three inherited from the base class. The proprietary properties are useful to manage the `DataSet` in its every aspect. We can divide the properties into two functionality groups. Within the first group all the properties that manage XML functionality are contained while in the second group there are properties to manage in-memory `DataSet` functionalities. So `Namespace` and `Prefix` properties are useful to specify a namespace and a prefix that will be used during XML document creation and tag comparison. In the in-memory group there are a couple of main properties: `Tables` and `Relations`. The former contains every table inside the `DataSet` that can be used to browse between the records. Instead, the latter contains every `DataRelation` object defined to relate two tables inside the `DataSet` object.

Let's begin with a brief description of the inherited properties continuing, then, with every proprietary property in more detail.

Property	Description
Container	This is a read-only property that retrieves the container for the `DataSet` object or a null reference (`Nothing` for VB.NET).
DesignMode	This is a read-only property that retrieves a Boolean value indicating whether the component is in design mode (`true`) or not (`false`).
Events	Retrieves a list of all the event's handlers attached to the `DataSet` object.

The CaseSensitive Property

VB.NET:

```
Public Property CaseSensitive As Boolean
```

C#:

```
public bool CaseSensitive {get; set;}
```

The `CaseSensitive` property either retrieves or sets a Boolean value indicating whether the searching, sorting, and filter operations applied to the `DataTable` records must consider the case-sensitive form (`true`) or not (`false`).

VB.NET:

```
Dim dbConn As New
SqlClient.SqlConnection("server=localhost;uid=sa;pwd=;database=pubs")

' Create a DataAdapter and fill the DataSet
Dim da As New SqlClient.SqlDataAdapter("SELECT au_fname,au_lname FROM authors",
dbConn)
Dim ds As New DataSet()
da.Fill(ds)

' How many records have found?
Console.WriteLine("Total number of records found: " &
ds.Tables(0).Rows.Count.ToString())

' Apply a filter without case-sensitive
Console.WriteLine("")
Console.WriteLine("-=-= Apply a filter without case-sensitive constraint -=-=")
Dim r() As DataRow = ds.Tables(0).Select("au_fname like 's%'")
Console.WriteLine("Total number of records found: " + r.Length.ToString())

' Apply a filter with case-sensitive
Console.WriteLine("")
Console.WriteLine("-=-= Apply a filter without case-sensitive constraint -=-=")
ds.CaseSensitive = True
r = ds.Tables(0).Select("au_fname like 's%'")
Console.WriteLine("Total number of records found: " + r.Length.ToString())
```

C#:

```
SqlConnection dbConn = new
SqlConnection("server=localhost;uid=sa;pwd=;database=pubs");

// Create a DataAdapter and fill the DataSet
SqlDataAdapter da = new SqlDataAdapter("SELECT au_fname,au_lname FROM
authors",dbConn);
DataSet ds = new DataSet();
da.Fill(ds);

// How many records have found?
Console.WriteLine("Total number of records found: " +
ds.Tables[0].Rows.Count.ToString());
```

```
// Apply a filter without case-sensitive
Console.WriteLine("\n-=-= Apply a filter without case-sensitive constraint -=-=");
DataRow[] r = ds.Tables[0].Select("au_fname like 's%'");
Console.WriteLine("Total number of records found: " + r.Length.ToString());

// Apply a filter with case-sensitive
Console.WriteLine("\n-=-= Apply a filter without case-sensitive constraint -=-=");
ds.CaseSensitive = true;
r = ds.Tables[0].Select("au_fname like 's%'");
Console.WriteLine("Total number of records found: " + r.Length.ToString());
```

The output for the example above is:

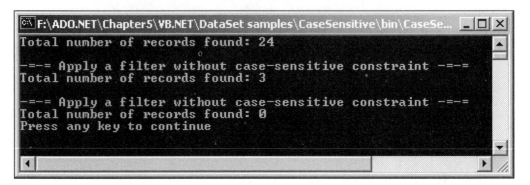

The `CaseSensitive` setting will be inherited from the tables contained inside the `DataSet`'s table collection. However, calling the `CaseSensitive` property exposed by the `DataTable` you can customize table per table your case-sensitive criteria.

The DataSetName Property

VB.NET:

```
Public Property DataSetName As String
```

C#:

```
public string DataSetName {get; set;}
```

This property either retrieves or sets the name associated to the `DataSet` object. The `DataSet` name will be used as root element inside the XML document that describes the data stored in the object.

VB.NET:

```
Dim ds As New DataSet()
Ds.DataSetName = "dsAuthors"
```

C#:

```
DataSet ds = new DataSet();
Ds.DataSetName = "dsAuthors";
```

The DefaultViewManager Property

VB.NET:

```
Public ReadOnly Property DefaultViewManager As DataViewManager
```

C#:

```
public DataViewManager DefaultViewManager {get;}
```

This property retrieves a reference to the DataViewManager object that contains methods and properties to create a DataView for each table contained in the DataSet. DefaultViewManager is useful whether you need to sort, filter, or search data inside the DataSet. Executing its method, CreateDataView() you can create a DataView having the schema build automatically to apply filter to. See the example below:

VB.NET:

```
' Create a DataSet
Dim ds As New DataSet()
sqlDataAdapter1.Fill(ds)

' Retrieve the DataViewManager
Dim dvm As DataViewManager = ds.DefaultViewManager

' Create the related DataView
Dim dv As DataViewManager  = dvm.CreateDataView(ds.Tables(0))

' Apply the filter
dv.RowFilter = "au_fname like 'f%'"

' Show in the grid the result
dataGrid1.DataSource = dv
```

C#:

```
// Create a DataSet
DataSet ds = new DataSet();
sqlDataAdapter1.Fill(ds);

// Retrieve the DataViewManager
DataViewManager dvm = ds.DefaultViewManager;

// Create the related DataView
DataView dv = dvm.CreateDataView(ds.Tables[0]);

// Apply the filter
dv.RowFilter = "au_fname like 'f%'";

// Show in the grid the result
dataGrid1.DataSource = dv;
```

As can be seen in this example, a DataAdapter has been populated from the pubs database from the SQL Server and the related default view has been assigned to a DataGrid object to show its content.

The EnforceConstraints Property

VB.NET:

```
Public Property EnforceConstraints As Boolean
```

C#:

```
public bool EnforceConstraints {get; set;}
```

The EnforceConstraints property either enables or disables the constraint rules check during the update processes. If a UniqueConstraint is defined and you insert duplicate values inside a primary key, a ConstraintException is raised. By setting this property to false, the default value is true, you avoid constraint exception execution and you can insert equal records in the table.

VB.NET:

```
' Read XML Schema containing table structure.
Dim ds As New DataSet("XMLDataSet")
ds.ReadXmlSchema("AuthorsSchema.XML")

' Add a unique constraint on the au_id column
ds.Tables(0).Constraints.Add("ConstraintID", ds.Tables(0).Columns("au_id"), True)

' Add the first record
Dim dr As DataRow = ds.Tables(0).NewRow()
dr("au_id") = "222-22-2222"
dr("au_fname") = "Fabio Claudio"
dr("au_lname") = "Ferracchiati"
dr("contract") = 1
ds.Tables(0).Rows.Add(dr)
ds.Tables(0).AcceptChanges()

' If you set this to true and then try to add the records
' below an exception will be raised. False value ignore the
' constraint rule for this table.
ds.EnforceConstraints = False

' I can insert another record with the same primary key
dr = ds.Tables(0).NewRow()
dr("au_id") = "222-22-2222"
dr("au_fname") = "Fabio Claudio"
dr("au_lname") = "Ferracchiati"
dr("contract") = 1
ds.Tables(0).Rows.Add(dr)
ds.Tables(0).AcceptChanges()
```

C#:

```
// Read XML Schema containing table structure.
DataSet ds = new DataSet("XMLDataSet");
ds.ReadXmlSchema("AuthorsSchema.XML");

// Add a unique constraint on the au_id column
ds.Tables[0].Constraints.Add("ConstraintID",ds.Tables[0].Columns["au_id"],true);
```

```
// Add the first record
DataRow dr = ds.Tables[0].NewRow();
dr["au_id"] = "222-22-2222";
dr["au_fname"] = "Fabio Claudio";
dr["au_lname"] = "Ferracchiati";
dr["contract"] = 1;
ds.Tables[0].Rows.Add(dr);
ds.Tables[0].AcceptChanges();

// If you set this to true and then try to add the records
// below an exception will be raised. False value ignore the
// constraint rule for this table.
ds.EnforceConstraints = false;

// I can insert another record with the same primary key
dr = ds.Tables[0].NewRow();
dr["au_id"] = "222-22-2222";
dr["au_fname"] = "Fabio Claudio";
dr["au_lname"] = "Ferracchiati";
dr["contract"] = 1;
ds.Tables[0].Rows.Add(dr);
ds.Tables[0].AcceptChanges();
```

The ExtendedProperties Property

VB.NET:

```
Public ReadOnly Property ExtendedProperties As PropertyCollection
```

C#:

```
public PropertyCollection ExtendedProperties {get;}
```

This property associates to the DataSet object one or more custom properties containing a value. You can pair custom information together with your object which is retrievable at any moment in your code by simply pointing to the element through its name.

VB.NET:

```
' Create a DataSet
Dim ds As New DataSet("DS")

' Add an extended property
ds.ExtendedProperties.Add("CreationDate",DateTime.Now)

' Print to video
Console.WriteLine(ds.ExtendedProperties("CreationDate").ToString())
```

C#:

```
// Create the DataSet
DataSet ds = new DataSet("DS");

// Add an extended property
```

```
ds.ExtendedProperties.Add("CreationDate",DateTime.Now);

// Print to video
Console.WriteLine(ds.ExtendedProperties["CreationDate"].ToString());
```

The HasErrors Property

VB.NET:

```
Public ReadOnly Property HasErrors As Boolean
```

C#:

```
public bool HasErrors {get;}
```

DataSet exposes this property to retrieve a Boolean value indicating whether any rows contained in any tables inside the DataSet has one or more errors. The HasErrors property is set to true by the RowError property of the DataRow object. Usually you go through each new record that has to be inserted in the DataSet and look for any possible error (duplicate values, null column, and so on). Anytime you find an error you can specify, for that specific row, the error description calling the RowError property. Finally, when you ask HasErrors whether at least an error has occurred it will return the related Boolean value. In the example below there are two DataSet objects, one filled with a XML schema to create the table schema and one filled from a XML data document. The data contained in the two datasets are the same so an error will be found.

VB.NET:

```
Module Module1

    Private Sub FindDuplicate(ByVal source As DataSet, ByVal dest As DataSet)
        Dim r() As DataRow
        Dim i As Integer

        For i = 0 To dest.Tables(0).Rows.Count - 1
            r = source.Tables(0).Select("au_id='" &
dest.Tables(0).Rows(i)("au_id") & "'")
            If r.Length > 0 Then
                dest.Tables(0).Rows(i).RowError = "Error, duplicate primary key
value"
            End If
        Next
    End Sub

    Sub PrintErrors(ByVal d As DataSet)
        Dim i As Integer
        For i = 0 To d.Tables(0).Rows.Count - 1
            If d.Tables(0).Rows(i).HasErrors Then
                Console.WriteLine(d.Tables(0).Rows(i).RowError.ToString())
            End If
        Next
    End Sub

    Sub Main()
        ' Read XML Schema containing table structure.
```

```vb
        Dim ds As New DataSet("DS")
        ds.ReadXmlSchema("AuthorsSchema.XML")

        ' Add a unique constraint on the au_id column
        ds.Tables(0).Constraints.Add("ConstraintID",
                            ds.Tables(0).Columns("au_id"), True)

        ' Add the first record
        Dim dr As DataRow = ds.Tables(0).NewRow()
        dr("au_id") = "222-22-2222"
        dr("au_fname") = "Fabio Claudio"
        dr("au_lname") = "Ferracchiati"
        dr("contract") = True
        ds.Tables(0).Rows.Add(dr)
        ds.Tables(0).AcceptChanges()

        ' Another DataSet filled with XML data
        Dim dsXML As New DataSet("XMLDataSet")
        dsXML.ReadXmlSchema("AuthorsSchema.XML")
        dsXML.ReadXml("Authors.XML")

        ' Looks for duplicated records
        FindDuplicate(ds, dsXML)

        ' If found errors, print out them
        ' Otherwise merge the dataset
        If (dsXML.HasErrors = False) Then
            ds.Merge(dsXML)
            Console.WriteLine("Merge done!")
        Else
            PrintErrors(dsXML)
        End If
    End Sub

End Module
```

C#:

```csharp
using System;
using System.Data;


namespace HasErrorExample
{
    class Class1
    {
        private static void FindDuplicate(DataSet source, DataSet dest)
        {
            DataRow[] r;

            for (int i=0;i<dest.Tables[0].Rows.Count;i++)
            {
                r = source.Tables[0].Select("au_id='" +
                    dest.Tables[0].Rows[i]["au_id"] + "'");
                if (r.Length > 0)
```

```
                {
                    dest.Tables[0].Rows[i].RowError = "Error,"
                    + "duplicate primary key value";
                }
            }
        }

        private static void PrintErrors(DataSet d)
        {
            for (int i=0;i<d.Tables[0].Rows.Count;i++)
            {
                if (d.Tables[0].Rows[i].HasErrors)
                {
                    Console.WriteLine(d.Tables[0].
                      Rows[i].RowError.ToString());
                }
            }
        }

        static void Main(string[] args)
        {
            // Read XML Schema containing table structure.
            DataSet ds = new DataSet("DS");
            ds.ReadXmlSchema("AuthorsSchema.XML");

            // Add a unique constraint on the au_id column
            ds.Tables[0].Constraints.Add("ConstraintID",
                        ds.Tables[0].Columns["au_id"],true);

            // Add the first record
            DataRow dr = ds.Tables[0].NewRow();
            dr["au_id"] = "222-22-2222";
            dr["au_fname"] = "Fabio Claudio";
            dr["au_lname"] = "Ferracchiati";
            dr["contract"] = true;
            ds.Tables[0].Rows.Add(dr);
            ds.Tables[0].AcceptChanges();

            // Another DataSet filled with XML data
            DataSet dsXML = new DataSet("XMLDataSet");
            dsXML.ReadXmlSchema("AuthorsSchema.XML");
            dsXML.ReadXml("Authors.XML");

            // Looks for duplicated records
            FindDuplicate(ds, dsXML);

            // If found errors, print out them
            // Otherwise merge the dataset
            if(!dsXML.HasErrors)
            {
                ds.Merge(dsXML);
                Console.WriteLine("Merge done!");
            }
            else
```

```
                         {
                                PrintErrors(dsXML);
                         }
                  }
           }
    }
```

The Locale Property

VB.NET:
```
   Public Property Locale As CultureInfo
```

C#:
```
   public CultureInfo Locale {get; set;}
```

This property either retrieves or sets the locale settings applied to the DataSet object. The Locale parameter has an influence over the string comparison, date managing, and number format. When you set a locale for the DataSet object, even the table will use the same locale setting. This property retrieves a CultureInfo object reference containing all the settings of the user machine. In order to set a locale you have to create a new CultureInfo object, using the System.Globalization namespace, and pass to the property.

VB.NET:
```
   Dim ds As New DataSet("DS")
   Dim ci As New CultureInfo("en-US",true)
   ds.Locale = ci
```

C#:
```
   DataSet ds = new DataSet("DS");
   CultureInfo ci = new CultureInfo("en-US",true);
   ds.Locale = ci;
```

The CultureInfo constructor receives a culture name string and a Boolean value indicating whether to use user culture settings (true) or the default culture settings.

The Namespace Property

VB.NET:
```
   Public Property Namespace As String
```
C#:
```
   public string Namespace {get; set;}
```

As you know DataSet is strictly tied to the XML technology offering a lot of functionalities to manage XML schema and data. This property allows either the retrieving or setting of a namespace that will be used by DataSet XML methods during data retrieving and data comparison. ReadXml() and WriteXml() use this property to retrieve and write the namespace associated to the DataSet, respectively.

Let's start from this simple XML document:

```
<?xml version="1.0" standalone="yes" ?>
<DS xmlns="http://www.wrox.com/Schema2001">
    <Table>
        <hire_date>2001-01-01T00:00:00.0000000+01:00</hire_date>
    </Table>
</DS>
```

Using the ReadXml() method to fill the DataSet, the namespace will be read from the XML document.

VB.NET:

```
Dim ds As New DataSet("DS")
ds.ReadXml("Date.xml")
Console.WriteLine(ds.Namespace)
```

C#:

```
DataSet ds = new DataSet("DS");
ds.ReadXml("Date.xml");
Console.WriteLine(ds.Namespace);
```

In this next example, the WriteXml() method will use the Namespace property to create the XML document:

VB.NET:

```
' Build a table with a datetime column
Dim dt As New DataTable("Table")
dt.Columns.Add(new DataColumn("hire_date",GetType(System.DateTime)))

' Add a new row and a new record
Dim r As DataRow = dt.NewRow()
r("hire_date") = "2001/01/01"
dt.Rows.Add(r)
dt.AcceptChanges()

' Build the Xml using the namespace
Dim ds As New DataSet("DS")
ds.Namespace = "myNamespace"
ds.Tables.Add(dt)

ds.WriteXml("Date.xml")
```

C#:

```
// Build a table with a datetime column
DataTable dt = new DataTable("Table");
dt.Columns.Add(new DataColumn("hire_date",typeof(System.DateTime)));

// Add a new row and a new record
DataRow r = dt.NewRow();
r["hire_date"] = "2001/01/01";
dt.Rows.Add(r);
```

```
dt.AcceptChanges();

// Build the Xml using the namespace
DataSet ds = new DataSet("DS");
ds.Namespace = "myNamespace";
ds.Tables.Add(dt);


ds.WriteXml("Date.xml");
```

The example above will create the `Date.xml` in the following way:

```
<?xml version="1.0" standalone="yes"?>
<DS xmlns="myNamespace">
  <Table>
    <hire_date>2001-01-01T00:00:00.0000000+01:00</hire_date>
  </Table>
</DS>
```

As you can see, the `Namespace` **myNamespace** has been used during XML document creation.

> **Note: If you set a namespace and then you read a XML document that contains another namespace, the `ReadXml()` method will try to understand the data. All the unrecognizable elements will be ignored.**

The Prefix Property

VB.NET:

```
Public Property Prefix As String
```

C#:

```
public string Prefix {get; set;}
```

The `Prefix` property either retrieves or sets a string value containing the namespace's prefix used in the XML Schema and in the XML document. In an XML document the prefix is used to define the tags contained in your namespace. In the following example, the `WriteXmlSchema()` method will create a schema containing both namespace and prefix values:

VB.NET:

```
' Build a table with a datetime column
Dim dt As New DataTable("Table")
dt.Columns.Add(New DataColumn("hire_date", GetType(System.DateTime)))

' Add a new row and a new record
Dim r As DataRow = dt.NewRow()
r("hire_date") = "01/01/2001"
dt.Rows.Add(r)
dt.AcceptChanges()

' Build the XmlSchema using the namespace and the prefix
Dim ds As New DataSet("DS")
```

```
ds.Namespace = "http://www.wrox.com/Schema2001"
ds.Prefix = "wrox"
ds.Tables.Add(dt)

ds.WriteXmlSchema("Schema.xml")
```

C#:

```csharp
// Build a table with a datetime column
DataTable dt = new DataTable("Table");
dt.Columns.Add(new DataColumn("hire_date",typeof(System.DateTime)));

// Add a new row and a new record
DataRow r = dt.NewRow();
r["hire_date"] = "01/01/2001";
dt.Rows.Add(r);
dt.AcceptChanges();

// Build the XmlSchema using the namespace and the prefix
DataSet ds = new DataSet("DS");
ds.Namespace = "http://www.wrox.com/Schema2001";
ds.Prefix = "wrox";
ds.Tables.Add(dt);

ds.WriteXmlSchema("Schema.xml");
```

The resulting schema contains the specified prefix:

```xml
<?xml version="1.0" standalone="yes"?>
<xsd:schema id="DS" targetNamespace="http://www.wrox.com/Schema2001"
xmlns="http://www.wrox.com/Schema2001"
xmlns:xsd="http://www.w3.org/2001/XMLSchema" xmlns:msdata="urn:schemas-microsoft-
com:xml-msdata" attributeFormDefault="qualified" elementFormDefault="qualified">
    <xsd:element name="DS" msdata:IsDataSet="true" msdata:Prefix="wrox">
      <xsd:complexType>
        <xsd:choice maxOccurs="unbounded">
          <xsd:element name="Table">
            <xsd:complexType>
              <xsd:sequence>
                <xsd:element name="hire_date" type="xsd:dateTime" minOccurs="0" />
              </xsd:sequence>
            </xsd:complexType>
          </xsd:element>
        </xsd:choice>
      </xsd:complexType>
    </xsd:element>
</xsd:schema>
```

As just mentioned, the `Prefix` property retrieves the string containing the namespace's prefix set previously in the code, or read from the XML document. In the following snippet of code the `ReadXml()` method will find the wrox prefix inside the document setting the property automatically:

```xml
<?xml version="1.0" standalone="yes"?>
<wrox:DS xmlns:wrox="http://www.wrox.com/Schema2001">
  <Table xmlns="http://www.wrox.com/Schema2001">
    <hire_date>2001-01-01T00:00:00.0000000+01:00</hire_date>
  </Table>
</wrox:DS>
```

VB.NET:

```
Dim ds As New DataSet("DS")
ds.ReadXml("Date.xml")
Console.WriteLine(ds.Prefix)
```

C#:

```
DataSet ds = new DataSet("DS");
ds.ReadXml("Date.xml");
Console.WriteLine(ds.Prefix);
```

The Relations Property

VB.NET:

```
Public ReadOnly Property Relations As DataRelationCollection
```

C#:

```
public DataRelationCollection Relations {get;}
```

This property retrieves a `DataRelationCollection` object reference containing every `DataRelation` object defined in the `DataSet`. A `DataRelation` defines a relation between two tables contained in the `DataSet` object. In Chapter 9 you'll find an exhaustive description of the `DataRelation` object.

In the following example, you can see the `Relations` property used to add a new relation inside the `DataSet` by its `Add()` method.

VB.NET:

```
' Insert a Relation among the tables
Dim dr As New DataRelation("AuthorsToPaymentRel", dcID, dcIDFK, True)

dsWrox.Relations.Add(dr)

' Print to video
Dim d As DataRow
Dim childRow As DataRow

For Each d In dsWrox.Tables("tabAuthors").Rows
    Console.WriteLine("Author: {0} {1}", d("Author_FirstName"),
d("Author_LastName"))
    For Each childRow In d.GetChildRows(dr)
        Console.WriteLine("Payment: {0}$", childRow("Payment"))
    Next
Next
```

C#:

```
// Insert a Relation among the tables
DataRelation dr = new DataRelation("AuthorsToPaymentRel",dcID,dcIDFK,true);

dsWrox.Relations.Add(dr);

// Print to video
foreach (DataRow d in dsWrox.Tables["tabAuthors"].Rows)
{
    Console.WriteLine("Author: {0}
{1}",d["Author_FirstName"],d["Author_LastName"]);
    foreach (DataRow childRow in d.GetChildRows(dr))
        Console.WriteLine("Payment: {0}$",childRow["Payment"]);
}
```

The Site Property

VB.NET:
```
Overrides Public Property Site As ISite
```
C#:
```
public override ISite Site {get; set;}
```

The Site property either retrieves or sets a reference to the ISite interface. It is useful to bind a component to a container enabling the communication and providing a way for the contained to manage the component.

The Table Property

VB.NET:
```
Public ReadOnly Property Tables As DataTableCollection
```

C#:
```
public DataTableCollection Tables {get;}
```

The Table property retrieves a DataTableCollection object reference containing every table inside the DataSet object. A DataTable is the in-memory counterpart of a database table and allows column and rows management, constraint rule application, and much more. When you add a new table to the collection without specifying its name, a default value will be assigned in the Table*n* format name, where *n* is an incremental number starting from zero. This can be seen in the example given under the Creating a Dataset section earlier in the chapter.

In Chapter 8 you'll find an exhaustive DataTable explanation.

DataSet Methods

DataSet exposes twenty-eight proprietary methods and eight inherited from MarshalByValueComponent and Object classes. The proprietary methods are really useful to manage XML documents and schemas and to synchronize database data with the in-memory one. In this part of the chapter you'll find every proprietary method analyzed in detail. Let's start with a brief explanation of the inherited methods:

Method	Description
Dispose	Release the resources used by the MarshalByValueComponent. There are two versions available: the first releases all the resources and don't want parameters, while the second accepts a Boolean value indicating whether the object has to release just the unmanaged resources (false) or both (true).
Equals	Return a Boolean value indicating whether two objects are equals (true) or not (false).
GetHashCode	Useful to hash algorithms and hash table, it retrieves a hash code associated to the object.
GetService	Retrieve the implementer of the IServiceProvider.
GetType	Get the type of the current object instance.
Finalize	It represents the destructor used by C#/C++ to free memory resources. In VB.NET it's called Finalize().
MemberwiseClone	Create an empty clone of the current object.
ToString	Returns a string containing the name of the class.

The AcceptChanges Method

VB.NET:

```
Public Sub AcceptChanges()
```

C#:

```
public void AcceptChanges();
```

The AcceptChanges() method commits in-memory every change made to the DataSet object since it was created or since the last time this method has been called. As was stated earlier, DataSet is an in-memory data representation and to every row, that the object contains, is assigned a state. In order to maintain a perfect alignment between in-memory data and data stored in the database you have to call this method after any operation that updates the records in the database. For example, each time you add new records to the DataSet you have some rows with the Added state value. You can call the GetChanges() method and pass the resulting rows to the Update() method of the DataAdapter object that will insert them in the database. If you don't call the AcceptChanges() at this time you'll have an in-memory data that isn't equal to the database counterpart because there are some rows appearing as new but that have been already inserted in the table. The example below shows this behaviour:

VB.NET:

```vbnet
Dim dbConn As New
SqlClient.SqlConnection("server=localhostuid=sapwd=database=pubs")
Dim da As New SqlClient.SqlDataAdapter("SELECT au_id,au_lname,au_fname,contract
FROM authors", dbConn)
Dim sql As New SqlClient.SqlCommandBuilder(da)

Dim ds As New DataSet("DS")

da.Fill(ds)

Dim dt As DataTable = ds.Tables(0).GetChanges(DataRowState.Added)
Console.WriteLine("Total number of Added records {0}", dt.Rows.Count)

' Insert a new row (IN-MEMORY)
Dim r As DataRow = ds.Tables(0).NewRow()
r("au_id") = "222-22-2222"
r("au_lname") = "Ferracchiati"
r("au_fname") = "Fabio Claudio"
r("contract") = True
ds.Tables(0).Rows.Add(r)

dt = ds.Tables(0).GetChanges(DataRowState.Added)
Console.WriteLine("Total number of Added records after adding a new row {0}",
dt.Rows.Count)

' Insert a new row (DATABASE)
da.Update(dt)

dt = ds.Tables(0).GetChanges(DataRowState.Added)
Console.WriteLine("Total number of Added records after the database table insert
{0}", dt.Rows.Count)

' Commit in-memory records
ds.AcceptChanges()

dt = ds.Tables(0).GetChanges(DataRowState.Added)
Console.WriteLine("Total number of Added records after the AcceptChanges() {0}",
dt.Rows.Count)
```

C#:

```csharp
SqlConnection dbConn = new
SqlConnection("server=localhost;uid=sa;pwd=;database=pubs");

SqlDataAdapter da = new SqlDataAdapter("SELECT au_id,au_lname,au_fname,contract
FROM authors",dbConn);
SqlCommandBuilder sql = new SqlCommandBuilder(da);

DataSet ds = new DataSet("DS");

da.Fill(ds);

DataTable dt = ds.Tables[0].GetChanges(DataRowState.Added);
Console.WriteLine("Total number of Added records {0}",dt.Rows.Count);
```

```
// Insert a new row (IN-MEMORY)
DataRow r = ds.Tables[0].NewRow();
r["au_id"] = "222-22-2222";
r["au_lname"] = "Ferracchiati";
r["au_fname"] = "Fabio Claudio";
r["contract"] = true;
ds.Tables[0].Rows.Add(r);

dt = ds.Tables[0].GetChanges(DataRowState.Added);
Console.WriteLine("Total number of Added records after adding a new row
{0}",dt.Rows.Count);

// Insert a new row (DATABASE)
da.Update(dt);

dt = ds.Tables[0].GetChanges(DataRowState.Added);
Console.WriteLine("Total number of Added records after the database table insert
{0}",dt.Rows.Count);

// Commit in-memory records
ds.AcceptChanges();

dt = ds.Tables[0].GetChanges(DataRowState.Added);
Console.WriteLine("Total number of Added records after the AcceptChanges()
{0}",dt.Rows.Count);
```

The output for the example will be:

`AcceptChanges()` called from a `DataSet` object will call the `AcceptChanges()` methods exposes by `DataTable` and `DataRow`, automatically.

The BeginInit and EndInit Methods

VB.NET:

```
NotOverridable Public Sub BeginInit()
```

```
NotOverridable Public Sub EndInit()
```

C#:

```
public void BeginInit();

public void EndInit();
```

These methods are used when the `DataSet` has to be initialized. `BeginInit()` ensures that accesses cannot be made from other components during the initialization phase. `EndInit()` restores the original situation allowing other components to use the `DataSet` object. Usually, these methods are used by the Visual Studio .NET design environment when you use the object inside a form.

The Clear Method

VB.NET:

```
Public Sub Clear()
```

C#:

```
public void Clear();
```

The `Clear()` method removes every row contained in every table inside the `DataSet` object. If you need to remove the tables and the relations, you can call the `Clear()` method exposed by the `DataTableCollection` and `DataRelationCollection` classes accessible from the `Tables` and `Relations` properties.

VB.NET:

```
Dim dbConn As New SqlConnection("server=localhost;uid=sa;pwd=;database=pubs")
Dim da As New SqlDataAdapter("SELECT au_id,au_lname,au_fname,contract FROM
authors", dbConn)

Dim ds As New DataSet("DS")

da.Fill(ds)

Console.WriteLine("Total rows: {0}", ds.Tables(0).Rows.Count)

ds.Clear()

Console.WriteLine("Total rows after the Clear(): {0}",
ds.Tables(0).Rows.Count.ToString())
```

C#:

```
SqlConnection dbConn = new
SqlConnection("server=localhost;uid=sa;pwd=;database=pubs");
SqlDataAdapter da = new SqlDataAdapter("SELECT au_id,au_lname,au_fname,contract
FROM authors",dbConn);

DataSet ds = new DataSet("DS");

da.Fill(ds);

Console.WriteLine("Total rows: {0}", ds.Tables[0].Rows.Count.ToString());
```

```
ds.Clear();

Console.WriteLine("Total rows after the Clear(): {0}", ds.Tables[0].Rows.Count);
```

The Clone Method

VB.NET:

```
Public Function Clone() As DataSet
```

C#:

```
public DataSet Clone();
```

This method retrieves a cloned version of the current `DataSet` object containing all the tables, relations, and constraint rules without the records contained in the tables. If you derive a new class from the `DataSet` and use this method, a clone will be released having the same derived class also. You can use the clone functionality when you need to do temporary operations and you don't want to operate on the master `DataSet` directly. You can always call the `Merge()` method should you need to group the new data with the original `DataSet`.

VB.NET:

```
...
Console.WriteLine("Total rows: {0}", ds.Tables(0).Rows.Count)

Dim dsCloned As DataSet = ds.Clone()

Console.WriteLine("Total rows after the Clone(): {0}",
dsCloned.Tables(0).Rows.Count)
```

C#:

```
...
Console.WriteLine("Total rows: {0}", ds.Tables[0].Rows.Count);

DataSet dsCloned = ds.Clone();

Console.WriteLine("Total rows after the Clone(): {0}",
dsCloned.Tables[0].Rows.Count);
```

The Copy Method

VB.NET:

```
Public Function Copy() As DataSet
```

C#:

```
public DataSet Copy();
```

183

Using the `Copy()` method you can copy the current `DataSet` in a new object duplicating both the structure and the data. You could use this method to generate a backup version of your `DataSet` before managing the data and structure in your original object. Another valuable use of this method is when you only need a part of the total records contained in the `DataSet`. You can copy it into a new object and remove the undesired records.

VB.NET:

```
...
Console.WriteLine("Total rows: {0}", ds.Tables(0).Rows.Count)

Dim dsCloned As DataSet = ds.Copy()

Console.WriteLine("Total rows after the Copy(): {0}",
dsCloned.Tables(0).Rows.Count)
```

C#:

```
...
Console.WriteLine("Total rows: {0}", ds.Tables[0].Rows.Count);

DataSet dsCloned = ds.Copy();

Console.WriteLine("Total rows after the Copy(): {0}",
dsCloned.Tables[0].Rows.Count);
```

The GetChanges Method

VB.NET:

```
Overloads Public Function GetChanges() As DataSet
```

```
Overloads Public Function GetChanges( _
    ByVal rowStates As DataRowState _
) As DataSet
```

C#:

```
public DataSet GetChanges();
```

```
public DataSet GetChanges(
    DataRowState rowStates
);
```

This method retrieves a reference to a `DataSet` object containing every change made to the current `DataSet`, either since its creation or `AcceptChanges()` last call. This method comes in two versions; the first version doesn't accept parameters and returns a reference to an object containing all the records that have been added, modified, or deleted. The second version of the method accepts a `RowState` value that filters the `DataSet`, returning only a subset of data having a row state with to one of the following values:

DataRowState value	Description
Added	All the rows with this state have been added to the `DataTable` but the `AcceptChanges()` still hasn't been called.
Deleted	All the rows with this state were deleted.
Detached	All the rows with this state have been created but not added to the table collection. Moreover, this value even identifies rows removed from the collection inside the table.
Modifies	All the rows with this state have been modified but the `AcceptChanges()` still hasn't been called.
Unchanged	All the rows with this state have not been modified either after their creation or after the last `AcceptChanges()` call.

In the following example you'll see the first version of the method in action:

VB.NET:

```
' Fill a DataSet with data from the pubs database
Dim dbConn As New SqlConnection("server=localhost;uid=sa;pwd=;database=pubs")
Dim da As New SqlDataAdapter("SELECT au_id,au_lname,au_fname,contract FROM
authors", dbConn)

Dim ds As New DataSet("DS")

da.Fill(ds)

' Insert a new row
Dim r As DataRow = ds.Tables(0).NewRow()
r("au_id") = "222-22-2222"
r("au_lname") = "Ferracchiati"
r("au_fname") = "Fabio Claudio"
r("contract") = True
ds.Tables(0).Rows.Add(r)

' Now modify the first row
ds.Tables(0).Rows(0)("au_fname") = "Fabio C."

' Print all the changes
Dim dsTemp As DataSet = ds.GetChanges()
Dim dr As DataRow
For Each dr In dsTemp.Tables(0).Rows
    Console.WriteLine("ID={0} And State={1}", dr("au_id"), dr.RowState)
Next
```

C#:

```
// Fill a DataSet with data from the pubs database
SqlConnection dbConn = new
SqlConnection("server-localhost;uid=sa;pwd=;database=pubs");
```

```
SqlDataAdapter da = new SqlDataAdapter("SELECT au_id,au_lname,au_fname,contract
FROM authors",dbConn);
DataSet ds = new DataSet("DS");
da.Fill(ds);

// Insert a new row
DataRow r = ds.Tables[0].NewRow();
r["au_id"] = "222-22-2222";
r["au_lname"] = "Ferracchiati";
r["au_fname"] = "Fabio Claudio";
r["contract"] = true;
ds.Tables[0].Rows.Add(r);

// Now modify the first row
ds.Tables[0].Rows[0]["au_fname"] = "Fabio C.";

// Print all the changes
DataSet dsTemp = ds.GetChanges();
foreach(DataRow dr in dsTemp.Tables[0].Rows)
{
    Console.WriteLine("ID={0} And State={1}", dr["au_id"], dr.RowState);
}
```

In this case a `DataSet` with two elements will be retrieved with both the `Added` and `Modified` row state. If you need to retrieve a subset of rows having a particular state, you have to use the second method's prototype:

VB.NET:

```
...
' Print only the Added rows
Dim dsTemp As DataSet = ds.GetChanges(DataRowState.Added)
Dim dr As DataRow
For Each dr In dsTemp.Tables(0).Rows
    Console.WriteLine("ID={0} And State={1}", dr("au_id"), dr.RowState)
Next
```

C#:

```
...
// Print only the Added rows
DataSet dsTemp = ds.GetChanges(DataRowState.Added);
foreach(DataRow dr in dsTemp.Tables[0].Rows)
{
    Console.WriteLine("ID={0} And State={1}", dr["au_id"], dr.RowState);
}
```

By specifying an enumeration value like the `Added` one, you can retrieve only the rows with that exact state.

The GetSchemaSerializable Method

VB.NET:

```
Overridable Protected Function GetSchemaSerializable()
    As XmlSchema
```

C#:

```
protected virtual XmlSchema GetSchemaSerializable();
```

This is a protected method that you can't use directly in your code. It retrieves an XmlTextReader useful for the IXmlSerializable implementation.

The GetSerializationData Method

VB.NET:

```
Protected Sub GetSerializationData( _
    ByVal info As SerializationInfo, _
    ByVal context As StreamingContext _
)
```

C#:

```
protected void GetSerializationData(
    SerializationInfo info,
    StreamingContext context
);
```

This is also a protected method not directly executable from the code. It retrieves serialization information behind the SerializationInfo object and a StreamingContext where either store or retrieve the serialized stream.

The GetXml and GetXmlSchema Methods

VB.NET:

```
Public Function GetXml() As String
```

```
Public Function GetXmlSchema() As String
```

C#:

```
public string GetXml();
```

```
public string GetXmlSchema();
```

The GetXml() and GetXmlSchema() methods retrieve a string containing the XML document and the XML schema for the current DataSet, respectively.

VB.NET:

```
' Create a connection object
Dim dbConn As New SqlConnection("server=localhost;uid=sa;pwd=;database=WroxDB")

' Create a DataAdapter
Dim da As New SqlDataAdapter("SELECT AuthorID, RTRIM(Author_FirstName) As
Author_FirstName, RTRIM(Author_LastName) As Author_LastName FROM tabAuthors",
dbConn)

' Create a DataSet
Dim dsAuthors As New DataSet("DS")

' Fill the DataSet
da.Fill(dsAuthors)

' Print to video
Console.WriteLine(dsAuthors.GetXml())
```

C#:

```
// Create a connection object
SqlConnection dbConn = new
SqlConnection("server=localhost;uid=sa;pwd=;database=WroxDB");

// Create a DataAdapter
SqlDataAdapter da = new SqlDataAdapter("SELECT AuthorID, RTRIM(Author_FirstName)
As Author_FirstName, RTRIM(Author_LastName) As Author_LastName FROM tabAuthors",
dbConn);

// Create a DataSet
DataSet dsAuthors = new DataSet("DS");

// Fill the DataSet
da.Fill(dsAuthors);

// Print to video
Console.WriteLine(dsAuthors.GetXml());
```

In the example above a simple query to the database has generated the following output:

The XML tag root is equal to the `DataSet` name specified during its creation, while the other tags are retrieved from the column names specified in the query. The `DataSet` object offers an XML document called Diffgram that persists both original and current row values with the corresponding row state values. The `GetXml()` method retrieves a Diffgram document whether at least one change has done to the `DataSet`:

VB.NET:

```
...
' Print to video
Console.WriteLine(dsAuthors.GetXmlSchema())
```

C#:

```
...
// Print to video
Console.WriteLine(dsAuthors.GetXmlSchema());
```

The resulting XML schema has the XML Schema Definition (XSD) language specification as you can see from the figure below:

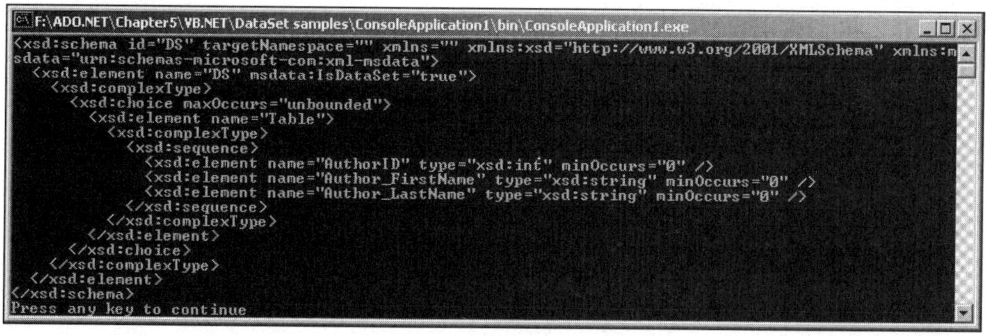

The HasChanges Method

VB.NET:

```
Overloads Public Function HasChanges() As Boolean
```

```
Overloads Public Function HasChanges( _
    ByVal rowStates As DataRowState _
) As Boolean
```

C#:

```
public bool HasChanges();
```

```
public bool HasChanges(
    DataRowState rowStates
);
```

This method retrieves a Boolean value indicating whether the records inside the `DataSet` have been changed. The first version of the method doesn't accept parameters and returns a true value whether at least one record has changed its value. Instead, the second version of this method accepts a `DataRowState` enumeration value in order to retrieve just a subset of records (for example only the modified rows). The `DataRowState` enumeration can assume one of the values as listed in the `GetChanges` method section.

VB.NET:

```
' Create a connection object
Dim dbConn As New
SqlClient.SqlConnection("server=localhost;uid=sa;pwd=;database=WroxDB")

' Create a DataAdapter
Dim da As New SqlClient.SqlDataAdapter("SELECT AuthorID, Author_FirstName,
Author_LastName FROM tabAuthors", dbConn)

' Create a DataSet
Dim dsAuthors As New DataSet("DS")

' Fill the DataSet
da.Fill(dsAuthors)

' Add a new record
Dim r As DataRow = dsAuthors.Tables(0).NewRow()

r("AuthorID") = 6
r("Author_FirstName") = "Mark"
r("Author_LastName") = "Seemann"

dsAuthors.Tables(0).Rows.Add(r)

' Print to video
Console.WriteLine(dsAuthors.HasChanges().ToString())
```

C#:

```
// Create a connection object
SqlConnection dbConn = new
SqlConnection("server=localhost;uid=sa;pwd=;database=WroxDB");

// Create a DataAdapter
SqlDataAdapter da = new SqlDataAdapter("SELECT AuthorID, Author_FirstName,
Author_LastName FROM tabAuthors", dbConn);

// Create a DataSet
DataSet dsAuthors = new DataSet("DS");

// Fill the DataSet
da.Fill(dsAuthors);

// Add a new record
DataRow r = dsAuthors.Tables[0].NewRow();

r["AuthorID"] = 6;
```

```
r["Author_FirstName"] = "Mark";
r["Author_LastName"] = "Seemann";

dsAuthors.Tables[0].Rows.Add(r);

// Print to video
Console.WriteLine(dsAuthors.HasChanges().ToString());
```

The HasSchemaChanged Method

VB.NET:

```
Overridable Protected Function HasSchemaChanged() As Boolean
```

C#:

```
protected virtual bool HasSchemaChanged();
```

This method retrieves a Boolean value indicating whether the DataSet's schema has changed after its creation. This is a protected overridable method so you can't call directly in your code but you have to use it in a DataSet derived class.

VB.NET:

```
' Create a connection object
Dim dbConn As New
SqlClient.SqlConnection("server=localhost;uid=sa;pwd=;database=WroxDB")

' Create a DataAdapter
Dim da As New SqlClient.SqlDataAdapter("SELECT AuthorID, Author_FirstName,
Author_LastName FROM tabAuthors", dbConn)

' Create a DataSet
Dim dsAuthors As New AuthorsDataSet()

' Fill the DataSet
da.Fill(dsAuthors)

' Add a table
dsAuthors.Tables.Add(New DataTable())

' Print to video
Console.WriteLine(dsAuthors.SchemaChanged().ToString())

Public Class AuthorsDataSet
    Inherits System.Data.DataSet

    Public Function SchemaChanged() As Boolean
        Return Me.HasSchemaChanged()
    End Function
End Class
```

C#:

```
// Create a connection object
```

```
SqlConnection dbConn = new
SqlConnection("server=localhost;uid=sa;pwd=;database=WroxDB");

// Create a DataAdapter
SqlDataAdapter da = new SqlDataAdapter("SELECT AuthorID, Author_FirstName,
Author_LastName FROM tabAuthors", dbConn);

// Create a DataSet
AuthorsDataSet dsAuthors = new AuthorsDataSet();

// Fill the DataSet
da.Fill(dsAuthors);

// Add a table
dsAuthors.Tables.Add(new DataTable());

// Print to video
Console.WriteLine(dsAuthors.SchemaChanged().ToString());

// Derive a new class in order to use the HasSchemaChanged() method
public class AuthorsDataSet : System.Data.DataSet
{
    public bool SchemaChanged()
    {
        return this.HasSchemaChanged();
    }
}
```

The InferXmlSchema Method

VB.NET:
```
Overloads Public Sub InferXmlSchema( _
    ByVal stream As Stream, _
    ByVal nsArray() As String _
)
```

```
Overloads Public Sub InferXmlSchema( _
    ByVal fileName As String, _
    ByVal nsArray() As String _
)
```

```
Overloads Public Sub InferXmlSchema( _
    ByVal reader As TextReader, _
    ByVal nsArray() As String _
)
```

```
Overloads Public Sub InferXmlSchema( _
    ByVal reader As XmlReader, _
    ByVal nsArray() As String _
)
```

C#:

```csharp
public void InferXmlSchema(
    Stream stream,
    string[] nsArray
);


public void InferXmlSchema(
    string fileName,
    string[] nsArray
);


public void InferXmlSchema(
    TextReader reader,
    string[] nsArray
);


public void InferXmlSchema(
    XmlReader reader,
    string[] nsArray
);
```

Whenever you receive an XML document without either a valid inline schema or an XSD schema you can try to infer the XML schema using one of the above versions of this method. The InferXmlSchema() follows some rules described below to infer a DataSet schema reading a valid XML document.

This method comes in four versions: the first accepts a Stream object containing the XML document; the second accepts a string with the complete path and filename of the XML document; the third accepts a TextReader object containing the XML document; and the fourth, and final version accepts a XmlReader object containing the XML document. Also, every version accepts a string array as a second parameter where you can specify the namespaces to be excluded during the infer operation.

The infer process starts looking for the elements in the XML document having the right characteristics to become a table in DataSet object. Every element that has at least one attribute will become a table:

```xml
<WroxDataSet>
    <Author firstname="Fabio Claudio"/>
</WroxDataSet>
```

Using the XML document above, the InferXmlSchema() method will produce an Author table having a column named firstname. Every element having at least a child element will be treated as a table:

```xml
<WroxDataSet>
    <Author>
        <AuthorID>1</AuthorID>
    </Author>
</WroxDataSet>
```

In this case the `Author` table will be created with a column called `AuthorID` containing the value 1. Finally, every repeated element inside the XML document will be inserted in the `DataSet` as a table:

```
<WroxDataSet>
    <AuthorID>1</AuthorID>
    <AuthorID>2</AuthorID>
</WroxDataSet>
```

By giving the above XML document to the `InferXmlSchema()` method, an `AuthorID` table will be created and a column named *element*_Text will contain the text between the corresponding tags (in the specific case is `AuthorID_Text` column name). There are cases where the final result is not the desired one, like when you treat an XML document like this:

```
<WroxDataSet xmlns:wrx="urn:schemas-wrox-com:wroxdata">
    <Author>
        <AuthorID wrx:type="int">1</AuthorID>
        <Author_FirstName wrx:maxLength="50" wrx:type="String">Fabio
Claudio</Author_FirstName>
        <Author_LastName
wrx:type="String">Ferracchiati</Author_LastName>
    </Author>
    <Book>
        <BookID wrx:type="int">1</BookID>
        <Title wrx:type="String">ADO.NET Programmer's
Reference</Title>
        <ISBN wrx:type="String">186100558X</ISBN>
    </Book>
</WroxDataSet>
```

Using the following code you'll receive unexpected results:

VB.NET:

```
' Create a DataSet
Dim dsAuthors As New DataSet()

' Infer the schema
dsAuthors.InferXmlSchema("Wrox.xml", Nothing)

' Print every table inferred
Dim t As DataTable
For Each t In dsAuthors.Tables
    Console.WriteLine(t.TableName)
Next

Console.WriteLine("-=-=-=-=-=-=-=-=-=-=-=-=-=-=-=-=-=")

' Create a new DataSet
Dim dsAuthors2 As New DataSet()

' Same XML document
dsAuthors2.InferXmlSchema("Wrox.xml", New String() {"urn:schemas-wrox-
com:wroxdata"})
```

```
' Different results
For Each t In dsAuthors2.Tables
    Console.WriteLine(t.TableName)
Next
```

C#:

```csharp
// Create a DataSet
DataSet dsAuthors = new DataSet();

// Infer the schema
dsAuthors.InferXmlSchema("Wrox.xml",null);

// Print every table inferred
foreach (DataTable t in dsAuthors.Tables)
    Console.WriteLine(t.TableName);

Console.WriteLine("-=-=-=-=-=-=-=-=-=-=-=-=-=-=-=-=-=-=-=");

// Create a new DataSet
DataSet dsAuthors2 = new DataSet();

// Same XML document
dsAuthors2.InferXmlSchema("Wrox.xml",new String[] {"urn:schemas-wrox-com:wroxdata"});

// Different results
foreach (DataTable t in dsAuthors2.Tables)
    Console.WriteLine(t.TableName);
```

As you can see from the following figure, if you don't specify the namespace to ignore, every element will be created as a table because they contain an attribute. If you specify a string array containing the namespace to exclude, just two tables will be created as we expect:

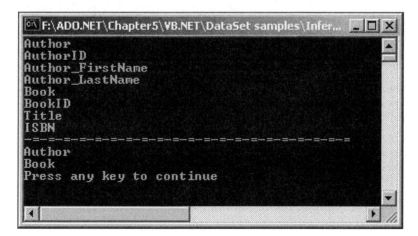

195

The Merge Method

VB.NET:

```
Overloads Public Sub Merge( _
    ByVal rows() As DataRow _
)


Overloads Public Sub Merge( _
    ByVal dataSet As DataSet _
)


Overloads Public Sub Merge( _
    ByVal table As DataTable _
)


Overloads Public Sub Merge( _
    ByVal dataSet As DataSet, _
    ByVal preserveChanges As Boolean _
)


Overloads Public Sub Merge( _
    ByVal rows() As DataRow, _
    ByVal preserveChanges As Boolean, _
    ByVal missingSchemaAction As MissingSchemaAction _
)


Overloads Public Sub Merge( _
    ByVal dataSet As DataSet, _
    ByVal preserveChanges As Boolean, _
    ByVal missingSchemaAction As MissingSchemaAction _
)


Overloads Public Sub Merge( _
    ByVal table As DataTable, _
    ByVal preserveChanges As Boolean, _
    ByVal missingSchemaAction As MissingSchemaAction _
)
```

C#:

```
public void Merge(
    DataRow[] rows
);


public void Merge(
    DataSet dataSet
);


public void Merge(
    DataTable table;
```

```
public void Merge(
    DataSet dataSet,
    bool preserveChanges
);
```

```
public void Merge(
    DataRow[] rows,
    bool preserveChanges,
    MissingSchemaAction missingSchemaAction
);
```

```
public void Merge(
    DataSet dataSet,
    bool preserveChanges,
    MissingSchemaAction missingSchemaAction
);
```

```
public void Merge(
    DataTable table,
    bool preserveChanges,
    MissingSchemaAction missingSchemaAction
);
```

This method merges the values provided through its parameters with the values inside the DataSet object. This method provides seven different versions:

❑ The first accepts an array of new DataRow objects to merge with the current ones

❑ The second method accepts a DataSet object to merge to the current ones

❑ The third accepts a DataTable object

❑ The fourth method adds a new parameter that represents a Boolean value indicating whether the changes made to the current DataSet have to be persisted (true) or not (false)

❑ The fifth to seventh methods add a third parameter that contains a MissingSchemaAction enumeration value indicating the action to undertake whether the schema has changed

For example, if you merge a DataSet having a new column with a DataSet having the same schema but not the new column, specifying the AddKey value for the MissingSchemaAction you'll create the new column in the original DataSet automatically. This parameter can assume one of the following values:

MissingSchemaAction values	Description
Error	If the original DataSet is not equal to the merged one a SystemException is generated.
Add	If the original DataSet has less columns of the merged one then these columns will be added.

Table continued on following page

MissingSchemaAction values	Description
AddWithKey	If the original DataSet has less columns than the merged one then these columns will be added, considering the primary keys also.
Ignore	If the original DataSet has less columns than the merged one then these columns will be ignored.

A typical use of this method is behind the **Submit** button of an HTML form where the client sends new information to add to the database. The middle-tier has to update the information in the database and returns a subset of information to the DataSet with every change that occurrs to the database from the last update.

When the Merge() method is called the two DataSets are compared in order to find any difference in the corresponding schemas. Actions based on the MissingSchemaAction value will be undertaken if some differences are found in the two schemas. After the schema comparison, the Merge() method looks for the data to merge into the original DataSet. There are two kinds of merge operations; the first is when you use the GetChanges() method to retrieve only the subset of data and the second is when a new DataSet, one loaded from a XML document, is merged to the original one. In the first case an internal unique identification number will be created for each row inside the original and generated DataSet. When changed row values are found, the unique id is used to update the original DataSet. In the second case, when both new rows and changed rows are found, the original DataSet primary key is used to find the correct value to update or to raise an error if the primary key already exists.

In the following example two DataSet objects are generated, one using the Fill() method, in order to retrieve data and schema from the database. The second contains only the schema in order to be used to add a new row that will be merged to the first DataSet.

VB.NET:

```
' Fill a DataSet with data from the pubs database
Dim dbConn As New
SqlClient.SqlConnection("server=localhost;uid=sa;pwd=;database=pubs")
Dim da As New SqlClient.SqlDataAdapter("SELECT au_id,au_lname,au_fname,contract
FROM authors", dbConn)
Dim ds As New DataSet("DS")
Dim ds2 As New DataSet("DS2")

' Fill with data and schema
da.Fill(ds)

' Only the schema for the other dataset
da.FillSchema(ds2, SchemaType.Source)

' Print the starting number of rows
Console.WriteLine("Starting number of rows: {0}", ds.Tables(0).Rows.Count)

' Add a new row
Dim r As DataRow
r = ds2.Tables(0).NewRow()
r("au_id") = "222-22-2222"
r("au_fname") = "Fabio Claudio"
r("au_lname") = "Ferracchiati"
```

```
r("contract") = True
ds2.Tables(0).Rows.Add(r)

' Merge the two DataSets
ds.Merge(ds2)

' Print the starting number of rows
Console.WriteLine("Number of rows after the Merge(): {0}",
ds.Tables(0).Rows.Count)
```

C#:

```
// Fill a DataSet with data from the pubs database
SqlConnection dbConn = new
SqlConnection("server=localhost;uid=sa;pwd=;database=pubs");
SqlDataAdapter da = new SqlDataAdapter("SELECT au_id,au_lname,au_fname,contract
FROM authors",dbConn);
DataSet ds = new DataSet("DS");
DataSet ds2 = new DataSet("DS2");

// Fill with data and schema
da.Fill(ds);

// Only the schema for the other dataset
da.FillSchema(ds2,SchemaType.Source);

// Print the starting number of rows
Console.WriteLine("Starting number of rows: {0}", ds.Tables[0].Rows.Count);

// Add a new row
DataRow r = ds2.Tables[0].NewRow();
r["au_id"] = "222-22-2222";
r["au_fname"] = "Fabio Claudio";
r["au_lname"] = "Ferracchiati";
r["contract"] = true;
ds2.Tables[0].Rows.Add(r);

// Merge the two DataSets
ds.Merge(ds2);

// Print the starting number of rows
Console.WriteLine("Number of rows after the Merge(): {0}",
ds.Tables[0].Rows.Count);
```

Note: During the merge process every RowState value will be preserved.

The OnPropertyChanging Method

VB.NET:

```
Overridable Protected Friend Dim Sub OnPropertyChanging( _
    ByVal pcevent As PropertyChangedEventArgs _
)
```

C#:

```
protected internal virtual void OnPropertyChanging(
    PropertyChangedEventArgs pcevent
);
```

This method used inside a derivated class can raise an event when a property is being changed from the DataSet object.

The OnRemoveRelation Method

VB.NET:

```
Overridable Protected Sub OnRemoveRelation( _
    ByVal relation As DataRelation _
)
```

C#:

```
protected virtual void OnRemoveRelation(
    DataRelation relation
);
```

This method, used inside a derived class, is the event handler for when a relation is being removed from the DataSet object.

The OnRemoveTable Method

VB.NET:

```
Overridable Protected Sub OnRemoveTable( _
    ByVal table As DataTable _
)
```

C#:

```
protected virtual void OnRemoveTable(
    DataTable table
);
```

This method, used inside a derived class, is the event handler for when a table is being removed from the DataSet object.

The RaisePropertyChanging Method

VB.NET:

```
Protected Friend Dim Sub RaisePropertyChanging( _
    ByVal name As String _
)
```

C#:

```
protected internal void RaisePropertyChanging(
    string name
);
```

This method sends a notification message that the specified property is changing.

The ReadXml Method

VB.NET:

```
Overloads Public Function ReadXml( _
    ByVal stream As Stream _
) As XmlReadMode


Overloads Public Function ReadXml( _
    ByVal fileName As String _
) As XmlReadMode


Overloads Public Function ReadXml( _
    ByVal reader As TextReader _
) As XmlReadMode


Overloads Public Function ReadXml( _
    ByVal reader As XmlReader _
) As XmlReadMode


Overloads Public Function ReadXml( _
    ByVal stream As Stream, _
    ByVal mode As XmlReadMode _
) As XmlReadMode


Overloads Public Function ReadXml( _
    ByVal fileName As String, _
    ByVal mode As XmlReadMode _
) As XmlReadMode


Overloads Public Function ReadXml( _
    ByVal reader As TextReader, _
    ByVal mode As XmlReadMode _
) As XmlReadMode
```

```
Overloads Public Function ReadXml( _
   ByVal reader As XmlReader, _
   ByVal mode As XmlReadMode _
) As XmlReadMode
```

C#:

```
public XmlReadMode ReadXml(
   Stream stream
);
```

```
public XmlReadMode ReadXml(
   string fileName
);
```

```
public XmlReadMode ReadXml(
   TextReader reader
);
```

```
public XmlReadMode ReadXml(
   XmlReader reader
);
```

```
public XmlReadMode ReadXml(
   Stream stream,
   XmlReadMode mode
);
```

```
public XmlReadMode ReadXml(
   string fileName,
   XmlReadMode mode
);
```

```
public XmlReadMode ReadXml(
   TextReader reader,
   XmlReadMode mode
);
```

```
public XmlReadMode ReadXml(
   XmlReader reader,
   XmlReadMode mode
);
```

This method reads from an XML document specified as a parameter and fills the DataSet with the data found. There are four ways to provide the XML document: by string with the path and filename, by Stream object, by TextReader object, and by XmlReader object.

VB.NET:

```
Dim ds As New DataSet()

' Read a XML using the string parameter
```

```
ds.ReadXml("Authors.xml")

' Read a XML using the XmlTextReader parameter
Dim fs As New IO.FileStream("Authors.xml", IO.FileMode.Open)
Dim xtr As New Xml.XmlTextReader(fs)
ds.ReadXml(xtr)
fs.Close()

' Read a XML using the TextReader parameter
Dim fs2 As New IO.FileStream("Authors.xml", IO.FileMode.Open)
Dim tr As IO.TextReader = New IO.StreamReader(fs2)
ds.ReadXml(tr)
fs2.Close()

' Read a XML using the Stream parameter
Dim fs3 As New IO.FileStream("Authors.xml", IO.FileMode.Open)
ds.ReadXml(fs3)
fs3.Close()
```

C#:

```
DataSet ds = new DataSet();

// Read a XML using the string parameter
ds.ReadXml("Authors.xml");

// Read a XML using the XmlTextReader parameter
FileStream fs = new FileStream("Authors.xml",FileMode.Open);
XmlTextReader xtr = new XmlTextReader(fs);
ds.ReadXml(xtr);
fs.Close();

// Read a XML using the TextReader parameter
FileStream fs2 = new FileStream("Authors.xml",FileMode.Open);
TextReader tr = new StreamReader(fs2);
ds.ReadXml(tr);
fs2.Close();

// Read a XML using the Stream parameter
FileStream fs3 = new FileStream("Authors.xml",FileMode.Open);
ds.ReadXml(fs3);
fs3.Close();
```

There is a second set of versions for this method that accept two parameters, the XML document to read from, and an XmlReadMode enumeration value. The last parameter can assume one of the following values:

XmlReadMode values	Description
Auto	This is the default value. If the XML document contains either a schema or an inline schema, the ReadXml() method will use the ReadSchema enumeration automatically. If the XML document doesn't contain a schema, the ReadXml() will try to infer it using the InferSchema value. Finally, if the XML document is a diffgram then the Diffgram enumeration value will be used by the method.
Diffgram	Reads data from an XML document containing original and current rows, together with the related row state.
Fragment	Reads data from an XML document containing the XDR schema. This one is typically retrieved from a SQL Server query with the FOR XML clause.
IgnoreSchema	Reads data from an XML document ignoring every inline schema different from the current DataSet schema.
InferSchema	Infers a schema reading an XML document and then load the corresponding data creating tables and columns automatically.
ReadSchema	Reads data from an XML document that contains a valid schema.

In the following example the Diffgram enumeration value will be used to retrieve a DataSet containing this data:

```xml
<?xml version="1.0" standalone="yes"?>
<diffgr:diffgram xmlns:msdata="urn:schemas-microsoft-com:xml-msdata"
xmlns:diffgr="urn:schemas-microsoft-com:xml-diffgram-v1">
  <DS>
    <Table diffgr:id="Table1" msdata:rowOrder="0">
...
    </Table>
    <Table diffgr:id="Table2" msdata:rowOrder="1" diffgr:hasChanges="modified">
...
    </Table>
...
...
    <Table diffgr:id="Table6" msdata:rowOrder="5" diffgr:hasChanges="inserted">
...
    </Table>
  </DS>
  <diffgr:before>
    <Table diffgr:id="Table2" msdata:rowOrder="1">
      <AuthorID>2</AuthorID>
      <Author_FirstName>Simon</Author_FirstName>
      <Author_LastName>Robinson</Author_LastName>
    </Table>
  </diffgr:before>
</diffgr:diffgram>
```

The Diffgram above contains a new row and a modified one. The DataSet we are retrieving will contain six records, one modified row, and a new record.

VB.NET:

```vb.net
' Create an empty dataset having the same schema as the XML document
Dim dbConn As New
SqlClient.SqlConnection("server=localhost;uid=sa;pwd=;database=WroxDB")
Dim da As New SqlClient.SqlDataAdapter("SELECT
AuthorID,Author_FirstName,Author_LastName FROM tabAuthors", dbConn)
Dim ds As New DataSet("DS")
da.FillSchema(ds, SchemaType.Source)

' Fill the DataSet using the Diffgram
ds.ReadXml("Diffgram.xml", XmlReadMode.DiffGram)

' Print to video
Console.WriteLine("Tables n. {0}", ds.Tables.Count)
Console.WriteLine("Rows n. {0}", ds.Tables(0).Rows.Count)

' Retrieve a subset of records for only the added and modified rows
Dim dv As New DataView(ds.Tables(0))
dv.RowStateFilter = DataViewRowState.Added
Console.WriteLine("Rows added n. {0}", dv.Count)
dv.RowStateFilter = DataViewRowState.ModifiedOriginal
Console.WriteLine("Rows modified n. {0}", dv.Count)
```

C#:

```csharp
// Create an empty dataset having the same schema as the XML document
SqlConnection dbConn = new
SqlConnection("server=localhost;uid=sa;pwd=;database=WroxDB");
SqlDataAdapter da = new SqlDataAdapter("SELECT
AuthorID,Author_FirstName,Author_LastName FROM tabAuthors",dbConn);
DataSet ds = new DataSet("DS");
da.FillSchema(ds, SchemaType.Source);

// Fill the DataSet using the Diffgram
ds.ReadXml("Diffgram.xml", XmlReadMode.DiffGram);

// Print to video
Console.WriteLine("Tables n. {0}",ds.Tables.Count);
Console.WriteLine("Rows n. {0}",ds.Tables[0].Rows.Count);

// Retrieve a subset of records for only the added and modified rows
DataView dv = new DataView(ds.Tables[0]);
dv.RowStateFilter = DataViewRowState.Added;
Console.WriteLine("Rows added n. {0}",dv.Count);
dv.RowStateFilter = DataViewRowState.ModifiedOriginal;
Console.WriteLine("Rows modified n. {0}",dv.Count);
```

The ReadXmlSchema Method

VB.NET:

```
Overloads Public Sub ReadXmlSchema( _
    ByVal stream As Stream _
)
```

```
Overloads Public Sub ReadXmlSchema( _
    ByVal fileName As String _
)
```

```
Overloads Public Sub ReadXmlSchema( _
    ByVal reader As TextReader _
)
```

```
Overloads Public Sub ReadXmlSchema( _
    ByVal reader As XmlReader _
)
```

C#:

```
public void ReadXmlSchema(
    Stream stream
);
```

```
public void ReadXmlSchema(
    string fileName
);
```

```
public void ReadXmlSchema(
    TextReader reader
);
```

```
public void ReadXmlSchema(
    XmlReader reader
);
```

This method creates an empty `DataSet` with tables, columns with related data types, relations and constraints loading information from an XML schema passed as parameter. The XML schema has to be written using the XSD standard. Usually, you use this method before calling the `ReadXml()` in order to prepare the `DataSet` to contain the data having that specific format.

The following XML schema has a valid XSD format and describes the authors table from the pubs database contained in the Microsoft SQL Server:

```
<?xml version="1.0" standalone="yes"?>
<xsd:schema id="NewDataSet" targetNamespace="" xmlns=""
xmlns:xsd="http://www.w3.org/2001/XMLSchema" xmlns:msdata="urn:schemas-microsoft-
com:xml-msdata">
  <xsd:element name="NewDataSet" msdata:IsDataSet="true">
    <xsd:complexType>
```

```
              <xsd:choice maxOccurs="unbounded">
                <xsd:element name="authors">
                  <xsd:complexType>
                    <xsd:sequence>
                      <xsd:element name="au_id" type="xsd:string" minOccurs="0" />
                      <xsd:element name="au_lname" type="xsd:string" minOccurs="0" />
                      <xsd:element name="au_fname" type="xsd:string" minOccurs="0" />
                      <xsd:element name="contract" type="xsd:boolean" minOccurs="0" />
                    </xsd:sequence>
                  </xsd:complexType>
                </xsd:element>
              </xsd:choice>
            </xsd:complexType>
          </xsd:element>
        </xsd:schema>
```

In the following example you'll see each version in action:

VB.NET:

```
Dim ds As New DataSet()

' Read an XML schema using the string parameter
ds.ReadXmlSchema("AuthorsSchema.xml")

' Read an XML schema using the XmlTextReader parameter
Dim fs As New IO.FileStream("AuthorsSchema.xml", IO.FileMode.Open)
Dim xtr As New Xml.XmlTextReader(fs)
ds.ReadXmlSchema(xtr)
fs.Close()

' Read an XML schema using the TextReader parameter
Dim fs2 As New IO.FileStream("AuthorsSchema.xml", IO.FileMode.Open)
Dim tr As IO.TextReader = New IO.StreamReader(fs2)
ds.ReadXmlSchema(tr)
fs2.Close()

' Read an XML schema using the TextReader parameter
Dim fs3 As New IO.FileStream("AuthorsSchema.xml", IO.FileMode.Open)
ds.ReadXmlSchema(fs3)
fs3.Close()
```

C#:

```
DataSet ds = new DataSet();

// Read an XML schema using the string parameter
ds.ReadXmlSchema("AuthorsSchema.xml");

// Read an XML schema using the XmlTextReader parameter
FileStream fs = new FileStream("AuthorsSchema.xml",FileMode.Open);
XmlTextReader xtr = new XmlTextReader(fs);
ds.ReadXmlSchema (xtr);
```

```
    fs.Close();

    // Read an XML schema using the TextReader parameter
    FileStream fs2 = new FileStream("AuthorsSchema.xml",FileMode.Open);
    TextReader tr = new StreamReader(fs2);
    ds.ReadXmlSchema (tr);
    fs2.Close();

    // Read an XML schema using the TextReader parameter
    FileStream fs3 = new FileStream("AuthorsSchema.xml",FileMode.Open);
    ds.ReadXmlSchema (fs3);
    fs3.Close();
```

The ReadXmlSerializable Method

VB.NET:

```
Overridable Protected Sub ReadXmlSerializable( _
    ByVal reader As XmlReader _
)
```

C#:

```
protected virtual void ReadXmlSerializable(
    XmlReader reader
);
```

This is a protected method used to retrieve XML serialization information to be used with an IXmlSerializable interface.

The RejectChanges Method

VB.NET:

```
Overridable Public Sub RejectChanges()
```

C#:

```
public virtual void RejectChanges();
```

This method rolls back every change made to the tables contained in the DataSet object even enforcing every constraint applied to the tables. You have to call this method when you find any error during database updates in order to come back to the original DataSet settings.

VB.NET:

```
Private Sub btnUndo_Click(ByVal sender As System.Object, ByVal e As
System.EventArgs) Handles btnUndo.Click
      ' Retrieve the dataset
      Dim ds As DataSet = CType(Session("ds"), DataSet)

      ' Reject its changes
      ds.RejectChanges()
```

```
        ' Update the DataGrid
        dgAuthors.DataBind()
    End Sub
```

C#:

```csharp
    private void btnUndo_Click(object sender, System.EventArgs e)
    {
        // Retrieve the dataset
        DataSet ds = (DataSet)Session["ds"];

        // Reject its changes
        ds.RejectChanges();

        // Update the DataGrid
        dgAuthors.DataBind();
    }
```

The example above is an extract from the **Example1** where the button **Undo** rolls back the `DataSet` to its original values.

The Reset Method

VB.NET:

```
    Overridable Public Sub Reset()
```

C#:

```csharp
    public virtual void Reset();
```

This method resets the `DataSet` object removing every table and relation contained within it. This method could be useful when you have finished using a `DataSet` and want to use the same object to retrieve other data.

VB.NET:

```vbnet
    ' Create an empty dataset having the same schema as the XML document
    Dim dbConn As New
    SqlClient.SqlConnection("server=localhost;uid=sa;pwd=;database=WroxDB")
    Dim da As New SqlClient.SqlDataAdapter("SELECT
    AuthorID,Author_FirstName,Author_LastName FROM tabAuthors", dbConn)
    Dim ds As New DataSet("DS")
    da.FillSchema(ds, SchemaType.Source)

    ' Print to video
    Console.WriteLine("Tables n. {0}", ds.Tables.Count)

    ' Reset DataSet
    ds.Reset()

    ' No more tables inside
```

```
Console.WriteLine("Tables n. {0}", ds.Tables.Count)
```

C#:

```csharp
// Create an empty dataset having the same schema as the XML document
SqlConnection dbConn = new
SqlConnection("server=localhost;uid=sa;pwd=;database=WroxDB");
SqlDataAdapter da = new SqlDataAdapter("SELECT
AuthorID,Author_FirstName,Author_LastName FROM tabAuthors",dbConn);
DataSet ds = new DataSet("DS");
da.FillSchema(ds, SchemaType.Source);

// Print to video
Console.WriteLine("Tables n. {0}",ds.Tables.Count);

// Reset DataSet
ds.Reset();

// No more tables inside
Console.WriteLine("Tables n. {0}",ds.Tables.Count);
```

The ShouldSerializeRelations Method

VB.NET:

```
Overridable Protected Function ShouldSerializeRelations() As Boolean
```

C#:

```csharp
protected virtual bool ShouldSerializeRelations();
```

This method retrieves a Boolean value indicating whether the relations contained in the DataSet have to be persisted (true) or not (false). Usually you'll use this method when you either create your own control that includes the DataSet and you want to know if the relations are changed or when you have created a designer for the DataSet.

The ShouldSerializeTables Method

VB.NET:

```
Overridable Protected Function ShouldSerializeTables() As Boolean
```

C#:

```csharp
protected virtual bool ShouldSerializeTables();
```

This method retrieves a Boolean value indicating whether the tables contained in the DataSet have to be persisted (true) or not (false). Usually you'll use this method when you either create your own control that include the DataSet and you want to know if the tables are changed or when you have created a designer for the DataSet.

The WriteXml Method

VB.NET:

```
Overloads Public Sub WriteXml( _
    ByVal stream As Stream _
)
```

```
Overloads Public Sub WriteXml( _
    ByVal fileName As String _
)
```

```
Overloads Public Sub WriteXml( _
    ByVal writer As TextWriter _
)
```

```
Overloads Public Sub WriteXml( _
    ByVal writer As XmlWriter _
)
```

```
Overloads Public Sub WriteXml( _
    ByVal stream As Stream, _
    ByVal mode As XmlWriteMode _
)
```

```
Overloads Public Sub WriteXml( _
    ByVal fileName As String, _
    ByVal mode As XmlWriteMode _
)
```

```
Overloads Public Sub WriteXml( _
    ByVal writer As TextWriter, _
    ByVal mode As XmlWriteMode _
)
```

```
Overloads Public Sub WriteXml( _
    ByVal writer As XmlWriter, _
    ByVal mode As XmlWriteMode _
)
```

C#:

```
public void WriteXml(
    Stream stream
);
```

```
public void WriteXml(
    string fileName
);
```

```
public void WriteXml(
    TextWriter writer
);
```

```
public void WriteXml(
    XmlWriter writer
);
```

```
public void WriteXml(
    Stream stream,
    XmlWriteMode mode
);
```

```
public void WriteXml(
    string fileName,
    XmlWriteMode mode
);
```

```
public void WriteXml(
    TextWriter writer,
    XmlWriteMode mode
);
```

```
public void WriteXml(
    XmlWriter writer,
    XmlWriteMode mode
);
```

This method writes the `DataSet` content in a specified XML document with or without the related XML schema. This method offers eight different versions. In the first four, you have to specify just a parameter that represents the XML document to write to.

VB.NET:

```
' Create a DataSet
Dim dbConn As New
SqlClient.SqlConnection("server=localhost;uid=sa;pwd=;database=WroxDB")
Dim da As New SqlClient.SqlDataAdapter("SELECT
AuthorID,Author_FirstName,Author_LastName FROM tabAuthors", dbConn)
Dim ds As New DataSet("DS")
da.Fill(ds)

' Write a XML using the string parameter
ds.WriteXml("WriteXmlString.xml")

' Write a XML using the TextWriter parameter
Dim fs As New IO.FileStream("WriteXmlTextWriter.xml", IO.FileMode.Create)
Dim tw As IO.TextWriter = New IO.StreamWriter(fs)
ds.WriteXml(tw)
fs.Close()

' Write a XML using the XmlWriter parameter
Dim fs2 As New IO.FileStream("WriteXmlXmlTextWriter.xml", IO.FileMode.Create)
Dim tw2 As IO.TextWriter = New IO.StreamWriter(fs2)
Dim xtw As New Xml.XmlTextWriter(tw2)
ds.WriteXml(xtw)
```

```
fs2.Close()

' Write a XML using the Stream parameter
Dim fs3 As New IO.FileStream("WriteXmlStream.xml", IO.FileMode.Create)
ds.WriteXml(fs3)
fs3.Close()
```

C#:

```
// Create a DataSet
SqlConnection dbConn = new
SqlConnection("server=localhost;uid=sa;pwd=;database=WroxDB");
SqlDataAdapter da = new SqlDataAdapter("SELECT
AuthorID,Author_FirstName,Author_LastName FROM tabAuthors",dbConn);
DataSet ds = new DataSet("DS");
da.Fill(ds);

// Write a XML using the string parameter
ds.WriteXml("WriteXmlString.xml");

// Write a XML using the TextWriter parameter
FileStream fs = new FileStream("WriteXmlTextWriter.xml", FileMode.Create);
TextWriter tw = new StreamWriter(fs);
ds.WriteXml(tw);
fs.Close();

// Write a XML using the XmlWriter parameter
FileStream fs2 = new FileStream("WriteXmlXmlTextWriter.xml", FileMode.Create);
TextWriter tw2 = new StreamWriter(fs2);
XmlTextWriter xtw = new XmlTextWriter(tw2);
ds.WriteXml(xtw);
fs2.Close();

// Write a XML using the Stream parameter
FileStream fs3 = new FileStream("WriteXmlStream.xml", FileMode.Create);
ds.WriteXml(fs3);
fs3.Close();
```

One of the resulting XML documents is shown below:

```
<?xml version="1.0" standalone="yes"?>
<DS>
  <Table>
    <AuthorID>1</AuthorID>
    <Author_FirstName>Fabio Claudio</Author_FirstName>
    <Author_LastName>Ferracchiati</Author_LastName>
  </Table>
  <Table>
    <AuthorID>2</AuthorID>
    <Author_FirstName>Simon</Author_FirstName>
    <Author_LastName>Robinson</Author_LastName>
  </Table>
  <Table>
    <AuthorID>3</AuthorID>
```

```
      <Author_FirstName>Alex</Author_FirstName>
      <Author_LastName>Homer</Author_LastName>
    </Table>
    <Table>
      <AuthorID>4</AuthorID>
      <Author_FirstName>Karen</Author_FirstName>
      <Author_LastName>Little</Author_LastName>
    </Table>
    <Table>
      <AuthorID>5</AuthorID>
      <Author_FirstName>Tim</Author_FirstName>
      <Author_LastName>Huckaby</Author_LastName>
    </Table>
  </DS>
```

The second group of versions accept the same first parameter adding an `XmlWriteMode` enumeration value that can assume one of the following values:

XmlWriteMode values	Description
Diffgram	Writes data into an XML document including original and current rows, together with the related row state. If you want to write only the changes that occurred to the `DataSet` you can call the `GetChanges()` after the method with the `Diffgram` parameter without calling the `AcceptChanges()` method before.
IgnoreSchema	Writes data into an XML document without the XML Schema.
WriteSchema	Writes data into an XML document with a XML schema having the XSD standard format.

In the following example the `WriteSchema` enumeration value is specified:

VB.NET:

```
' Create a DataSet
Dim dbConn As New
SqlClient.SqlConnection("server=localhost;uid=sa;pwd=;database=WroxDB")
Dim da As New SqlClient.SqlDataAdapter("SELECT
AuthorID,Author_FirstName,Author_LastName FROM tabAuthors", dbConn)
Dim ds As New DataSet("DS")
da.Fill(ds)

' Write a XML with the schema
ds.WriteXml("WriteXmlStringWithSchema.xml", XmlWriteMode.WriteSchema)
```

C#:

```csharp
// Create a dataset
SqlConnection dbConn = new
SqlConnection("server=localhost;uid=sa;pwd=;database=WroxDB");
SqlDataAdapter da = new SqlDataAdapter("SELECT
AuthorID,Author_FirstName,Author_LastName FROM tabAuthors",dbConn);
DataSet ds = new DataSet("DS");
da.Fill(ds);

// Write a XML with the schema
ds.WriteXml("WriteXmlStringWithSchema.xml", XmlWriteMode.WriteSchema);
```

The following XML document will be generated:

```xml
<?xml version="1.0" standalone="yes"?>
<DS>
  <xsd:schema id="DS" targetNamespace="" xmlns=""
xmlns:xsd="http://www.w3.org/2001/XMLSchema" xmlns:msdata="urn:schemas-microsoft-
com:xml-msdata">
    <xsd:element name="DS" msdata:IsDataSet="true">
      <xsd:complexType>
        <xsd:choice maxOccurs="unbounded">
          <xsd:element name="Table">
            <xsd:complexType>
              <xsd:sequence>
                <xsd:element name="AuthorID" type="xsd:int" minOccurs="0" />
                <xsd:element name="Author_FirstName" type="xsd:string"
minOccurs="0" />
                <xsd:element name="Author_LastName" type="xsd:string"
minOccurs="0" />
              </xsd:sequence>
            </xsd:complexType>
          </xsd:element>
        </xsd:choice>
      </xsd:complexType>
    </xsd:element>
  </xsd:schema>
  <Table>
    <AuthorID>1</AuthorID>
    <Author_FirstName>Fabio Claudio</Author_FirstName>
    <Author_LastName>Ferracchiati</Author_LastName>
  </Table>
  <Table>
    <AuthorID>2</AuthorID>
    <Author_FirstName>Simon</Author_FirstName>
    <Author_LastName>Robinson</Author_LastName>
  </Table>
  <Table>
    <AuthorID>3</AuthorID>
    <Author_FirstName>Alex</Author_FirstName>
    <Author_LastName>Homer</Author_LastName>
  </Table>
  <Table>
    <AuthorID>4</AuthorID>
```

```
      <Author_FirstName>Karen</Author_FirstName>
      <Author_LastName>Little</Author_LastName>
    </Table>
    <Table>
      <AuthorID>5</AuthorID>
      <Author_FirstName>Tim</Author_FirstName>
      <Author_LastName>Huckaby</Author_LastName>
    </Table>
  </DS>
```

The WriteXmlSchema Method

VB.NET:
```
Overloads Public Sub WriteXmlSchema( _
   ByVal stream As Stream _
)
```

```
Overloads Public Sub WriteXmlSchema( _
   ByVal fileName As String _
)
```

```
Overloads Public Sub WriteXmlSchema( _
   ByVal writer As TextWriter _
)
```

```
Overloads Public Sub WriteXmlSchema( _
   ByVal writer As XmlWriter _
)
```

C#:
```
public void WriteXmlSchema(
   Stream stream
);
```

```
public void WriteXmlSchema(
   string fileName
);
```

```
public void WriteXmlSchema(
   TextWriter writer
);
```

```
public void WriteXmlSchema(
   XmlWriter writer
);
```

This method writes an XML schema for the current `DataSet` inside the specified file. The method provides four versions: a string to indicate the full path and filename, a TextWriter object, an XmlWriter object, and a Stream object. The XML schema will contain every table, relation, and constraint present in the `DataSet` and it will follow the XSD standard specification.

VB.NET:

```
' Create a DataSet
Dim dbConn As New
SqlClient.SqlConnection("server=localhost;uid=sa;pwd=;database=WroxDB")
Dim da As New SqlClient.SqlDataAdapter("SELECT
AuthorID,Author_FirstName,Author_LastName FROM tabAuthors", dbConn)
Dim ds As New DataSet("DS")
da.Fill(ds)

' Write a XML using the string parameter
ds.WriteXmlSchema("WriteXmlSchema.xml")

' Write a XML using the TextWriter parameter
Dim fs As New IO.FileStream("WriteXmlSchemaTextWriter.xml", IO.FileMode.Create)
Dim tw As IO.TextWriter = New IO.StreamWriter(fs)
ds.WriteXmlSchema(tw)
fs.Close()

' Write a XML using the XmlWriter parameter
Dim fs2 As New IO.FileStream("WriteXmlSchemaXmlTextWriter.xml",
IO.FileMode.Create)
Dim tw2 As IO.TextWriter = New IO.StreamWriter(fs2)
Dim xtw As New Xml.XmlTextWriter(tw2)
ds.WriteXmlSchema(xtw)
fs2.Close()

' Write a XML using the Stream parameter
Dim fs3 As New IO.FileStream("WriteXmlSchema.xml", IO.FileMode.Create)
ds.WriteXmlSchema(fs3)
fs3.Close()
```

C#:

```
// Create a DataSet
SqlConnection dbConn = new
SqlConnection("server=localhost;uid=sa;pwd=;database=WroxDB");
SqlDataAdapter da = new SqlDataAdapter("SELECT
AuthorID,Author_FirstName,Author_LastName FROM tabAuthors",dbConn);
DataSet ds = new DataSet("DS");
da.Fill(ds);

// Write a XML using the string parameter
ds.WriteXmlSchema("WriteXmlSchema.xml");

// Write a XML using the TextWriter parameter
FileStream fs = new FileStream("WriteXmlSchemaTextWriter.xml", FileMode.Create);
TextWriter tw = new StreamWriter(fs);
ds.WriteXmlSchema(tw);
fs.Close();
```

```
// Write a XML using the XmlWriter parameter
FileStream fs2 = new FileStream("WriteXmlSchemaXmlTextWriter.xml",
FileMode.Create);
TextWriter tw2 = new StreamWriter(fs2);
XmlTextWriter xtw = new XmlTextWriter(tw2);
ds.WriteXmlSchema(xtw);
fs2.Close();

// Write a XML using the Stream parameter
FileStream fs3 = new FileStream("WriteXmlSchemaStream.xml", FileMode.Create);
ds.WriteXmlSchema(fs3);
fs3.Close();
```

The code above retrieves some data from the WroxDB database and fills the file with the corresponding XML schema:

```
<?xml version="1.0" standalone="yes"?>
<xsd:schema id="DS" targetNamespace="" xmlns=""
xmlns:xsd="http://www.w3.org/2001/XMLSchema"
xmlns:msdata="urn:schemas-microsoft-com:xml-msdata">
  <xsd:element name="DS" msdata:IsDataSet="true">
    <xsd:complexType>
      <xsd:choice maxOccurs="unbounded">
        <xsd:element name="Table">
          <xsd:complexType>
            <xsd:sequence>
              <xsd:element name="AuthorID" type="xsd:int"
minOccurs="0" />
              <xsd:element name="Author_FirstName" type="xsd:string"
minOccurs="0" />
              <xsd:element name="Author_LastName" type="xsd:string"
minOccurs="0" />
            </xsd:sequence>
          </xsd:complexType>
        </xsd:element>
      </xsd:choice>
    </xsd:complexType>
  </xsd:element>
</xsd:schema>
```

DataSet Events

DataSet provides just one event: MergeFailed. This event is raised when attempting to merge two DataSets fails. Let's examine in detail how to treat the event.

The MergeFailed Event

VB.NET:

```
Public Event MergeFailed As MergeFailedEventHandler
```

C#:

```
public event MergeFailedEventHandler MergeFailed;
```

This event is raised when a `Merge()` operation generates an error, usually when two rows have the same primary key value. You can manage this event in order to reconcile errors and let the merge operation finish successfully. The following snippet of code shows an example of how to call the related delegate function in order to manage the event:

VB.NET:

```
' Fill a DataSet with data from the pubs database
Dim dbConn As New
SqlClient.SqlConnection("server=localhost;uid=sa;pwd=;database=pubs")
Dim da As New SqlClient.SqlDataAdapter("SELECT au_id,au_lname,au_fname,contract
FROM authors", dbConn)
Dim ds As New DataSet("DS")
Dim ds2 As New DataSet("DS2")

' Fill with data and schema
da.Fill(ds)

' Only the schema for the other dataset
da.FillSchema(ds2, SchemaType.Source)

' Print the starting number of rows
Console.WriteLine("Starting number of rows: {0}", ds.Tables(0).Rows.Count)

' Add a new row
Dim r As DataRow
r = ds2.Tables(0).NewRow()
r("au_id") = "222-22-2222"
r("au_fname") = "Fabio Claudio"
r("au_lname") = "Ferracchiati"
r("contract") = True
ds2.Tables(0).Rows.Add(r)

' Add the event handler to manage merge failures
AddHandler ds.MergeFailed, New MergeFailedEventHandler(AddressOf OnMergeFailed)

' Merge the two DataSets
ds.Merge(ds2)

' Print the starting number of rows
Console.WriteLine("Number of rows after the Merge(): {0}",
ds.Tables(0).Rows.Count)

. . .
```

```vbnet
Private Sub OnMergeFailed(ByVal sender As Object, ByVal args As
MergeFailedEventArgs)
      ' Here manage the errors
      . . .
End Sub
```

C#:

```csharp
// Fill a DataSet with data from the pubs database
SqlConnection dbConn = new
SqlConnection("server=localhost;uid=sa;pwd=;database=pubs");
SqlDataAdapter da = new SqlDataAdapter("SELECT au_id,au_lname,au_fname,contract
FROM authors",dbConn);
DataSet ds = new DataSet("DS");
DataSet ds2 = new DataSet("DS2");

// Fill with data and schema
da.Fill(ds);

// Only the schema for the other dataset
da.FillSchema(ds2,SchemaType.Source);

// Print the starting number of rows
Console.WriteLine("Starting number of rows: {0}", ds.Tables[0].Rows.Count);

// Add a new row
DataRow r = ds2.Tables[0].NewRow();
r["au_id"] = "222-22-2222";
r["au_fname"] = "Fabio Claudio";
r["au_lname"] = "Ferracchiati";
r["contract"] = true;
ds2.Tables[0].Rows.Add(r);

// Add the event handler to manage merge failures
ds.MergeFailed += new MergeFailedEventHandler(OnMergeFailed);

// Merge the two DataSets
ds.Merge(ds2);

// Print the starting number of rows
Console.WriteLine("Number of rows after the Merge(): {0}",
ds.Tables[0].Rows.Count);

. . .

protected static void OnMergeFailed(Object sender, MergeFailedEventArgs args)
{
      // Here manage the errors
      . . .
}
```

If the new record is already contained in the DataSet, the MergeFailed event will be raised. The argument passed to the delegate function contains the following properties:

Argument	Description
Conflict	Returns the merge conflict description.
Table	Returns the Table name where the merge error occurred.

Summary

With its strict tie in with the XML language, and its disconnected characteristic, DataSet is the most powerful object in ADO.NET. We can use DataSet to manage our data inside both Internet/Intranet and client/server applications.

In this chapter, we have analyzed every way to fill a DataSet object and every property and method exposed by it. Thanks to the new XSD.EXE application, we can transform our untyped DataSet into a typed one in order to have a more useful object and a more readable code.

Finally, its perfect integration with the DataAdapter object allows easy DataSet schema and data retrieval, with relations and constraints.

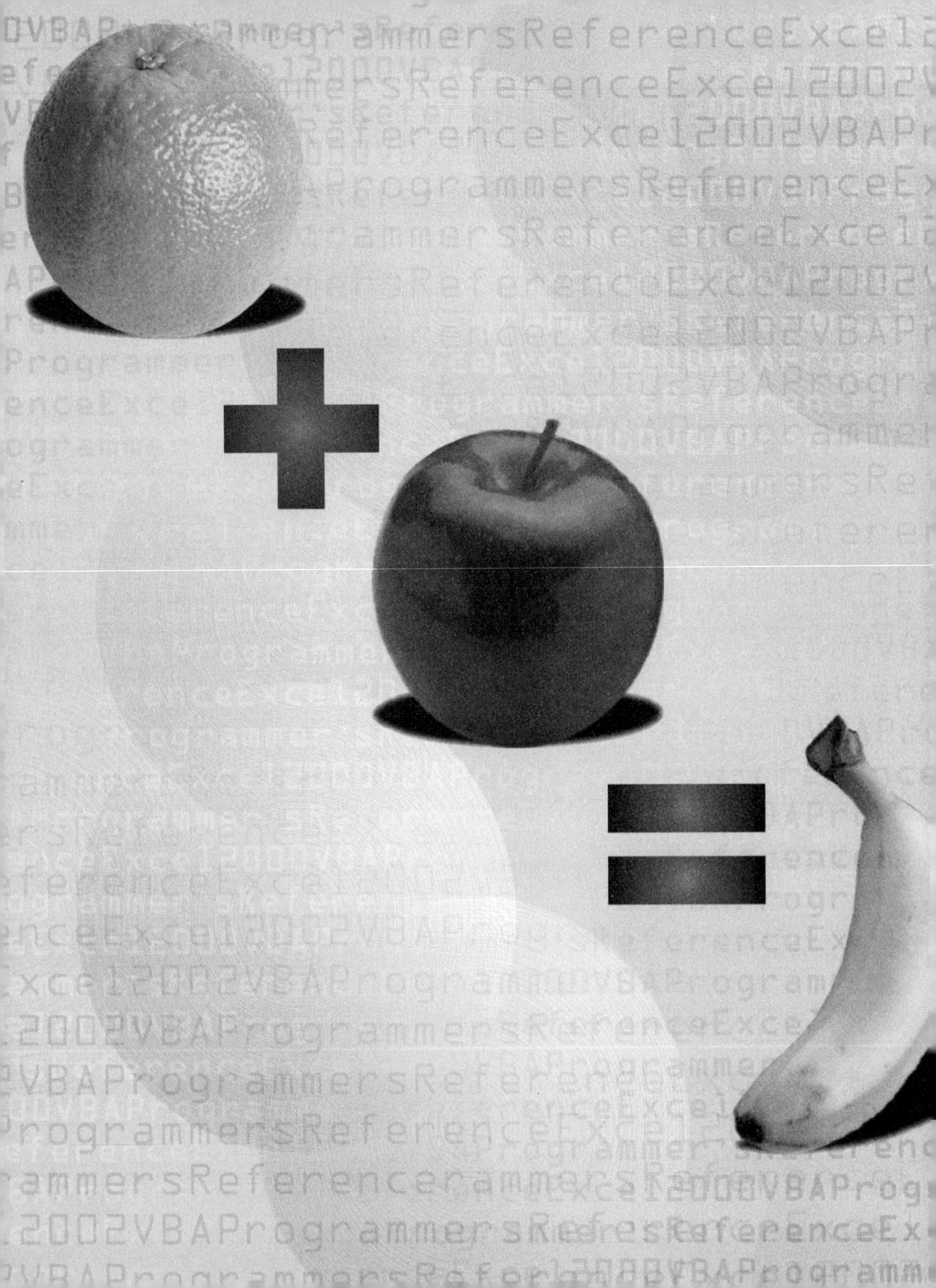

The DataReader Object

The DataReader object is used for accessing data from the data store and is one of the two mechanisms that ADO.NET provides. The other mechanism, using a DataAdapter object to transfer the data to a DataSet, will be discussed in the next chapter.

> The **DataReader** object provides a read only, forward only, high performance mechanism to retrieve data from a data store as a data stream, while staying connected with the data source.

The DataReader is restricted but highly optimized. It is important to keep the following characteristics of the DataReader in mind before deciding which mechanism to use in an application for data access:

❑ Access to the data source is on a per record basis – only one record at a time is in the DataReader object's memory:

❑ Records can be accessed only in a forward direction. This means that we cannot perform complex operations on the records such as sorting or directly accessing specific records:

❑ The record in a DataReader object is read only:

❑ While we are reading the records from the data source, the DataReader object remains connected to the database. No other action can be performed on the connection while the DataReader object is reading the records. Therefore the application should close the DataReader after it has finished reading all of the records so that the connection with the database is released for other uses

The .NET framework provides data providers for SQL Server (version 7.0 and higher), native OLE DB providers and native ODBC drivers:

❑ SqlDataReader (defined in the System.Data.SqlClient namespace)

❑ OleDbDataReader (defined in the System.Data.OleDb namespace)

❑ OdbcDataReader (defined in the System.Data.Odbc namespace)

These three data providers provide access to the data managed by the most commonly used databases in the industry. As always, there are exceptions. There may be some applications that use their own proprietary legacy databases for which there are no OLE DB providers or ODBC drivers available. This would mean that the database would need to provide its own .NET data provider to manipulate the information.

> For a managed provider to provide its own `DataReader` it must provide a class that
> inherits from the `MarshalByRefObject` class and implements
> `IDataReader, IDataRecord, IEnumerable` and `IDisposable` interfaces.

Here are the Visual Basic definitions of the three native .NET managed provider `DataReader` classes:

```
NotInheritable Public Class OleDbDataReader
    Inherits MarshalByRefObject
    Implements IDataReader, IDataRecord, IEnumerable, IDisposable
```

```
NotInheritable Public Class SqlDataReader
    Inherits MarshalByRefObject
    Implements IDataReader, IDataRecord, IEnumerable, IDisposable
```

```
NotInheritable Public Class OdbcDataReader
    Inherits MarshalByRefObject
    Implements IDataReader, IDataRecord, IEnumerable, IDisposable
```

The `IDataReader` and `IDataRecord` interfaces are defined in the `System.Data` namespace, the
`IEnumerable` interface is defined in the `System.Collections` namespace and the `IDisposable`
interface is defined in the `System` namespace.

The `SqlDataReader` object supports all of the methods and properties of the `OleDbDataReader` and
`OdbcDataReader` objects, and also has additional methods that are especially designed for utilizing
SQL Server specific data types.

> Inheriting `DataReader` classes from `MarshalByRefObject` class makes it possible
> for these objects to be marshaled across assembly boundaries.

Inheriting an object from `MarshalByRefObject` class signifies that the object is `AppDomain` bound
and it is passed by reference when it is remoted. If the `DataReader` objects are not inherited from the
`MarshalByRefObject` that would mean that you could not pass this object outside the context of your
`AppDomain` as a method parameter, because it will not be able to leave its `AppDomain`. Therefore if you
have a multi-tier architecture, the `DataReader` would need to be processed in the data access layer and
all records would need to be cached in an object that can be passed across application domains.

Fortunately this is not the case – the `DataReader` objects are remotable so they can be passed across
`AppDomains` as method parameters. When the `DataReader` object is marshaled, the clients receive a
reference to the `DataReader` object in their own `AppDomain`. When the client invokes methods on the
remoted `DataReader` object, the calls gets marshaled back to the server where the `DataReader` was created.

The `DataReader` keeps the connection with the database open as long as the `Close` method is not
called. Therefore if your application is passing the `DataReader` object across `AppDomains` it is very
important that database connections do not get tied up for periods longer than required, otherwise the
scalability of the application will suffer.

> For remoted `DataReader` objects, the server side implementation should not call the `Close`
> method to free up the database connection. Instead it should call the `ExecuteReader`
> method on the `Command` object with `CommandBehavior.CloseConnection` as a
> parameter. This means that when the client calls `Close` on the `DataReader` object, the
> database connection associated with it will also be closed.

The following code shows an implementation where the server fetches the `OleDbDatareader` object by calling `ExecuteReader` method, and then passes a reference to the `OleDbDataReader` object as a return value of the method called from the presentation layer of the application.

The following method would be part of a class called `CustomerDataAccess` that acts as the server:

C#:

```csharp
public OleDbDataReader GetCustomerRecord (String strID)
{
    StringBuilder strQuery = new StringBuilder ("SELECT * FROM CUSTOMERS
                                    WHERE CustomerId='");
    strQuery.Append(strID);
    strQuery.Append("'");

    // Create OleDbCommand using already opened database connection.
    OleDbCommand oledbCmd = new OleDbCommand (strQuery.ToString (),
                                    m_OleDbConnection);

    // Execute the command with CommandBehavior.CloseConnection as
    // method parameter. This way we can be sure that when caller calls
    // Close method on the DataReader object, the associated database
    // connection also gets closed.
    OleDbDataReader dtReader = null;
    try
    {
      dtReader = oledbCmd.ExecuteReader (CommandBehavior.CloseConnection);
    }
    catch (OleDbException ex)
    {
        Trace.WriteLine (ex.Message);
    }

    return dtReader;
}
```

The following method creates an instance of the `CustomerDataAccess` class and uses it to obtain a `DataReader` object:

C#:

```csharp
private void DisplayCustomer (String strID)
{
    // Create a new instance of data access class.
    CustomerDataAccess data = new CustomerDataAccess ();

    // Initialize the connection.
    data.Intialize ();

    // Call GetCustomer method on the DataAccess layer object
    // to fetch the DataReader object for the given customer
    // ID.
    OleDbDataReader dtReader = data.GetCustomerRecord (strID);
    if (null != dtReader)
    {
        // Make sure to call Read method on Datareader object so
        // that the DataReader's pointer is positioned at first record.
        dtReader.Read ();
```

```
        int iOrdinal = dtReader.GetOrdinal ("ContactName");
        String strName = dtReader.GetString (iOrdinal);
        // Set the retrieved value in the edit control.
        m_wndContactName.Text = strName;

        // Make sure to call Close method on DataReader object. This will
        // also close the associated database connection.
        dtReader.Close ();
    }
}
```

In the example above, the GetCustomer method is a member of the CustomerDataAccess class in the data access layer of a multi-tier application. It fetches the OleDbDataRecord object for the customer record corresponding to strID. If the call succeeds then the fetched OleDbDataReader is passed to the caller of the method. Pay attention to the fact that the Close method is not called on the fetched OleDbDataReader object. The DisplayCustomer is a method in the presentation layer, which calls the GetCustomer method on the CustomerDataAccess class. If the call returns a valid OleDbDatareader object then the record information is fetched from the DataReader. To keep things brief the example only shows fetching the ContactName column. The returned value is written to the m_wndContactName edit control. After the record has been retrieved, the Close method is called on the OleDbDataReader object, which also closes the database connection.

The DataReader provides a very good mechanism for reading a large amount of data from the data source because it keeps only one record in memory at any time. Therefore there is little memory overhead involved with the use of a DataReader object. No records are cached except for the current row that the DataReader reads. All of these factors make the DataReader object fast and light. However since it is a forward only reader, if our application needs to cache all the records for later use we must store them in an ArrayList or some other enumerable collection object.

Choosing the right data access mechanism is very important for the success of your application. In applications where thousands of users may be accessing the data concurrently, scalability of the data access layer is particularly important. The DataReader is geared more towards performance than providing a lot of functionality. It is very useful if you need to make a single pass through the data.

The DataReader does not provide the capability to get the number of records that it contains. If you need to find out the record count, you can follow two approaches. The first one is to increment a counter in the loop used to read all the records from the DataReader object. The second approach is by using multiple SELECT query statements as shown below.

SQL:

```
SELECT Count (*) As RecordCount FROM CUSTOMERS; SELECT * FROM CUSTOMERS
```

The above query will return a DataReader with two result sets. The first result set will contain only one row with one field, RecordCount. The value for this field will give the number of records that are returned. We can then call the NextResult method to move to the second result set which will return the data rows. The following example shows the second approach in action:

C#:

```
string strStatement =
            "SELECT COUNT(*) AS RecordCount FROM Customers;SELECT * FROM
Customers";
```

```
OleDbCommand oledbCmd = new OleDbCommand (strStatement, m_ADOConnection);

// Execute the command.
OleDbDataReader dtReader = oledbCmd.ExecuteReader
(CommandBehavior.CloseConnection);
int nCount = 0;

while (dtReader.Read ())
{
    nCount = (int)(dtReader.GetValue (0));
}

if (dtReader.NextResult ())
{
    while (dtReader.Read ())
    {
      // Read all the fields.
    }
}
```

As mentioned earlier the .NET framework provides three `DataReader` objects corresponding to the three managed providers: `SqlDataReader`, `OleDbDataReader`, and `OdbcDataReader`. All three classes support very much the same properties/methods/events with a few exceptions. For most of this chapter all the three classes will be referred to as the `DataReader` class except where it is necessary to distinguish.

Data Type Mapping

Before we discuss the fields, properties, methods, and events of the `DataReader` object it is important to explore how the different databases such as **Microsoft SQL Server**, **Microsoft Access**, **Oracle**, **DB2**, and **MySQL** save the field data in their own data formats. Although most of the data formats used by these databases are very similar there are some exceptions. When you call the `Item` property of the `DataReader` object, it presents the data to the caller in .NET native formats such as `String`, `Int32`, `Decimal`, and `Boolean`. The back end database may not have a direct correspondence to these native formats. In those cases the .NET framework converts them to the closest native format. For example the strings are stored as `varchar`, `nvarchar`, and so on. in SQL Server. When you call the `Item` property on the `DataReader` object, this data type is returned as `String` object. Similarly the SQL Server `bit` data type is returned as a .NET `Boolean` object.

The following table shows the mapping between database specific and .NET native data formats, and the `Get` methods that should be used to get the field value (we will discuss `Get` methods later in the chapter):

Oracle	Microsoft Access 2000	SQL Server 2000	.NET Framework Native Types	Get Method
	Number	int	Int32	GetInt32
NVARCHAR2	Text	nvarchar	String	GetString
	Hyperlink	ntext	String	GetString
BFILE	OLE Object	image	Byte[]	GetBytes

Table continued on following page

Oracle	Microsoft Access 2000	SQL Server 2000	.NET Framework Native Types	Get Method
NCHAR		nchar	String	GetString
DATE	Date/Time	datetime	DateTime	GetDateTime
	Integer	smallint	Short	GetInt16
	Currency	money	Decimal	GetDecimal
	Yes/No	bit	Boolean	GetBoolean
NUMBER(p)		real	Single	GetInt32
CHAR			String	GetString
	Double	float	Double	GetDouble
	Memo		String	GetString
VARCHAR2		varchar	String	GetString
	Single		Single	GetInt32
		uniqueidentifier	Guid	GetGuid
LONG		bigint	Long	GetInt64
BLOB		binary	Byte[]	GetBytes
		char	String	GetString
		decimal	Decimal	GetDecimal
NUMBER(p,s)		numeric	Decimal	GetDecimal
		smalldatetime	DateTime	GetDateTime
		sql_variant	Object	GetValue
		text	String	GetString
		timestamp	Byte[]	GetBytes
		tinyint	Byte	GetByte
		varbinary	Byte[]	GetBytes
LONG RAW			Byte[]	GetBytes

The DataReader Object Members

This section discusses properties, methods and events that are common to the OleDbDataReader, OdbcDataReader, and SqlDataReader. Additional facilities provided by the SqlDataReader are discussed in a separate section later in the chapter.

DataReader Constructors

There are no constructors for the `DataReader` class. The only way to create a `DataReader` object is by calling the `ExecuteReader` method on the `Command` object. The class is marked with the `NonInheritable` attribute meaning that you cannot inherit any class from any of the `DataReader` classes.

C#:

```
OleDbCommand oledbCmd = new OleDbCommand ();
oledbCmd.Connection = oledbConn;
oledbCmd.CommandText = "SELECT * FROM EMPLOYEES";
OleDbDataReader dtReader = oledbCmd.ExcuteReader
(CommandBehavior.ConnectionClose);
```

The above example creates an `OleDbCommand` object. A valid SQL statement for selecting all records from the `EMPLOYEES` table is assigned to the `CommandText` property and a valid, open `OleDbConnection` is assigned to the command object. The example then calls the `Command` object's `ExecuteReader` method. The method is passed `CommandBehavior.ConnectionClose` as the argument, which will make sure that when `Close` method is called on the `DataReader` object the associated database connection also closes. For more details on the `ExecuteReader` method, refer to Chapter 4, Command Object.

DataReader Properties

The Depth Property

Returns an integer indicating how deeply nested the current row is in a data shaping query.

VB.NET:

```
Overridable Public ReadOnly Property Depth As Integer
```

C#:

```
public int Depth {get;}
```

This property is read-only and returns the number of levels between the current row in `DataRead` object and the root of the table's hierarchy. If the given table is at the root of hierarchy, it has a `Depth` value of zero.

This property is of interest if you are using a query that returns multidimensional or hierarchical results. Microsoft Data Access Components (MDAC) ships with an OLE DB provider for data shaping commonly referred to as `MSDataShape`. This data provider returns the data in hierarchical tables. For example the following Transact-SQL query returns data as two-dimensional data tables.

SQL:

```
SHAPE   {SELECT * FROM CUSTOMERS WHERE CustomerID='ALFKI'} AS Customers
 APPEND ({SELECT * FROM ORDERS WHERE CustomerID=?} AS Orders
 RELATE CustomerID TO PARAMETER 0) As OrdersGrid
```

229

This is a hierarchical query. It retrieves the customer record with `CustomerID='ALFKI'` from the `CUSTOMERS` table. It uses this `CustomerID` value to retrieve only the records from the `ORDERS` table that match this `CustomerID`. Finally the relation is established between the two tables based on the `CustomerID` value.

When this query is executed, the `DataReader` object appends an extra data column at the end of the table returning `CUSTOMERS` data. For example if the `CUSTOMERS` table has 11 fields, an additional field at ordinal 11 gets appended in the returned `DataReader` object. This appended field contains another `DataReader` object that retrieves the data rows from the `ORDERS` table.

The `DataReader` object resulting from the above query has data tables at two levels. The data rows corresponding to the parent query `SELECT * FROM CUSTOMERS` are at the top level. Therefore if you get the `Depth` property for this `DataReader`, it will be 0. The data rows corresponding to child query `SELECT * FROM ORDERS` are at the child level and the `Depth` property value for this `DataReader` object will be 1. For deeper nested child queries the `DataReader` objects will be added at depth levels 2, 3 and so on.

The following code illustrates how the `MSDataShape` OLE DB provider can be used to retrieve hierarchical `data` from the database.

VB.NET:

```vbnet
Dim strQuery As String = "SHAPE{SELECT * FROM Customers} As Customers" & _
                         " APPEND({SELECT * FROM Orders} AS Orders " & _
                         " RELATE CustomerID TO CustomerID) As Orders"

Dim strConn As String = "Provider=MSDataShape.1;Data Provider=SQLOLEDB.1;" & _
                        " Database=Northwind;Server=localhost;uid=sa;pwd="
Dim oledbConn As OleDbConnection
Try
    'Open the connection with database.
    oledbConn = New OleDbConnection(strConn)
    oledbConn.Open()
    'Create command object to execute SQL query.
    Dim oledbCmd As New OleDbCommand(strQuery, oledbConn)
    'Get the hierarchical Datareader object
    Dim custDtReader As OleDbDataReader = oledbCmd.ExecuteReader()
    Dim ordersDtReader As OleDbDataReader
    Dim iFieldCount As Integer = custDtReader.FieldCount
    Dim idx As Integer
    While custDtReader.Read()
        iFieldCount = custDtReader.FieldCount
        'The last data field in the DataReader for Customers
      'table contains the DataReader object for Orders
      'table. Get that field and cast it to OleDbDataReader
      'type object.
        ordersDtReader = custDtReader.GetValue(iFieldCount - 1)
        Dim iDepth As Integer = custDtReader.Depth
        Trace.WriteLine("Customer Depth = " + iDepth.ToString())
        While (ordersDtReader.Read())
          ' Fetch all the data rows from Orders table for
          ' the current CustomerID in custDtReader DataReader
          ' object.
        End While
      ' Make sure to close the child DataReader object.
      ordersDtReader.Close()
        End While
```

```
        'Now close the parent DataReader.
        CustDtReader.Close()
Catch ex As OleDbException
        Trace.WriteLine(ex.Message)
Catch e As Exception
        Trace.WriteLine(e.Message)
End Try
' Close the database connection.
oledbConn.Close()
```

C#:

```
string strQuery = "SHAPE {SELECT * FROM Customers WHERE " +
                "CustomerID='ALFKI'} As Customers" +
            " APPEND ({SELECT * FROM Orders WHERE " +
            "CustomerID=?} AS Orders " +
            " RELATE CustomerID TO PARAMETER 0) As OrdersGrid";

string strConn = "Provider=MSDataShape.1;Data Provider=SQLOLEDB.1;" +
            " Database=Northwind;Server=localhost;uid=sa;pwd=";

OleDbConnection oledbConn = null;
OleDbDataReader custDtReader = null;
OleDbDataReader ordersDtReader = null;
try
{
    oledbConn = new OleDbConnection (strConn);
    oledbConn.Open ();
    OleDbCommand oledbCmd = new OleDbCommand (strQuery, oledbConn);
    custDtReader = oledbCmd.ExecuteReader ();
    int iCustFldCount = custDtReader.FieldCount;
    int iDepth = 0;
    while (custDtReader.Read ())
    {
      // The last data field in the DataReader for Customers
      // table contains the DataReader object for Orders
      // table. Get that field and cast it to OleDbDataReader
      // type object.
      ordersDtReader = (OleDbDataReader) custDtReader.GetValue (iCustFldCount -
1);
      iDepth = dtCustReader.Depth;
      Trace.WriteLine ("Depth of Customer Table = " + iDepth.ToString ());
      while (ordersDtReader.Read ())
      {
          // Fetch all the data rows from Orders table for
          // the current CustomerID in custDtReader DataReader
          // object.
      }
      // Make sure to close the child DataReader object.
      ordersDtReader.Close ();
    }
    //      Now close the parent DataReader.
    custDtReader.Close ();
}
catch (OleDbException ex)
{
    Trace.WriteLine (ex.Message);
}
catch (Exception e)
{
```

```
        Trace.WriteLine (e.Message);
    }
    // Close the database connection.
    oledbConn.Close ();
```

In the connection string the `MSDataShape` OLE DB provider is assigned to the `Provider` parameter and the SQLOLEDB provider has been assigned to the `Data Provider` clause in the connection string.

The code opens a connection with the Northwind database and then calls the `ExecuteReader` method on a `Command` object. The `FieldCount` property of the parent `DataReader` object, `custDtReader`, is used to determine the location of the child `DataReader`. The code calls the `GetValue` method on the parent `DataReader` to get the child `DataReader` object. The child `DataReader` object, `dtOrdReader`, will retrieve the ORDER records corresponding to the `CustomerId` of the current parent `row`, `custDtReader`. After all the rows have been fetched, the child and parent `DataReader` objects are closed.

It is necessary to close the child `DataReader` before the parent `DataReader`. Otherwise `System.InvalidOperationException` exception is thrown with this message: "There is a hierarchical `DataReader` open on this `DataReader` which must be closed first."

The FieldCount Property

Indicates the number of fields in the current record. This is a read-only property.

VB.NET:
```
    Overridable Public ReadOnly Property FieldCount As Integer
```

C#:
```
    public int FieldCount {get;}
```

This property is defined by the `IDataReader` interface. It returns the number of fields or columns present in the current record fetched by the `DataReader` object. For example:

VB.NET:
```
    Dim iNumOfFields As Integer = dtReader.FieldCount
```

C#:
```
    int iNumOfFields = dtReader.FieldCount;
```

We can use this property to get the number of fields in a result set, and each field's name. Based on this information we can dynamically resize or modify the GUI used to display the data retrieved by the `DataReader` object. The `FieldCount` property is important for dynamically sizing and building the ASP.NET pages. Because the `DataReader` objects can be passed across `AppDomain` boundaries, the presentation layer can access information about the field count and field names directly from the `DataReader`.

The following code in the presentation layer of an application gets the `DataReader` object from the data access layer (represented by the `data` object with the method `GetCustomerRecord`) and then builds a list of field names for later use.

VB.NET:

```
' Call GetCustomer method on the DataAccess layer object
' to fetch the DataReader object for the given customer
' ID.
Dim dtReader As OleDbDataReader = data.GetCustomerRecord(strID)
' Make sure to call Read method on Datareader object so
' that the DataReader's pointer is positioned at first record.
dtReader.Read()
Dim iNumFields As Integer = dtReader.FieldCount
Dim strFldNameArr As New ArrayList()
Dim idx As Integer
For idx = 0 To idx < iNumFields
    ' Get the names of the data columns and store
    ' them in the ArrayList.
    strFldNameArr.Add(dtReader.GetName(idx))
Next idx

' Make sure to call Close method on DataReader object. This will
' also close the associated database connection.
dtReader.Close()
```

C#:

```
// Call GetCustomer method on the DataAccess layer object
// to fetch the DataReader object for the given customer
// ID.
OleDbDataReader dtReader = data.GetCustomerRecord (strID);
if (null != dtReader)
{
    // Make sure to call Read method on Datareader object so
    // that the DataReader's pointer is positioned at first record.
    dtReader.Read ();
    int iNumFields = dtReader.FieldCount;
    ArrayList strFldNameArr = new ArrayList ();
    for (int idx = 0; idx < iNumFields; idx++)
    {
        // Get the names of the data columns and store
        // them in the ArrayList.
        strFldNameArr.Add (dtReader.GetName (idx));
    }
    // Make sure to call Close method on DataReader object. This will
    // also close the associated database connection.
    dtReader.Close ();
}
```

The IsClosed Property

The `IsClosed` property indicates whether the `OleDbDataReader` object is closed. This is a read-only property.

VB.NET:

```
NotOverridable Public ReadOnly Property IsClosed As Boolean
```

C#:

```
public bool IsClosed {get;}
```

After you have fetched all records, the framework does not close the DataReader object by itself. Based on the value returned from this property, we can call the Close method to close the data reader object, if it is still open, so that it releases its associated database connection with the data source.

VB.NET:

```
If Not (dtReader.IsClosed) Then
      dtReader.Close()
End If
```

C#:

```
if (!dtReader.IsClosed)
      dtReader.Close();
```

It is very important that the data reader object closes, one of the best places to use this property can be in exception handler. In the finally section of a try...catch block add code to check if data reader is closed and close it if it is still open. The following code shows how try/catch/finally blocks can be used to make sure that the DataReader object gets closed even if the data access operation throws an exception.

VB.NET:

```
Dim dtReader As SqlDataReader = Nothing
Dim sqlConnection As SqlConnection
Dim sqlCmd As SqlCommand
Dim strConnection As String
Dim strQuery As String

Try
    strConnection = "server=NETSDK;uid=sa;pwd=;database=northwind"
    strQuery = "SELECT * FROM Employees"
    sqlConnection = New SqlConnection(strConnection)
    'Create new command object.
    sqlCmd = New SqlCommand(strQuery, sqlConnection)
    'Open the conection with database.
    sqlConnection.Open()
    'Execute the SQL command to retrieve data from Employee
    'tables in DataReader object.
    dtReader = sqlCmd.ExecuteReader
    'Read each record of the data source.
    While (dtReader.Read)
       'Access the fields for each row.
    End While

Catch e As Exception
    Trace.Write(e.Message)
Catch sqlEx As SqlException
    Dim err As SqlError
    Dim errors As SqlErrorCollection = sqlEx.Errors
    For Each err In errors
```

```
        Trace.WriteLine(err.Message)
    Next
Finally
    'Close the connection of data reader object with DB connection
    If Not (dtReader Is Nothing) AndAlso Not (dtReader.IsClosed) Then
        dtReader.Close()
    End If
    'Close the DB connection.
    sqlConnection.Close()
End Try
```

This property is also useful if you wish to perform an operation on a DataReader but are not sure if the DataReader is open. Most DataReader operations will raise an exception if attempted on a closed DataReader so we can use this property to check, before we attempt an operation that it will not raise an exception.

The Item Property

The Item property gets the value of the specified data column as a .NET Object. This is a read-only property and is defined by IDataRecord interface.

The Item property is set as the DefaultMemberAttribute attribute of the DataReader class. Therefore, if we access the DataReader without providing any member name, the framework will invoke the Item property. In C#, this property provides the indexer for the DataReader class.

There are two overloaded implementations of the Item property, one takes the name of the data column as its argument and the other takes the ordinal position of the column in the result set. Ordinal numbering of the columns starts from zero.

The Item (String) Property

This overloaded implementation gets the value of the named data column as a .NET object.

VB.NET:

```
Overloads NotOverridable Public Default ReadOnly Property _
    Item(ByVal name As String) As Object
```

C#:

```
public object this[string name] {get;}
```

The name that is used to access the field value may not be the same as the name in the source database that you are querying. If the Transact-SQL SELECT statement specifies an alias for a column, using an AS clause, then the value for that column should be accessed by specifying only the alias name. The following code illustrates the usage of this overloaded Item property. It implements a method that retrieves all the product names from the PRODUCTS table and stores them in ArrayList object (defined in the System.Collections namespace). The SELECT statement used, retrieves the data for the ProductName column into a field with alias name Store Product Name. Therefore, to fetch the value for this field from the DataReader, the Item property is accessed with "Store Product Name" as the parameter.

VB.NET:

```
Public Function GetListOfProducts(ByRef prodList As ArrayList) As Integer
    Dim strConn As String = "Provider= SQLOLEDB.1; Data Source=localhost; uid=sa;"
& _
                        "pwd=sa; Initial Catalog=Northwind"
    Dim strQuery As String = "SELECT ProductName As 'Store Product Name' FROM
PRODUCTS"

    ' Create Connection object and Open it.
    Dim oledbConn As New OleDbConnection(strConn)
    oledbConn.Open()

    ' Create the Command object to get DataReader for the
    ' PRODUCTS table.
    Dim oledbCmd As New OleDbCommand(strQuery, oledbConn)
    Dim prodDtReader As OleDbDataReader = _
            oledbCmd.ExecuteReader(CommandBehavior.CloseConnection)
    While prodDtReader.Read()
        prodList.Add(prodDtReader("Store Product Name"))
    End While
    'Close the DataReader.
    prodDtReader.Close()
    Return prodList.Count
End Function
```

C#:

```
public int GetListOfProducts (out ArrayList prodList)
{
    prodList = null;
    string strConn = "Provider= SQLOLEDB.1; Data Source=localhost; uid=sa;"+
                "pwd=; Initial Catalog=Northwind";
    string strQuery = "SELECT ProductName As 'Store Product Name'FROM PRODUCTS";

    // Create Connection object and Open it.
    OleDbConnection oledbConn = new OleDbConnection (strConn);
    oledbConn.Open ();

    // Create the Command object to get DataReader for the
    // PRODUCTS table.
    OleDbCommand oledbCmd = new OleDbCommand (strQuery, oledbConn);
    OleDbDataReader prodDtReader = oledbCmd.ExecuteReader(
                            CommandBehavior.CloseConnection);
    prodList = new ArrayList ();
    while (prodDtReader.Read ())
    {
      prodList.Add (prodDtReader["Store Product Name"]);
    }
    // Close the DataReader object.
    prodDtReader.Close ();
    return prodList.Count;
}
```

If the Item property is called with a data column name that does not exist, the framework will raise a System.IndexOutOfRange exception.

The Item (Int32) Property

This read-only property gets the value of the specified data column in a .NET native format when it is accessed by its zero based ordinal position in the table.

VB.NET:

```
Overloads NotOverridable Public Default ReadOnly Property Item( _
    ByVal index As Integer _
) As Object
```

C#:

```
public object this[int index] {get;}
```

Accessing a column by ordinal position will be faster than accessing it by name.

The following table describes the parameter for this implementation of the property:

Parameter	Type	Description
Index	Int32	Zero based ordinal position of the data column in the result set.

The ordinal position value that is passed as the argument to access the field value is zero based, in other words the first data column in the table will be accessed by passing zero as parameter.

VB.NET:

```
Dim fldVal As Object = dtReader.Item(0)
```

C#:

```
object fldVal = dtReader[0];
```

If your application needs to access the column by its ordinal position, then you can call the GetOrdinal method (discussed later in the chapter) to get the ordinal position for a particular named field and then call Item property with this ordinal value.

The following code shows how to obtain the ContactName field's ordinal position in the Customers table of the Nothwind database, and then use that ordinal value to get the value of the field.

VB.NET:

```
Public Function GetContactName(ByVal strID As String) As String
    Dim strConn As String = "Provider= SQLOLEDB.1; Data Source=localhost; uid=sa;"
& _
                        "pwd=; Initial Catalog=Nothwind"
    Dim strQuery As StringBuilder = New StringBuilder()
    strQuery.Append("SELECT * FROM Customers WHERE CudtomerId= '")
    strQuery.Append(strID)
```

```
        strQuery.Append("'")

        ' Create Connection object and Open it.
        Dim oledbConn As New OleDbConnection(strConn)
        oledbConn.Open()

        ' Create the Command object to get DataReader for the
        ' Customers table.
        Dim strFldVal As String
        Dim oledbCmd As New OleDbCommand(strQuery.ToString(), oledbConn)
        Dim custDtReader As OleDbDataReader = _
                oledbCmd.ExecuteReader(CommandBehavior.CloseConnection)
        While custDtReader.Read()
            strFldVal = custDtReader.Item(custDtReader.GetOrdinal("ContactName"))
        End While
        ' Close the DataReader to release the database connection
        custDtReader.Close()
        Return strFldVal
    End Function
```

C#:

```
    public string GetContactName (string strID)
    {
        string strConn = "Provider= SQLOLEDB.1; Data Source=localhost;" +
                    "uid=sa; pwd=; Initial Catalog=Northwind";
        StringBuilder strQuery = new StringBuilder ();
        strQuery.Append ("SELECT * FROM Customers WHERE CustomerId='");
        strQuery.Append (strID);
        strQuery.Append ("'");

        // Create Connection object and Open it.
        OleDbConnection oledbConn = new OleDbConnection (strConn);
        oledbConn.Open ();

        // Create the Command object to get DataReader for the
        // Customers table.
        string strFldVal = "";
        OleDbCommand oledbCmd = new OleDbCommand (strQuery.ToString (), oledbConn);
        OleDbDataReader custDtReader = oledbCmd.ExecuteReader (
                            CommandBehavior.CloseConnection);
        while (custDtReader.Read ())
        {
            strFldVal = (string)custDtReader[custDtReader.GetOrdinal("ContactName")];
        }
        // Close the DataReader to release the database connection.
        custDtReader.Close ();
        return strFldVal;
    }
```

When the column is accessed by name, the DataReader object calls GetOrdinal method to get the ordinal position of the named column. Then that ordinal value is used to get the value for the specified column. Therefore if we are accessing the same column repeatedly it is more efficient to obtain the ordinal position using the GetOrdinal method and from then on use this value to reference the column. Be careful when hard-coding ordinal positions since a change to the database or to the SQL command string can change the position in which columns appear.

If the column name or ordinal does not match the one in the data source's schema, the property raises `System.IndexOutOfRangeException` exception.

The RecordsAffected Property

This property indicates the number of rows modified, added or deleted by the execution of a SQL statement.

VB.NET:

```
Overridable Public ReadOnly Property RecordsAffected As Integer
```

C#:

```
public int RecordsAffected {get;}
```

After executing a SELECT SQL statement, a value of –1 is always retuned. For other query types, if none of the rows are affected by the SQL statement execution then the property returns a value 0.

This is one of only two properties that can be called after the `DataReader` object has been closed, the other one being the `IsClosed` property.

This property is not much use for SELECT queries but the `ExecuteReader` method is not just called for selecting records into the `DataReader`. `ExecuteReader` can also be used for DELETE, INSERT, and UPDATE operations. In these cases it is useful to know how many rows have been affected by the command. The `DataReader` object returned for these update queries does not return the affected records, but we can find the number of records affected using this property.

The following example deletes a record from the EMPLOYEES table of the `Northwind` database by executing a DELETE query. The value returned by the `RecordsAffected` property is used to check if the record actually got deleted. For sake of brevity, the `EmployeeId` of the record is hard coded and no exception handling code is including.

VB.NET:

```
Dim strConn As String = "Provider= SQLOLEDB.1; Data Source=localhost; uid=sa;" & _
                        "pwd=; Initial Catalog=Northwind;"
Dim strQuery As String = "DELETE FROM EMPLOYEES WHERE EmployeeId = '9'"

' Create Connection object and Open it.
Dim oledbConn As New OleDbConnection(strConn)
oledbConn.Open()

' Create the Command object to execute DELETE statement
Dim oledbCmd As New OleDbCommand(strQuery.ToString(), oledbConn)
Dim empDtReader As OleDbDataReader = _
        oledbCmd.ExecuteReader(CommandBehavior.CloseConnection)
' Check if any record has been affected or not.
If empDtReader.RecordsAffected <= 0 Then
    Trace.WriteLine("ERROR: No record has been deleted")
End If
empDtReader.Close()
```

C#:

```
string strConn = "Provider= SQLOLEDB.1; Data Source=localhost;" +
            " uid=sa; pwd=; Initial Catalog=Northwind";
string strQuery = "DELETE FROM EMPLOYEES WHERE EmployeeId='9'";
// Create Connection object and Open it.
OleDbConnection oledbConn = new OleDbConnection (strConn);
oledbConn.Open ();

// Create the Command object to execute DELETE statement
OleDbCommand oledbCmd = new OleDbCommand (strQuery, oledbConn);
OleDbDataReader empDtReader = oledbCmd.ExecuteReader
(CommandBehavior.CloseConnection);
// Check if any record has been affected or not.
If (empDtReader.RecordsAffected <= 0)
{
    Trace.WriteLine ("ERROR: No record has been deleted");
}
empDtReader.Close ();
```

DataReader Methods

The Close Method

This method closes the DataReader object, therefore releasing the connection for other operations or to close.

VB.NET:

```
NotOverridable Public Sub Close ()
```

C#:

```
public void Close();
```

The Close method is defined by the IDataReader interface. The DataReader object keeps the connection open with the database as long as we are reading records from it. As long as the DataReader is using the connection, we cannot do any other operations with it. Therefore it is important that the DataReader is closed as soon as possible.

> We should call the Close method on DataReader object as soon as we have finished reading all of the records. A System.InvalidOperationException exception will be thrown if an attempt is made to close the Connection before calling the Close method on the DataReader object.

This method will release the open Connection object for other operations. The following code builds an OleDbCommand object using a SELECT query statement and the OleDbConnection object, oledbConn. The ExecuteReader method is called on the Command to get the DataReader for the CUSTOMERS table. After all the records have been read, the Close method is called on the DataReader. Now the connection associated with the DataReader is free to be used for other operations. In this example the Close method is called on the OleDbConnection object to release the connection with the Microsoft Access database.

VB.NET:

```
Dim strSelectQuery As String = "SELECT * FROM CUSTOMERS"
Dim strConn As String = "Provider=Microsoft.Jet.OLEDB.4.0;Data
Source=C:\\Northwind.mdb"
Dim oledbConn As New OleDbConnection(strConn)
oledbConn.Open()
Dim oledbCmd As New OleDbCommand(strSelectQuery, oledbConn)
' Call ExecuteReader method specifying the DataReader to receive the results
Dim custDtReader As OleDbDataReader = oledbCmd.ExecuteReader()
While custDtReader.Read ()
    ' Get the record's fields
End While
' Close the DataReader
custDtReader.Close()
oledbConn.Close()
```

C#:

```
string strSelectQuery = "SELECT * FROM CUSTOMERS";
string strConn = "Provider=Microsoft.Jet.OLEDB.4.0;Data Source=C:\\Northwind.mdb";
OleDbConnection oledbConn = new OleDbConnection (strConn)
oledbConn.Open ()
OleDbCommand oledbCmd = new OleDbCommand (strSelectQuery, oledbConn);
OleDbDataReader custDtReader = oledbCmd.ExecuteReader();
while (custDtReader.Read()) {
    // Get the record's fields
}
// Close the DataReader
custDtReader.Close();
oledbConn.Close();
```

In the above code, to close the database connection, the `Close` method has been called on the `Connection` object explicitly. If the `ExecuteReader` method is passed `CommandBehavior.CloseConnection` as a parameter then you don't have to call the `Close` method on the `Connection` object because when the `DataReader` is closed, the associated database connection also gets closed automatically.

The Read Method

If there is a next record available then this method reads it into the `DataReader` object and returns true, otherwise it returns false.

VB.NET:

```
NotOverridable Public Function Read() As Boolean
```

C#:

```
public bool Read();
```

Unlike the `Recordset` in ADO, the `DataReader` object's pointer is not placed at the first record right after the `Command` object has successfully obtained it. You will have to explicitly call the `Read` method to move the `DataReader` to first record. Failing to call the `Read` method before trying to access the data will raise the `System.InvalidCastException` exception. For example, the following code will throw such an exception:

VB.NET:

```
Dim dtReader As OleDbDataReader = oledbCmd.ExecuteReader()
Dim fld As Object = dtReader.Item (0) ' System.InvalidCastException is thrown
```

C#:

```
OleDbDataReader dtReader = oledbCmd.ExecuteReader ();
object fld = dtReader[0];      // System.InvalidCastException is thrown
```

The Read method call serves two purposes: first it moves the pointer to the next record; second it reads the row data. If we call the Read method but there is no next record to read (we have already read the last one, or there were no records returned) then the method returns false. If there is another record then the Read method reads it and returns true.

The Read method is often used with a while loop, so that while the Read method returns true we know that it has another record and we can perform the required operations on it inside the loop block.

The following example uses a while loop to read all process all of the records returned by the query. The Read method acts as the condition for the loop and also loads the next record into memory.

VB.NET:

```
Dim strConnection As String = "Provider=Microsoft.JET.OleDb.4.0;" & _
                  "Data Source=C:\Northwind.mdb"
'Create new connection object.
Dim oledbConn As New OleDbConnection(strConnection)
'Create new command object.
Dim oledbCmd As New OleDbCommand()
'Set the atributes of the command.
With oledbCmd
    .Connection = oledbConn
    .CommandText = "SELECT * FROM Suppliers"
End With
'Open the conection with database.
oledbConn.Open()
'Execute the command to retrieve data DataReader object.
Dim suppDtReader As OleDbDataReader = _
                oledbCmd.ExecuteReader(CommandBehavior.CloseConnection)
'Read each record of the data source.
While suppDtReader.Read ()
    'Read each field of the fetched data row.
End While

'Close the connection of data reader object with DB connection
suppDtReader.Close()
'Close the DB connection.
oledbConn.Close()
```

If the connection is not open before the ExecuteReader method call, the
System.InvalidOperationException gets thrown with the message
'ExecuteReader requires an open and available Connection (state=Closed).'

The Get Methods

The `DataReader` object provides a number of methods beginning `Get`, such as `GetBoolean`, `GetInt32`, and `GetDecimal`. Most of these methods take the ordinal position of a given data column as the method parameter and return the field's value in the specified data type. What this means is that if we know that a data column is of type Integer, then the `GetInt32` will return the field value as an `Integer`. This will be more efficient than using the `Item` property because it does not need to perform such complex data conversions.

All three `DataReader` objects (`SqlDataReader`, `OleDbDataReader` and `OdbcDataReader`) provide the following methods that work in this way:

- ❑ `GetBoolean`
- ❑ `GetByte`
- ❑ `GetChar`
- ❑ `GetDateTime`
- ❑ `GetDecimal`
- ❑ `GetDouble`
- ❑ `GetFloat`
- ❑ `GetGUID`
- ❑ `GetInt16`
- ❑ `GetInt32`
- ❑ `GetInt64`
- ❑ `GetString`
- ❑ `GetTimeSpan`

The above methods all take the following parameter:

Parameter	Type	Description
Ordinal	Integer	Ordinal position of the data column in the table, starting from zero for the first column

It is essential that we call the appropriate `GetXXX` method because the .NET framework will not perform any data type conversions in case of data type mismatch. For example we should obtain a data column that stores values of type `Boolean` using the `GetBoolean` method. If any other `Get` method is called to get this field value, `System.InvalidCastException` will be thrown.

These strongly typed methods can improve the performance of the application because there is no overhead associated with data type conversions. These methods should only be used if you have complete knowledge of the native data types specified for the various data columns in the database otherwise your application will end up throwing exceptions because of data type mismatches.

The following example gets the ordinal position of the field `IsInStock`, which is of type Boolean, and then gets its value from the `DataReader`.

VB.NET:

```
Dim iOrdinal As Integer = dtReader.GetOrdinal("IsInStock")
Dim bVal As Boolean = dtReader.GetBoolean(iOrdinal)
```

C#:

```
int iOrdinal = dtReader.GetOrdinal("IsInStock");
bool bVal = dtReader.GetBoolean (iOrdinal);
```

There are a few methods like `GetBytes`, `GetChars` etc. that take more than one parameter. These methods will be described in their respective sections later in the chapter.

Refer to the Data Type Mapping section earlier in this chapter for a table that explains which method should be called for various database data types.

The GetBoolean Method

This method gets the value of the data column as a `Boolean` data type. The value of the data column must be stored as a Boolean value in the database.

Refer to the section on The Get Methods for further information.

The GetByte Method

This method gets the value of the data column for which the field value is stored as `byte` data type in the database.

Refer to the section on The Get Methods for further information.

The GetBytes Method

This method gets the value of the specified data column where the field value is stored as a `byte` array. For example in the `Employees` table of the Northwind database, the images stored in the `Photo` column are returned as a `byte` array.

VB.NET:

```
NotOverridable Public Function GetBytes( _
    ByVal ordinal As Integer, ByVal dataIndex As Long, _
    ByVal buffer() As Byte, ByVal bufferIndex As Integer, _
    ByVal length As Integer _
) As Integer
```

C#:

```
public int GetBytes(
    int ordinal, long dataIndex, byte[] buffer,
    int bufferIndex, int length
);
```

The following table describes the parameters for this method:

Parameter	Type	Description
Ordinal	Integer	Zero-based data column ordinal position.
DataIndex	Long	Index in the source byte array, in the data source, where copying begins.
Buffer	Byte array	Buffer where field's data will be copied.
BufferIndex	Integer	Index in the destination buffer, provided by the caller, where copying begins.
Length	Integer	Maximum number of byte elements that will be copied to the data buffer.

This method copies the specified number of bytes of data from the data source into the buffer supplied by the caller. The return value from this method is the actual number of bytes that were copied to destination buffer. If you don't want to copy all of the data from the data source, specify the length parameter to the maximum number of bytes that your buffer can handle. See below for a way to find the required buffer size to obtain the entire array.

The source and destination arrays should be one-dimensional. Depending on the values specified for different method parameters, the GetBytes method could throw following exceptions:

Exception Type	Condition
InvalidCastException	The source data is not of type Byte
IndexOutOfRangeException	The supplied buffer size if insufficient
ArgumentOutOfRangeException	Caused by one of the following: ❑ dataIndex is less than the source data array's lower bound ❑ bufferIndex is less than the destination array's lower bound ❑ length is less than zero ❑ The sum of dataIndex and length is greater than the number of elements in source byte array ❑ The sum of bufferIndex and length is greater than the number of elements in allocated in destination byte array

You can get the required buffer size by specifying the buffer parameter as null (Nothing in Visual Basic). The method returns the size of the buffer that will be required to copy all of the elements from the source array. You can use this returned value to allocate the buffer size, and then call the GetBytes method again.

This example gets data from the Photo column of the Employees table in the Northwind database. The **SQL Server** stores this data as its native type image, which corresponds to a Byte array in the .NET framework.

The first time the GetBytes method is called the Buffer parameter is null, because we are only interested in obtaining the size of the array. In the second GetBytes call the value returned from the first GetBytes call is used to get all of the bytes for the photo.

VB.NET:

```
Dim iOrdinal As Integer = empDtReader.GetOrdinal("Photo")
' Get the size required for the bye array to store the picture.
Dim lSize As Long = empDtReader.GetBytes(iOrdinal, 0, Nothing, 0, 0)
' Allocate the byte array
Dim btValArr(lSize) As Byte
' Get the Photo field value from the database in allocated
' byte array
empDtReader.GetBytes(iOrdinal, 0, btValArr, lSize, 0)
```

C#:

```
int iOrdinal = empDtReader.GetOrdinal("Photo");
// Get the size required for the bye array to store the picture.
long lSize = empDtReader.GetBytes(iOrdinal, 0, null, 0 , 0);
// Allocate the byte array
byte [] btValArr = new byte[lSize];
// Get the Photo field value from the database in allocated
// byte array
long lRetVal = empDtReader.GetBytes(iOrdinal, 0, btValArr, 0, (int)lSize);
```

The GetChar Method

Gets the value from the specified data column as a character.

Refer to the section on the Get Methods for further information.

The GetChars Method

Gets the value of the specified data column as an array of characters.

VB.NET:

```
NotOverridable Public Function GetChars( _
     ByVal ordinal As Integer, ByVal dataIndex As Long, _
     ByVal buffer() As Char, ByVal bufferIndex As Integer, _
     ByVal length As Integer _
) As Integer
```

C#:

```
public int GetChars(
     int ordinal, long dataIndex, char[] buffer,
     int bufferIndex, int length
);
```

The following table describes the parameters for this method:

Parameter	Type	Description
ordinal	Integer	Zero-based data column ordinal position
dataIndex	Integer	Index in the source array where copying begins
buffer	Byte	Buffer where the field's data will be copied
bufferIndex	Integer	Index in the destination buffer, provided by the caller, where copying begins
length	Integer	Maximum number of character elements that will be copied to the data buffer

This method is like the GetBytes method, with the difference that the source data type should be a character array instead of a byte array. The two methods follow the same rules as far as the method parameters are concerned. For details refer to the GetBytes method.

The GetData Method

Gets the data for the specified data column as an OleDbDataReader object.

VB.NET:

```
NotOverridable Public Function GetData ( _
    ByVal ordinal As Integer _
) As OleDbDataReader
```

C#:

```
public OleDbDataReader GetData (
    int ordinal
);
```

This method is not supported in the Beta 2 release of the .NET SDK. The GetValue method can be used instead.

The GetDataTypeName Method

This method gets the name of the database data type for the specified data column.

VB.NET:

```
NotOverridable Public Function GetDataTypeName ( _
    ByVal index As Integer _
) As String
```

C#:

```
public string GetDataTypeName (
    int index
);
```

The returned value is the data source's native data type name and not the .NET data type. These data types may not be the same as the data types that the framework supports. For example with SQL Server as the backend database you will get data type names like int, nvarchar, datetime, image, and ntext. In Oracle the data type names that are returned are NVARCHAR2, BLOB, LONG, and so on.

The following code gets the data type name for the first data column in the table.

VB.NET:

```
Dim strName As String = dtReader.GetDataTypeName(0)
```

C#:

```
string strName = dtReader.GetDataTypeName(0);
```

The GetDateTime Method

This method gets the value of a data column in the table as a DateTime object.

Refer to the section on The Get Methods for further information.

The GetDecimal Method

This method gets the value of the specified data column which stores the values as Double type. For example if you access the values for data columns storing values as *money*, *smallmoney*, *numeric*, and *decimal* types, this method will return these field values as Decimal objects.

Refer to the section on The Get Methods for further information.

The GetDouble Method

This method gets the value of the specified data column whose value is stored as a Double type in the table of the database. For example in SQL Server the data column that stores values of type float will return the value as a Double type.

Refer to the section on The Get Methods for further information.

The GetFieldType Method

This method gets the data type of the data for a specified column.

VB.NET:

```
NotOverridable Public Function GetFieldType ( _
    ByVal ordinal As Integer _
) As Type
```

C#:

```
public Type GetFieldType (
    int ordinal
);
```

Parameter	Type	Description	Default
Ordinal	Integer	Data Column's Ordinal	

This returns the Type representing the type of Object that would be returned if we used the Item property of GetValue method to obtain this column's data. We can use this method to optimize data retrieval by first checking the data type and then calling the corresponding strongly typed method. When we access the Item property or call the GetValue method, all the information is returned as type Object. To do this, the internal implementation gets the data type and based on this selects the correct strongly typed Get method. Finally it returns the value as an object. If we are accessing the same column repeatedly it will be more efficient to get and store the field type for the column, and from then on use the correct strongly typed Get method.

If the specified column index value is outside the range of zero to one less than FieldCount, the framework will throw a System.IndexOutOfRangeException exception.

Refer to the Data Type Mapping section for details of which data type GetFieldType will return for different native database types.

The following code gets the data type for the data column at ordinal position zero. The returned value is of type Type.

VB.NET:

```
Dim dtType As Type = dtReader.GetFieldType(0)
```

C#:

```
Type dtType = dtReader.GetFieldType(0);
```

The GetFloat Method

This method gets the value of the specified data column as a single-precision floating-point number in a Float object.

VB.NET:

```
NotOverridable Public Function GetFloat ( _
    ByVal ordinal As Integer _
) As Single
```

C#:

```
public float GetFloat (
    int ordinal
);
```

If you look at the signature of this method, you will notice that the Visual Basic code returns the value as type `Single` whereas the C# code returns the value as type `float`. This does not mean that the precision of the field value changes based on the language – the data type is the same but in C# it is given a different alias.

Refer to the section on The Get Methods for further information.

The GetGuid Method

This method gets the value of the specified data column as a globally unique identifier (GUID). For example the `uniqueidentifier` type data columns in SQL Server return the field values as `System.Guid` objects.

Refer to the section on The Get Methods for further information.

The GetInt16 Method

This method gets the value of the specified column as a 16-bit signed integer. For example in a Microsoft Access database the field value stored as `Integer` and in a SQL Server database the field values stored as `smallint` both return the value as `System.Int16` data type.

Refer to the section on The Get Methods for further information.

The GetInt32 Method

This method gets the value of the specified column as a 32-bit signed integer. The underlying data for the column should be of the type `Integer` for successful execution of this method.

Refer to the section on The Get Methods for further information.

The GetInt64 Method

This method gets the value of the specified column as a 64-bit signed integer. The underlying data for the specified column must be stored as a `Long` type, for example `LONG` in Oracle and `bigint` in SQL Server.

Refer to the section on The Get Methods for further information.

The GetName Method

This `method` gets the name of the data column in String format.

VB.NET:

```
NotOverridable Public Function GetName ( _
    ByVal ordinal As Integer _
) As String
```

C#:

```
public string GetName (
    int ordinal
);
```

Usually the name returned by the method is the same as the name of the data column in the database. But if the SELECT query uses AS clauses to alias the retrieved column names, then the name returned by the method is the alias specified in the statement. For example the following Transact-SQL statement fetches the records from `Shippers` table of the `Northwind` database. The query uses an AS clause to get the `CompanyName` column as `Shipping Company`. The `GetName` method call will return the name as `Shipping Company` and not `CompanyName`.

SQL:

```
SELECT CompanyName As 'Shipping Company' FROM SUPPLIERS
```

The following code gets the name of the field returned by execution of the above SQL query.

VB.NET:

```
Dim strColName As String = shipperDtReader.GetName (0)
```

C#:

```
string strColName = shipperDtReader.GetName (0);
```

Sometimes you will be using join queries to retrieve data from more than one table into the `DataReader`. If the join query is performed on tables that have one or more data columns with the same name then the `DataReader` may have one or more columns with the same names. For example the following join query on the `Northwind` database in SQL Server results in two columns with name `EmployeeId`.

SQL:

```
"SELECT * FROM Orders, Employees WHERE Orders.EmployeeId = Employees.EmployeeId"
```

But if you use the same query for the `Northwind` database in **Microsoft Access 2000** database, the names of the two `EmployeeId` columns are not the same in the `DataReader`. The names are fully qualified by the name of the table – the names for the two data columns show as `Orders.EmployeeId` and `Employees.EmployeeId`.

The names of the data columns resulting from join queries vary with OLE DB providers for various databases. To avoid confusion and conflicts resulting from this kind of situation it is always best to use AS clauses in the query to alias the conflicting column names.

The GetOrdinal Method

This method gets the ordinal position for the given data column name in the result set.

VB.NET:

```
NotOverridable Public Function GetOrdinal ( _
    ByVal name As String _
) As Integer
```

C#:

```
public int GetOrdinal (
    string name
);
```

The following table describes the parameter for this method:

Parameter	Type	Description
Name	String	The name of the data column whose ordinal position needs to found

The framework throws System.IndexOutOfRangeException if the name of the specified column does not exist in the table's schema.

Referencing a column by name is resource intensive since a series of string comparisons must be performed in order to obtain the correct column. Using an ordinal reference is far faster. Therefore if we need to obtain data from a given column several times it is more efficient to obtain the ordinal position using this method and subsequently always reference the column by number instead of name.

The following example retrieves the ordinal position of the data column ContactTitle in the Customers table of the Northwind database.

VB.NET:

```
Dim iOrdinal As Integer = dtReader.GetOrdinal("ContactTitle")
```

C#:

```
int iOrdinal = dtReader.GetOrdinal("ContactTitle");
```

Depending on the OLE DB provider, the join queries can result in some conflicting column names. This provider specific behavior can affect the return value of the GetOrdinal method. For example in case of the OLE DB provider for SQL Server, the execution of the following join query will return a DataReader that has two data columns called EmployeeId.

SQL:

```
SELECT * FROM Orders, Employees WHERE Orders.EmployeeId =
    Employees.EmployeeId
```

If we try to get the ordinal position of the EmployeeId data column, it will always return the ordinal position of EmployeeId column of the Orders table and not the Employees table. The EmployeeId column is at ordinal position 2 in the Orders table and is at ordinal position 0 in the Employees table. Therefore this method will always return the ordinal position value as 2 because the Orders table will be the first table in the result set. If the Employees was first in the result set then zero will be returned when the GetOrdinal method is called with EmployeeId as the parameter.

The JET OLE DB provider returns different names for the two `EmployeeID` columns in the above query. If we try to call the `GetOrdinal` method with `EmployeeId` as the parameter, `System.IndexOutOfRangeException` gets thrown. The following example shows how to obtain the ordinal position of the `EmployeeId` data column in this case.

VB.NET:

```
Dim ordtblOrdinal As Integer = dtReader.GetOrdinal("Orders.EmployeeId")
Dim emptblOrdinal As Integer = dtReader.GetOrdinal("Employees.EmployeeId")
```

C#:

```
int ordtblOrdinal = dtReader.GetOrdinal("Orders.EmployeeId");
int emptblOrdinal = dtReader.GetOrdinal("Employees.EmployeeId");
```

However, since this behavior differs between providers, it is best to avoid the problem by using the SQL `AS` clause to create an alias for duplicate column names.

The GetSchemaTable Method

This method is used to get the schema for data held in the `DataReader` object's result set.

VB.NET:

```
NotOverridable Public Function GetSchemaTable () As DataTable
```

C#:

```
public DataTable GetSchemaTable();
```

The `IDataReader` interface, which every `DataReader` class implements, defines this method. This method gets the complete schema information of the result set that the `DataReader` object is reading. The `DataTable` returned by the method is populated with rows and columns containing the schema information. Each row in the `DataTable` represents a field in the result set; each column in the `DataTable` represents the attributes that are set for the data field.

The schema information can be obtained while the `DataReader` object is open. A `System.InvalidOperationException` exception will be thrown if the method is called on a closed `DataReader` object.

The following code calls this method on an open `DataReader`.

VB.NET:

```
Dim dtTable As DataTable = dtReader.GetSchemaTable()
```

C#:

```
DataTable dtTable = dtReader.GetSchemaTable();
```

The following C# code can be used to dump the schema information of a table.

```
DataTable schemaTable = dtReader.GetSchemaTable ();
foreach (DataRow dtRow in schemaTable.Rows)
{
      foreach (DataColumn dtCol in schemaTable.Columns)
      {
            Trace.Write (dtCol + ": ");
            Trace.WriteLine (dtRow[dtCol]);
      }
      Trace.WriteLine ("**************************");
}
```

The output from the above code for the `CompanyName` column of the `CUSTOMER` table in the `Northwind` database is as follows:

```
**************************
ColumnName: CompanyName
ColumnOrdinal: 2
ColumnSize: 40
NumericPrecision: 255
NumericScale: 255
DataType: System.String
ProviderType: 202
IsLong: False
AllowDBNull: False
IsReadOnly: False
IsRowVersion: False
IsUnique: False
IsKey: False
IsAutoIncrement: False
BaseSchemaName:
BaseCatalogName:
BaseTableName:
BaseColumnName:
**************************
```

This method can be useful for applications that dynamically build their SQL queries. Using the meta-data information returned by the method, you can check what kinds of values are allowed for a particular data column and what constraints it needs to satisfy. If the value specified for that data column does not match the table's schema, then the method that is building the query can prompt the user to specify the right kind of information.

The schema information returned by this method can also help to dynamically assign attributes to the controls of windows forms and ASP.NET pages. For example if the schema of the table indicates that a particular column is `ReadOnly`, you can set the control representing that column's value as `ReadOnly`, which will indicate to the users of the application that they are not allowed to modify this value.

This method is the counterpart of the OLE DB `IColumnsRowset::GetColumnsRowSet` method. The following table explains the columns returned by this method, and shows how they map to OLE DB column ids:

DataReader Column	OLE DB Column ID	Description	Default
ColumnName	DBCOLUMN_NAME	Name of the column as defined in the data source or the alias given in the SQL command string. If the method fails to retrieve this attribute, a null value is returned.	null
ColumnOrdinal	DBCOLUMN_NUMBER	Data column's ordinal number, with the first column being number 1. For bookmark data fields this property returns 0.	
ColumnSize	DBCOLUMN_ COLUMNSIZE	Maximum possible length of the field.	
NumericPrecision	DBCOLUMN_ PRECISION	For numeric data, this column represents the maximum precision for the field value.	
NumericScale	DBCOLUMN_SCALE	For data types DBTYPE_DECIMAL and DBTYPE_NUMERIC, this property returns the maximum number of digits to the right of the decimal point. For other data types, it returns a null value.	
DataType		Maps to common language runtime type of DbType.	
DbType	DBCOLUMN_TYPE	Indicates column's data type. If field contains different types of data in different columns, then the property returns Object. The value of this property cannot be null.	
IsLong	DBCOLUMNFLAGS_ ISLONG	True if the data type of the field is Binary Long Object (BLOB). Every managed provider has its own definition of a very long data type.	
AllowDBNull	DBCOLUMNFLAGS_ ISNULLABLE	This property is set to true if the field can accept a Null value.	

Table continued on following page

DataReader Column	OLE DB Column ID	Description	Default
IsReadOnly	DBCOLUMNFLAGS_WRITE	This attribute returns `true` if the data column value cannot be edited, otherwise it returns `false`.	
IsRowVersion	DBCOLUMNFLAGS_ISROWID	This property is `true` if the field represents a persistent row identifier that cannot be written to. It does nothing useful except identify the row.	
IsUnique	DBCOLUMN_ISUNIQUE	This property is set to `VARIANT_TRUE` if no two rows can contain the same value in this column. If the value does not need to remain unique, the property is set to `VARIANT_FALSE`.	VARIANT_FALSE
IsKeyColumn	DBCOLUMN_KEYCOLUMN	Set to `true` if the data column uniquely identifies a data row on its own or as a part of set of columns.	VARIANT_FALSE
IsAutoIncrement	DBCOLUMN_ISAUTOINCRMENT	The property is set to `VARIANT_TRUE` if new records are automatically assigned a value for this column in fixed increments. Otherwise the property is set to `VARIANT_FALSE`.	VARIANT_FALSE
BaseSchemaName	DBCOLUMN_BASESCHEMANAME	The name of the schema that contains the given data column. Failure to retrieve this value sets the property to `null`.	null
BaseCatalogName	DBCOLUMN_BASECATALOGNAME	The name of the catalog in the back end database that contains the given data column. Failure to retrieve this value sets the property to `null`.	null
BaseTableName	DBCOLUMN_BASETABLENAME	The name of the table or view in the back end database that contains the given data column. Failure to retrieve this value sets the property to `null`.	null

DataReader Column	OLE DB Column ID	Description	Default
BaseColunName	DBCOLUMN_ BASECOLUMNNAME	The name of the data column as specified in the data source. If an alias is used to retrieve a column, then this value is different than the one returned in the ColumnName column. Failure to retrieve this value sets the property to `null`.	`null`

The GetString Method

This method gets the value of the specified data column, in a data table, as a `string`.

Refer to the section on The Get Methods for further information.

The GetTimeSpan Method

This method gets the value of the specified data column as a `TimeSpan` object. `TimeSpan` objects represent a period of time (for example 2 hours), which is different to a Date/Time value, which identifies a particular moment in history or the future (for example 2pm). However few databases currently use `TimeSpan` data types.

Refer to the section on The Get Methods for further information on using this method.

The GetValue Method

This method gets the value of the specified data column as a .NET `Object`. This method provides generic access to the data for a given column without the restrictions of the strongly typed access methods such as `GetInt32`, `GetString`.

VB.NET:

```
Overloads Public Function GetValue (_
     ByVal ordinal As Integer _
) As Object
```

C#:

```
public object GetValue (
     int ordinal
);
```

It has been mentioned earlier that to get the maximum performance out of your data access layer it is best to use the strongly typed data access functions. The `GetValue` method is useful for accessing data columns when we are not sure about the underlying data type.

Strongly typed access methods are best. The `GetValue` method needs to do a lot more work than a strongly typed method because it must return the field value as type `Object`. This means that irrespective of the underlying data type, the return value has to be converted to type `Object`. This is often done using boxing.

> **Boxing is a technique where the values are implicitly converted to type Object. A new instance of Object is created and data of the value type variable is copied in to this new Object.**

The implementation of the `GetValue` method includes a huge switch statement that checks the underlying data type from the table's schema. Based on the type information returned it calls the appropriate method of the `BitConverter` class to get the value of the field. For example if the underlying data if of type Integer, then the `BitConverter.ToInt32` method is called to convert the data stream for the data column. Finally the returned value is boxed to `Object`.

When you call `GetInt32` method, the implementation does need have to go through these switch statements to decide what internal function to use.

However there are cases when it is necessary to use `GetValue`. Two field types will always return objects. Firstly, if we use the `DataReader` to access hierarchical data then the `DataReader` corresponding to the child tables of the hierarchy are stored in the last column as an `Object`. We can use `GetValue` to return this object, and no boxing will need to be performed.

Secondly, SQL Server allows the data to be stored as of type `sql_variant`. The field values of these columns will return the value as an `Object`. Therefore if we call a strongly typed access method for these data columns, an exception will be thrown. We need to use the `GetValue` method to access the data.

The Item property also calls this method to get the field values.

Here are a few recommendations about using this method:

❑ Use this method if the under lying data in the table is of type `Object` (for exampe `sql_variant` and `DataReader`).

❑ Use this method if you are not sure about the under lying data type. It is better to take a slight performance hit than to bring the application to halt because of the exception thrown by data type mismatch.

❑ If the data type of a column is known then call the corresponding typed method rather than calling this generic `GetValue` method or using the `Item` property.

The GetValues Method

This method gets the values of all the data columns for the current record of the `DataReader` object.

VB.NET:

```
NotOverridable Public Function GetValues ( _
    ByVal values() Object _
) As Integer
```

C#:

```
public int GetValues (
    object[] values
);
```

The following table describes the parameter for the method:

Parameter	Type	Description
values	Object	An Object array to copy the attribute fields into

Successful execution of this method populates the array with a number of field values. The size of the object array that is passed to the method does not have to be the same as the number of columns in the result set, but it must not be a null reference. If the specified buffer is less than the number of columns in the result set then only the number of fields that can fit into the buffer get copied; if the supplied buffer size is larger than the number of columns in the result set, the extra elements in the array are set to null references.

This method is advantageous in the sense that all the field values are retrieved in one call instead of getting them individually. This prompts the question, why do we need to access individual column values, using various Get methods, when all the values can be fetched with one call? To answer this it is necessary to see how this method returns the data.

The field values are returned in a zero based object array. And the indices of this array correspond to the ordinal positions of the columns in the DataReader. The first data column will be saved in the array element at index zero; the second data column will be saved in the array element at index one and so on. The object array does not contain any information about the column names.

This method will definitely give a performance boost to your application if you are accessing the fields by the ordinal positions and these ordinals will not change over the time. In this case you can fetch all of the data columns in one call.

The following code gets the value of the FieldCount property of an open DataReader and creates an object array of the appropriate size. It then calls the GetValues method to get values of all data fields for that particular record in the table. This implementation assumes that the implementer of the data access layer knows the ordinal position corresponding to each data column's name.

VB.NET:

```
Dim iNumFields As Integer = dtReader.FieldCount
' Allocate the exact buffer size for array that will
' return the field values. This is very important to get data
' for all the columns. If null reference is supplied as buffer
' an exception will be thrown by framework with a message that
' "Invalid Buffer Size" has been provided.
Dim fldValues(iNumFields) As Object
While (dtReader.Read)
    dtReader.GetValues(fldValues)
    ' do something with the data
End While
```

C#:

```
int iNumFields = dtReader.FieldCount;
// Allocate the exact buffer size for array that will
// return the field values. This is very important to get data
// for all the columns. If null reference is supplied as buffer
// an exception will be thrown by framework with a message that
// "Invalid Buffer Size" has been provided.
object [] fldValues = new object[iNumFields];
while (dtReader.Read ())
```

```
{
    dtReader.GetValues (fldValues);
    // do something with the data
}
```

The IsDBNull Method

This method is used to check if the value of the specified data column is Null or not.

VB.NET:
```
NotOverridable Public Function IsDBNull ( _
        ByVal ordinal As Integer _
) As Boolean
```

C#:
```
public bool IsDBNull (
        int ordinal
);
```

The method takes the ordinal position of the data column as a parameter. If the value of the field for the specified column ordinal is of type System.DBNull, this method will return True. Otherwise it will return False.

The DBNull value is not the same as Nothing in Visual Basic or null in C#. It is a valid object, defined in System namespace, which indicates that the value for a particular data column is not initialized. An empty string, of length zero, is not the same as DBNull.

The database schema specifies if a particular field in a table can have Null value. For example, the following Transact-SQL statement creats a table named ADDRESS. In the schema it assigns **NOT NULL** attributes to the columns AddressID, State, and PostalCode, and the rest of the columns have **NULL** attribute. This means that the data columns that have **NOT NULL** attributes will always have some valid value stored in them, but the rest of the columns can be left without values.

SQL:
```
CREATE TABLE Address
{
AddressIS int NOT NULL,
StreetName nvarchar(50) NULL,
City nvarchar(50) NULL,
State char(10) NOT NULL,
Country nvarchar(50) NULL,
PostalCode char(10) NOT NULL
}
```

If we get the value of the StreetName field from this table, it may return value of type DBNull indicating that no value has been assigned to this field. If we try to assign this value to a variable of type String, the framework will throw System.InvalidCastException.

This method can help to avoid run time exceptions by checking if the value for a data column is of type DBNull before obtaining the value.

The following code implements a method in the data access layer of an application. It is used to return the price of products for which the ProductID is specified as the method parameter. After getting the DataReader object, the method checks if the value for UnitPrice column is DBNull or not. If it is a valid Decimal value, it returns the value in the out parameter.

VB.NET:

```
Public Function GetProductPrice _
            (ByVal strID As String, ByRef prodPrice As Decimal) As Integer
    prodPrice = 0
    Dim strConn As String = _
            "Provider= SQLOLEDB.1; Data Source=localhost; uid=sa;" & _
            "pwd=; Initial Catalog=Northwind;"
    Dim strQuery As StringBuilder = New StringBuilder()
    strQuery.Append _
            ("SELECT ProductName, UnitPrice FROM PRODUCTS WHERE " & _
            "ProductId='")
    strQuery.Append(strID)
    strQuery.Append("'")

    ' Create Connection object and Open it.
    Dim oledbConn As New OleDbConnection(strConn)
    oledbConn.Open()

    ' Create the Command object to get a DataReader for the
    ' PRODUCTS table.
    Dim oledbCmd As New OleDbCommand(strQuery.ToString(), oledbConn)
    Dim prodDtReader As OleDbDataReader = _
            oledbCmd.ExecuteReader(CommandBehavior.CloseConnection)
    While prodDtReader.Read()
        ' Get ordinal position for UnitPrice column.
        Dim iOrdinal As Integer = prodDtReader.GetOrdinal("UnitPrice")

        ' Make sure that there is a valid price specified for the
        ' product. If not then return -1 to the user indicating that
        ' price for the product is unknown. Otherwise get the value of
        ' the field and return it in the prodPrice parameter.
        If prodDtReader.IsDBNull(iOrdinal) Then
            Trace.WriteLine("Price of the product is Unknown")
            prodDtReader.Close()
            Return -1
        End If

        prodPrice = prodDtReader.GetDecimal(iOrdinal)
    End While
    prodDtReader.Close()
    Return prodPrice
End Function
```

C#:

```
public int GetProductPrice (string strID, out decimal prodPrice)
{
    prodPrice = 0.0M;
    string strConn = "Provider= SQLOLEDB.1; Data Source=localhost;" +
```

```
          " uid=sa; pwd=; Initial Catalog=Northwind";
      StringBuilder strQuery = new StringBuilder ();
      strQuery.Append
          ("SELECT ProductName, UnitPrice FROM PRODUCTS WHERE ProductId='");
      strQuery.Append (strID);
      strQuery.Append ("'");

      // Create Connection object and Open it.
      OleDbConnection oledbConn = new OleDbConnection (strConn);
      oledbConn.Open ();

      // Create the Command object to get DataReader for the
      // PRODUCTS table.
      OleDbCommand oledbCmd = new OleDbCommand (strQuery.ToString (),
          oledbConn);
      OleDbDataReader prodDtReader = oledbCmd.ExecuteReader(
                          CommandBehavior.CloseConnection);
      while (prodDtReader.Read ())
      {
          int iOrdinal = prodDtReader.GetOrdinal("UnitPrice");
          // Make sure that there is a valid price specified for the
          // product. If not then return -1 to the user indicating that
          // price for the product is unknown. Otherwise get the value
          // the field and return it in the prodPrice parameter.
          if (prodDtReader.IsDBNull (iOrdinal))
          {
              Trace.WriteLine ("Price of the product is Unknown");
              prodDtReader.Close ();
              return -1;
          }

          prodPrice = prodDtReader.GetDecimal(iOrdinal);
      }
      prodDtReader.Close ();
      return prodPrice;
  }
```

If the `IsDBNull` method is not called in the above code and the value returned is `DBNull`, then an exception gets thrown when the value returned by the `GetDecimal` method is assigned to variable `prodPrice`.

The NextResult Method

When a batch SQL statement is used to retrieve multiple result sets from a database, this method is used to advance the `DataReader` to the next result set. Once the `DataReader` is advanced to the next result set, we cannot move back to the previous one.

VB.NET:

```
NotOverridable Public Function NextResult () As Boolean
```

C#:

```
public bool NextResult ();
```

This method is equivalent to the `Recordset` object's `NextRecordset` method in ADO. Not all databases support the execution of batch SQL statements returning multiple tables. For example Microsoft SQL Server and Oracle databases support the batch statements, whereas Microsoft Access database does not support it. Therefore you should refer to the documentation of your database to check whether batch statement processing is supported.

The following stored procedure in the `Northwind` database in **SQL Server 2000** returns a `DataReader` that contains two result sets. The first result set returns the rows from the `SUPPLIERS` table and the second returns rows from the `SHIPPERS` table:

```
CREATE PROCEDURE GetSuppliersAndShippers As
     SELECT * FROM SUPPLIERS
     SELECT * FROM SHIPPERS
GO
```

The number of result sets returned in the `DataReader` object depends on the number of `SELECT` statements specified in the batch SQL query. Successful execution of the `ExecuteReader` method on the `DataCommand` object places the cursor of `DataReader` object on the first result set. To move to the next result set it is necessary to call the `NextResult` method. This method returns one of the following two values:

❑ `True` – The `DataReader` object has been moved to the next result set successfully

❑ `False` – The `DataReader` object failed to move to next result set or there are no more result sets to be retrieved from the data source

The next example uses this method to read the multiple result sets returned the following stored procedure created in the `Northwind` database.

SQL:

```
CREATE PROCEDURE
     GetRegionAndTerritories
AS
     SELECT * FROM REGION
     SELECT * FROM TERRITORIES
GO
```

The code creates an `OleDbCommand` object. It assigns the name of the stored procedure, `GetRegionAndTerritories`, to the `CommandText` property and `CommandType.StoredProcedure` to the `CommandType` property. Calling the `ExecuteReader` method returns a `DataReader` object that contains two result sets. The first `Read` loop reads all of the records from the first result set containing the `REGION` table records. After the loop finishes, indicated by `false` being returned by the `Read` method, the outer `while` loop calls the `NextResult` method. Because there is another result set in the `DataReader`, the method will return `true` and the `DataReader` object advances to the next result set, which contains records from `TERRITORIES` table. Then the `Read` loop reads the records from second result set. After reading all the record rows from `TERRITORIES` table, the call to `NextResult` method returns `false`, indicating that there are no more result sets in the `DataReader`. Finally the `Close` method is called on the `DataReader` to release the connection with the database.

VB.NET:

```
Dim strConn As String = _
     "Provider= SQLOLEDB.1; Data Source=localhost; uid=sa;pwd=;" & _
     "Initial Catalog=Northwind "
' Create Connection object and Open it.
Dim oledbConn As New OleDbConnection(strConn)
'Open the database connection.
oledbConn.Open()
```

```
' Create the Command object to execute stored procedure.
Dim oledbCmd As New OleDbCommand()
With oledbCmd
    .Connection = oledbConn
    .CommandText = "GetRegionAndTerritories"
    .CommandType = CommandType.StoredProcedure
End With

' Call ExecuteReader method to get the result sets.
Dim dtReader As OleDbDataReader = _
        oledbCmd.ExecuteReader(CommandBehavior.CloseConnection)
Do
    ' Display all rows
    While (dtReader.Read ())
        ' Read the row fields
        Dim iFldIdx As Integer
        For iFldIdx = 0 To (dtReader.FieldCount - 1)
            Console.Write(dtReader.Item(iFldIdx).ToString() & ",")
        Next
        Console.WriteLine()
    End While
    ' Load up the next table if there is another
    Console.WriteLine("** End of Table **")
Loop While (dtReader.NextResult())
'Close the DataReader.
dtReader.Close()
```

C#:

```
string strConn = "Provider= SQLOLEDB.1; Data Source=localhost;" +
                 "uid=sa; pwd=; Initial Catalog=Northwind";
// Create Connection object and Open it.
OleDbConnection oledbConn = new OleDbConnection (strConn);
oledbConn.Open ();

// Create the Command object to execute stored procedure.
OleDbCommand oledbCmd = new OleDbCommand ();
oledbCmd.Connection = oledbConn;
oledbCmd.CommandText = "GetRegionAndTerritories";
oledbCmd.CommandType = CommandType.StoredProcedure;
// Call ExecuteReader method to get the result sets
OleDbDataReader dtReader = oledbCmd.ExecuteReader
(CommandBehavior.CloseConnection);
do
{
    // Display all rows
    while (dtReader.Read ())
    {
        // Read the row fields
        for (int iFldIdx = 0; iFldIdx < dtReader.FieldCount; iFldIdx++)
        {
            Console.Write(dtReader[iFldIdx].ToString());
        }
        Console.WriteLine();
    }
    // Load up the next table if there is another
    Console.WriteLine("** End of Table **");
```

```
    } while (dtReader.NextResult ());

    // Close the DataReader.
    dtReader.Close ();
```

The above example has shown how a stored procedure that uses batch SQL statements returns multiple result sets. This does not mean that the `DataReader` object returns multiple result sets for only stored procedures. You can specify a batch of valid SQL statement while creating the `OleDbCommand` object. Calling the `ExecuteReader` method on this command will also return a `DataReader` containing multiple result sets. The results obtained above code can also be obtained if the `CommandText` of the `OleDbCommand` object is set to the following string:

SQL:

```
    "SELECT * FROM REGION; SELECT * FROM TERRITORIES"
```

The following code illustrates the use of above batch query.

C#:

```
    string strSquery = "SELECT * FROM REGION; SELECT * FROM TERRITORIES";
    OleDbCommand oledbCmd = new OleDbCommand (strQuery, oledbConn);
    OleDbDataReader dtReader = oledbCmd.ExecuteReader ();
```

The batch query is submitted as one query to the database, which returns multiple result sets to the `DataReader`.

> If the **Close** method is called on the **DataReader** after reading the first result set then that **DataReader** cannot be used to read the remaining result sets. If we call the **NextResult** method after closing the **DataReader**, the framework throws **System.InvalidOperationExecption**.

The SqlDataReader Object

This data provider is used exclusively for accessing data from SQL Server version 7.0 and higher. This class implements the same interfaces as implemented by other two `DataReader` classes, `OleDbDataReader` and `OdbcDataReader`. There are are two main reasons to differentiate between this class and the other `DataReader` classes:

❏   The most important feature of the class is that the data provider's interface with the SQL Server is not through an OLE DB provider or ODBC driver. It uses the Tabular Data Stream (**TDS**) protocol for communication with the server. TDS is the data stream protocol used by SQL Server to communicate with clients. Whenever a query needs to be executed on the server by the `SqlDataReader` object, it is packaged in a **TDS** packet and sent to the server, which then sends the result back to the application using TDS. Since there is no intermediate provider involved, the data access is faster and more efficient.

❑   This class implements some data access methods such as `GetSqlBinary` and `GetSqlDouble` that return the values as SQL Server native data types such as `SqlBinary` and `SqlDouble`. These SQL Server specific data types are defined in the `System.Data.SqlTypes` namespace. Use of these data types prevents any precision loss that may occur when the SQL Server data types are converted to .NET native types. Since no data type conversion takes place for these strongly typed methods, it provides faster access to the field values.

Accessing the backend through a generic managed provider, such as `OleDbDataReader` and `OdbcDataReader`, always adds an extra layer of OLE DB or ODBC code that results in some inefficiency. Therefore it is better to use a native managed provider, if available, for a particular database. If your application will always be using SQL Server as its backend database, use the managed provider objects for SQL Server. If you use the `SqlCommand` object, the `ExecuteReader method` will automatically return an `SqlDataReader`.

This section will discuss the methods provided by the `SqlDataReader` that are not supported by other varieties of `DataReader`. The `SqlDataReader` does not implement any additional properties.

SqlDataReader Constructors

There is no constructor for the `SqlDataReader` class. This class is defined in the `System.Data.SqlClient` namespace. The only way to create an `SqlDataReader` object is by calling the `ExecuteReader` method on a `SqlCommand` object. The following example creates a `SqlConnection` object and opens it. It then creates a `SqlCommand` object and assigns the SELECT statement to its `CommandText` property. Finally it calls the `ExecuteReader` method to get the `SqlDataReader` that will be used to get records from the EMPLOYEES table.

VB.NET:
```
Dim strConn As String = "Server=localhost;uid=sa;pwd=;database=Northwind"
Dim sqlConn As New SqlConnection(strConn)
Dim sqlCmd As SqlCommand = New SqlCommand ()
With sqlCmd
    .Connection = sqlConn
    .CommandText = "SELECT * FROM EMPLOYEES"
End With
Dim dtReader As SqlDataReader = sqlCmd.ExecuteReader()
```

C#:
```
string strConn = "Server=localhost;uid=sa;pwd=;database=Northwind";
SqlConnection sqlConn = new SqlConnection(strConn);
SqlCommand sqlCmd = new SqlCommand ();
sqlCmd.Connection = sqlConn;
sqlCmd.CommandText = "SELECT * FROM EMPLOYEES";
SqlDataReader dtReader = sqlCmd.ExecuteReader();
```

There are no objects from the `System.Data.OleDb` namespace used in this implementation because only objects defined in `System.Data.SqlClient` are used for SQL Server specific data access. Therefore you will use `SqlConnection` and `SqlCommand` classes to create the `Connection` and `Command` objects.

In the connection string no data provider has been specified. This class can only be used for accessing SQL Server so we do not need to specify a provider. See the chapter on The Connection Object (Chapter 3) for further information.

SqlDataReader Methods

The GetSqlxxx Methods

This class implements some GetSqlxxx accessor methods in addition to the GetXXX methods implemented by OleDbDataReader and OdbcDataReader classes. These GetSqlxxx methods return the column values as the SQL Server native data types. It is recommended that if you know the underlying data type in the SQL Server database's table then use these strongly typed methods to access the data column values. It will improve the efficiency of the application because no overheads are involved converting the data type from SQL Server native types to Common Language Runtime (CLR) types.

The following table presents the mapping of SQL Server native types, .NET native types and the GetSqlxxx methods to be used to access corresponding data columns:

SQL Server native types	.NET Framework SqlType	GetSqlxxx Method
binary	SqlBinary	GetSqlBinary
bigint	SqlInt64	GetSqlInt64
bit	SqlBit	GetSqlBoolean
char	SqlString	GetSqlString
datetime	SqlDateTime	GetSqlDateTime
decimal	SqlDecimal	GetSqlDecimal
float	SqlDouble	GetSqlDouble
image	SqlBinary	GetSqlBinary
int	SqlInt32	GetSqlInt32
money	SqlMoney	GetSqlMoney
nchar	SqlString	GetSqlString
ntext	SqlString	GetSqlString
nvarchar	SqlString	GetSqlString
numeric	SqlNumeric	GetSqlDecimal
real	SqlSingle	GetSqlSingle
smalldatetime	SqlDateTime	GetSqlDateTime
smallint	SqlInt16	GetSqlInt16
smallmoney	SqlMoney	GetSqlMoney
sql_variant	Object	GetSqlValue

Table continued on following page

SQL Server native types	.NET Framework SqlType	GetSqlxxx Method
text	SqlString	GetSqlString
timestamp	SqlBinary	GetSqlBinary
tinyint	SqlByte	GetSqlByte
varbinary	SqlBinary	GetSqlBinary
varchar	SqlString	GetSqlString
uniqueidentifier	SqlGuid	GetSqlGuid

If the data in the SQL Server is not stored as correct type for the method then `System.InvalidCastException` will be thrown. For example if we call `GetSqlString` for a data column that stores Integer values then the exception will be thrown, no attempt at conversion will take place.

All of these access methods take only one parameter, the zero based ordinal position of the data column in the `SqlDataReader` object. The following table describes the parameter that is passed to these `Get` methods:

Parameter	Type	Description
ordinal	Integer	Zero-based ordinal position of the data column in the table

The GetSqlBinary Method

This method gets the value of the specified data column as a variable-length stream of binary data. For example if you get the `logo` field in the `pub_info` table of the `Pubs` database, it will be returned as `SqlBinary` type data.

VB.NET:

```
NotOverridable Public Function GetSqlBinary( _
    ByVal ordinal As Integer _
) As SqlBinary
```

C#:

```
public SqlBinary GetSqlBinary(
    int ordinal
);
```

The following code gets the data stored in the `logo` data column.

VB.NET:

```
Dim picData As SqlBinary = dtReader.GetSqlBinary(dtReader.GetOrdinal("logo"))
```

C#:
```
SqlBinary picData = dtReader.GetSqlBinary(dtReader.GetOrdinal("logo"));
```

The GetSqlBoolean Method

This method gets the value of the specified data column as an `SqlBoolean` object, which has a value that is either `true` or `false`.

VB.NET:
```
NotOverridable Public Function GetSqlBoolean( _
    ByVal ordinal As Integer _
) As SqlBit
```

C#:
```
public SqlBit GetSqlBoolean(
    int ordinal
);
```

The following code gets the value of the `Discontinued` field in the PRODUCTS table of the Northwind database.

VB.NET:
```
Dim bDiscontinued As SqlBoolean = _
    dtReader.GetSqlBoolean(dtReader.GetOrdinal("Discontinued"))
```

C#:
```
SqlBoolean bDiscontinued = _
    dtReader.GetSqlBoolean(dtReader.GetOrdinal("Discontinued"));
```

The GetSqlByte Method

This method gets the value of the specified data column as an `SqlByte` object – an 8-bit unsigned integer. For example the `min_lvl` and `max_lvl` fields in the JOBS table of the pubs database store the values as `tinyint`. These fields will return their values as `SqlByte`.

VB.NET:
```
NotOverridable Public Function GetSqlByte( _
    ByVal ordinal As Integer _
) As SqlByte
```

C#:
```
public SqlByte GetSqlByte(
    int ordinal
);
```

The following code gets the value stored in the `min_lvl` field from the `JOBS` table.

VB.NET:

```
Dim minLevel As SqlByte = dtReader.GetSqlByte(dtReader.GetOrdinal("min_lvl"))
```

C#:

```
SqlByte minLevel = dtReader.GetSqlByte(dtReader.GetOrdinal("min_lvl"));
```

The GetSqlDateTime Method

This method gets the value of the specified data column as a `SqlDateTime` object. For example the `ord_date` field in the `SALES` table of the `pubs` database stores the values as `datetime`. This method will get the value of this field as `SqlDateTime`. The values stored as `smalldatetime` are also returned as `SqlDateTime`.

VB.NET:

```
NotOverridable Public Function GetSqlDateTime( _
    ByVal ordinal As Integer _
) As SqlDateTime
```

C#:

```
public SqlBinary GetSqlDateTime(
    int ordinal
);
```

The following code gets the value of the `ord_date` field from the `DataReader`.

VB.NET:

```
Dim orderDate As SqlDateTime = dtReader.GetSqlDateTime
(dtReader.GetOrdinal("ord_date"))
```

C#:

```
SqlDateTime orderDate = dtReader.GetSqlDateTime (dtReader.GetOrdinal("ord_date"));
```

The GetSqlDouble Method

This method gets the value of the specified data column as a `SqlDouble` object. Values that are stored in SQL Server as float are returned as `SqlDouble`.

VB.NET:

```
NotOverridable Public Function GetSqlDouble( _
    ByVal ordinal As Integer _
) As SqlDouble
```

C#:

```
public SqlDouble GetSqlDouble(
    int ordinal
);
```

The following code gets the value of data column `TotalVolume` that stores total volume of various containers in the `Storage` table of a warehouse database.

VB.NET:

```
Dim totalVolume As SqlDouble = dtReader.GetSqlDouble
(dtReader.GetOrdinal("TotalVolume"))
```

C#:

```
SqlDouble totalVolume = dtReader.GetSqlDouble
(dtReader.GetOrdinal("TotalVolume"));
```

The GetSqlGuid Method

This method gets the value of the specified data column as a `SqlGuid` object. This data type corresponds to data columns that store their values as a `uniqueidentifier`.

VB.NET:

```
NotOverridable Public Function GetSqlGuid( _
    ByVal ordinal As Integer _
) As SqlGuid
```

C#:

```
public SqlGuid GetSqlGuid(
    int ordinal
);
```

The following code gets the value of the `ProductId` field of the table.

VB.NET:

```
Dim prodID As SqlGuid = dtReader.GetSqlGuid(GetOrdinal("ProductId"))
```

C#:

```
SqlGuid prodID = dtReader.GetSqlGuid(GetOrdinal("ProductId"));
```

The GetSqlInt16 Method

This method gets the value of the specified data column as an `SQLInt16` object – a 16-bit signed integer value. Values stored as `smallint` are returned as `SqlInt16` objects.

VB.NET:

```
NotOverridable Public Function GetSqlInt16( _
    ByVal ordinal As Integer _
) As SQLInt16
```

C#:

```
public SQLInt16 GetSqlInt16(
    int ordinal
);
```

The following example gets the value of the qty field in SALES table of pubs database.

VB.NET:

```
Dim disVal As SqlInt16 = dtReader.GetSqlInt16(dtReader.GetOrdinal("qty"))
```

C#:

```
SqlInt16 disVal = dtReader.GetSqlInt16(dtReader.GetOrdinal("qty"));
```

The GetSqlInt32 Method

This method gets the value of the specified data column as an SqlInt32 object – a 32-bit signed integer value. Values stored as int in the tables are returned as a SqlInt32 objects.

VB.NET:

```
NotOverridable Public Function GetSqlInt32( _
    ByVal ordinal As Integer _
) As SqlInt32
```

C#:

```
public SqlInt32 GetSqlInt32(
    int ordinal
);
```

The following code gets the value of the royaltyper field of the TITLEAUTHOR table of the pubs database.

VB.NET:

```
Dim iRoyalty As SqlInt32 = dtReader.GetSqlInt32(dtReader.GetOrdinal("royaltyper"))
```

C#:

```
SqlInt32 iRoyalty = dtReader.GetSqlInt32(dtReader.GetOrdinal("royaltyper"));
```

The GetSqlInt64 Method

This method gets the value of the specified data column as an `SqlInt64` object – a 64-bit signed integer value. Values stored as `bigint` are returned as a `SqlInt64` object.

VB.NET:

```
NotOverridable Public Function GetSqlInt64( _
    ByVal ordinal As Integer _
) As SqlInt64
```

C#:

```
public SqlInt64 GetSqlInt64(
    int ordinal
);
```

The following table gets the value of the column `Population,` which stores the value of the population of a country.

VB.NET:

```
Dim lPopultation As Long = dtReader.GetInt64(dtReader.GetOrdinal("Population"))
```

C#:

```
long lPopultation = dtReader.GetInt64(dtReader.GetOrdinal("Population"));
```

The GetSqlMoney Method

This method gets the value of the specified data column as an `SqlMoney` object. Data columns storing values as `money` and `smallmoney` return their value as a `SqlMoney` object.

VB.NET:

```
NotOverridable Public Function GetSqlMoney( _
    ByVal ordinal As Integer _
) As SqlMoney
```

C#:

```
public SqlMoney GetSqlMoney(
    int ordinal
);
```

The following code gets the value of the `Freight` data column from the `ORDERS` table of the Northwind database.

VB.NET:

```
Dim freightVal As SqlMoney = dtReader.GetSqlMoney (dtReader.GetOrdinal("Freight"))
```

C#:

```
SqlMoney freightVal = dtReader.GetSqlMoney (dtReader.GetOrdinal("Freight"));
```

The GetSqlNumeric Method

This method gets the value of the specified data column as a SqlNumeric object. This method should be used for data columns that store values as numeric and decimal types.

VB.NET:

```
NotOverridable Public Function GetSqlNumeric( _
    ByVal ordinal As Integer _
) As SqlNumeric
```

C#:

```
public SqlNumeric GetSqlNumeric(
    int ordinal
);
```

The following example gets the value of the discount field in the DISCOUNTS table of the pubs database.

VB.NET:

```
Dim disVal As SqlNumeric = _
    dtReader.GetSqlNumeric(dtReader.GetOrdinal("discount"))
```

C#:

```
SqlNumeric disVal = _
    dtReader.GetSqlNumeric(dtReader.GetOrdinal("discount "));
```

The GetSqlSingle Method

This method gets the value of the specified data column as a SqlSingle object. This method should be used for data columns that store data of type real.

VB.NET:

```
NotOverridable Public Function GetSqlSingle( _
    ByVal ordinal As Integer _
) As SqlSingle
```

C#:

```
public SqlSingle GetSqlSingle(
    int ordinal
);
```

The following code gets the value of data column `TotalVolume` that stores total volume of various containers in the Storage table of a warehouse database.

VB.NET:

```
Dim totalVolume As SqlSingle = dtReader.GetSqlSingle _
    (dtReader.GetOrdinal("TotalVolume"))
```

C#:

```
SqlDouble totalVolume = dtReader.GetSqlDouble _
    (dtReader.GetOrdinal("TotalVolume"));
```

The GetSqlString Method

This method gets the value of the specified data column as an `SqlString` object. This method should be used for data columns that store string data for example `char`, `varchar`, `nvarchar`.

VB.NET:

```
NotOverridable Public Function GetSqlString( _
    ByVal ordinal As Integer _
) As SqlString
```

C#:

```
public SqlString GetSqlString(
    int ordinal
);
```

The following code gets the value of the `au_lname` column of the `AUTHORS` table in the `pubs` database.

VB.NET:

```
Dim strLName As SqlString = dtReader.GetSqlString(dtReader.GetOrdinal("au_lname"))
```

C#:

```
SqlSingle strLName = dtReader.GetSqlString(dtReader.GetOrdinal("au_lname"));
```

The GetSqlValue Method

This method gets the value of the specified data column as SQL Server native format object. It provides generic access to the data. It is equivalent to the `GetValue` method discussed in the `OleDbDataReader` class with the difference that the returned `Object` represents the SQL Server specific data types. For example if you call the `GetType` method on the `Object` returned by this method, it will be of type `System.SqlString` if the specified column stores the value in one of the string formats. For more detail refer to the discussion of the `GetValue` method in the `OleDbDataReader` class.

VB.NET:

```
NotOverridable Public Function GetSqlValue( _
    ByVal ordinal As Integer, _
) As Object
```

C#:

```
public object GetSqlValue(
    int ordinal,
);
```

The following code gets the value of the data column at ordinal position 1.

VB.NET:

```
Dim fldVal As Object = dtReader.GetSqlValue(1)
```

C#:

```
object fldVal = dtReader.GetValue(1);
```

The GetSqlValues Method

This method gets the values of all the data columns for the current record in the `SqlDataReader` object.

VB.NET:

```
NotOverridable Public Function GetSqlValues( _
    ByVal values () As Object _
) As Integer
```

C#:

```
public int GetSqlValues(
    object[] values
);
```

The following table describes the parameter for this method:

Parameter	Type	Description
Values	Object	An `Object` array to copy the attribute fields into

This method is similar to `GetValues` method discussed in `OleDbDataReader` section. The only difference is that field values are returned as strongly typed SQL Server specific data type objects. Refer to the discussion of the `GetValues` method in the `OleDbDataReader` class for more details on this method.

The following code illustrates the use of this property.

VB.NET:

```
Dim fldValues (dtReader.FieldCount) As Object
dtReader.GetSqlValues(fldValues)
```

C#:

```
object [] fldValues = new object [dtReader.FieldCount];
dtReader.GetSqlValues(fldValues);
```

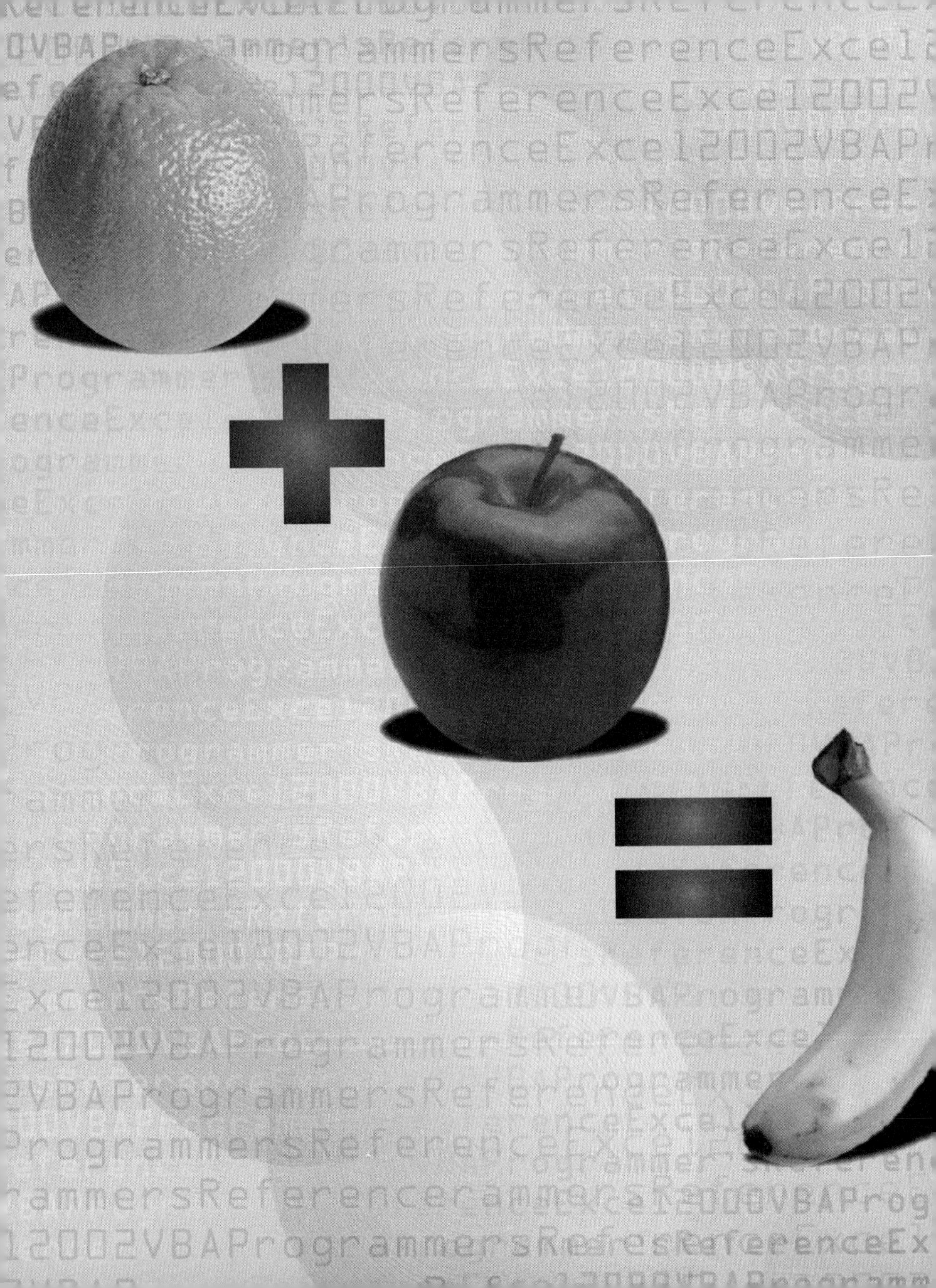

7

The DataAdapter Object

The `DataAdapter` object is used to retrieve data from a data source and populate the `DataTable` objects in a `DataSet`. It provides a conduit between the data source and the `DataSet`. Unlike the `DataReader` object discussed in the previous chapter, the `DataAdapter` keeps the connection open with the data store only long enough that the command gets executed and the `DataSet` gets populated with data. This follows the scalability design pattern of obtaining the resources as late as possible and releasing them as soon as possible. If the connection is open prior to calling `Fill` method, the `DataAdapter` does not close it after finishing the execution. After the execution of `DataAdapter`, it maintains no link with the `DataSet` it populates. Therefore, the same `DataAdapter` object can be used to populate multiple instances of `DataSet` objects.

Unlike the `DataReader`, which is targeted more towards performance than functionality, the `DataAdapter` provides a lot of functionality. This does not mean that the `DataAdapter` objects do not provide a good performance and there is no use for it. The two data access mechanisms have their own pros and cons. There are certain situations where the `DataReader` is more suited than the `DataAdapter`. For example, if we want to access the data only for displaying the records, where no updating of the records will be done, then the use of the `DataReader` is a more efficient approach. The `DataAdapter` uses the `DataReader` internally to populate the `DataSet`. It reads the records one at a time and caches them in memory.

These are some of the situations in which we might think of using the `DataAdapter`:

- ❑ If we need to navigate back and forth through the records, use the `DataAdapter`. The `DataReader` cannot be used in this case because it provides a forward only access.

- ❑ If we need to update the data and a number of records at a time. Although the `DataReader` can be used to update the records but it is not very efficient.

- ❑ If we need to access relational tables. The `DataReader` does provide any direct functionality to establish relations between the in-memory data tables.

- ❑ If we need to read and write the data from and to an XML file. The `DataSet` populated by the `DataAdapter` can be used to directly write the records into XML files using `DataSet` class's `WriteXml` method and the `ReadXml` method can be used to populate the `DataSet` from an XML file. Refer to Chapter 5, The DataSet Object, for more details on these methods.

The `DataAdapter` object also provides properties, such as `InsertCommand`, `UpdateCommand`, and `DeleteCommand` that can be used to commit the changes, made to the records in the `DataTable` objects in the `DataSet`, to the data source. This is accomplished by calling the `Update` method on the `DataAdapter` object. The `DataAdapter` also supports some very useful events such as `RowUpdating` and `RowUpdated`. An application can provide event handlers for these events to have finer control over the data access flow.

The `DataAdapter` objects, `SqlDataAdapter`, `OleDbDataAdapter`, and `OdbcDataAdapter`, inherit from `DbDataAdapter` class, which is defined in `System.Data.Common` namespace. All the `DataAdapter` classes implement two interfaces, `IDbDataAdapter` (defined in `System.Data` namespace) and `ICloneable` (defined in `System` namespace). The definitions of these `DataAdapter` objects are as follows:

```
Public Class SqlDataAdapter
      Inherits DbDataAdapter
      Implements ICloneable, IDbDataAdapter
```

```
Public Class OleDbDataAdpater
      Inherits DbDataAdapter
Implements ICloneable, IDbDataAdapter
```

```
Public Class OdbcDataAdapter
Inherits DbDataAdapter
Implements ICloneable, IDbDataAdapter
```

The DataAdapter

This is the base class for all the `DataAdapater` classes and is defined in `System.Data.Common` namespace.

VB.NET:
```
MustInherit Public Class DataAdapter
      Inherits Component
      Implements IDataAdapter
```

C#:
```
public abstract class DataAdapter : Component, IDataAdpater
```

This class implements `IDataAdapter` interface (defined in `System.Data` namespace), which provides the definitions of common set of properties and methods that every `DataAdapater` class, for example, `SqlDataAdapter`, `OleDbDataAdapter`, and `OdbcDataAdapter`, must implement. A client cannot directly create an instance of this abstract class. The classes that inherit from this abstract class can override the implementation of this class's properties and methods and provide some extra set of managed provider specific functionality.

The `DataAdapter` class provides the building blocks for disconnected data access mechanism from a data source. It serves as bridge between the `DataSet` and the data source for retrieving and updating data. The class provides two very useful methods, `Fill` and `Update`, which can be used to keep the records in the `DataSet` and data source up to date. These are the two methods that serve as the transportation mechanism for the traffic between `DataSet` and the data source.

The DataAdapter Constructor ()

This is the default constructor for DataAdapter class:

VB.NET:

```
Protected Sub New()
```

C#:

```
protected DataAdapter();
```

When a new instance of a derived DataAdapter class is created, this base class constructor initializes values of the following properties:

❑ AcceptChangesDuringFill set to true

❑ MissingMappingAction set to MissingMappingAction.Passthrough

❑ MissingSchemaAction set to MissingSchemaAction.Add

❑ TableMappings set to an array of TableMappings objects

These properties control the behavior of the Fill method, which is used to retrieve the records from the data source. The constructor initializes these properties to the values that correspond to the very commonly encountered way of accessing data. For details on these properties refer to the respective property's section.

DataAdapter Properties

The AcceptChangesDuringFill Property

Gets or sets the Boolean flag which indicates whether the AcceptChanges method will be called on DataRow while it is being added to DataTable during Fill method.

VB.NET:

```
Public Property AcceptChangesDuringFill As Boolean
```

C#:

```
public bool AcceptChangesDuringFill {get; set;}
```

When the Fill method is called on the DataAdapter, this property plays a very crucial role in populating and updating the information in DataTable objects. After the data has been retrieved from a data source, the BeginLoadData method is called on the DataTable, which in turn calls LoadDataRow method to populate the DataRow object for the data row being loaded.

The second parameter for this method is the Boolean flag, indicating whether the AcceptChanges method will be called on this DataRow object or not. By default the AcceptChangesDuringFill property value is set to true. It means that if there is any DataRow present in the DataTable before Fill method is called, the current data and the data source will be compared. If any changes are also detected, AcceptChanges method will be invoked to commit all the changes. This will set the RowSatate property value of the DataRow to DataRowState.Unchanged. If the property value is also set to false, AcceptChanges method will not be called during Fill, and newly added rows will be treated as inserted rows with the RowState set to Added.

The MissingMappingsAction Property

Gets or sets the action to be taken if there is no matching table or column available in the `DataSet` for the data from the data source.

VB.NET:

```
Public Property MissingMappingAction As _ MissingMappingAction
```

C#:

```
public MissingMappingAction MissingMappingAction {get; set;}
```

The `DataSet` object passed to `Fill` method may or may not have and `DataTable` object added to it. Even if there is a `DataTable` object associated, its schema may not match with the data coming from the data source. In case this mapping is missing, there are three options that a client has. These options are also specified through this property by specifying the `MissingMappingAction` enumeration. This has the following possible values:

- ❑ `Error` – Don't continue with the operation, and raise the appropriate `SystemException` exception

- ❑ `Ignore` – This option will make the `Fill` operation ignore the table for which mapping is missing and continue on with the rest of the tables, if any

- ❑ `Passthrough` – If any data column or table is missing, managed provider will create that and add it to `DataSet` object

`MissingMappingAction.Passthrough` is the default value set for the property when a new `DataAdapter` object is created. The following code will raise a `SystemException` exception, because the value of this property has been set to `MissingMappingAction.Error`, and `DataTable` object does not map to the `Customers` table in the data source.

VB.NET:

```
Dim sqlCmd As SqlCommand = new SqlCommand()
sqlCmd.CommandText = "SELECT * FROM Customers"
Dim dtAdapater As SqlDataAdapter = new SqlDataAdapter ()
DataAdapter.SelectCommand = sqlCmd
' If the mapiing is missing, raise the error.
dtAdapter.MissingMappingAction = MissingMappingAction.Error
' Create new DataTable object and invoke Fill method.
Dim dtTable = new DataTable()
Dim iNumRecords As Integer = dtAdapter.Fill (dtTable)
```

C#:

```
SqlCommand sqlCmd = new SqlCommand ();
sqlCmd.CommandText = "SELECT * FROM Customers";
SqlDataAdapter dtAdapter = new SqlDataAdapter ();
dtAdapter.SelectCommand = sqlCmd;
// If the table mapping is missing, raise exception.
dtAdapter.MissingMappingAction = MissingMappingAction.Error;
// Create new DataTable object and invoke Fill method.
DataTable dtTable = new DataTable ();
int iNumRecords = dtAdapter.Fill (dtTable);
```

It is recommended that the value of this property should be set to
`MissingMappingAction.Passthrough` unless you have complete information about the data
source's table to insert a new `DataTable` object before invoking `Fill` method. If you are loading the
table's schema information from an **XSD** (XML Schema Defintion) or an XML file, and you don't want
the `DataAdapter` to alter it, then you definitely should set this property's value to
`MissingMappingAction.Error`. This indicates to the `DataAdapter` that it does not need to fetch
any schema information from the data source to populate the schema table, because the caller has
already provided it.

The MissingSchemaAction Property

Gets or sets the action to be taken when existing `DataSet` schema does not match with the schema of
the incoming data.

VB.NET:

```
Overridable Public Property MissingSchemaAction As _
MissingSchemaAction
```

C#:

```
public MissingSchemaAction MissingSchemaAction {get; set;}
```

The execution of `Fill` method checks if the `DataSet` or `DataTable` object passed to it has any
column schema information present in it. Based on whether or not this information is present, four
courses of action might be taken. The `MissingSchemaAction` property sets one of these options as a
`MissingSchemaAction` enumeration value. The enumeration can have one of the following values:

❑ `Error` – The `Fill` operation is not completed, and a `SystemException` exception is thrown

❑ `Ignore` – This value indicates that the `Fill` operation should add only those data columns to
the `DataTable` for which schema information is present, and ignored the rest of the columns

❑ `Add` – If the `DataTable` in the `DataSet` object passed to the `Fill` method has no information
about the columns, the necessary data columns will be added to the `DataTable`, based on the
schema it retrieves from the data source

❑ `AddWithKey` – This value indicates that if the `DataSet` does not contain any schema
information for the data columns of `DataTable`, then it should be added, using the schema
information obtained from the data source

This action sounds very much like the previous enumeration value: `Add`. But there is a big difference
between the two. If the `MissingSchemaAction` property value is set to `Add`, the `Fill` method
populates the `DataSet` with data rows and columns, and no information about the primary key and
constraints is added to the `DataTable`. Whereas setting the property value to `AddWithKey`, checks if
there is any primary key or unique columns present in the data source. If it is, then this information is
also populated in the `DataTable` object in the `DataSet`.

> If the data source has an auto-incrementing column, the `Fill` method with
> `MissingSchemaAction` property value set to `MissingSchemaAction.AddWithKey`
> will add that data column to `DataTable` with `AutoIncrement` property value set to
> true. But the values of `AutoIncrementSeed` and `AutoIncrementStep` will not be
> set by `Fill` operation. These values need to be set explicitly after the call.

The following example shows how to set the value of `MissingSchemaAction` property to `MissingSchemaAction.Error` and set the column information in `DataTable` before calling `Fill` method. Addition of new columns to the `Columns` collection of the `DataTable` explicitly adds the columns mappings for `RegionID` and `RegionDescription` fields.

VB.NET:

```
Dim strCmd As String = "SELECT * FROM REGION"
Dim oledbCmd As New OleDbCommand(strCmd)
Dim dtAdapter As OleDbDataAdapter  = New OleDbDataAdapter ()
dtAdapter.SelectCommand = oledbCmd
dtAdapter.MissingMappingAction = MissingMappingAction.Passthrough
dtAdapter.MissingSchemaAction = MissingSchemaAction.Error
Dim dtTable As DataTable  = New DataTable ()
dtTable.Columns.Add ("RegionID")
dtTable.Columns.Add ("RegionDescription")
Dim iNumRecords As Integer = dtAdapter.Fill (dtTable)
```

C#:

```
string strCmd = "SELECT * FROM REGION";
OleDbCommand oledbCmd = new OleDbCommand (strCmd);
OleDbDataAdapter dtAdapter = new OleDbDataAdapter ();
dtAdapter.SelectCommand = oledbCmd;
dtAdapter.MissingMappingAction = MissingMappingAction.Passthrough;
dtAdapter.MissingSchemaAction = MissingSchemaAction.Error;
DataTable dtTable = new DataTable ();
dtTable.Columns.Add ("RegionID");
dtTable.Columns.Add ("RegionDescription");
int iNumRecords = dtAdapter.Fill (dtTable);
```

In the code above, if `RegionID` and `RegionDescription` data columns are not added to `DataTable` before calling `Fill` method, a `SystemException` exception will be thrown. This is because `MissingSchemaAction` property is set to `Error`, and so column information is expected in the `DataTable`.

The TableMappings Property

Gets the `TableMappingsCollection` object describing the master mapping between the data source tables and the `DataTable` objects in `DataSet`.

VB.NET:

```
Public ReadOnly Property TableMappings As _
    DataTableMappingCollection
```

C#:

```
public DataTableMappingCollection TableMappings {get;}
```

When the `Fill` method retrieves the data from the back end data source, it checks if there is any table mapping provided in the `DataSet`. This table mapping dictates how the incoming data tables will be mapped to the `DataTable` objects in the `DataSet`. If no table mappings are provided, the framework maps the incoming data table to default table name `Table`. Also if there are multiple incoming tables then the tables are mapped to `Table`, `Table1`, `Table2`, and so on.

We can use this property to get the `DataTableMappingsCollection` for the `DataAdapter`, and then remove or add our own `DataTableMapping` objects in the collection using properties and methods of the `DataTableMappingsCollection` class. Each object in this collection can be accessed using the `Item` property.

The following code shows how the `DataTableMapping` objects can be added to the `DataTableMappingCollection` of a `DataAdapter`. It is specifying that the `Customers` table from the data source should be mapped to the table `MyCustomers`. The execution of `Fill` method creates a new `DataTable` named `MyCustomers` and populates it with the records. If the table mappings is not provides, the `Fill` method will create `DataTable` with default name `Table`.

VB.NET:

```
Dim DataAdapter as dtAdapter = new DataAdapter ()
dtAdapter.TableMappings.Add ("Customers", "MyCustomers")
```

C#:

```
DataAdapter dtAdapter = new DataAdapter ();
dtAdapter.TableMappings.Add ("Customers", "MyCustomers");
```

The `DataTableMapping` class has the following properties that can be used to completely define the one to one relation between the source data table and the `DataTable` in the `DataSet`:

Property	Description
SourceTable	This property indicates the case-sensitive name of the data table coming from data source.
DataSetTable	This property indicates the name of the `DataTable` in `DataSet` to which `SourceTable` data table from source will be mapped.
ColumnMappings	This returns the `DataColumnMappings` collection object for a given `DataTable`. This collection can be used to access individual `DataColumnMapping` objects that specify how the data columns from the source table are mapped to the columns in `DataTable` of the `DataSet`.

These properties of the `DataTableMapping` object can also be set directly through the constructor that takes these parameters as arguments. For example:

```
Dim orderTblMapping As DataTableMapping _
  = New DataTableMapping ("Orders", "MyOrders")
Dim detailTblMapping As DataTableMapping
  = New DataTableMapping("OrderDetails", "MyOrderDetails")
Dim dtAdapter As New DataAdapter ()
dtAdapter.TableMappings.Add (orderTblMapping)
dtAdapter.TableMapping.Add (detailTblMapping)
```

If no `DataColumnMapping` is specified, then the `DataSet` adds the columns as provided by the source. If the `Fill` operation encounters any duplicate column names it generates pseudo names for the subsequent columns by adding numeric suffixes at the end of the original column name. For example, if there are three `Address` columns in the data source then these will be mapped to `Address`, `Address1`, and `Address2` columns in `DataTable`.

The `DataColumnMapping` class provides the following properties to completely specify the column mapping for a `DataTable`:

Property	Description
SourceColumn	This property gets/sets the case-sensitive name of the source column that will be mapped
DataSetColumn	This property gets/sets the name of the column in `DataTable` to which `SourceColumn` will be mapped to

The following example shows how the column mapping collection can be added to a `DataTableMapping` object for `Region` table of `NorthWind` database:

```
// Create column mapping for RegionId column
DataColumnMapping idColMap = new DataColumnMapping
    ("RegionId", "MyRegionID");
// Create column mapping for description column
DataColumnMapping desColMap = new DataColumnMapping
    ("RegionDescription", "MyDescription");
// Create table mapping to map Region table to MyRegion table
DataTableMapping dtTblMapping = new DataTableMapping
    ("Region", "MyRegion");
// Add the column mappings to DataColumnMappings collection
dtTblMapping.ColumnMappings.Add (idColMap);
dtTblMapping.ColumnMappings.Add (desColMap);
// Add this DataTableMapping object to DataAdapter.
DataDapter dtAdapter = new DataAdapter ();
dtAdapter.TableMappings.Add (dtTblMapping);
```

DataAdapter Methods

The CloneInternals Method

The method creates a copy of this instance of `DataAdapter` object.

VB.NET:
```
Overridable Protected Function CloneInternals() As DataAdapter
```

C#:
```
protected virtual DataAdapter CloneInternals();
```

This is a **protected** method that all the derived `DataAdapter` classes can override to provide their own implementation. The derived class must call the base class's `CloneInternals` method. This method clones all the properties except the connection object that the original `DataAdapter` object uses to connect to data source. The cloned `DataAdapter` object shares the connection with the original object.

The following C# code shows the high-level pseudo implementation of this method in the base class. It starts with creation of a new instance of `DataAdapter` class object. Then the properties associated with original object are copied over to the new `DataAdapter` object. The method does a shallow copy of the associated connection object:

```
protected virtual DataAdapter CloneInternals ()
{
    Type dtType = GetType ();
    Object ob = Activator::CreateInstance(dtType);
    DataAdapter dtAdapter = (DataAdapter)ob;
    // Clone the AcceptChangesDuringFill property value
    dtAdapter.AcceptChangesDuringFill = this.AcceptChangesDuringFill;
    // Clone the MissingMappingAction property value.
    dtAdapter.MissingMappingAction = this.MissingMappingAction;
    // Clone the MissingSchemaAction property value.
    dtAdapter.MissingSchemaAction = this.MissingSchemaAction;
    // Clone the TableMappings property value by enumerating
    // each entry in this TableMapping and setting them in
    // newly created DataAdapter object.
    IEnumerator en = this.TableMappings.GetEnumerator ();
    while (en.MoveNext ())
    {
        dtAdapter.TableMappings.Add (((DataTableMapping)en.Current).Clone ());
    }

    dtAdapter.SelectCommand.Connection = this.SelectCommand.Connection;
    return dtAdapter;
}
```

The CreateTableMappings Method

The method creates a new `DataTableMappingCollection` object for `DataAdapter` object.

VB.NET:

```
Overridable Protected Function CreateTableMappings() As _
DataTableMappingCollection
```

C#:

```
protected virtual DataTableMappingCollection CreateTableMappings();
```

This method is called when we call the `TableMappings` property on the `DataAdapter` object to get the table mapping collection, if one already does not exist. The implementation of `TableMappings` property calls an internal method, `get_TableMappings`. This method first checks if the internal `tableMappings` variable is a valid object or not. If it is not, it calls the virtual method `CreateTableMappings` to create new instance of the table mapping. This is a virtual method that every derived `DataAdapter` class can override.

The Fill Method

Populates the `DataSet` or `DataTable` with new or updated records from the data source, and, if necessary, creates the default `DataTable` named `Table` in the `DataSet`.

VB.NET:

```
MustOverride Public Function Fill( _
    ByVal dataSet As DataSet _
) As Integer
```

C#:

```
public abstract int Fill(
    DataSet dataSet
);
```

Parameter	Type	Description
dataset	DataSet	DataSet to be populated with data records

This is an abstract method, and the base class does not provide any implementation for it. The derived class must provide the managed provider specific or generic implementation for this method. For details refer to discussion of Fill method in DbDataAdapter and OleDbDataAdapter sections.

The FillSchema Method

Populates the DataSet with the tables containing schema information received from the data source. If no table mapping is provided to DataAdapter, the newly created DataTable will have the default name Table. The discussion of this method in DbDataAdapter class provides a detailed example showing the usage.

VB.NET:

```
MustOverride Public Function FillSchema( _
ByVal dataSet As DataSet, _
ByVal schemaType As SchemaType _
) As DataTable()
```

C#:

```
public abstract DataTable[] FillSchema(
DataSet dataSet,
SchemaType schemaType
);
```

The following table describes the parameters of this method:

Parameters	Type	Description
dataSet	DataSet	DataSet that will be populated with data table's schema information
schemaType	SchemaType	The value for this enumeration specifies how to treat the existing schema in the DataSet when new schema information is populated from data source

The SchemaType enumeration can have one of the following values:

❑ Source – Specifying this value for the SchemaType indicates that FillSchema should ignore all the existing table mappings in DataSet, and should return new set of DataTable objects, describing schemas, without applying any transformations to the schema obtained from data source. The DataTables returned in the DataSet will have default names Table, Table1, and so on.

❑ Mapped – This is the recommended value to be set for SchemaType variable. This value indicates to framework that if there is any existing table mapping set for the DataAdapter, use that to populate the DataSet. For example, if there is a table mapping that maps source table SrcTable to DtTable, then the table returned by FillSchema method will have the name DtTable and same schema as was set prior to method call.

This is an abstract method; therefore, every derived `DataAdapter` must provide its implementation. All three managed providers do not provide separate implementations: they use the generic implementation provides by their base class `DbDataAdapter`. For details, refer to this method's discussion in `DbDataAdapter` class.

The GetFillParameters Method

The method gets the stored procedure and/or return parameters used by the SQL `SELECT` command during the `Fill` method.

VB.NET:

```
MustOverride Public Function GetFillParameters() As IDataParameter()
```

C#:

```
public abstract IDataParameter[] GetFillParameters();
```

The method returns an array of `IDataPatameter` objects. Each of these `IDataParameter` objects contains the complete information about the input and output parameters for the stored procedure, used by the SQL `SELECT` command, set in the `connection` object of the `DataAdapter`.

This is an abstract method and every derived `DataAdapter` class must provide the implementation for it. The managed providers, `SqlDataAdapter`, `OleDbDataAdapter`, and `OdbcDataAdapter`, use the implementation of this method provided by their base class `DbDataAdapter`.

The following code sets one input and three output parameters for `GetEmployeeInfo` stored procedure for `Employees` data table in the `Northwind` database. After the successful execution of the `Fill` method, the `GetFillParameters` method is called to get the values returned in output parameters:

```
CREATE PROCEDURE GetEmployeeInfo
 @FirstName varchar(255) Output,
 @LastName varchar(255) Output,
 @BirthDate datetime Output,
 @EmployeeID INT
AS
SELECT
 @FirstName = FirstName,
 @LastName = LastName,
 @BirthDate = BirthDate
FROM Employees WHERE EmployeeId = @EmployeeID
RETURN 0
GO
```

The implementation creates a new `OleDbConnection` by specifying the connection string as the constructor parameter. Although the `Open` method has been called exclusively on the connection, it is not essential for using the `DataAdapter`. As it has been mentioned in the introduction of chapter that the `DataAdapter` will open the connection by itself if it is in the closed state. All the input and out parameters for the stored procedure are added to the Parameters collection of the `OleDbCommand`. Successful execution of the Fill method returns three data column values as output parameter of the stored procedure. To get the values of these parameters, the `GetFillParameters` method is called.

VB.NET:

```
Dim strConn As String = "Provider= SQLOLEDB.1; Data Source=localhost;" & _
                         " Initial Catalog=NorthWind; User ID=sa; Pwd=;"
Dim oledbConn As New OleDbConnection(strConn)
' Open the connection with database.
oledbConn.Open()
' Create a new command to retrieve records.
Dim cmd As New OleDbCommand()
With cmd
    .CommandType = CommandType.StoredProcedure
    .Connection = oledbConn
    .CommandTimeout = 60
    .CommandText = "GetEmployeeInfo"
End With

' Create and add stored procedure parameters to the command object.
Dim fnameParam As New OleDbParameter("@FirstName", OleDbType.VarChar, 255)
fnameParam.Direction = ParameterDirection.Output

Dim lnameParam As New OleDbParameter("@LastName", OleDbType.VarChar, 255)
lnameParam.Direction = ParameterDirection.Output

Dim bdateParam As New OleDbParameter("@BirthDate", OleDbType.Date)
bdateParam.Direction = ParameterDirection.Output

Dim empidParam As New OleDbParameter("@EmployeeID", OleDbType.Integer)
empidParam.Direction = ParameterDirection.Input
empidParam.Value = 2

cmd.Parameters.Add(empidParam)
cmd.Parameters.Add(fnameParam)
cmd.Parameters.Add(lnameParam)
cmd.Parameters.Add(bdateParam)

' Create SqlDataAdapter object for exceution of SELECT query.
Dim dtAdapter As New OleDbDataAdapter()
dtAdapter.SelectCommand = cmd
' Execute the command by calling Fill method
Dim dtTable As New DataTable()
dtAdapter.Fill(dtTable)
' Get the output patameters returned by execution of procedure.
Dim oledbParams() As IDataParameter = dtAdapter.GetFillParameters()
Dim strFirstName As String = oledbParams(1).Value
```

C#:

```
string strConn = "Provider= SQLOLEDB.1; Data Source=localhost;
  Initial Catalog=NorthWind; User ID=sa; Pwd=;";
OleDbConnection oledbConn = new OleDbConnection (strConn);
// Open the connection with database.
oledbConnection.Open ();
// Create a new command to retrieve records.
OledbCommand cmd= new OledbCommand ();
cmd.CommandType = CommandType.StoredProcedure;
cmd.CommandTimeout = 60;
```

```
cmd.Connection = oledbConn;
cmd.CommandText = "GetEmployeeInfo";
// Create and add stored procedure parameters to the command object.
OleDbParameter fnameParam = new OleDbParameter ("@FirstName",
        OleDbType.VarChar, 255);
fnameParam.Direction = ParameterDirection.Output;

OleDbParameter lnameParam = new OleDbParameter ("@LastName",
      OleDbType.VarChar, 255);
lnameParam.Direction = ParameterDirection.Output;

OleDbParameter bdateParam = new OleDbParameter ("@BirthDate",
      OleDbType.Date);
bdateParam.Direction = ParameterDirection.Output;

OleDbParameter empidParam = new OleDbParameter ("@EmployeeID",
      OleDbType.Integer);
empidParam.Direction = ParameterDirection.Input;
empidParam.Value = 2;

cmd.Parameters.Add (empidParam);
cmd.Parameters.Add (fnameParam);
cmd.Parameters.Add (lnameParam);
cmd.Parameters.Add (bdateParam);

// Create SqlDataAdapter object for exceution of SELECT query.
OleDbDataAdapter dtAdapter = new OleDbDataAdapter ();
dtAdapter.SelectCommand = cmd;
// Execute the command by calling Fill method
DataTable dtTable = new DataTable ();
dtAdapter.Fill (dtTable);
// Get the output patameters returned by execution of procedure.
IDataParameter [] oledbParams = dtAdapter.GetFillParameters ();
string strFirstName = oledbParams[1].Value;
```

The ShouldSerializeTableMappings Method

The method gets the `Boolean` flag indicating if one or more `TableMapping` objects are present in the `DataSet` of `DataAdapter`. The value returned, also indicates if the table mappings can be persisted or not.

VB.NET:

```
Overridable Protected Function ShouldSerializeTableMappings() As _
    Boolean
```

C#:

```
protected virtual bool ShouldSerializeTableMappings();
```

The method returns `true` if there is one or more table mappings set for the `DataAdapter`, otherwise it returns `false`. If there is no `TableMapping` object in the `DataAdapter`, then there is no need to serialize the table mappings. This is a protected method. A third party data provider `DataAdapter` that derives from this method can make use of this method. If the provider decides to support serialization, then based on the value returned by this method s/he can decide if the table mappings need to be serialized or not.

291

This method could be very helpful if you are creating your own control that incorporates the `DataAdapter` object. When you persist the control, then based on the value returned by this method, you can persist the table mappings so that these can be reinstated when the control is read from the persisted state.

The Update Method

The method calls the `INSERT`, `UPDATE` or `DELETE` SQL statement depending on the `RowState` property value of each `DataRow` contained in the `DataSet`.

VB.NET:

```
MustOverride Public Function Update( _
    ByVal dataSet As DataSet _
    ) As Integer
```

C#:

```
public abstract int Update(
DataSet dataSet
);
```

The following table describes the parameter of this method:

Parameter	Type	Description
dataSet	DataSet	The DataSet containing the updated records

The method returns the number of data rows that were updated successfully during this `Update` operation. This is an abstract method and every derived class must provide its implementation. For details, refer to discussion of this method in `DbDataAdapter` class.

The DbDataAdapter

The `DbDataAdpater` class provides the base class functionality for the entire managed provider specific `DataAdapter` classes.

VB.NET:

```
MustInherit Public Class DBDataAdapter
        Inherits DataAdapter
```

C#:

```
public abstract class DBDataAdapter : DataAdapter
```

This class is derived from `DataAdapter` class and provides most of the generic implementation used by the two managed provider classes, `OleDbDataAdapter` and `SqlDataAdapter`. You cannot create a new instance of this class directly, because this is an abstract class. The public members of this class can be accessed through the `OleDbDataAdapter`, `SqlDataAdapter` or any class derived from this class. The derived classes must implement all the abstract class members and override the implementation of virtual members to provide managed provider specific features.

DbDataAdapter Constructor

The DbDataAdapter Constructor ()

This is the default constructor for the DbDataAdapter class.

VB.NET:

```
Protected Sub New()
```

C#:

```
protected DataAdapter();
```

This is a **protected** constructor for this class. Therefore, the consumers of the DataAdapter class cannot directly create a new instance of this class. The public members of this class can be accessed through the derived class provided for each managed provider. For SQL Server managed provider SqlDataAdapter class provides the access, for OLE DB managed provider OleDbDataAdapter class provides the access and for native ODBC drivers the OdbcDataAdapter class provides the access to the public members. This derived class's constructor calls the base class DataAdapter constructor, which initializes the properties MissingMappingAction, MissingSchemaAction, and AcceptChangesDuring to their default values Passthrough, Add, and True respectively.

DbDataAdapter Properties

The DbDataAdapter class inherits all the properties from the base class DataAdapter and does not define any new properties. For details, refer to the properties of the DataAdapter class.

DbDataAdapter Methods

The CreateRowUpdatedEvent Method

Creates a new instance of the RowUpdatedEventArgs class.

VB.NET:

```
MustOverride Protected Function CreateRowUpdatedEvent( _
ByVal dataRow As DataRow, _
ByVal command As IDbCommand, _
ByVal statementType As StatementType, _
ByVal tableMapping As DataTableMapping _
) As RowUpdatedEventArgs
```

C#:

```
protected abstract RowUpdatedEventArgs CreateRowUpdatedEvent(
DataRow dataRow,
IDbCommand command,
StatementType statementType,
DataTableMapping tableMapping
);
```

The following table describes the parameters of this method:

Parameter	Type	Description
dataRow	DataRow	The DataRow that updated the record in the data source
command	IDbCommand	The command object that was executed by the Update method to update the row
statementType	StatementType	The type of command that updated the row. This could be either SELECT, UPDATE, DELETE, or INSERT
tableMapping	DataTableMapping	The DataTableMapping that provides the master mapping between a source data table and the DataTable in the DataSet

This is an abstract method and every derived DataAdapter class needs to provide the implementation for it. If the derived class inherits from a base class that provides the implementation of this method then the derived class must call the base class's implementation for this method. If you inherit directly from DbDataAdapter class, however there is no base class implementation that you can call. Due to the protected access, a consumer of the DataAdapter cannot call this method.

When the Update method is called on the DataAdapter object, if data record for a DataRow in the table gets updated, the CreateRowUpdatedEvent is called in order to create a new instance of RowUpdatedEventArgs object to pass to event handler delegate for RowUpdatedEvent. This method is called after the row has been updated. The RowUpdatedEventArgs is an abstract class. This being the case, every derived DataAdapter provides a derived class for this event argument class. The SQL Server Managed Provider creates a new instance of SqlRowUpdatedEventArgs class and OLE DB managed provider creates a new instance of OleDbRowUpdatedEventArgs class when CreateRowUpdatedEvent method gets called during Update method.

Following code shows how a derived DataAdapter class can provide implementation for this method to return the managed provider specific event arguments object. The method does not call the base class implementation, because this class has been derived directly from DbDataAdapter, which does not have any implementation of this method.

VB.NET:
```
Protected Overrides Function RowUpdatedEventArgs CreateRowUpdatedEvent ( _
                              dataRow As DataRow,
                              command As IdbCommand,
                              statementType As StatementType,
                              tableMapping As DataTableMapping)
     Return New WroxRowUpdatedEventArgs( dataRow, command, _
                              StatementType, tableMapping)
  End Function
```

C#:
```
override protected RowUpdatedEventArgs CreateRowUpdatedEvent(
                              DataRow dataRow,
                              IDbCommand command,
                              StatementType statementType,
```

```
                                        DataTableMapping tableMapping)
    {
        return new WroxRowUpdatedEventArgs(dataRow, command,
                                    statementType, tableMapping);
    }
```

In the above sample code `Wrox` is a derived data provider.

The CreateRowUpdatingEvent Method

The method creates a new instance of the `RowUpdatingEventArgs` class.

VB.NET:

```
MustOverride Protected Function CreateRowUpdatingEvent( _
    ByVal dataRow As DataRow, _
    ByVal command As IDbCommand, _
    ByVal statementType As StatementType, _
    ByVal tableMapping As DataTableMapping _
) As RowUpdatingEventArgs
```

C#:

```
protected abstract RowUpdatingEventArgs CreateRowUpdatingEvent(
    DataRow dataRow,
    IDbCommand command,
    StatementType statementType,
    DataTableMapping tableMapping
);
```

This method has the same parameters as `CreateRowUpdatedEvent` method. Refer to the previous section for explanation of the parameters.

Like the `CreateRowUpdatedEvent` method, this is an abstract method and every derived `DataAdapter` class needs to provide the implementation for it. It follows the same rules for calling the base class implementation.

This method, like `CreateRowUpdatedEvent`, gets called during an `Update` operation, with the difference that it is called before any changes are made to the `DataRow`, whereas the `CreateRowUpdatedEvent` method is called after the data row has been updated. Like `RowUpdatedEventArgs` class, the `RowUpdatingEventArgs` is also an abstract class. SQL Server managed provider creates a new instance of `SqlRowUpdatingEventArgs` class and OLE DB managed provider creates a new instance of `OleDbRowUpdatingEventArgs` class, when the `Update` method is called on the `DataAdapter` object.

The following code shows how a derived `DataAdapter` class can provide implementation for this method to return the managed provider specific event arguments object.

VB.NET:

```
Protected Overrides Function RowUpdatingEventArgs CreateRowUpdatingEvent ( _
                            dataRow As DataRow,
                            command As IdbCommand,
```

```
                                        statementType As StatementType,
                                        tableMapping As DataTableMapping)
        Return New WroxRowUpdatingEventArgs( dataRow, command, _
                                        StatementType, tableMapping)
    End Function
```

C#:

```
override protected RowUpdatingEventArgs CreateRowUpdatingEvent(
                            DataRow dataRow,
                            IDbCommand command,
                            StatementType statementType,
                            DataTableMapping tableMapping)
{
    return new WroxRowUpdatingEventArgs(dataRow, command,
                            statementType, tableMapping);
}
```

In the above sample code, Wrox is a derived data provider having the following definition:

```
public class WroxDataAdapter : DbDataAdapter, ICloneable, IDbDataAdapter
```

The Fill Method

The Fill method adds or updates the rows of data in the DataSet object and creates DataTable if none have been created in the DataSet. This method acts the data flow conduit that transports the records from the data source to the DataSet. Therefore, it is very important to understand this operation and how the values of various properties can effect the operation. The DbDataAdapter class provides eight overloaded implementations of this method. Of these eight implementations only four have the public access attribute. The other protected implementations are used internally by the public Fill method implementations to retrieve the data from the data source. The syntax and parameters for all the overloaded methods are presented at the end of this method's discussion.

All implementations of the Fill method provide the mechanism of retrieving the data from a data source, and populating the DataSet and the DataTable that has been provided by the caller. This method not only fetches the records data, but also retrieves the table schema from the data source. To query the data it uses the SELECT SQL query statement set in the command object (SqlCommand or OleDbCommand) associated with the DataAdapter. The DataSet populated by this method does not keep any reference to the connection object that was associated with SelectCommand used to query the result sets. The DataSet returned by the method is very much like disconnected Recordset in ADO, meaning that after the data has been retrieved, the DataSet does not stay connected with the data source.

Now lets look at how this method is supposed to work and what functionality it provides. As mentioned earlier this method adds or updates the records in the DataSet. This action is largely dependent on the values of the various properties; MissingSchemaAction, MissingMappingAction, and so on, of the DataAdapter.

The method checks the state of connection (OleDbConnection or SqlConnection) at the start of implementation. If the connection is open before the call, after the successful retrieval of data, it will leave it open. If the connection is also in a Closed state before the call, the method call the Open method on the IDbConnection object associated with the DataAdapter, and, after the data has been retrieved, the Close method is called to put the connection back to Closed state.

The values of the `MissingSchemaAction` and `MissingMappingAction` properties play a very crucial role when the tables and record rows are added to the `DataSet` or `DataTable` object. By default these properties are set to `MissingSchemaAction.Add` and `MissingMappingAction.Passthrough` respectively.

When the `DataTable` and `DataColumn` objects are added to the `DataSet`, the following strategies are implemented:

- ❑ If there is no table mapping specified for the `DataAdapter`, and `MissingMappingAction` is set to `Passthrough`, the new `DataTable` objects are created with default names:

    - ❑ If there is only one source table, it is mapped to `DataTable` with name `Table`.

    - ❑ If the `SELECT` query returns multiple tables, then a separate `DataTable` object is created for each one of them, and the table names are generated by putting a numeric suffix to the default name `Table`, for example `Table`, `Table1`, `Table2`, `Table3`, and so on.

- ❑ If no column mapping is provided, then the `DataColumn` objects are mapped to the source column names. The framework gets the metadata of the table from the data source. From this metadata information, it extracts the column names, as defined in the data source, and uses them to create `DataColumn` objects in the `DataTable`.

    - ❑ If there are columns with duplicate names, then the subsequent columns are named by adding a numeric suffix to the original column name, for example `Phone`, `Phone1`, `Phone2`, and so on. This kind of situation can commonly arise whenever the join queries are used to get data from multiple tables. These multiple tables may have columns with same name. To avoid this kind of situation it is a best practice to use AS clause in the queries to alias the column names.

    - ❑ If the source table has unnamed data columns, or for some reason the schema fails to get the names for the data columns, then those columns are added with names generated by putting a numeric suffix to their names: `Column1`, `Column2`, `Column3`, and so on.

- ❑ If the `MissingSchemaAction` property is set to `AddWithKey`, then the `PrimaryKey` and `Constriants` properties are also set for the `DataTable`, depending on whether the source table provides primary key and constraint information. For more details on how this information is populated, refer to the `FillSchema` method of this class.

- ❑ Calling `Fill` method for the same data source on the same `DataTable` can either merge the matching records or append new rows. It depends on the presence of primary key information in the `DataTable`. If the primary key is created in the schema of the `DataTable`, then the matching data rows get merged with the one that are already present in the `DataTable` otherwise rows will be appended to the `DataTable`.

- ❑ If the `DataSet` contains multiple `DataTable` objects with the names that differ only by case, then the method performs a case sensitive search on table names for mapping the tables with those in data source. If the search fails, then new `DataTable` objects are created for that table and populated with records. If there is only one `DataTable` in the `DataSet` whose name differs by case only, then that `DataTable` gets updated by the records from data source.

Based on the above guidelines there are a couple of recommendations that should be taken into consideration:

❑ Avoid creating `DataTable` or `DataColumn` mappings with numeric suffixes. This could create some very unexpected results when names for duplicate or unnamed data columns and multiple result sets are generated.

❑ Set the `MissinggSchemaAction` property value to `AddWithKey`. This will create the primary key information in `DataTable`, and subsequent calls to `Fill` method will not add duplicate data rows to the table.

The following table describes the effect of values of `MissingSchemaAction` and `AcceptChangesDuringFill` properties on the `Fill` operation:

MissingSchemaAction	AcceptChanges DuringFill	Action
Add	false	The primary key constraint will not be added to the `DataSet`. The duplicate rows will be added to the `DataSet` if the `Fill` method is called again with same SELECT query. Every `DataRow` that is added to the `DataSet` will have its `RowState` property set to `DataRowState.Added`.
Add	true	The primary key constraint will not be added to the `DataSet`. The duplicate rows will be added to the `DataSet` if the `Fill` method is called again with same SELECT query. Due to the fact that `AcceptChanges` will be called after row has been retrieved, every `DataRow` will have its `RowState` property set to `DataRowState.Unchanged`.

MissingSchemaAction	AcceptChanges DuringFill	Action
AddWithKey	false	The primary key constraint will be added when data is retrieved from the data source. This makes sure that no duplicate records get added to the DataSet. AcceptChanges will not be called during Fill operation therefore, every fetched DataRow will have its RowState property value set to DataRowSatate.Added. If you will call Fill method again with same SELECT query, the framework will throw ConstraintException exception and if you event handler for FillError event, this error will show up there. The same exception will also be thrown if the row data changes in the data source during subsequent Fill method calls.
AddWithKey	true	The primary key constraint is added to the DataSet; therefore no duplicate records will get added if Fill method is called again with same SELECT query. Every fetched row will have its RowState property value set to DataRowState.Unchanged because AcceptChanges will be called by the method. If the record is changed in the data source, the subsequent Fill method will update the record in the DataSet without throwing any exception.

The following code snippet calls the Fill method to retrieve 10 records, starting from the starting position of source table the records from Products table of the NorthWind database.

VB.NET:

```
' Create new instance of DataAdapter object and assign the SelectCommand
' Also set the MissingSchemaAction property to create primary key
' information in the DataTable.
Dim dtAdapter As New OleDbDataAdapter ()
```

```
With dtAdapter
   .SelectCommand = New OleDbCommand ("SELECT * FROM Products")
   .SelectCommand.Connection = oledbConn
   .MissingSchemaAction = MissingSchemaAction.AddWithKey
End With
' Create new DataSet object to pass to Fill method.
Dim dtSet As New DataSet("ProductsData")
' Call the Fill method to populate the DataSet with 10 records from start.
Dim iCount As Integer = dtAdapter.Fill(dtSet, 0, 10, "ProductsTable")
```

C#:

```
// Create new instance of DataAdapter object and assign the SelectCommand
// Also set the MissingSchemaAction property to create primary key
// information in the DataTable.
OleDbDataAdapter dtAdapter = new OleDbDataAdapter ();
dtAdapter.SelectCommand = new OleDbCommand ("SELECT * FROM Products");
dtAdapter.MissingSchemaAction = MissingSchemaAction.AddWithKey;
// Create new DataSet object to pass to Fill method.
DataSet dtSet = new DataSet("ProductsData");
// Call the Fill method to populate the DataSet with 10 records from start.
int iCount = dtAdapter.Fill(dtSet, 0, 10, "ProductsTable");
```

If the SELECT query does not return any records, then the method does not raise any exception, returns a value of 0, and no DataRow is added to the DataTable or DataSet. In case some error occurs during the Fill operation, the returned DataSet contains all the records prior to the occurrence of error. Also if an error occurs for a SELECT query returning multiple tables, the process terminates at the result set that generated the error, and the rest of the tables are skipped.

Based on the above discussion you can see that it is very important to understand how the Fill method works and how the values of all the properties, MissingSchemaAction, MissingMappingAction, TableMapping, and AcceptChangesDuringFill can affect the output of this method. The **ILDASM** tool can be utilized to look at IL Code for the actual implementation of this method. The following points will summarize the highlights of the algorithm used by this method:

1. The DataAdapter calls the ExecuteReader method on the SelectCommand associated with it. It checks the state of the connection associated with this command. If this connection is closed, the framework explicitly opens it and the ExecuteReader method is called with CommandBehavior.CloseConnection parameter. This will make sure that connection is closed after the call. If the connection is open prior to calling Fill method, it kept open after the execution of the method.

2. If the client has not provides any schema and/or table mapping information, it obtains that information from the data source. Based on the metadata, the DataTable is created if there is none already. DataColumn objects are also set up in this DataTable. If the MissingSchemaAction property value is set to AddWithKey, the constraints are also set up in the DataTable.

3. The DataAdapter uses the DataReader to fetches all the records that were returned by the SELECT query. Refer to Chapter 6 for more information on how it works.

4. All the records that are obtained from the `DataReader`, are then used to populate the `DataRow` objects in the `DataTable`. If the `AcceptChangesDuringFill` property is set to true, the `AcceptChanges` method is called on the `DataTable`. When the `DataSet` and `DataTable` are populated with the records, all the rules that are discussed earlier are followed to set up the names of `DataColumn` and `DataTable`. If the `SELECT` query returns multiple results then multiple `DataTable` objects are created in the `DataSet` and then populated with records.

Following are the syntax and parameter description of all eight overloaded implementations of `Fill` method.

The Fill (DataSet) Method

This overloaded implementation populates the caller provided `DataSet` object with records from the data source. If the `DataSet` does not contain any `DataTable` object, it creates one with the default name `Table`. The method returns the number of records retrieved from the data source.

VB.NET:

```
Overrides Overloads Public Function Fill( _
   ByVal dataSet As DataSet _
) As Integer
```

C#:

```
public override int Fill(
   DataSet dataSet
);
```

The following table describes the parameters for this overloaded implementation of the method:

Parameter	Type	Description
dataset	DataSet	The `DataSet` that will get populated with rows of records and schema

The Fill (DataTable) Method

This overloaded implementation populates the `DataTable` object; passed in as method parameter, object with records from the data source. The method returns the number of records retrieved from the data source.

VB.NET:

```
Overloads Public Function Fill( _
   ByVal dataTable As DataTable _
) As Integer
```

C#:

```
public int Fill(
   DataTable dataTable
);
```

The following table describes the parameters for this overloaded implementation of the method:

Parameter	Type	Description
dataTable	DataTable	The DataTable that will get populated with rows of records and schema

The Fill (DataSet, String) Method

This overloaded implementation populates the caller provided DataSet object with records from the data source. If the DataSet does not contain any DataTable object, it creates one and maps to the name of the source table name provided by the caller. For example, if the srcTable parameter value is set to EmployeeData, then the name of the DataTable created in the DataSet object will be EmployeeData and not the default name Table. The method returns the number of records retrieved from the data source.

VB.NET:

```
Overloads Public Function Fill( _
    ByVal dataSet As DataSet, _
    ByVal srcTable As String _
) As Integer
```

C#:

```
public int Fill(
    DataSet dataSet,
    string srcTable
);
```

The following table describes the two parameters that the caller of this method needs to supply:

Parameter	Type	Description
dataset	DataSet	The DataSet that will get populated with rows of records and schema
srcTable	String	The name of the source table that will be mapped to the DataTable

If you have used this overloaded method to populate a DataTable and want to pick up the changes in the data source for the same DataTable, then make sure that you specify the same name string as was supplied for the first call. If you specify a different name or failed to supply any name, then you will end up with a new DataTable along with the one that already exists in the DataSet. The reason for this behavior is that when you call the Fill method second time, it looks in the DataSet to check if there is a DataTable with the same name, as specified as method parameter. If there is no name specified or it is different, then the test fails and a new DataTable is created in the DataSet.

For example, the following code will end up with two tables in the DataSet because the second Fill method call did not specify any table name.

VB.NET:

```
Dim strQuery As String = "SELECT * FROM ORDERS"
Dim strConn As String = "Data Source = localhost; uid=sa; pwd=;" & _
                        " Initial Catalog=Northwind;"
' Create the connection
Dim sqlConn As New SqlConnection(strConn)
' Create the command object by specifying the already created connection object.
Dim selectCmd As New SqlCommand(strQuery, sqlConn)
' Create the DataAdapter to get the records.
Dim orderDtAdapter As New SqlDataAdapter(selectCmd)
' Call the Fill methods and specify the table name to be used.
Dim orderSet As New DataSet()
orderDtAdapter.Fill(orderSet, "Customer Orders")

' Call the fill method again to pick up any changes in the database.
orderDtAdapter.Fill(orderSet) ' This will generate a new table in the DataSet.
```

C#:

```
string strQuery = "SELECT * FROM ORDERS";
string strConn = "Data Source = localhost; uid=sa; pwd=; Initial
Catalog=Northwind;";
// Create the connection
SqlConnection sqlConn = new SqlConnection (strConn);
// Create the command object by specifying the already created connection object.
SqlCommand selectCmd = new SqlCommand(strQuery, sqlConn);
// Create the DataAdapter to get the records.
SqlDataAdapter orderDtAdapter = new SqlDataAdapter(selectCmd);
// Call the Fill methods and specify the table name to be used.
DataSet orderSet = new DataSet ();
orderDtAdapter.Fill (orderSet, "Customer Orders");

// Call the fill method again to pick up any changes in the database.
orderDtAdapter.Fill(orderSet); // This will generate a new table in the DataSet.
```

The Fill (DataTable, IDataReader) Method

This is a protected access overloaded implementation of the method. This method can be used internally by a derived `DataAdapter` classes to retrieve the records from the data source by providing the `DataReader` object. The data reader accesses each record sequentially in connected mode and populates the `DataTable` provides by caller of this method. The implementation of this method calls the private access function `Fill (Object, String, Int32, DataReader, Int32)` to get the data records from source.

VB.NET:

```
Overridable Overloads Protected Function Fill( _
   ByVal dataTable As DataTable, _
   ByVal dataReader As IDataReader _
) As Integer
```

C#:

```
protected virtual int Fill(
```

303

```
        DataTable dataTable,
        IDataReader dataReader
    );
```

The following table describes the parameters of this method that the caller should supply:

Parameter	Type	Description
dataTable	DataTable	The DataTable that will get populated with rows of records and schema
dataReader	IDataReader	The DataReader object that retrieves the records from the data source in connected mode

The Fill (DataTable, IDbCommand, CommandBehavior) Method

This is a protected access overloaded implementation of the method. The implementation of the public access method Fill (DataTable) calls this method to populate the user supplied DataTable object.

VB.NET:

```
Overridable Overloads Protected Function Fill( _
    ByVal dataTable As DataTable, _
    ByVal command As IDbCommand, _
    ByVal behavior As CommandBehavior _
) As Integer
```

C#:

```
protected virtual int Fill(
    DataTable dataTable,
    IDbCommand command,
    CommandBehavior behavior
);
```

Parameter	Type	Description
dataTable	DataTable	The DataTable that will get populated with rows of records and schema.
command	IDbCommand	This is the Command (OleDbCommand, SqlCommand or OdbcCommand depending on the choice of data provider) object that is created by specifying the SELECT query. The method uses this query to retrieve the records from the data source.

Parameter	Type	Description
behavior	CommandBehavior	This is a bitwise flag specified by a combination of CommandBehavior enumeration values. It describes the affect of query command. The possible values of this enumeration are CloseConnection, SchemaOnly, KeyInfo, SequentialAccess, SingleResult, and SingleRow.

The Fill (DataSet, Int32, Int32, String) Method

This overloaded implementation populates the caller provided DataSet object with records from the data source.

VB.NET:

```
Overloads Public Function Fill( _
    ByVal dataSet As DataSet, _
    ByVal startRecord As Integer, _
    ByVal maxRecords As Integer, _
    ByVal srcTable As String _
) As Integer
```

C#:

```
public int Fill(
    DataSet dataSet,
    int startRecord,
    int maxRecords,
    string srcTable
);
```

The following table describes the parameters for this over loaded implementation of this method. These are the parameters that the caller needs to supply for execution of Fill method:

Parameter	Type	Description
dataset	DataSet	The DataSet that will get populated with rows of records and schema
startRecord	Integer	This is the zero-based record number in the complete list of records from the population of the DataSet will start
maxRecords	Integer	The maximum number of records that should be retrieved from data source and stuffed in the DataSet
srcTable	String	The name of the source table that will be mapped to the DataTable

This implementation provides extra control on the number of records and the position from where to start copying the records from a source table into the DataSet. The startRecord parameter value must be a valid index, as must the maxRecords value:

```
0 <= startRecord < total number of source records
0 < maxRecords <= total number of source records
```

If the `DataSet` does not contain any `DataTable` object, it creates one and maps to the name of the source table name provided by the caller. For example, if the `srcTable` parameter value is set to `EmployeeData`, then the name of the `DataTable` created in the `DataSet` object will be `EmployeeData` and not the default name `Table`. The method returns the number of records retrieved from the data source.

The Fill (DataSet, String, IDataReader, Int32, Int32) Method

This is a protected access overloaded implementation of the method. The method can be used by a derived `DataAdapter` class to retrieve the records from the data source by providing the `DataReader` object. The implementation of this method calls the private access function `Fill (Object, String, IDataReader, Int32, Int32)` to get the data records from source.

VB.NET:

```
Overridable Overloads Protected Function Fill( _
    ByVal dataSet As DataSet, _
    ByVal srcTable As String, _
    ByVal dataReader As IDataReader, _
    ByVal startRecord As Integer, _
    ByVal maxRecords As Integer _
) As Integer
```

C#:

```
protected virtual int Fill(
    DataSet dataSet,
    string srcTable,
    IDataReader dataReader,
    int startRecord,
    int maxRecords
);
```

This method has one more parameter than the previous overloaded implementation. The following table describes the extra parameter that it takes. For description of rest of the parameters refer to the previous implementation:

Parameter	Type	Description
dataReader	IDataReader	The DataReader object that retrieves the records from the data source in connected mode

The Fill (DataSet, Int32, Int32, String, IDbCommand, CommandBehavior) Method

This is a protected access overloaded implementation of the method. The implementation of the public access methods `Fill (DataSet)`, `Fill (DataSet, String)` & `Fill (DataSet, Int32, Int32, String)` call this method to populate the user supplied `DataSet` object. The implementation of this private method internally calls the private access function `Fill (Object, Int32, Int32, String, -IDbCommand, CommandBehavior)` to retrieve the data.

VB.NET:

```
Overridable Overloads Protected Function Fill( _
    ByVal dataSet As DataSet, _
    ByVal startRecord As Integer, _
    ByVal maxRecords As Integer, _
    ByVal srcTable As String, _
    ByVal command As IDbCommand, _
    ByVal behavior As CommandBehavior _
) As Integer
```

C#:

```
protected virtual int Fill(
    DataSet dataSet,
    int startRecord,
    int maxRecords,
    string srcTable,
    IDbCommand command,
    CommandBehavior behavior
);
```

The following table describes the parameters for this overloaded implementation of `Fill` method:

Parameter	Type	Description
dataset	DataSet	The `DataSet` that will get populated with rows of records and schema.
startRecord	Integer	This is the zero-based record number in the complete list of records from the population of the `DataSet` will start.
maxRecords	Integer	The maximum number of records that should be retrieved from data source and stuffed in the `DataSet`.
srcTable	String	The name of the source table that will be mapped to the `DataTable`.
command	IDbCommand	The `SELECT` query that is set as in the command object for retrieving the records from source.

Parameter	Type	Description
behavior	CommandBehavior	This is bitwise flag specified by combination of CommandBehavior enumeration values and describes the affect of query command. The possible values of this enumeration are CloseConnection, SchemaOnly, KeyInfo, SequentialAccess, SingleResult, and SingleRow.

The FillSchema Method

This method adds the schema of a DataTable to a DataSet, and synchronizes it with a data source schema. The DbDataAdapter class provides five overloaded implementations of this method. Out of these five implementations, two are protected methods that are used internally by other three method implementations.

The three public access overloaded implementations of this method are as follows:

❑ FillSchema(DataSet, SchemaType)

❑ FillSchema(DataTable, SchemaType)

❑ FillSchema(DataSet, SchemaType, String)

The following table describes the parameters for the FillSchema methods with public access attribute:

Parameter	Type	Description
dataSet	DataSet	DataSet that will be populated with data table's schema information.
dataTable	DataTable	DataTable that will be populated with data table's schema information.
schemaType	SchemaType	The value for this enumeration specifies how to treat the existing schema in the DataSet when new schema information is populated from data source. The two possible values for this parameter are SchemaType.Mapped or SchemaType.Source.
srcTable	String	Name of the table in data source that will be used for table mapping.

This method is like the Fill method that is used to retrieve the data records from data source with the difference that it does not retrieve the records. Instead, it is used to retrieve the metadata of the table. The DataTable returned by this method contains the rows and columns that completely define all the attributes of the fields for that table.

The method uses the SQL SELECT query in the SelectCommand to fetch the schema information. The connection object associated with the DataAdapter does not have to be open when FillSchema method is called. Like Fill, this method also checks the state of the connection object. If the connection is closed before execution of this method, it is opened, and, after retrieving the information from the data source, it is closed by the managed provider. If the connection is open before the call to the FillSchema method, it is left open after the execution of the method.

After retrieving schema information from the data source, this method checks the value of SchemaType parameter that has been specified by the caller. The value of this parameter can be either SchemaType.Mapped or SchemaType.Source. For more details on these values, refer to the discussion of FillSchema in the DataAdapter class. Depending on the value of this parameter, a DataTable is added to the DataSet that needs to be populated. Then information about each data column's schema is added to the DataTable. A new instance of DataColumn object is created for each data field in the source table. The following properties of the DataColumn are then set, depending on information returned from the data source:

❑ AllowDBNull – Specifies whether NULL values are allowed for the data field or not.

❑ Unique – Is the value of this data field unique throughout the data table?

❑ AutoIncrement – Specifies whether the value of this field will be auto incremented or not when a new row gets added to the table. The AutoIncrementStep and AutoIncrement property values are not set by the FillSchema method. These values will have to be set after the DataTable containing schema has been returned by the method.

❑ ReadOnly – Specifies whether the value in the data field can be modified or not after it gets added to the table.

❑ MaxLength – Specifies the maximum length of the text field that this field can save.

The method not only sets the various DataColumn properties, but also populates the DataTable with PrimaryKey and Constraint information (if there is any) in the data source for that table. The constraint information is only added if the MissingSchemaAction property value is set to MissingSchemaAction.AddWithKey. The following rules are followed the PrimaryKey and Constraints properties are added to the DataTable:

❑ If the data table has a primary key column or set of columns defining the primary key, then these are set in the DataTable as primary key columns.

❑ If the data table has no primary key columns, then whether there are any data columns with Unique property set is checked. If any are found, the next condition that is checked is whether all of these columns are nonnullable: in other words, the value of the AllowDBNull property for these columns is set as **false**. If both of these conditions are satisfied, these data columns are set as PrimaryKey property in the DataTable. And if any of these Unique data columns can have NULL values, then the PrimaryKey property is not set for the DataTable. Instead, UniqueConstraint is set as the Constraint property for the DataTable.

❑ If the data source has both primary key and unique columns, then the primary key columns are set in the DataColumnCollection for the PrimaryKey property of the DataTable.

The population of the schema information in the `DataSet` follows the following rules to deal with special conditions that may arise because of kind of information returned from the data source:

❑ If the `SELECT` query returns multiple data tables, the schema information for each table is placed in separate `DataTable` objects in the `DataSet`. If there is no table mapping provided for the `DataAdapter`, or the `SchemaType` enumeration value is set to `SchemaType.Source`, then each table is named by appending a numeric value at the end of default name for the first table. For example, if the query returns 3 result sets then the schema will be placed in data tables named `Table`, `Table1` and `Table2`. The following code shows an example of a SQL `SELECT` query, returning schema for multiple tables. The schema for source table `Shippers` will be configured in the `DataTable` called `Table`, and that for source table `Suppliers` will be configured in `DataTable` called `Table1`.

VB.NET:

```
Dim conn As New SqlConection ( _
    "Data Source=localhost;  Initial Catalog=NorthWind; _
    User ID=sa; Pwd=")
' Create new instance of command object
Dim cmd As New SqlCommand( _
    "SELECT * FROM Shippers, Suppliers", conn)
' Create new instance of DataAdapter object
Dim dtAdapter As New SqlDataAdapter(cmd)
' Call FillSchema method to retrieve schema information of two tables
Dim dtSet As New DataSet()
Dim dtTables As DataTable() = dtAdapter(dtSet, SchemaType.Source)
```

C#:

```
SqlConnection conn = new SQLConnection(
    "Data Source=localhost;  Initial Catalog=NorthWind;
    User ID=sa; Pwd="
    );
SqlCommand cmd = new SqlCommand(
    "SELECT * FROM Shippers, Suppliers", conn);
dtAdapter = new SqlDataAdapter(cmd);
// Call the FillSchema method to retrieve the schema of the two tables.
DataSet dtSet = new DataSet();
DataTable [] dtTables = dtAdapter.FillSchema(dtSet, SchemaType.Source);
```

❑ If the `SELECT` query returns unnamed data columns, they are added to the `DataTable` with columns named `Column1, Column2`, and so on.

❑ If the `SELECT` query returns columns with duplicate names, then the method generates artificial names for the columns by placing a numeric suffix to the original data column's name. For example, if the query returns two `Phone` data columns, then the first column will be added to the `DataSet` with name `Phone`, and the second one will be added with name `Phone1`. The following code shows how a `SELECT` query can return data columns `CompanyName` with duplicate names.

VB.NET:

```
Dim strConn As String = "Provider = SQLOLEDB.1; Data Source=localhost; " & _
                        "uid=sa; pwd=; Initial Catalog=Northwind"
Dim strQuery As String = "SELECT SupplierId, Suppliers.CompanyName," & _
                        "ShipperID, Shippers.CompanyName " & _
                    "FROM Suppliers, Shippers WHERE " & _
```

```
                                   "Suppliers.CompanyName = 'Microsoft' AND " & _
                                   "Suppliers.CompanyName = Shippers.CompanyName"
    ' Create the connection object.
    Dim oledbConn As New OleDbConnection(strConn)
    ' Create the command object which will be used as SELECT command
    ' for the DataAdapter.
    Dim oledbCmd As New OleDbCommand(strQuery, oledbConn)
    Dim dtAdapter As New OleDbDataAdapter(oledbCmd)
    Dim dtSet As New DataSet()
    dtAdapter.FillSchema(dtSet, SchemaType.Mapped)
```

C#:

```
    string strConn = "Provider = SQLOLEDB.1; Data Source=localhost; " +
                "uid=sa; pwd=; Initial Catalog=Northwind";
    string strQuery = "SELECT SupplierId, Suppliers.CompanyName," +
                "ShipperID, Shippers.CompanyName " +
                "FROM Suppliers, Shippers WHERE " +
                "Suppliers.CompanyName = 'Microsoft' AND " +
                "Suppliers.CompanyName = Shippers.CompanyName";
    // Create the connection object.
    OleDbConnection oledbConn = new OleDbConnection (strConn);
    // Create the command object which will be used as SELECT command
    // for the DataAdapter.
    OleDbCommand oledbCmd= new OleDbCommand (strQuery, oledbConn);
    OleDbDataAdapter dtAdapter = new OleDbDataAdapter (oledbCmd);
    DataSet dtSet = new DataSet ();
    dtAdapter.FillSchema (dtSet, SchemaType.Mapped);
```

The example above puts the Suppliers.CompanyName in the DataColumn called CompanyName, and the Shippers.CompanyName in the DataColumn called CompanyName1.

> It is highly recommended that application should try not to map the source table and column names to **DataTable** and **DataColumn** objects with names having numerical suffixes. This may cause conflict with the artificial names generated by framework in case of duplicates.

When the FillSchema method is executed for the SQL Server managed provider, a FOR BROWSE clause is appended to the SELECT query. This turns on the SET FMTONLY permission signifying that this SELECT query will return only the metadata to the client and no rows of data is to be returned. This is an optimization added by the data provider, because the only information this method is interested in is getting the schema information and nothing else. For example, a simple query:

```
SELECT * FROM Customers
```

Is sent to the SQL Server database as:

```
SET FMTONLY ON
SELECT * FROM Customers
```

Therefore, you should be aware of the limitation of adding a FOR BROWSE clause to the SELECT query. Some of the potential restrictions are as follows:

❑ FOR XML can't coexist with FOR BROWSE.

❑ FOR BROWSE uses the optimistic concurrency controls, which do not lock the data being read. Therefore, a SELECT query should not have the locking hint HOLDLOCK specified. The use of SQL query SELECT * FROM Orders WITH (HOLDLOCK) will generate an error with the FillSchema method.

❑ The SELECT query should not consist of statements joined by a UNION operator, as FOR BROWSE does not work in that mode.

For batch SQL statements returning multiple record sets, the OLE DB providers return schema for only the first data table. The best bet in this case, is the use of the Fill method with the MissingSchemaAction property value set to AddWithKey. If this value is not set, then schema returned will not populate the PrimaryKey and Constraints properties of the DataTable schema.

The following output shows the schema information obtained from PRODUCTS table of Northwind database. The first row displays the name of the table. The subsequent rows then display the column information Caption, Ordinal, DataType, MaxLength, AutoIncrement, AutoIncrementSeed, AutoIncrementStep, AllowDBNull, and ReadOnly.

```
Table: Products
ProductID:0,System.Int32,-1,True,True,0,1,False,True
ProductName:1,System.String,40,False,False,0,1,False,False
SupplierID:2,System.Int32,-1,False,False,0,1,True,False
CategoryID:3,System.Int32,-1,False,False,0,1,True,False
QuantityPerUnit:4,System.String,20,False,False,0,1,True,False
UnitPrice:5,System.Decimal,-1,False,False,0,1,True,False
UnitsInStock:6,System.Int16,-1,False,False,0,1,True,False
UnitsOnOrder:7,System.Int16,-1,False,False,0,1,True,False
ReorderLevel:8,System.Int16,-1,False,False,0,1,True,False
Discontinued:9,System.Boolean,-1,False,False,0,1,False,False
```

I used the following utility functions to dump this information in a trace log.

C#:

```csharp
public void DumpSchemaInformation (DataTable schemaTable)
{
    Trace.WriteLine ("Table: " + schemaTable.TableName);
    foreach (DataColumn dtCol in schemaTable.Columns)
    {
        DumpColumnInformation (dtCol);
    }
    Trace.WriteLine ("**************************");
}

public void DumpColumnInformation(DataColumn dtCol)
{
    Trace.Write (dtCol.Caption + ":");
    Trace.Write (dtCol.Ordinal + ",");
```

```
        Trace.Write (dtCol.DataType + ",");
        Trace.Write (dtCol.MaxLength + ",");
        Trace.Write (dtCol.Unique + ",");
        Trace.Write (dtCol.AutoIncrement + ",");
        Trace.Write (dtCol.AutoIncrementSeed + ",");
        Trace.Write (dtCol.AutoIncrementStep + ",");
        Trace.Write (dtCol.AllowDBNull + ",");
        Trace.WriteLine (dtCol.ReadOnly);
    }
```

The GetFillParameters Method

Gets the stored procedure and/or return parameters used by the SELECT command during the Fill method.

VB.NET:

```
    Overrides Public Function GetFillParameters() As IDataParameter()
```

C#:

```
    public override IDataParameter[] GetFillParameters();
```

The method returns an array of IDataParameter objects, which provide complete information about the output and input stored procedure parameters. For detailed information on how parameters are set in command object, refer to Parameters property in of Command class in Chapter 4.

This method is defined in the base class DataAdapter and every derived class must provide the implementation. The managed providers for SQL Server, OLE DB providers and native ODBC drivers, use the generic implementation provided by this class. For more details on this topic, refer to the GetFillParameter method's discussion in DataAdapter class.

The OnFillError Method

This method raises the FillError event during Fill operation.

VB.NET:

```
    Overridable Protected Sub OnFillError( _
        ByVal value As FillErrorEventArgs _
    )
```

C#:

```
    protected virtual void OnFillError(
        FillErrorEventArgs value
    );
```

This is a protected method that every derived DataAdapter class can override to provide their own implementation to raise the FillError event when there is an error during Fill method. It is very important that the derived class should call the base class's OnFillError method so that any information that is added by the base class to the FillErrorEventArgs parameter is available to it. This method gets the list of all the event handlers that have been added to the DataAdapter object. The reason it is necessary to get this list is because there can be more than one event handlers listening for this event. The DataAdpater enumerates over this list and invokes the FillError event through the FillErrorEventHandler delegate for each one of the listeners.

313

The managed providers OleDbDataAdapter, SqlDataAdapter and OdbcDataAdapter use the base class implementation of this method.

The OnRowUpdatedMethod

This method raises the RowUpdated event during Update operation.

VB.NET:
```
MustOverride Protected Sub OnRowUpdated( _
    ByVal value As RowUpdatedEventArgs _
)
```

C#:
```
protected abstract void OnRowUpdated(
    RowUpdatedEventArgs value
);
```

This is a protected abstract method, and every derived DataAdapter class must provide the managed provider specific implementation for it. This method raises RowUpdated event after a data row has been updated during an Update operation. For more details refer to the respective derived classes, OleDbDataAdapter, SqlDataAdapter and OdbcDataAdapter. It gives a chance to the event handler to take appropriate action based on the values of the properties of RowUpdatedEventArgs object that is passed to the event handler function.

The OnRowUpdating Method

This method raises RowUpdating event during Update operation.

VB.NET:
```
MustOverride Protected Sub OnRowUpdating( _
    ByVal value As RowUpdatingEventArgs _
)
```

C#:
```
protected abstract void OnRowUpdating(
    RowUpdatingEventArgs value
);
```

This is a protected abstract method and every derived DataAdapter class must provide the managed provider specific implementation for it. This method raises a RowUpdating event just *before* the Fill operation tries to update a data row. It gives a chance to the event handler to take appropriate action, based on the values of the properties of the RowUpdatingEventArgs object that is passed to the event handler function.

The Update Method

The Update Method calls INSERT, UPDATE, or DELETE for each inserted, updated, or deleted record in DataTable called Table of the DataSet. The DbDataAdapter class provides five overloaded implementations of this method.

The Update (DataRow[]) Method

VB.NET:
```
Overloads Public Function Update( _
   ByVal dataRows() As DataRow _
) As Integer
```

C#:
```
public int Update(
   DataRow[] dataRows
);
```

Parameter	Type	Description
dataRows	DataRow []	An array of DataRow objects that will be used to update the data source records

The Update (DataSet) Method

VB.NET:
```
Overrides Overloads Public Function Update( _
   ByVal dataSet As DataSet _
) As Integer
```

C#:
```
public override int Update(
   DataSet dataSet
);
```

Parameter	Type	Description
dataset	DataSet	The DataSet, containing the DataRow objects with updated data, which will be used to update the data source records

The Update (DataTable) Method

VB.NET:
```
Overloads Public Function Update( _
   ByVal dataTable As DataTable _
) As Integer
```

C#:
```
public int Update(
   DataTable dataTable
);
```

Parameter	Type	Description
dataTable	DataTable	The DataTable containing the updated data rows

The Update (DataRow[], DataTableMapping) Method

This method has protected access is called by the Update(DataTable) and Update(DataRow[]) methods internally to update the records in data source.

VB.NET:

```
Overridable Overloads Protected Function Update( _
    ByVal dataRows() As DataRow, _
    ByVal tableMapping As DataTableMapping _
) As Integer
```

C#:

```
protected virtual int Update(
    DataRow[] dataRows,
    DataTableMapping tableMapping
);
```

Parameter	Type	Description
dataRows	DataRow []	An array of DataRow objects that contain the updated records
tableMapping	DataTableMapping	The table mapping information that the Update operation will use to identify which source table is mapped to which DataTable in the DataSet

The Update (DataSet, String) Method

This method has protected access is called by the Update(DataSet) method internally to update the records in data source.

VB.NET:

```
Overloads Public Function Update( _
    ByVal dataSet As DataSet, _
    ByVal srcTable As String _
) As Integer
```

C#:

```
public int Update(
    DataSet dataSet,
    string srcTable
);
```

Parameter	Type	Description
dataset	DataSet	The DataSet that contains the DataRow objects with updated data
srcTable	String	The name of the source table that will be mapped to DataTable in the DataSet

The consumers of the DataAdapter objects call the Update method to submit all the cached changes in the DataSet object to the data source. A successful execution of the Fill method returns a DataSet object with records from the data source. The records in this DataSet can be modified, deleted, or new rows may be added. Since the DataSet objects functions in a disconnected mode, the changes are not submitted to the data source until the Update method is called.

The DataSet keeps track of all the data manipulations and accordingly modifies the value of the RowState property of each modified DataRow object. For example, if a row is deleted using the Delete method on a DataRow, the state of that row is changed to DataRowState.Deleted, and for the unchanged data rows this value is set to DataRowState.Unchnaged.

When the Update method is called, the action queries (INSERT, UPDATE, or DELETE) are issued to the database to perform the appropriate update action. The order in which these SQL queries are executed follows no particular order. The framework looks at the status of each row in the table and issues the action query based on that status.

For example, if the first row in the table has a status value of DataRowState.Modified, the UPDATE command will be executed and if the next row has status value of DataRowState.Deleted, the DELETE command will be executed. This process of execution continues until all the data rows in the data set have been updated. If the status values corresponding to the rows in the data set are in random order then the update operation will happen in random order too.

> This random order of execution of commands adds a degree of inefficiency and slows down the execution. Therefore it is suggested that rows with similar **DataRowStatus** property values should be grouped together before calling the **Update** method.

This update order can be controlled by calling GetChanges method on the DataTable object to get an array of DataRow objects, which have a similar status, and then pass the returned DataRow objects to the Update method call. The following code illustrates how this ordered update could be accomplished:

VB.NET:

```
' Call Fill method to get the data from source.
dtAdapter.FillData (dtSet)
Dim dtTable As DataTable = dtSet.Table("Employees")
' Manipulate the DataRows in this table by adding new rows
' updating some and deleting couple of them

' First get all the rows that have been modified.
Dim updatedTable As DataTable = dtTable.GetChanges()

' Now get the rows that have been added since last AcceptChanges call
```

```
' and call Update to update data source records.
Dim newRows () As DataRow = _
    updatedTable.Select(Nothing, Nothing, DataViewRowState.Added)
dtAdapter.Update(newRows)

' Now get the rows that have been deleted since last AcceptChanges call
' and call Update to update data source records.
Dim deletedRows () As DataRow = _
    updatedTable.Select(Nothing, Nothing, DataViewRowState.Deleted)
dtAdapter.Update(deletedRows)
```

C#:

```
// Call Fill method to get the data from source.
dtAdapter.FillData (dtSet);
DataTable  dtTable = dtSet.Table("Employees");
// Manipulate the DataRows in this table by adding new rows
// updating some and deleting couple of them

// First get all the rows that have been modified.
DataTable updatedTable = dtTable.GetChanges();

// Now get the rows that have been added since last AcceptChanges call
// and call Update to update data source records.
DataRow[] newRows =
    updatedTable.Select(null, null, DataViewRowState.Added);
dtAdapter.Update(newRows);

// Now get the rows that have been deleted since last AcceptChanges call
// and call Update to update data source records.
DataRow[] deletedRows =
    updatedTable.Select(null, null, DataViewRowState.Deleted);
dtAdapter.Update(deletedRows);
```

The ordered Update operation not only improves efficiency, but it is also sometimes necessary that certain update operations be carried out in a certain order to maintain the referential integrity of the table.

The DataAdapter class has InsertCommand, DeleteCommand and UpdateCommand properties that it uses to assign the provider specific command objects (OleDbCommand or SqlCommand) which update the data source records. Based on the value of the DataRowStatus property value of an updated row, the method checks if the command property corresponding to that operation has been set by the caller or not.

For example, if a new row has been added, the method will look for the value of the InsertCommand property. If that particular command is not set, the managed provider will throw a System.InvalidOperatioException exception. A nice feature is that these commands for the DataAdapter are automatically generated. We can create an OleDbCommandBuilder or SqlCommandBuilder object and assign the DataAdapter object to it.

The CommandBuilder will not generate commands if any of the following conditions are not met:

❑ The DataTable used to update the data source must be generated from single table and should not be related to any other DataTable in the DataSet

❑ A primary key column should be present in the DataTable that it will use to specify the WHERE clause in the SQL statement

❑ The data source table or column names must not contain any special characters like spaces, periods, quotation marks or any other non-alphanumeric characters

We must explicitly specify the InsertCommand, DeleteCommand, or UpdatCommand if any of the above conditions are not satisfied. Otherwise, the method throws an InvalidOperationException or SqlException exception, depending on the type of violation, and terminates the operation.

The following code illustrates the use of OleDbCommandBuilder for automatic generation of update commands.

VB.NET:

```
Dim dtSet  As New DataSet ()
dtAdapter.Fill (dtSet)
Dim dtRow As DataRow = dtSet.Tables(0).Rows(0)
dtRow("LastName") = "Mutombo"
Dim cmdBldr As New OleDbCommandBuilder (dtAdapter);
Dim iNumUpdated As Integer = dtAdapter.Update(dtSet)
```

C#:

```
DataSet dtSet = new DataSet ();
dtAdapter.Fill (dtSet);
DataRow dtRow = dtSet.Tables[0].Rows[0];
dtRow["LastName"] = "Mutombo";
OleDbCommandBuilder cmdBldr = new OleDbCommandBuilder(dtAdapter)
int iNumUpdated = dtAdapter.Update(dtSet);
```

> To improve the efficiency of the **Update** method, it is highly recommended that you provide these update commands (**InsertCommand, UpdateCommand**, and **DeleteCommand**) explicitly instead of using **SqlCommandBuilder, OleDbCommandBuilder** or **OdbcCommandBuilder**. The **CommandBuilder** registers itself as a listener for the **RowUpdating** event.
>
> Whenever a row is to be updated, the **DataAdapter** will fire the **RowUpdating** event and then **CommandBuilder** will diagnose the row values and create the action query. By explicitly specifying the update queries, you can avoid an extra level of *Detect & React* mechanism layer added by event handlers of the **CommandBuilder** object.

When the Update method modifies the data source record it gives the caller a chance to terminate or skip the operation, before and after the update takes place, by raising OnRowUpdating and OnRowUpdated events. If the OnRowUpdating and OnRowUpdated event handlers do not vote on terminating the operation (by setting the Status value to UpdateStatus.Continue), the changes are submitted to the data source and the RowState for every row is set to DataRowState.Unchanged. For details on handling these update events, refer to the RowUpdating and RowUpdating events in the OleDbDataAdapter and SqlDataAdapter class sections.

The following code sets the `DeleteCommand` explicitly to delete a data row from the `Territories` table of the `Northwind` database:

VB.NET:

```
Dim sqlCmd As New SqlCommand ()
sqlCmd.Connection = sqlConnection
sqlCmd.CommandText = "SELECT * FROM Territories WHERE TerritoryID = 48084'"

' Set the SelectCommand and call Fill method to get the data row
dtAdapter.SelectCommand = sqlCmd
Dim dtTable As New DataTable ()
dtAdapter.Fill (dtTable)

' Set the selected row to Deleted status.
dtTable.Rows(0).Delete ()

' Set the delete command and call Update method to commit changes.
dtAdapter.DeleteCommand.CommandText = _
    "DELETE FROM Territories WHERE TerritoryID = '48084'"
dtAdapter.DeleteCommand.Connection = sqlConnection
dtAdapter.Update (dtTable)
```

C#:

```
SqlCommand sqlCmd= new SqlCommand ();
sqlCmd.Connection = sqlConnection;
sqlCmd.CommandText = "SELECT * FROM Territories WHERE TerritoryID = '48084'";

// Set the SelectCommand and call Fill method to get data
dtAdapter.SelectCommand = sqlCmd;
DataTable dtTable = new DataTable ();
dtAdapter.Fill (dtTable);

// Set the selected row to Deleted status.
DataRow dtRow = dtTable.Rows[0];
dtRow.Delete ();

// Set the delete command and call Update to commit changes.
string strCmd = "DELETE FROM TERRITORIES WHERE TerritoryID = '48084'";
dtAdapter.DeleteCommand = new SqlCommand (strCmd);
dtAdapter.DeleteCommand.Connection = sqlConnection;
dtAdapter.Update (dtTable);
```

DbDataAdapter Events

The FillError Event

This event gets raised when there is an error during the execution of the `Fill` method.

VB.NET:

```
Public Event FillError As FillErrorEventHandler
```

C#:

```
public event FillErrorEventHandler FillError;
```

During the execution of the Fill method, the managed provider maintains the data and referential integrity in the DataSet receiving the data from the data source. If any error occurs during this operation, a FillError event is raised, providing an opportunity to take appropriate action: either to continue or terminate the operation.

The error during the Fill operation can occur due to number of reasons. For example, if the incoming data violates the constraints established for DataTable schema, or there is a data type mismatch between DataTable's column and data source's column, or the managed provider fails to convert the data source native format to .NET data format. This event is not raised in case any error occurs at the data source. For example, if you supply an invalid SELECT query, the Fill method will definitely fail but there will be no FillError event. The framework will report this error by throwing an exception. Similarly if the client loses the network connection while Fill error is being executed,

When an error occurs, that dataRow is not added to the DataTable. The FillError event is raised, and the FillErrorEventArgs object is passed to the event handler. Based on the values of the properties of FillErrorEventArgs object, the application can take one of the following actions:

❑ Rectify the problem with the operation and continue with addition of that row to the DataTable

❑ Ignore the error and continue the operation without adding that row to the DataTable

❑ Terminate the Fill operation completely

The FillErrorEventArgs class, providing the data for FillError event, has the following properties:

❑ Errors – This property gets the error that raised the event. The information is passed as an Exception object.

❑ Values – This property gets the object array containing the value of the columns for the row that encountered error during Fill operation. The array has an index based on zero, and these indices represent the order in which the columns were being added to the row in DataTable.

❑ DataTable – This property gets is the DataTable object that was being fetched when error occurred.

❑ Continue – This property sets the Boolean flag indicating what action to take when the error occurred. Setting this value to true indicates that ignore the error and continue with Fill operation. And setting this property value to false will terminate the Fill operation by throwing an exception.

The following code shows how to add the event handler for the FillError event, and how to set the value of the Continue property in the event handler to take appropriate action in cases of the event being raised:

```
SqlDataAdapter dtAdapter = new SqlDataAdapter ();
dtAdapter.SelectCommand = sqlCmd;
// Add the event handler for FillError event.
dtAdapter.FillError += new FillErrorEventHandler (FillErrorHandler);
```

```
// Execute the command by calling Fill method from baseclass
// DbDataAdapter class.
DataTable dtTable = new DataTable ();
int iNumRecords = dtAdapter.Fill (dtTable);

protected static void FillErrorHandler(object sender, FillErrorEventArgs args)
{
    // Get the name of the table throwing error.
    string strTable = args.DataTable.ToString ();
    Console.WriteLine ("Table with error : " + strTable);
    // Get the type of exception thrown.
    Type excpType = args.Errors.GetType ();
    Console.WriteLine ("Exception type: " + excpType.ToString ());
    Console.WriteLine ("Number of values=" + args.Values.Length);
    // Based on the exception thow, set the value for Continue  property.
    else if (excpType == typeof (System.OverflowException))
    {
        args.Continue = true;
    }
}
```

The OleDbDataAdapter

VB.NET:

```
NotInheritable Public Class OleDbDataAdapter
     Inherits DbDataDapter
     Implements ICloneable, IDbDataAdapter
```

C#:

```
public sealed class OleDbDataAdapter :
     DbDataDapter,
     ICloneable, IDbDataAdapter
```

The OleDbDataAdapter provides the public access class for OLE DB managed provider DataAdapter object. It is inherited from DbDataAdapter class and provides the implementation for abstract properties, SelectCommand, InsertCommand, DeleteCommand, and UpdateCommand, defined in IDbDataAdapter interface. In addition to the four overloaded forms of Fill method, discussed in DbDataAdapter class, this class also provides two overloaded implementations of the Fill method that help in fetching data from the ADO Recordset or Record object.

OleDbDataAdapter Constructor

OleDbDataAdapter Constructor ()

Initializes a new instance of the OleDbDataAdapter class.

VB.NET:

```
Overloads Public Sub New()
```

C#:

```
public OleDbDataAdapter();
```

This is the default constructor for this class. When a new instance of this object is created, the properties of this class get initialized to their default values. These default values of properties can be changed by accessing individual read/write properties of the class.

VB.NET:

```
Dim dtDapter As New OleDbDataAdapter ()
dtAdapter.MissingSchemaAction = MissingSchemaAction.AddWithKey
```

C#:

```
OleDbDataAdapter dtAdapter = new OleDbDataAdapter ();
dtAdapter. MissingSchemaAction = MissingSchemaAction.AddWithKey;
```

OleDbDataAdapter Constructor (OleDbCommand)

Initializes a new instance of the OleDbDataAdapter class with the specified OleDbCommand object.

VB.NET:

```
Overloads Public Sub New( _
    ByVal selectCommand As OleDbCommand _
)
```

C#:

```
public OleDbDataAdapter(
    OleDbCommand selectCommand
);
```

The query associated with the OleDbCommand should be a valid SQL SELECT statement. The constructor associates this command object to SelectCommand of the DataAdapter. This constructor first calls the default constructor of the base class DbDataAdapter that initializes the properties of this DataAdapter object to its default value.

VB.NET:

```
Dim oledbCmd As New OleDbCommand ("SELECT * FROM Products")
Dim dtAdapter As New OleDbDataAdapter (oledbCmd)
```

C#:

```
OleDbCommand oledbCmd = new OleDbCommand ("SELECT * FROM Products");
OleDbDataAdapter dtAdapter = new OleDbDataAdapter (oledbCmd);
```

OleDbDataAdapter Constructor (String, OleDbConnection)

Initializes a new instance of the OleDbDataAdapter class with the specified command text string and an OleDbConnection object.

VB.NET:

```
Overloads Public Sub New( _
    ByVal selectCommandText As String, _
    ByVal selectConnection As OleDbConnection _
)
```

C#:

```
public OleDbDataAdapter(
    string selectCommandText,
    OleDbConnection selectConnection
);
```

The command text string must be a valid SQL SELECT statement. This constructor first calls the default constructor of the base class DbDataAdapter that initializes the properties of this DataAdapter object to its default value. It then calls the OleDbCommand (string, OleDbConnection) class constructor, which sets the command string as CommandText and connection object for the command object. This created OleDbCommand object is set as SelectCommand for the DataAdapter.

VB.NET:

```
Dim strConn = "Provider=Microsoft.JET.OLEDB.4.0;" & _
    "Data Source=Northwind.mdb"
Dim oledbConn As New OleDbConnection (strConnection)
Dim strCmd = "SELECT * FROM Products"
Dim dtAdapter As New OleDbDataAdapter (strCmd, oledbConn)
dtAdapter.MissingSchemaAction = MissingSchemaAction.AddWithKey
```

C#:

```
string strConn = "Provider=Microsoft.JET.OLEDB.4.0;" +
    "Data Source=Northwind.mdb";
OleDbConnection oledbConn = new OleDbConnection (strConn);
string strCmd = "SELECT * FROM Products";
OleDbDataAdapter dtAdapter = new OleDbDataAdapter (strCmd, oledbConn);
dtAdapter.MissingSchemaAction = MissingSchemaAction.AddWithKey;
```

OleDbDataAdapter Constructor (String, String)

Initializes a new instance of the OleDbDataAdapter class with the specified command text string and a connection string.

VB.NET:

```
Overloads Public Sub New( _
    ByVal selectCommandText As String, _
    ByVal selectConnectionString As String _
)
```

C#:

```
public OleDbDataAdapter(
    string selectCommandText,
    string selectConnectionString
);
```

The selectCommandText string must be a valid SQL SELECT statement and the selectConnectionString string must be a valid connection string. This constructor first calls the default constructor of the base class DbDataAdapter, which initializes the properties of this DataAdapter object to its default value. Next it calls OleDbConnection (string) class constructor, which sets the selectConnectionString as ConnectionString for the connection object. This created OleDbConnection along with command string is then passed to OleDbCommand (string, OleDbConnection) class constructor to create a new instance of the command object which gets set as SelectCommand for the DataAdapter:

```
Dim strConn = "Provider=Microsoft.JET.OLEDB.4.0;" & _
    "Data Source=Northwind.mdb"
Dim strCmd = "SELECT * FROM Products"
Dim dtAdapter As New OleDbDataAdapter (strCmd, strConn)
dtAdapter.MissingSchemaAction = MissingSchemaAction.AddWithKey
```

```
string strConn = "Provider=Microsoft.JET.OLEDB.4.0;" +
    "Data Source=Northwind.mdb";
string strCmd = "SELECT * FROM Products";
OleDbDataAdapter dtAdapter = new OleDbDataAdapter (strCmd, strConn);
dtAdapter.MissingSchemaAction = MissingSchemaAction.AddWithKey;
```

OleDbDataAdapter Properties

The DeleteCommand Property

Gets or sets the command for deleting the records from the specified data set. This property is inherited from the base class `DataAdapter`.

VB.NET:

```
Public Property DeleteCommand As OleDbCommand
```

C#:

```
public OleDbCommand DeleteCommand {get; set;}
```

This property is set as an instance of `OleDbCommand` object. It is used during `Update` operation for deleting the records corresponding to the `DataRow` objects with `RowStatus` property set to `Deleted`. If the caller does not explicitly set this command property, it can be automatically generated during the `Update` operation provided that a valid `SelectCommand` has been specified, a primary key is present in the table, and an `OleDbCommandBuilder` is associated with the `DataAdapter`.

To improve efficiency of `Update` operation, we should always set this command property explicitly.

The following code illustrates how this property can be set to delete a record from the table. It first fetches the record from the database by calling `Fill` method and then call `Delete` method on the retrieved `DataRow`. This sets the `RowState` property of the `DataRow` to `Deleted`. The `Update` method is then called to commit all the changes made in the `DataSet` to the data source. For the sake of brevity, no exception handling and event handling has been implemented for this method.

VB.NET:

```
Public Function DeleteContact(ByVal strID As String)
    Dim strConn As String = "Data Source=localhost;uid=sa;pwd=;Initial
Catalog=Northwind"
    Dim strDelCmd As New StringBuilder()
    Dim strQuery As New StringBuilder()
    strQuery.Append("SELECT * FROM CONTACTS WHERE ContactId = '")
    strQuery.Append(strID + "'")
    strDelCmd.Append("DELETE FROM CONTACTS WHERE ContactId = '")
    strDelCmd.Append(strID + "'")
```

```
      ' Create Connection object.
      Dim sqlConn As New SqlConnection(strConn)
      ' Create the Command object to get DataReader for the
      ' CONTACTS table.
      Dim selectCmd As New SqlCommand(strQuery.ToString(), sqlConn)
      ' Create the DataAdapter object to fetch and update records.
      Dim dtAdapter As New SqlDataAdapter(selectCmd)
      ' Set the MissingSchemaAction property to so that constraint
      ' information is created in the table.
      dtAdapter.MissingSchemaAction = MissingSchemaAction.AddWithKey
      Dim contactSet As New DataSet()
      dtAdapter.Fill(contactSet, "Contacts")
      ' Attach the DeleteCommand to the DataAdapter
      dtAdapter.DeleteCommand = New SqlCommand(strDelCmd.ToString(), sqlConn)
      ' Delete the record row from table.
      contactSet.Tables(0).Rows(0).Delete()
      ' Update the data source.
      dtAdapter.Update(contactSet, "Contacts")
   End Function
```

C#:

```
   public void DeleteContact(string strID)
   {
       string strConn = "Data Source=localhost;uid=sa; pwd=; Initial
   Catalog=Northwind";
       StringBuilder strDelCmd = new StringBuilder ();
       StringBuilder strQuery = new StringBuilder ();
       strQuery.Append ("SELECT * FROM CONTACTS WHERE ContactId = '");
       strQuery.Append (strID + "'");
       strDelCmd.Append ("DELETE FROM CONTACTS WHERE ContactId = '");
       strDelCmd.Append (strID + "'");
       // Create Connection object.
       SqlConnection sqlConn = new SqlConnection (strConn);
       // Create the Command object to get DataReader for the
       // CONTACTS table.
       SqlCommand selectCmd = new SqlCommand (strQuery.ToString (), sqlConn);
       // Create the DataAdapter object to fetch and update records.
       SqlDataAdapter dtAdapter = new SqlDataAdapter (selectCmd);
       // Set the MissingSchemaAction property to so that constraint
       // information is created in the table.
       dtAdapter.MissingSchemaAction = MissingSchemaAction.AddWithKey;
       DataSet contactSet = new DataSet ();
       dtAdapter.Fill (contactSet, "Contacts");
       // Attach the DeleteCommand to the DataAdapter
       dtAdapter.DeleteCommand = new SqlCommand (strDelCmd.ToString (), sqlConn);
       // Delete the record row from table.
       contactSet.Tables[0].Rows[0].Delete ();
       // Update the data source.
       dtAdapter.Update (contactSet, "Contacts");
   }
```

When we delete records for tables that are related to other tables in the data set, care must be taken to maintain the referential integrity of the database. Before we delete any parent row, we must make sure that it is not referencing a row in the child table. If it does, then we should delete the child rows before deleting the parent row.

If an attempt is made to delete a row that has foreign key constraint with column of another data table, then the framework throws an exception with the message:

```
DELETE STATEMENT conflicted with COLUMN REFERENCE constrints <constraintname>
```

For example, EMPLOYEE table's OrderId column has foreign key relationship with OrderId column of ORDERS table. Deleting any employee record will violate the referential integrity of the tables. The framework does not let this happen unless you specify the appropriate action to be taken to satisfy the constraint, which could be cascading or deleting the parent-child rows in bottom up fashion in other words submitting the delete action for the child first and then deleting the parent rows.

Before any update action is carried out the OnRowUpdating events is fired. You can register as many event handlers as you want for different tables in the dataSet. For example, if you have hierarchical tables in the DataSet, you can register separate event handlers for separate tables and provide table specific processing in these handler. This event handler provides you access to the row that is being updated. From this DataRow object, you can complete information about the parent and child rows that are in the delete action. From there you can decide if the referential integrity is being maintained or not. To catch the problems early, you can even register event handlers for RowDeleting and RowDeleted events for every table. These events will be fired when you call Delete method on the DataRow. If the DeleteRule on the DataRelation has been set to Rule.Cascade, you can make sure that all the required parent-child rows are getting their status set to DataRowState.Deleted before the Update method is even called.

Before accessing any properties of the DataRow, check that its RowState property value is not DataRowState.Deleted. The framework will throw a DeletedRowInaccesibleException exception if you try to access the deleted row.

The following code demonstrates the delete action on hierarchical data rows of ORDERS and ORDERDETAILS tables of Northwind database. These tables have foreign key constraint established on OrderId data column. The implementation performs the following steps:

1. Creates a SqlConnection object by specifying the connection string as constructor argument.

2. Builds the batch query for SELECT and DELETE action. Notice that in DELETE query, the record from ORDERDETAILS is being deleted first otherwise the Update method fails, because of referential integrity getting broken if ORDER records are deleted first.

3. Retrieves the records from two tables by calling Fill method. Notice that before the Fill call, the TableMapping has been added for the two tables. The records from ORDERS table will be populated in Orders DataTable and records from ORDERDETAILS will be populated in OrderDetails DataTable instead of the DataTable objects with default names Table and Table1.

4. Next, a ForeignKeyConstraint object is created. The parent-child columns are passed in as the constructor arguments. The DeleteRule property of the constraint is set to Rule.Cascade, and a new DataRelation is added to the table.

5. To handle the row delete and update events, the event handlers are added for the DataAdpater as well as for the two tables. These event handlers have not been shown in the code. Refer to the RowUpdated and RowUpdating events section for more details.

6. The row returned by Fill method is deleted by calling Delete method on the DataRow.

7. And finally Update method is called to commit the changes to the data source.

C#:

```csharp
public bool DeleteOrder (string strID)
{
    bool bRetVal = true;
    string strConn = "Data Source=localhost; uid=sa; pwd=; Initial
Catalog=Northwind";
    StringBuilder strDelCmd = new StringBuilder ();
    StringBuilder strQuery = new StringBuilder ();

    // Construct the SELECT query
    strQuery.Append ("SELECT OrderId FROM ORDERS WHERE OrderId = '");
    strQuery.Append (strID + "';");
    strQuery.Append ("SELECT OrderId FROM ORDERDETAILS WHERE OrderId = '");
    strQuery.Append (strID + "'");

    // Construct the DELETE query.
    strDelCmd.Append ("DELETE FROM ORDERDETAILS WHERE OrderId = '");
    strDelCmd.Append (strID + "';");
    strDelCmd.Append ("DELETE FROM ORDERS WHERE OrderId = '");
    strDelCmd.Append (strID + "'");

    try
    {
      SqlConnection sqlConn = new SqlConnection (strConn);
      SqlCommand selectCmd = new SqlCommand (strQuery.ToString (), sqlConn);
      SqlDataAdapter dtAdapter = new SqlDataAdapter (selectCmd);
      // Set the MissingSchemaAction property to so that constraint
      // information is created in the table.
      dtAdapter.MissingSchemaAction = MissingSchemaAction.AddWithKey;
      // Add event handler to handle errors during Fill operation.
      dtAdapter.FillError += new FillErrorEventHandler (FillErrorEvtHndlr);
      // Add the event handlers to get the events before the rows are
      // updated and aftet the row has been updated.
      dtAdapter.RowUpdated += new SqlRowUpdatedEventHandler(OnRowUpdatedEvtHndlr);
      dtAdapter.RowUpdating += new
SqlRowUpdatingEventHandler(OnRowUpdatingEvtHndlr);

      // Add the table mapping for the two tables that will be returned by
      // the batch SELECT query.
      dtAdapter.TableMappings.Add ("Table", "Orders");
      dtAdapter.TableMappings.Add ("Table1", "OrderDetails");

      DataSet ordersSet = new DataSet ();
      // Call Fill method to fetch the records.
      dtAdapter.Fill (ordersSet);

      // Add the Foreign Key constrinat to the table.
      ForeignKeyConstraint fkcOrderId = new ForeignKeyConstraint
 ("OrderIDConstraint",
                           ordersSet.Tables["Orders"].Columns["OrderId"],
                           ordersSet.Tables["OrderDetails"].Columns["OrderId"]);
      // Specify the DeleteRule for constraint to Cascade.
      fkcOrderId.DeleteRule = Rule.Cascade;
```

```
      //Add the constraint to the OrderDetails table
      ordersSet.Tables["OrderDetails"].Constraints.Add(fkcOrderId);

      // Add the this relation to the DataSet before any updates are done.
      DataRelation rel = new DataRelation ("OrderIDRelation",
            new DataColumn [] {ordersSet.Tables["Orders"].Columns["OrderId"]},
            new DataColumn []
{ordersSet.Tables["OrderDetails"].Columns["OrderId"]});
      ordersSet.Relations.Add (rel);

      // Attach the DeleteCommand to the DataAdapter
      dtAdapter.DeleteCommand = new SqlCommand (strDelCmd.ToString(), sqlConn);

      // Add the event handler for row deletion operation on the DataTable.
      ordersSet.Tables["Orders"].RowDeleted +=
            new DataRowChangeEventHandler (OrdersRowDeleted);
      ordersSet.Tables["Orders"].RowDeleting +=
            new DataRowChangeEventHandler (OrdersRowDeleting);
      ordersSet.Tables["OrderDetails"].RowDeleted +=
            new DataRowChangeEventHandler (DetailsRowDeleted);
      ordersSet.Tables["OrderDetails"].RowDeleting +=
            new DataRowChangeEventHandler (DetailsRowDeleting);

      // Delete the record row from table. This call will raise the events
      // on the table.
      ordersSet.Tables[0].Rows[0].Delete ();
      // Update the data source.
      int iRecsDeleted = dtAdapter.Update (ordersSet);
      Console.WriteLine ("Number of records deleted = {0}", iRecsDeleted);
    }
    catch (SqlException ex)
    {
      bRetVal = false;
      foreach (SqlError err in ex.Errors)
      {
          Console.WriteLine ("SQLERROR: {0}", err.Message);
      }
    }
    catch (Exception ex)
    {
      bRetVal = false;
      Console.WriteLine ("ERROR: {0}", ex.Message);
    }

    return bRetVal;
}
```

The InsertCommand Property

Gets or sets the command for inserting new records to the data source during Update operation.

VB.NET:
```
Public Property InsertCommand As OleDbCommand
```

C#:
```
public OleDbCommand InsertCommand {get; set;}
```

This property is set as an instance of OleDbCommand object. It is used during the Update operation for inserting new records corresponding to the DataRow objects with RowStatus property set to Added. If the caller does not explicitly set this command property then it can be automatically generated during the Update operation provided that a valid SelectCommand has been specified, a primary key is present in the table, and an OleDbCommandBuilder is associated with the DataAdapter.

The following code makes use of the SqlCommandBuilder to automatically generate InsertCommand to insert the records into the database. The code implements a public method in the data access layer to add a publisher's information into the PUBS database. It adds the information into two tables: PUBLISHERS and PUB_INO. The method also demonstrates the use of FileStream and BinaryReader to read the bitmap file from the disk and insert the byte array value into the logo field of PUB_INFO table. These two classes are defined in System.IO namespace.

VB.NET:
```
Public Function AddPublisherInfo(ByVal strID As String, ByVal strName As String, _
        ByVal strCity As String, ByVal strState As String, _
        ByVal strCountry As String, ByVal strPrInfo As String, _
        ByVal strLogoFile As String)
    Dim strConn As String = "Data Source = ADONET;" & _
                        " uid=sa; pwd=; Initial Catalog = pubs"
    Dim strPubSelect As String = "SELECT * FROM PUBLISHERS;"
    Dim strPubInfoSelect As String = "SELECT * FROM PUB_INFO"
    Try
      ' Create the connection.
        Dim sqlConn As New SqlConnection(strConn)
        ' Create the DataAdapter call Fill method to get the record.
        Dim pubDtAdapter As New SqlDataAdapter(strPubSelect, sqlConn)
        Dim pubinfoDtAdapter As New SqlDataAdapter(strPubInfoSelect, sqlConn)
        pubDtAdapter.MissingSchemaAction = MissingSchemaAction.AddWithKey
        pubinfoDtAdapter.MissingSchemaAction = MissingSchemaAction.AddWithKey

        Dim pubDtTable As New DataTable("PublisherInfo")
        pubDtAdapter.Fill(pubDtTable)

        Dim pubinfoDtTable As New DataTable("PublisherInfo")
        pubinfoDtAdapter.Fill(pubinfoDtTable)

        ' Create a new row in PUBLISHER table.
        Dim pubRow As DataRow = pubDtTable.NewRow()
        ' Create new row in pub_info table.
        Dim pubinfoRow As DataRow = pubinfoDtTable.NewRow()
```

```vb
            ' Populate the information for Publisher table.
            pubRow("pub_id") = strID
            pubRow("pub_name") = strName
            pubRow("city") = strCity
            pubRow("state") = strState
            pubRow("country") = strCountry
            ' Add this row to the table.
            pubDtTable.Rows.Add(pubRow)

            ' Populate the information for pub_info table row.
            pubinfoRow("pub_id") = strID
            pubinfoRow("pr_info") = strPrInfo

            Dim st As FileStream = File.Open(strLogoFile, FileMode.Open)
            Dim br As New BinaryReader(st)
            pubinfoRow("logo") = br.ReadBytes(CType(br.BaseStream.Length, Integer))
            ' Add this row to the table.
            pubinfoDtTable.Rows.Add(pubinfoRow)

            Dim pubCB As New SqlCommandBuilder(pubDtAdapter)
            Dim pubinfoCB As New SqlCommandBuilder(pubinfoDtAdapter)

            ' Commit the changes made to the datasource.
            Dim iRecsUpdated As Integer = pubDtAdapter.Update(pubDtTable)
            Console.WriteLine("Number of records updated = {0}", iRecsUpdated)
            iRecsUpdated = pubinfoDtAdapter.Update(pubinfoDtTable)
            Console.WriteLine("Number of records updated = {0}", iRecsUpdated)

    Catch ex As OleDbException
        Trace.WriteLine("OLEDBEXCEPTION: " + ex.Message)
    Catch ex As Exception
        Trace.WriteLine("EXCEPTION: " + ex.Message)
    End Try
End Function
```

C#:

```csharp
public void AddPublisherInfo (string strID, string strName,
    string strCity, string strState, string strCountry,
    string strPrInfo, string strLogoFile)
{
    string strConn = "Data Source = ADONET;" +
                " uid=sa; pwd=; Initial Catalog = pubs";
    string strPubSelect = "SELECT * FROM PUBLISHERS;";
    string strPubInfoSelect = "SELECT * FROM PUB_INFO";
    try
    {
    // Create the connection.
    SqlConnection sqlConn = new SqlConnection(strConn);
    // Create the DataAdapter call Fill method to get the record.
    SqlDataAdapter pubDtAdapter = new SqlDataAdapter (strPubSelect, sqlConn);
    SqlDataAdapter pubinfoDtAdapter = new SqlDataAdapter (strPubInfoSelect,
sqlConn);
    pubDtAdapter.MissingSchemaAction = MissingSchemaAction.AddWithKey;
    pubinfoDtAdapter.MissingSchemaAction = MissingSchemaAction.AddWithKey;
```

```
    // Fill the publishers table
    DataTable pubDtTable = new DataTable("PublisherInfo");
    pubDtAdapter.Fill (pubDtTable);

    // Fill the pub_info table.
    DataTable pubinfoDtTable = new DataTable("PublisherInfo");
    pubinfoDtAdapter.Fill (pubinfoDtTable);

    // Create a new row in PUBLISHER table.
    DataRow pubRow = pubDtTable.NewRow ();
    // Create new row in pub_info table.
    DataRow pubinfoRow = pubinfoDtTable.NewRow ();

    // Populate the information for Publisher table.
    pubRow["pub_id"] = strID;
    pubRow["pub_name"] = strName;
    pubRow["city"] = strCity;
    pubRow["state"] = strState;
    pubRow["country"] = strCountry;
    // Add this row to the table.
    pubDtTable.Rows.Add (pubRow);

    // Populate the information for pub_info table row.
    pubinfoRow["pub_id"] = strID;
    pubinfoRow["pr_info"] = strPrInfo;

    // Open the image file to create the stream.
    FileStream st = File.Open (strLogoFile, FileMode.Open);
    BinaryReader br = new BinaryReader(st);
    pubinfoRow["logo"] = br.ReadBytes ((int)br.BaseStream.Length);
    // Add this row to the table.
    pubinfoDtTable.Rows.Add (pubinfoRow);

    SqlCommandBuilder pubCB = new SqlCommandBuilder (pubDtAdapter);
    SqlCommandBuilder pubinfoCB = new SqlCommandBuilder (pubinfoDtAdapter);

    // Commit the changes made to the datasource.
    int iRecsUpdated = pubDtAdapter.Update (pubDtTable);
    Trace.WriteLine ("Number of records updated = " + iRecsUpdated);

    iRecsUpdated = pubinfoDtAdapter.Update (pubinfoDtTable);
    Trace.WriteLine ("Number of records updated = " + iRecsUpdated);
}
catch (OleDbException ex)
{
  Trace.WriteLine ("OLEDBEXCEPTION: " + ex.Message);
}
catch (Exception ex)
{
  Trace.WriteLine ("EXCEPTION: " + ex.Message);
}
}
```

Like other Update commands, care must be taken to maintain the integrity of the database records. If there is a parent child relation between the tables, then the rows in the parent table should be added before the child rows could be added. For example, in the PUBS database the TITLES and PUBLISHERS tables have a foreign key relation on the pub_id column. If you are entering a new record into TITLES table, either the corresponding publisher's record should be present in the PUBLISHERS table or you have to insert a new record in that data table.

Notice the SELECT statement appended to the INSERT statement. When a new record is added to the data source, the auto-incremented identity column's value is not returned in the DataSet. To overcome this problem, the SELECT statement is added to return the record for which the identity column was auto-incremented. The @@IDENTITY value returns the last auto-generated value.

> **If we specify the source table name for mapping source during the Fill method, then we need to make sure that the same name is provided during the Update method call. Failure to do so, will result in an ArgumentNullException exception being thrown.**

The following code shows the implementation that would throw an exception:

```
DataAdapter.Fill (dtSet, "MyTable")
' Inset a new data row to the data set and call update.
DataAdapter.Update (dtSet);
```

The reason why this Update call is faulty is that it is looking for the default name Table for mapping, and the supplied DataSet is mapped to the MyTable DataTable. This requirement applies to all the update commands: InsertCommand, DeleteCommand, UpdateCommand, and SelectCommand.

The SelectCommand Property

Gets or sets the command for retrieving records based on the SQL statement set as the command text.

VB.NET:
```
Public Property SelectCommand As OleDbCommand
```

C#:
```
public OleDbCommand SelectCommand {get; set;}
```

This property is set as an instance of the OleDbCommand object. It gets set by the SQL SELECT statement that is either explicitly set in the command object property, or passed in as the class constructor for the DataAdapter. None of the Fill and Update operations succeed unless this command property has been set. A successful execution of SelectCommand returns a single data table or multiple data tables, depending on the type of query issued by the command. If the query fails to fetch any records, the DataSet is not populated with any record and the call does not raise any exception.

VB.NET:
```
Dim strConn = "Provider=Microsoft.JET.OLEDB.4.0;" & _
    "Data Source=Northwind.mdb"
Dim strCmd = "SELECT * FROM OrderDetails"
```

```
Dim oledbConn As New OleDbconnection(strConn)
Dim dtAdapter As New OleDbDataAdapter ()
With dtAdapter
    .SelectCommand = new OleDbCommand (strCmd)
    .SelectCommand.Connection = oledbConn
End With
Dim dtDeatilsSet As New DataSet ()
dtAdapter.Fill (dtDeatilsSet)
```

C#:

```
string strConn = "Provider=Microsoft.JET.OLEDB.4.0;" +
        "Data Source=Northwind.mdb";
string strCmd = "SELECT * FROM OrderDetails";
OleDbConnection oledbConn = new OleDbconnection(strConn);
OleDbDataAdapter dtAdapter = new OleDbDataAdapter ();
dtAdapter.SelectCommand = new OleDbCommand (strCmd, oledbConn);
DataSet dtDeatilsSet = new DataSet ();
DtAdapter.Fill (dtDeatilsSet);
```

The UpdateCommand Property

The UpdateCommand property gets or sets the command object to update the records in the data source.

VB.NET:

```
Public Property UpdateCommand As OleDbCommand
```

C#:

```
public OleDbCommand UpdateCommand {get; set;}
```

This property is set as an instance of OleDbCommand object. It is used during the Update operation for updating records corresponding to the DataRow objects with RowStatus property set to Modified. If the caller does not explicitly set this command property it can be automatically generate during the Update operation, provided that a valid SelectCommand has been specified, a primary key is present in the table, and an OleDbCommandBuilder is associated with the DataAdapter.

If the update action involves only one DataTable in the DataSet, then using the CommandBuilder object, OleDbCommandBuilder, SqlCommandBuilder or OdbcCommandBuilder, can automatically generate the UpdateCommand for you. Use of CommandBuilder introduces some performance hit but it makes the coding process easy. The CommandBuilder has to make round trips to the database to get the metadata and build the update action query dynamically. To improve efficiency of the Update operation, we should always set this command property explicitly

The following show the implementation of a method in the data access tier that is used to update the record in AUTHORS table in the PUBS database. The method uses the CommandBuilder to build the UpdateCommand for committing the changes using the Update method on the DataAdapter.

VB.NET:

```
Public Function UpdateAuthor(ByVal strID As String, ByVal strLastName As String, _
        ByVal strFirstName As String, ByVal phone As String, _
        ByVal strAddress As String, ByVal strCity As String, _
        ByVal strState As String, ByVal strZip As String, _
        ByVal bContract As Boolean) As Boolean
    Dim bRetVal As Boolean = True
    Dim strConn As String = "Provider = SQLOLEDB.1; Data Source = ADONET;" & _
                " uid=sa; pwd=; Initial Catalog = pubs"
    Dim strSelectCmd As String = "SELECT * FROM AUTHORS WHERE au_id='" & _
                            strID + "'"
    Try
        ' Create the connection.
        Dim oledbConn As New OleDbConnection(strConn)
        ' Create the DataAdapter call Fill method to get the record.
        Dim dtAdapter As New OleDbDataAdapter(strSelectCmd, oledbConn)
        dtAdapter.MissingSchemaAction = MissingSchemaAction.AddWithKey
        Dim dtSet As New DataSet("Authors DataSet")
        dtAdapter.Fill(dtSet, "Authors")

        ' Update the record in the table.
        Dim authorRec As DataRow = dtSet.Tables("Authors").Rows(0)
        authorRec("au_lname") = strLastName
        authorRec("au_fname") = strFirstName
        authorRec("phone") = phone
        authorRec("address") = strAddress
        authorRec("city") = strCity
        authorRec("state") = strState
        authorRec("zip") = strZip
        If bContract Then
            authorRec("contract") = 1
        Else
            authorRec("contract") = 0
        End If

        ' Attach the DataAdapter to CommandBuilder for automatic
        ' generation of UpdateCommand.
        Dim cmdBldr As New OleDbCommandBuilder(dtAdapter)

        ' Commit the changes made to the datasource.
        Dim iRecsUpdated As Integer = dtAdapter.Update(dtSet, "Authors")
        Trace.WriteLine("Number of records updated = " + iRecsUpdated)

    Catch ex As OleDbException
        bRetVal = False
        Trace.WriteLine("OLEDBEXCEPTION: " + ex.Message)
    Catch ex As Exception
        bRetVal = False
        Trace.WriteLine("EXCEPTION: " + ex.Message)
    End Try

    Return bRetVal
End Function
```

C#:

```csharp
public bool UpdateAuthor (string strID, string strLastName,
                    string strFirstName, string phone,
                    string strAddress, string strCity,
                    string strState, string strZip,
                    bool bContract)
{
    bool bRetVal = true;
    string strConn = "Provider = SQLOLEDB.1; Data Source = ADONET;" +
                " uid=sa; pwd=; Initial Catalog = pubs";
    string strSelectCmd = "SELECT * FROM AUTHORS WHERE au_id='" +
                    strID + "'";
    try
    {
      // Create the connection.
      OleDbConnection oledbConn = new OleDbConnection(strConn);
      // Create the DataAdapter call Fill method to get the record.
      OleDbDataAdapter dtAdapter = new OleDbDataAdapter (strSelectCmd, oledbConn);
      dtAdapter.MissingSchemaAction = MissingSchemaAction.AddWithKey;
      DataSet dtSet = new DataSet("Authors DataSet");
      dtAdapter.Fill (dtSet, "Authors");

      // Update the record in the table.
      DataRow authorRec = dtSet.Tables["Authors"].Rows[0];
      authorRec["au_lname"] = strLastName;
      authorRec["au_fname"] = strFirstName;
      authorRec["phone"] = phone;
      authorRec["address"] = strAddress;
      authorRec["city"] = strCity;
      authorRec["state"] = strState;
      authorRec["zip"] = strZip;
      authorRec["contract"] = (bContract == true) ? 1 : 0;
      // Attach the DataAdapter to CommandBuilder for automatic
      // generation of UpdateCommand.
      OleDbCommandBuilder cmdBldr = new OleDbCommandBuilder (dtAdapter);

      // Commit the changes made to the datasource.
      int iRecsUpdated = dtAdapter.Update (dtSet, "Authors");
      Trace.WriteLine ("Number of records updated = " + iRecsUpdated);
    }
    catch (OleDbException ex)
    {
     bRetVal = false;
     Trace.WriteLine ("OLEDBEXCEPTION: " + ex.Message);
    }
    catch (Exception ex)
    {
     bRetVal = false;
     Trace.WriteLine ("EXCEPTION: " + ex.Message);
    }
    return bRetVal;
}
```

Updating a record in the data source is one of the most important actions that the data access layer performs and is source of lot of errors. If the process of record update is not very clear to the implementer, it could lead to very anomalous results.

Developing an application for a single user is relatively a simple task. But in the new world it is not the case anymore. Most of the applications have thousands and some have millions of users accessing the database to retrieve the information. This is where the things start becoming a little complex.

It has been mentioned in the introduction of this chapter that the `DataSet` populated by the `Fill` method works in disconnected from the database, like the disconnected `Recordset` in ADO. All the results of the query are cached in the `DataSet` object's memory. ADO.Net does not let us specify the lock on the record. It works on the principle of optimistic locking, which means that after the query has returned the record to a caller, any other client can fetch it for any purpose. This locking mechanism decides how the records will be updated. Optimistic locking is very useful for building scalable applications because the records or tables are not locked while one client is working on it. Multiple users can retrieve the same record. Although optimistic locking introduces more effort on part of the client application, at the end, it overweighs the advantages we get by scalability and performance.

Let's consider the example of updating the author information in the PUBS database. After we have grabbed the record from a table, we might make some changes to some fields. In the meantime, a second employee in the company fetched the same author's record and updated the phone number, corresponding to phone field in the table. We next submit the changes. The framework throws an exception with the message "CONCURRENCY VIOLATION: the Update Command affected 0 record."

There are two possible solutions to this case. First, is that the update action could have overwritten the changes made by the other client. Second, is that the update action fails, and an error is returned to the caller. What happened in this case is that whoever commits the changes first will succeed in updating the record, and the other client's changes will be rejected. This way, ADO.NET avoids anybody from unintentionally overwriting the changes made by others.

Let's look at the UPDATE statement that was submitted to the SQL Server for this update action:

```
UPDATE "AUTHORS"
SET "address" = @P1 , "contract" = @P2
WHERE
  ( "au_id" = @P3 AND "au_lname" = @P4 AND
    "au_fname" = @P5 AND "phone" = @P6 AND
    "address" = @P7 AND "city" = @P8 AND
    "state" = @P9 AND "zip" = @P10 AND
    "contract" = @P11
  )',
 N'@P1 varchar(34),@P2 bit,@P3 varchar(22),
   @P4 varchar(12),@P5 varchar(12),@P6 char(24),
   @P7 varchar(22),@P8 varchar(28),@P9 char(4),
   @P10 char(10),@P11 bit',
   '67 Seventh Avenue', 1, '998-72-3567', 'Ringer',
   'Albert', '801 826-0752             ', '67 Seventh ',
   'Salt Lake City', 'UT ',
   '84512      ', 0
```

The `CommandBuilder` is smart enough to figure out what fields were changed and it only submits changes for those fields only. For example, in the above example, we changed address and contract field information only. Before the updates were submitted to the database, another client changed the contract field value to 1.

Pay attention to parameter P11 in the above UPDATE query. It has a value of 0 that corresponds to the field value when the record was fetched. The WHERE clause is checking on all the fields of the table to make sure that the record that is being updated is the same as the one that was originally retrieved from the database. The CommandBuilder builds this query by checking the DataRowVersion.Current and DataRowVersion.Orginal version values of all the fields in the row. The following C# codes shows how these different values can be obtained by using the appropriate DataRowVersion enumeration value:

```
string originalValue = (string)authorRec["address", DataRowVersion.Original];
string currentValue = (string)authorRec["address", DataRowVersion.Current];
bool bValueChanged = (string.Compare (originalValue, currentValue) != 0);
```

Since the original field value for the contract field did not match the one that is currently in the database, therefore the UpdateCommand fails and throws an exception indicating that update action failed.

The automatic command generation using the CommandBuilder fails if there is no primary key or unique column in the table. The CommandBuilder obtains the metadata information dynamically from the database. In the absence of the primary key or unique column, the Update method will throw an exception indicating that there is no primary key in the table. The only alternative, if there is no primary key in the table, is to explicitly specify the UPDATE query in the UpdateCommand of the DataAdapter instead of using the CommandBuilder. For more information, refer to the chapter on CommandBuilder classes (chapter 4).

If it is absolutely essential for an application to overwrite the changes made by others, then you can accomplish this by explicitly specifying the UPDATE command and not comparing the current values in the database with the original values that DataSet has. The following code shows explicit creation of UpdateCommand that may overwrite other user's changes:

```
string updateCmd = "UPDATE AUTHORS SET au_lname = '" +
            strLastName +
            "' WHERE au_id = '" +
            strID + "'";
dtAdapter.UpdateCommand = new OleDbCommand (updateCmd, oledbConn);

// Commit the changes made to the datasource.
int iRecsUpdated = dtAdapter.Update (dtSet, "Authors");
Trace.WriteLine ("Number of records updated = " + iRecsUpdated);
```

For updating the hierarchical records follow the same approach as discussed in DeleteCommand section.

Successful execution of UpdateCommand returns the number of records that were updated by the Update method. If the update action fails, the return value is zero. The possible reason for the update action to fail could be one of the following:

❑ Another user modified the record that you are trying to update. This happens due to optimistic updating conflict.

❑ Invalid data supplied for one or more columns.

❑ Constraints set up for the tables are not being satisfied. This would happen in case of relational data tables.

❑ Some internal error in the DataAdapter like server loosing connection with database or due to some bug in the implementation.

OleDbDataAdapter Methods

The Fill Method

In addition to the `Fill` methods discussed in `DbDataAdapter` class, the `OleDbDataAdapter` class provides two overloaded implementations of `Fill` method that take an ADO `Recordset` or `Record` object as input parameter and populates the `DataSet` with the records extracted from these ADO objects.

The Fill (DataTable, Object) Method

VB.NET:

```
Overloads Public Function Fill( _
    ByVal dataTable As DataTable, _
    ByVal adodb As Object _
) As Integer
```

C#:

```
public int Fill(
    DataTable dataTable,
    object adodb
);
```

Parameter	Type	Description
dataTable	DataTable	The caller provided DataSet object to fill records and schema in
adodb	Object	The Recordset or Record object to retrieve data from

The Fill (DataSet, Object, String) Method

VB.NET:

```
Overloads Public Function Fill( _
    ByVal dataSet As DataSet, _
    ByVal adodb As Object, _
    ByVal srcTable As String _
) As Integer
```

C#:

```
public int Fill(
    DataSet dataSet,
    object adodb,
    string srcTable
);
```

Parameter	Type	Description
dataSet	DataSet	The caller provided DataSet object to fill records and schema in
adodb	Object	The Recordset or Record object to retrieve data from
srcTable	String	The name of the source table that will be mapped to DataTable in the DataSet

These two overloaded implementations of the Fill method facilitate the retrieval of data records from an ADO Recordset or Record object. We can use .NET COM **Interop** services to access the ADO object model to fetch data from Recordset objects. For more details on use of **Interop** services for data access, refer to Chapter 16.

The methods take an already populated Recordset or Record object as Input parameter and use **Interop** services to call the methods on the ADO object to iterate over each recordset and record and add it to the caller provided DataSet.

> **This data flow between ADO and ADO.Net object works only in one direction i.e. from ADO to ADO.Net. The DataSet cannot update the data in the Recordset. All the update operations must be taken care of explicitly either by ADO.Net or ADO objects.**

This overloaded implementation of the Fill method follows the same rules for populating the DataSet as the other implementations in DbDataAdapter class. The only difference is that in this case the data source is a Recordset or Record object instead of a backend database. If the MissingSchemaAction property value is set to AddWithKey, then the primary key and constraints are created in the DataTable. If the record set has a primary key then the subsequent calls to this method will update the data rows that match the primary keys, otherwise the rows are appended to the DataTable. The PrimaryKey property can also be set by calling FillSchema method for that table, or it can be explicitly set in the DataTable object, as shown in the following sample:

```
Dim dtTable As New DataTable ()
Dim pkCol(2) As DataColumn
Dim pkAuIdKey As New DataColumn ()

' Set data type and column name for author id
With pkAuIdKey
    .DataType = System.String.GetType()
    .ColumnName = "au_id"
End With

' Add the two columns to DataTable
dtTable.Columns.Add (pkAuIdKey)

' Add the column to array of PrimaryKeys
pkCol(0) = pkAuIdKey

' Set the primary keys for table.
```

```
dtTable.PrimaryKey = pkCol

' Create DataSet and add the table to it.
Dim dtSet As New DataSet ()
dtSet.Tables.Add (dtTable)

' Call Fill method to populate DataSet from Recordset object.
dtAdapter.Fill (dtSet, adoRecSet)
```

When the `DataTable` and `DataColumn` objects are added to the `DataSet`, the method follows the same guidelines as described in the `Fill` method section of the `DbDataAdapter` class. For more details, refer to the discussion of `Fill` method in the `DbDataAdapter` class.

The following code populates a `DataSet` from an ADO `Recordset`. The `Recordset` object, `adoRecSet`, is an ADO object that an application received from a COM server, implementing the data access tier of an application, using **Interop**:

```
Dim dtAdapter As New OleDbDataAdapter ()
Dim dtSet As New DataSet ()
dtAdapter.Fill (dtSet, adoRecSet, "Customers")
```

```
OleDbDataAdapter dtAdapter = new OleDbDataAdapter ();
DataSet dtSet = new DataSet ();
DtAdapter.Fill (dtSet, adoRecSet, "Customers");
```

The data types of each field in the `Record` object are converted to the CLR types for storing the values in the `DataColumn` objects. The following table shows this data mapping between ADO and ADO.Net CLR data types:

ADO Data Type	.NET CLR Data Type
adEmpty	null
adBoolean	Int16
adTinyInt	SByte
adSmallInt	Int16
adInteger	Int32
adBigInt	Int64
adUnsignedTinyInt	promoted to Int16
adUnsignedSmallInt	promoted to Int32
adUnsignedInt	promoted to Int64
adUnsignedBigInt	promoted to Decimal
adSingle	Single
adDouble	Double
adCurrency	Decimal
adDecimal	Decimal
adNumeric	Decimal
adDate	DateTime
adDBDate	DateTime
adDBTime	DateTime
adDBTimeStamp	DateTime

Table continued on following page

341

ADO Data Type	.NET CLR Data Type
adFileTime	DateTime
adGUID	Guid
adError	ExternalException
adIUnknown	object
adIDispatch	object
adVariant	object
adPropVariant	object
adBinary	byte[]
adChar	string
adWChar	string
adBSTR	string
adChapter	object
adUserDefined	not supported
adVarNumeric	not supported

The OnRowUpdated Method

Raises OnRowUpdated event passing RowUpdatedEventArgs object to event handler.

VB.NET:

```
Overrides Protected Sub OnRowUpdated( _
    ByVal value As RowUpdatedEventArgs _
)
```

C#:

```
protected override void OnRowUpdated(
    RowUpdatedEventArgs value
);
```

Parameter	Type	Description
value	RowUpdatedEventArgs	The object containing the event data

The managed providers, OleDbDataAdapter, SqlDataAdapter, and OdbcDataAdapter, override the implementation provided in the base class DbDataAdapter. For more information, refer to this event in DbDataAdapter class.

The OnRowUpdating Method

Raises OnRowUpdating event passing RowUpdatingEventArgs object to event handler.

VB.NET:

```
Overrides Protected Sub OnRowUpdating( _
    ByVal value As RowUpdatingEventArgs _
)
```

C#:

```
protected override void OnRowUpdating(
    RowUpdatingEventArgs value
);
```

Parameter	Type	Description
value	RowUpdatingEventArgs	The object containing the event data

The managed providers, OleDbDataAdapter, SqlDataAdapter, and OdbcDataAdapter, override the implementation provided in the base class DbDataAdapter. For more information refer to this event in DbDataAdapter class.

OleDbDataAdapter Events

The RowUpdated Event

This event is raised during execution of Update method against the data source. The event is raised only if after a data row has been changed during execution.

VB.NET:

```
Public Event RowUpdated As OleDbRowUpdatedEventHandler
```

C#:

```
public event OleDbRowUpdatedEventHandler RowUpdated;
```

This event gets raised when one of the update commands (InsertCommand, UpdateCommand, and DeleteCommand) has changed a data row in the DataSet. The OleDbRowUpdatedEventHandler delegate invokes the event handler and passes the OleDbRowUpdatedEventArgs object as the parameter to the event handler for this event. We can add or remove the event handlers for this event to the DataAdapter object before the Update method is invoked.

VB.NET:

```
Dim dtAdpater As New OleDbDataAdapter(strQuery, strConn)
' Add the event handler to recieve the events after a data row
' has been updated.
AddHandler dtAdapter.RowUpdated, _
    New OleDbRowUpdatedEventHandler(AddressOf OnRowUpdatedEvtHndlr)
```

C#:

```
OleDbDataAdapter dtAdapter = new OleDbDataAdapter (strQuery, strConn);
dtAdapter.RowUpdated += new OleDbRowUpdatedEventHandler (
                            OnRowUpdatedEvtHandler);
```

The OleDbRowUpdatedEventArgs object has the following properties that provide the complete information of the data related to the update event:

❑ Command – This is the command object that performed the Update operation on the row.

❑ Row – This is the DataRow containing the updated information for the record.

❑ StatementType – This property corresponds to StatementType enumeration indicating what type of SQL statement was executed by the Update method. This property can have one of the four enumeration values:

    ❑ SELECT – A SQL SELECT query statement.

343

- ❏ INSERT – A SQL INSERT statement.

- ❏ DELETE – A SQL DELETE statement.

- ❏ UPDATE – A SQL UPDATE statement.

- ❏ Status – This property gets/sets the UpdateStatus value of the command object. It can have one of the following four enumeration values:

  - ❏ Continue – The DataAdapter will continue with the Update operation.

  - ❏ ErrorsOccured – The Update of the data row encountered some errors and row was not updated.

  - ❏ SkipCurrentRow – The Update operation will not update the current data row and skip to the next record.

  - ❏ SkipAllRemainingRows – The Update operation will not update the current and any remaining rows.

- ❏ TableMapping – Gets the table mapping associated with the DataAdapter.

- ❏ RecordsAffected – This property gets the number of the rows that were modified by the Update method. If no data row was modified, the returned value is 0. In the case of a SELECT query, this property returns a value of –1.

- ❏ Errors – Gets the errors generated during the Update method. This information is returned as an Exception object.

The Status property value indicates if any error occurred during the Update operation. Then, depending on the nature of the error and information provided by other properties, we can modify the value of this property to one of the possible four values. If we set the value to ErrorsOcuured, the Update method will terminate and throw an exception that is set in the Errors property.

We can provide our own exception in this property to provide more information to the exception handler. The following code shows the implementation of the event handler function. For sake of brevity, this method is not checking the details of the values that were received in OleDbRowUpdatedEventArgs parameter. The function checks that if there was any error encountered during the update operation, simply the update of current row but don't terminate the whole Update process. This behavior is different from setting the status value as UpdateStatus.Continue. In the later case, the update operation will continue which may succeed if you have fixed the errors in the error handler. Otherwise the update operation will fail.

VB.NET:

```
Private Shared Sub OnRowUpdatedEvtHandler ( _
    sender As Object, args As OleDbRowUpdatedEventArgs)
    ' If error occurred, skip the current row.
    If args.Status = UpdateStatus.ErrorsOccurred
        args.Status = UpdateStatus.SkipCurrentRow
    End If
End Sub
```

C#:

```
private static void OnRowUpdatedEvtHandler(
    object sender, OleDbRowUpdatedEventArgs args)
```

```
    {
        // If error occurred skip the current row.
        if (args.Status == UpdateStatus.ErrorsOccurred)
        {
            args.Status = UpdateStatus.SkipCurrentRow;
        }
    }
}
```

The `SqlDataAdapter` provides a similar implementation for this event with the difference that `SqlRowUpdatedEventHandler` delegate invokes the event handler and the `SqlRowUpdatedEventArgs` object is passed as argument to the event handler method. This object has the same properties as `OleDbRowUpdatedEventArgs` class has.

VB.NET:

```
' Create SqlDataAdapter object for excecution of SELECT query.
Dim dtAdapter As New SqlDataAdapter(sqlSelCmd, sqlConn)

' Add the event handler to recieve the events after a data row
' has been updated.
AddHandler dtAdapter.RowUpdated, _
            New SqlRowUpdatedEventHandler(AddressOf OnRowUpdatedEvtHndlr)
```

C#:

```
// Create SqlDataAdapter object for excecution of SELECT query.
SqlDataAdapter dtAdapter = new SqlDataAdapter (strCmd, sqlConn);

// Add the event handler to recieve the events after a data row
// has been updated.
dtAdapter.RowUpdated += new SqlRowUpdatedEventHandler (
                                OnRowUpdatedEvtHandler);
```

The RowUpdating Event

This event is raised during execution of the `Update` method against the data source. The event is raised before any changes are made to a data row.

VB.NET:

```
Public Event RowUpdating As OleDbRowUpdatingEventHandler
```

C#:

```
public event OleDbRowUpdatingEventHandler RowUpdating;
```

This event gets raised when one of the update commands is called (`InsertCommand`, `UpdateCommand`, and `DeleteCommand`) just before a `dataRow` is about to be changed in the `DataSet`. The `OleDbRowUpdatingEventHandler` delegate invokes the event handler and passes the `OleDbRowUpdatingEventArgs` object as the parameter to the event handler for this event. We can add or remove the event handlers for this event to the `DataAdapter` object before the `Update` method is invoked:

```
' Create SqlDataAdapter object for exceution of SELECT query.
Dim dtAdapter As New OleDbDataAdapter(oledbSelCmd, oledbConn)

' Add an event handler to receive the events before a data row
' is updated.
AddHandler dtAdapter.RowUpdating, _
            New OleDbRowUpdatingEventHandler(AddressOf OnRowUpdatingEvtHndlr)
```

```
' Create SqlDataAdapter object for exceution of SELECT query.
OleDbDataAdapter dtAdapter = new OleDbDataAdapter (oledbSelCmd, oledbConn);
' Add an event handler to receive the events before a data row
' is updated.
dtAdapter.RowUpdated += new  OleDbRowUpdatingEventHandler (
                               OnRowUpdatingEvtHandler);
```

The `OleDbRowUpdatingEventArgs` object provides the same properties as `OleDbRowUpdatedEventArgs` except `RowsAffected`. No change has been made at this stage, therefore there is no way of knowing how many rows have been modified. Refer to the discussion of `RowUpdated` event for details on other properties.

Depending on the value of `Status` property and information provided by the rest of the property values of `OleDbRowUpatingEventArgs`, we can set the `Status` property value to indicate what action needs to be taken after the event handler returns control to the `Update` method. The implications of setting this value are the same as has been discussed in the `RowUpdated` event. A very common case of the `RowUpdatingEventArgs.Status` value being set to `ErrorOccured` is if one or more field values have a data type that does not match the one in metadata of the table:

```
Private Shared Sub OnRowUpdatingEvtHandler ( _
    sender As Object, args As SqlRowUpdatingEventArgs)
  ' If error occurred, skip the current row.
  If args.Status = UpdateStatus.ErrorsOccurred
      args.Status = UpdateStatus.SkipCurrentRow
  End If
End Sub
```

```
protected static void OnRowUpdatingEvtHandler(
    object sender, SqlRowUpdatingEventArgs args)
{
  // If error occurred skip the current row.
  if (args.Status == UpdateStatus.ErrorsOccurred)
  {
     args.Status = UpdateStatus.SkipCurrentRow;
  }
}
```

The `SqlDataAdapter` provides the similar implementation for this event with the difference that the `SqlRowUpdatingEventHandler` delegate invokes the event handler and the `SqlRowUpdatingEventArgs` object is passed as the argument to the event handler method. This object has the same properties as `SqlRowUpdatedEventArgs` class.

VB.NET:

```
' Create SqlDataAdapter object for excecution of SELECT query.
Dim dtAdapter As New SqlDataAdapter (strCmd, strConn)

' Add an event handler to receive the events before a data row
' is updated.
AddHandler dtAdapter.RowUpdating, _
          New SqlRowUpdatingEventHandler(AddressOf OnRowUpdatingEvtHndlr)
```

C#:

```
SqlDataAdapter dtAdapter = new SqlDataAdapter (strCmd, strConn);
DtAdapter.RowUpdated += new SqlRowUpdatingEventHandler (_
                                 OnRowUpdatedEvtHandler);
```

The SqlDataAdapter

VB.NET:

```
NotInheritable Public Class OleDbDataAdapter
     Inherits DbDataAdapter
     Implements ICloneable, IDbDataAdapter
```

C#:

```
public sealed class SqlDataAdapter :
     DbDataDapter,
     ICloneable, IDbDataAdapter
```

The `SqlDataAdapter` provides the public access class for SQL Server managed provider `DataAdapter` object. It is inherited from `DbDataAdapter` class and provides the implementation for abstract properties, `SelectCommand`, `InsertCommand`, `DeleteCommand`, and `UpdateCommand`, defined in `IDbDataAdapter` interface. For the rest of the class members, it inherits the implementation from base class `DbDataAdapter` and `DataAdapter`. For accessing and manipulating data for SQL Server 7.0 and higher, it is highly recommended that you use classes provided in `System.Data.SqlClient` namespace, because the SQL Server managed provider does not go through OLE DB layer to connect to data source. Instead, it uses SQL Server specific transport mechanism, which is very efficient.

SqlDataAdapter Constructors

SqlDataAdapter Constructor ()

Initializes a new instance of the `SqlDataAdapter` class.

VB.NET:

```
Overloads Public Sub New()
```

C#:

```
public SqlDataAdapter();
```

This is the default constructor for this class. When a new instance of this object is created, the properties of this class get initialized to their default values. These default values of properties can be changed by accessing individual read/write properties of the class.

VB.NET:

```
Dim dtDapter As New SqlDataAdapter ()
dtAdapter.MissingSchenaAction = MissingSchemaAction.AddWithKey
```

C#:

```
SqlDataAdapter dtAdapter = new SqlDataAdapter ();
dtAdapter.MissingSchemaAction = MissingSchemaAction.AddWithKey;
```

SqlDataAdapter Constructor (SqlCommand)

Initializes a new instance of the `SqlDataAdapter` class with the specified `SQLCommand` object.

VB.NET:

```
Overloads Public Sub New( _
    ByVal selectCommand As SqlCommand _
)
```

C#:

```
public SqlDataAdapter(
    SqlCommand selectCommand
);
```

The query associated with the `SqlDbCommand` should be a valid SQL `SELECT` statement. The constructor associates this command object to `SelectCommand` of the `DataAdapter`. This constructor first calls the default constructor of the base class `DbDataAdapter` that initializes the properties of this `DataAdapter` object to their default values.

VB.NET:

```
Dim sqlCmd As New SqlCommand ("SELECT * FROM Products")
Dim dtAdapter As New SqlDataAdapter (sqlCmd)
```

C#:

```
SqlCommand sqlCmd = new SqlCommand ("SELECT * FROM Products");
SqlDataAdapter dtAdapter = new SqlDataAdapter (sqlCmd);
```

SqlDataAdapter Constructor (String, SqlConnection)

Initializes a new instance of the `SqlDataAdapter` class with the specified command text string and an `SQLConnection` object.

VB.NET:

```
Overloads Public Sub New( _
    ByVal selectCommandText As String, _
    ByVal selectConnection As SqlConnection _
)
```

C#:

```
public SqlDataAdapter(
    string selectCommandText,
    SqlConnection selectConnection
);
```

The command text string must be a valid SQL SELECT statement. This constructor first calls the default constructor of the base class DbDataAdapter that initializes the properties of this DataAdapter object to default value. It then calls the SqlCommand (string, SqlConnection) class constructor, which sets the command string as CommandText and connection object for the command object. This then created SqlDbCommand object is set as SelectCommand for the DataAdapter.

VB.NET:

```
Dim strConn = "Data Source = localhost; Intial Catalog=Northwind; " & _
    "User ID=sa; Pwd="
Dim sqlConn As New SqlConnection (strConnection)
Dim strCmd = "SELECT * FROM Products"
Dim dtAdapter As New SqlDataAdapter (strCmd, sqlConn)
dtAdapter.MissingSchemaAction = MissingSchemaAction.AddWithKey
```

C#:

```
string strConn = "Data Source = localhost; Intial Catalog=Northwind; " +
    "User ID=sa; Pwd=";
SqlConnection sqlConn = new SqlConnection (strConn);
string strCmd = "SELECT * FROM Products";
SqlDataAdapter dtAdapter = new SqlDataAdapter (strCmd, sqlConn);
dtAdapter.MissingSchemaAction = MissingSchemaAction.AddWithKey;
```

SqlDataAdapter Constructor (String, String)

Initializes a new instance of the SqlDataAdapter class with the specified command text string and a connection string.

VB.NET:

```
Overloads Public Sub New( _
    ByVal selectCommandText As String, _
    ByVal selectConnectionString As String _
)
```

C#:

```
public SqlDataAdapter(
    string selectCommandText,
    string selectConnectionString
);
```

349

The selectCommandText string must be a valid SQL SELECT statement and the selectConnectionString string must be a valid connection string. This constructor first calls the default constructor of the base class DbDataAdapter that initializes the properties of this DataAdapter object to their default values. Next it calls SqlConnection (string) class constructor, which sets the selectConnectionString as ConnectionString for the connection object. This SqlConnection, along with the command string, is then passed to SqlCommand (string, SqlConnection) class constructor to create new instance of the command object, which gets set as SelectCommand for the DataAdapter.

VB.NET:

```
Dim strConn = "Data Source = localhost; Intial Catalog=Northwind; " & _
    "User ID=sa; Pwd="
Dim strCmd = "SELECT * FROM Products"
Dim dtAdapter As New SqlDataAdapter (strCmd, strConn)
dtAdapter.MissingSchemaAction = MissingSchemaAction.AddWithKey
```

C#:

```
string strConn = "Data Source = localhost; Intial Catalog=Northwind; " +
    "User ID=sa; Pwd=";
string strCmd = "SELECT * FROM Products";
SqlDataAdapter dtAdapter = new SqlDataAdapter (strCmd, strConn);
dtAdapter.MissingSchemaAction = MissingSchemaAction.AddWithKey;
```

SqlDataAdapter Properties

The DeleteCommand Property

Gets or sets the command for deleting the records from the specified data set. This property is inherited from the base class DataAdapter.

VB.NET:

```
Public Property DeleteCommand As SqlCommand
```

C#:

```
public SqlCommand DeleteCommand {get; set;}
```

The implementation and usage of this method is same as in OleDbDataAdapter with the difference that the command property is set as SqlCommand object instead of OleDbCommand object. Refer to DeleteCommand section in OleDbDataAdapter class for more details.

VB.NET:

```
Dim dtAdapter As New SqlDataAdapter (strCmd, strConn)
dtAdapter.DeleteCommand = New SqlCommand (strDelCmd)
```

C#:

```
SqlDataAdapter dtAdapter = new SqlDataAdapter (strCmd, strConn);
dtAdapter.DeleteCommand = new SqlCommand (strDelCmd);
```

The InsertCommand Property

The InsertCommand property gets or sets the command for inserting new records to the data source during Update operation.

VB.NET:

```
Public Property InsertCommand As SqlCommand
```

C#:

```
public SqlCommand InsertCommand {get; set;}
```

The implementation and usage of this method is the same as in OleDbDataAdapter with the difference that the command property is set as SqlCommand object instead of OleDbCommand object. Refer to InsertCommand section in OleDbDataAdapter class for more details.

VB.NET:

```
Dim dtAdapter As New SqlDataAdapter (strCmd, strConn)
dtAdapter.InsertCommand = New SqlCommand (strInsCmd)
```

C#:

```
SqlDataAdapter dtAdapter = new SqlDataAdapter (strCmd, strConn);
dtAdapter.InsertCommand = new SqlCommand (strInsCmd);
```

The SelectCommand Property

The SelectCommand Property gets or sets the command for retrieving records based on the SQL statement set as the command text.

VB.NET:

```
Public Property SelectCommand As SqlCommand
```

C#:

```
public SqlCommand SelectCommand {get; set;}
```

The implementation and usage of this method is same as in OleDbDataAdapter with the difference that the command property is set as SqlCommand object instead of OleDbCommand object. Refer to SelectCommand section in OleDbDataAdapter class for more details.

VB.NET:

```
Dim dtAdapter As New SqlDataAdapter ()
dtAdapter.InsertCommand = New SqlCommand (strSelCmd)
```

C#:

```
SqlDataAdapter dtAdapter = new SqlDataAdapter ();
dtAdapter.SelectCommand = new SqlCommand (strSelCmd);
```

The UpdateCommand Property

The UpdateCommand Property gets or sets the command object to update the records in the data source.

VB.NET:

```
Public Property UpdateCommand As SqlCommand
```

C#:

```
public SqlCommand UpdateCommand {get; set;}
```

The implementation and usage of this method is same as in OleDbDataAdapter with the difference that the command property is set as SqlCommand object instead of OleDbCommand object. Refer to UpdateCommand section in OleDbDataAdapter class for more details.

VB.NET:

```
Dim dtAdapter As New SqlDataAdapter (strCmd, strConn)
dtAdapter.UpdateCommand = New SqlCommand (strUpdCmd)
```

C#:

```
SqlDataAdapter dtAdapter = new SqlDataAdapter (strCmd, strConn);
dtAdapter.UpdateCommand = new SqlCommand (strUpdCmd);
```

SqlDataAdapter Methods

SqlDataAdapter class implements all the methods that OleDbDataAdapter class implements with only one exception. It uses the Fill method's implementation provided by the base class, DbDataAdapter. For discussion of the methods of this class, refer to methods of OleDbDataAdapter class.

SqlDataAdapter Events

SqlDataAdapter class supports exactly the same events as the OleDbDataAdapter class. For details on these events, refer to the Events section of the OleDbDataAdapter class.

The OdbcDataAdapter

VB.NET:

```
NotInheritable Public Class OdbcDataAdapter
     Inherits DbDataAdapter
     Implements ICloneable, IDbDataAdapter
```

C#:

```
public sealed class OdbcDataAdapter :
    DbDataDapter,
    ICloneable, IDbDataAdapter
```

This is the data provider that uses the native ODBC drivers to communicate with the data source. It is implemented in `OdbDataAdapter` class. This class is defined in `System.Data.Odbc` namespace. To ink to this namespace you need to refer to `System.Data.Odbc.dll` in your project. The following example, shows the command line compilation of a C# source file, `EmpDataAccess.cs` and a VB.Net source file, `EmpDataAccess.vb` that uses the `OdbcDataAdapter` to retrieve records from a database into the `DataSet`.

VB.NET:

```
vbc /r:System.Data.Odb.dll EmpDataAccess.vb
```

C#:

```
csc /r:System.Data.Odbc.dll EmpDataAccess.cs
```

The following code uses the ODBC driver for Microsoft Access database to get records from the database file `Northwind.mdb`. Notice that the only difference between this code and the code that was discussed on `OleDbDataAdapter` and `SqlDataAdapter` is the connection string.

VB.NET:

```
Dim strConn As String = "Driver={Microsoft Access Driver (*.mdb)};" & _
                        "DBQ=C:\\Northwind.mdb"
Dim strQuery As String = "SELECT * FROM PRODUCTS"
' Create Connection object and Open it.
Dim odbcConn As New OdbcConnection(strConn)

' Create the Command object
Dim odbcCmd As New OdbcCommand(strQuery, odbcConn)

'Create the DataAdapter to fetch records from PRODUCTS table.
Dim prodDtAdapter As New OdbcDataAdapter(odbcCmd)
Dim prodDtSet As New DataSet()

' Call Fill method to get the records.
prodDtAdapter.Fill(prodDtSet)
```

C#:

```
string strConn = "Driver={Microsoft Access Driver (*.mdb)};" +
                       "DBQ=C:\\Northwind.mdb";
string strQuery = "SELECT * FROM PRODUCTS";
// Create Connection object and Open it.
OdbcConnection odbcConn = new OdbcConnection(strConn);

// Create the Command object
OdbcCommand odbcCmd = new OdbcCommand(strQuery, odbcConn);
```

```
// Create the DataAdapter to fetch records from PRODUCTS table.
OdbcDataAdapter prodDtAdapter = new OdbcDataAdapter(odbcCmd);
DataSet prodDtSet = new DataSet();

// Call Fill method to get the records.
prodDtAdapter.Fill(prodDtSet);
```

The public access members for this class are the same as provided by other two DataAdapter classes. For more details, refer to the OleDbDataAdapter and SqlDataAdapter classes.

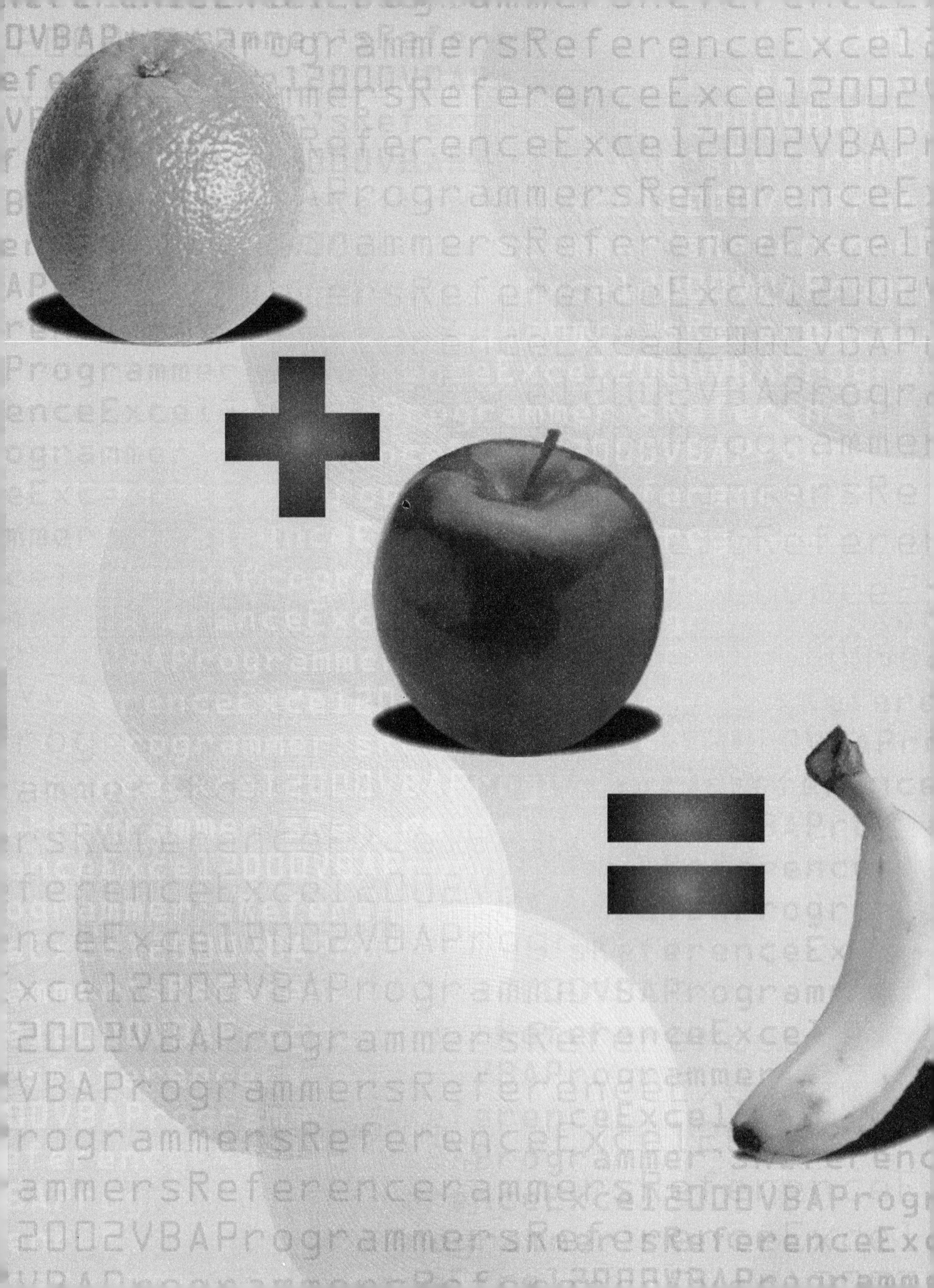

8

The DataTable object

The `DataTable` represents the ADO.NET counterpart of a generic database table. It contains columns and rows, constraint rules, relations between tables, and all the functionality needed to manage a generic database table. Usually, a `DataTable` schema is created by a `DataAdapter` object when its `FillSchema()` method is called, and a SQL command is executed, for example:

VB.NET:

```
Dim dbConn As New
SqlClient.SqlConnection("server=localhost;uid=sa;pwd=;database=WroxDB")

Dim daAuthors As New SqlClient.SqlDataAdapter("SELECT AuthorID, Author_FirstName,
Author_LastName FROM tabAuthors", dbConn)
Dim dtAuthors As New DataTable("Authors")

' Create the table schema automatically
daAuthors.FillSchema(dtAuthors,SchemaType.Source)
```

C#:

```
SqlConnection dbConn = new
SqlConnection("server=localhost;uid=sa;pwd=;database=WroxDB");

SqlDataAdapter daAuthors = new SqlDataAdapter("SELECT AuthorID, Author_FirstName,
Author_LastName FROM tabAuthors",dbConn);
dtAuthors = new DataTable("dtAuthors");

// Create the table schema automatically
daAuthors.FillSchema(dtAuthors,SchemaType.Source);
```

The `DataTable` however exposes methods and properties to create the table schema from scratch. We will start by creating columns, assign data types to them, and adding the column to the `Columns` collection contained in the `DataTable` object:

VB.NET:

```
Dim dtAuthors As New DataTable("dtAuthors")
```

```
' Define the primary key column
Dim dcAuthorID As New DataColumn("AuthorID")
dcAuthorID.AllowDBNull = False
dcAuthorID.Unique = True
dcAuthorID.DataType = GetType(System.Int32)

' Add the primary key
dtAuthors.Columns.Add(dcAuthorID)

' Define the First name column, no null, max 50 chars
Dim dcAuthorFirstName As New DataColumn("Author_FirstName")
dcAuthorFirstName.AllowDBNull = False
dcAuthorFirstName.DataType = GetType(System.String)
dcAuthorFirstName.MaxLength = 50

' Add the FirstName column
dtAuthors.Columns.Add(dcAuthorFirstName)
. . .
. . .
```

C#:

```
DataTable dtAuthors = new DataTable("dtAuthors");

// Define the primary key column
DataColumn dcAuthorID = new DataColumn("AuthorID");
dcAuthorID.AllowDBNull = false;
dcAuthorID.Unique = true;
dcAuthorID.DataType = typeof(System.Int32);

// Add the primary key column
dtAuthors.Columns.Add(dcAuthorID);

// Define the First name column, no null, max 50 chars
DataColumn dcAuthorFirstName = new DataColumn("Author_FirstName");
dcAuthorFirstName.AllowDBNull = false;
dcAuthorFirstName.DataType = typeof(System.String);
dcAuthorFirstName.MaxLength = 50;

// Add the FirstName column
dtAuthors.Columns.Add(dcAuthorFirstName);


. . .
. . .
```

After that, we can insert values inside the columns in order to form a row. This row will be added to the Rows collection of the DataTable:

VB.NET:

```
. . .
. . .

' Add a row to the table
Dim dtNewRow As DataRow
```

```
dtNewRow = dtAuthors.NewRow()
dtNewRow("AuthorID") = 1
dtNewRow("Author_FirstName") = "Fabio Claudio"

dtAuthors.Rows.Add(dtNewRow)
```

C#:

```
.  .  .
.  .  .

// Add a row to the table
DataRow dtNewRow = dtAuthors.NewRow();
dtNewRow["AuthorID"] = 1;
dtNewRow["Author_FirstName"] = "Fabio Claudio";

dtAuthors.Rows.Add(dtNewRow);
```

If we have defined a primary key in the table, we can create a `UniqueConstraint` and add it to the `Constraints` collection exposed by the `DataTable`, in order to inform the object that the specified column must contain unique values. This method is equal to setting the Boolean `true` value for the `Unique` property of the `DataColumn` object:

VB.NET:

```
.  .  .
.  .  .

' Define a UniqueConstraint for the column ID
Dim ucID As New UniqueConstraint("ConstraintOnAuthorID", dcAuthorID)

' Add to the constraints collection
dtAuthors.Constraints.Add(ucID);

' Try to insert again the same record
dtNewRow = dtAuthors.NewRow()
dtNewRow("AuthorID") = 1
dtNewRow("Author_FirstName") = "Fabio Claudio"

dtAuthors.Rows.Add(dtNewRow)
```

C#:

```
.  .  .
.  .  .

// Define a UniqueConstraint for the column ID
UniqueConstraint ucID = new UniqueConstraint("ConstraintOnAuthorID",dcAuthorID);

// Add to the constraints collection
dtAuthors.Constraints.Add(ucID);

// Try to insert again the same record
dtNewRow = dtAuthors.NewRow();
dtNewRow["AuthorID"] = 1;
```

```
dtNewRow["Author_FirstName"] = "Fabio Claudio";

dtAuthors.Rows.Add(dtNewRow);
```

The code above terminates trying to insert the same record in the table after attempting to violate the constraint. As we can see, an appropriate exception has been thrown:

```
F:\ADO.NET\Chapter8\C#\DataTable samples\ConsoleApplication2\bin\Debug\ConsoleApplication2.exe  _ □ X

Unhandled Exception: System.Data.ConstraintException: Column 'AuthorID' is const
rained to be unique.  Value '1' is already present.
    at System.Data.DataTable.InsertRow(DataRow row, Int32 proposedID, Int32 pos)
    at System.Data.DataRowCollection.Add(DataRow row)
```

These are just a few of the ways in which the DataTable object may be used, and in this chapter we'll see how to implement them in code, together with all the other properties and methods.

The DataTable Object

The DataTable object inherits from the MarshalByValueComponent and Object classes. The latter implements basic functionalities valid for each object inside the .NET object hierarchy. The former provides the base implementation for a remote marshal mechanism, using a copy of the object (ByValue). Moreover, DataTable implements a few interfaces that add serialization functionalities (ISerializable), batch initialization features (ISupportInitialize), and automatic binding processes between the object and the data source (IListSource).

Each of these objects provides its own set of functionalities accessible from inherited properties and methods. This chapter will give a brief description of them focusing on proprietary properties and methods.

DataTable Constructors

The following excerpts indicate the various ways of instantiating the DataTable, in both VB and C#:

VB.NET:

```
Public Sub New()

Public Sub New(ByVal tableName As String)

Protected Sub New( _
   ByVal info As SerializationInfo, _
   ByVal context As StreamingContext)
```

C#:

```
public DataTable();

public DataTable(string tableName);

protected DataTable(
   SerializationInfo info,
   StreamingContext context);
```

The `DataTable` has three constructors. The default constructor lets us create a blank copy of a `DataTable` object, initializing each internal structure to their default values.

VB.NET:

```
Dim dtAuthors As New DataTable()
```

C#:

```
System.Data.DataTable dtAuthors = new System.Data.DataTable();
```

The second version of the constructor takes the source table name as a parameter. The name is useful to access a specific table when more `DataTable` objects are created.

VB.NET:

```
Dim dtAuthors As New DataTable("Authors")
```

C#:

```
System.Data.DataTable dtAuthors = new System.Data.DataTable("Authors");
```

The third and last constructor is a protected method so it cannot be used directly. It is used by the `ISerializable` interface during serialization processes.

DataTable Properties

The `DataTable` object exposes eighteen of its own properties, and three inherited from the `MarshalByValueComponent` class. Thanks to these properties, we can define all the columns that comprise the table, define a primary key, retrieve the rows contained in the table, and perform a variety of other things. In this section, we'll analyze each property.

Before looking at the properties that are specific to the `DataTable`, we'll take a very brief look at the inherited properties:

Property	Description
Container	This is a read-only property that retrieves the container for the `DataTable` object or a null reference (`Nothing` in VB)
DesignMode	This is a read-only property that retrieves a Boolean value indicating whether the component is in design mode
Events	This is a read-only property that retrieves an `EventHandlerList` containing a list of the component's delegates

The CaseSensitive Property

The `CaseSensitive` property gets or sets a `Boolean` value, indicating whether string comparisons will be case-sensitive. The `DataTable` object uses string comparison when methods, such as `Select` are called. The default value is false, but if the `DataTable` object is contained within a `DataSet`, then it assumes its own `CaseSensitive` value.

VB.NET:

```
Public Property CaseSensitive As Boolean
```

C#:

```
public bool CaseSensitive {get; set;}
```

The following example fills the `DataTable` object with three columns from the `authors` table in the `pubs` database. There is a record in the table with the `au_lname` column containing "Karsen". The code searches for "karsen", with non case-sensitive comparison, so the "Karsen" record is found and written to the console. Next, the `DataTable CaseSensitive` property is set to true, and the same search takes place. This time no record is found. The program reports this by writing a message to the console.

VB.NET:

```
Dim dbConn As New SqlClient.SqlConnection _
    ("server=localhost;uid=sa;pwd=;database=pubs")
Try
    ' Create Authors DataTable
    Dim dtAuthors As New DataTable("Authors")

    ' Create a DataAdapter to fill the table
    Dim daAuthors As New SqlClient.SqlDataAdapter("SELECT
                        au_id,au_fname,au_lname FROM authors", dbConn)

    daAuthors.Fill(dtAuthors)

    ' Search without case-sensitive comparison
    dtAuthors.CaseSensitive = False
    Dim r() As DataRow
    r = dtAuthors.Select("au_lname = 'karsen'")

    ' Write result to console
    If r.Length > 0 Then
        Console.WriteLine("Found: " + r(0)("au_lname"))
    Else
        Console.WriteLine("Nothing found")
    End If

    ' Search with case-sensitive comparison
    dtAuthors.CaseSensitive = True
    r = dtAuthors.Select("au_lname = 'karsen'")

    ' Write result to console
    If r.Length > 0 Then
        Console.WriteLine("Found: " + r(0)("au_lname"))
    Else
        Console.WriteLine("Nothing found")
    End If

Catch e As Exception
    Console.WriteLine(e.Message)
Finally
    If dbConn.State = ConnectionState.Open Then dbConn.Close()
End Try
```

C#:

```csharp
SqlConnection dbConn = new
    SqlConnection("server=localhost;uid=sa;pwd=;database=pubs");

try
{
    // Create Authors DataTable
    DataTable dtAuthors = new DataTable("Authors");

    // Create a DataAdapter to fill the table
    SqlDataAdapter daAuthors = new SqlDataAdapter("SELECT
                    au_id,au_fname,au_lname FROM authors",dbConn);

    daAuthors.Fill(dtAuthors);

    // Search without case-sensitive comparison
    dtAuthors.CaseSensitive = false;
    DataRow[] r = dtAuthors.Select("au_lname = 'karsen'");

    // Write to console
    if (r.Length > 0)
        Console.WriteLine("Found: " + r[0]["au_lname"]);
    else
        Console.WriteLine("Nothing found");

    // Search with case-sensitive comparison
    dtAuthors.CaseSensitive = true;
    r = dtAuthors.Select("au_lname = 'karsen'");

    // Write to console
    if (r.Length > 0)
        Console.WriteLine("Found: " + r[0]["au_lname"]);
    else
        Console.WriteLine("Nothing found");
}
catch (Exception e)
{
    Console.WriteLine(e.Message);
}
finally
{
    if (dbConn.State == ConnectionState.Open)
        dbConn.Close();
}
```

The output will look like this:

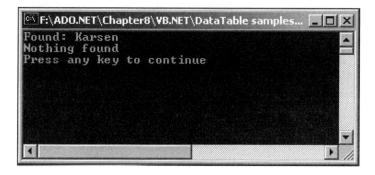

The ChildRelations Property

VB.NET:

```
Public ReadOnly Property ChildRelations As DataRelationCollection
```

C#:

```
public DataRelationCollection ChildRelations {get;}
```

ChildRelations is a read-only property that retrieves a collection of DataRelation objects. A DataRelation object contains parent/child relations between two tables. Thanks to this property, we can retrieve every child relation for this DataTable. There is full explanation for this object in Chapter 9.

The Columns Property

VB.NET:

```
Public ReadOnly Property Columns As DataColumnCollection
```

C#:

```
public DataColumnCollection Columns {get;}
```

This property is read-only, and it retrieves a DataColumnCollection object containing a collection of all the columns forming a table. We'll study this object in more depth next in this chapter. For now, all we have to know is that the DataColumnCollection has all the properties and methods to manage the columns describing a table.

VB.NET:

```
Dim dbConn As New SqlConnection("server=localhost;uid=sa;pwd=;database=pubs")

' Create Authors DataTable
Dim dtAuthors As New DataTable("Authors")

' Create a DataAdapter to fill the table
Dim daAuthors As New SqlClient.SqlDataAdapter("SELECT au_id,au_fname,au_lname FROM
authors", dbConn)

daAuthors.Fill(dtAuthors)

' Retrieve the first column from the collection
Dim dcAuthorID As DataColumn
dcAuthorID = dtAuthors.Columns("au_id")

' Print to video
Console.WriteLine(dcAuthorID.DataType)
```

C#:

```
SqlConnection dbConn = new
SqlConnection("server=localhost;uid=sa;pwd=;database=pubs");
```

```
// Create Authors DataTable
DataTable dtAuthors = new DataTable("Authors");

// Create a DataAdapter to fill the table
SqlDataAdapter daAuthors = new SqlDataAdapter("SELECT au_id,au_fname,au_lname FROM
authors",dbConn);

daAuthors.Fill(dtAuthors);

// Retrieve the first column from the collection
DataColumn dcAuthorID = dtAuthors.Columns["au_id"];

// Print to video
Console.WriteLine(dcAuthorID.DataType);
```

The Constraints Property

This property gets a `ConstraintCollection` object that contains a collection of `Constraint` objects for the current `DataTable`. We'll examine in detail `Constraint` and `ConstraintCollection` objects in the next chapter. For now, we have just to consider that with `Constraint` functionalities, we can define column rules in order to maintain the integrity of the data in the table. For example, joining two tables by a primary and a foreign key, we can define a constraint in order to delete every related `row` in both the tables.

VB.NET:

```
Public ReadOnly Property Constraints As ConstraintCollection
```

C#:

```
public ConstraintCollection Constraints {get;}
```

The DataSet Property

VB.NET:

```
Public ReadOnly Property DataSet As DataSet
```

C#

```
public DataSet DataSet {get;}
```

This is a read-only property that retrieves the `DataSet` object that contains the `DataTable`.

VB.NET:

```
Dim dbConn As New
SqlClient.SqlConnection("server=localhost;uid=sa;pwd=;database=pubs")

Dim dsAuthors As New DataSet("Authors")

' Create Authors DataTable
Dim dtAuthors As DataTable

' Create a DataAdapter to fill the DataSet
```

```
Dim daAuthors As New SqlClient.SqlDataAdapter("SELECT au_id,au_fname,au_lname FROM
authors", dbConn)

' Fill the DataSet
daAuthors.Fill(dsAuthors)

' Retrieve the table contained in DataSet
dtAuthors = dsAuthors.Tables(0)

' Check if they are equals
If dsAuthors.Equals(dtAuthors.DataSet) Then
    Console.WriteLine("Yes, we are equals")
End If
```

C#:

```
SqlConnection dbConn = new
SqlConnection("server=localhost;uid=sa;pwd=;database=pubs");

// Create a DataSet
DataSet dsAuthors = new DataSet("Authors");

// Create a DataAdapter to fill the DataSet
SqlDataAdapter daAuthors = new SqlDataAdapter("SELECT au_id,au_fname,au_lname FROM
authors",dbConn);

// Fill the DataSet
daAuthors.Fill(dsAuthors);

// Retrieve the table contained in DataSet
DataTable dtAuthors = dsAuthors.Tables[0];

// Check if they are equals
if (dsAuthors.Equals(dtAuthors.DataSet))
    Console.WriteLine("Yes, we are equals");
```

In the example above, the Equals() method retrieves a Boolean value indicating whether the two objects are equal.

The DefaultView Property

VB.NET:

```
Public ReadOnly Property DefaultView As DataView
```

C#:

```
public DataView DefaultView {get;}
```

This is a read-only property that retrieves the default DataView object associated with the DataTable. As we see in Chapter 10, a DataView is similar to a view based on a table, that shows only certain columns, or performs some particular operation, such as filtering or sorting.

366

VB.NET:

```vbnet
' Create the connection object
Dim dbConn As New
SqlClient.SqlConnection("server=localhost;uid=sa;pwd=;database=pubs")

' Create Authors DataTable
Dim dtAuthors As New DataTable("Authors")

' Create a DataAdapter to fill the table
Dim daAuthors As New SqlClient.SqlDataAdapter("SELECT
au_id,au_fname,au_lname,contract FROM authors", dbConn)
daAuthors.Fill(dtAuthors)

' Set the DataSource to point to data contained
' in the DataView object
dgAuthors.DataSource = dtAuthors.DefaultView
```

C#:

```csharp
SqlConnection dbConn = new
SqlConnection("server=localhost;uid=sa;pwd=;database=pubs");

// Create Authors DataTable
DataTable dtAuthors = new DataTable("Authors");

// Create a DataAdapter to fill the table
SqlDataAdapter daAuthors = new SqlDataAdapter("SELECT
au_id,au_fname,au_lname,contract FROM authors",dbConn);
daAuthors.Fill(dtAuthors);

// Set the DataSource to point to data contained
// in the DataView object
dgAuthors.DataSource = dtAuthors.DefaultView;
```

The DisplayExpression Property

VB.NET:

```vbnet
Public Property DisplayExpression As String
```

C#:

```csharp
public string DisplayExpression {get; set;}
```

This method can either retrieve or set a `DisplayExpression` string that we can use to do particular tasks on the data. We'll look in more detail at this when looking at the `Expression` property of the `DataColumn` object.

VB.NET:

```vbnet
Dim dbConn As New
SqlClient.SqlConnection("server=localhost;uid=sa;pwd=;database=pubs")

' Create Authors DataTable
Dim dtAuthors As New DataTable("Authors")
```

```
' Create a DataAdapter to fill the DataSet
Dim daAuthors As New SqlClient.SqlDataAdapter("SELECT
au_id,au_fname,au_lname,contract FROM authors", dbConn)

' Fill the DataSet
daAuthors.Fill(dtAuthors)

' Set the DisplayExpression
dtAuthors.DisplayExpression = "au_id = '222-22-2222'"

' Get the DisplayExpression
Console.WriteLine(dtAuthors.DisplayExpression)

' DisplayExpression doesn't filter the rows.
Console.WriteLine("Number of rows: {0}", dtAuthors.Rows.Count)
```

C#:

```
SqlConnection dbConn = new
SqlConnection("server=localhost;uid=sa;pwd=;database=pubs");

// Create Authors DataTable
DataTable dtAuthors = new DataTable("Authors");

// Create a DataAdapter to fill the table
SqlDataAdapter daAuthors = new SqlDataAdapter("SELECT
au_id,au_fname,au_lname,contract FROM authors",dbConn);
daAuthors.Fill(dtAuthors);

// Set the DisplayExpression

dtAuthors.DisplayExpression = "au_id = '222-22-2222'";

// Get the DisplayExpression

Console.WriteLine(dtAuthors.DisplayExpression);

// DisplayExpression doesn't filter the rows.
Console.WriteLine("Number of rows: {0}", dtAuthors.Rows.Count);
```

The ExtendedProperties Property

VB.NET:

```
Public ReadOnly Property ExtendedProperties As PropertyCollection
```

C#:

```
public PropertyCollection ExtendedProperties {get;}
```

ExtendedProperties is a read-only method that retrieves a collection of custom information. In fact, PropertyCollection contains a Property objects collection where we can add our own data not belonging to the database.

VB.NET:

```
Dim dtAuthors As New DataTable("Authors")

' Add a custom property
dtAuthors.ExtendedProperties.Add("CreationDate", DateTime.Now)

' Print its content
MessageBox.Show("The object has been created at " &
                dtAuthors.ExtendedProperties("CreationDate"))
```

C#:

```
DataTable dtAuthors = new DataTable("Authors");

// Add a custom property
dtAuthors.ExtendedProperties.Add("CreationDate", DateTime.Now);

// Print its content
MessageBox.Show("The object has been created at " +
                dtAuthors.ExtendedProperties["CreationDate"]);
```

In the above example, we store the object creation date inside the collection with the item key `CreationDate`, before generating an appropriate message box:

The HasErrors Property

VB.NET:

```
Public ReadOnly Property HasErrors As Boolean
```

C#:

```
public bool HasErrors {get;}
```

`HasErrors` is a read-only property indicating whether an error occurred during `DataTable` management operations (`true`), or whether all the data inside the table is valid (`false`). Before we update the database with new records contained in the `DataTable`, it is a good thing to check if there was an error during table data population. If you use a `DataSet` to manage your records, you can go through all the tables and use this property to validate the data.

VB.NET:

```
' DataSet pre-loaded with data from pubs
dsPubs.GetChanges()

' Check each table's HasErrors property.
```

```
Dim dtPubTables As DataTable

For Each dtPubTables In dsPubs.Tables
    If dtPubTables.HasErrors Then
        ' Stop
    End If
Next
```

C#:

```
// DataSet pre-loaded with data from pubs
dsPubs.GetChanges();

// Check each table's HasErrors property.
DataTable dtPubTables;

foreach (dtPubTables in dsPubs.Tables)
{
    if (dtPubTables.HasErrors)
        // Stop
}
```

The Locale Property

VB.NET:

```
Public Property Locale As CultureInfo
```

C#:

```
public CultureInfo Locale {get; set;}
```

This property either gets or sets `CultureInfo` object attributes. The object lets us know locale attributes to use inside our code when we compare two strings or when we check the date format. If no `CultureInfo` attributes are set and `DataTable` is contained inside a `DataSet`, then it will use parent locale information.

The MinimumCapacity Property

VB.NET:

```
Public Property MinimumCapacity As Integer
```

C#:

```
public int MinimumCapacity {get; set;}
```

The `MinimumCapacity` property is useful when you need to get or to set the initial table size in rows. The default value is 25 rows, but we can change this, giving a new value for this property. This value is used by the system during initialization processes, and it reserves memory space to contain the rows. If you have critical memory situation, you can adapt the value of this property to improve performance. For example, if you know that you will use a `DataTable` to retrieve only a row from the database, you can improve the performance setting this property to one.

VB.NET:

```
Dim dtPubTables As DataTable
dtPubTables.MinimumCapacity = 1
```

C#:

```
DataTable dtPubTables;
dtPubTables.MinimumCapacity = 1;
```

The Namespace Property

VB.NET:

```
Public Property Namespace As String
```

C#:

```
public string Namespace {get; set;}
```

This property retrieves or sets the XML namespace string used in the XML representation of the data stored inside the DataTable object.

VB.NET:

```
Dim dtPubTables As DataTable
dtPubTables.Namespace = "urn:schemas-wrox-com:pub"
```

C#

```
DataTable dtPubTables;
dtPubTables.Namespace = "urn:schemas-wrox-com:pub";
```

After the namespace settings, your XML schema associated to the DataTable will contain your namespace:

```
<?xml version="1.0" standalone="yes"?>
<xsd:schema id="dsAuthors" targetNamespace="" xmlns=""
xmlns:xsd="http://www.w3.org/2001/XMLSchema" xmlns:msdata="urn:schemas-microsoft-
com:xml-msdata" xmlns:app1="urn:schemas-wrox-com:pub">
  <xsd:import namespace="urn:schemas-wrox-com:pub" schemaLocation="app1_NS.xsd" />
  <xsd:element name="dsAuthors" msdata:IsDataSet="true" msdata:Locale="it-IT">
    <xsd:complexType>
      <xsd:choice maxOccurs="unbounded" />
    </xsd:complexType>
  </xsd:element>
</xsd:schema>
```

The ParentRelations Property

VB.NET:

```
Public ReadOnly Property ParentRelations As DataRelationCollection
```

C#:

```
public DataRelationCollection ParentRelations {get;}
```

This is a read-only property that retrieves a collection of `DataRelation` objects. A `DataRelation` object contains parent/child relations between two tables. Thanks to this property, we can get every parent relation for a particular `DataTable`. There is a detailed explanation of this object in Chapter 9.

The Prefix Property

VB.NET:

```
Public Property Prefix As String
```

C#:

```
public string Prefix {get; set;}
```

The `Prefix` method retrieves or sets the XML namespace prefix string used in the XML representation of the data stored inside the `DataTable` object.

VB.NET:

```
Dim dtPubTables As DataTable
dtPubTables.Prefix = "pub"
```

C#:

```
DataTable dtPubTables;
dtPubTables.Prefix = "pub";
```

If we set a prefix to the XML document, it will prefix each tag with the value specified:

```xml
<?xml version="1.0" standalone="yes"?>
<dsAuthors>
  <pub:Table xmlns:pub="urn:schemas-wrox-com:pub">
    <au_id xmlns="urn:schemas-wrox-com:pub">172-32-1176</au_id>
    <au_fname xmlns="urn:schemas-wrox-com:pub">Johnson</au_fname>
    <au_lname xmlns="urn:schemas-wrox-com:pub">White</au_lname>
    <contract xmlns="urn:schemas-wrox-com:pub">true</contract>
  </pub:Table>
</dsAuthors>
```

The PrimaryKey Property

VB.NET:

```
Public Property PrimaryKey As DataColumn ()
```

C#:

```
public DataColumn[] PrimaryKey {get; set;}
```

The `PrimaryKey` method retrieves or sets a `DataColumn` objects array that represents all the `DataTable` primary keys. It could be used in the following way:

VB.NET:

```
Dim dbConn As New
SqlClient.SqlConnection("server=localhost;uid=sa;pwd=;database=pubs")
```

```
' Create Authors DataTable
Dim dtAuthors As New DataTable("Authors")

' Create a DataAdapter to fill the table
Dim daAuthors As New SqlClient.SqlDataAdapter("SELECT au_id,au_fname,au_lname FROM
authors", dbConn)
daAuthors.Fill(dtAuthors)

' Set PrimaryKey to au_id column
Dim keys(1) As DataColumn
keys(0) = dtAuthors.Columns("au_id")
dtAuthors.PrimaryKey = keys

' Print to video
Console.WriteLine(dtAuthors.PrimaryKey.Length.ToString())
```

C#:

```
SqlConnection dbConn = new
SqlConnection("server=localhost;uid=sa;pwd=;database=pubs");

// Create Authors DataTable
DataTable dtAuthors = new DataTable("Authors");

// Create a DataAdapter to fill the table
SqlDataAdapter daAuthors = new SqlDataAdapter("SELECT au_id,au_fname,au_lname FROM
authors",dbConn);
daAuthors.Fill(dtAuthors);

// Set PrimaryKey to au_id column
DataColumn[] keys = new DataColumn[1];
keys[0] = dtAuthors.Columns["au_id"];
dtAuthors.PrimaryKey = keys;

// Print to Console
Console.WriteLine(dtAuthors.PrimaryKey.Length.ToString());
```

The Rows Property

VB.NET:

```
Public ReadOnly Property Rows As DataRowCollection
```

C#:

```
public DataRowCollection Rows {get;}
```

The Rows property retrieves a DataRowCollection object containing each row comprising a
DataTable record. As we see in the next chapter, a DataRowCollection manages every row,
represented by a DataRow object, contained in the DataTable, enabling us to add new rows, delete
records, and so on.

After having changed some records, we have to call the AcceptChanges() method from the
DataTable methods:

373

VB.NET:

```
Dim dbConn As New
SqlClient.SqlConnection("server=localhost;uid=sa;pwd=;database=pubs")

' Create Authors DataTable
Dim dtAuthors As New DataTable("Authors")

' Create a DataAdapter to fill the table
Dim daAuthors As New SqlClient.SqlDataAdapter("SELECT au_id,au_fname,au_lname FROM
authors", dbConn)
daAuthors.Fill(dtAuthors)

' Retrieve rows collection
Dim drcAuthors As DataRowCollection
drcAuthors = dtAuthors.Rows

' Print to video first row and first column
Console.WriteLine(drcAuthors(0)("au_id"))
```

C#:

```
SqlConnection dbConn = new
SqlConnection("server=localhost;uid=sa;pwd=;database=pubs");

// Create Authors DataTable
DataTable dtAuthors = new DataTable("Authors");

// Create a DataAdapter to fill the table
SqlDataAdapter daAuthors = new SqlDataAdapter("SELECT au_id,au_fname,au_lname FROM
authors",dbConn);
daAuthors.Fill(dtAuthors);

// Retrieve rows collection
DataRowCollection drcAuthors = dtAuthors.Rows;

// Print to video first row and first column
Console.WriteLine(drcAuthors[0]["au_id"]);
```

The Site Property

VB.NET:

```
Overrides Public Property Site As ISite
```

C#:

```
public override ISite Site {get; set;}
```

This property retrieves or sets a `System.ComponentModel.ISite` interface that allows binding a
component and a container, enabling a communication mechanism.

The TableName Property

VB.NET:

```
Public Property TableName As String
```

C#:

```
public string TableName {get; set;}
```

TableName is a property that you can use either to set or to get a virtual table name. This is not the real database table name, but a unique name that identifies the object inside a `DataTableCollection` object. As we have seen in Chapter 5, the object exposes a property called `Tables` that contains each table present in the `DataSet` object. You can refer just to a specific table inside the collection using its table name. Usually, this property is used when you have called the default constructor, and then you want to specify a table name.

VB.NET:

```
' Create Authors DataTable
Dim dtAuthors As New DataTable()
dtAuthors.TableName = "Authors"
```

C#:

```
// Create Authors DataTable
DataTable dtAuthors = new DataTable();
dtAuthors.TableName = "Authors";
```

DataTable Methods

The `DataTable` provides twenty-six of its own methods, and eight inherited from the `MarshalByValueComponent` and `Object` classes. As you can imagine, we can do a lot of things with all of these methods. For example, we can add new rows to the `DataTable`, sort, filter, and go through each record inside the table, and so on.

The following table gives a brief explanation of the inherited methods:

Method	Description
Dispose	Releases resources used by the `MarshalByValueComponent`. It comes in two versions: the first releases all the resources, and doesn't require parameters, while the second accepts a Boolean value indicating whether to release only the unmanaged resources (`false`) or both the managed and unmanaged resources (`true`).
Equals	Returns a Boolean value indicating whether two objects are equal (`true`) or not (`false`).
GetHashCode	Useful to hash algorithms and hash table, it retrieves a hash code associated with the object.

Table continued on following page

Method	Description
GetService	Retrieves the implementer of the `IServiceProvider`.
GetType	Gets the type of the current object instance.
Finalize	Represents the destructor used by C#/C++ to free memory resources. In VB.NET: it's called `Finalize`.
MemberwiseClone	Creates an empty clone of the current object.

Now we can start to examine each of the `DataTable` methods in turn.

The AcceptChanges Method

VB.NET:

```
Public Sub AcceptChanges()
```

C#:

```
public void AcceptChanges();
```

This method is used to commit every change effected, since the last call, to the records in the `DataTable`. If any errors are thrown, you can either try to reconcile them, or call the `RejectChanges()` method to rollback the record changes.

VB.NET:

```
Dim dbConn As New
SqlClient.SqlConnection("server=localhost;uid=sa;pwd=;database=pubs")

Try
    ' Create Authors DataTable
    Dim dtAuthors As New DataTable("Authors")

     Create a DataAdapter to fill the table
    Dim daAuthors As New SqlClient.SqlDataAdapter("SELECT
au_id,au_fname,au_lname,contract FROM authors", dbConn)
    daAuthors.Fill(dtAuthors)

    ' Create a command builder to implement SQL insert command
    ' automatically
    Dim sqlCB As New SqlClient.SqlCommandBuilder(daAuthors)

    ' Create a new row
    Dim drNewAuthor As DataRow

    ' It has the same table schema
    drNewAuthor = dtAuthors.NewRow()
    drNewAuthor("au_id") = "222-22-2222"
    drNewAuthor("au_fname") = "Fabio Claudio"
    drNewAuthor("au_lname") = "Ferracchiati"
    drNewAuthor("contract") = 1
```

```
        ' Add the new row to the collection contained
        ' in the DataTable
        dtAuthors.Rows.Add(drNewAuthor)

        ' Update the database records
        daAuthors.Update(dtAuthors)

        ' Accept DataTable changes
        dtAuthors.AcceptChanges()
Catch e As Exception

        Console.WriteLine(e.Message)
Finally
        dbConn.Close()
End Try
```

C#:

```
SqlConnection dbConn = new
SqlConnection("server=localhost;uid=sa;pwd=;database=pubs");

try
{
    // Create Authors DataTable
    DataTable dtAuthors = new DataTable("Authors");

    // Create a DataAdapter to fill the table
    SqlDataAdapter daAuthors = new SqlDataAdapter("SELECT
                    au_id,au_fname,au_lame,contract FROM
                    authors",dbConn);
    daAuthors.Fill(dtAuthors);

    // Create a command builder to implement SQL insert command
    // automatically
    SqlCommandBuilder sqlCB = new SqlCommandBuilder(daAuthors);

    // Create a new row
    DataRow drNewAuthor;
    drNewAuthor = dtAuthors.NewRow()

    // It has the same table schema
    drNewAuthor["au_id"] = 222-22-2222";
    drNewAuthor["au_fname"] = "Fabio Claudio";
    drNewAuthor["au_lname"] = "Ferracchiati";
    drNewAuthor["contract"] = 1;

    // Add the new row to the collection contained
    // in the DataTable
    dtAuthors.Rows.Add(drNewAuthor);

    // Update the database records
    daAuthors.Update(dtAuthors);

    // Accept DataTable changes
    dtAuthors.AcceptChanges();
```

```
    )

catch (Exception e)_
(
       Console.WriteLine(e.Message);
)
```

It's very important to call this method after you have updated the database records using the `Update()` method exposed by the `DataAdapter` object, as `AcceptChanges()` method changes how any rows are marked, (for example from deleted to orginial). This in turn can affect how the table and its data is managed in the database. Also, this method affects the `RowState` property of the `DataRow` object by changing its state with one of the values listed below:

DataViewRowState value	Description
Added	All the new rows will be retrieved.
CurrentRows	All the current rows will be retrieved. A current row identifies unchanged, new and modified rows.
Deleted	All the deleted rows will be retrieved.
ModifiedCurrent	All the current modified rows will be retrieved.
ModifiedOriginal	All the original records that have been modified will be retrieved.
None	No records will be retrieved.
OriginalRows	All the original rows will be retrieved.
Unchanged	All the unchanged rows will be retrieved.

The BeginInit and EndInit Methods

VB.NET:

```
NotOverridable Public Sub BeginInit()
NotOverridable Public Sub EndInit()
```

C#:

```
public void BeginInit();
public void EndInit();
```

These two methods are complementary and they indicate that an initialization to the object has started and ended, respectively. This prevents the object from being used during initialization process. These methods have been produced mainly to work with Visual Studio .NET to avoid the situation where other objects or window forms could gain access during initialization stage.

The BeginLoadData, LoadDataRow and EndLoadData Methods

VB.NET:

```
Public Sub BeginLoadData()

Public Function LoadDataRow( _
   ByVal values() As Object, _
   ByVal fAcceptChanges As Boolean _
) As DataRow

Public Sub EndLoadData()
```

C#:

```
public void BeginLoadData();

public DataRow LoadDataRow(
   object[] values,
   bool fAcceptChanges
);

public void EndLoadData();
```

These are three complementary methods useful either to update or add rows inside the table. The first method, `BeginLoadData()` turns off constraints rules, indexes maintenance, and notifications. The second retrieves either an update or new `DataRow` object formed from the input parameters. It needs an object array containing the values to either update or add to the table and a Boolean value indicating whether to accept the changes (`true`) or not (`false`). The last one, `EndLoadData()`, completes the process by restoring the situation to one similar to the one before the `BeginLoadData()` method was called.

In the following example, a new row is created but not accepted to the table, due to the Boolean value for `LoadDataRow` being set to `False`:

VB.NET:

```
...
      Create a DataAdapter to fill the table
      Dim daAuthors As New SqlClient.SqlDataAdapter("SELECT
au_id,au_fname,au_lname,phone,address,city,state,zip,contract FROM authors",
dbConn)
      daAuthors.Fill(dtAuthors)

      ' Create a command builder to implement SQL insert command
      ' automatically
      Dim sqlCB As New SqlClient.SqlCommandBuilder(daAuthors)

      ' Create a new row
      Dim drNewAuthor As DataRow
      Dim objNewAuthor(9) As Object

      objNewAuthor(0) = "222-22-2222"
      objNewAuthor(1) = "Fabio Claudio"
      objNewAuthor(2) = "Ferracchiati"
      objNewAuthor(3) = ""
```

```
        objNewAuthor(4) = ""
        objNewAuthor(5) = ""
        objNewAuthor(6) = ""
        objNewAuthor(7) = "00100"
        objNewAuthor(8) = 1

      dtAuthors.BeginLoadData()
      drNewAuthor = dtAuthors.LoadDataRow(objNewAuthor, False)
      dtAuthors.EndLoadData()

      ' Update the database records
      daAuthors.Update(dtAuthors)
...
```

C#:

```
...
      // Create a DataAdapter to fill the table
      SqlDataAdapter daAuthors = new SqlDataAdapter("SELECT
au_id,au_fname,au_lname,phone,address,city,state,zip,contract FROM
authors",dbConn);
      daAuthors.Fill(dtAuthors);

      // Create a command builder to implement SQL insert command
      // automatically
      SqlCommandBuilder sqlCB = new SqlCommandBuilder(daAuthors);

      // Create a new row
      DataRow drNewAuthor;

      Object[] objNewAuthor = new Object[9];

      objNewAuthor[0] = "222-22-2222";
      objNewAuthor[1] = "Fabio Claudio";
      objNewAuthor[2] = "Ferracchiati";
      objNewAuthor[3] = "";
      objNewAuthor[4] = "";
      objNewAuthor[5] = "";
      objNewAuthor[6] = "";
      objNewAuthor[7] = "00100";
      objNewAuthor[8] = 1;

      dtAuthors.BeginLoadData();
      drNewAuthor = dtAuthors.LoadDataRow(objNewAuthor,false);
      dtAuthors.EndLoadData();

      // Update the database records
      daAuthors.Update(dtAuthors);
...
```

The Clear Method

VB.NET:

```
Public Sub Clear()
```

C#:

```
public void Clear();
```

This method clears all the data contained in the `DataTable` object.

VB.NET:

```
...
' Create a DataAdapter to fill the table
Dim daAuthors As New SqlClient.SqlDataAdapter("SELECT au_id,au_fname,au_lname FROM
authors", dbConn)
daAuthors.Fill(dtAuthors)

Console.WriteLine("Total records before the Clear() call: " &
dtAuthors.Rows.Count)

dtAuthors.Clear()

Console.WriteLine("Total records after the Clear()  call: " &
dtAuthors.Rows.Count)
```

C#:

```
...
// Create a DataAdapter to fill the table
SqlDataAdapter daAuthors = new SqlDataAdapter("SELECT
au_id,au_fname,au_lname,contract FROM authors",dbConn);
daAuthors.Fill(dtAuthors);

Console.WriteLine("Total records before the Clear() call: " +
dtAuthors.Rows.Count);

dtAuthors.Clear();

Console.WriteLine("Total records after the Clear()  call: " +
dtAuthors.Rows.Count);
```

The example above gives the following output due to the data being cleared from the table:

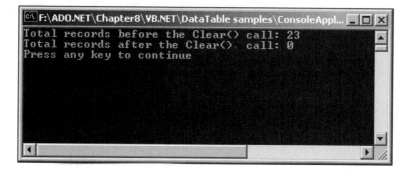

The Clone and Copy Methods

VB.NET:

```
Public Function Clone() As DataTable
Public Function Copy() As DataTable
```

C#:

```
public DataTable Clone();
public DataTable Copy();
```

Both of these methods create a new `DataTable` object. The difference is that `Copy()` produces an object with the same table schema, relations, constraints, and data, while `Clone()` generates only an empty object with the same `DataTable` object structure.

VB.NET:

```
...
' Fill a DataSet
Dim dsAuthors As New DataSet("dsAuthors")
daAuthors.Fill(dsAuthors)

' Retrieve the data table contained in the DataSet
' and clone and copy it.
dtAuthors = dsAuthors.Tables(0)

Dim dtCopyAuthors As DataTable
Dim dtCloneAuthors As DataTable

dtCopyAuthors = dtAuthors.Copy()
dtCloneAuthors = dtAuthors.Clone()

' Print to video some results
Console.WriteLine("Total records before the Clear() call: " &
dtAuthors.Rows.Count)

dtAuthors.Clear()

Console.WriteLine("Total records after the Clear() call: " &
dtAuthors.Rows.Count)

Console.WriteLine("Total records after the Clear() call for cloned table: " &
dtCloneAuthors.Rows.Count)

Console.WriteLine("Total records after the Clear() call for copied table: " &
dtCopyAuthors.Rows.Count)
```

C#:

```
...
// Fill a DataSet
DataSet dsAuthors = new DataSet("dsAuthors");
daAuthors.Fill(dsAuthors);

// Retrieve the data table contained in the DataSet
// and clone and copy it.
```

```
DataTable dtCloneAuthors;
DataTable dtCopyAuthors;

dtAuthors = dsAuthors.Tables[0];
dtCopyAuthors = dtAuthors.Copy();
dtCloneAuthors = dtAuthors.Clone();

// Print to video some results.
Console.WriteLine("Total records before the Clear() call: " +
dtAuthors.Rows.Count);

dtAuthors.Clear();

Console.WriteLine("Total records after the Clear()  call: " +
dtAuthors.Rows.Count);

Console.WriteLine("Total records after the Clear() call for cloned table: "+
dtCloneAuthors.Rows.Count);

Console.WriteLine("Total records after the Clear()  call for copied table: " +
dtCopyAuthors.Rows.Count);
```

In the example above, a table contained in the DataSet has been cloned and copied. After the Clear() calls, the cloned table is empty, because the method creates only the table structure, while the copied table maintains table records. This can be seen from the following output as the copied table has the same number of records as the initial table before it was cleared:

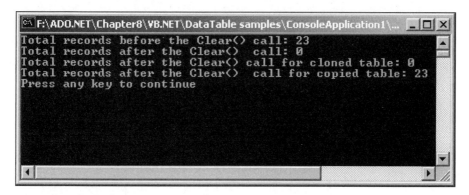

The GetChanges Method

VB.NET:

```
Overloads Public Function GetChanges() As DataTable

Overloads Public Function GetChanges( _
   ByVal rowStates As DataRowState _
) As DataTable
```

C#:

```
public DataTable GetChanges(
   DataRowState rowStates
);

public DataTable GetChanges();
```

383

GetChanges() comes in two versions; with each method retrieving a DataTable object containing all the changes made to the table, either after its creation, or after the last AcceptChanges() call. The first version retrieves only the records where DataRowState is not equal to Unchanged. In the latter version, you can choose a DataRowState in order to retrieve a particular set of data like the Added or Deleted rows.

DataRowState can assume one of the values described in the AcceptChanges section.

VB.NET:

```
. . .

Dim dtAuthors As New DataTable()

' Create a new row
Dim drNewAuthor As DataRow
drNewAuthor = dtAuthors.NewRow()

' It has the same table schema
drNewAuthor("au_id") = "222-22-2222"
drNewAuthor("au_fname") = "Fabio Claudio"
drNewAuthor("au_lname") = "Ferracchiati"
drNewAuthor("contract") = 1

' Add the new row to the collection contained
' in the DataTable
dtAuthors.Rows.Add(drNewAuthor)

' Merge the DataSet data with all the rows that are changed
dsAuthors.Merge(dtAuthors.GetChanges())

. . .
```

C#:

```
. . .

DataTable dtAuthors = new DataTable();

// Create a new row
DataRow drNewAuthor;
drNewAuthor = dtAuthors.NewRow();

// It has the same table schema
drNewAuthor["au_id"] = "222-22-2222";
drNewAuthor["au_fname"] = "Fabio Claudio";
drNewAuthor["au_lname"] = "Ferracchiati";
drNewAuthor["contract"] = 1;

// Add the new row to the collection contained
// in the DataTable
dtAuthors.Rows.Add(drNewAuthor);

// Merge the DataSet data with all the rows that are changed
dsAuthors.Merge(dtAuthors.GetChanges());

. . .
```

The GetErrors Method

VB.NET:

```
Public Function GetErrors() As DataRow()
```

C#:

```
public DataRow[] GetErrors();
```

With this method a `DataRow` object array containing all the records having an error are retrieved. In this case, an error doesn't mean that the record has, for example, a column with a wrong type specified, but that it doesn't respect a specific rule. There could be cases where you can't validate all the data that an application passes to the database from your user interface (for example retrieving data from a XML document). This is the classic situation where you could use this method in conjunction with the `RowError` property of the `DataRow` object and the `RowChanged` event.

VB.NET:

```
Sub PrintErrors(ByVal t As DataTable)
      Dim r() As DataRow = t.GetErrors()
      Dim i As Integer

      For i = 0 To r.Length - 1
            Console.WriteLine("AuthorID: " + r(i)("AuthorID") + " - " +
r(i).RowError)
      Next
End Sub
```

C#:

```
private static void PrintErrors(DataTable t)
{
      DataRow[] r = t.GetErrors();

      for(int i=0;i<r.Length;i++)
      {
            Console.WriteLine("AuthorID: " + r[i]["AuthorID"] + " - " +
r[i].RowError);
      }
}
```

The snippet of code above is extracted from the `Example1`, that comes with the download for the book. The example retrieves new records from an XML file and tries to store them in the related table in the database. If duplicate records are found, then an error message is associated to the row and inside the routine above, the `AuthorID` of the error row is printed together with the error cause.

The GetRowType Method

VB.NET:

```
Overridable Protected Function GetRowType() As Type
```

C#:

```
protected virtual Type GetRowType();
```

This is a protected method useful to retrieve the `Type` object of a specific `DataRow` contained in the `DataTable`. Recall that you can't call a protected method directly using an instance of the object. This method is used internally by the class.

The HasSchemaChanged Method

VB.NET:

```
Overridable Protected Function HasSchemaChanged() As Boolean
```

C#:

```
protected virtual bool HasSchemaChanged();
```

This protected method is also used internally to retrieve a Boolean value indicating whether a `DataTable` schema has changed (`true`) or not (`false`).

The ImportRow Method

VB.NET:

```
Public Sub ImportRow( _
    ByVal row As DataRow _
)
```

C#:

```
public void ImportRow(
    DataRow row
);
```

This method imports a row inside the `DataRowCollection`, including its `DataRowState` value, errors, original, and current value.

VB.NET:

```
Dim dbConn As New
SqlClient.SqlConnection("server=localhost;uid=sa;pwd=;database=pubs")

' Create DataAdapter
Dim da As New SqlClient.SqlDataAdapter("SELECT au_id,au_fname,au_lname FROM
authors", dbConn)

' An empty table with just the table schema
Dim dt As New DataTable("Authors")
da.FillSchema(dt, SchemaType.Source)

' A filled table
Dim dtTemp As New DataTable("Temp")
da.Fill(dtTemp)

Dim r As DataRow = dtTemp.Rows(0)

Console.WriteLine("Before ImportRow: " & dt.Rows.Count.ToString())

' Import one row
dt.ImportRow(r)

Console.WriteLine("After ImportRow: " & dt.Rows.Count.ToString())
```

C#:

```csharp
SqlConnection dbConn = new
SqlConnection("server=localhost;uid=sa;pwd=;database=pubs");

// Create DataAdapter
SqlDataAdapter da = new SqlDataAdapter("SELECT au_id,au_fname,au_lname FROM
authors",dbConn);

// An empty table with just the table schema
DataTable dt = new DataTable("Authors");
da.FillSchema(dt,SchemaType.Source);

// A filled table
DataTable dtTemp = new DataTable("Temp");
da.Fill(dtTemp);

DataRow r = dtTemp.Rows[0];

Console.WriteLine("Before ImportRow: " + dt.Rows.Count.ToString());

// Import one row
dt.ImportRow(r);

Console.WriteLine("After ImportRow: " + dt.Rows.Count.ToString());
```

In the above example, 1 row was imported into a new table, as can be seen by the output generated by this example:

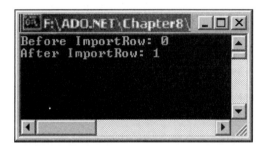

The NewRow Method

VB.NET:

```
Public Function NewRow() As DataRow
```

C#:

```csharp
public DataRow NewRow();
```

NewRow() creates a new row inside the rows collection contained in the DataTable object, having the same schema as the table. When you need to add a record to the database, you have to use this method, then you can insert the values into each column. Finally, call the Add() method of the DataRowCollection object retrieved from the Rows property of the DataTable, as is shown in the following example:

387

VB.NET:

```
...
    ' Create a new row
    Dim drNewAuthor As DataRow

    ' It has the same table schema
    drNewAuthor = dtAuthors.NewRow()
    drNewAuthor("au_id") = "222-22-2222"
    drNewAuthor("au_fname") = "Fabio Claudio"
    drNewAuthor("au_lname") = "Ferracchiati"
    drNewAuthor("contract") = 1

    ' Add the new row to the collection contained
    ' in the DataTable
    dtAuthors.Rows.Add(drNewAuthor)

    ' Update the database records
    daAuthors.Update(dtAuthors)
...
```

C#:

```
...
    // Create a new row
    DataRow drNewAuthor;
    drNewAuthor = dtAuthors.NewRow();

    // It has the same table schema
    drNewAuthor["au_id"] = "222-22-2222";
    drNewAuthor["au_fname"] = "Fabio Claudio";
    drNewAuthor["au_lname"] = "Ferracchiati";
    drNewAuthor["contract"] = 1;

    // Add the new row to the collection contained
    // in the DataTable
    dtAuthors.Rows.Add(drNewAuthor);

    // Update the database records
    daAuthors.Update(dtAuthors);
...
```

The OnColumnChanged and OnColumnChanging Method

VB.NET:

```
Overridable Protected Sub OnColumnChanged( _
   ByVal e As DataColumnChangeEventArgs _
)
```

```
Overridable Protected Sub OnColumnChanging( _
   ByVal e As DataColumnChangeEventArgs _
)
```

C#:

```
protected virtual void OnColumnChanged(
   DataColumnChangeEventArgs e
);
```

```
protected virtual void OnColumnChanging(
   DataColumnChangeEventArgs e
);
```

These are two methods that raise the `ColumnChanged` and `ColumnChanging` events respectively. The latter is fired before the former, as you can see from the following example:

VB.NET:

```
...
      daAuthors.Fill(dtAuthors)

      AddHandler dtAuthors.ColumnChanged, New
               DataColumnChangeEventHandler(AddressOf OnColumnChanged)

      AddHandler dtAuthors.ColumnChanging, New
               DataColumnChangeEventHandler(AddressOf OnColumnChanging)

      ' Create a new row
      Dim drNewAuthor As DataRow

      ' It has the same table schema
      drNewAuthor = dtAuthors.NewRow()
      drNewAuthor("au_id") = "222-22-2222"
      drNewAuthor("au_fname") = "Fabio Claudio"
      drNewAuthor("au_lname") = "Ferracchiati"
      drNewAuthor("contract") = 1

End Sub

Private Sub OnColumnChanged(ByVal sender As Object, ByVal args As
                        DataColumnChangeEventArgs)
      Console.WriteLine("Column " + args.Column.ToString() + " has changed")
End Sub

Private Sub OnColumnChanging(ByVal sender As Object, ByVal args As
                        DataColumnChangeEventArgs)
      Console.WriteLine("Column " + args.Column.ToString() + " is changing")
```

C#:

```
...
daAuthors.Fill(dtAuthors);

dtAuthors.ColumnChanged += new
      DataColumnChangeEventHandler(OnColumnChanged);
dtAuthors.ColumnChanging += new
      DataColumnChangeEventHandler(OnColumnChanging);
```

```
// Create a new row
DataRow drNewAuthor;
drNewAuthor = dtAuthors.NewRow();

// It has the same table schema
drNewAuthor["au_id"] = "222-22-2222";
drNewAuthor["au_fname"] = "Fabio Claudio";
drNewAuthor["au_lname"] = "Ferracchiati";
drNewAuthor["contract"] = 1;

protected static void OnColumnChanged(Object sender, DataColumnChangeEventArgs
args)
{
    Console.WriteLine("Column " + args.Column.ToString() + " has
                      changed");
}

protected static void OnColumnChanging(Object sender, DataColumnChangeEventArgs
args)
{
    Console.WriteLine("Column " + args.Column.ToString() + " is
                      changing");
}
```

Giving the following output for this example:

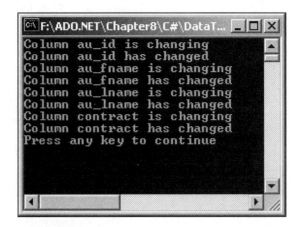

The OnPropertyChanging Method

VB.NET:

```
Overridable Protected Friend Dim Sub OnPropertyChanging( _
    ByVal pcevent As PropertyChangedEventArgs _
)
```

C#:

```
protected internal virtual void OnPropertyChanging(
    PropertyChangedEventArgs pcevent
);
```

Using this method, you can raise the `PropertyChanging` method. This event is fired each time a `DataTable` property is changing its value. This is not a method you can use directly from the `DataTable` object however, due to its protection level. You have to derive a new class that overrides this method remembering to call the parent inside the body of the method's code.

The OnRemoveColumn Method

VB.NET:

```
Overridable Protected Friend Dim Sub OnRemoveColumn( _
    ByVal column As DataColumn _
)
```

C#:

```
protected internal virtual void OnRemoveColumn(
    DataColumn column
);
```

Similar to the previous methods, this method, used inside a derived class, can raise an event when a column is being removed from the `DataTable` object.

VB.NET:

```
Sub Main()
    Dim dbConn As New
SqlClient.SqlConnection("server=localhost;uid=sa;pwd=;database=pubs")

    ' Create Authors DataTable
    Dim dtAuthors As New AuthorsDataTable()

    ' Create a DataAdapter to fill the DataSet
    Dim daAuthors As New SqlClient.SqlDataAdapter("SELECT
au_id,au_fname,au_lname,contract FROM authors", dbConn)

    ' Fill the DataSet
    daAuthors.Fill(dtAuthors)

    dtAuthors.Columns.Remove("contract")

End Sub


Public Class AuthorsDataTable
    Inherits DataTable

    Protected Overrides Sub OnRemoveColumn(ByVal column As DataColumn)
        Console.WriteLine("The column {0} has been removed",
column.ColumnName())
    End Sub
End Class
```

C#:

```
static void Main(string[] args)
{
    SqlConnection dbConn = new
```

```
        SqlConnection("server=localhost;uid=sa;pwd=;database=pubs");

        // Create Authors DataTable
        AuthorsDataTable dtAuthors = new AuthorsDataTable();

        // Create a DataAdapter to fill the table
        SqlDataAdapter daAuthors = new SqlDataAdapter("SELECT
        au_id,au_fname,au_lname,contract FROM authors",dbConn);
        aAuthors.Fill(dtAuthors);

        dtAuthors.Columns.Remove("contract");
    }

public class AuthorsDataTable : DataTable
{
    protected override void OnRemoveColumn(DataColumn column)
    {
        Console.WriteLine("The column {0} has been removed",
                        column.ColumnName);
    }
}
```

The OnRowChanged and OnRowChanging Methods

VB.NET:

```
Overridable Protected Sub OnRowChanged( _
    ByVal e As DataRowChangeEventArgs _
)

Overridable Protected Sub OnRowChanging( _
    ByVal e As DataRowChangeEventArgs _
)
```

C#:

```
protected virtual void OnRowChanged(
    DataRowChangeEventArgs e
);

protected virtual void OnRowChanging(
    DataRowChangeEventArgs e
);
```

These methods allow the implementation of the RowChanged and RowChanging event handlers. These events are fired when the row is changed or changing respectively inside the DataTable. They are very useful in conjunction with the RowError property of the DataRow object because they let us check each row and decide whether to associate an error to it.

VB.NET:

```
    ...
        daAuthors.Fill(dtAuthors)

        AddHandler dtAuthors.RowDeleted, New
```

```
        DataRowChangeEventHandler(AddressOf OnRowChanged)
    AddHandler dtAuthors.RowDeleting, New
        DataRowChangeEventHandler(AddressOf OnRowChanging)


    ' Change the first row
    dtAuthors.Rows(0)("au_id") = "222-22-2222"


    . . .
End Sub

Private Sub OnRowChanging(ByVal sender As Object, ByVal args As
DataRowChangeEventArgs)
    Console.WriteLine("The row is being changed")
End Sub

Private Sub OnRowChanged(ByVal sender As Object, ByVal args As
DataRowChangeEventArgs)
    Console.WriteLine("The row has been changed")
```

C#:

```
...
daAuthors.Fill(dtAuthors);

dtAuthors.RowChanging += new DataRowChangeEventHandler(OnRowChanging);
dtAuthors.RowChanged += new DataRowChangeEventHandler(OnRowChanged);

// Change the first row
dtAuthors.Rows[0]["au_id"] = "222-22-2222";
. . .

protected static void OnRowChanging(Object sender, DataRowChangeEventArgs args)
{
    Console.WriteLine("The row is being changed");
}

protected static void OnRowChanged(Object sender, DataRowChangeEventArgs args)
{
    Console.WriteLine("The row has been changed");
}
```

The OnRowDeleted and OnRowDeleting Methods

VB.NET:

```
Overridable Protected Sub OnRowDeleted( _
    ByVal e As DataRowChangeEventArgs _
)

Overridable Protected Sub OnRowDeleting( _
    ByVal e As DataRowChangeEventArgs _
)
```

C#:

```
protected virtual void OnRowDeleted(
    DataRowChangeEventArgs e
);

protected virtual void OnRowDeleting(
    DataRowChangeEventArgs e
);
```

The `RowDeleted` and `RowDeleting` event handlers are implemented by these methods. The events are fired when the row has been deleted from the row collection inside the `DataTable` object, and when the row is being deleted, respectively. These events could be useful when you need to remove records bounded with the processing ones. You can check if a particular row is being deleted and remove some other records from the database.

VB.NET:

```
    ...
        daAuthors.Fill(dtAuthors)

        AddHandler dtAuthors.RowDeleted, New
            DataRowChangeEventHandler(AddressOf OnRowDeleted)
        AddHandler dtAuthors.RowDeleting, New
            DataRowChangeEventHandler(AddressOf OnRowDeleting)

        dtAuthors.Rows.Remove(drNewAuthor)

        . . .
    End Sub

Private Sub OnRowDeleted(ByVal sender As Object, ByVal args As
DataRowChangeEventArgs)
        Console.WriteLine("The row has been deleted")
End Sub

Private Sub OnRowDeleting(ByVal sender As Object, ByVal args As
DataRowChangeEventArgs)
        Console.WriteLine("The row is being deleted")
End Sub
```

C#:

```
...
daAuthors.Fill(dtAuthors);

dtAuthors.RowDeleted += new DataRowChangeEventHandler(OnRowDeleted);
dtAuthors.RowDeleting += new DataRowChangeEventHandler(OnRowDeleting);

DataRow drNewAuthor;

dtAuthors.Rows.Remove(drNewAuthor);

. . .
```

```
protected static void OnRowDeleted(Object sender, DataRowChangeEventArgs args)
{
    Console.WriteLine("The row has been deleted");
}

protected static void OnRowDeleting(Object sender, DataRowChangeEventArgs args)
{
    Console.WriteLine("The row is being deleted");
}
```

The RejectChanges Method

VB.NET:

```
Public Sub RejectChanges()
```

C#:

```
public void RejectChanges();
```

This method implements a rollback mechanism that avoids accepting the changes occurred to the `DataTable` object. This method is the opposite of `AcceptChanges()`. Usually, the code you implement checks whether the table has an error with the `HasError` property, and then it decides whether to commit the data with the `AcceptChanges()` or rollback them with `RejectChanges()`.

VB.NET:

```
' If no errors found Update the table
' otherwise print the errors
If bErrors = False Then
    da.Update(dt)
    dt.AcceptChanges()
    Console.WriteLine("Records are stored successfully")
Else
    PrintErrors(dt)
    dt.RejectChanges()
End If
```

C#:

```
// If no errors found Update the table
// otherwise print the errors
if(!bErrors)
{
    da.Update(dt);
    dt.AcceptChanges();
    Console.WriteLine("Records are stored successfully");
}
else
{
    PrintErrors(dt);
    dt.RejectChanges();
}
```

The Select Method

VB.NET:

```
Overloads Public Function Select() As DataRow()
```

```
Overloads Public Function Select( _
    ByVal filterExpression As String _
) As DataRow()
```

```
Overloads Public Function Select( _
    ByVal filterExpression As String, _
    ByVal sort As String _
) As DataRow()
```

```
Overloads Public Function Select( _
    ByVal filterExpression As String, _
    ByVal sort As String, _
    ByVal recordStates As DataViewRowState _
) As DataRow()
```

C#:

```
public DataRow[] Select();
```

```
public DataRow[] Select(
    string filterExpression
);
```

```
public DataRow[] Select(
    string filterExpression,
    string sort
);
```

```
public DataRow[] Select(
    string filterExpression,
    string sort,
    DataViewRowState recordStates
);
```

This method is one of the most useful because it lets you sort, filter, and select records inside the table. As shown above, it comes in four versions with every one returning an array of `DataRow` objects representing a set of records queried from the table. The first version doesn't require parameters and returns all the records contained in the `DataTable` object.

VB.NET:

```
...
daAuthors.Fill(dtAuthors)

' Retrieve all the records
Dim dbRows() As DataRow
dbRows = dtAuthors.Select()
```

```
Dim I As Integer
For I = 0 To dbRows.Length - 1
    Console.WriteLine(dbRows(I)("au_lname"))
Next
```

C#:

```
...
daAuthors.Fill(dtAuthors);

// Retrieve all the records
DataRow[] dbRows;
dbRows = dtAuthors.Select();

for (int i=0;i<dbRows.Length;i++)
    Console.WriteLine(dbRows[i]["au_lname"].ToString());
```

The second version of this method accepts a filter expression string to filter records inside the DataTable object. The following example filters all the records returning only the ones starting with the *S* letter:

VB.NET:

```
...
daAuthors.Fill(dtAuthors)

' Retrieve all the records
Dim dbRows() As DataRow

' Selects all the Authors with names starting with S
dbRows = dtAuthors.Select("au_lname LIKE 'S%'")

Dim I As Integer
For I = 0 To dbRows.Length - 1
    Console.WriteLine(dbRows(I)("au_lname"))
Next
```

C#:

```
...
daAuthors.Fill(dtAuthors);

// Retrieve all the records
DataRow[] dbRows;

// Selects all the Authors with names starting with S
dbRows = dtAuthors.Select("au_lname LIKE 'S%'");

for (int i=0;i<dbRows.Length;i++)
    Console.WriteLine(dbRows[i]["au_lname"].ToString());
```

The third method accepts two strings representing the filter rule and the sort directive, respectively. In this third example, the filter is again the letter S and the sort directive is DESC to represent descending order:

397

VB.NET:

```
...
daAuthors.Fill(dtAuthors)

' Retrieve all the records
Dim dbRows() As DataRow

' Select all Authors with names beginning with S and list in
' descending order
dbRows = dtAuthors.Select("au_lname LIKE 'S%'", "au_lname DESC")

Dim I As Integer
For I = 0 To dbRows.Length - 1
    Console.WriteLine(dbRows(I)("au_lname"))
Next
```

C#:

```
...
daAuthors.Fill(dtAuthors);

// Retrieve all the records
DataRow[] dbRows;

// Select all Authors with names beginnning with S and list in
// descending order
dbRows = dtAuthors.Select("au_lname LIKE 'S%'", "au_lname DESC");

for (int i=0;i<dbRows.Length;i++)
    Console.WriteLine(dbRows[i]["au_lname"].ToString());
```

The fourth and last version of the method accepts three parameters; the first is the filter string, the second is the sort string, while the third is the DataViewRowState enum value. This version retrieves all the records inside the DataTable object having the specified row state and the applied filtering and sorting rules. In this case, the first two parameters are the same as previous, and the third is CurrentRows, which is explained in the table below the example.

VB.NET:

```
...
daAuthors.Fill(dtAuthors)

' Retrieve all the records
Dim dbRows() As DataRow
dbRows = dtAuthors.Select("au_lname LIKE 'S%'", "au_lname DESC",
    DataViewRowState.CurrentRows)

Dim I As Integer
For I = 0 To dbRows.Length - 1
    Console.WriteLine(dbRows(I)("au_lname"))
Next
```

C#:

```
...
daAuthors.Fill(dtAuthors);

// Retrieve all the records
DataRow[] dbRows;
dbRows = dtAuthors.Select("au_lname LIKE 'S%'", "au_lname DESC",
    DataViewRowState.CurrentRows);

for (int i=0;i<dbRows.Length;i++)
    Console.WriteLine(dbRows[i]["au_lname"].ToString());
```

The `recordStates` parameter can assume either one of the the values or a bitwise combination of them as listed in the `AcceptChanges()` section.

The ToString Method

VB.NET:

```
Overrides Public Function ToString() As String
```

C#:

```
public override string ToString();
```

This method can retrieve the table name and the `DisplayExpression` string if present.

VB.NET:

```
Dim dbConn As New
SqlClient.SqlConnection("server=localhost;uid=sa;pwd=;database=pubs")

' Create Authors DataTable
Dim dtAuthors As New DataTable("Authors")

' Create a DataAdapter to fill the table
Dim daAuthors As New SqlClient.SqlDataAdapter("SELECT
au_id,au_fname,au_lname,contract FROM authors", dbConn)
daAuthors.Fill(dtAuthors)

Console.WriteLine(dtAuthors.ToString())
```

C#

```
SqlConnection dbConn = new
SqlConnection("server=localhost;uid=sa;pwd=;database=pubs");

// Create Authors DataTable
DataTable dtAuthors = new DataTable("Authors");

// Create a DataAdapter to fill the table
SqlDataAdapter daAuthors = new SqlDataAdapter("SELECT
au_id,au_fname,au_lname,contract FROM authors",dbConn);
daAuthors.Fill(dtAuthors);

Console.WriteLine(dtAuthors.ToString());
```

DataTable Events

Events are fired by .NET framework when specific circumstances are verified. In the case of the `DataTable` object, they are verified when either a column or a row changes its state so we can use events fired during a row-deleting phase, column's changing, and so on. In this section each event will be listed with a description of when it will be fired. If you need to study some examples, please refer to the previous section, `DataTable` methods, where they are covered in greater detail.

`DataTable` inherits its events from the `MarshalByValueComponent` class:

VB.NET:

```
NotOverridable Public Event Disposed As EventHandler
```

C#:

```
public event EventHandler Disposed;
```

This is fired when the `Dispose` method is called.

The ColumnChanged Event

VB.NET:

```
Public Event ColumnChanged As DataColumnChangeEventHandler
```

C#:

```
public event DataColumnChangeEventHandler ColumnChanged;
```

This event is fired when a column contained in the `DataTable` has changed its value. The `DataColumnChangeEventArgs` parameter will contain one of the following arguments:

Argument	Description
Column	Retrieve the `DataColumn` object containing the changed value
ProposedValue	Retrieve or set a `ProposedValue` object
Row	Retrieve the `DataRow` object containing the changed value

The ColumnChanging Event

VB.NET:

```
Public Event ColumnChanging As DataColumnChangeEventHandler
```

C#:

```
public event DataColumnChangeEventHandler ColumnChanging;
```

This event is fired when a column contained in the `DataTable` is being changed in value. The `DataColumnChangeEventArgs` parameter will contain one of the following arguments:

Argument	Description
Column	Retrieve the `DataColumn` object containing the changed value
ProposedValue	Retrieve or set a `ProposedValue` object
Row	Retrieve the `DataRow` object containing the changed value

The RowChanged Event

VB.NET:

```
Public Event RowChanged As DataRowChangeEventHandler
```

C#:

```
public event DataRowChangeEventHandler RowChanged;
```

This event is fired when a row contained in the `DataTable` has changed its value. The `DataRowChangeEventArgs` parameter will contain one of the following arguments:

Argument	Description
Action	Retrieve the action description for the changed row. It can assume one of the following values: `Add`: the row has been added to the `DataTable`. `Change`: the row has been changed. `Commit`: the row has been committed. `Delete`: the row has been deleted. `Nothing`: no changes to the row. `Rollback`: the changes have been rolled back.
Row	Retrieve the `DataRow` object containing the changed value.

The RowChanging Event

VB.NET:

```
Public ReadOnly Property Row As DataRow
```

C#:

```
public DataRow Row {get;}
```

This event is fired when a row contained in the `DataTable` is being changed in value. The `DataRowChangeEventArgs` parameter will contain one of the arguments as listed above.

The RowDeleted Event

VB.NET:

```
Public Event RowDeleted As DataRowChangeEventHandler
```

C#:

```
public event DataRowChangeEventHandler RowDeleted;
```

This event is fired when a row has been removed from the rows contained in the `DataTable`. The `DataRowChangeEventArgs` parameter will contain one of the arguments listed previously.

The RowDeleting Event

VB.NET:

```
Public Event RowDeleting As DataRowChangeEventHandler
```

C#:

```
public event DataRowChangeEventHandler RowDeleting;
```

This event is fired when a row is being removed from the rows contained in the `DataTable` and contains one of the arguments for the `DataRowChangeEventArgs` parameter.

The Sub-Objects

As we have seen in the first part of this chapter, `DataTable` is a class that contains all the functionalities of a generic table defined in a generic database. Microsoft Framework .NET is well structured and, mainly, object-oriented, so every functionality that affects a table has been split into sub-functionalities all contained within their respective classes. For instance, a database table contains columns declared with various data types. The `DataTable` class provides a collection of `DataColumns` that you can use to define all the columns that comprise your table specifying the data type that they will contain. Usually, at least one column within your table will contain unique values that you define as a primary key. As such, `DataTable` contains a `Constraint` objects collection that defines constraint rules to avoid column value duplication. Moreover, in a database all the records are contained in a table and you can access them by quering a set of rows. `DataTable` also contains a `DataRowCollection` objects collection containing all the rows making up your queried record set. Each aspect for managing your tables has been implemented and well defined. In this part of Chapter 8 the sub-objects contained inside the `DataTable` are going to be analyzed in further detail.

The DataColumn Object

The `DataColumn` object represents a column inside the collection contained in the `DataTable`. To configure your table schema, you have to start creating columns specifying their type, for example, whether they are unique, which is the primary key, and so on. `DataColumn` gives all the functionalities to manage this kind of situation. In this section, each property, method, and event belonging to the `DataColumn` object will be examined.

DataColumn Constructors

VB.NET:

```
Public Sub New()
```

```
Public Sub New( _
    ByVal columnName As String _
)
```

```
Public Sub New( _
    ByVal columnName As String, _
    ByVal dataType As Type _
)
```

```
Public Sub New( _
    ByVal columnName As String, _
    ByVal dataType As Type, _
    ByVal expr As String _
)
```

```
Public Sub New( _
    ByVal columnName As String, _
    ByVal dataType As Type, _
    ByVal expr As String, _
    ByVal type As MappingType _
)
```

C#:

```
public DataColumn();
```

```
public DataColumn(
    string columnName
);
```

```
public DataColumn(
    string columnName,
    Type dataType
);
```

```
public DataColumn(
    string columnName,
    Type dataType,
    string expr
);
```

```
public DataColumn(
    string columnName,
    Type dataType,
    string expr,
    MappingType type
);
```

As was shown above, the `DataColumn` object has five versions of its constructor. The first is the default constructor; it doesn't accept parameters and creates an empty object initializing all the internal data to default values.

VB.NET:

```
' Create AuthorID column
Dim dcAuthorID As New DataColumn()
```

C#:

```
// Create AuthorID column
DataColumn dcAuthorID = new DataColumn();
```

The second constructor version accepts a `columnName` string parameter that represents the column name, for example `au_id`, to associate to the object.

VB.NET:

```
' Create AuthorID column
Dim dcAuthorID As New DataColumn("au_id")
```

C#:

```
// Create AuthorID column
DataColumn dcAuthorID = new DataColumn("au_id");
```

The third version of the constructor allows a column name and the column type to be specified directly during the object's creation, `au_id` and `String` type:

VB.NET:

```
' Create AuthorID column
Dim dcAuthorID As New DataColumn("au_id", GetType(System.String))
```

C#:

```
// Create AuthorID column
DataColumn dcAuthorID = new DataColumn("au_id",typeof(System.String));
```

The fourth version allows the creation of a `DataColumn` object specifying a column name, a column type, and an expression. The latter parameter can be set with a mathematical operation in order to calculate the column value programmatically, as is shown below:

VB.NET:

```
' Create a SalesTotal column
Dim dcSalesTotal As New DataColumn("SalesTotal", GetType(System.String), "qty *
price")
```

C#:

```
// Create a SalesTotal column
DataColumn dcAuthorID = new DataColumn("SalesTotal", GetType(System.String), "qty
* price");
```

Finally, the fifth and last version of the constructor accepts a column name parameter, a column type, an expression string, and a `MappingType` enum value. The latter sets how the column will be translated in a XML document when the `WriteXML` method is called. The `MappingType` enum value can assume one of the following values (you can find more information about it in the `ColumnMapping` property section):

Value	Description
Attribute	The column will be represented with a XML attribute
Element	The column will be represented with a XML element
Hidden	The column will be hidden inside an internal structure
SimpleContent	The column will be mapped to a XMLTest class element

Below, a `DataColumn` similar to the previous ones is being created with the added argument that it will be represented by an XML attribute:

VB.NET:

```
' Create a SalesTotal column
Dim dcSalesTotal As New DataColumn("SalesTotal", GetType(System.String), "qty *
price", MappingType.Attribute)
```

C#:

```
// Create a SalesTotal column
DataColumn dcAuthorID = new DataColumn("SalesTotal", GetType(System.String), "qty
* price", MappingType.Attribute);
```

DataColumn Properties

The `DataColumn` object exposes eighteen of its own properties and four inherited ones. Thanks to its properties, we can define a column type and a column name, implement an expression, auto increment its value, and so on. Before we start to examine each property let's list the inherited ones:

Property	Description
Container	Retrieves the `IContainer` associated to the `DataColumn` object, which provides all the functionality needed by this objects components
DesignMode	Retrieves a Boolean value indicating whether the object is in design mode
Site	Either retrieves or sets the site for the component
Events	Retrieves a list of event handlers for this object

Now we can start to examine the properties.

The AllowDBNull Property

VB.NET:

```
Public Property AllowDBNull As Boolean
```

C#:

```
public bool AllowDBNull {get; set;}
```

This property allows the specification of the column that will accept null values (`true`) or not (`false`). If you indicate a required column value and you don't provide it to the table, an exception will be thrown. The following example shows the creation of a new column, `ID`, that does not accept null values:

VB.NET:

```
' Create a required column
Dim dcID As New DataColumn("ID", GetType(System.Int32))
dcID.AllowDBNull = False
```

C#:

```
// Create a required column
DataColumn dcID = new DataColumn("ID", typeof(System.Int32));
myColumn.AllowDBNull = false;
```

The AutoIncrement, AutoIncrementSeed and AutoIncrementStep Properties

VB.NET:

```
Public Property AutoIncrement As Boolean
```

```
Public Property AutoIncrementSeed As Long
```

```
Public Property AutoIncrementStep As Long
```

C#:

```
public bool AutoIncrement {get; set;}
```

```
public long AutoIncrementSeed {get; set;}
```

```
public long AutoIncrementStep {get; set;}
```

`AutoIncrement` sets or retrieves a `Boolean` value indicating whether it is an auto-increment column type. This kind of column increments itself each time a record is added to the table. The second property lets you choose which is the starting value for the column, while the latter is used to decides the subsequent increment, step, value (default is 1).

In the following example, the column is set to increment itself automatically by a value of 10 starting at 0:

VB.NET:

```
' Create a required column with a starting value 0, and a step increment of
' 10
Dim dcID As New DataColumn("ID", GetType(System.Int32))
dcID.AllowDBNull = False
dcID.AutoIncrement = True
dcID.AutoIncrementSeed = 0
dcID.AutoIncrementStep = 10
```

C#:

```
// Create a required column with a starting value 0, and a step increment of
// 10
DataColumn dcID = new DataColumn("ID", typeof(System.Int32));
dcID.AllowDBNull = false;
dcID.AutoIncrement = true;
dcID.AutoIncrementSeed = 0;
dcID.AutoIncrementStep = 10;
```

The Caption Property

VB.NET:

```
Public Property Caption As String
```

C#:

```
public string Caption {get; set;}
```

Using this property, you can set a caption label visible in windows components able to show it (in other words DataGrid component).

VB.NET:

```
' Set the caption
Dim dcID As New DataColumn("ID", GetType(System.Int32))
dcID.Caption = "ID"
```

C#:

```
// Set the caption
DataColumn dcID = new DataColumn("ID", typeof(System.Int32));
dcID.Caption = "ID";
```

The ColumnMapping Property

VB.NET:

```
Overridable Public Property ColumnMapping As MappingType
```

C#:

```
public virtual MappingType ColumnMapping {get; set;}
```

We have already seen this property when we were looking at one of the constructor versions available. You can specify a `MappingType` enum value to the column that will be used during the XML document creation, by the `WriteXML()` method of the `DataSet` object. The `ColumnMapping` property can assume one of the following values:

Value	Description
Attribute	The column will be represented with a XML attribute
Element	The column will be represented with a XML element
Hidden	The column will be hidden inside an internal structure
SimpleContent	The column will be mapped to a XMLTest class element

In the following examples, each value is going to be shown in turn, starting with `Attribute`:

VB.NET:

```
' Create a column
Dim dcID As New DataColumn("ID", GetType(System.Int32))

' Set the Attribute enum value
dcID.ColumnMapping = MappingType.Attribute

' Add the column to the table
Dim dtAuthors As New DataTable("Authors")
dtAuthors.Columns.Add(dcID)

' Create a DataSet and add the table to it
Dim dsAuthors As New DataSet("dsAuthors")
dsAuthors.Tables.Add(dtAuthors)

' Add a new row to the table
Dim drNewRow As DataRow

drNewRow = dtAuthors.NewRow()
drNewRow("ID") = 1

dtAuthors.Rows.Add(drNewRow)
dtAuthors.AcceptChanges()

' Write the XML Schema of this table
dsAuthors.WriteXml("C:\dataAttribute.xml")
```

C#:

```
// Create a column
DataColumn dcID = new DataColumn("ID", typeof(System.Int32));

// Set the Attribute enum value
dcID.ColumnMapping = MappingType.Attribute;

// Add the column to the table
```

```
DataTable dtAuthors = new DataTable("Authors");
dtAuthors.Columns.Add(dcID);

// Create a DataSet and add the table to it
DataSet dsAuthors = new DataSet("dsAuthors");
dsAuthors.Tables.Add(dtAuthors);

// Add a new row to the table
DataRow drNewRow;

drNewRow = dtAuthors.NewRow();
drNewRow["ID"] = 1;

dtAuthors.Rows.Add(drNewRow);
dtAuthors.AcceptChanges();

// Write the XML Schema of this table
dsAuthors.WriteXml("C:\\dataAttribute.xml");
```

With an `Attribute` value, the code will generate this XML document:

```
<?xml version="1.0" standalone="yes"?>
<dsAuthors>
  <Authors ID="1" />
</dsAuthors>
```

By changing the `MappingType` to the `Element` value, the following XML document will be generated:

```
<?xml version="1.0" standalone="yes"?>
<dsAuthors>
  <Authors>
    <ID>1</ID>
  </Authors>
</dsAuthors>
```

With the `Hidden` value, no tags will be generated:

```
<?xml version="1.0" standalone="yes"?>
<dsAuthors>
  <Authors />
</dsAuthors>
```

Finally, using the last attribute, `SimpleContent`, we will get the following output:

```
<?xml version="1.0" standalone="yes"?>
<dsAuthors>
  <Authors>1</Authors>
</dsAuthors>
```

The ColumnName Property

VB.NET:

```
Public Property ColumnName As String
```

C#:

```
public string ColumnName {get; set;}
```

Using this property you can either retrieve or set the column name of the `DataColumn` object contained inside the `DataColumnCollection` collection. Usually, you'll use this property to set the name after having created the column using the default constructor.

VB.NET:

```
' Set the caption
Dim dcID As New DataColumn()
dcID.ColumnName = "ID"
```

C#:

```
// Set the caption
DataColumn dcID = new DataColumn();
dcID.ColumnName = "ID";
```

The DataType Property

VB.NET:

```
Public Property DataType As Type
```

C#:

```
public Type DataType {get; set;}
```

This property can either get or set a column type. A possible list of valid type values is shown below:

- ❏ `Byte`
- ❏ `Char`
- ❏ `DateTime`
- ❏ `Decimal`
- ❏ `Double`
- ❏ `Int16`
- ❏ `Int32`
- ❏ `Int64`
- ❏ `SByte`
- ❏ `Single`
- ❏ `String`
- ❏ `TimeSpan` (not supported by VB.NET)

❑   `UInt16` (not supported by VB.NET)

❑   `UInt32` (not supported by VB.NET)

❑   `UInt64` (not supported by VB.NET)

Below, our `ID` column is being set to a type of `Int32`:

VB.NET:

```
' Set the type
Dim dcID As New DataColumn()
dcID.ColumnName = "ID"
dcID.DataType = GetType(System.Int32)
```

C#:

```
// Set the type
DataColumn dcID = new DataColumn();
dcID.ColumnName = "ID";
dcID.DataType = typeof(System.Int32);
```

The DefaultValue Property

VB.NET:

```
Public Property DefaultValue As Object
```

C#:

```
public object DefaultValue {get; set;}
```

The `DefaultValue` property allows you to choose a default value to associate to the column when a new record will be created.

VB.NET:

```
' Set a default value
Dim dcContract As New DataColumn()
dcContract.ColumnName = "contract"
dcContract.DataType = GetType(System.Boolean)
dcContract.DefaultValue = False
```

C#:

```
// Set a default value
DataColumn dcContract = new DataColumn();
dcContract.ColumnName = "contract";
dcContract.DataType = typeof(System.Boolean);
dcContract.DefaultValue = false;
```

The Expression Property

VB.NET:

```
Public Property Expression As String
```

C#:

```
public string Expression {get; set;}
```

411

The `Expression` property adds a great functionality to `DataColumn` object. It allows the creation of a column where results from aggregate functions, Boolean operations, filtering of records, and much more can be stored. To begin with, let's look at one of the simplest uses of the `Expression` property:

VB.NET:

```
' Create some columns
Dim dcID As New DataColumn("ID", GetType(System.Int32))
Dim dcQty As New DataColumn("Qty", GetType(System.Int32))
Dim dcPrice As New DataColumn("Price", GetType(System.Int32))
Dim dcTotalPrice As New DataColumn("TotalPrice", GetType(System.Int32))

' Add the columns to the table
Dim dtAuthors As New DataTable("Authors")
dtAuthors.Columns.Add(dcID)
dtAuthors.Columns.Add(dcQty)
dtAuthors.Columns.Add(dcPrice)
dtAuthors.Columns.Add(dcTotalPrice)

' Create a DataSet and add the table to it
Dim dsAuthors As New DataSet("dsAuthors")
dsAuthors.Tables.Add(dtAuthors)

' Add three records to the table
Dim drNewRow As DataRow

drNewRow = dtAuthors.NewRow()
drNewRow("ID") = 1
drNewRow("Qty") = 10
drNewRow("Price") = 120
dtAuthors.Rows.Add(drNewRow)

drNewRow = dtAuthors.NewRow()
drNewRow("ID") = 2
drNewRow("Qty") = 20
drNewRow("Price") = 240
dtAuthors.Rows.Add(drNewRow)

drNewRow = dtAuthors.NewRow()
drNewRow("ID") = 3
drNewRow("Qty") = 30
drNewRow("Price") = 360
dtAuthors.Rows.Add(drNewRow)

dtAuthors.AcceptChanges()

' Create a TotalPrice column
dsAuthors.Tables(0).Columns("TotalPrice").Expression = "Qty * Price"

Dim r As DataRow

For Each r In dsAuthors.Tables(0).Rows
     Console.WriteLine(r("TotalPrice"))
Next
```

C#:

```csharp
// Create some columns
DataColumn dcID = new DataColumn("ID", typeof(System.Int32));
DataColumn dcQty = new DataColumn("Qty", typeof(System.Int32));
DataColumn dcPrice = new DataColumn("Price", typeof(System.Int32));
DataColumn dcTotalPrice = new DataColumn("TotalPrice", typeof(System.Int32));

// Add the columns to the table
DataTable dtAuthors = new DataTable("Authors");
dtAuthors.Columns.Add(dcID);
dtAuthors.Columns.Add(dcQty);
dtAuthors.Columns.Add(dcPrice);
dtAuthors.Columns.Add(dcTotalPrice);

// Create a DataSet and add the table to it
DataSet dsAuthors = new DataSet("dsAuthors");
dsAuthors.Tables.Add(dtAuthors);

// Add three records to the table
DataRow drNewRow;

drNewRow = dtAuthors.NewRow();
drNewRow["ID"] = 1;
drNewRow["Qty"] = 10;
drNewRow["Price"] = 120;
dtAuthors.Rows.Add(drNewRow);

drNewRow = dtAuthors.NewRow();
drNewRow["ID"] = 2;
drNewRow["Qty"] = 20;
drNewRow["Price"] = 240;
dtAuthors.Rows.Add(drNewRow);

drNewRow = dtAuthors.NewRow();
drNewRow["ID"] = 3;
drNewRow["Qty"] = 30;
drNewRow["Price"] = 360;
dtAuthors.Rows.Add(drNewRow);

dtAuthors.AcceptChanges();

// Create a TotalPrice column
dsAuthors.Tables[0].Columns["TotalPrice"].Expression = "Qty * Price";

foreach (DataRow r in dsAuthors.Tables[0].Rows)
    Console.WriteLine(r["TotalPrice"]);
```

In the example above, the expression calculates the total price that an imaginary client has to pay and stores the final result into the column. If we examine the code, we will see that the `TotalPrice` column has never been assigned directly in the code, but it is the result of the expression. This property is very powerful, isn't it? It can also do a lot of other things. Let's continue to examine it with another example:

VB.NET:

```
' Create some columns
Dim dcID As New DataColumn("ID", GetType(System.Int32))
Dim dcQty As New DataColumn("Qty", GetType(System.Int32))
Dim dcPrice As New DataColumn("Price", GetType(System.Int32))
Dim dcTotalRecords As New DataColumn("TotalRecords", GetType(System.Int32))

. . .

' Create a TotalPrice column
dsAuthors.Tables(0).Columns("TotalRecords").Expression = "Count(ID)"

. . .
```

C#:

```
// Create some columns
DataColumn dcID = new DataColumn("ID", typeof(System.Int32));
DataColumn dcQty = new DataColumn("Qty", typeof(System.Int32));
DataColumn dcPrice = new DataColumn("Price", typeof(System.Int32));
DataColumn dcTotalRecords = new DataColumn("TotalRecords", typeof(System.Int32));

. . .

// Create a TotalPrice column
dsAuthors.Tables[0].Columns["TotalRecords"].Expression = "Count(ID)";

. . .
```

In the example above, the expression defines an aggregate function retrieving the number of records and storing it into the column.

In this final example, you can see that the expression can even accept filter rules. In this case, the column will contain a `Boolean` value indicating which row has been filtered (`false`) and which not (`true`).

VB.NET:

```
' Create some columns
Dim dcID As New DataColumn("ID", GetType(System.Int32))
Dim dcQty As New DataColumn("Qty", GetType(System.Int32))
Dim dcPrice As New DataColumn("Price", GetType(System.Int32))
Dim dcExpression As New DataColumn("Expression", GetType(System.Boolean))

' Add the columns to the table
Dim dtAuthors As New DataTable("Authors")
dtAuthors.Columns.Add(dcID)
dtAuthors.Columns.Add(dcQty)
dtAuthors.Columns.Add(dcPrice)
dtAuthors.Columns.Add(dcExpression)

' Create a DataSet and add the table to it
Dim dsAuthors As New DataSet("dsAuthors")
dsAuthors.Tables.Add(dtAuthors)

' Add three records to the table
```

```vbnet
Dim drNewRow As DataRow

drNewRow = dtAuthors.NewRow()
drNewRow("ID") = 1
drNewRow("Qty") = 10
drNewRow("Price") = 120
dtAuthors.Rows.Add(drNewRow)

drNewRow = dtAuthors.NewRow()
drNewRow("ID") = 2
drNewRow("Qty") = 20
drNewRow("Price") = 240
dtAuthors.Rows.Add(drNewRow)

drNewRow = dtAuthors.NewRow()
drNewRow("ID") = 3
drNewRow("Qty") = 30
drNewRow("Price") = 360
dtAuthors.Rows.Add(drNewRow)

dtAuthors.AcceptChanges()

' Create a TotalPrice column
dsAuthors.Tables(0).Columns("Expression").Expression = "Qty>=30"

Dim r As DataRow

For Each r In dsAuthors.Tables(0).Rows
    Console.WriteLine("ID" & r("ID") & ": " & r("Expression"))
Next
```

C#:

```csharp
// Create some columns
DataColumn dcID = new DataColumn("ID", typeof(System.Int32));
DataColumn dcQty = new DataColumn("Qty", typeof(System.Int32));
DataColumn dcPrice = new DataColumn("Price", typeof(System.Int32));
DataColumn dcExpression = new DataColumn("Expression", typeof(System.Boolean));

// Add the column to the table
DataTable dtAuthors = new DataTable("Authors");
dtAuthors.Columns.Add(dcID);
dtAuthors.Columns.Add(dcQty);
dtAuthors.Columns.Add(dcPrice);
dtAuthors.Columns.Add(dcExpression);

// Create a DataSet and add the table to it
DataSet dsAuthors = new DataSet("dsAuthors");
dsAuthors.Tables.Add(dtAuthors);

// Add a new row to the table
DataRow drNewRow;

drNewRow = dtAuthors.NewRow();
```

```
drNewRow["ID"] = 1;
drNewRow["Qty"] = 10;
drNewRow["Price"] = 120;
dtAuthors.Rows.Add(drNewRow);

drNewRow = dtAuthors.NewRow();
drNewRow["ID"] = 2;
drNewRow["Qty"] = 20;
drNewRow["Price"] = 240;
dtAuthors.Rows.Add(drNewRow);

drNewRow = dtAuthors.NewRow();
drNewRow["ID"] = 3;
drNewRow["Qty"] = 30;
drNewRow["Price"] = 360;
dtAuthors.Rows.Add(drNewRow);

dtAuthors.AcceptChanges();

dsAuthors.Tables[0].Columns["Expression"].Expression = "Qty>=30";

foreach (DataRow r in dsAuthors.Tables[0].Rows)
    Console.WriteLine("ID" + r["ID"] + ": " + r["Expression"]);
```

The only record that has the quantity value equal or greater than 30, is the third. In the expression column you'll find a `false` value for the first and second row, while you'll find a `true` for the last one. This can be seen in the next figure:

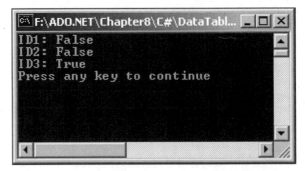

If you have a `DataSet` object containing more than one table related to each other, you could have the necessity to aggregate two or more values not present in the same table. In this case, you can use `Child` and `Parent` prefixes to point to a column present in the child table and parent table respectively.

For example, if you have an order description in the `Orders` table that is related to the `Customers` parent table, you can use the `Child.OrdersDescription` instruction to retrieve it. If your column contains a reserved character, listed below, you will have to wrap it in two square brackets:

❑   \n (newline)

❑   \t (tab)

❑   \r (carriage return)

❑   ~ ( ) # \ / = > < + - * % & | ^ ' " [ ]

If your column name contains square brackets however, you have to escape them with a forward slash character.

Finally, the `Expression` property can also accept a few generic SQL functions with a list of them following:

Function	Description	Example
CONVERT (expression,type)	Converts a given expression to a specified type	objCol.Expression = "CONVERT(QTY,System.String)"
LEN(expression)	Retrieves the length of the string	objCol.Expression = "LEN(FirstName)"
ISNULL(expression , replaceval)	Replaces a null expression with a given value	objCol.Expression = "ISNULL(QTY,0)"
IIF(condition, truepart, falsepart)	If the condition is true then retrieves the truepart else retrieves the falsepart	objCol.Expression = "IIF(QTY>40,'ONE FREE','DISCOUNT')"
TRIM (expression)	Removes all leading and trailing blank characters	objCol.Expression = "TRIM(Phone)"
SUBSTRING (expression, start, length)	Retrieves a substring of the specified length starting from the start position	objCol.Expression = "SUBSTRING(LastName,1,8)"

You can reset an expression property by either setting a null value or an empty string to it.

The ExtendedProperties Property

VB.NET:

```
Public ReadOnly Property ExtendedProperties As PropertyCollection
```

C#:

```
public PropertyCollection ExtendedProperties {get;}
```

This method is useful to associate extra information to the column. Practically, it is a dictionary object associated with the `DataColumn` object. Using this property, you can populate a `PropertyCollection` object specifying your own data. In the following example, the date when the contract was created is stored:

VB.NET:

```
' Set a default value
Dim dcContract As New DataColumn()
dcContract.ColumnName = "contract"
dcContract.DataType = GetType(System.Boolean)
dcContract.DefaultValue = False
' Store the object creation date
dcContract.ExtendedProperties.Add("CreationDate", DateTime.Now)
```

C#:

```
// Set a default value
DataColumn dcContract = new DataColumn();
dcContract.ColumnName = "contract";
dcContract.DataType = typeof(System.Boolean);
dcContract.DefaultValue = false;

// Store the object creation date
dcContract.ExtendedProperties.Add("CreationDate", DateTime.Now);
```

The MaxLength Property

VB.NET:

```
Public Property MaxLength As Integer
```

C#:

```
public int MaxLength {get; set;}
```

This property either retrieves or sets the maximum length that a string column can assume. In the following case, it is setting a length of 30 to the LastName column, thereby restricting how long the name can be that is entered into the column:

VB.NET:

```
Dim dcContract As New DataColumn()
dcContract.ColumnName = "LastName"
dcContract.DataType = GetType(System.String)
dcContract.MaxLength = 30
```

C#:

```
DataColumn dcContract = new DataColumn();
dcContract.ColumnName = "LastName";
dcContract.DataType = typeof(System.String);
dcContract.MaxLength = 30;
```

The Namespace and Prefix Properties

VB.NET:

```
Public Property Namespace As String
```

```
Public Property Prefix As String
```

C#:

```
public string Namespace {get; set;}
```

```
public string Prefix {get; set;}
```

Both properties define the column representation inside an XML document. Namespace retrieves or sets a namespace to use inside the XML schema, while Prefix retrieves or sets the prefix to be used.

> **Note: these methods work like the DataTable object counterpart as we have seen at the beginning of the chapter.**

The Ordinal Property

VB.NET:

```
Public ReadOnly Property Ordinal As Integer
```

C#:

```
public int Ordinal {get;}
```

This property retrieves the zero-based ordinal position of the DataColumn object inside the collection, or −1 if it is not contained in it.

VB.NET:

```
' Create some columns
Dim dcID As New DataColumn("ID", GetType(System.Int32))
Dim dcQty As New DataColumn("Qty", GetType(System.Int32))
Dim dcPrice As New DataColumn("Price", GetType(System.Int32))

' Add the columns to the table
Dim dtAuthors As New DataTable("Authors")
dtAuthors.Columns.Add(dcID)
dtAuthors.Columns.Add(dcQty)
dtAuthors.Columns.Add(dcPrice)

' Create a DataSet and add the table to it
Dim dsAuthors As New DataSet("dsAuthors")
dsAuthors.Tables.Add(dtAuthors)

Console.WriteLine(dcPrice.Ordinal.ToString())
```

C#:

```
// Create some columns
DataColumn dcID = new DataColumn("ID", typeof(System.Int32));
DataColumn dcQty = new DataColumn("Qty", typeof(System.Int32));
DataColumn dcPrice = new DataColumn("Price", typeof(System.Int32));

// Add the column to the table
DataTable dtAuthors = new DataTable("Authors");
dtAuthors.Columns.Add(dcID);
dtAuthors.Columns.Add(dcQty);
dtAuthors.Columns.Add(dcPrice);

Console.WriteLine(dcPrice.Ordinal.ToString());
```

419

The ReadOnly Property

VB.NET:

```
Public Property ReadOnly As Boolean
```

C#:

```
public bool ReadOnly {get; set;}
```

This property either returs or accepts a `Boolean` value indicating whether the column is read-only. When a column has the read-only flag (`true`), it cannot be modified.

VB.NET:

```
' Set the type
Dim dcID As New DataColumn()
dcID.ColumnName = "ID"
dcID.ReadOnly = True
```

C#:

```
// Set the type
DataColumn dcID = new DataColumn();
dcID.ColumnName = "ID";
dcID.ReadOnly = true;
```

The Table Property

VB.NET:

```
Public ReadOnly Property Table As DataTable
```

C#:

```
public DataTable Table {get;}
```

This method retrieves the `DataTable` object that contains the column object.

VB.NET:

```
' Create some columns
Dim dcID As New DataColumn("ID", GetType(System.Int32))
Dim dcQty As New DataColumn("Qty", GetType(System.Int32))
Dim dcPrice As New DataColumn("Price", GetType(System.Int32))

' Add the columns to the table
Dim dtAuthors As New DataTable("Authors")
dtAuthors.Columns.Add(dcID)
dtAuthors.Columns.Add(dcQty)
dtAuthors.Columns.Add(dcPrice)

Console.WriteLine(dcPrice.Table.TableName)
```

C#:

```
// Create some columns
DataColumn dcID = new DataColumn("ID", typeof(System.Int32));
DataColumn dcQty = new DataColumn("Qty", typeof(System.Int32));
```

```
DataColumn dcPrice = new DataColumn("Price", typeof(System.Int32));

// Add the column to the table
DataTable dtAuthors = new DataTable("Authors");
dtAuthors.Columns.Add(dcID);
dtAuthors.Columns.Add(dcQty);
dtAuthors.Columns.Add(dcPrice);

Console.WriteLine(dcPrice.Table.TableName);
```

The Unique Property

VB.NET:

```
Public Property Unique As Boolean
```

C#:

```
public bool Unique {get; set;}
```

The Unique property either gets or sets a Boolean value indicating whether the value contained in the column has to be unique (true) or not (false). In the following example, the data found in the ID column has to be unique (true) or, cannot be duplicated:

VB.NET:

```
' Set the type
Dim dcID As New DataColumn()
dcID.ColumnName = "ID"
dcID.Unique = True
```

C#:

```
// Set the type
DataColumn dcID = new DataColumn();
dcID.ColumnName = "ID";
dcID.Unique = true;
```

The DataColumn Methods

The DataColumn object has just one proprietary method and eight inherited from MarshalByValueComponent and Object classes.

Let's start with a brief description of the inherited methods:

Method	Description
Dispose	Releases the resources used by the MarshalByValueComponent. It comes in two versions; the first releases all the resources and doesn't want parameters, while the second accepts a Boolean value indicating whether to release just the unmanaged resources (false) or both (true).
Equals	Returns a Boolean value indicating whether two objects are equals (true) or not (false).
GetHashCode	Useful to hash algorithms and hash table, it retrieves a hash code associated to the object.
GetService	Retrieves the implementer of the IServiceProvider.
GetType	Gets the type of the current object instance.
Finalize	It represents the destructor used by C#/C++ to free memory resources. In VB.NET: it's called Finalize.
MemberwiseClone	Creates an empty clone of the current object.

The ToString Method

VB.NET:

```
Overrides Public Function ToString() As String
```

C#:

```
public override string ToString();
```

This is the only owned method of the DataColumn object. As shown in the examples below, it retrieves a string containing the column name and the expression, if present.

VB.NET:

```
' Create a column
Dim dcExpression As New DataColumn("Expression", GetType(System.Boolean))

' Add the columns to the table
Dim dtAuthors As New DataTable("Authors")
dtAuthors.Columns.Add(dcExpression)

' Create a TotalPrice column
dsAuthors.Tables(0).Columns("Expression").Expression = "Qty>=30"

Console.WriteLine(dsAuthors.Tables[0].Columns["Expression"].ToString())
```

C#:

```
// Create a column
DataColumn dcExpression = new DataColumn("Expression", typeof(System.Boolean));
```

```
// Add the column to the table
DataTable dtAuthors = new DataTable("Authors");
dtAuthors.Columns.Add(dcExpression);


dsAuthors.Tables[0].Columns["Expression"].Expression = "Qty>=30";

Console.WriteLine(dsAuthors.Tables[0].Columns["Expression"].ToString());
```

The DataRow Object

The DataRow object is derived only from the Object class, and it represents a record contained in the DataTable. This object lets you manage a row in every aspect. Using DataRow methods and properties you can easily add a new row, modify a row, delete one, and a lot of other functionalities that will be explored through the next pages.

DataRow doesn't provide a constructor so you'll never use the new keyword to instantiate the object but simply just declare it:

VB.NET:

```
Dim drAuthor As DataRow
```

C#:

```
DataRow drAuthors;
```

DataRow Properties

DataRow exposes six properties useful to retrieve data from a DataTable object. The classic Item property will let you point to a particular column value contained in the row, while RowError and RowState will allow error managing and row state retrieval operations. In the following sections, we will analyze each property provided by the object.

Note: No inherited properties are available.

The HasErrors Property

VB.NET:

```
Public ReadOnly Property HasErrors As Boolean
```

C#:

```
public bool HasErrors {get;}
```

This property retrieves a Boolean value indicating whether one or more columns contained in the DataRow have errors. During the validation phase you can specify that a particular column in a specific row has an error, also with an error description.

VB.NET:

```
If drAuthor.HasError Then dcColsErr = drAuthor.GetColumnsInError()
```

C#:

```
if(drAuthor.HasError)
    dcColsErr = drAuthor.GetColumnsInError();
```

The Item Property

VB.NET:

```
Overloads Public Default Property Item( _
    ByVal columnName As String _
) As Object
```

```
Overloads Public Default Property Item( _
    ByVal column As DataColumn _
) As Object
```

```
Overloads Public Default Property Item( _
    ByVal columnIndex As Integer _
) As Object
```

```
Overloads Public Default ReadOnly Property Item( _
    ByVal columnName As String, _
    ByVal version As DataRowVersion _
) As Object
```

```
Overloads Public Default ReadOnly Property Item( _
    ByVal column As DataColumn, _
    ByVal version As DataRowVersion _
) As Object
```

```
Overloads Public Default ReadOnly Property Item( _
    ByVal columnIndex As Integer, _
    ByVal version As DataRowVersion _
) As Object
```

C#:

```
public object this[
    string columnName
] {get; set;}
```

```
public object this[
    DataColumn column
] {get; set;}
```

```
public object this[
    int columnIndex
] {get; set;}
```

```
public object this[
    string columnName,
    DataRowVersion version
] {get;}
```

```
public object this[
    DataColumn column,
    DataRowVersion version
] {get;}
```

```
public object this[
    int columnIndex,
    DataRowVersion version
] {get;}
```

The syntax above shows that the Item property comes with six different versions. The first three are useful to retrieve or set a column value contained in the DataRow. The last three are useful to retrieve a column value specifying a DataRowVersion enumeration value for the specified row.

As you can see from the following examples, the Item property is designated by the square brackets and round brackets in C# and VB.NET respectively without the need to write its name. In this first example, we are setting a column value:

VB.NET:

```
DrAuthor("au_id") = "222-22-2222"
Console.WriteLine(drAuthor(dcID))
DrAuthor(0) = "222-22-2222"
```

C#:

```
drAuthor["au_id"] = "222-22-2222";
Console.WriteLine(drAuthor[dcID]);
drAuthor[0] = "222-22-2222";
```

In this next example, we are using the DataRowVersion to specify values for the rows:

VB.NET:

```
Console.WriteLine(drAuthor("au_id",DataRowVersion.Current))
Console.WriteLine(drAuthor(dcID,DataRowVersion.Original))
Console.WriteLine(drAuthor(0, DataRowVersion.Default))
```

C#:

```
Console.WriteLine(drAuthor["au_id",DataRowVersion.Current]);
Console.WriteLine(drAuthor[dcID,DataRowVersion.Original]);
Console.WriteLine(drAuthor[0, DataRowVersion.Default]);
```

The DataRowVersion enumeration can assume one of four values, which can be found in the Item property section.

The ItemArray Property

VB.NET:

```
Public Property ItemArray As Object ()
```

C#:

```
public object[] ItemArray {get; set;}
```

The ItemArray property either retrieves or sets an array of values associated with the columns contained in the DataRow object. With this example, we are retrieving an array of the values associated with the specified row, drNewAuthor:

VB.NET:

```
Dim dbConn As New
SqlClient.SqlConnection("server=localhost;uid=sa;pwd=;database=pubs")

Try
    ' Create Authors DataTable
    Dim dtAuthors As New DataTable("Authors")

    ' Create a DataAdapter to fill the table
    Dim daAuthors As New SqlClient.SqlDataAdapter("SELECT
au_id,au_fname,au_lname,contract FROM authors", dbConn)
    daAuthors.Fill(dtAuthors)

    ' Create a new row
    Dim drNewAuthor As DataRow

    ' It has the same table schema
    drNewAuthor = dtAuthors.NewRow()
    drNewAuthor("au_id") = "222-22-2222"
    drNewAuthor("au_fname") = "Fabio Claudio"
    drNewAuthor("au_lname") = "Ferracchiati"
    drNewAuthor("contract") = 1

    ' Retrieve an array with the value inside the row
    Dim items() As Object
    items = drNewAuthor.ItemArray

    ' Print to video
    Console.WriteLine("AuthorID = " & items(0))
    Console.WriteLine("FirstName = " & items(1))
    Console.WriteLine("LastName = " & items(2))
    Console.WriteLine("Contract = " & items(3))

Catch e As Exception
    Console.WriteLine(e.Message)
End Try
```

C#:

```
SqlConnection dbConn = new
SqlConnection("server=localhost;uid=sa;pwd=;database=pubs");
```

```
try
{
    // Create Authors DataTable
    DataTable dtAuthors = new DataTable("Authors");

    // Create a DataAdapter to fill the table
    SqlDataAdapter daAuthors = new SqlDataAdapter("SELECT
au_id,au_fname,au_lname,contract FROM authors",dbConn);
    daAuthors.Fill(dtAuthors);

    // Create a new row
    DataRow drNewAuthor;
    drNewAuthor = dtAuthors.NewRow();

    // It has the same table schema
    drNewAuthor["au_id"] = "222-22-2222";
    drNewAuthor["au_fname"] = "Fabio Claudio";
    drNewAuthor["au_lname"] = "Ferracchiati";
    drNewAuthor["contract"] = 1;

    // Retrieve an array with the value inside the row
    Object[] items;
    items = drNewAuthor.ItemArray;

    // Print to video
    Console.WriteLine("AuthorID = " + items[0]);
    Console.WriteLine("FirstName = " + items[1]);
    Console.WriteLine("LastName = " + items[2]);
    Console.WriteLine("Contract = " + items[3]);
}
catch (Exception e)
{
    Console.WriteLine(e.Message);
}
```

The RowError Property

VB.NET:

```
Public Property RowError As String
```

C#:

```
public string RowError {get; set;}
```

This property simply retrieves the string with the error description for the specific row. Moreover, if you need to specify a string for the error in the row you can use this property. Usually, this property is used in conjuction with the HasError property.

VB.NET:

```
If dtAuthors.Rows(0).HasErrors Then
    MessageBox.Show(dtAuthors.Rows(0).RowError.ToString())
```

C#:

```
if (dtAuthors.Rows[0].HasErrors)
    MessageBox.Show(dtAuthors.Rows[0].RowError.ToString());
```

The RowState Property

VB.NET:

```
Public ReadOnly Property RowState As DataRowState
```

C#:

```
public DataRowState RowState {get;}
```

The RowState property retrieves a DataRowState enumeration value for the specific row contained in the DataRowCollection inside the DataTable.

DataRowState can assume one of five values listed and described in the AcceptChanges() method section.

In this example, the actual value for the state of the row is being written, example Default:

VB.NET:

```
Console.WriteLine("The RowState is: " & drNewAuthor.RowState.ToString())
```

C#:

```
Console.WriteLine("The RowState is: " + drNewAuthor.RowState.ToString());
```

The Table Property

VB.NET:

```
Public ReadOnly Property Table As DataTable
```

C#:

```
public DataTable Table {get;}
```

This property retrieves the DataTable object that contains the specific DataRow, in this case drNewAuthor:

VB.NET:

```
Console.WriteLine("The Table name of the DataTable is: " &
drNewAuthor.Table.TableName)
```

C#:

```
Console.WriteLine("The Table name of the DataTable is: " +
drNewAuthor.Table.TableName);
```

The DataRow Methods

`DataRow` exposes eighteen proprietary methods and six inherited from its base class. All the methods are useful to manage data contained in a row inside the `DataTable`, so you can accept and reject changes, delete a row, edit its content, and so on. Before we start to analyze all the provided methods let's look at the inherited ones:

Method	Description
Equals	Returns a `Boolean` value indicating whether two objects are equal (`true`) or not (`false`).
GetHashCode	Useful to hash algorithms and hash table, it retrieves a hash code associated to the object.
GetType	Gets the type of the current object instance.
Finalize	It represents the destructor used by C#/C++ to free memory resources. In VB.NET: it's called Finalize.
MemberwiseClone	Creates an empty clone of the current object.
ToString	Retrieves a string that represents the object.

Throughout the rest of this section, we are going to examine the proprietary methods for the `DataRow` object.

The AcceptChanges and RejectChanges Methods

VB.NET:

```
Public Sub AcceptChanges()
```

```
Public Sub RejectChanges()
```

C#:

```
public void AcceptChanges();
```

```
public void RejectChanges();
```

These two methods allow you to either commit or roll back all the changes made to the `DataRow` object respectively. If you use the first method, an implicit call to the `EndEdit()` method will be done while each time you use the second method the `CancelEdit()` will be executed implicitly. It is important to remember that when you roll back the situation, the `DataRow` object will be removed from the row collection inside the `DataTable`.

VB.NET:

```
' Create a new row
Dim drNewAuthor As DataRow
drNewAuthor = dtAuthors.NewRow()

' It has the same table schema
```

```
drNewAuthor("au_id") = "222-22-2222"
drNewAuthor("au_fname") = "Fabio Claudio"
drNewAuthor("au_lname") = "Ferracchiati"
drNewAuthor("contract") = 1

dtAuthors.Rows.Add(drNewAuthor)

Console.WriteLine("After the Add: n." + dtAuthors.Rows.Count.ToString())

drNewAuthor.RejectChanges()

Console.WriteLine("After the RejectChanges(): n." &
dtAuthors.Rows.Count.ToString())

dtAuthors.Rows.Add(drNewAuthor)
drNewAuthor.AcceptChanges()

Console.WriteLine("After the AcceptChanges(): n." &
dtAuthors.Rows.Count.ToString())
```

C#:

```
// Create a new row
DataRow drNewAuthor;
drNewAuthor = dtAuthors.NewRow();

// It has the same table schema
drNewAuthor["au_id"] = "222-22-2222";
drNewAuthor["au_fname"] = "Fabio Claudio";
drNewAuthor["au_lname"] = "Ferracchiati";
drNewAuthor["contract"] = 1;

dtAuthors.Rows.Add(drNewAuthor);

Console.WriteLine("After the Add: n." + dtAuthors.Rows.Count.ToString());

drNewAuthor.RejectChanges();

Console.WriteLine("After the RejectChanges(): n." +
dtAuthors.Rows.Count.ToString());

dtAuthors.Rows.Add(drNewAuthor);
drNewAuthor.AcceptChanges();

Console.WriteLine("After the AcceptChanges(): n." +
dtAuthors.Rows.Count.ToString());
```

This example will give the following output, showing a new row was added and removed through the RejectChanges() method and then added again but accepted with the AcceptChanges() method:

The BeginEdit, CancelEdit, and EndEdit Methods

VB.NET:

```
Public Sub BeginEdit()

Public Sub CancelEdit()

Public Sub EndEdit()
```

C#:

```
public void BeginEdit();

public void CancelEdit();

public void EndEdit();
```

These methods manage the DataRow object's content. The BeginEdit() method blocks access from the other objects and until the EndEdit() is called, even the events will not fire. This is very useful when you need to change a group of rows inside the table. In this way, you can put the changes between the BeginEdit() and EndEdit() in order to be sure that no operation will be done from any other objects. The CancelEdit() cancels the edit operation on the row, rolling back all the data to their original values.

VB.NET:

```
drNewRow.BeginEdit()

. . .

If drNewRow.HasErrors Then
    drNewRow.CancelEdit();
Else
    drNewRow.EndEdit();
End If
```

C#:

```
drNewRow.BeginEdit();

. . .

if(drNewRow.HasErrors)
    drNewRow.CancelEdit();
else
    drNewRow.EndEdit();
```

431

As stated earlier, when the `AcceptChanges()` method is called, an implicit call to the `EndEdit()` method is done, while the `RejectChanges()` method calls the `CancelEdit()` method implicitly.

The ClearErrors Method

VB.NET:

```
Public Sub ClearErrors()
```

C#:

```
public void ClearErrors();
```

This method clears each error message associated with a row using the `RowError` property and `GetColumnError` method, which is discussed later in this section.

VB.NET:

```
If drNewRow.HasError Then
      ' Retrieve the columns containing wrong values
      arrCols = drNewRow.GetColumnsInError()

      ' Print to video error messages
      Dim I As Integer
      For I=0 To arrCols.Length-1
            Console.WriteLine(drNewRow.GetColumnError(I))
      Next
End If

' Clear the error messages
drNewRow.ClearErrors()
```

C#:

```
if(drNewRow.HasError)
{
      // Retrieve the columns containing wrong values
      arrCols = drNewRow.GetColumnsInError();

      // Print to video error messages
      for(int I=0; I < arrCols.Length;I++)
            Console.WriteLine(drNewRow.GetColumnError(I));
}

// Clear the error messages
drNewRow.ClearErrors();
```

The above example shows how an error message can be retrieved, viewed, and then cleared from the table.

The Delete Method

VB.NET:

```
Public Sub Delete()
```

C#:

```
public void Delete();
```

This method simply deletes a row, removing it from the table. The RowState will contain the Deleted value, but the row is not physically removed from the row until the AcceptChanges() method of the DataTable is called. You can get back deleted rows calling the RejectChanges() method before the AcceptChanges() ones.

VB.NET:

```
' Create a new row
Dim drNewAuthor As DataRow
drNewAuthor = dtAuthors.NewRow()


' It has the same table schema
drNewAuthor["au_id"] = "222-22-2222"
drNewAuthor["au_fname"] = "Fabio Claudio"
drNewAuthor["au_lname"] = "Ferracchiati"
drNewAuthor["contract"] = 1

dtAuthors.Rows.Add(drNewAuthor)

Console.WriteLine("After the Add: n." & dtAuthors.Rows.Count.ToString())

drNewAuthor.Delete()

Console.WriteLine("After the Delete(): n." & dtAuthors.Rows.Count.ToString())
```

C#:

```
// Create a new row
DataRow drNewAuthor;
drNewAuthor = dtAuthors.NewRow();

// It has the same table schema
drNewAuthor["au_id"] = "222-22-2222";
drNewAuthor["au_fname"] = "Fabio Claudio";
drNewAuthor["au_lname"] = "Ferracchiati";
drNewAuthor["contract"] = 1;

dtAuthors.Rows.Add(drNewAuthor);

Console.WriteLine("After the Add: n." + dtAuthors.Rows.Count.ToString());

drNewAuthor.Delete();

Console.WriteLine("After the Delete(): n." + dtAuthors.Rows.Count.ToString());
```

The GetChildRows Method

VB.NET:

```
Overloads Public Function GetChildRows( _
    ByVal relation As DataRelation _
) As DataRow()
```

```
Overloads Public Function GetChildRows( _
    ByVal relationName As String _
) As DataRow()
```

```
Overloads Public Function GetChildRows( _
    ByVal relation As DataRelation, _
    ByVal version As DataRowVersion _
) As DataRow()
```

```
Overloads Public Function GetChildRows( _
    ByVal relationName As String, _
    ByVal version As DataRowVersion _
) As DataRow()
```

C#:

```csharp
public DataRow[] GetChildRows(
    DataRelation relation
);
```

```csharp
public DataRow[] GetChildRows(
    string relationName
);
```

```csharp
public DataRow[] GetChildRows(
    DataRelation relation,
    DataRowVersion version
);
```

```csharp
public DataRow[] GetChildRows(
    string relationName,
    DataRowVersion version
);
```

The GetChildRows methods retrieve a DataRow objects array containing every child row related to the current row. The first two methods accept a DataRelation object and a data relation name respectively. The final two need to receive the DataRowVersion of the row and one of the values found in the Item property section can be used with this method.

VB.NET:

```
For Each drRelation In dtAuthor.ChildRelations
    For Each drRow In dtAuthor.Rows
        arrRows = drRow.GetChildRows(drRelation)
```

```
                  For i = 0 To arrRows.GetUpperBound(0)
                     For Each dcColumn in dtAuthor.Columns
                          Console.WriteLine(arrRows(i)(dcColumn))
                     Next myColumn
              Next i
         Next drRow
    Next drRelation
```

C#:

```
DataRow[] arrRows;
foreach(DataRelation drRelation in dtAuthor.ChildRelations)
{
     foreach(DataRow drRow in dtAuthor.Rows)
     {
          arrRows = drRow.GetChildRows(drRelation);

          for(int i = 0; i < arrRows.Length; i++)
          {
               foreach(DataColumn dcColumn in dtAuthor.Columns)
               {
                    Console.WriteLine(arrRows[i][dcColumn]);
               }
          }
     }
}
```

The code above loops through each relation inside the table, looking for child rows that will be displayed to video.

The GetColumnError and SetColumnError Methods

VB.NET:

```
Overloads Public Function GetColumnError( _
   ByVal column As DataColumn _
) As String
```

```
Overloads Public Function GetColumnError( _
   ByVal columnIndex As Integer _
) As String
```

```
Overloads Public Function GetColumnError( _
   ByVal columnName As String _
) As String
```

```
Overloads Public Sub SetColumnError( _
   ByVal column As DataColumn, _
   ByVal error As String _
)
```

```
Overloads Public Sub SetColumnError( _
   ByVal columnIndex As Integer, _
   ByVal error As String _
)
```

```
Overloads Public Sub SetColumnError( _
   ByVal columnName As String, _
   ByVal error As String _
)
```

C#:

```
public string GetColumnError(
   DataColumn column
);
```

```
public string GetColumnError(
   int columnIndex
);
```

```
public string GetColumnError(
   string columnName
);
```

```
public void SetColumnError(
   DataColumn column,
   string error
);
```

```
public void SetColumnError(
   int columnIndex,
   string error
);
```

```
public void SetColumnError(
   string columnName,
   string error
);
```

The GetColumnError() method retrieves an error description for the specified column. It comes in three versions because it lets you choose the parameter to identify the column. You can pass to it a DataColumn object, an index with the position of the column, and a string with the column name. SetColumnError() sets an error description associating the specified string to a column. Similarly, this method has three versions for the same reasons as the first ones. Usually, you use SetColumnError() to store error messages retrieved by GetColumnError() during the validation phase, as is shown below:

VB.NET:

```
dtAuthors.Rows(0).SetColumnError("au_id","Error: Wrong type")

   . . .

   ' During validation
   If dtAuthors.Rows(0).HasErrors Then
       MessageBox.Show(dtAuthors.Rows(0).GetColumnError("au_id").ToString())
```

C#:

```
dtAuthors.Rows[0].SetColumnError("au_id","Error: Wrong type");

. . .

// During validation
if (dtAuthors.Rows[0].HasErrors)
    MessageBox.Show(dtAuthors.Rows[0].GetColumnError("au_id").ToString());
```

The GetColumnsInError Method

VB.NET:

```
Public Function GetColumnsInError() As DataColumn()
```

C#:

```
public DataColumn[] GetColumnsInError();
```

This method retrieves a `DataColumn` array with all the values that have generated the errors. Usually, this method is used to clean the `DataColumnCollection` object inside the `DataRow` in order to add, modify, or delete only the valid rows inside the table.

VB.NET:

```
If dtAuthors.Rows(0).HasErrors Then
    ' Array of column with errors
    Dim dcBadColumns() As DataColumn

    ' Retrieve bad cols
    dcBadColumns = dtAuthors.Rows(0).GetColumnsInError()

    ' Print to video bad values
    Dim strMsg As String
    Dim i As Integer

    For i = 0 To dcBadColumns.Length - 1
        strMsg = dtAuthors.Rows(0)(dcBadColumns(i)).ToString()
        MessageBox.Show(strMsg)
    Next
End If
```

C#:

```
if (dtAuthors.Rows[0].HasErrors)
{
    // Array of column with errors
    DataColumn[] dcBadColumns;

    // Retrieve bad cols
    dcBadColumns = dtAuthors.Rows[0].GetColumnsInError();

    // Print to video bad values
    string strMsg;
    for (int i=0;i < dcBadColumns.Length;i++)
    {
        strMsg = dtAuthors.Rows[0][dcBadColumns[i]].ToString();
        MessageBox.Show(strMsg);
    }
}
```

The GetParentRow and GetParentRows Methods

VB.NET:

```
Overloads Public Function GetParentRow( _
    ByVal relation As DataRelation _
) As DataRow
```

```
Overloads Public Function GetParentRow( _
    ByVal relationName As String _
) As DataRow
```

```
Overloads Public Function GetParentRow( _
    ByVal relation As DataRelation, _
    ByVal version As DataRowVersion _
) As DataRow
```

```
Overloads Public Function GetParentRow( _
    ByVal relationName As String, _
    ByVal version As DataRowVersion _
) As DataRow
```

```
Overloads Public Function GetParentRows( _
    ByVal relation As DataRelation _
) As DataRow()
```

```
Overloads Public Function GetParentRows( _
    ByVal relationName As String _
) As DataRow()
```

```
Overloads Public Function GetParentRows( _
    ByVal relation As DataRelation, _
    ByVal version As DataRowVersion _
) As DataRow()
```

```
Overloads Public Function GetParentRows( _
    ByVal relationName As String, _
    ByVal version As DataRowVersion _
) As DataRow()
```

C#:

```
public DataRow GetParentRow(
    DataRelation relation
);
```

```
public DataRow GetParentRow(
    string relationName
);
```

```
public DataRow GetParentRow(
   DataRelation relation,
   DataRowVersion version
);
```

```
public DataRow GetParentRow(
   string relationName,
   DataRowVersion version
);
```

```
public DataRow[] GetParentRows(
   DataRelation relation
);
```

```
public DataRow[] GetParentRows(
   string relationName
);
```

```
public DataRow[] GetParentRows(
   DataRelation relation,
   DataRowVersion version
);
```

```
public DataRow[] GetParentRows(
   string relationName,
   DataRowVersion version
);
```

These two methods retrieve either a DataRow, or an array of DataRow objects containing all the parent rows. They need to know which is the DataRelation object or its name to retrieve the parent rows. If you retrieve a DataTable inside a DataSet, then you can use the ParentRelations property in order to get a collection of DataRelation objects to use inside these methods.

In the following example, we are retrieving the parent row throught the use of the DataRelation object:

VB.NET:

```
' Retrieve the table and its relation.
Dim dtAuthors As DataTable
dtAuthors = dsAuthors.Tables("Authors")

Dim relation As DataRelation
relation = dtAuthors.ParentRelations(0)

' Retrieve parent row and print to video
Dim parentRow As DataRow
Dim r As DataRow
For Each r In dtAuthors.Rows
     parentRow = r.GetParentRow(relation)
     Console.WriteLine("Parent row: " & parentRow(0))
Next
```

C#:

```
// Retrieve the table and its relation.
DataTable dtAuthors = dsAuthors.Tables["Authors"];
DataRelation relation = dtAuthors.ParentRelations[0];

// Retrieve parent row and print to video
DataRow parentRow;
foreach(DataRow r in dtAuthors.Rows)
{
     parentRow = r.GetParentRow(relation);
     Console.WriteLine("Parent row: " + parentRow[0]);
}
```

There are even two versions of the method that accept a DataRowVersion enumeration value also. In that way, you can retrieve either a row or an array of rows containing only the parent row having specific characteristics. The DataRowVersion can assume one of four values, which are listed and explained in the Item property section.

In this next example, we are again retrieving the parent row using the DataRelation object, but we are asking for the default common values for the rows by using the DataRowVersion.Default enumeration type:

VB.NET:

```
' Retrieve the table and its relation.
Dim dtAuthors As DataTable
dtAuthors = dsAuthors.Tables("Authors")

Dim relation As DataRelation
relation = dtAuthors.ParentRelations(0)

' Retrieve parent row and print to video
Dim parentRow As DataRow
Dim r As DataRow
For Each r In dtAuthors.Rows
     parentRow = r.GetParentRow(relation, DataRowVersion.Default)
     Console.WriteLine("Parent row: " & parentRow(0))
Next
```

C#:

```
// Retrieve the table and its relation.
DataTable dtAuthors = dsAuthors.Tables["Authors"];
DataRelation relation = dtAuthors.ParentRelations[0];

// Retrieve parent row and print to video
DataRow parentRow;
foreach(DataRow r in dtAuthors.Rows)
{
     parentRow = r.GetParentRow(relation, DataRowVersion.Default);
     Console.WriteLine("Parent row: " + parentRow[0]);
}
```

The HasVersion Method

VB.NET:

```
Public Function HasVersion( _
    ByVal version As DataRowVersion _
) As Boolean
```

C#:

```
public bool HasVersion(
    DataRowVersion version
);
```

This method retrieves a `Boolean` value indicating whether a specificated `DataRowVersion` exists for the row. This is useful when you use methods requiring a `DataRowVersion` parameter to avoid thrown exceptions when a particular value is not found for the row.

VB.NET:

```
' Retrieve the table and its relation.
Dim dtAuthors As DataTable
dtAuthors = dsAuthors.Tables("Authors")

Dim relation As DataRelation
relation = dtAuthors.ParentRelations(0)

' Retrieve parent row and print to video
Dim parentRow As DataRow
Dim r As DataRow
For Each r In dtAuthors.Rows
    If r.HasVersion(DataRowVersion.Default) Then
            parentRow = r.GetParentRow(relation, DataRowVersion.Default)
            Console.WriteLine("Parent row: " & parentRow(0))
    End If
Next
```

C#:

```
// Retrieve the table and its relation.
DataTable dtAuthors = dsAuthors.Tables["Authors"];
DataRelation relation = dtAuthors.ParentRelations[0];

// Retrieve parent row and print to video
DataRow parentRow;
foreach(DataRow r in dtAuthors.Rows)
{
    if (r.HasVersion(DataRowVersion.Default))
    {
            parentRow = r.GetParentRow(relation, DataRowVersion.Default);
            Console.WriteLine("Parent row: " + parentRow[0]);
    }
}
```

Above, the `HasVersion` is being used to determine if the rows in the specified table has a default common value for its `DataRowVersion` enumeration. A `DataRowVersion` enumeration can assume one of the values listed and described in the `Item` property section.

The IsNull Method

VB.NET:

```
Overloads Public Function IsNull( _
   ByVal column As DataColumn _
) As Boolean
```

```
Overloads Public Function IsNull( _
   ByVal columnIndex As Integer _
) As Boolean
```

```
Overloads Public Function IsNull( _
   ByVal columnName As String _
) As Boolean
```

```
Overloads Public Function IsNull( _
   ByVal column As DataColumn, _
   ByVal version As DataRowVersion _
) As Boolean
```

C#:

```
public bool IsNull(
   DataColumn column
);
```

```
public bool IsNull(
   int columnIndex
);
```

```
public bool IsNull(
   string columnName
);
```

```
public bool IsNull(
   DataColumn column,
   DataRowVersion version
);
```

The IsNull method again retrieves a Boolean value, but this time it indicates whether the specified column has a null value. There are three possibilities available to pass the column to this method: column name, DataColumn, or index position. The last version of this method accepts an additional DataRowVersion parameter that can assume one of the values listed in the Item property section.

VB.NET:

```
' Check for null values
For Each r In dtAuthors.Rows
    For Each c In dtAuthors.Columns
            If r.IsNull(c) Then Console.WriteLine("A null value has been found!")
    Next
Next
```

C#:

```
// Check for null values
foreach (DataRow r in dtAuthors.Rows)
{
        foreach (DataColumn c in dtAuthors.Columns)
        {
                if (r.IsNull(c))
                        Console.WriteLine("A null value has been found!");
        }
}
```

The SetNull Method

VB.NET:

```
Protected Sub SetNull( _
   ByVal column As DataColumn _
)
```

C#:

```
protected void SetNull(
   DataColumn column
);
```

This is a protected method that sets a null value to the specified DataColumn object.

The SetParentRow Method

VB.NET:

```
Overloads Public Sub SetParentRow( _
   ByVal parentRow As DataRow _
)
```

```
Overloads Public Sub SetParentRow( _
   ByVal parentRow As DataRow, _
   ByVal relation As DataRelation _
)
```

C#:

```
public void SetParentRow(
   DataRow parentRow
);
```

```
public void SetParentRow(
   DataRow parentRow,
   DataRelation relation
);
```

This method indicates a new parent row for a specified one. It accepts either a DataRow with the parent row to bind to, or a parent row with a DataRelation object reference. In the following case, the new parent row is being set to Customer Orders within the Northwind database:

VB.NET:

```
Dim childRow As DataRow
Dim parentRow As DataRow

' Get a ParentRow and a ChildRow from a DataSet.
childRow = dsNorthwind.Tables("Orders").Rows(1)
parentRow = dsNorthwind.Tables("Customers").Rows(2)

' Set the parent row of a DataRelation.
childRow.SetParentRow(parentRow, dsNorthwind.Relations("CustomerOrders"))
```

C#:

```
DataRow childRow;
DataRow parentRow;

// Get a ParentRow and a ChildRow from a DataSet.
childRow = dsNorthwind.Tables["Orders"].Rows[1];
parentRow = dsNorthwind.Tables["Customers"].Rows[2];

// Set the parent row of a DataRelation.
childRow.SetParentRow(parentRow, dsNorthwind.Relations["CustomerOrders"]);
```

The SetUnspecified Method

VB.NET:

```
Public Sub SetUnspecified( _
    ByVal column As DataColumn _
)
```

C#:

```
public void SetUnspecified(
    DataColumn column
);
```

This method sets the column value, specified either by a `DataColumn` object or by a column name, to `Unspecified`.

VB.NET:

```
' Set all the columns to unspecified
Dim r As DataRow
Dim c As DataRow

For Each r In dtAuthors.Rows
    For Each c in dtAuthors.Columns
            r.SetUnspecified(c)
    Next
Next
```

C#:

```csharp
// Set all the columns to unspecified
foreach (DataRow r in dtAuthors.Rows)
{
    foreach (DataColumn c in dtAuthors.Columns)
    {
        r.SetUnspecified(c);
    }
}
```

Relevant Collection Objects

In this final part of Chapter 8 we will describe the three collection objects contained in the `DataTable`: `DataColumnCollection`, `DataRowCollection`, and `ConstraintCollection`. A collection is a list of items managed dynamically inside our code. Using a collection object we will be able to add, modify and delete objects, loop through each item contained inside it, and so on.

Each collection contained in the `DataTable` inherits base functionalities from the `InternalDataCollection` base class. It implements generic properties and methods that you'll find when you write your code. The most important are `Count` and `List` that retrieve the number of items contained in the collection and a list of them, respectively. Each collection class exposes properitary properties and methods like the `Add()` method that adds an item to the collection or the `RemoveAt()` that removes an item with a specific index.

Let's start with a brief explanation of these objects.

The DataColumnCollection Object

When you fill a `DataTable` object with data, coming from a database, using a `DataAdapter` object, the `Fill()` method automatically fills the `DataTable` with data and table schema. Internally, the method will create a `DataColumn` object for each column present in the table. In order to associate these columns to the table object, `DataTable` exposes a property called `Columns`. The `Add()` and `Fill()` methods of the `DataAdapter` object will add the column to the table forming a collection of `DataColumn` objects. Then, the `Columns` property, a `DataColumnCollection` object, is contained and created by `DataTable`. It provides all the properties and methods to manage columns contained within that table, including the following:

Property	Description
Count	Retrieves the total number of items inside the collection.
IsReadOnly	True if the collection is read-only, otherwise false.
IsSynchronized	True if the collection is synchronized, otherwise false.
Item	Retrieves an item from the collection. It's possible to specify either an index position or the column name.
SyncRoot	Retrieves an object that can be used to synchronize the collection.
List	It is a protected property that retrieves a list of the items inside the collection.

Method	Description
Add	Adds an item to the collection.
AddRange	Adds an array of objects at the end of the collection.
CanRemove	Checks whether the specified column can be removed from the collection (true) or not (false)
Clear	Clears the collection removing every item.
Contains	Checks whether the collection contains a column with the specified name.
CopyTo	Copies each item in the collection to a specified array.
Equals	Returns a Boolean value indicating whether two objects are equal (true) or not (false).
GetEnumerator	Retrieves a reference to the IEnumerator interface.
GetHashCode	Useful to hash algorithms and hash table, it retrieves a hash code associated to the object.
GetType	Gets the type of the current object instance.
IndexOf	Retrieves the index for a column inside the collection specifying its column name.
Remove	Removes an item from the collection.
RemoveAt	Removes an item at the specified index position.
ToString	Retrieves a string that represents the object.
Finalized	It represents the destructor used by C#/C++ to free memory resources. In VB.NET: it's called Finalize.
MemberwiseClone	Creates an empty clone of the current object.
OnCollectionChanged	Raises the OnCollectionChanged event fired when an item in the collection has been changed.
OnCollectionChanging	Raises the OnCollectionChanging event fired when an item in the collection is being changed.

Event	Description
CollectionChanged	It is fired when an item is either added or deleted from the collection. A CollectionChangeEventArgs is passed to the event handler containing the action on the item and the element changed.

446

The DataRowCollection Object

When the application uses a `DataAdapter` to fill the `DataTable` object and launches a query to a database using its `SqlCommand` object, the `DataTable` is filled with the resulting set of records. The `Fill()` method will create a row for each record retrieved by the query to the database. Each row, then, is added to the `DataRowCollection` object contained in the `DataTable` and accessible through the `Rows` property.

The properties for the `DataRowCollection` object, are the same as for the `DataColumnCollection` object, which were listed in the previous section. All the methods provided by `DataRowCollection` to manage rows are contained in the table below:

Method	Description
Add	Adds an item to the collection.
Clear	Clears the collection removing every item.
Contains	Checks whether the collection contains a column with the specified name.
CopyTo	Copies each item in the collection to a specified array.
Equals	Returns a `Boolean` value indicating whether two objects are equal (`true`) or not (`false`).
Find	Retrieves a DataRow object found inside the collection specifying one or more primary key values.
GetEnumerator	Retrieves a reference to the IEnumerator interface.
GetHashCode	Useful to hash algorithms and hash table, it retrieves a hash code associated to the object.
GetType	Gets the type of the current object instance.
InsertAt	Inserts a DataRow item in the collection at the specified position.
Remove	Removes an item from the collection.
RemoveAt	Removes an item at the specified index position.
ToString	Retrieves a string that represents the object.
Finalized	It represents the destructor used by C#/C++ to free memory resources. In VB.NET: it's called `Finalize`.
MemberwiseClone	Creates an empty clone of the current object.

The ConstraintCollection Object

The `DataTable` also exposes the `Constraints` property. It is a `ConstraintCollection` object containing both `UniqueConstraint` and `ForeignConstraint` objects, which is defined and added using its methods inside the `DataTable`. By adding a `DataRelation` object to the `DataSet` in order to set a relation between two tables, will cause these constraint objects to be created and added to the collection automatically.

Again, the properties of the ConstraintCollection object are the same as the previous two collection objects. The methods and events associated with it are listed below:

Method	Description
Add	Adds an item to the collection.
AddRange	Adds an array of objects at the end of the collection.
CanRemove	Checks whether the specified constraint can be removed from the collection (`true`) or not (`false`).
Clear	Clears the collection removing every item.
Contains	Checks whether the collection contains a constraint with the specified name.
CopyTo	Copies each item in the collection to a specified array.
Equals	Returns a `Boolean` value indicating whether two objects are equal (`true`) or not (`false`).
GetEnumerator	Retrieves a reference to the `IEnumerator` interface.
GetHashCode	Useful to hash algorithms and hash table, it retrieves a hash code associated to the object.
GetType	Gets the type of the current object instance.
IndexOf	Retrieves the index for a constraint inside the collection specifying its constraint name.
Remove	Removes an item from the collection.
RemoveAt	Removes an item at the specified index position.
ToString	Retrieves a string that represents the object.
Finalized	It represents the destructor used by C#/C++ to free memory resources. In VB.NET: it's called `Finalize`.
MemberwiseClone	Creates an empty clone of the current object.
OnCollectionChanged	Raises the `OnCollectionChanged` event fired when an item in the collection has been changed.

Event	Description
CollectionChanged	It is fired when an item is either added or deleted from the collection. A CollectionChangeEventArgs is passed to the event handler containing the action on the item and the element changed.

Summary

In this chapter, we have studied the DataTable object together with its sub-objects. In real situations, it will be very unlikely that you'll use these objects directly in your code to create a table schema. It's much more useful to delegate this job to objects like the DataAdapter and DataSet. The DataTable and sub-objects, however, are essentials during the managing phase where you have to check data consistency, add or delete records, or other such operations.

We also looked at the collection objects involved with the DataTable object, finishing with the ConstraintCollection object.

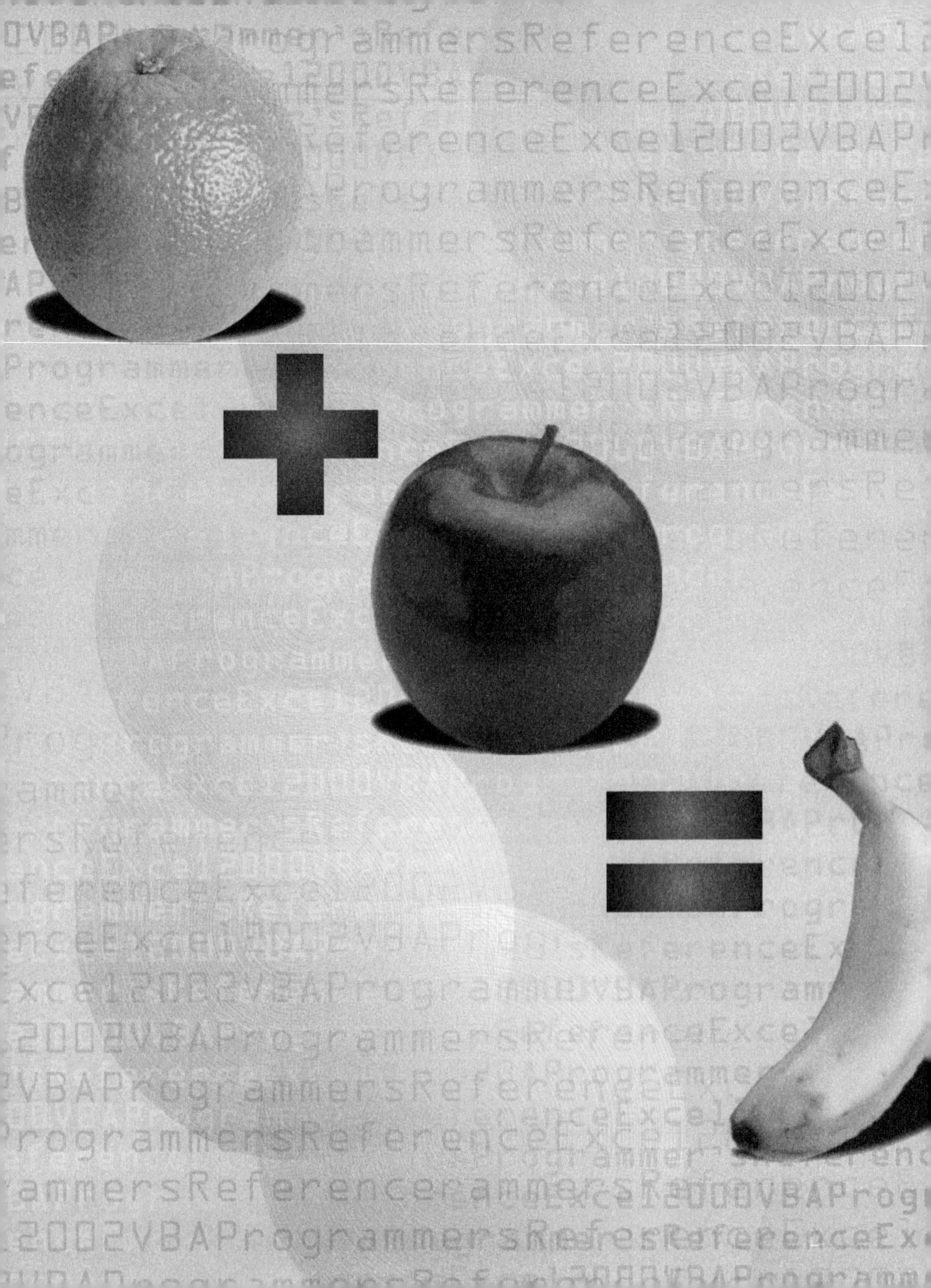

DataRelations

Understanding Table Relationships

Maintaining table relationships is new in ADO.NET. We can now create entire in-memory data structures complete with tables, relationships, triggers, and constraints. Using table relationships we can maintain referential integrity at the client level, enforcing constraints, and performing cascade triggers before the data is sent to the data source.

A relationship is created between a parent table and a child table. Usually the relationship is one-to-many, meaning one record in a parent table has many corresponding records in a child table. The relationship between two tables is defined with columns – one or more columns in a parent table (parent columns) relate to one or more columns in a child table (child columns).

Relationship Integrity

Table relationships help with data integrity. For example, a relationship between an order record and an order details record helps to prevent a situation where order details records exists without a parent order record (this is known as 'orphaned records'). Most data sources allow relationships to be forced at four occasions:

❑ Relationship creation – occurs when the relationship is created; the data source validates existing data to ensure in complies with the relation; if not, the relationship is not created

❑ Inserts – occurs when a row is inserted into the parent or child table; the newly inserted row is checked to verify complicity with the relationship

❑ Updates – occurs when a row in a parent table is updated; the actions invoked on the child table are specified using the cascade update trigger (cascading triggers are discussed next)

❑ Deletes – occurs when a row in a parent table is deleted; the actions invoked on the child table are specified using the cascade delete trigger (cascading triggers are discussed next)

Cascading Triggers

Maintaining relationships often requires the use of cascading triggers. Cascading triggers mean that when a table changes, it triggers a cascade of changes to other tables. There are two cascading triggers used to manage related rows:

❑ **Cascade Update** – manages the updates to child records performed on related rows in a child table when rows in a parent table are modified or deleted

❑ **Cascade Delete** – manages the deletion of related rows in a child table when rows in a parent table are modified or deleted

DataRelation Components

In ADO.NET relationships, the parent table, child table, parent columns, and child columns correspond to the same components in database table relationships described above. The `UniqueConstraint` defines a column (or a combination of columns) that has unique values in the parent table. The primary key of the parent table, for example, automatically carries a `unique constraint`. The `ForeignKeyConstraint` identifies the Cascade Update and Cascade Delete triggers.

Here is a diagram of a set of relationships in the Northwind database. The `DataRelation` components are identified below (the Foreign Key Constraints are not visible in the diagram):

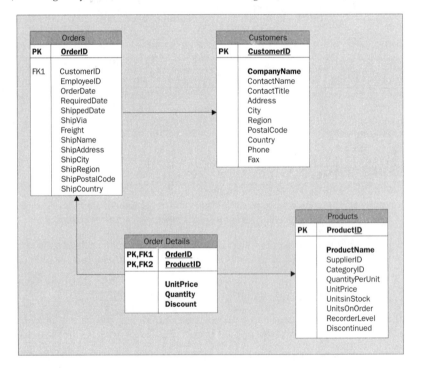

The following table describes the relationships between the above tables.

	Customers -> Orders	Orders -> OrderDetails	Products -> OrderDetails
Parent Table	Customers	Orders	Products
Child Table	Orders	OrderDetails	OrderDetails
Parent Column	CustomerID	OrderID	ProductID
Child Column	CustomerID	OrderID	ProductID
Parent Table Unique Constraint	CustomerID (PK)	OrderID (PK)	ProductID (PK)
Child Table Unique Constraint	OrderID (PK)	OrderID, ProductID (PK)	OrderID, ProductID (PK)

An example of a multi-column `UniqueConstraint` can be seen in the `OrderDetails` table, which has a primary key comprising of the `OrderID` and `ProductID` columns. This means that while there can be many detail items in a single order (rows with the same `OrderID`) and many orders with the same product (rows with the same `ProductID`), there cannot be more than one detail item for a specific product in an order (rows with the same `OrderID`/`ProductID` combination).

Unique constraints are not only useful for maintaining relationship integrity. They can also ensure that data within a table maintains integrity. For example, in an employee database the email address may not be a key field but it is important not to assign two employees the same email address. Here a `UniqueConstraint` would not be maintaining relationship integrity, but it would maintain data integrity and add an extra level of usefulness to the system.

A `DataRelation` object and its associated `ForeignKeyConstraint` object have properties reference many of the same components. The diagrams below show a `DataSet` containing an `Orders` and a `Customers` table. It identifies the objects returned for several of the `DataRelation` and `ForeignKeyConstraint` properties, and we will see that there is a great deal of overlap. The tables are linked with a `DataRelation` called `relCo`, which links two column pairs: the parent columns are `CustomerID` and `Cust_OrderID` from the `Customers` table; the child columns are `OrdID` and `Ord_CustomerID` from the `Orders` table. The `ForeignKeyConstraint` on the `Orders` table, called `fkeyOrders`, helps to maintain the `DataRelation`.

Objects returned by `DataRelation` properties are:

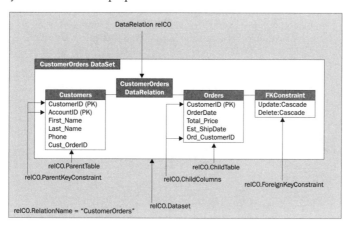

Objects returned by `ForeignKeyConstraint` properties are:

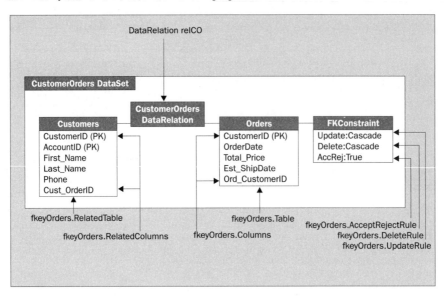

Changes From ADO 2.6

Relationships were maintained in ADO 2.6 using SHAPE commands, where related records were stored in a `recordset` and placed in a field in the parent record the ADO.NET `DataReader` now employs a similar approach to shaped data. The ability to create an entire data structure new in ADO.NET, so virtually everything in this chapter is new material.

The DataRelation Class

The `DataRelation` object represents a single relationship built between two `DataTable` objects. This relationship can be one-to-one, one-to-many and many-to-many. The `DataRelation` is quite flexible in that it allows for multiple relations to exist between tables and each relation can contain multiple columns.

All of the `DataRelation` objects within a `DataSet` are stored in the `DataRelationCollection` object. The `DataRelationCollection` object is accessible through the `DataSet` object (via the `Relations` property) or through a related `DataTable` object (via the `ChildRelations` or `ParentRelations` property).

DataRelation Constructors

The `DataRelation` constructors use various parameters to initialize the new `DataRelation` object.

Create the relation by providing a name, a single parent column, and a single child column.

VB.NET:

```
Public Sub New(
      ByVal relationName As String,
      ByVal parentColumn As DataColumn,
      ByVal childColumn As DataColumn)
```

C#:

```
public DataRelation(
      string relationName,
      DataColumn parentColumn,
      DataColumn childColumn);
```

Create the relation by providing a name, an array of parent columns and an array of child columns.

VB.NET:

```
Public Sub New(
      ByVal relationName As String,
      ByVal parentColumns() As DataColumn,
      ByVal childColumns() As DataColumn)
```

C#:

```
public DataRelation(
      string relationName,
      DataColumn[] parentColumns,
      DataColumn[] childColumns);
```

Create the relation by providing a name, a single parent column, a single child column, and whether or not to automatically create constraints.

VB.NET:

```
Public Sub New(
      ByVal relationName As String,
      ByVal parentColumn As DataColumn,
      ByVal childColumn As DataColumn,
      ByVal createConstraints As Boolean)
```

C#:

```
public DataRelation(
      string relationName,
      DataColumn parentColumn,
      DataColumn childColumn,
      bool createConstraints);
```

Create the relation by providing a name, an array of parent columns, an array of child columns, and whether or not to automatically create constraints.

VB.NET:

```
Public Sub New(
        ByVal relationName As String,
        ByVal parentColumns() As DataColumn,
        ByVal childColumns() As DataColumn,
        ByVal createConstraints As Boolean)
```

C#:

```
public DataRelation(
        string relationName,
        DataColumn[] parentColumns,
        DataColumn[] childColumns,
        bool createConstraints);
```

Create the relation by providing a name, the parent table name, an array of parent column names, an array of child column names, and whether or not the relation is nested.

VB.NET:

```
Public Sub New(
        ByVal relationName As String,
        ByVal parentTableName As String,
        ByVal childTableName As String,
        ByVal parentColumnNames() As String,
        ByVal childColumnNames() As String,
        ByVal nested As Boolean)
```

C#:

```
public DataRelation(
        string relationName,
        string parentTableName,
        string childTableName,
        string[] parentColumnNames,
        string[] childColumnNames,
        bool nested);
```

It is important to remember the following points when constructing a `DataRelation`:

❏ There must be the same number of child columns as parent columns. The pairings go by index, so the first parent column is related to the first child column.

❏ Parent columns and child columns must have the same data type.

❏ You should not reference the same column twice in a parent column or child column collection.

❏ There is no check to guarantee the parent columns exist in the parent table, or that the child columns exist in the child table.

❏ If the `CreateConstraints` setting is true, a `ForeignKeyConstraint` will be created.

❏ If we want to allow orphaned records, we can. However, orphaned records cause problems when enforcing constraints. For example, if an orphaned `OrderDetail` record exists (it contains an `OrderID` that the `Orders` table does not), an exception is thrown when the constraint is created.

456

DataRelation Properties

Most of the properties of the `DataRelation` class provide access to the different components of a table relationship, as discussed in the introduction.

The ChildColumns Property

The `ChildColumns` property returns an array of `DataColumn` objects that form the child side of the `DataRelation` object.

VB.NET:

```
Overridable Public ReadOnly Property ChildColumns As DataColumn ()
```

C#:

```
public virtual DataColumn[] ChildColumns {get;}
```

The ChildKeyConstraint Property

The `ChildKeyConstraint` property returns the `ForeignKeyConstraint` object for the `DataRelation`.

VB.NET:

```
Overridable Public ReadOnly Property ChildKeyConstraint As ForeignKeyConstraint
```

C#:

```
public virtual ForeignKeyConstraint ChildKeyConstraint {get;}
```

The ChildTable Property

The `ChildTable` property returns the child `DataTable` of the current `DataRelation` object.

VB.NET:

```
Overridable Public ReadOnly Property ChildTable As DataTable
```

C#:

```
public virtual DataTable ChildTable {get;}
```

The DataSet Property

The `DataSet` property returns the `DataRelation` object's parent `DataSet`.

VB.NET:

```
Overridable Public ReadOnly Property DataSet As DataSet
```

C#:

```
public virtual DataSet DataSet {get;}
```

The Nested Property

The `Nested` property gets and sets whether the current `DataRelation` object will be persisted as nested or non-nested XML.

VB.NET:

```
Overridable Public Property Nested As Boolean
```

C#:

```
public virtual bool Nested {get; set;}
```

There are two ways that a `DataSet` containing `DataRelation` objects can be persisted to XML: the parent and child records can be listed separately and grouped by table, or the child records can listed within their parent record.

For example, consider a relationship between an `Orders` table and an `OrderDetails` table. If the `Nested` property were set to `false`, the XML generated would like this:

```
<OrdersAndDetails>
    <Orders>
        <Order ID>1</OrderID>
        <EmployeeID>34</EmployeeID>
    </Orders>
    <Orders>
        <Order ID>2</OrderID>
        <EmployeeID>62</EmployeeID>
    </Orders>

    <OrderDetails>
        <OrderDetailID>287</OrderDetailID>
        <OrderID>1</OrderID>
        <ProductID>834</ProductID>
    </OrderDetails>
    <OrderDetails>
        <OrderDetailID>288</OrderDetailID>
        <OrderID>1</OrderID>
        <ProductID>987</ProductID>
    </OrderDetails>
    <OrderDetails>
        <OrderDetailID>325</OrderDetailID>
        <OrderID>2</OrderID>
        <ProductID>951</ProductID>
    </OrderDetails>
    <OrderDetails>
        <OrderDetailID>358</OrderDetailID>
        <OrderID>1</OrderID>
        <ProductID>753</ProductID>
    </OrderDetails>
    <OrderDetails>
        <OrderDetailID>387</OrderDetailID>
        <OrderID>2</OrderID>
        <ProductID>159</ProductID>
    </OrderDetails>
<OrdersAndDetails>
```

If the Nested property were set to true, the XML would be like this:

```
<OrdersAndDetails>
    <Orders>
        <Order ID>1</OrderID>
        <EmployeeID>34</EmployeeID>
        <OrderDetails>
            <OrderDetailID>287</OrderDetailID>
            <OrderID>1</OrderID>
            <ProductID>834</ProductID>
        </OrderDetails>
        <OrderDetails>
            <OrderDetailID>288</OrderDetailID>
            <OrderID>1</OrderID>
            <ProductID>987</ProductID>
        </OrderDetails>
        <OrderDetails>
            <OrderDetailID>358</OrderDetailID>
            <OrderID>1</OrderID>
            <ProductID>753</ProductID>
        </OrderDetails>
    </Orders>
    <Orders>
        <Order ID>2</OrderID>
        <EmployeeID>62</EmployeeID>
        <OrderDetails>
            <OrderDetailID>325</OrderDetailID>
            <OrderID>2</OrderID>
            <ProductID>951</ProductID>
        </OrderDetails>
        <OrderDetails>
            <OrderDetailID>387</OrderDetailID>
            <OrderID>2</OrderID>
            <ProductID>159</ProductID>
        </OrderDetails>
    </Orders>
</OrdersAndDetails>
```

The ParentColumns Property

The ParentColumns property returns a DataColumn array of the DataRelation object's parent DataColumns.

VB.NET:

```
Overridable Public ReadOnly Property ParentColumns As DataColumn ()
```

C#:

```
public virtual DataColumn[] ParentColumns {get;}
```

The ParentKeyConstraint Property

The `ParentKeyConstraint` property returns the `UniqueConstraint` of the current `DataRelation` object

VB.NET:

```
Overridable Public ReadOnly Property ParentKeyConstraint As UniqueConstraint
```

C#:

```
public virtual UniqueConstraint ParentKeyConstraint {get;}
```

The ParentTable Property

The `ParentTable` property returns the `DataRelation` object's parent `DataTable`.

VB.NET:

```
Overridable Public ReadOnly Property ParentTable As DataTable
```

C#:

```
public virtual DataTable ParentTable {get;}
```

The RelationName Property

The `RelationName` property gets and sets the name of the current `DataRelation` object in the parent `DataRelationCollection` object.

VB.NET:

```
Overridable Public Property RelationName As String
```

C#:

```
public virtual string RelationName {get; set;}
```

DataRelation Methods

The CheckStateForProperty Method

The `CheckStateForProperty` method validates the `DataRelation` object; this is a protected method.

VB.NET:

```
Protected Sub CheckStateForProperty()
```

C#:

```
protected void CheckStateForProperty();
```

Exceptions:

❑ `DataException` – failure of any of the three validations described below

The `CheckStateForProperty` Method ensures the following three validations:

❑ The `DataTable` objects referenced by `ParentTable` and `Table` properties belong to the same `DataSet` object

❑ The `ParentColumns` and `ChildColumns` do not have a pair which contain different data types

❑ The `ParentColumns` and `ChildColumns` do not have a pair that references the same `DataColumn`

If you will be building an application where the user can form relations, it's a good idea to check that the `DataColumn` objects also exist in the appropriate `DataTable` objects – something that `CheckStateForProperty` does not validate.

The Constraint Class

The `Constraint` class is the base class for the `ForeignKeyConstraint` and `UniqueConstraint` objects. It is an abstract class so it cannot be instantiated, but it does contain the generic properties and methods used by `ForeignKeyConstraint` and `UniqueConstraint`. A constraint is a rule that helps maintain database integrity. For example, we can define rules that delete all child records when the parent is deleted, or that indicate that a value in a column must remain unique.

The `DataTable` object possesses a `Constraint` collection. We can use the `Constraints` property of the `DataTable` object to retrieve a reference to the `ConstraintCollection` that manages the constraint rules.

Constraint Constructor

VB.NET:

```
Protected Sub New()
```

C#:

```
protected Constraint();
```

The default constructor is used only in a derived class's constructor. A call to the `Constraint` constructor allows the class to initialize and assign default values.

Constraint Properties

The `Constraint` class has only two properties. The first retrieves the constraint name contained in the `DataTable` object's `ConstraintCollection`, while the second retrieves the `DataTable` to which the constraint applies.

The ConstraintName Property

VB.NET:

```
Overridable Public Property ConstraintName As String
```

C#:

```
public virtual string ConstraintName {get; set;}
```

This property is used either to get or to set the constraint name assigned to the Constraint object, contained in the ConstraintCollection, inside the DataTable object.

VB.NET:

```
Dim cs As UniqueConstraint
For Each cs In  dtAuthors.Constraints
    Console.WriteLine(cs.ConstraintName)
Next
```

C#:

```
foreach(Constraint cs in dtAuthors.Constraints)
{
    Console.WriteLine(cs.ConstraintName);
}
```

The Table Property

VB.NET:

```
MustOverride Public ReadOnly Property Table As DataTable
```

C#:

```
public abstract DataTable Table {get;}
```

This property retrieves a reference to the Constraint object's DataTable.

VB.NET:

```
Console.WriteLine(cs.Table.TableName)
```

C#:

```
Constraint cs;
Console.WriteLine (cs.Table.TableName);
```

Constraint Methods

The `Constraint` object overrides the `ToString` method to return the constraint name. The other methods are all inherited from the `Object` class, which are described briefly here:

Method	Description
Equals	Return a `Boolean` value indicating whether two objects are equal
GetHashCode	Useful to hash algorithms and hash table, it retrieves a hash code associated to the object
GetType	Get the type of the current object instance
Finalize	It represents the destructor used by C#/C++ to free memory resources. In VB.NET it's called `Finalize`
MemberwiseClone	Create an empty clone of the current object

The ToString Method

VB.NET:

```
Overrides Public Function ToString() As String
```

C#:

```
public override string ToString();
```

This simple method retrieves a string variable with the constraint name.

VB.NET:

```
Dim cs As Constraint
Console.WriteLine(cs.ToString)
```

C#:

```
Constraint cs;
Console.WriteLine(cs.ToString());
```

The UniqueConstraint Object

`UniqueConstraint` object is derived from both the `Constraint` and `Object` classes and it exposes methods and properties to define a unique constraint rule on one or more columns inside a table. When you define a unique constraint rule for a table you prohibit duplicate records from being inserted. As we'll see in this part of the chapter we use the `Columns` property to define the columns belonging to the unique constraint rule.

Sometimes we will define a unique constraint on a set of columns, at other times we may have several unique constraints in a single table. It is important to understand the difference.

Consider a table containing an email_address and a full_name column. If we define a single unique constraint that includes both columns, then the table can contain the same full name several times, and the same email address several times (for example, different people can share the same email address), but the same full name and email address cannot appear within more than one record. If we instead defined two unique constraints, one for full_name and one for email_address, then the same name can never appear more than once in the table, and the same email address can never appear more than once in the table.

UniqueConstraint Constructor

There are five constructors for the UniqueConstraint object. Each version allows creating a unique constraint rule associated with a column or set of columns. There is no default constructor – all of them require parameters.

The first constructor accepts a single DataColumn object to which the constraint will apply:

VB.NET:

```
' Retrieve the column ID contained in the DataTable
Dim dcID As DataColumn
dcID = dtAuthors.Columns("au_id")

' Apply the constraint
Dim ucID As New UniqueConstraint(dcID)
```

C#:

```
// Retrieve the column ID contained in the DataTable
DataColumn dcID;
dcID = dtAuthors.Columns["au_id"];

// Apply the constraint
UniqueConstraint ucID = new UniqueConstraint(dcID);
```

The second constructor needs an array of DataColumn objects. This version of the constructor is useful when a table has more then one column defined as the primary key. In the example below a DataTable object has been filled with data contained in the OrderDetails table from the **Northwind** database available with SQL Server, which has two primary keys.

VB.NET:

```
' Retrieve the column IDs contained in the DataTable
Dim dcPrimaryKeys(2) As DataColumn
dcPrimaryKeys(0) = dtOrderDetails.Columns("OrderID")
dcPrimaryKeys(1) = dtOrderDetails.Columns("ProductID")

' Apply the constraint
Dim ucID As New UniqueConstraint(dcPrimaryKeys)
```

C#:

```
// Retrieve the column IDs contained in the DataTable
DataColumn[] dcPrimaryKeys = new DataColumn[2];
dcPrimaryKeys[0] = dtOrderDetails.Columns["OrderID"];
dcPrimaryKeys[1] = dtOrderDetails.Columns["ProductID"];

// Apply the constraint
UniqueConstraint ucID = new UniqueConstraint(dcPrimaryKeys);
```

The third constructor allows us to give the unique constraint a name. This will be useful when we need to retrieve the constraint object from the collection contained in the `DataTable`.

VB.NET:

```
' Retrieve the column ID contained in the DataTable
Dim dcPrimaryKeys As DataColumn
dcPrimaryKeys = dtOrderDetails.Columns("OrderID")

' Apply the constraint
Dim ucID As New UniqueConstraint("OrderIDConstraint", dcPrimaryKeys)
```

C#:

```
// Retrieve the column ID contained in the DataTable
DataColumn dcPrimaryKeys;
dcPrimaryKeys = dtOrderDetails.Columns["OrderID"];

// Apply the constraint
UniqueConstraint ucID = new UniqueConstraint("OrderIDConstraint",dcPrimaryKeys);
```

The fourth constructor accepts a string parameter containing the constraint name and an array of `DataColumn` objects.

VB.NET:

```
' Retrieve the column IDs contained in the DataTable
Dim dcPrimaryKeys(2) As DataColumn
dcPrimaryKeys(0) = dtOrderDetails.Columns("OrderID")
dcPrimaryKeys(1) = dtOrderDetails.Columns("ProductID")

' Apply the constraint
Dim ucID As New UniqueConstraint("OrderIDConstraint", dcPrimaryKeys)
```

C#:

```
// Retrieve the column IDs contained in the DataTable
DataColumn[] dcPrimaryKeys = new DataColumn[2];
dcPrimaryKeys[0] = dtOrderDetails.Columns["OrderID"];
dcPrimaryKeys[1] = dtOrderDetails.Columns["ProductID"];

// Apply the constraint
UniqueConstraint ucID = new UniqueConstraint("OrderIDConstraint", dcPrimaryKeys);
```

The fifth constructor takes as parameters a string constraint name, a DataColumn array and a Boolean enabling us to specify whether the constraint applies to the primary key.

VB.NET:

```
' Array of column names
Dim columns(1) As String
columns(0) = "OrderID"
columns(1) = "ProductID"

' Apply the constraint
Dim ucID As New UniqueConstraint("OrderIDConstraint", columns, True)
```

C#:

```
// Array of column names
String[] columns = new String[2];
columns[0] = "OrderID";
columns[1] = "ProductID";

// Apply the constraint
UniqueConstraint ucID = new UniqueConstraint("OrderIDConstraint",columns,true);
```

UniqueConstraint Properties

UniqueConstraint exposes three of its own properties and one inherited from the Constraint class. The most useful is the Columns property because it enables us to retrieve an array of the DataColumns comprising the constraint rule.

The inherited property is as follows:

Property	Description
ConstraintName	It allows either retrieving or setting the constraint name for the UniqueConstraint object

We will now discuss the properties defined by the UniqueConstraint object.

The Columns Property

VB.NET:

```
Overridable Public ReadOnly Property Columns As DataColumn ()
```

C#:

```
public virtual DataColumn[] Columns {get;}
```

This property retrieves an array of DataColumn objects that comprise the constraint rule.

VB.NET:

```
Dim dcPrimaryKeys(1) As DataColumn
dcPrimaryKeys(0) = dtOrderDetails.Columns("OrderID")
dcPrimaryKeys(1) = dtOrderDetails.Columns("ProductID")
```

```
' Apply the constraint
Dim ucID As New UniqueConstraint(dcPrimaryKeys)
Dim dcColumns() As DataColumn
dcColumns = ucID.Columns

' Write to console how many column are contained in the constraint rule
Console.WriteLine(dcColumns.Length.ToString())
```

C#:

```
DataColumn[] dcPrimaryKeys = new DataColumn[2];
dcPrimaryKeys[0] = dtOrderDetails.Columns["OrderID"];
dcPrimaryKeys[1] = dtOrderDetails.Columns["ProductID"];

// Apply the constraint
UniqueConstraint ucID = new UniqueConstraint(dcPrimaryKeys);

// Retrieve DataColumn composing the constraint
DataColumn[] dcColumns;
dcColumns = ucID.Columns;

// Write to console how many column are contained in the constraint rule
Console.WriteLine(dcColumns.Length.ToString());
```

The IsPrimaryKey Property

VB.NET:

```
Public ReadOnly Property IsPrimaryKey As Boolean
```

C#:

```
public bool IsPrimaryKey {get;}
```

This property retrieves a `Boolean` value indicating whether the constraint is on a primary key.

VB.NET:

```
Dim dcPrimaryKeys(1) As DataColumn
dcPrimaryKeys(0) = dtOrderDetails.Columns("OrderID")
dcPrimaryKeys(1) = dtOrderDetails.Columns("ProductID")

' Apply the constraint
Dim ucID As New UniqueConstraint(dcPrimaryKeys)

' Write to console
Console.WriteLine(ucID.IsPrimaryKey.ToString())
```

C#:

```
DataColumn[] dcPrimaryKeys = new DataColumn[2];
dcPrimaryKeys[0] = dtOrderDetails.Columns["OrderID"];
dcPrimaryKeys[1] = dtOrderDetails.Columns["ProductID"];

// Apply the constraint
UniqueConstraint ucID = new UniqueConstraint(dcPrimaryKeys);

// Write to console
Console.WriteLine(ucID.IsPrimaryKey.ToString());
```

The Table Property

VB.NET:

```
Overrides Public ReadOnly Property Table As DataTable
```

C#:

```
public override DataTable Table {get;}
```

This property retrieves a reference to the `UniqueConstraint` object's `DataTable`.

VB.NET:

```
Dim dcPrimaryKeys(1) As DataColumn
dcPrimaryKeys(0) = dtOrderDetails.Columns("OrderID")
dcPrimaryKeys(1) = dtOrderDetails.Columns("ProductID")

' Apply the constraint
Dim ucID As New UniqueConstraint(dcPrimaryKeys)

' Write to console
Console.WriteLine(ucID.Table.TableName)
```

C#:

```
DataColumn[] dcPrimaryKeys = new DataColumn[2];
dcPrimaryKeys[0] = dtOrderDetails.Columns["OrderID"];
dcPrimaryKeys[1] = dtOrderDetails.Columns["ProductID"];

// Apply the constraint
UniqueConstraint ucID = new UniqueConstraint(dcPrimaryKeys);

// Write to console
Console.WriteLine(ucID.Table.TableName);
```

UniqueConstraint Methods

`UniqueConstraint` object overrides two methods from `Object` and inherits four methods from base classes. The inherited methods are:

Method	Description
ToString	Retrieve a string that represents the object.
MemberwiseClone	Create an empty clone of the current object.
GetType	Get the type of the current object instance.
Finalize	It represents the destructor used by C#/C++ to free memory resources. In VB.NET it's called Finalize.

The overridden methods will be discussed in more detail.

The Equals Method

VB.NET:

```
Overrides Public Function Equals( _
    ByVal key2 As Object _
) As Boolean
```

C#:

```
public override bool Equals(
    object key2
);
```

This method retrieves a `Boolean` value indicating whether an object passed as a parameter is equal to the `UniqueConstraint`. This will return `true` if the two `UniqueConstraints` are on the same columns – it does not need to be the same object.

VB.NET:

```
Dim dcPrimaryKeys(1) As DataColumn
dcPrimaryKeys(0) = dtOrderDetails.Columns("OrderID")
dcPrimaryKeys(1) = dtOrderDetails.Columns("ProductID")

' Apply the constraint
Dim ucID As New UniqueConstraint(dcPrimaryKeys)
Dim ucID2 As New UniqueConstraint(dcPrimaryKeys)

' Write to console
Console.WriteLine(ucID.Equals(ucID2).ToString())
```

C#:

```
DataColumn[] dcPrimaryKeys = new DataColumn[2];
dcPrimaryKeys[0] = dtOrderDetails.Columns["OrderID"];
dcPrimaryKeys[1] = dtOrderDetails.Columns["ProductID"];

// Apply the constraint
UniqueConstraint ucID = new UniqueConstraint(dcPrimaryKeys);
UniqueConstraint ucID2 = new UniqueConstraint(dcPrimaryKeys);

// Write to console
Console.WriteLine(ucID.Equals(ucID2).ToString());
```

The GetHashCode Method

VB.NET:

```
Overrides Public Function GetHashCode() As Integer
```

C#:

```
public override int GetHashCode();
```

This method retrieves a 32-bit signed Integer variable containing the hash code for the `UniqueConstraint` object.

VB.NET:

```
Dim dcPrimaryKeys(1) As DataColumn
dcPrimaryKeys(0) = dtOrderDetails.Columns("OrderID")
dcPrimaryKeys(1) = dtOrderDetails.Columns("ProductID")

' Apply the constraint
Dim ucID As New UniqueConstraint(dcPrimaryKeys)

' Write to console
Console.WriteLine(ucID.GetHashCode().ToString())
```

C#:

```
DataColumn[] dcPrimaryKeys = new DataColumn[2];
dcPrimaryKeys[0] = dtOrderDetails.Columns["OrderID"];
dcPrimaryKeys[1] = dtOrderDetails.Columns["ProductID"];

// Apply the constraint
UniqueConstraint ucID = new UniqueConstraint(dcPrimaryKeys);

// Write to console
Console.WriteLine(ucID.GetHashCode().ToString());
```

The ForeignKeyConstraint Object

The `ForeignKeyConstraint` object controls actions performed on a table's child record(s) when a parent table's contents change. It can be used to enforce referential integrity at the client level, before attempting to post the data to the data source.

You'll notice that the `ChildColumns` and `ParentColumns` properties of the `DataRelation` object are analogous to the `Columns` and `RelatedColumns` properties of the `ForeignKeyConstraint` object. This is because the `ForeignKeyConstraint` object is built upon the `Constraint` object and the property naming convention follows. The same can be said when comparing `ChildTable`/`ParentTable` properties of the `DataRelation` object and `RelatedTable`/`Table` properties of the `ForeignKeyConstraint` object

ForeignKeyConstraint Behavior

The presence of a constraint allows for navigation and prevents the existence of orphaned records. No actions are undertaken during updates and deletes unless the constraint is enforced (set the `EnforceConstraints` property of the `DataSet` to `True`).

The actions undertaken can conflict with constraint enforcement. For example, a `DeleteRule` of `None` and an enforced constraint will generate an exception when we attempt to delete a parent row that still has child rows. This is because the constraint `DeleteRule` does nothing to the child rows when the parent row is deleted but the constraint requires that a parent row cannot be deleted before the child rows are deleted. Therefore, the exception is thrown. We can get around this by either changing the `DeleteRule`, not enforcing the constraint, or manually checking for and/or deleting child records before deleting the parent.

ForeignKeyConstraint Constructors

The `ForeignKeyConstraint` has five constructors.

The first constructor takes a single parent column and a single child column as parameters.

VB.NET:

```
Public Sub New(
    ByVal parentColumn As DataColumn,
    ByVal childColumn As DataColumn)
```

C#:

```
public ForeignKeyConstraint(
    DataColumn parentColumn,
    DataColumn childColumn);
```

The second constructor takes an array of parent columns and an array of child columns as its parameters.

VB.NET:

```
Public Sub New(
    ByVal parentColumns() As DataColumn(),
    ByVal childColumns() As DataColumn())
```

C#:

```
public ForeignKeyConstraint(
    DataColumn[] parentColumns,
    DataColumn[] childColumns);
```

The third constructor takes a name, a single parent column, and a single child column as its parameters.

VB.NET:

```
Public Sub New(
    ByVal constraintName As String,
    ByVal parentColumn As DataColumn,
    ByVal childColumn As DataColumn)
```

C#:

```
public ForeignKeyConstraint(
    string constraintName,
    DataColumn parentColumn,
    DataColumn childColumn);
```

The fourth constructor takes a name, an array of parent columns, and an array of child columns, and its parameters.

VB.NET:

```
Public Sub New(
      ByVal constraintName As String,
      ByVal parentColumns() As DataColumn,
      ByVal childColumns() As DataColumn)
```

C#:

```
public ForeignKeyConstraint(
      string constraintName,
      DataColumn[] parentColumns,
      DataColumn[] childColumns);
```

The fifth constructor takes a name for the constraint, the parent table name, an array of parent column names, an array of child column names, the `AcceptRejectRule`, `DeleteRule`, and `UpdateRule` settings as parameters.

VB.NET:

```
Public Sub New(
      ByVal constraintName As String,
      ByVal parentTableName As String,
      ByVal parentColumnNames() As String,
      ByVal childColumnNames() As String,
      ByVal acceptRejectRule As AcceptRejectRule,
      ByVal deleteRule As Rule,
      ByVal updateRule As Rule)
```

C#:

```
public ForeignKeyConstraint(
      string constraintName,
      string parentTableName,
      string[] parentColumnNames,
      string[] childColumnNames,
      AcceptRejectRule acceptRejectRule,
      Rule deleteRule,
      Rule updateRule);
```

In the example at the end of this section, we use several different constructors to create new `ForeginKeyConstraint` objects.

ForeignKeyConstraint Properties

The properties of the `ForeginKeyConstraint` class provide access to the different components of a table relationship as discussed in the introduction, or set the actions to take in response to cascade triggers – deletion of a record, insertion of a new record, and changes to an existing record.

The AcceptRejectRule Property

This property gets and sets what to do if a column in the constraint has `AcceptChanges` called on it.

VB.NET:

```
Overridable Public Property AcceptRejectRule As AcceptRejectRule
```

C#:

```
public virtual AcceptRejectRule AcceptRejectRule {get; set;}
```

The `AcceptRejectRule` property determines how an `AcceptChanges` command is handled. Once the `ForeignKeyConstraint` is activated, if the constrained column changes and the `AcceptChanges` method is called then we can use one of these values to determine what to do:

❑ Cascade – the changes cascade across the related rows

❑ None – no action is taken

The Columns Property

This property returns a `DataColumn` array of the `ForeignKeyConstraint` object's child columns.

VB.NET:

```
Overridable Public ReadOnly Property Columns As DataColumn ()
```

C#:

```
public virtual DataColumn[] Columns {get;}
```

The ConstraintName Property

This property gets and sets the name of the current `ForeignKeyConstraint` object in the parent `ConstraintCollection` object.

VB.NET:

```
Overridable Public Property ConstraintName As String
```

C#:

```
public virtual string ConstraintName {get; set;}
```

The DeleteRule Property

This property gets and sets how a row deletion is handled in the current `ForeignKeyConstraint` object.

VB.NET:

```
Overridable Public Property DeleteRule As Rule
```

C#:

```
public virtual Rule DeleteRule {get; set;}
```

The `DeleteRule` property determines how deleted rows in a parent table are handled. The `Rule` enumeration constants are:

- ❏   `Cascade` – all related rows are deleted
- ❏   `None` – no action is taken
- ❏   `SetDefault` – set related columns to their default value
- ❏   `SetNull` – set related columns to Null

The RelatedColumns Property

This property returns a `DataColumn` array of the `ForeignKeyConstraint` object's parent `columns`.

VB.NET:

```
Overridable Public ReadOnly Property RelatedColumns As DataColumn ()
```

C#:

```
public virtual DataColumn[] RelatedColumns {get;}
```

The RelatedTable Property

This property returns the `ForeignKeyConstraint` object's parent `DataTable`.

VB.NET:

```
Overridable Public ReadOnly Property RelatedTable As DataTable
```

C#:

```
public virtual DataTable RelatedTable {get;}
```

The Table Property

The property returns the `ForeignKeyConstraint` object's child `DataTable`.

VB.NET:

```
Overrides Public ReadOnly Property Table As DataTable
```

C#:

```
public override DataTable Table {get;}
```

The UpdateRule Property

This proerty gets and sets how a row update is handled in the current `ForeignKeyConstraint` object.

VB.NET:

```
Overridable Public Property UpdateRule As Rule
```

C#:

```
public virtual Rule UpdateRule {get; set;}
```

The `UpdateRule` Property determines how changed rows in a parent table are handled. The `Rule` enumeration constants are:

- ❑ `Cascade` – all related columns are updated
- ❑ `None` – no action is taken
- ❑ `SetDefault` – set related columns to their default value
- ❑ `SetNull` – set related columns to Null

Example

We have three tables: `Employees`, `Addresses`, and `Accounts`. Each `Account` is assigned an `Employee` (`AccountEmployee` relation), and each `Employee` has one or more `Addresses` (`EmployeeAddress` relation). The `AccountEmployee` relation should update any child columns when there are changes made to the `Employee` record, but it should *not* delete any related `Account` records. If we remove an employee, we want to keep the account and reassign it. So we implement a `SetDefault` rule and assign it to the Account Manager's ID. The `EmployeeAddress` relation should update any child columns when employee updates occur *and* delete any related records when employee deletions occur.

VB.NET:

```
Private Sub InitializeTableConstraints()
    Dim cnst As ForeignKeyConstraint
    Dim colParent As DataColumn
    Dm colChild As DataColumn

    ' Create the AccountEmployee constraint
    colParent = MyDataSet.Tables("Employees").Columns("ID")
    colChild = MyDataSet.Tables("Accounts").Columns("EmployeeID")
    cnst = New ForeignKeyConstraint(colParent, colChild)
    With cnst
        .ConstraintName = "AccountEmployee"
        .DeleteRule = Rule.SetDefault
        .UpdateRule = Rule.Cascade
        .AcceptRejectRule = AcceptRejectRule.Cascade
    End With
    ' Add the constraint
    myDataSet.Tables("Employees").Constraints.Add(cnst)

    ' Create the EmployeeAddress constraint
    colParent = MyDataSet.Tables("Employees").Columns("ID")
    colChild = MyDataSet.Tables("Addresses").Columns("EmployeeID")
    cnst = New ForeignKeyConstraint(colParent, colChild)
    With cnst
        .ConstraintName = "EmployeeAddress"
        .DeleteRule = Rule.Cascade
        .UpdateRule = Rule.Cascade
        .AcceptRejectRule = AcceptRejectRule.Cascade
```

```
        End With
        ' Add the constraint
        myDataSet.Tables("Employees").Constraints.Add(cnst)

        ' Enforce the contsraints
        myDataSet.EnforceConstraints = True
    End Sub
```

C#:

```csharp
private void InitializeTableConstraints()
    {
        ForeignKeyConstraint cnst;
        DataColumn colParent;
        DataColumn colChild;

        // Create the AccountEmployee constraint
        colParent = MyDataSet.Tables("Employees").Columns("ID");
        colChild = MyDataSet.Tables("Accounts").Columns("EmployeeID");
        cnst = new ForeignKeyConstraint(colParent, colChild);
        cnst.ConstraintName = "AccountEmployee";
        cnst.DeleteRule = Rule.SetDefault;
        cnst.UpdateRule = Rule.Cascade;
        cnst.AcceptRejectRule = AcceptRejectRule.Cascade;
        // Add the constraint
        myDataSet.Tables("Employees").Constraints.Add(cnst);

        // Create the EmployeeAddess constraint
        colParent = MyDataSet.Tables("Employees").Columns("ID");
        colChild = MyDataSet.Tables("Addresses").Columns("EmployeeID");
        cnst = new ForeignKeyConstraint(colParent, colChild);
        cnst.ConstraintName = "EmployeeAddress";
        cnst.DeleteRule = Rule.Cascade;
        cnst.UpdateRule = Rule.Cascade;
        cnst.AcceptRejectRule = AcceptRejectRule.Cascade;
        // Add the constraint
        myDataSet.Tables("Employees").Constraints.Add(cnst);

        // Enforce the contsraints
        myDataSet.EnforceConstraints = true;
    }
```

DataRelationCollection Class

The DataRelationCollection class stores all of the DataRelation objects in a DataSet. The class performs all of the normal duties of a Collection, and some others:

❑ Validating the DataRelation objects before they are appended or deleted

❑ Importing and exporting an array of DataRelation items

❑ Raising change events

This is an abstract class. The DataRelation class uses its hidden subclasses, DataSetRelationCollection and DataTableRelationCollection.

DataRelationCollection Properties

The Count Property

The Count property returns the number of DataRelation objects in the DataRelationCollection object

VB.NET:

```
Overridable Public ReadOnly Property Count As Integer
```

C#:

```
public virtual int Count {get;}
```

The IsReadOnly Property

The IsReadOnly property indicates whether the DataRelationCollection object can be modified.

VB.NET:

```
Public ReadOnly Property IsReadOnly As Boolean
```

C#:

```
public bool IsReadOnly {get;}
```

The IsSynchronized Property

The IsSynchronized property indicates whether the DataRelationCollection object is thread-safe.

VB.NET:

```
Public ReadOnly Property IsSynchronized As Boolean
```

C#:

```
public bool IsSynchronized {get;}
```

The Item Property

The Item property returns a specific DataRelation object in the current DataRelationCollection object, specified by name or index position.

VB.NET:

```
MustOverride Overloads Public Default ReadOnly Property Item(
    ByVal name As String) As DataRelation

MustOverride Overloads Public Default ReadOnly Property Item(
    ByVal index As Integer) As DataRelation
```

C#:

```
public abstract DataRelation this[string name] {get;}

public abstract DataRelation this[int index] {get;}
```

The List Property

The List property returns all of the DataRelation objects in the DataRelationCollection object as a list; this is a protected property.

VB.NET:

```
Overridable Protected ReadOnly Property List As ArrayList
```

C#:

```
protected virtual ArrayList List {get;}
```

The List property returns the relations in an ArrayList object, which is similar to an array, but its bounds are dynamically controlled by adding and removing items.

The SyncRoot Property

This property returns an object that can be used to synchronize (make thread-safe) the DataRelationCollection object.

VB.NET:

```
Public ReadOnly Property SyncRoot As Object
```

C#:

```
public object SyncRoot {get;}
```

DataRelationCollection Methods

The Add Method

The Add method adds a DataRelation object to the current DataRelationCollection object. There are several ways to add a DataRelation object to a DataRelationCollection.

Adding an Existing DataRelation

We can add an existing DataRelation object to the collection:

VB.NET:

```
Overloads Public Sub Add(
    ByVal relation As DataRelation)
```

C#:

```
public void Add(
    DataRelation relation);
```

Doing this can raise the following exceptions:

❑ ArgumentNullException – the relation parameter is Null.

❑ ArgumentException – the DataRelation belongs to another Collection or is a member of the current collection

❑ DuplicateNameException – a DataRelation of the same name already exists in the current collection. (This is a case-sensitive comparison).

❑ InvalidConstraintException – the DataRelation is invalid

This method will fire a CollectionChanged event if the Add is successful.

Adding a New Single-Column Relation

We can create and add a DataRelation to collection by providing a single parent column and a single child column.

VB.NET:

```
Overridable Overloads Public Function Add(
     ByVal parentColumn As DataColumn
     ByVal childColumn As DataColumn) As DataRelation
```

C#:

```
public virtual DataRelation Add(
     DataColumn parentColumn
     DataColumn childColumn);
```

Doing this can raise the following exceptions:

❑ ArgumentException – the DataRelation belongs to another collection or is a member of the current collection

❑ InvalidConstraintException – the DataRelation is invalid (a DataRelation cannot be created with the DataColumns passed)

Doing this will fire a CollectionChanged event if the Add is successful.

Adding a New Multiple-Column Relation

We can create and add a DataRelation by providing an array of parent columns and an array of child columns.

VB.NET:

```
Overridable Overloads Public Function Add(
     ByVal parentColumns() As DataColumn,
     ByVal childColumns() As DataColumn) As DataRelation
```

C#:

```
public virtual DataRelation Add(
     DataColumn[] parentColumns,
     DataColumn[] childColumns);
```

479

Doing this can raise the following exceptions:

- ❑ ArgumentException – the DataRelation belongs to another collection or is already a member of the current collection

- ❑ InvalidConstraintException – the DataRelation is invalid (a DataRelation cannot be created with the DataColumns passed)

Doing this will fire a CollectionChanged event if the Add is successful.

Adding a New Named Single-Column Relation

We can create and add a DataRelation providing a name, a single parent column and a single child column.

VB.NET:

```
Overridable Overloads Public Function Add(
    ByVal name As String,
    ByVal parentColumn As DataColumn,
    ByVal childColumn As DataColumn) As DataRelation
```

C#:

```
public virtual DataRelation Add(
    string name,
    DataColumn parentColumn,
    DataColumn childColumn);
```

We can also create and add a DataRelation by providing a name, a single parent column, a single child column and whether or not to automatically create constraints

VB.NET:

```
Overridable Overloads Public Function Add(
    ByVal name As String,
    ByVal parentColumn As DataColumn,
    ByVal childColumn As DataColumn,
    ByVal createConstraints As Boolean) As DataRelation
```

C#:

```
public virtual DataRelation Add(
    string name,
    DataColumn parentColumn,
    DataColumn childColumn,
    bool createConstraints);
```

Doing this can raise the following exceptions:

- ❑ ArgumentException – the DataRelation belongs to another collection or is a member of the current collection

- ❑ DuplicateNameException – a DataRelation of the same name already exists in the current collection (this is a case-sensitive comparison)

- ❑ InvalidConstraintException – the DataRelation is invalid (a DataRelation cannot be created with the DataColumns passed)

Doing this will fire the CollectionChanged event if the Add is successful.

Adding a New Named Multiple-Column Relation

We can create and add a DataRelation by providing a name, an array of parent columns, and an array of child columns.

VB.NET:

```
Overridable Overloads Public Function Add(
    ByVal name As String,
    ByVal parentColumns() As DataColumn,
    ByVal childColumns() As DataColumn) As DataRelation
```

C#:

```
public virtual DataRelation Add(
    string name,
    DataColumn[] parentColumns,
    DataColumn[] childColumns);
```

We can also create and add a DataRelation providing a name, an array of parent columns, an array of child columns and whether or not to automatically create constraints.

VB.NET:

```
Overridable Overloads Public Function Add(
    ByVal name As String,
    ByVal parentColumns() As DataColumn,
    ByVal childColumns() As DataColumn,
    ByVal createConstraints As Boolean) As DataRelation
```

C#:

```
public virtual DataRelation Add(
    string name,
    DataColumn[] parentColumns,
    DataColumn[] childColumns,
    bool createConstraints);
```

Doing this can raise the following exceptions:

❑ `ArgumentException` – the `DataRelation` belongs to another collection or is a member of the current collection

❑ `DuplicateNameException` – a `DataRelation` of the same name already exists in the current collection. (this is a case-sensitive comparison)

❑ `InvalidConstraintException` – the `DataRelation` is invalid (a `DataRelation` cannot be created with the `DataColumns` passed)

Doing this will fire the `CollectionChanged` event if the Add is successful.

Further Notes on the Add Method

The Add Method appends a new or existing `DataRelation` object to the collection. Exceptions fire if the `DataRelation` cannot be created as requested, or if a `DataRelation` of the same name already exists. With no name provided, the `DataRelation` objects are named sequentially: Relation1, Relation2, and so on.

We will now build a `DataRelationCollection` using several different constructors. The `DataRelationCollection` for an existing `DataSet` called `MyDataSet` is used. This `DataRelationCollection` will then be referenced in the subsequent code examples to illustrate basic collection behaviors.

VB.NET:

```
Dim relAccountContacts as DataRelation
Dim relOrderDetails as DataRelation
Dim relProductSuppliers as DataRelation
Dim arrRelations() as DataRelation
Dim arrParents() as DataColumn
Dim arrChildren() as DataColumn
Dim colDataRelations as DataRelationCollection

' get the DataRelationCollection reference
colDataRelations = MyDataSet.Relations

' add customer orders by providing a name, and parent and child column
' arrays
arrParents (0)=MyDataSet.Tables("Accounts").Columns("AccountID")
arrParents (1)=MyDataSet.Tables("Accounts").Columns("AccManagerID")
arrChildren (0)=MyDataSet.Tables("Contacts").Columns("AccountID")
arrChildren (1)=MyDataSet.Tables("Contacts").Columns("AccManagerID")
relCustomerOrders = _
    New DataRelation("AccountContacts",colParents,colChildren)
colDataRelations.Add(relCustomerOrders)

' add order details by providing a name and parent and child columns
relOrderDetails = colDataRelations.Add("OrderDetails", _
    MyDataSet.Tables("Orders").Columns("OrderID"), _
    MyDataSet.Tables("OrderDeatils").Columns("OrderID"))

' add product suppliers by providing parent and child columns
relProductSuppliers = colDataRelations.Add _
```

```
          (MyDataSet.Tables("Products").Columns("ProductID"), _
          MyDataSet.Tables("Suppliers").Columns("SupplierID"))
    ' rename the new relation
    relProductSuppliers.RelationName = "ProductSuppliers"

    ' output the collection contents
    For t = 1 to colDataRelations.Count-1
        Debug.Write(t & ": " & colDataRelations(t-1).RelationName & vbCrLf)
    Next t
```

C#:

```
    DataRelation relAccountContacts;
    DataRelation relOrderDetails;
    DataRelation relProductSuppliers;
    DataRelation[] arrRelations;
    DataColumn[] arrParents;
    DataColumn[] arrChildren;
    DataRelationCollection colDataRelations;

    // get the DataRelationCollection reference
    colDataRelations = MyDataSet.Relations;

    // add customer orders by providing a name, and parent and child column
    // arrays
    arrParents (0) = MyDataSet.Tables("Accounts").Columns("AccountID");
    arrParents (1) = MyDataSet.Tables("Accounts").Columns("AccManagerID");
    arrChildren (0) = MyDataSet.Tables("Contacts").Columns("AccountID");
    arrChildren (1) = MyDataSet.Tables("Contacts").Columns("AccManagerID");
    relCustomerOrders = New
        DataRelation("AccountContacts",colParents,colChildren);
    colDataRelations.Add(relCustomerOrders);

    // add order details by providing a name and parent and child columns
    relOrderDetails = colDataRelations.Add("OrderDetails",
        MyDataSet.Tables("Orders").Columns("OrderID"),
        MyDataSet.Tables("OrderDeatils").Columns("OrderID"))'

    // add product suppliers by providing parent and child columns
    relProductSuppliers =
        colDataRelations.Add(MyDataSet.Tables("Products").Columns("ProductID"),
        MyDataSet.Tables("Suppliers").Columns("SupplierID"));
    // rename the new relation
    relProductSuppliers.RelationName = "ProductSuppliers";

    //   output the collection contents
    for (int t = 1; t <= colDataRelations.Count-1; t++)
        Debug.Write(t & ": " & colDataRelations(t-1).RelationName & vbCrLf);
```

The output is:

1: OrderDetails
2: AccountContacts
3: ProductSuppliers

The AddRange Method

The AddRange method appends an array of DataRelation objects to the current DataRelationCollection object.

VB.NET:

```
Overridable Public Sub AddRange (
    ByVal relations() As DataRelation)
```

C#:

```
public virtual void AddRange(
    DataRelation[] relations);
```

The DataRelation objects are appended at the end of the collection.

The Clear Method

Clears the contents of the current DataRelationCollection object

VB.NET:

```
Overridable Public Sub Clear()
```

C#:

```
public virtual void Clear();
```

The Contains Method

The Contains method determines whether a named DataRelation object exists in the current DataRelationCollection object.

VB.NET:

```
Overridable Public Function Contains(
    ByVal name As String) As Boolean
```

C#:

```
public virtual bool Contains(
    string name);
```

The comparison is case-sensitive.

The CopyTo Method

The CopyTo method populates an array (starting at a specified array index) with the DataRelation objects from the current DataRelationCollection object.

VB.NET:

```
NotOverridable Public Sub CopyTo(
    ByVal ar As Array,
    ByVal index As Integer)
```

C#:

```
public void CopyTo(
    Array ar,
    int index);
```

The GetEnumerator Method

The GetEnumerator Method returns an IEnumerator for the current DataRelationCollection object (used for iterating)

VB.NET:

```
NotOverridable Public Function GetEnumerator() As IEnumerator
```

C#:

```
public IEnumerator GetEnumerator();
```

The GetEnumerator Method is equivalent to the _NewEnum method you would use to iterate through a wrapped VB collection object using For...Next loops.

The Remove Method

The Remove method removes a specified DataRelation object from the current DataRelationCollection object. There are several ways to remove a DataRelation object from the current collection, two of which use overloaded versions of the Remove method:

We can remove the DataRelation object passed in the parameter.

VB.NET:

```
Overloads Public Sub Remove(
    ByVal relation As DataRelation)
```

C#:

```
public void Remove(
    DataRelation relation);
```

Doing this can raise the following exceptions:

❑ ArgumentNullException – the relation parameter is Null

❑ ArgumentException – the DataRelation is not a member of the collection

We can remove the DataRelation object whose name is provided.

VB.NET:

```
Overloads Public Sub Remove(
    ByVal name As String)
```

C#:

```
public void Remove(
    string name);
```

This will throw an `IndexOutOfRange` exception if no `DataRelation` of the given name exists in the collection.

Doing this will fire a `CollectionChanged` event if the `Remove` is successful.

The RemoveAt Method

Removes the `DataRelation` object from the current `DataRelationCollection` object at a given index.

VB.NET:

```
Public Sub RemoveAt(
    ByVal index As Integer)
```

C#:

```
public void RemoveAt(
    int index);
```

Exceptions:
- ❑ `IndexOutOfRange` – no `DataRelation` exists in the current collection at that index

Events:
- ❑ `CollectionChanged` – fired if the `Remove` is successful

Example of Removing and Adding Relations

In the example collection, we will remove the `OrderDetails` and `AccountContacts DataRelation` objects from the collection, then put them together in an array and append them.

VB.NET:

```
' remove the OrderDetails
colDataRelations.RemoveAt(2)
' verify the removal worked
Debug.Write("OrderDetails " & _
    IIf(colDataRelations.Contains("OrderDetails"),"does","does not") & _
    " exist in this collection." & vbCrLf)

' remove the AccountContacts
colDataRelations.Remove("AccountContacts")

' add them back as an array
Dim arrRelations(1) as DataRelation
arrRelations(0)=relAccountContacts
arrRelations(1)=relOrderDetails
colDataRelactions.AddRange(arrRelations)

' output the contents of the collection
Dim relCollectionMember As DataRelationCollection
For Each relCollectionMember in colDataRelations
    Debug.Write(t & ": " & relCollectionMember.RelationName & _
        ControlChars.cr)
Next t
```

C#:

```
// remove the OrderDetails
colDataRelations.RemoveAt(2);
// verify the removal worked
Debug.Write("OrderDetails " & _
    IIf(colDataRelations.Contains("OrderDetails"),"does","does not") & _
    " exist in this collection." & vbCrLf);

// remove the AccountContacts
colDataRelations.Remove("AccountContacts");

// add them back as an array
DataRelation[] arrRelations;
arrRelations[0]=relAccountContacts;
arrRelations[1]=relOrderDetails;
colDataRelactions.AddRange(arrRelations);

// output the contents of the collection
foreach (DataRelationCollection relCollectionMember in colDataRelations)
{
    Debug.Write(t + ": " + relCollectionMember.RelationName +
        ControlChars.cr);
}
```

The output is:

OrderDetails does not exist in this collection.

1: ProductSuppliers
2: OrderDetails
3: AccountContacts

The AddCore and RemoveCore Protected Methods

These methods are used by the Add and Remove methods for validating DataRelation objects.

The AddCore Method

Verifies the table; this is a protected method.

VB.NET:

```
Overridable Protected Sub AddCore(
    ByVal relation As DataRelation)
```

C#:

```
protected virtual void AddCore(
    DataRelation relation);
```

This method can throw the following exceptions:

❑ ArgumentNullException – the relation parameter is Null

❑ ArgumentExcpetion – the DataRelation belongs to another Collection or is a member of the current collection

❑ DuplicateNameException – a DataRelation of the same name already exists in the current collection (this is a case-sensitive comparison).

The `AddCore` Method validates the `DataRelation` object passed to it. It validates that the passed `DataRelation` is not null, that it does not belong to another Collection, that it is not already a member of the current Collection and that another `DataRelation` of the same name does not exist in the current collection.

The `AddCore` method is used by the `Add` method for validation before appending the relation to the collection. The exceptions fired by the `Add` method originate in `AddCore`.

The RemoveCore Method

Verifies the relation; this is a protected method.

VB.NET:

```
Overridable Protected Sub RemoveCore(
    ByVal relation As DataRelation)
```

C#:

```
protected virtual void RemoveCore(
    DataRelation relation);
```

Exceptions:

- ❑ `ArgumentNullException` – the relation parameter is Null

- ❑ `ArgumentExcpetion` – the `DataRelation` is not a member of the current collection

The `RemoveCore` method validates the `DataRelation` object passed to it. It ensures that the passed `DataRelation` is not null, and that it is a member of the current collection.

The `RemoveCore` method is used by the `Remove` method. The exceptions fired by the `Remove` method originate in `RemoveCore`.

Summary

Maintaining table relationships is new in ADO.NET. Relationships are managed using the following three objects:

- ❑ `DataRelation` object – identifies the tables and columns involved

- ❑ `UniqueConstraint` object – identifies the primary key of the parent table, or maintains uniqueness of some other column

- ❑ `ForeignKeyConstraint` object – identifies how updates and deletes are handled in the related child rows

Constraints need to be enforced explicitly by setting the `EnforeConstraints` property of the `DataSet` to `True`. Remember that enforcing certain constraints can cause exceptions when the constraint instructions result in row relations that violate the constraint.

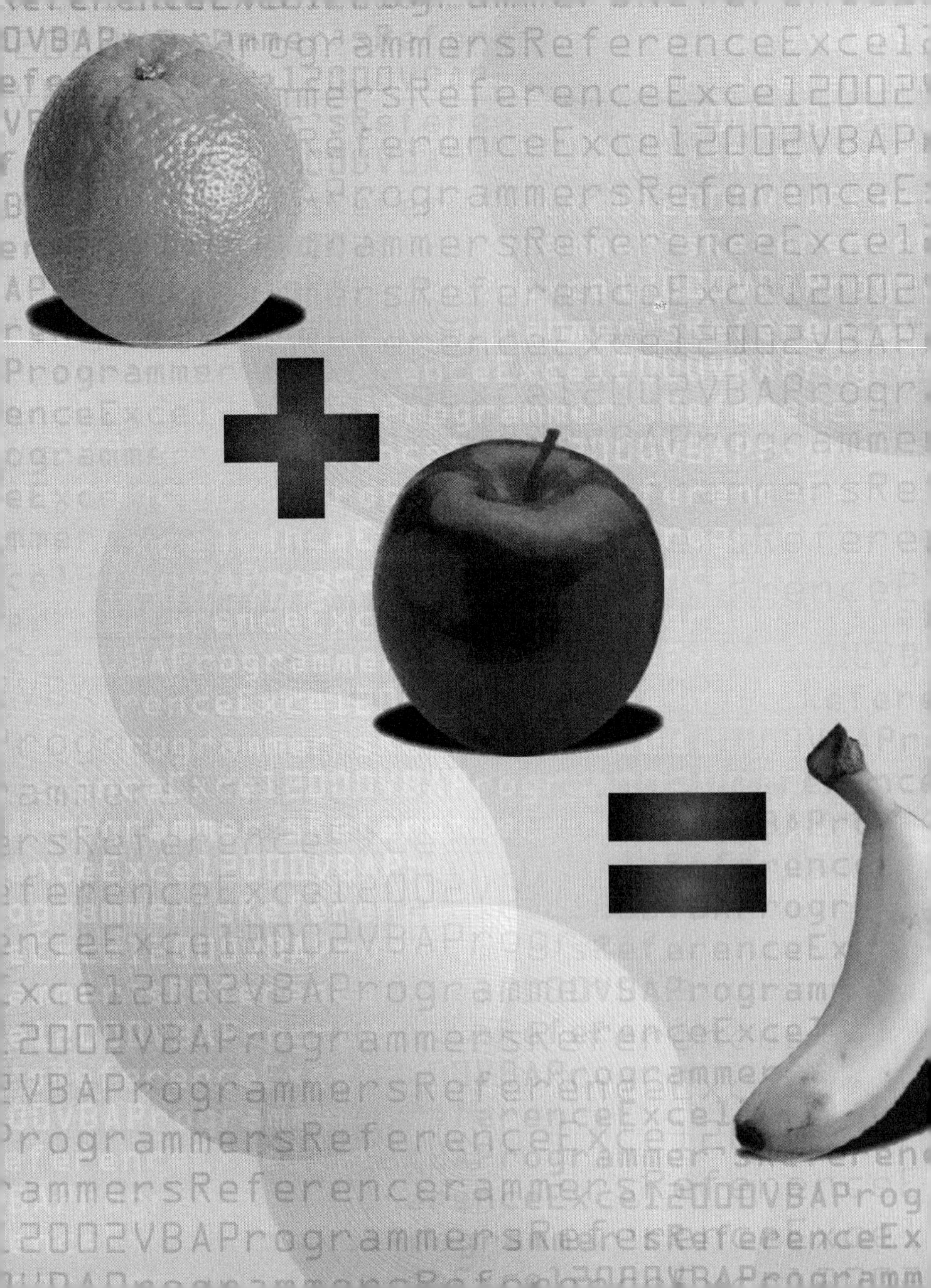

Using DataViews

The `DataView` object provides us with an easy to use yet powerful method for creating a custom view of a `DataTable`. A primary purpose of the `DataView` object is to provide a binding mechanism between GUI components and data. That doesn't mean we can't have a `DataView` without a GUI though. All the methods that a GUI would use to manipulate the `DataTable` underlying the `DataView` are easily accessible to us programmatically – we could just as easily have a console application.

It is possible to have several `DataView` objects for a single `DataTable`.

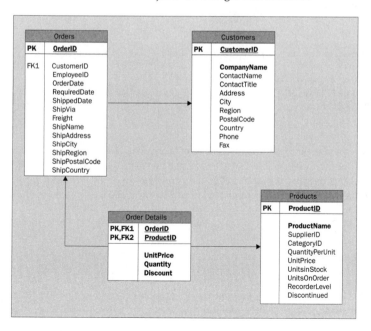

This shows a `DataTable` with numerous views over it. Each view maintains its own filter and sort settings – it's completely independent from any other views that may exist. What happens at the presentation layer is up to us; we might bind one view to a `DataGrid`, one to a `ListView`, and the final one to a `TextBox`. Of course we might not want to bind the views to anything.

It's important to note that the DataView object isn't the same as a data view created using, for example, CREATE SQL VIEW. A view created in this manner may contain columns from one or many related tables. We could modify the contents of the view and any modifications would be reflected in the underlying data tables. The DataView, however, is different. This object is only concerned with presenting a view for a single DataTable. It cannot be used to re-order, add or remove columns from the view. The DataView directly reflects the schema of the DataTable, if there's a requirement to show only selected columns from a table in a view then a DataTable containing only the required columns must be created.

That's fine if we have a single DataTable that we need to create a view for, but what happens if we have something more complex? Like several tables in a DataSet? Wouldn't it be nice if we had some way of managing all those views in one place? This is precisely what the DataViewManager is for.

Unlike the DataView, which is only concerned with one DataTable, the DataViewManager deals with entire DataSets. As you're probably already aware, a DataSet can contain many tables and can be used to manage relationships between them.

When we work with a DataViewManager, we don't directly interact with DataView objects. Instead, we use DataViewSetting objects. These aren't as complex as DataViews in that they deal only with sorting and filtering, whereas with a DataView we can also specify whether rows can be edited, added, or deleted. The DataViewManager maintains a collection of these objects, one per DataTable in the DataSet. We can retrieve a DataViewSetting object for a given table from the DataViewManager and customize it as required.

We'll quickly compare the uses of the DataView and DataViewManager object. Both examples bind a filtered view to a DataGrid, but they achieve this in slightly different ways. The first example shows how to use the DataView.

C#:

```
public void CreateAndBind(DataTable dataTable, DataGrid dataGrid)
{
    DataView newView = DataView(dataTable);
    newView.RowFilter = "USER_ID > 10";
    dataGrid.SetDataBinding(newView, "");
}
```

The above code shows a simple method called CreateAndBind. Into this method we pass both DataTable and DataGrid objects. First of all, we create a DataView, the DataTable is associated with the DataView by providing it in the DataView constructor. Next, we set a simple filter that will inlude all users with a USER_ID greater than 10 and finally bind the DataView to the DataGrid.

Alternatively, we could use the DataViewManager:

```
public void CreateAndBind(DataSet dataSet, DataGrid dataGrid,
                                                string tableName)
{
    DataViewManager dvm = new DataViewManager(dataSet);
    dvm.DataViewSettings[tableName].RowFilter = "USER_ID > 10";
    dataGrid.SetDataBinding(dvm, tableName);
}
```

It's slightly more complicated but still relatively straightforward. This time we've passed in a `DataSet` to the `CreateAndBind` method rather than a `DataTable`. We still pass in the `DataGrid`, but there's also a third parameter. This parameter (`tableName`) is the name of the table we want to view in the `DataGrid`.

So, we create the `DataViewManager` for this `DataSet`, and then we set the filter for the table we're interested in. Remember that the `DataViewManager` is looking after the views for all the tables in the `DataSet`. We could have more than one table therefore, we need to tell the `DataViewManager` which table we're interested in. We pass the table name to the collections indexer to do this. Finally, we bind the `DataViewManager` to the `DataGrid`, making use of the second parameter, and pass through the name of the table we wish to view (again, because we potentially have more than one table in the `DataSet`).

In a real application, we probably wouldn't create the `DataViewManager` as a local variable in a method like this. It would be somewhere more accessible, where we could repeatedly bind different GUI controls to the object.

We have already discussed the `DataView` and `DataViewManager` objects. There will be two more objects that will also be covered in this chapter:

❑ `DataViewSetting` – this maintains view settings for each `DataTable` in the `DataSet` associated with the `DataViewManager`.

❑ `DataViewSettingCollection` – this is used by the `DataViewManager` to manage all its `DataViewSetting` objects.

Preliminaries

As we work through this chapter, I'll try to illustrate how we create, customize, and bind to our `DataView` object. To do this we will refer to data obtained from the Northwind database, specifically a `DataTable` based on the following query:

SQL:

```
SELECT customerid, companyname, contactname, city FROM customers
```

We will then use `DataView` objects to filter and sort this table in various ways. If you wish to follow these examples, then this section will help you to set up a suitable demonstration application. If you do not wish to follow the examples, then feel free to skip this section.

The procedure will be very similar in C# and VB.NET, so choose the language that you are most familiar with.

Creating a Form

In Visual Studio.NET, create a new Windows application (we've called ours `DataViewDemo`). Now open `Form1` in the designer so you can see an empty form in the center of the screen. Using the Toolbox (which you can open by selecting **View | Toolbox** from the main menu), place two `DataGrid` objects and a `Button` control onto the Form. You should now have a form something like this (notice the button is labeled "Fill", in order to do this right click on the button and select Properties, find the Text property and change it from "button1" to "Fill"):

Variable and Procedure Declarations

Include the following in the form's declarations (double click anywhere on the form to bring up the code view, then in VB select Declarations from the right hand drop down list):

VB.NET:

```
Private m_userTable As DataTable
```

C#:

```
private DataTable m_userTable;
```

This declares the `DataTable` object that we will be using for the examples. Immediately below this declaration, include the following:

VB.NET:

```
Private Sub BuildTable()
    Dim sqlConn As SqlConnection = New _
            SqlConnection("server=localhost;uid=sa;pwd=;database=northwind")
    Dim sqlComm As SqlCommand = New _
            SqlCommand("select customerid, companyname, contactname, " & _
            "city from customers", sqlConn)
    Dim ad As New SqlDataAdapter(sqlComm)
    m_userTable = New DataTable("USERS")
    sqlConn.Open()
    ad.Fill(m_userTable)
End Sub
```

C#:

```
private void BuildTable() {
    SqlConnection sqlConn = new
            SqlConnection("server=localhost;uid=sa;pwd=;database=northwind");
    SqlCommand sqlComm = new
            SqlCommand("select customerid, companyname, contactname, " +
            "city from customers", sqlConn);
    SqlDataAdapter ad = new SqlDataAdapter(sqlComm);
    m_userTable = new DataTable("USERS");
    sqlConn.Open();
    ad.Fill(m_userTable);
}
```

This declares a method `BuildTable` that will populate our `DataTable` with data from the Northwind database.

Calling the BuildTable Method

Finally, find the form's constructor, and include the line given in bold below. In C#, simply find the code block beginning `public Form1()`. In VB.NET you will need to expand the "Windows Form Designer generated code" region and find the block beginning `Public Sub New()`.

VB.NET:

```
Public Sub New()
    MyBase.New()

    'This call is required by the Windows Form Designer.
    InitializeComponent()

    BuildTable ()
End Sub
```

C#:

```
public Form1()
{
    InitializeComponent();

    BuildTable();
}
```

This means that when the form initializes, our `DataTable` will be populated automatically.

Binding the Table to the DataGrid Objects

OK, nearly there now, we just need to bind this table to the `DataGrid` objects we added earlier. Return to the form view, double click the button, and add the following code:

VB.NET:

```
Private Sub button1_Click(ByVal sender As System.Object, ByVal e As
                        System.EventArgs) Handles button1.Click
    DataGrid1.SetDataBinding(m_userTable, "")
    DataGrid2.SetDataBinding(m_userTable, "")
End Sub
```

C#:

```csharp
private void button1_Click(object sender, System.EventArgs e)
{
    dataGrid1.SetDataBinding(m_userTable, "");
    dataGrid2.SetDataBinding(m_userTable, "");
}
```

Not surprisingly, this piece of code creates a simple binding between the `DataTable` and the `DataGrids`.

Now, build the project and run it! We should be presented with a form showing an empty `DataGrid` and a button. Click the button, and we should get something like this:

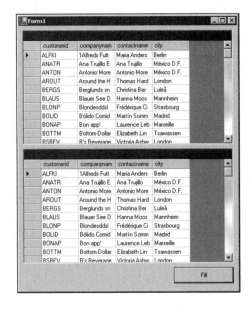

It's time to move on now, and look at what a `DataView` can do for us.

The DataView Object

In this section, we're going to look at using the `DataView` object. The `DataView` object provides us with a method for creating a customizable view for a single `DataTable`. We can sort and filter the view as well as specifying what editing operations can be performed on the view's data.

A `DataView` does not let us present custom views over a table's schema, that is the view will only show columns that are already in the table, it can't add or remove them.

DataView Constructors

There are two constructors for the `DataView` object.

VB.NET:

```
Public Sub New()

Public Sub New(DataTable)
```

C#:

```
public DataView();

public DataView(DataTable);
```

The parameterless constructor returns a `DataView` that has no `DataTable` associated with it and therefore isn't ready for using.

VB.NET:

```
Dim newView As DataView

newView = New DataView()
```

C#:

```
DataView newView = new DataView ();
```

Before we can use the `DataView`, it must be associated with a `DataTable`. We do this by setting the `Table` property of the `DataView` to a valid `DataTable`. In order to do this, we'd write something such as:

VB.NET:

```
Public Function CreateView(ByVal dataTable As DataTable) As DataView

    Dim dataView As New DataView()

    dataView.Table = dataTable

    Return dataView

End Function
```

The above code creates a `DataView` with no associated `DataTable` by using the default constructor. We then associate the `DataTable` with the view by using the `Table` property on the second line. The second constructor takes a `DataTable` as it's only argument.

VB.NET:

```
Public Function CreateView ( ByVal dataTable as DataTable ) As DataView
Dim newView As DataView()

    newView = New DataView ( dataTable )

    Return newView
End Function
```

C#:

```csharp
public DataView CreateView ( DataTable dataTable )
{
    DataView newView = new DataView ( dataTable );

    return newView;
}
```

When a `DataView` is created using this constructor, we have an object that can be used immediately.

Let's add a `DataView` to our fledgling application then. Firstly, we need to add a private `DataView` member.

VB.NET:

```vbnet
Private m_userView As DataView
```

C#:

```csharp
private DataView m_userView;
```

Next, we need to create our `DataView` object. We'll use the constructor that takes a `DataTable` object. In the forms constructor, add this code (in VB this will be inside the **Windows Forms Designer Generated Code** region):

VB.NET:

```vbnet
Public Sub New()
    MyBase.New()

    'This call is required by the Windows Form Designer.
    InitializeComponent()

    m_userTable = New DataTable("USERS")

    BuildTable()

    m_userView = New DataView(m_userTable)
End Sub
```

C#:

```csharp
public Form1 ()
{
    InitializeComponent ();

    m_userTable = new DataTable ( "USERS" );

    BuildTable ();

    m_userView = new DataView ( m_userTable );
}
```

Now we should be able to bind the `DataGrid` objects to our new `DataView` object. Find the button click handler we added at the start and change:

VB.NET:

```
DataGrid1.SetDataBinding(m_userTable, "")
```

C#:

```
dataGrid1.SetDataBinding(m_userTable, "");
```

So that it reads:

VB.NET:

```
DataGrid1.SetDataBinding(m_userView, "")
```

C#:

```
dataGrid1.SetDataBinding(m_userView, "");
```

Only change the binding for the `dataGrid1` member, this will provide us with a useful way of comparing the effects of filters and sorts on a view over that of binding directly to a `DataTable` Now build and run the project. When we click the button, we should see the same data as before, but internally the data is now coming via a `DataView`.

DataView Properties

In this section we're going to look at the properties of the `DataView` object.

The AllowDelete Property

The `AllowDelete` property indicates whether rows can be deleted from the `DataTable` using the `DataView`.

VB.NET:

```
Public Property AllowDelete As Boolean
```

C#:

```
public bool AllowDelete {get; set;}
```

Setting this property to true allows us to delete rows from the `DataTable` assigned to the `DataView`.

VB.NET:

```
DataView.AllowDelete = True
DataView.Delete(0)
```

C#:

```
dataView.AllowDelete = true;
dataView.Delete(0);
```

The above example enables deletion of rows and then deletes the first row from the `DataTable`. We stop rows being deleted by setting the value to false:

499

VB.NET:

```
DataView.AllowDelete = False

' this raises an exception
DataView.Delete ( 0 )
```

C#:

```
dataView.AllowDelete = false;

// this raises an exception
dataView.Delete ( 0 );
```

This code would cause the DataView to throw an exception. Be aware that this only stops us deleting rows from the table via the DataView object – we can still access the DataTable directly and delete the rows from there.

Lets add some more code to our application. We'll add a new method now where we can play with the views properties as much as we want. So add this new method to the form class:

VB.NET:

```
Private Function CustomizeView()
    m_userView.AllowDelete = False
End Function
```

C#:

```
private void CustomizeView ()
{
    m_userView.AllowDelete = false;
}
```

Now call this method from the forms constructor:

VB.NET:

```
Public Sub New()

    'previous code omitted for brevity

    m_userView = New DataView(m_userTable)

    CustomizeView ()
End Sub
```

C#:

```
public Form1 ()
{
    // previous code omitted for brevity
    m_userView = new DataView ( m_userTable );

    CustomizeView ();
}
```

In the `CustomizeView` method, add `m_userView.AllowDelete = false` and start up the application. Once you've populated the grid, try selecting a row and pressing delete. The `datagrid1` won't allow you to delete any of the rows, whereas `datagrid2`, which is directly bound to the `DataTable`, will allow deletions. If you set this property to `true`, the `DataGrid` will allow rows to be deleted again.

The AllowEdit Property

Indicates whether rows in the `DataTable` can be edited.

VB.NET:

```
Public Property AllowEdit As Boolean
```

C#:

```
public bool AllowEdit {get; set;}
```

In order to enable editing of the `DataTable` via the `DataView`, we set the property to true.

VB.NET:

```
dataView.AllowEdit = True
Dim drv As DataRowView = dataView(0)
drv.BeginEdit()
drv("contactname ") = "bob"
drv.EndEdit()
```

C#:

```
dataView.AllowEdit = true;
DataRowView drv = dataView[0];
drv.BeginEdit();
drv["contactname" ] = "bob";
drv.EndEdit();
```

The example shows the `AllowEdit` property being set to true. We then get the first row from the `DataView` using it's indexer. We let the row know we intend to edit it by calling `BeginEdit`, we then set the `contactname` column to 'bob', and call `EndEdit` to let the row know we've finished.

If we set `AllowEdit` to `false` and tried the same code again, then the line `drv [ " contactname " ] = "bob"` would raise an exception. Calling `BeginEdit` or `EndEdit` while `AllowEdit` is set to `false` won't cause an exception to be raised. Calling `CancelEdit` on the `DataRowView` object can roll back any changes that have been made. No exception is raised if `CancelEdit` is called when `AllowEdit` is false.

We can try out this property by adding it to our `CustomizeView` method and setting its value. A `false` value stops us editing the cell contents, while `true` enables the cells, again compare this with the behavior to the `DataTable` bound grid.

The AllowNew Property

Indicates whether new rows can be added to the `DataTable`.

VB.NET:

```
Public Property AllowNew As Boolean
```

C#:

```
public bool AllowNew {get; set;}
```

To allow new rows to be added to the `DataTable` via the `DataView` set the property to true.

C#:

```
dataView.AllowNew = true;
```

Setting the property to `false` will stop the `DataView` from allowing new rows to be added. Again, it doesn't stop new rows being added to directly to the underlying `DataTable`.

We could try to add a new row programmatically:

C#:

```
dataView.AllowNew = false;
DataRowView newRow = dataView.AddNew ();          // raise exception
```

As soon as we attempt to add the new row to the `DataView` object, an exception will be thrown.

Try setting the property in the `CustomizeView` method to see how it affects the `DataGrid`. With `AllowNew` set to true, then we'd be able to add a new row by pressing the down cursor when it's on the last row in the grid. With a value of false, the `DataGrid` won't let us add new rows.

The ApplyDefaultSort Property

Indicates whether the default sort should be used on the view.

VB.NET:

```
Public Property ApplyDefaultSort As Boolean
```

C#:

```
public bool AppyDefaultSort {get;set;}
```

C# example:

```
dataView.ApplyDefaultSort = true;

bool defaultSort = dataView.ApplyDefaultSort;
```

The default sort to be applied to the view is determined in this order:

- ❏ Regardless of whether `ApplyDefaultSort` is true or false if a sort string has been explicitly set using the `Sort` property then this is deemed to be the default sort.

- ❏ If no sort has been explicitly set and `ApplyDefaultSort` is true, then the view attempts to create a default sort using the `DataTables`' primary key or keys. If `ApplyDefaultSort` is false, then the view is unsorted.

- ❏ If the `DataTable` doesn't contain any primary keys and a sort hasn't been specified, then the sort is undefined. This simply means that the rows aren't sorted in the view and setting `ApplyDefaultSort` to true or false has no effect on the view.

It might help to illustrate this with a concrete example so let's add some more code to the application.

Find the `BuildTable` method and add the following code at the end of the method:

VB.NET:

```
Private Sub BuildTable ()
{_
    Dim columns(1) As DataColumn

    columns(0) = userNameCol

    m_userTable.PrimaryKey = columns
End Sub
```

C#:

```
private void BuildTable ()
{
    // create an array of one to hold our primary key
    DataColumn []columns = new DataColumn [ 1 ];

    // add the customer id column to the array
    columns[0] = userNameCol;

    // and set the primary key columns on the table
    m_userTable.PrimaryKey = columns;
}
```

Briefly, this code creates an array of `DataColumns` with one element. We add the user column to the array, and assign the array to the `PrimaryKey` property of the `DataTable`. If we wished to, we could create a larger array and use more than one column as a primary key (if you try this then use a column such as USER_NAME because all the values in there are unique – if we used the USER_TYPE column then an exception would be raised because there are duplicate values in the column). Of course I wouldn't recommend using the USER_NAME column as a primary key, but this makes the following example clearer.

Now let's move to the `CustomizeView` method. Here we'll set the `ApplyDefaultSort` property to false. If you've been jumping about this chapter, make sure that there are no sort strings set on the `Sort` property. So type this code:

C# code (VB.NET code identical, just leave off the semi-colon):

```
m_userView.ApplyDefaultSort = false;
```

Build and run the application. When we hit the button we should see datagrid1 with the rows (apparently) sorted on USER_ID. In reality, the view isn't sorted, what you're seeing is the rows in the order they were added to the DataTable. We can also tell the view isn't sorted because none of the column headers contain the • symbol.

Now set the ApplyDefaultSort to true and run the application again. We should now see a completely different view; ordered on the USER_NAME column. Apart from the obvious difference in the order of the rows, also notice that next to the USER_NAME column header we can now see the • symbol.

Finally, if we were to add a sort string using the Sort property, we could see how this affects the view. So in the CustomizeView method add:

C# code (VB.NET code identical, just leave off the semi-colon):

```
m_userView.Sort = "FULL_NAME";
```

Now try setting ApplyDefaultSort to true or false. Regardless of the setting the view will always be sorted on the FULL_NAME column. The Sort property is discussed at length later in the chapter.

The Count Property

Returns the number of rows currently in the DataView.

VB.NET:
```
Public ReadOnly Property Count As Integer
```

C#:
```
public int Count {get;}
```

We'd use this property in the following way:

VB.NET:
```
Dim rowCount = m_userView.Count
```

C#:
```
int rowCount = dataView.Count;
```

The rowCount variable will contain the number of rows in the DataView. This doesn't always correspond to the number of rows in the DataTable – if a filter has been applied to the DataView, then there may be rows in the DataTable that the DataView isn't required to show.

The DataViewManager Property

A read-only property that returns the `DataViewManager` object that was used to create the `DataView`.

VB.NET:

```
Public ReadOnly Property DataViewManager As DataViewManager
```

C#:

```
public DataViewManager DataViewManager {get;}
```

If the `DataView` wasn't created using a `DataViewManager`, then a null reference will be returned.

VB.NET:

```
Dim viewManager = m_userView.DataViewManager
```

C#:

```
DataViewManager viewManager = dataView.DataViewManager;
```

We will discuss the `DataViewManager` in detail later in the chapter.

The Item Property

Returns a `DataRowView` at a given index in the `DataView`.

VB.NET:

```
Public Default ReadOnly Property Item( ByVal recordIndex As Integer)
                                   As DataRowView
```

C#:

```
public DataViewRow this [ int recordIndex ];
```

We would use the property in the following way:

VB.NET:

```
Dim drv = dataView ( 7 )
```

C#:

```
DataRowView drv = dataView [ 7 ];
```

When accessing any rows contained in the `DataView`, it is important to ensure that the row is in the `DataView` and not only the underlying `DataTable`. If the view has a filter applied, then it may not contain all the rows of the `DataTable`.

A more robust method of using the property would be to write something like:

VB.NET:

```
Private Function GetRow(ByVal dataView As DataView, ByVal rowIndex As Int32)
                       As DataRowView

    If (rowIndex >= 0 & rowIndex < dataView.Count) Then
      Return dataView(rowIndex)
    Else
        Return Nothing
    End If
End Function
```

C#:

```
private DataRowView GetRow(DataView dataView, int rowIndex)
{
    if (rowIndex >= 0 && rowIndex < dataView.Count)
        return dataView[rowIndex];
    else
        return null;
}
```

Using this method ensures that we never attempt to access the row collection of the `DataView` out of bounds.

The RowFilter Property

A filter applied to the `DataView` that defines the rows the `DataView` should contain.

VB.NET:

```
Overridable Public Property RowFilter As String
```

C#:

```
public virtual string RowFilter{get;set;}
```

For example, we could create a filter to only include people with the name "Bob":

C#:

```
dataView.RowFilter = "NAME = 'Bob'";
```

The filter should be a string that evaluates as a `Boolean` value. If it helps, think of a filter as a SQL select but with the `SELECT` keyword missing.

A table showing the general formatting rules for filters is shown below:

Type	Format	Explanation
string	SURNAME='Smith'	All string values to be used in filters should be in single quotes.
int, long etc	AGE=50	Numeric values should be unquoted.
date (SqlDateTime)	DOB=#10/22/1974#	Date values should be enclosed in hash brackets. Note then when using a date as a filter, the date format in the filter string must be the same as the format in the column.

VB.NET:

```
dataView.RowFilter = "DOB=#10/22/1974#"
```

C#:

```
dataView.RowFilter = "SURNAME='Smith'";
```

The following comparison operators are valid in `DataView` filters:

Comparison Operators	Example	Explanation
`<`, `>`, `<=`, `>=`, `<>`, `=`	`USER_ID<10, USER_ID <=35, USER_ID <>101`	Standard equality, less than and greater than operators.
`IN`	`USER_ID IN (1,5,6)`	Selects all rows who's USER_ID is 1, 5 or 6.
`LIKE`	`FULL_NAME='*Stevenson'`	Enables us to include a wildcard '*' in our filters. This filter searches through the `FULL_NAME` column and returns any record that ends in `'Stevenson'`.

The use of the wildcard is extremely useful although it does have limitations. For example, we can't use the wild card in the middle of words. Searching for `'Steven*son'` would cause a format exception to be raised.

Another useful part of filter is to be able to include Boolean operators in them:

Operator	Example	Explanation
`AND`	`USER_NAME='Smith' AND USER_ID=50`	Filter all rows where the user name is Smith and user ID equals 50
`OR`	`USER_NAME='SmithT' OR USER_NAME ='JonesF'`	Filter all rows where the user name is SmithT or JonesF
`NOT`	`USER_NAME='SmithT' AND NOT USER_ID=50`	Filter all rows where the user name is SmithT and the user ID isn't 50

Of course, we can also include parentheses in the filters as well to clarify our intentions. The following examples use parentheses to change the meaning of a filter:

C#:

```
// finds all records with user_name Smitht that do not have a User ID of 50
dataView.RowFilter = "(NOT USER_ID=50) AND USER_NAME='SmithT';
```

```
// finds all records that do not have user_name SmithT and do not have
// user_id of 50
dataView.RowFilter = "NOT (USER_ID = 50 AND USER_NAME ='SmithT');
```

We can also embed functions into our filters:

Function	Example	Explanation
LEN()	LEN(PASSWORD<6)	Returns true if a password is less than 6 characters.
ISNULL()	ISNULL(PASSWORD,USER_NAME)	If password is null, then user name is returned.
IIF()	IIF(USER_TYPE='Administrator', USER_NAME=DICKINSONP, USER_NAME='ODELLS')	Essentially an if / then / else function. If the user is an administrator, then show records with user name DICKINSONP, otherwise show records with the user name ODELLS.
TRIM()	TRIM(PASSWORD)	Removes all characters like \n, \t, \r from the string.
SUBSTRING()	SUBSTRING(PASSWORD, 0, 3)	Extracts the first 3 characters from the PASSWORD.

Let's try some filters in our application now we've had a look at them. In the `CustomizeView` method, try out these various filters.

The following filter will include records where the contact name is longer than 15 characters:

```
m_userView.RowFilter = "LEN(contactname) > 15";
```

This one will return records where the `companyname` begins with F and the city is London, and every contact in Berlin:

```
m_userView.RowFilter =
            "IIF(contactid LIKE 'F*',city='London', city='Berling')";
```

Finally, if a filter has been applied but doesn't appear to be working, it's worth checking that the `sort` property is valid. If an invalid `sort` has been specified then the filter won't work, and all rows will be displayed.

The RowStateFilter Property

The `RowStateFilter Property` filters the rows allowed in the `DataView` based on the rows' state.

VB.NET:
```
Public Property RowStateFilter As DataViewRowState
```

C#:
```
public DataViewRowState RowStateFilter {get;set;}
```

We can use this property like this:

VB.NET:

```
dataView.RowStateFilter = DataViewRowState.CurrentRows
Dim dvrs = dataView.RowStateFilter
```

C#:

```
dataView.RowStateFilter = DataViewRowState.CurrentRows;
DataViewRowState dvrs = dataView.RowStateFilter;
```

Valid states are part of the `DataViewRowState` enumeration. All allowable values are shown below:

DataViewRowState	Explanation
Added	Includes newly added rows.
CurrentRows	Includes all rows except deleted rows.
Deleted	Includes only deleted rows.
ModifiedCurrent	Includes any rows that have been modified. Any rows in a view with this filter will have the modified version of the data.
ModifiedOriginal	Includes the original version of rows that have been modified. Any rows in a view with this filter will have the original data and not the modified version.
None	Includes no rows at all.
OriginalRows	Includes the original version of all rows in the underlying table. That is, even if a row is modified only the original row data will be displayed.
Unchanged	Includes only rows that haven't been modified.

When we talk about modified rows, we mean the contents of the row have changed. A row that has been modified and then deleted is no longer considered modified – it is deleted. Deleted rows do not appear in views that only include modified rows.

We can combine filters to provide more complex views:

VB.NET:

```
dataView.RowStateFilter = DataViewRowState.Added or _
    DataViewRowState.Deleted
```

C#:

```
dataView.RowStateFilter = DataViewRowState.Added | DataViewRowState.Deleted;
```

This creates a view for us that can be used to view rows that have been added or deleted.

A few of the row states are mutually exclusive – it makes no sense to combine them. A list of some of these invalid combinations is shown below:

```
DataViewRowState.CurrentRows | DataViewRowState.OriginalRows
```

```
DataViewRowState.ModifiedCurrent | DataViewRowState.ModifiedOriginal

DataViewRowState.ModifiedCurrent | DataViewRowState.OriginalRows
```

This is in not an exhaustive list; there are many more combinations that cause the `DataView` to cry out! If you do attempt an invalid combination, then `DataView` will throw an exception to tell you what's wrong.

These filters need to be used carefully. Consider this example:

VB.NET:

```
m_userView.RowStateFilter = DataViewRowState.Deleted Or _
                            DataViewRowState.CurrentRows
```

C#:

```
m_userView.RowStateFilter = DataViewRowState.Deleted |
                            DataViewRowState.CurrentRows;
```

If we use this combination and delete a row, the row will continue to be present in the `DataView`. If we then try to delete that row again, the `DataView` will raise an exception, because it is already marked as deleted – it cannot be deleted again.

In a real world application, we would probably highlight any rows that had been deleted and stop the user trying to delete them twice. We would also need to catch the exception thrown if the user did try to delete a deleted row.

The Sort Property

Sets or gets a string defining the columns that `DataView` is sorted on, and the sort order. Similar to a SQL `ORDER BY` clause.

VB.NET:

```
Public Property Sort As String
```

C#:

```
public string Sort {get; set;}
```

Any `DataView` can be sorted on one or more columns in the underlying `DataTable`. To sort a `DataView` we'd write something like:

VB.NET:

```
dataView.Sort = "contactid"
```

This would sort the view based on the `contactid` column of the table. To sort on multiple columns we'd use:

VB.NET:

```
dataView.Sort = "contactname, companyname"
```

This will sort the view on the `contactname` and `companyname` columns. A comma must separate each column name in the sort string.

By default columns are sorted in ascending order. When defining the sort we could be explicit and append the string "ASC".

C#:

```
dataView.Sort = "contactid ASC";
dataView.Sort = "contactname, companyname ASC";
```

Similarly, to sort in descending order we append the string "DESC".

C#:

```
dataView.Sort = "contactid DESC";
dataView.Sort = "contactname, companyname DESC";
```

There is no validation on the sort string, so it's possible to specify columns that don't exist in the table. This doesn't cause an exception to be raised, so it's quite a simple error to miss. If we set filters on the view and they don't appear to work, it could be because the `Sort` property is invalid.

The Table Property

Sets or gets the `DataTable` that `DataView` is based on.

VB.NET:

```
Public Property Table As DataTable
```

C#:

```
public DataTable Table {get;set;}
```

Property usage:

VB.NET:

```
Dim t As DataTable = dataView.Table
dataView.Table = New DataTable()
```

C#:

```
DataTable t = dataView.Table;
dataView.Table = new DataTable();
```

This allows us to access the `DataTable`. If the view hasn't yet been associated with a table, then a null reference is returned. Otherwise a reference to the `DataTable` will be returned.

Refer to Chapter 8 for details of the `DataTable` object.

The IsOpen Property

Indicates whether the DataView currently has a DataTable associated with it, and is providing a view over the table.

VB.NET:

```
Protected ReadOnly Property IsOpen As Boolean
```

C#:

```
protected bool IsOpen {get;}
```

This property is only accessible to objects that inherit from the DataView object. The value of this property can only be altered by using the protected Open and Close methods.

The Site Property

The Site property gets or sets the ISite interface of the site where the DataView component may be sited.

VB.NET:

```
Overridable Public Property Site As ISite
```

C#:

```
public virtual ISite Site {get; set;}
```

VB.NET:

```
Dim site = dataView.Site
```

C#:

```
ISite site = dataView.Site;
```

The value returned from this property depends on whether the DataView has been sited, that is added to a container. If the view has not been added to the container, then a null reference will be returned. If the control has been added to a container then an ISite interface should be returned.

We would generally use this property to provide access to services and other components in the site.

The Container Property

The Container property returns an object implementing the IContainer interface representing the container that the DataView might have been added to.

VB.NET:

```
Overridable Public ReadOnly Property Container As IContainer
```

C#:

```
public virtual IContainer Container {get;}
```

VB.NET:

```
Dim container = dataView.Container
```

C#:

```
IContainer container = dataView.Container;
```

If the view has been added to a container, then this property will return an object implementing the IContainer interface, otherwise a null reference will be returned.

Using this property, we can add or remove components from the container.

The DesignMode Property

Returns a value indicating whether the DataView is in design mode.

VB.NET:

```
Overridable Public ReadOnly Property DesignMode As Boolean
```

C#:

```
public virtual bool DesignMode {get;}
```

This property indicates whether the component is currently in design mode. If the component hasn't been sited then this method always returns false.

This property is generally used at design time and doesn't have much use at run-time.

The Events Property

Gets the event handlers that have been subscribed to the DataView component.

VB.NET:

```
Protected ReadOnly Property Events As EventHandlerList
```

C#:

```
protected EventHandlerList Events {get;}
```

This property is only available to classes inherited from DataView. This property returns the contents of the events collection in the base class MarshalByValueComponent. Unless we expose some new events from the DataView object, which we then add to the base classes event collection, this property will usually only return the event handlers for the Disposed event (assuming any have been added).

VB.NET:

```
Dim eventHandler As EventHandlerList = this.Events
```

C#:

```
EventHandlerList eventHandler = this.Events
```

DataView Methods

The AddNew Method

Adds a new `DataRow` to the view's `DataTable`.

VB.NET:

```
Overridable Public Function AddNew() As DataRowView
```

C#:

```
public virtual DataRowView AddNew();
```

Before attempting to use this method, the `AllowNew` property must be set to `true`. If we don't, then an exception will be raised.

If the view is bound to a GU I object like in our application then we never need call this method. The framework takes care of everything.

If we wanted to use this method we'd write something like this:

VB.NET:

```
dataView.AllowEdit = True
Dim newRow As DataViewRow = dataView.AddNew()
newRow.BeginEdit()
newRow("contactid") = "OREC"
newRow.EndEdit()
```

C#:

```
dataView.AllowEdit = true;
DataViewRow newRow = dataView.AddNew();
newRow.BeginEdit();
newRow["contactid"] = "OREC";
newRow.EndEdit();
```

First of all, we make sure that `AllowEdit` is true. We then call the `AddNew` method that internally adds a new `DataRow` object to its `DataTable` and then wraps it in an object called a `DataViewRow`, this is then returned to us. We then call `BeginEdit` to let the row know we intend to alter its contents, we then set the `contactid` column, and finally, call `EndEdit` to confirm the changes.

If we were to write this code:

```
DataRowState rowState = newRow.Row.RowState;
```

Before calling `EndEdit`, we'd see that value is `Detached`. All rows that are added using the `AddNew` method are returned in a `Detached` state. This means that the row currently isn't part of the `DataTables` row collection. In order to make sure it's added to the collection, we must call `EndEdit`.

Note that if we set the `RowStateFilter` property to `DataViewRowState.Added`, then as soon as we call `AddNew`, the row will appear in the `DataView`. The row hasn't been added to the `DataTable` however until we call `EndEdit` (or add the row to the `DataTable` row collection directly).

The BeginInit Method

Called by the framework when the `DataView` is bound to a form or another component.

VB.NET:

```
NotOverridable Public Sub BeginInit()
```

C#:

```
public void BeginInit();
```

The framework uses this method to ensure that the bound form or component is fully initialized before it's used. This initialization is called at run time.

Internally, this method sets the `DataView` state to indicate that the controlling object is currently initializing. Any filters or sorts applied after `BeginInit` is called, but before `EndInit`, will not be applied until `EndInit` is called.

The EndInit Method

Called by the framework when the `DataView` is bound to a form or another component.

VB.NET:

```
NotOverridable Public Sub EndInit()
```

C#:

```
public void EndInit ();
```

This method notifies the `DataView` that the object that it is bound to has finished initializing.

This method sets its' state to indicate that the controlling object has finished initialization. Once this has occurred, then any filters or sorts that are required for the view are applied.

The Delete Method

Deletes a specified row from the `DataTable`.

VB.NET:

```
Public Sub Delete(ByVal index As Integer)
```

C#:

```
public void Delete(int index);
```

Method usage:

C#:

```
DataView.Delete (rowIndex);
```

Before calling this method, the `AllowDelete` property must be set to `true`. Calling `Delete` when this property isn't true will cause a `DataException`.

The row index must correspond to a valid row index, in other words a number between 0 and `DataView.Count`. For example:

VB.NET:

```
If (rowIndex >= 0 & rowIndex < DataView.Count) Then
    dataView.Delete(rowIndex)
End If
```

It's important to remember that the index being passed is the index of the row's location in the `DataView`, not the index of the row's location in the `DataTable`.

Any rows that are deleted have their state modified to `DataViewRowState.Deleted`. So, in the usual manner we can roll back any deletions by calling `RejectChanges` on the `DataTable`. This rolls back any changes made to the `DataTable`, since `AcceptChanges` was last called.

It's important to note that when we use `Delete` on a `DataView`, the actual entry in the `DataView` is removed completely. This means we can't write code like this:

C#:

```
dataView.Delete(3);
dataView[3].Row.RejectChanges();
```

This is deleting the row at index three, which marks the row for deletion in the `DataTable` and completely removes the row from the `DataView`. So when we call the `RejectChanges` on the row like this, one of two things will happen: we'll either reject any changes we've made to another row or get an exception, because there are no longer three rows in the `DataView`.

The Find Method

Finds a row in the `DataTable` with the specified primary key.

VB.NET:

```
Overloads Public Function Find(Object) As Integer
Overloads Public Function Find(Object()) As Integer
```

C#:

```
public int Find (object key);
public int Find (object[] keys);
```

The following examples illustrate how the `Find` method may be used:

VB.NET:

```
Dim rowNumber = dataView.Find(1)

Dim keys(2) As Object

keys(0) = 1
keys(1) = "DICKINSONP"

Dim rowNumber = dataView.Find(keys)
```

C#:

```
int rowNumber = dataView.Find(1);
object[] keys = new object[] {1, "DICKINSONP"};
rowNumber = dataView.Find(keys);
```

The main points of both these methods are:

❑ Both methods return the index of the row that matches the keys in the `DataView`. This is not the row index of the row in the `DataTable`.

❑ If no row matches the specified keys then –1 is returned by both methods.

The find method has two implementations, one takes a single `Object` that represents a key, the second takes an array of `Objects` that represents multiple keys. Both methods take `Objects`, because a database's primary key can be of any type, and the `Find` method must support this.

This flexibility means that we must be careful. When we pass an object or objects to these methods, they must either match the column type or be able to safely cast to the column type. If the table is sorted on a column of type `long`, then we must either pass through a `long`, another numeric that can be safely cast to a `long`, or a `string`. The method will convert a string to a long if required.

The following example illustrates this, where USER_ID is numeric:

```
dataView.Sort = "USER_ID";    // sort on a numeric column
int rowIndex = dataView.Find ( 5 );    // ok, we've passed a numeric value
rowIndex = dataView.Find ( "5" ); // ok, a string representing a numeric
rowIndex = dataView.Find ( "DICKINSONP" );    // exception thrown, can't
                                               // cast to a numeric value
```

The first two method calls are fine. The third method call can't convert the string "DICKINSONP" into a numeric value, so it will cause an exception.

If the user is able to control the `Sort` property of the `DataView` – say through the column headings of a `DataGrid` – it is necessary to check what columns the data is being sorted on before performing the Find. It is also easy to forget how the table is being sorted if the table has one or more primary keys, we haven't explicitly set a sort and we've set `ApplyDefaultSort` to true. Awareness of these issues should enable you to avoid many common pitfalls.

The following example sorts the table on the numeric column USER_ID and then attempts to find the user with ID 5.

VB.NET:

```
"_"dataView.Sort = "USER_ID"
int rowIndex = dataView.Find(5)
```

C#:

```
dataView.Sort = "USER_ID";
int rowIndex = dataView.Find(5);
```

Let's look at a slightly more complex example using the `Find(object[])` method:

VB.NET:

```
dataView.Sort = "USER_ID, USER_NAME"
Dim FindArray As Object(2)
FindArray(0) = 1
FindArray(1) = "DICKINSONP"
Dim rowIndex As Integer = dataView.Find (FindArray);
```

C#:

```
dataView.Sort = "USER_ID, USER_NAME";
int rowIndex = dataView.Find ( new object[] {1, "DICKINSONP"} );
```

This sets the view to sort first on the USER_ID column and then the USER_NAME column. The `Find` method then takes an object array containing the values 1 and "DICKINSONP". The values correspond to the USER_ID and USER_NAME column respectively.

The order of the values in the object array must match the order of the columns in the default sort. If they do not, then you will get either undesired search results or an exception as the runtime tries to cast your objects to invalid types.

The GetEnumerator Method

Provides an enumerator to iterate over the views DataRowView objects.

VB.NET:

```
NotOverridable Public Function GetEnumerator() As IEnumerator
```

C#:

```
public IEnumerator GetEnumerator ();
```

This is one of those methods that we very rarely call directly. Generally, we'll let the framework call `GetEnumerator` in the `foreach` statement.

The following example shows how we'd iterate over each DataRowView object in the DataView. What we actually do with the object is then up to us. In the example, the contents of the object is printed out.

C#:

```
foreach (DataRowView dataRowView in dataView)
{
    int numCols = dataView.Table.Columns.Count;

    for (int colIndex = 0; colIndex < numCols; colIndex++)
    {
        Console.WriteLine(dataRowView [ colIndex ]);
    }
}
```

If the DataView contains no DataRowView, then content of the `foreach` loop will not be executed.

The Open Method

The Open method opens the DataView and begins presenting a view over the DataViews ~ object's table.

VB.NET:

```
Protected Sub Open()
```

C#:

```
protected void Open();
```

Before using this method, a DataTable must have been associated with the DataView. The method refreshes the internal row cache that the DataView maintains and raises a ListChanged event.

This method is protected so it can only be called in derived classes. Deriving a class from DataView and including the following method would allow other objects to call the Open method. It's not generally a good idea to expose the Open method to the world, but this is how we could:

C#:

```
public void ExposeOpen ()
{
    base.Open ();
}
```

If this method is bound to a GUI object, such as a DataGrid, then the DataGrid will be able to display the view.

The Close Method

The Close method closes the DataView and stops the view being presented over the view's DataTable.

VB.NET:

```
Protected Sub Close()
```

C#:

```
protected void Close();
```

We could expose this protected method in the following way:

C#:

```
public void ExposeClose ()
{
    if (base.IsOpen)
        base.Close ();
}
```

This example ensures that the view is open before attempting to perform the close. This destroys the DataView object's internal row cache, which stops the view being presented. If this view were bound to a control such as a DataGrid, calling this method would clear the contents of the grid.

The ColumnCollectionChanged Method

The `ColumnCollectionChanged` method is called when the underlying `DataTable` changes. It is a protected method, but by defining our own subclass of `DataView`, we can override the default with a custom handler.

VB.NET:

```
Overridable Protected Sub ColumnCollectionChanged(ByVal sender As Object, _
                    ByVal e As CollectionChangeEventArgs)
```

C#:

```
protected virtual void ColumnCollectionChanged(object sender,
CollectionChangeEventArgs e);
```

The following code demonstrates how to override this method in a derived class:

C#:

```
override protected void ColumnCollectionChanged(object sender,
CollectionChangeEventArgs e)
{
      // place your code in here
}
```

Parameter	Type	Description
sender	object	The object that raised the event
E	CollectionChangeEventArgs	The event arguments for the collection object

The default implementation of this method raises the `ListChanged` event by calling the protected method `OnListChanged`.

This method is an ideal place to restrict which changes raise the `ListChanged` event. If we take the example where we have a table named "User" containing columns, such as user name, password, and permissions. These are details that need to be stored in the database even when the user isn't logged in to our application. There are some details that are definitely only stored at run time though, perhaps a session cookie. To store this session cookie we may add a runtime only column to the user table called "SESSION". The SESSION value will be meaningless in most applications, therefore it seems reasonable not to raise a ListChanged event just because this column has been added. We may write something like this:

C#:

```
override protected void ColumnCollectionChanged (object sender,
CollectionChangeEventArgs e)
{
      DataColumn dc = (DataColumn) e.Element;

      if (dc.ColumnName != "SESSION")
            base.ColumnCollectionChanged(sender, e);
}
```

Of course we can write more sophisticated methods here. For example we may wish to raise different events depending on the details of the change. The above code demonstrates the principle.

The IndexListChanged Method

The IndexListChanged executes when the data in a DataView changes – when a row is changed, added, or removed.

VB.NET:

```
Overridable Protected Sub IndexListChanged(ByVal sender As Object, _
                                ByVal e As ListChangedEventArgs)
```

C#:

```
protected virtual void IndexListChanged (object sender,
                            ListChangedEventArgs e);
```

The following code demonstrates how to override this method in a subclass of DataView:

C#:

```
override protected void IndexListChanged (object sender, ListChangedEventArgs e)
{
    // your code here
}
```

The parameters are as follows:

Parameter	Type	Description
sender	object	The object that raised the event.
E	ListChangedEventArgs	The event arguments for the list object. From this we can work out how the list was modified.

The default implementation causes the ListChanged event to be raised by calling OnListChanged.

If all work with data is done through a DataView, then this method might be quite a good place to add some auditing facility. We might write something like:

C#:

```
override protected void IndexListChanged(object sender,
ListChangedEventArgs e)
{
    string auditLog = "";
    switch(e.ListChangedType)
    {
        case ListChangedType.ItemAdded:
            auditLog = "New item added. Index : " +
            e.NewIndex.ToString();
```

```
            break;

        case ListChangedType.ItemChanged:
              auditLog = "Row modified. Old index : " +
              e.OldIndex.ToString() + " new index : " +
            e.NewIndex.ToString();
        break;

        default:
              auditLog = "Unknown modification.";
        break;
    }
    SignLog(auditLog);
}
```

This simple example shows how we might create a text log each time the DataView content changes. The imaginary SignLog method might show the user the log entry and get them to electronically sign it. There are a lot more enumerated values in the ListChangedType enumeration than shown here, so we could implement more powerful handling here.

The OnListChanged Method

The OnListChanged method raises the ListChanged event.

VB.NET:

```
Overridable Protected Sub OnListChanged(ByVal e As ListChangedEventArgs)
```

C#:

```
protected virtual void OnListChanged(ListChangedEventArgs e);
```

Method usage:

C#:

```
override protected void OnListChanged(ListChangedEventArgs e)
{
    // new code here
}
```

This method is called when the internal cache of the DataView is modified. In this method, we can choose whether or not we wish to raise an event to indicate that the cache has altered. The default implementation will raise the ListChanged event.

It's possible to be skeptical about the usefulness of overriding this method. If the DataView is bound to a DataGrid and we delete a row from the grid, then our overridden OnListChanged isn't called. Instead, the protected UpdateIndex method explicitly calls the OnListChanged method of the base class – it completely bypasses our method. As a matter of fact, the only action that seems to call our method from the DataGrid is that of adding a new row. Editing a row causes the OnListChanged method of the base class to be called as well.

So, if you override this method and find it's not been called when you expect, then that's probably why.

The Reset Method

The Reset method causes the DataView row cache to reset itself.

VB.NET:

```
Protected Sub Reset()
```

C#:

```
protected void Reset();
```

Calling this method when the IsOpen property is false has no effect on the view contents. Otherwise, the method resets the rows that the view has stored in its internal cache.

As this is a protected method if we wish to call it from another object we must create a DataView subclass and include a new method to expose the Reset method:

C#:

```
public void ExposeReset()
{
    base.Reset();
}
```

The UpdateIndex Method

The UpdateIndex method is called internally when a view state alters.

VB.NET:

```
Protected Sub UpdateIndex()

Overridable Protected Sub UpdateIndex(force As Boolean)
```

C#:

```
protected void UpdateIndex();

protected virtual void UpdateIndex(bool force);
```

The DataView maintains an internal index of the records it's currently displaying. This method ensures that the index is kept in sync with any changes made to the view. Generally, we should never need to use this method directly – it's called internally when the view state alters. This might be because of a new filter or sort, or the view being opened.

There are two implementations of the method. To expose the parameter less method we could write:

C#

```
public void ExposeUpdateIndex()
{
    base.UpdateIndex();
}
```

This causes the view's index to update if the view is currently closed, but a request to open the view has been made. This method simply calls UpdateIndex(false).

523

The second implementation of `UpdateIndex` takes a `bool` value. In order to use it we could write:

VB.NET:
```
Public Sub ExposeUpdateIndex(ByVal force As Boolean)
    Me.UpdateIndex(force)
End Sub
```

If we pass true to this method the internal index will be updated if either of these conditions are true:

❑ The view is already open but a request has been made to open the view again

❑ The view is currently closed but a request has been made to open the view

Passing false is functionally equivalent to using the parameter less method.

It's possible to override the `UpdateIndex(bool)` method, but I'd be very wary about doing this. Classes internal to the .net framework use this method in several places. Obviously, it's important that the method behaves as these classes expect. If you are curious, have a look at the `RelatedView` class in the `System.Data` namespace. The class is private so you'll have to delve in to IL to see how it uses the `UpdateIndex(bool)` method.

The Dispose Method

Disposes of resources that the `DataView` is using.

VB.NET:
```
Overloads Overrides Public Sub Dispose()
Overloads Overridable Protected Sub Dispose(Boolean)
```

C#:
```
public override void Dispose();
protected virtual void Dispose(bool);
```

This method explicitly disposes both the components own resources and any other resources that it may be using.

VB.NET:
```
dataView.Dipose(False)
```

C#:
```
dataView.Dispose ();
```

The above example would only release the components own resources; this is useful if the component is sharing unmanaged resources with other components. Obviously, we wouldn't want to destroy resources that are still in use elsewhere. Calling this method with true is the equivalent of calling the `Dispose` method with no parameters.

The GetService Method

Attempts to return a service from the components site.

VB.NET:
```
Overridable Public Function GetService(ByVal service As Type) _
                              As Object
```

C#:
```
public virtual object GetService(Type service);
```

The default implementation of this method in `MarshalByValueComponent` attempts to return the requested service from the `DataView` object's container (or **site** as it's more properly known). This being the case, unless the `GetService` method is overridden, a null reference will always be returned unless the `DataView` has been added to a container that provides the requested service.

The following example illustrates how we might use the `GetService` method. To start with we create a `Container` object and then add the `DataView` to the container. This sets the container as the site for the `DataView`. Finally, we use `GetService` to request a service of type `IContainer`, and this returns us the `IContainer` interface for the `DataView` object's site.

C#:
```
System.ComponentModel.Container container = new Container();
container.Add(dataView);
IContainer iCont = (IContainer) dataView.GetService(typeof(IContainer));
```

The `GetService` method can be used to retrieve any service that the `DataViews'` container (site) implements. If a service is requested that the container doesn't implement, then a null reference is returned.

Adding the `DataView` to a `Container` object is of questionable use, because it's a very simple class that has no database specific services. To do something more meaningful, we'd derive our own class from `Container` and then implement a more useful interface on this class. We could then add the `DataView` to our own container class and use `GetService` to request our own interfaces.

DataView Events

In this section, we'll go through the events found on the `DataView` object.

The Disposed Event

The `Disposed` event is raised when the `DataView` object is disposed of.

VB.NET:
```
NotOverridable Public Event Disposed As EventHandler
```

C#:
```
public event EventHandler Disposed;
```

C#:

```
dataView.Disposed += new EventHandler(DisposedHandler);
```

This method can be used to notify subscribers that the component has been disposed of. In order for the `Disposed` event to be raised, the `DataView` must have been added to a container, that is its `Site` property must be returning a value other than a null reference.

The code below illustrates the steps taken to cause the event to be raised:

C#:

```
Container container = new Container();
container.Add(dataView);
dataView.Disposed += new EventHandler(DisposedEvent);
dataView.Dispose();
```

The code above creates a new container control and adds the `DataView` to its collection of components. We then register an event handler for the `Disposed` event, this will be called when the `DataView` is disposed of. Finally, we call the `Dispose method`, which will cause the `Disposed` event to be raised.

In order to handle the event, our event handler would look like this:

C#

```
private void DisposedEvent(object sender, EventArgs args)
{
    // some useful code
}
```

What we do in the event handler is up to us. It's often useful to perform some additional housekeeping in response to this event.

The ListChanged Event

The `ListChanged` Event is raised when the `DataView object's` row cache changes.

VB.NET:

```
NotOverridable Public Event ListChanged As ListChangedEventHandler
```

C#:

```
public event ListChangedEventHandler ListChanged;
```

If the `OnListChangedMethod` hasn't been overridden in order to stop this event being raised, this event should be raised every time a row or column is removed or added.

To cause the event to be raised we'd write something like this:

C#:

```
dataView.ListChanged += new ListChangedEventHandler(ListChangedHandler);
dataView.Delete(0);
```

The code above registers the event handler and then deletes the first row from the view. Of course, the DataView must be associated with a DataTable containing at least one row. Our event handler would look something like this:

C#:

```
private void ListChangedHandler ( object sender, ListChangedEventArgs args )
{
    // something useful here
}
```

Through the `ListChangedEventArgs` parameter we can find out how the list was modified and what row in particular was affected.

The DataViewManager Object

In the following section, we're going to take a look at using the `DataViewManager`. As we've seen already, a `DataView` corresponds to a single `DataTable`. The `DataViewManager` works with many `DataTables`, which must be contained in a `DataSet`. The key differences and points between the `DataView` and the `DataViewManager` object are:

❑   The `DataViewManager` provides a view per `DataTable` stored in a `DataSet`

❑   We set properties on a view contained in the `DataViewManager` using the `DataViewSetting` object

❑   The `DataViewManager` has a `DataViewSetting` object for each `DataTable` in the `DataSet`

❑   The `DataViewSetting` objects are contained in a `DataViewSettingCollection` object

The `DataViewManager` doesn't provide more than one view per table. In other words, we can't have two or three views in the `DataViewManager` for a single `DataTable`.

In this section, we'll modify our little application to use a `DataViewManager` instead of a `DataView`. The `DataViewManager` shares the same `System.Data` namespace with the `DataView`.

DataViewManager Constructors

There are two constructors for the `DataViewManager` object.

VB.NET:

```
Public Sub New()
Public Sub New(DataSet)
```

C#:

```
public DataViewManager();
public DataViewManager ( DataSet );
```

The parameterless constructor allows us to create a `DataViewManager` without having a `DataSet` object first. Before we can use the `DataViewManager` However ,we need to associate it with a `DataSet` object. Passing a `DataSet` through to a `DataViewManager` constructor returns an object that we can use for managing views straight away.

If you're following the example, we'll now add a `DataViewManager` to our application. We'll also need to create a `DataSet` to hold our `USERS` table.

So, let's add these two new members first.

VB.NET:

```
Private m_dataSet As DataSet
Private m_dvm as DataViewManager
```

C#:

```
private DataSet m_dataSet;
private DataViewManager m_dvm;
```

Now we have to create them in our constructors, so add this code (in VB this code will be inside the **Windows Forms Generated Code** region):

VB.NET:

```
Public Sub New()
     ' code omitted for brevity
   BuildTable()

     ' create the DataSet object
   m_ds = New DataSet()

     ' create the DataViewManager object with the DataSet
   m_dvm = New DataViewManager(m_ds)

   End Sub
```

C#:

```
public Form1()
{
    // code omitted for brevity
    BuildTable();

    // create the DataSet object
    m_ds = new DataSet();

    // create the DataViewManager with the DataSet
    m_dvm = new DataViewManager(m_ds);
}
```

Now we've created a `DataViewManager` object and associated it with a `DataSet`. In order to make the `DataViewManager` useful, we now need to add our table to the `DataSet`. So add this code just beneath the code we've added.

VB.NET:

```
m_ds.Tables.Add ( m_userTable )
```

C#:

```
m_ds.Tables.Add ( m_userTable );
```

Finally, we just need to bind this `DataViewManager` to the `DataGrids`, so find the button click handler and replace any code in there with this:

VB.NET:

```
DataGrid1.SetDataBinding(m_dvm, "USERS")
DataGrid2.SetDataBinding(m_dvm, "USERS")
```

C#:

```
dataGrid1.SetDataBinding ( m_dvm, "USERS" );
dataGrid2.SetDataBinding ( m_dvm, "USERS" );
```

Notice that we're passing the name of the `DataTable` through as the second parameter. This is because we need to explicitly tell the `DataGrid` which table in the `DataViewManager` we want to view. This is necessary because the `DataViewManager` can have many views (dependent on the number of `DataTables` in its `DataSet`).

If you build and run the application you should see both `DataGrids` fill up with exactly the same information. This is obviously because we only have one table and both grids are using that data.

In order to illustrate how the `DataViewManager` works with multiple tables, we'll add a bit more code. We'll first of all duplicate the original table, then rename it and then alter its contents.

VB.NET:

```
Private Function CopyTable ()

    ' make a copy of the table
    Dim copiedTable = m_userTable.Copy ()

    ' rename the table
    copiedTable.TableName = "USERS_2"

    ' now modify some of its' data
    copiedTable.Rows(0)("customerid") = "BARNS"
    copiedTable.Rows(0)("companyname") = "Barnes Co."
    copiedTable.Rows(0)("contactname") = "David Barnes"
    copiedTable.Rows(0)("city") = "Birmingham"

    ' customize any more rows as you wish
    ' .....

    'finally add the table to the dataset
    m_ds.Tables.Add ( copiedTable )

End Function
```

C#:

```
private void CopyTable ()
{
    // make a copy of the table
    DataTable copiedTable = m_userTable.Copy ();

    // rename the table
    copiedTable.TableName = "USERS_2";

    // now modify some of its' data
    copiedTable.Rows[0]["customerid"] = "BARNS";
    copiedTable.Rows[0]["companyname"] = "Barnes Co.";
    copiedTable.Rows[0]["contactname"] = "David Barnes";
    copiedTable.Rows[0]["city"] = "Birmingham";

    // customize any more rows as you wish
    // .....

    //add the table to the dataset
    m_ds.Tables.Add ( copiedTable );
}
```

In the code above we started by taking a copy of the table. This copies the schema and contents of the table. We've then renamed the table to "USERS_2". Next, we change the contents of row 0, you can do this for all the rows in the table if you wish – simply increment the number in brackets. Finally, we've added the copied table to the DataSet. This means we now have two DataTables to view.

Call this new CopyTable method in your constructor after the code that adds m_userTable to the DataSet.

Now all that's left is to bind this new DataTable to the second grid in our GUI. So find the button click handler and replace the line:

C#:

```
dataGrid2.SetDataBinding ( m_dvm, "USERS" );
```

With:

C#:

```
dataGrid2.SetDataBinding ( m_dvm, "USERS_2" );
```

Run the application. When you click on the button, you should now see the top data grid showing the original USERS table showing the USERS_2 table.

This illustrates how we can dynamically add DataTables to the DataSet, and how the DataViewManager will provide us with a view for that table straight away.

DataViewManager Properties

In this section, we'll discuss the properties of the `DataViewManager`.

The DataSet Property

The `DataSet` property returns the `DataSet` object associated with the `DataViewManager`.

VB.NET:

```
Public Property DataSet As DataSet
```

C#:

```
public DataSet DataSet {get; set;}
```

VB.NET:

```
Dim dataSet = dataViewManager.DataSet
dataViewManager.DataSet = dataSet
```

C#:

```
DataSet dataSet = dataViewManager.DataSet;
dataViewManager.DataSet = dataSet;
```

Before a `DataViewManager` object can be used, it needs to be associated with a `DataSet` object. If the intention isn't to bind a control to the `DataViewManager`, but to use it to create `DataViews`, using the `CreateDataView` method then it isn't necessary for the `DataSet` to contain any tables.

It's fine to associate the `DataSet` with the `DataViewManager` and add tables to the `DataSet` later on, just prior to binding the `DataViewManager` to a control.

VB.NET:

```
Private Function BindTable(ByVal dataTable As DataTable, _
                           ByVal dataGrid As DataGrid)

    ' create the new dataset
    Dim dataSet = New DataSet()

    ' create a new view manager
    Dim dvm = New DataViewManager()

    ' associate the DataSet with our view manager
    dvm.DataSet = dataSet

    ' add the table to the dataset
    dvm.DataSet.Tables.Add(dataTable)

    ' now bind the view to the dataset
    dataGrid.SetDataBinding(dvm, dataTable.TableName)
End Function
```

C#:

```
private void BindTable(DataTable dataTable, DataGrid dataGrid)
{
    // create the new dataset
    DataSet dataSet = new DataSet();

    // create a new view manager
    DataViewManager dvm = new DataViewManager();

    // associate the DataSet with our view manager
    dvm.DataSet = dataSet;

    // add the table to the dataset
    dvm.DataSet.Tables.Add(dataTable);

    // now bind the view to the dataset
    dataGrid.SetDataBinding(dvm, dataTable.TableName);
}
```

This simple example illustrates how we can bind a DataViewManager to a DataGrid and then add tables to the DataSet property of the DataViewManager. Most of the code is self-explanatory except the DataGrid.SetDataBinding method call, which we will look at now. The first parameter is the DataViewManager object, the second the name of the table. This is because unlike the DataView object, which is for a specific table, the DataViewManager deals with views for one or many tables. When we bind to the DataGrid we need to tell it which table in the DataViewManager (or more accurately the DataSet) we wish to view.

The DataViewSettingCollectionString Property

The DataViewSettingCollectionString property returns an XML representation of the DataViewSettings collection belonging to the DataViewManager.

VB.NET:

```
Public Property DataViewSettingCollectionString As String
```

C#:

```
public string DataViewSettingCollectionString {get; set;}
```

VB.NET:

```
StringViewSettingXML = dataViewManager.DataViewSettingsCollectionString
```

This method is used for persisting the DataView. When called it will return an XML string similar to this:

XML:

```
<DataViewSettingCollectionString>
    <People Sort="ID" RowFilter="AGE>'23'" RowStateFilter="CurrentRows"/>
    <Addresses Sort="" RowFilter="" RowStateFilter="CurrentRows"/>
</DataViewSettingCollectionString>
```

In this particular `DataViewManager` we have two tables: `People` and `Addresses`. We can see that the `People` table is sorted on `ID`, is filtered to display only people older than 23, and is displaying rows with the current row status.

The DataViewSettings Property

The `DataViewSettings` property returns a `DataViewSettingCollection` object.

VB.NET:

```
Public ReadOnly Property DataViewSettings As DataViewSettingCollection
```

C#:

```
public DataViewSettingCollection DataViewSettings {get;}
```

C#:

```
DataViewSettingCollection dvsc = dataViewManager.DataViewSettings;
```

The collection returned contains all the settings for each view on each table stored in the `DataSet` associated with the `DataViewManager`. If there are no `DataTables` in the associated `DataSet` then the collection returned will have no items.

We may use this property like this:

VB.NET:

```
Dim dvs As DataViewSetting
For Each dvs In dataViewManager.DataViewSettings
    dvs.Sort = GetTablesPrimaryKey(dvs.Table)
Next
```

The code would sort each view on the table's primary key. It does this by iterating over the settings for each of the `DataTables` and then calling an imaginary method that returns a string containing the table's primary key.

As well as giving us the ability to iterate over the settings for each table, we can also use the collections indexer (the `Item` property). Let's look at a brief example of this:

VB.NET:

```
m_dvm.DataViewSettings("USERS").Sort = " companyname"
```

C#:

```
m_dvm.DataViewSettings["USERS"].Sort = "companyname";
```

The example uses the `Item` property (which is the default property for a collection so we don't need to name it) to access the `DataViewSettings` for a specific table in the `DataSet`. It then sets the `USERS` table to sort on `companyname`. Using `DataViewSettings` and the indexer, we can get at all the settings for the view and customize it as we wish.

The above example is equivalent to writing:

```
dataView.Sort = " companyname";
```

With a `DataView`, we have direct access to the settings and with a `DataViewManager` we have to go through the `DataViewSettings` collection to access the settings that we require.

The Container Property

Refer to the `DataView` `Container` property for more information on this property.

The DesignMode Property

Refer to the `DataView` `DesignMode` property for more information on this property.

The Site Property

Refer to the `DataView` `Site` property for more information on this property.

The Events Property

Refer to the `DataView` `Events` property for more information on this property.

DataViewManager Methods

This section will illustrate the methods of the `DataViewManager` object.

The CreateDataView Method

The `CreateDataView` method creates a `DataView` for a given `DataTable`.

VB.NET:
```
Public Function CreateDataView(ByVal table As DataTable) As DataView
```

C#:
```
public DataView CreateDataView(DataTable table);
```

We can use it in the following way:

VB.NET:
```
Dim dataView = dataViewManager.CeateDataView(dataTable)
```

C#:
```
DataView dataView = dataViewManager.CreateDataView(dataTable);
```

The returned object is a fully initialized `DataView` with default settings. It can be used as soon as it's created.

Using this method doesn't alter the `DataViewManager` state in any way. It simply creates a new `DataView` object and passes it back to us. The new `DataViewSettings` for the table aren't added to the `DataViewSettingCollection` and the table isn't added to the `DataSet`. I highlight this because it's easy to think something complicated is going on under the covers. If you try to use this method without having set the `DataSet` property, then an exception is thrown. This is strange, since the `DataSet` isn't used in any way to create the new `View`.

The OnListChanged Method

The `OnListChanged` method is called when either the `DataTable` or `DataRelation` collection of the `DataSet` changes.

VB.NET:

```
Overridable Protected Sub OnListChanged(ByVal e As ListChangedEventArgs)
```

C#:

```
protected virtual void OnListChanged(ListChangedEventArgs e);
```

This method is only available to classes inherited from `DataViewManager`. The default implementation raises the `ListChanged` event to notify event subscribers that one of the `DataSet` collections has altered.

The RelationCollectionChanged Method

Called when the `DataRelation` of the `DataSet` collection changes.

VB.NET:

```
Overridable Protected Sub RelationCollectionChanged( _
                          ByVal sender As Object, _
                          ByVal e As CollectionChangeEventArgs )
```

C#:

```
protected virtual void RelationCollectionChanged(object sender,
                          CollectionChangeEventArgs e);
```

This method is only available to classes inherited from `DataViewManager`. The default implementation calls the `OnListChanged` method. To cause this method to be called, we could write something like this:

VB.NET:

```
Dim dvm As new DataViewManager(dataSet)
Dim dr As New DataRelation("test", _
                          userTable.Columns("contactid"), _
                          backupTable.Columns("contactid_ref"))
dataSet.Relations.Add(dr)
```

Again, if we removed a `DataRelation` from the `DataSet` relations collection, then this method would be called.

The TableCollectionChanged Method

Called when the `DataSets` object's `DataTable` collection changes.

VB.NET:

```
Overridable Protected Sub TableCollectionChanged(ByVal sender As
Object, _
                         ByVal e As CollectionChangeEventArgs)
```

C#:

```
protected virtual void TableCollectionChanged(object sender,
                            CollectionChangeEventArgs e );
```

This method is only available to classes inherited from inherited `DataViewManager`. The default implementation calls the `OnListChanged` method.

C#:

```
DataViewManager dvm = new DataViewManager(dataSet);
dataSet.Tables.Remove("USERS");
```

The above example removes the `USERS` `DataTable` from the `DataViewManagers` `DataSet`. This would cause the `TableCollectionChanged` method to be called. Adding a new `DataTable` to the `DataSet` would also call the method.

The GetService Method

Refer to the `DataView` `GetService` method for more information on this method.

The Dispose Method

Refer to the `DataView` `Dispose` method for more information on this method.

DataViewManager Events

This section will cover the events of the `DataViewManager` object.

The Disposed Event

Refer to the `DataView` `Disposed` event for more information on this event.

The ListChanged Event

The `ListChanged` event is raised when either the `DataSets'` `DataTable` or `DataRelation` collections change.

VB.NET:
```
NotOverridable Public Event ListChanged As _
                                    ListChangedEventHandler
```

C#:
```
public event ListChangedEventHandler ListChanged;
```

In the default implementation this event is raised by the `OnListChanged` method, which in turn is called by either of the `TableCollectionChanged` or `RelationCollectionChanged` methods.

To subscribe to the event we'd write this:

C#:
```
dataViewManager.ListChanged += new ListChangedEventHandler (MyHandler)
```

Where the actual handler for the method would look like this:

C#:
```
private void MyHandler (object sender, ListChangedEventArgs args)
```

In the handler, we'd use the `args` parameter to work out how the list had changed.

The DataViewSetting Object

In order to allow customization of the views in the `DataViewManager`, we use this `DataViewSetting` object rather than using a `DataView` object directly. As we'll see, this object's properties are very similar to those on the `DataView` object, and we will frequently refer back to them.

In order to access these objects, we use the `DataViewSettings` property on the `DataViewManager`.

The following code will return a `DataViewSetting` object containing the settings for the `Users` table:

C#:
```
DataViewSetting dvs = m_dvm.DataViewSettings["USERS"];
```

By using the properties of the returned object we'll be able to customize the view in the same way we'd customize a `DataView` object.

DataViewSetting Constructors

We can't create a `DataViewSetting` directly; we have to use the `DataViewSettings` property on the `DataViewManager` object.

VB.NET:
```
Dim dvs As dataViewManager.DataViewSetting("USERS")
```

C#:
```
DataViewSetting dvs = dataViewManager.DataViewSetting["USERS"];
```

This will give us the `DataViewSetting` object for the `People` table.

DataViewSetting Properties

This section will discuss the properties of the `DataViewSetting` object. Most properties correspond to properties on the `DataView` object so I'll refer you back to them.

The ApplyDefaultSort Property

See the `ApplyDefaultSort` property on the `DataView` for more information.

The DataViewManager Property

The `DataViewManager` property returns the `DataViewManager` object that was used to create the `DataViewSetting`.

VB.NET:
```
Public ReadOnly Property DataViewManager As DataViewManager
```

C#:
```
public DataViewManager DataViewManager {get;}
```

We can call the method in the following way:

```
DataViewManager dvm = dataViewSetting.DataViewManager;
```

There's no way of creating a `DataViewSetting` object without using a `DataViewManager` so a valid object (in other words not a null reference) should always be returned.

The RowFilter Property

See the `RowFilter` property on the `DataViewManager` object for more information.

The RowStateFilter Property

See the `RowStateFilter` property on the `DataViewManager` object for more information.

The Sort Property

See the `Sort` property on the `DataViewManager` object for more information.

The Table Property

See the `Table` property on the `DataViewManager` object for more information.

DataViewSetting Methods

The DataViewSetting object only possesses methods inherited methods from object, which will not be covered here.

The DataViewSettingCollection Object

Each `DataTable` stored in the `DataSet` associated with the `DataViewManager` has a `DataViewSetting` object associated with its view. In order to manage these objects, the `DataViewManager` uses the `DataViewSettingCollection` object.

The contents of this collection object are managed internally, we can only enumerate over the collection – we can't modify it in any way.

DataViewSettingCollection Constructors

There are no public constructors for the `DataViewSettingCollection`. The `DataViewSettings` property on the `DataViewManager` is a `DataViewSettingCollection` object.

DataViewSettingCollection Properties

This section will deal with the properties on the `DataViewSettingCollection` object.

The Count Property

The Count property returns the number of `DataViewSetting` objects currently in the collection.

VB.NET:
```
Overridable Public ReadOnly Property Count As Integer
```

C#:
```
public virtual int Count {get;}
```

We could use this in the following way:

C#:
```
int count = dataViewManager.DataViewSettings.Count;
```

There is a `DataViewSetting` object for each DataTable in the `DataSet` associated with the `DataViewManager`.

The IsReadOnly Property

The IsReadOnly property returns a value indicating whether the DataViewSettingCollection is read-only. For a DataViewSettingCollection it will always return true.

VB.NET:

```
Public ReadOnly Property IsReadOnly As Boolean
```

C#:

```
public bool IsReadOnly {get;}
```

The DataViewSettingCollection is readonly – we can't add or remove objects from the collection. The collections contents are maintained internally. This being the case IsReadOnly always returns true.

The Item Property

The Item property returns a specified DataViewSetting object from the collection.

VB.NET:

```
Overloads Overridable Public Default Property Item(DataTable) _
                                                As DataViewSetting
Overloads Overridable Public Default ReadOnly Property Item(String) _
                                                As DataViewSetting
Overloads Overridable Public Default Property Item(Integer) _
                                                As DataViewSetting
```

C#:

```
public virtual DataViewSetting this[DataTable] {get; set;}
public virtual DataViewSetting this[string] {get;}
public virtual DataViewSetting this[int] {get; set;}
```

The following examples, show how we can retrieve the DataViewSetting object using its index, the table it's been created for or the name of the table. We can choose the one most suitable to our needs.

VB.NET:

```
Dm dvs = dataViewManager.DataViewSettings(0)
dvs = dataViewManager.DataViewSettings(dataTable)
dvs = dataViewManager.DataViewSettings("USERS")
```

C#:

```
DataViewSetting dvs = dataViewManager.DataViewSettings[0];
dvs = dataViewManager.DataViewSettings[dataTable];
dvs = dataViewManager.DataViewSettings["USERS"];
```

If we know the index of the table in the DataSets' Tables collection then we can use that to retrieve its' settings:

C#:

```
DataViewSetting dvs = dataViewManager.DataViewSettings [ 0 ];
```

Another way of getting the `DataViewSettings` is to pass through the `DataTable` object that you want the settings for.

VB.NET:

```
Dim dvs = dataViewManager.DataViewSettings ( dataTable )
```

There's a word of caution here though. If we pass a `DataTable` object that doesn't exist in the `DataViewSettingCollection`, we will still get returned a `DataViewSetting` object. This can be a little confusing: if we ask for an object from a collection we don't expect one to be created and returned if it doesn't already exist. In this case, however, the `DataViewManager` creates a `DataViewSetting` object for our table, adds it to the `DataViewSettingCollection` and then returns it to us.

This leads me onto the last way of getting `DataTable` settings from this property – by using the name of the table.

VB.NET:

```
Dim dvs = dataViewManager.DataViewSettings("USERS")
```

If we want to make sure that we're getting the data view settings for the correct table then this indexer can be most useful. We pass the name of the table, in this case `USER`, and if the table doesn't exist in the `DataSet`, then a null reference is returned, otherwise we get the appropriate `DataViewSetting` object.

The IsSynchronized Property

The `IsSynchronized` property returns a value indicating whether the collection is synchronized in other words thread-safe.

VB.NET:

```
Public ReadOnly Property IsSynchronized As Boolean
```

C#:

```
public bool IsSynchronized {get;}
```

The default implementation always returns false indicating that the collection is not thread-safe. This shouldn't be a problem however, because the `DataViewManager` maintains the collection internally.

The SyncRoot Property

The `SyncRoot` property returns an object that we can use to synchronize access to the `DataViewSettingCollection`.

VB.NET:

```
Public ReadOnly Property SyncRoot As Object
```

C#:

```
public object SyncRoot {get;}
```

C#:

```
object o = dataViewManager.DataViewSettings.SyncRoot;
DataViewSettingCollection dvsc = (DataViewSettingCollection) o;
```

Using the `SyncRoot` property simply returns a reference the `DataViewSettings` object itself – the object returned is no more thread-safe than the object we already have!

There's no need to worry too much about this collection being thread-safe though because its contents are all internally managed anyway.

DataViewSettingCollection Methods

This section will cover the methods on the `DataViewSettingCollection` object.

The CopyTo Method

The `CopyTo` method copies the `DataViewSetting` objects from the collection to an array.

VB.NET:

```
NotOverridable Public Sub CopyTo( ByVal ar As Array, ByVal index As Integer)
```

C#:

```
public void CopyTo(Array ar, int index);
```

This example shows how to use the `CopyTo` method. First of all we create an array of `DataViewSetting` objects. We know how big the array should be by using the `Count` property on the collection. Then the copy is performed passing the array and a value indicating the start index of the array.

C#:

```
DataViewSetting []settings = new DataViewSetting
                                [DataViewManager.DataViewSettings.Count];
dataViewManager.DataViewSettings.CopyTo(settings, 0);
```

The `CopyTo` method's parameters are:

Parameter	Type	Explanation
ar	Array	The array where the `DataViewSettings` should be copied.
index	int	The start index of the destination array. In most cases this will be 0 but in VB.NET it's possible to define the start index of an array.

As usual, we can iterate over the array and alter the object's properties:

C#:

```csharp
foreach (DataViewSetting dvs in settings)
{
    dvs.ApplyDefaultSort = true;
}
```

The method name `CopyTo` is a bit of a misnomer – the `DataViewSettings` in the new array aren't copies of the original objects, they're actually references to the objects. This means any changes made to the objects in the array will be reflected in the `DataViewSettingCollection`. Removing an object from the array or setting it to null doesn't affect the contents of the `DataViewSettingCollection` though.

The GetEnumerator Method

Provides an enumerator to iterate over the views `DataViewSetting` objects.

VB.NET:

```vbnet
NotOverridable Public Function GetEnumerator() As IEnumerator
```

C#:

```csharp
public IEnumerator GetEnumerator ();
```

In this example, `GetEnumerator` isn't actually called. This is because the framework calls the method – we should never have to call `GetEnumerator` directly. The example shows how we'd iterate over each `DataViewSetting` object in the collection. In this example we then set each view to use the default sort.

VB.NET:

```vbnet
Dim dvs As DataViewSetting

For Each dvs In dvm.DataViewSettings
    dvs.ApplyDefaultSort = True
Next
```

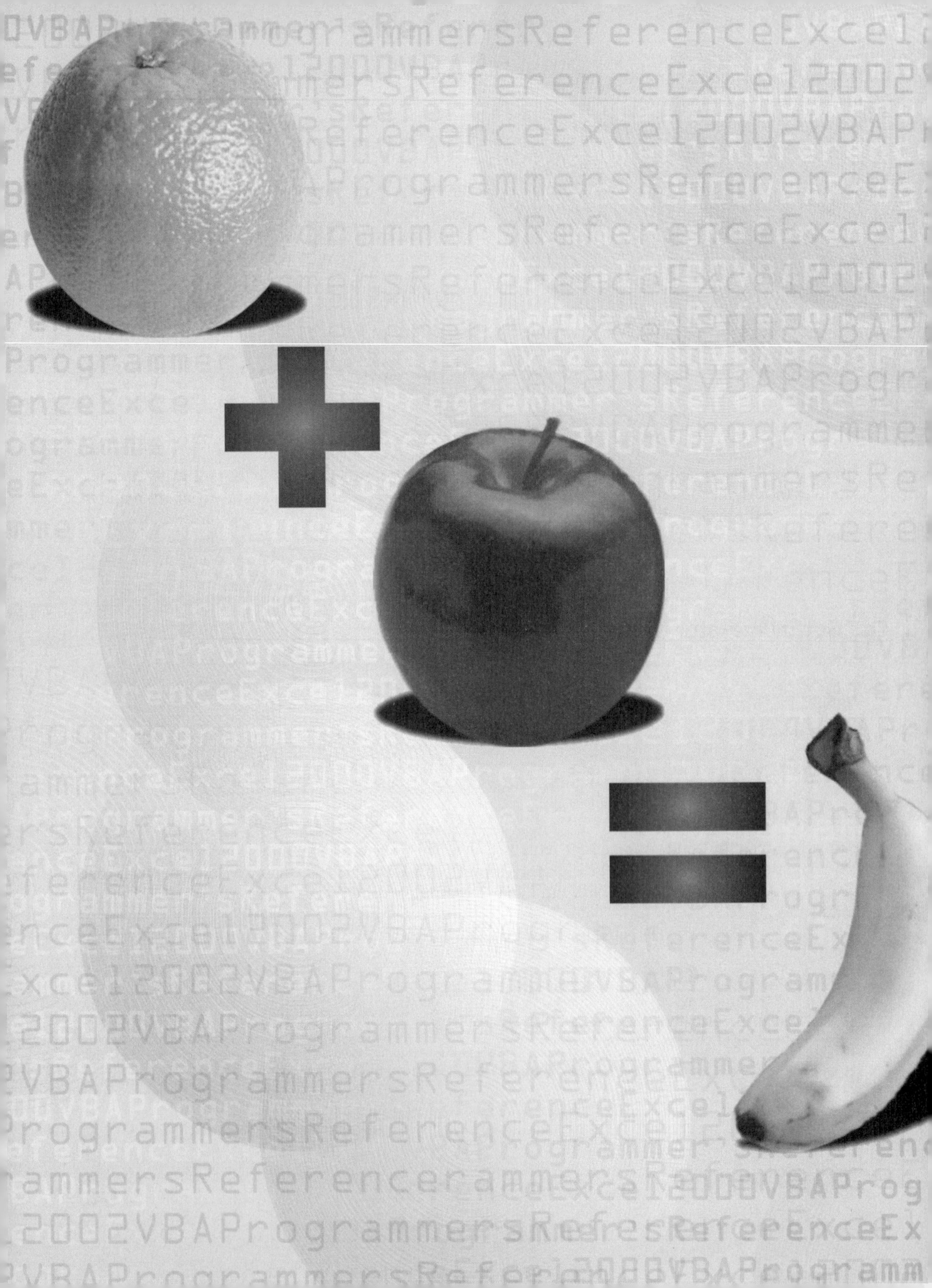

Mapping

Mapping objects are a new set of classes that allow mapping columns and tables from a data source, to either a DataSet or a DataTable object. As such, we can give more significant names to columns and tables so we can improve the code readability. Moreover, you could fill a DataSet with an XML schema that is not name-compatible with your data source columns. In this kind of situation, you have to use these objects in order to link the DataSet columns to the data source ones. In this chapter, we'll analyze all the methods and properties exposed by the DataTableMapping and DataColumnMapping classes showing how they integrate themselves in the ADO.NET's context. At the end of chapter, we will study DataTableMappingCollection and DataColumnMappingCollection classes that like the name suggests, are a collection of objects you can use with particular DataAdapter's methods and properties.

The Mapping Mechanism

The DataAdapter's Fill() method fills a DataSet object with records retrieved from a data source, previously defined by a connection using the SqlConnection object contained in its SelectCommand property. During the filling process, the DataAdapter object looks for a table mapping definition and if it doesn't find one, it uses the same columns name as the data source ones. So, in order to access to these data, you have to use exactly the same columns name in the DataTable object. Let's look at a simple example:

VB.NET:

```
Dim dbConn As New SqlClient.SqlConnection()

Try
' Create a connection to the Pubs database
dbConn.ConnectionString = "server=localhost;uid=sa;pwd=;database=pubs"

' Create a DataAdapter to retrieve data from pubs database
Dim AuthorsAdapter As New SqlClient.SqlDataAdapter("SELECT au_lname,
au_fname FROM authors", dbConn)

' Create a DataSet to manage records
Dim dsAuthors As New DataSet("dsAuthors")

' Fill the DataSet
AuthorsAdapter.Fill(dsAuthors)
```

```
' Print to video the records
Dim r As Data.DataRow
For Each r In dsAuthors.Tables(0).Rows
Console.WriteLine(r("au_lname") & " " & r("au_fname"))
Next
Catch ex As Exception
' An error occurred, print it to video
Console.WriteLine(ex.ToString)
Finally
' Close the connection to the database
If dbConn.State = ConnectionState.Open Then dbConn.Close()
End Try
```

C#:

```
SqlConnection dbConn = new System.Data.SqlClient.SqlConnection();

try
{
// Create a connection to the Pubs database
dbConn.ConnectionString = "server=localhost;uid=sa;pwd=;database=pubs";

// Create a DataAdapter to retrieve data from pubs database
SqlDataAdapter AuthorsAdapter = new
System.Data.SqlClient.SqlDataAdapter("SELECT au_lname, au_fname FROM
authors",dbConn);
// Create a DataSet to manage records
DataSet dsAuthors = new System.Data.DataSet("dsAuthors");

// Fill the DataSet
AuthorsAdapter.Fill(dsAuthors);

// Print to video the records
foreach (System.Data.DataRow r in dsAuthors.Tables[0].Rows)
Console.WriteLine(r["au_lname"].ToString() + " " +
r["au_fname"].ToString());
}
catch (Exception e)
{
// An error occured, print it to video
Console.WriteLine (e.Message);
}
finally
{
// If the connection was open then close it
if (dbConn.State == ConnectionState.Open)
dbConn.Close();
}
```

In this example, columns name are a bit contorted and it is really difficult to remember their names through all of the application code. You have to spend a lot of time to check their exact names from the table definition in your database or choose a different method, like the ordinal reference ones, to access to the information with all the disadvantages it procures. It could be very useful to create a table mapping mechanism in order to change column names with more significant ones.
DataTableMapping object lets you implement just a table mapping system from the data source tables to the DataSet ones. Through TableMappings collection exposed by DataAdapter object, you can add your table-mapped columns, previously defined in your code and use the new ones during the application code.

VB.NET:

```
SqlConnection dbConn = new System.Data.SqlClient.SqlConnection();

try
{
// Create a connection to the Pubs database
dbConn.ConnectionString =
"server=localhost;uid=sa;pwd=;database=pubs";

// Create an array of DataColumnMapping to define the new column names
DataColumnMapping[] dcmAuthors = {new
System.Data.Common.DataColumnMapping("au_lname","Author_LastName"),
newSystem.Data.Common.DataColumnMapping("au_fname","Author_FirstName")};

// Create a DataTableMapping object containing the column array
DataTableMapping dtmAuthors = new
System.Data.Common.DataTableMapping("Table","authors",dcmAuthors);

// Create a DataAdapter to retrieve data from pubs database
SqlDataAdapter AuthorsAdapter = new
System.Data.SqlClient.SqlDataAdapter("SELECT au_lname, au_fname FROM
authors",dbConn);

// Associate it to the DataAdapter
AuthorsAdapter.TableMappings.Add(dtmAuthors);

// Create a DataSet to manage records
DataSet dsAuthors = new System.Data.DataSet("dsAuthors");

// Fill the DataSet
AuthorsAdapter.Fill(dsAuthors);

// Now I can use the new column names
foreach (System.Data.DataRow r in dsAuthors.Tables[0].Rows)
Console.WriteLine(r["Author_LastName"].ToString() + " " +
r["Author_FirstName"].ToString());
}
catch (Exception e)
{
// An error occured, print it to video
Console.WriteLine (e.Message);
}
finally
{
// If the connection was open then close it
if (dbConn.State == ConnectionState.Open)
dbConn.Close();
}
```

C#:

```
Dim dbConn As New SqlClient.SqlConnection()

Try
    ' Create a connection to the Pubs database
```

```
        dbConn.ConnectionString = "server=localhost;uid=sa;pwd=;database=pubs"

        ' Create an array of DataColumnMapping to define the new column names
        Dim dtmAuthors As New System.Data.Common.DataTableMapping("Table",
        "authors", New System.Data.Common.DataColumnMapping() {New
        System.Data.Common.DataColumnMapping("au_lname", "Author_LastName"),
        New System.Data.Common.DataColumnMapping("au_fname",
                        Author_FirstName")})

        ' Create a DataAdapter to retrieve data from pubs database
        Dim AuthorsAdapter As New SqlClient.SqlDataAdapter("SELECT au_lname,
                        au_fname FROM authors", dbConn)

        ' Associate it to the DataAdapter
        AuthorsAdapter.TableMappings.Add(dtmAuthors)

        ' Create a DataSet to manage records
        Dim dsAuthors As New DataSet("dsAuthors")

        ' Fill the DataSet
        AuthorsAdapter.Fill(dsAuthors)

        ' Print to video the records
        Dim r As Data.DataRow
        For Each r In dsAuthors.Tables(0).Rows
            Console.WriteLine(r("Author_LastName") & " " &
                    r("Author_FirstName"))
        Next
    Catch ex As Exception
        ' An error occurred, print it to video
        Console.WriteLine(ex.ToString)
    Finally
        ' Close the connection to the database
        If dbConn.State = ConnectionState.Open Then dbConn.Close()
    End Try
```

In this way you could use more readable column names, during records extraction, from the data source. As you can see from the code above, you have to follow a few steps to implement table-mapping mechanism:

1. You have to create an array of `DataColumnMapping` objects which define the new name-relation between the data source and the `DataSet` object source.

2. Create a `DataTableMapping` object that contains the `DataColumnMapping` array and specifies which data source table the columns are contained within.

3. Use the `TableMappings` collection exposed by the `DataAdapter` derived class to inform that a new table mapping system has to be used between data source columns and `DataSet` ones.

4. Reference the columns using the new mapped names. It means using the new `DataSet` tables to select and update the data source ones.

Another significant use of `DataTableMapping` object is when you retrieve data using a `DataSet` object, filled with an XML schema, having different characteristics to your data source. For example, you could have a BizTalk XML schema that defines BizTalk message characteristics and you want to process the incoming messages and store them in the database. You can load the BizTalk schema in the `DataSet` object, retrieve the data from the BizTalk message, and use `DataTableMapping` object to link `DataSet` column names to the database ones. Then you can call the `Update()` method exposed by the `DataAdapter` class in order to add records to the data source.

For example, imagine we receive the following XML document:

```
<?xml version="1.0" standalone="yes"?>
<Authors>
  <authors>
    <Author_ID>222-22-2222</Author_ID>
    <Author_FirstName>Fabio Claudio</Author_FirstName>
    <Author_LastName>Ferracchiati</Author_LastName>
    <Author_Contract>true</Author_Contract>
  </authors>
</Authors>
```

This document contains new authors that we need to add to our database. Our table has different columns (table authors from pubs database) however, so we have to implement a mapping mechanism. We have to specify that `Author_ID` will be mapped to `au_id` in your database, and so on for the other columns:

VB.NET:
```
' Create an array of DataColumnMapping to define the new column names
Dim dtmAuthors As New System.Data.Common.DataTableMapping("Table",
    "authors", New System.Data.Common.DataColumnMapping()
    {New System.Data.Common.DataColumnMapping("au_id", "Author_ID"),
    New System.Data.Common.DataColumnMapping("au_fname",
        "Author_FirstName"),
    New System.Data.Common.DataColumnMapping("au_lname",
        "Author_LastName"),
    New System.Data.Common.DataColumnMapping("contract",
        "Author_Contract")})

' Create a DataAdapter to retrieve data from pubs database
Dim AuthorsAdapter As New SqlClient.SqlDataAdapter("SELECT au_id, au_lname,
au_fname, contract FROM authors", dbConn)
```

C#:
```
// Create an array of DataColumnMapping to define the new column names
DataColumnMapping[] dcmAuthors = {                              new
DataColumnMapping("au_id","Author_ID"),
            new DataColumnMapping("au_lname","Author_LastName"),
            new DataColumnMapping("au_fname","Author_FirstName"),
            new DataColumnMapping("contract","Author_Contract")
                };

// Create a DataTableMapping object containing the column array
DataTableMapping dtmAuthors = new DataTableMapping("Table","authors",dcmAuthors);
```

After that, we can inform the `DataAdapter` object that we want use the new mapping columns:

VB.NET:

```
' Create a DataAdapter to retrieve data from pubs database
Dim AuthorsAdapter As New SqlClient.SqlDataAdapter("SELECT au_id, au_lname,
au_fname, contract FROM authors", dbConn)

' Associate it to the DataAdapter
AuthorsAdapter.TableMappings.Add(dtmAuthors)
```

C#:

```
// Create a DataAdapter to retrieve data from pubs database
SqlDataAdapter AuthorsAdapter = new SqlDataAdapter("SELECT au_id, au_fname,
au_lname, contract FROM authors",dbConn);

// Associate it to the DataAdapter
AuthorsAdapter.TableMappings.Add(dtmAuthors);
```

Now we have to fill a `DataSet` object with the source database records in order to create automatically an internal `DataSet` schema:

VB.NET:

```
' Create a DataSet to manage records
Dim dsAuthors As New DataSet("dsAuthors")

' Fill the DataSet
AuthorsAdapter.Fill(dsAuthors)
```

C#:

```
// Create a DataSet to manage records
DataSet dsAuthors = new DataSet("Authors");
AuthorsAdapter.Fill(dsAuthors);
```

At this time, we can retrieve new data through loading from the XML document. We can use the `ReadXml()` method exposed by the `DataSet` object passing a filename directly:

VB.NET:

```
' Fill a new DataSet with XML document data
Dim dsNewAuthors As New DataSet("NewAuthors")
dsNewAuthors.ReadXml("authors_schema_and_data.xml")
```

C#:

```
// Fill a new DataSet with XML document data
DataSet dsNewAuthors = new DataSet("NewAuthors");
dsNewAuthors.ReadXml("authors_schema_and_data.xml");
```

Now we have two objects having the same internal schema, so they could be merged in a unique `DataSet` object formed with the total of the data:

VB.NET:

```
' Merge DataSet generated from database with DataSet
' generated from XML document
dsAuthors.Merge(dsNewAuthors, True, MissingSchemaAction.Ignore)
```

C#:

```
// Merge DataSet generated from database with DataSet
// generated from XML document
dsAuthors.Merge(dsNewAuthors,true,MissingSchemaAction.Ignore);
```

Finally, we can store the DataSet in the database:

VB.NET:

```
' Create an InsertCommand SQL command
Dim sb As New SqlClient.SqlCommandBuilder(AuthorsAdapter)

' Insert new records
AuthorsAdapter.Update(dsAuthors)

' Print to video final result
Console.WriteLine("New authors have been added to the database.")
```

C#:

```
// Create an InsertCommand SQL command
SqlCommandBuilder sb = new SqlCommandBuilder(AuthorsAdapter);

// Insert new records
AuthorsAdapter.Update(dsAuthors);

// Print to video final result
Console.WriteLine("New authors have been added to the database.");
```

It is important to note that all the objects, methods, and properties within this chapter are defined in the System.Data.Common namespace.

The DataTableMapping Object

The DataTableMapping object contains a collection of mapped columns that define the link from the physical tables contained in the database, to the virtual ones present in the DataSet. When a DataSet object is filled by the DataAdapter, a mapping mechanism starts; it looks for a DataTableMapping object collection associated with the DataAdapter. If no objects were found, then original names will be used to create the DataSet schema, otherwise new column names will be used instead. To associate a new DataTableMapping object to the DataAdapter, you have to use either the Add() or AddRange() methods exposed by the DataTableMappingCollection object contained as a property in the DataAdapter object. You can learn more about that in Chapter 7. If you want learn more about DataTableMappingCollection objects, you can find it at the end of this chapter.

DataTableMapping Constructor

DataTableMapping is a class derived from MarshallByRefObject, and from Object classes that implements two interfaces: ITableMapping and ICloneable. The former is the interface that allows an inheriting class to implement the Table Mapping mechanism. The latter implements clone functionality to the inheriting class. In that way, it will be possible create a new class with the same values as the cloned one.

The Default Constructor

Let's start to examine its simplest constructor:

VB.NET:
```
Public Sub New()
```

C#:
```
public DataTableMapping();
```

The default constructor initializes all class attributes to the default values. Let's see an example:

VB.NET:
```
Dim dtmAuthors As New DataTableMapping
```

C#:
```
System.Data.Common.DataTableMapping dtmAuthors = new
System.Data.Common.DataTableMapping();
```

The Second Constructor

You can use this constructor to define the source data table and DataSet table directly during DataTableMapping object creation.

VB.NET:
```
Public Sub New( _
    ByVal sourceTable As String, _
    ByVal dataSetTable As String _
)
```

C#:
```
public DataTableMapping(
    string sourceTable,
    string dataSetTable
);
```

The sourceTable parameter represents the case-sensitive source table name from the data source, while the dataSetTable, is the table name from a DataSet to map to. In the following example, a DataTableMapping will be created in order to link from a Northwind's Products table to a DataSet table:

VB.NET:

```
Dim dtmProducts As New Data.Common.DataTableMapping("Products","dsProducts")
```

C#:

```
System.Data.Common.DataTableMapping dtmProducts = new
System.Data.Common.DataTableMapping("Products","dsProducts");
```

Pay attention to the first parameter, which has to be exactly the same as the source table name.

The Third Constructor

You can use this constructor to define the source data table, `DataSet` table, and an array of `DataColumnMapping` objects directly, during `DataTableMapping` object creation.

VB.NET:

```
Public Sub New( _
    ByVal sourceTable As String, _
    ByVal dataSetTable As String, _
    ByVal columnMappings() As DataColumnMapping _
)
```

C#:

```
public DataTableMapping(
    string sourceTable,
    string dataSetTable,
    DataColumnMapping[] columnMappings
);
```

The first and second parameter are the same as we have seen before, while `columnMappings` is an array of `DataColumnMapping` objects, with each one containing a link between a source column name from a data source, and a `DataTable` column name. Look this snippet of code:

VB.NET:

```
Dim dtmProducts As New System.Data.Common.DataTableMapping("Table", "Products",
New System.Data.Common.DataColumnMapping() {New
System.Data.Common.DataColumnMapping("ProductID", "ID"), New
System.Data.Common.DataColumnMapping("ProductName", "Name")})
```

C#:

```
System.Data.Common.DataTableMapping dtmProducts = new
System.Data.Common.DataTableMapping("Table", "Products", new
System.Data.Common.DataColumnMapping[] {new
System.Data.Common.DataColumnMapping("ProductID", "ID"), new
System.Data.Common.DataColumnMapping("ProductName", "Name")});
```

As you can see, it's really easy to define an array of columns directly, during the object creation.

DataTableMapping Properties

In this section, we will examine the three properties used by a `DataTableMapping` object to get/set protected information, such as the source table, and the `DataSetTable` names. We'll also show how to retrieve a reference to a `DataTableMappingCollection` object.

The DataSetTable Property

VB.NET:

```
Public Property DataSetTable As String
```

C#:

```
public string DataSetTable {get; set;}
```

Use this property to either get or set the `DataSetTable` name that will be used to create a `DataTable` object inside a `DataSet` ones.

VB.NET:

```
Dim dtmAuthors As New System.Data.Common.DataTableMapping()

' Set the property
dtmAuthors.DataSetTable = "dtmAuthors"

' Get the property
Console.WriteLine(dtmAuthors.DataSetTable.ToString())
```

C#:

```
System.Data.Common.DataTableMapping dtmAuthors = new
System.Data.Common.DataTableMapping();

// Set the property
dtmAuthors.DataSetTable = "dtmAuthors";

// Get the property
Console.WriteLine(dtmAuthors.DataSetTable.ToString());
```

This property is typically used when you create a `DataTableMapping` object, using its default constructor, and you need to specify which `DataSet` table to map to.

The SourceTable Property

VB.NET:

```
Public Property SourceTable As String
```

C#:

```
public string SourceTable {get; set;}
```

You can use this property, to either get or set the source table case-sensitive name, from a data source.

VB.NET:

```
Dim dtmAuthors As New System.Data.Common.DataTableMapping()

' Set the property
dtmAuthors.SourceTable = "Authors"

' Get the property
Console.WriteLine(dtmAuthors.SourceTable.ToString())
```

C#:

```
System.Data.Common.DataTableMapping dtmAuthors = new
System.Data.Common.DataTableMapping();

// Set the property
dtmAuthors.SourceTable = "Authors";

// Get the property
Console.WriteLine(dtmAuthors.SourceTable.ToString());
```

This property is also used when you create a `DataTableMapping` object from its default construct.

The ColumnMappings Property

VB.NET:

```
Public ReadOnly Property ColumnMappings As _
    DataColumnMappingCollection
```

C#:

```
public DataColumnMappingCollection ColumnMappings {get;}
```

Use this property to retrieve a `DataColumnMappingCollection` object associated with a `DataTableMapping` object. We've seen that when we create a `DataTableMapping` object, we can specify a `DataColumnMapping` array. Internally, a `DataColumnMappingCollection` will be created to contain just the columns previously created. You can use this property to retrieve a reference to the column collection in order to manage its content.

VB.NET:

```
' Create a DataTableMapping object containing the column array
Dim dtmAuthors As New System.Data.Common.DataTableMapping("Table", "Authors", New
System.Data.Common.DataColumnMapping() {New
System.Data.Common.DataColumnMapping("au_fname", "Author_FirstName"), New
System.Data.Common.DataColumnMapping("au_lname", "Author_LastName")})

' Create a DataColumnMappingCollection object
Dim dcmcAuthors As New System.Data.Common.DataColumnMappingCollection()

' Retrieve the column collection
dcmcAuthors = dtmAuthors.ColumnMappings
```

```
' Print to video the number of column inside the collection
Console.WriteLine(dcmcAuthors.Count.ToString())
```

C#:

```
// Create an array of DataColumnMapping to define the new column names
System.Data.Common.DataColumnMapping[] dcmAuthors = {new
System.Data.Common.DataColumnMapping("au_lname","Author_LastName"),
new System.Data.Common.DataColumnMapping("au_fname","Author_FirstName")};

// Create a DataTableMapping object containing the column array
System.Data.Common.DataTableMapping dtmAuthors = new
System.Data.Common.DataTableMapping("Table","authors",dcmAuthors);

// Create a DataColumnMappingCollection object
System.Data.Common.DataColumnMappingCollection dcmcAuthors = new
System.Data.Common.DataColumnMappingCollection();

// Retrieve the column collection
dcmcAuthors = dtmAuthors.ColumnMappings;

// Print to video the number of column inside the collection
Console.WriteLine (dcmcAuthors.Count.ToString());
```

The output of this example will be like the column added to the `DataTableMapping` object at the beginning of the code. At the end of this chapter, we will examine, in more detail, the `DataColumnMappingCollection` object, together with the `DataTableMappingCollection` that represents a tables collection contained inside the `DataAdapter` object.

DataTableMapping Methods

Now we take a look to methods provided by `DataTableMapping` objects. There are just three proprietary methods, and a few others inherited from MarshallByRefObject and Object classes. In this paragraph, we will examine all these methods focusing our attention on the proprietary ones.

The Proprietary Methods

DataTableMapping provides three proprietary methods: GetColumnMappingBySchemaAction(), GetDataTableBySchemaAction(), and ToString(). Let's start to examine each of them in some detail.

The GetColumnMappingBySchemaAction Method

VB.NET:

```
Public Function GetColumnMappingBySchemaAction( _
    ByVal sourceColumn As String, _
    ByVal mappingAction As MissingMappingAction _
) As DataColumnMapping
```

C#:

```
public DataColumnMapping GetColumnMappingBySchemaAction(
    string sourceColumn,
    MissingMappingAction mappingAction
);
```

This method allows us to retrieve a `DataColumnMapping` object by specifying its name in `sourceColumn` method's parameter. The second parameter, `mappingAction`, is an `enum` type variable that can assume one of the following values:

MissingMappingAction values	Description
Error	If you specify this value and the column you are looking for is missing in the collection, then a `SystemException` object will be returned.
Ignore	If you specify this value and the column you are looking for is missing in the collection, then a null reference will be returned. In VB.NET language it will return a `Nothing` value.
Passthrough	If you specify this value and the column you are looking for is missing in the collection, then a `DataColumn` object will be created and added to the `DataSet` using the name you passed to the first parameter.

You can use this method when you need to check whether a particular column is mapped to a source data column in the `DataTable` object filled by a `DataAdapter` object or when you need to add a new mapped-column to the `DataSet` object. Let's look at three examples, one for each `MissingMappingAction` value:

VB.NET:

```
' Create a connection to the Pubs database
Dim dbConn As New
System.Data.SqlClient.SqlConnection("server=localhost;uid=sa;pwd=;database=pubs")

' Create a DataAdapter to retrieve data from pubs database
Dim daAuthors As New System.Data.SqlClient.SqlDataAdapter("SELECT au_fname,
au_lname, au_id FROM Authors", dbConn)

' Create a DataTableMapping object containing the column array
daAuthors.TableMappings.AddRange(New System.Data.Common.DataTableMapping() {New
System.Data.Common.DataTableMapping("Table", "Authors", New
System.Data.Common.DataColumnMapping() {New
System.Data.Common.DataColumnMapping("au_fname", "Author_FirstName"), New
System.Data.Common.DataColumnMapping("au_lname", "Author_LastName")})})

' Create a DataSet to manage records
Dim dsAuthors As New Data.DataSet("dsAuthors")

' Fill the DataSet
daAuthors.Fill(dsAuthors)

' Retrieve DateTableMapping object from the collection
Dim dtmAuthor As New System.Data.Common.DataTableMapping()
dtmAuthor = daAuthors.TableMappings.GetByDataSetTable("Authors")

' Retrieve DataColumnMapping object from the collection
```

```vb
' If it doesn't exist the method will create it
Dim dcmAuthor As New System.Data.Common.DataColumnMapping()
dcmAuthor = dtmAuthor.GetColumnMappingBySchemaAction("Author_ID",
MissingMappingAction.Passthrough)

' Because Author_ID was not declared before it has been created
' by method. So we have to add to the collection and to create
' again the DataSet
dcmAuthor.SourceColumn = "au_id"
dtmAuthor.ColumnMappings.Add(dcmAuthor)
daAuthors.TableMappings.Clear()
daAuthors.TableMappings.Add(dtmAuthor)
daAuthors.Fill(dsAuthors)

' Print to video the new mapped-column values
Dim r As System.Data.DataRow
For Each r In dsAuthors.Tables(0).Rows
   Console.WriteLine(r("Author_ID"))
Next
```

C#:

```csharp
// Create a connection to the Pubs database
System.Data.SqlClient.SqlConnection dbConn = new
System.Data.SqlClient.SqlConnection("server=localhost;uid=sa;pwd=;database=pubs");

// Create an array of DataColumnMapping to define the new column names
System.Data.Common.DataColumnMapping[] dcmAuthors = {new
System.Data.Common.DataColumnMapping("au_lname","Author_LastName"),
new System.Data.Common.DataColumnMapping("au_fname","Author_FirstName")};

// Create a DataTableMapping object containing the column array
System.Data.Common.DataTableMapping dtmAuthors = new
System.Data.Common.DataTableMapping("Table","authors",dcmAuthors);

// Create a DataAdapter to retrieve data from pubs database
System.Data.SqlClient.SqlDataAdapter daAuthors = new
System.Data.SqlClient.SqlDataAdapter("SELECT au_fname, au_lname, au_id FROM
Authors", dbConn);

// Associate it to the DataAdapter
daAuthors.TableMappings.Add(dtmAuthors);

// Create a DataSet to manage records
System.Data.DataSet dsAuthors = new System.Data.DataSet("Authors");

// Fill the DataSet
daAuthors.Fill(dsAuthors);

// Retrieve DateTableMapping object from the collection
System.Data.Common.DataTableMapping dtmAuthor =
daAuthors.TableMappings.GetByDataSetTable("Authors");

// Retrieve DataColumnMapping object from the collection
// If it doesn't exist, method will create it
```

```
System.Data.Common.DataColumnMapping dcmAuthor =
dtmAuthor.GetColumnMappingBySchemaAction("Author_ID",MissingMappingAction.Passthro
ugh);

// Because Author_ID was not declared before it has been created
// by method. So we have to add to the collection and to create
// again the DataSet
dcmAuthor.SourceColumn = "au_id";
dtmAuthor.ColumnMappings.Add(dcmAuthor);
daAuthors.TableMappings.Clear();
daAuthors.TableMappings.Add(dtmAuthor);
daAuthors.Fill(dsAuthors);

// Print to video the new mapped-column values
foreach (System.Data.DataRow r in dsAuthors.Tables[0].Rows)
    Console.WriteLine (r["Author_ID"].ToString());
```

In this example, you can see the `Passthrough` value utilization. The
`GetColumnMappingBySchemaAction()` method looks for the `Author_ID` column in the `DataSet`
object filled previously by the `DataAdapter`'s `Fill()` method. As it was not declared and because we
chose the `Passthrough` value, a new `DataColumn` with a `DataSetColumn` set to "`Author_ID`"
will be created. This new object isn't present in the `DataTableMapping` collection contained in the
`DataAdapter` object so we have to remove the old one and add back the new collection. In that way it
will be possible to fill the `DataSet` object using the new column also. The final result shows that:

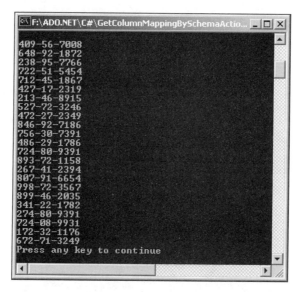

If we chose to change the `MissingMappingAction` value to `Error`, in the following way:

VB.NET:

```
dcmAuthor = dtmAuthor.GetColumnMappingBySchemaAction("Author_ID",
MissingMappingAction.Error)
```

559

C#:

```csharp
System.Data.Common.DataColumnMapping dcmAuthor =
dtmAuthor.GetColumnMappingBySchemaAction("Author_ID",MissingMappingAct
ion.Error);
```

A `SystemException` will be raised and the following error will be shown:

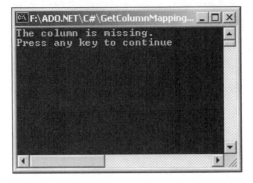

Finally, by changing the `MissingMappingAction` to the `Ignore` value, a null reference will be returned:

VB.NET:

```vbnet
dcmAuthor = dtmAuthor.GetColumnMappingBySchemaAction("Author_ID",
MissingMappingAction.Ignore)
If dcmAuthor Is Nothing Then
    Console.WriteLine("The column is missing...")
    Exit Sub
End If
```

C#:

```csharp
System.Data.Common.DataColumnMapping dcmAuthor =
dtmAuthor.GetColumnMappingBySchemaAction("Author_ID",MissingMappingAction.Ignore);

if (dcmAuthor == null)
{
    Console.WriteLine("The column is missing…");
    return;
}
```

Then the output will be:

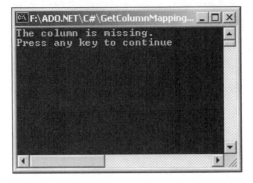

Otherwise, if you look for a preloaded mapped column in the collection, the
`GetColumnMappingBySchemaAction()` method will return a valid `DataColumnMapping` object:

VB.NET:

```
dcmAuthor = dtmAuthor.GetColumnMappingBySchemaAction("au_fname",
MissingMappingAction.Ignore)
If dcmAuthor Is Not Nothing Then
   Console.WriteLine("The column is missing...")
Else
    Console.WriteLine("The column was founded and it is mapped to "
            & dcmAuthor.DataSetColumn & " value")
End If

Exit Sub
```

C#:

```
System.Data.Common.DataColumnMapping dcmAuthor =
dtmAuthor.GetColumnMappingBySchemaAction("au_fname",MissingMappingAction.Ignore);

if (dcmAuthor != null)
{
   Console.WriteLine("The column was founded and it is mapped to" +
           dcmAuthor.DataSetColumn + " value");
   return;
}
```

The output for the new code will be:

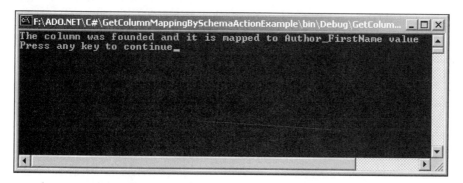

The GetDataTableBySchemaAction Method

VB.NET:

```
Public Function GetDataTableBySchemaAction( _
   ByVal dataSet As DataSet, _
   ByVal schemaAction As MissingSchemaAction _
) As DataTable
```

C#:

```
public DataTable GetDataTableBySchemaAction(
    DataSet dataSet,
    MissingSchemaAction schemaAction
);
```

This method allows retrieving a `DataTable` object contained in a `DataSet` object previously filled by the `DataAdapter`'s `Fill()` method. You have to pass a `DataSet` object to the first parameter and a `MissingSchemaAction` enum value to the second one. The latter parameter could assume one of these values:

MissingSchemaAction values	Description
Error	If you specify this value and the table you are looking for is missing in the `DataSet`, then a `SystemException` object will be returned.
Add	If you specify this value and the table you are looking for is missing in the `DataSet`, then the necessary columns will be added to the `DataSet` schema.
AddWithKey	If you specify this value and the table you are looking for is missing in the `DataSet`, then the necessary columns will also be added to the `DataSet` schema with primary key information.
Ignore	If you specify this value and the table you are looking for is missing in the `DataSet`, then a null reference will be returned. In VB.NET it will return a `Nothing` value.

In the following section of code, you will see how use this method to retrieve a `DataTable` object contained in a `DataSet` just filled previously by `Fill()` method.

VB.NET:

```
' Create a connection to the Pubs database
Dim dbConn As New
System.Data.SqlClient.SqlConnection("server=localhost;uid=sa;pwd=;database=pubs")

' Create a DataAdapter to retrieve data from pubs database
Dim daAuthors As New System.Data.SqlClient.SqlDataAdapter("SELECT au_fname,
au_lname, au_id FROM Authors", dbConn)

' Create a DataTableMapping object containing the column array
Dim dtmAuthors As New System.Data.Common.DataTableMapping("Table", "Authors", New
System.Data.Common.DataColumnMapping() {New
System.Data.Common.DataColumnMapping("au_fname", "Author_FirstName"), New
System.Data.Common.DataColumnMapping("au_lname", "Author_LastName")})

daAuthors.TableMappings.AddRange(New System.Data.Common.DataTableMapping()
{dtmAuthors})
```

```vbnet
' Create a DataSet to manage records
Dim dsAuthors As New Data.DataSet("dsAuthors")

' Fill the DataSet
daAuthors.Fill(dsAuthors)

Dim dtAuthors As New System.Data.DataTable()

' Retrieve DataTable contained into the DataSet
dtAuthors = dtmAuthors.GetDataTableBySchemaAction(dsAuthors, _
                        MissingSchemaAction.Error)

' Print to video its records
Dim r As System.Data.DataRow
For Each r In dtAuthors.Rows
    Console.WriteLine(r("Author_FirstName") & " " & r("Author_LastName"))
Next
```

C#:

```csharp
// Create a connection to the Pubs database
System.Data.SqlClient.SqlConnection dbConn = new
System.Data.SqlClient.SqlConnection("server=localhost;uid=sa;pwd=;database=pubs");

// Create an array of DataColumnMapping to define the new column names
System.Data.Common.DataColumnMapping[] dcmAuthors = {new
System.Data.Common.DataColumnMapping("au_lname","Author_LastName"),
new System.Data.Common.DataColumnMapping("au_fname","Author_FirstName")};

// Create a DataTableMapping object containing the column array
System.Data.Common.DataTableMapping dtmAuthors = new
System.Data.Common.DataTableMapping("Table","authors",dcmAuthors);

// Create a DataAdapter to retrieve data from pubs database
System.Data.SqlClient.SqlDataAdapter daAuthors = new
System.Data.SqlClient.SqlDataAdapter("SELECT au_fname, au_lname, au_id FROM
Authors", dbConn);

// Associate it to the DataAdapter
daAuthors.TableMappings.Add(dtmAuthors);

// Create a DataSet to manage records
System.Data.DataSet dsAuthors = new System.Data.DataSet("Authors");

// Fill the DataSet
daAuthors.Fill(dsAuthors);

// Retrieve DataTable contained into the DataSet
System.Data.DataTable dtAuthors = new System.Data.DataTable();
dtAuthors =
dtmAuthors.GetDataTableBySchemaAction(dsAuthors,System.Data.MissingSchemaAction.Er
ror);

// Print to video its records
```

```
foreach (System.Data.DataRow r in dtAuthors.Rows)
{
    Console.WriteLine (r["Author_FirstName"].ToString() + " " +
            r["Author_LastName"].ToString());
}
```

When you need to use AddWithKey value, you should pay attention to the SQL Server .NET Data Provider, that appends a FOR BROWSE clause to your query. This behavior could bring some side effects; for example, if you use some instructions like SET FMTONLY ON that let you retrieve just column information and no data, your code could be not work like you aspect. Moreover, you have to check that your OLE DB .NET Data Provider can accept DBPROP_UNIQUEROWS property in order to retrieve the primary key information.

The ToString Method

VB.NET:

```
Overrides Public Function ToString() As String
```

C#:

```
public override string ToString();
```

This method simply converts the source table name to a string value.

VB.NET:

```
' Create a DataTableMapping object containing the column array
Dim dtmAuthors As New System.Data.Common.DataTableMapping("Table", "Authors", New
System.Data.Common.DataColumnMapping() {New
System.Data.Common.DataColumnMapping("au_fname", "Author_FirstName"), New
System.Data.Common.DataColumnMapping("au_lname", "Author_LastName")})

' Print to video DataTableMApping source table name
Console.WriteLine(dtmAuthors.ToString())
```

C#:

```
// Create an array of DataColumnMapping to define the new column names
System.Data.Common.DataColumnMapping[] dcmAuthors = {new
System.Data.Common.DataColumnMapping("au_lname","Author_LastName"),
new System.Data.Common.DataColumnMapping("au_fname","Author_FirstName")};

// Create a DataTableMapping object containing the column array
System.Data.Common.DataTableMapping dtmAuthors = new
System.Data.Common.DataTableMapping("Table","authors",dcmAuthors);

// Print to video DataTableMapping source table name
Console.WriteLine(dtmAuthors.ToString());
```

When you use DataTableMapping object like a string parameter inside a method, such as the WriteLine() one, the ToString() method could be omitted because it will be called automatically. So the last code line could be:

VB.NET:

```
' Print to video DataTableMApping source table name
Console.WriteLine(dtmAuthors)
```

C#:

```
// Print to video DataTableMapping source table name
Console.WriteLine(dtmAuthors);
```

The final result will be the same.

The MarshallByRefObject Inherited Methods

There are few methods directly inherited from both `Object` and `MarshallByRefObject` classes. There are common methods to each class, having a similar kind of hierarchy to the `DataAdapter` ones. Let's start examining the `MarshallByRefObject` inherited methods.

The CreateObjRef Method

VB.NET:

```
Overridable Public Function CreateObjRef( _
    ByVal requestedType As Type _
) As ObjRef
```

C#:

```
public virtual ObjRef CreateObjRef(
    Type requestedType
);
```

You can create an object reference by calling this method and passing the requested object's type.

The GetLifetimeService Method

VB.NET:

```
NotOverridable Public Function GetLifetimeService() As Object
```

C#:

```
public object GetLifetimeService();
```

Usually, this method retrieves an `ILease` object interface that manages the lifetime policy for the `DateTableMapping` object. By getting a lifetime service object, you can manipulate the lease time for the object in order to either increment or decrement the default time.

The InitializeLifetimeService Method

VB.NET:

```
Overridable Public Function InitializeLifetimeService() As Object
```

C#:
```
public virtual object InitializeLifetimeService();
```

You can override this function, in order to provide your own lease time, initializing a new and customized, lifetime service object.

The Object Inherited Methods

As you know, the Object class is the root of the hierarchy, and it supports all the .NET Framework classes. It contains a few generic methods useful for each class composing the hierarchy. Using its methods, it will be possible check if two objects are equal, copy an object, and so on. Let's examine each method.

The Equal Method

VB.NET:
```
Overridable Overloads Public Function Equals( _
    ByVal obj As Object _
) As Boolean
```

C#:
```
public virtual bool Equals(
    object obj
);
```

The first of the two versions of this method lets you check if the DataTableMapping object you are using is equal to another object you pass to the method. If they are equal, the method returns a true Boolean value, otherwise it returns a false value.

VB.NET:
```
Overloads Public Shared Function Equals( _
    ByVal objA As Object, _
    ByVal objB As Object _
) As Boolean
```

C#:
```
public static bool Equals(
    object objA,
    object objB
);
```

The second version of the method checks if an object is equal to another one both passed to the method like parameters. Yet, if they are equal the method returns a true Boolean value otherwise it returns a false value.

The GetHashCode Method

VB.NET:

```
Overridable Public Function GetHashCode() As Integer
```

C#:

```
public virtual int GetHashCode();
```

Use this method if you need a hash code that represents your DataTableMapping through all of the objects lifetime.

The GetType Method

VB.NET:

```
Public Function GetType() As Type
```

C#:

```
public Type GetType();
```

If you need to know which is the Type of a particular object you can call this method.

The Finalize Method

VB.NET:

```
Overrides Protected Sub Finalize()
```

C#:

```
~Object();
```

This method is automatically called before the DataTableMapping object gets out from the function scope, and before it's reclaimed by the garbage collector.

The MemberwiseClone Method

VB.NET:

```
Protected Function MemberwiseClone() As Object
```

C#:

```
protected object MemberwiseClone();
```

Use this method if you need to clone the DataTableMapping object, but recall that will be provided an empty object without references to other objects. You can implement an ICloneable interface in the derived class however, if you need enhanced clone functionality.

The DataColumnMapping Object

During `DataTableMapping` explanation, we have just encountered the `DataColumnMapping` object when we have seen how to map columns from source data to `DataSet` object. It is possible however, to use this object to create mapped-columns linked to a `DataTable` object without interrogating `DataSet` methods. In this paragraph will see each method and property with more details focusing just on this new `DataColumnMapping` aspect.

The object with its methods and properties is defined in the `System.Data.Common` namespace.

DataColumnMapping Constructor

`DataColumnMapping` is a class derived from `MarshallByRefObject` and from `Object` classes that implements two interfaces: `IColumnMapping` and `ICloneable`. The former allows an inheriting class to implement `ColumnMapping` functionalities. The latter implements clone functionality to the inheriting class. In that way, it will be possible to create a new class with the same values as the cloned one.

The Default Constructor

DataColumnMapping object comes with just two constructors, a default one to create an empty object and two parameters; one to set values inside its two properties. Here we see the default constructor:

VB.NET:
```
Public Sub New()
```

C#:
```
public DataColumnMapping();
```

The default constructor initializes all class attributes to the default values. Let's see an example:

VB.NET:
```
Dim dcmAuthors As New DataColumnMapping()
```

C#:
```
System.Data.Common.DataColumnMapping dcmAuthors = new System.Data.Common.
DataColumnMapping();
```

The Second Constructor

You can use this constructor to define the source data column and `DataSet` column directly during `DataColumnMapping` object creation.

VB.NET:

```
Public Sub New( _
    ByVal sourceColumn As String, _
    ByVal dataSetColumn As String _
)
```

C#:

```
public DataColumnMapping(
    string sourceColumn,
    string dataSetColumn
);
```

sourceColumn parameter represents the case-sensitive source column name from the data source, while the dataSetColumn is the column name from a DataSet to map to. In the following example a DataColumnMapping will be created in order to link from a Northwind's Products column to a DataSet ones:

VB.NET:

```
Dim dcmProducts As New Data.Common.DataColumnMapping("ProductID", "ID")
```

C#:

```
System.Data.Common.DataColumnMapping dcmProducts = new System.Data.Common.
DataColumnMapping("ProductID","ID");
```

Again, pay attention to the first parameter that has to be exactly the same as the source column name.

DataColumnMapping Properties

In this paragraph, we'll be examining the two properties used by a DataColumnMapping object to get/set protected information such as the source column and the DataSet column names.

The DataSetColumn Property

VB.NET:

```
Public Property DataSetColumn As String
```

C#:

```
public string DataSetColumn {get; set;}
```

Use this property either to get or to set the DataSetColumn name that will be used by a DataSet object to map to the source column.

VB.NET:

```
Dim dcmAuthors As New System.Data.Common.DataColumnMapping()

' Set the property
dcmAuthors.DataSetColumn = "Author_LastName"

' Get the property      Console.WriteLine(dcmAuthors.DataSetColumn.ToString())
```

C#:

```
System.Data.Common.DataColumnMapping dcmAuthors = new System.Data.Common.
DataColumnMapping();

// Set the property
dcmAuthors.DataSetColumn = "Author_LastName";

// Get the property
Console.WriteLine(dcmAuthors.DataSetColumn.ToString());
```

Usually, this property is used when you create a `DataColumnMapping` object using its default constructor and you need to specify which is the `DataSet` column to map to.

The SourceColumn Property

VB.NET:

```
Public Property SourceColumn As String
```

C#:

```
public string SourceColumn {get; set;}
```

Use this property either to get or to set the source column case-sensitive name from a data source.

VB.NET:

```
Dim dcmAuthors As New System.Data.Common.DataColumnMapping()

' Set the property
dcmAuthors.SourceColumn = "au_lname"

' Get the property
Console.WriteLine(dcmAuthors.SourceColumn.ToString())
```

C#:

```
System.Data.Common.DataColumnMapping dcmAuthors = new
System.Data.Common.DataColumnMapping();

// Set the property
dcmAuthors.SourceColumn = "au_lname";

// Get the property
Console.WriteLine(dcmAuthors.SourceColumn.ToString());
```

Also, this property is usually used when you create a `DataTableMapping` object from its default construct.

DataColumnMapping Methods

Even the `DataColumnMapping` inherit the same methods as the `DataTableMapping` ones, because both are derived from the same classes. Below, you'll find a brief description of these methods, but for more information, please consult the `DataTableMapping's` methods:

Method	Description
Equals	Returns a Boolean value indicating whether two objects are equal (`true`) or not (`false`).
GetHashCode	Useful to hash algorithms and hash table, it retrieves a hash code associated with the object.
GetLifetimeService	Usually this method retrieves an `ILease` object interface that manages the lifetime policy for the `DateColumnMapping` object.
GetType	Gets the type of the current object instance.
InitializeLifeTimeService	Overriding this method you can provide your own lease time to the object.
Finalize	Represents the destructor used by C#/C++ to free memory resources. In VB.NET it's called `Finalize`.
MemberwiseClone	Creates an empty clone of the current object.

`DataColumnMapping` provides just two proprietary methods, one to retrieve a string containing the column name and the other to retrieve a `DataColumn` object from a `DataTable`.

The GetDataColumnBySchemaAction Method

VB.NET:

```
Public Function GetDataColumnBySchemaAction( _
   ByVal dataTable As DataTable, _
   ByVal dataType As Type, _
   ByVal schemaAction As MissingSchemaAction _
) As DataColumn
```

C#:

```
public DataColumn GetDataColumnBySchemaAction(
    DataTable dataTable,
    Type dataType,
    MissingSchemaAction schemaAction
);
```

You can use this method when you need to retrieve a DataColumn object contained in a specified DataTable object. The dataTable parameter represents exactly the DataTable that contains the column needed, dataType is the type of the column (integer, string, and so on) while the last parameter is a MissingSchemaAction enum value that can assume one of the following values:

MissingSchemaAction values	Description
Error	If you specify this value and the column you are looking for is missing in the DataTable, then a SystemException object will be returned.
Add	If you specify this value and the column you are looking for is missing in the DataTable, then the necessary columns will be added to the schema.
AddWithKey	If you specify this value and the column you are looking for is missing in the DataTable, then the necessary columns will be added to the schema with primary key information also.
Ignore	If you specify this value and the table you are looking for is missing in the DataTable, then a null reference will be returned. In VB.NET language it will return a Nothing value.

Let's see a snippet of code to demonstrate this method:

VB.NET:

```
' Create a connection to the Northwind database
Dim dbConn As New
SqlClient.SqlConnection("server=localhost;uid=sa;pwd=;database=Northwind")

' Create a DataTableMapping object containing the column array
Dim dtmProducts As New System.Data.Common.DataTableMapping("Table", "Products", _
New System.Data.Common.DataColumnMapping() {New _
System.Data.Common.DataColumnMapping("ProductID", "ID"), New _
System.Data.Common.DataColumnMapping("ProductName", "Name")})

' Create a DataAdapter to retrieve data from Northwind database
Dim ProductsAdapter As New SqlClient.SqlDataAdapter("SELECT ProductID, ProductName _
FROM Products", dbConn)

' Associate it to the DataAdapter
ProductsAdapter.TableMappings.Add(dtmProducts)

' Create a DataSet to manage records
Dim dsProducts As New DataSet("Products")
```

```
' Fill the DataSet
ProductsAdapter.Fill(dsProducts)

' Retrieve the table Products from the DataSet
Dim dtProducts As New DataTable()
dtProducts = dtmProducts.GetDataTableBySchemaAction(dsProducts,
MissingSchemaAction.Error)

' Retrieve the DataColumn object from the DataColumnMapping that contains
' the ProductID
Dim dcProductID As New DataColumn()
dcProductID =
dtmProducts.ColumnMappings("ProductID").GetDataColumnBySchemaAction(dtProducts,
GetType(System.Int32), MissingSchemaAction.Error)

' Print to video its caption
Console.WriteLine(dcProductID.Caption)
```

C#:

```
using System;
using System.Data;
using System.Data.Common;
using System.Data.SqlClient;

. . .

// Create a connection to the Northwind database
SqlConnection dbConn = new SqlConnection();
dbConn.ConnectionString = "server=localhost;uid=sa;pwd=;database=Northwind";

// Create an array of DataColumnMapping to define the new column names
DataColumnMapping[] dcmProducts = {new DataColumnMapping("ProductID","ID"),
new DataColumnMapping("ProductName","Name")};

// Create a DataTableMapping object containing the column array
DataTableMapping dtmProducts = new
DataTableMapping("Table","Products",dcmProducts);

// Create a DataAdapter to retrieve data from Northwind database
SqlDataAdapter ProductsAdapter = new SqlDataAdapter("SELECT ProductID, ProductName
FROM Products",dbConn);

// Associate it to the DataAdapter
ProductsAdapter.TableMappings.Add(dtmProducts);

// Create a DataSet to manage records
DataSet dsProducts = new DataSet("Products");

// Fill the DataSet
ProductsAdapter.Fill(dsProducts);

// Retrieve the table Products from the DataSet
DataTable dtProducts = new DataTable();
```

```
dtProducts = dtmProducts.GetDataTableBySchemaAction(dsProducts,
System.Data.MissingSchemaAction.Error);

// Retrieve the DataColumn object from the DataColumnMapping that contains
// the ProductID
DataColumn dcProductID =
dtmProducts.ColumnMappings["ProductID"].GetDataColumnBySchemaAction(dtProducts,typ
eof(System.Int32),MissingSchemaAction.Error);

// Print to video its caption
Console.WriteLine(dcProductID.Caption);
```

The code above simply retrieves a `DataColumn` object from a `DataTable` contained into a `DataSet` filled previously by the `Fill()` method, and subsequently print, on video its caption. As you aspect the column name will be "ID" as shown in the following picture:

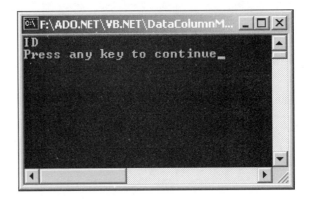

The ToString Method

VB.NET:

```
Overrides Public Function ToString() As String
```

C#:

```
public override string ToString();
```

This method simply converts the source column name to a string value.

VB.NET:

```
' Create a DataColumnMapping object
Dim dcmAuthors As New System.Data.Common.DataColumnMapping("au_fname",
"Author_FirstName")

' Print to video its source column name
Console.WriteLine(dcmAuthors.ToString())
```

C#:

```
// Create a DataColumnMapping object
System.Data.Common.DataColumnMapping dcmAuthors = new
System.Data.Common.DataColumnMapping("au_lname","Author_LastName");

// Print to video its source column name
Console.WriteLine(dcmAuthors.ToString());
```

Even this method like the DataTableMapping ones is automatically used when the DataColumnMapping is passed to a method like a string parameter.

The DataTableMappingCollection Object

In a lot of the examples we have seen in this chapter, we have often encountered the Add() method exposed by the TableMappings property of the DataAdapter object. Well, what we have used is just a DataTableMappingCollection returned by the property's call. If you have used a collection before you'll know that it is used to manage an array of objects. You can simply count how many objects the collection contains, you can add and remove one of them, plus a lot more. The final part of this chapter, is dedicated to examining the collections provided for DataTableMapping and DataColumnMapping objects. Let's start with the former.

DataTableMappingCollection Constructor

The DataTableMappingCollection object is derived from MarshallByRefObject class and from the Objects class and it implements a few of interface that characterize its collection functionalities. They are: ITableMappingCollection, IList, Icollection, and IEnumerable. The first is the core interface, because it allows implementing DataTableMapping collection functionalities. The second represents the abstract base class present in each collection object. The third is an interface that defines the size of the collection, the synchronization methods. It is derived from the fourth interface that implements the enumerate functionality.

The Default Constructor

VB.NET:
```
Public Sub New()
```

C#:
```
public DataTableMappingCollection();
```

The unique constructor available for this object allows creating an empty DataTableMappingCollection variable, initializing each of its objects to a null reference.

VB.NET:

```
Dim dtmcAuthors As New DataTableMappingCollection
```

C#:

```
System.Data.Common.DataTableMappingCollection dtmcAuthors = new
System.Data.Common.DataTableMappingCollection();
```

DataTableMappingCollection Properties

This object provides just two properties, one to count its own elements, and the other to point to a specific element in the collection. Let's examine both.

The Count Property

VB.NET:

```
Public ReadOnly Property Count As Integer
```

C#:

```
public int Count {get;}
```

You can use this property to retrieve the number of `DataTableMapping` objects contained in the collection. This is a read-only property, so no settings are permitted. In the following example, we are counting the number of Tables and writing the result to the console:

VB.NET:

```
Dim dtmcAuthors As New Common.DataTableMappingCollection()

dtmcAuthors.Add("Table", "Authors")
dtmcAuthors.Add("NewTable", "NewAuthors")

Console.WriteLine("Count={0}", dtmcAuthors.Count.ToString())
```

C#:

```
using System;
using System.Data.Common;

DataTableMappingCollection dtmcAuthors = new DataTableMappingCollection();

dtmcAuthors.Add("Table","Authors");
dtmcAuthors.Add("NewTable","NewAuthors");

Console.WriteLine("Count={0}",dtmcAuthors.Count.ToString());
```

The output of this simple example will be:

Count=2

The Item Property

VB.NET:

```
Overloads Public Default Property Item( ByVal index As Integer _
) As DataTableMapping

Overloads Public Default Property Item( ByVal sourceTable As String _
) As DataTableMapping
```

C#:

```
public DataTableMapping this[int index
] {get; set;}

public DataTableMapping this[string sourceTable
] {get; set;}
```

The Item property is used to retrieve a DataTableMapping object contained in the collection passing either a numeric index or a source table name string. You can also point to a specific element in the collection in order to change its content.

VB.NET:

```
Dim dtmcAuthors As New Common.DataTableMappingCollection()

dtmcAuthors.Add("Table", "Authors")
dtmcAuthors.Add("NewTable", "NewAuthors")

Console.WriteLine(dtmcAuthors("Table").DataSetTable)
Console.WriteLine(dtmcAuthors(1).DataSetTable)
```

C#:

```
using System;
using System.Data.Common;

DataTableMappingCollection dtmcAuthors = new DataTableMappingCollection();

dtmcAuthors.Add("Table","Authors");
dtmcAuthors.Add("NewTable","NewAuthors");

Console.WriteLine (dtmcAuthors["Table"].DataSetTable);
Console.WriteLine (dtmcAuthors[1].DataSetTable);
```

In this case the output will be:

Authors
NewAuthors

As you can see from the code above, you'll never find the `Item` property written through the script lines. To access the `Item` property you have to use square brackets in C# and brackets in VB.NET.

DataTableMappingCollection Methods

The `DataTableMappingCollection` object allows managing collection's elements through the use of its own methods. You can add a `DataTableMapping` object; remove an old one, insert an object in a specific position, and remove it from a specific position. You have all the tools to manage a collection efficiently.

As you can see from hierarchy, `DataTableMappingCollection` is derived from `IMarshallByRefObject` interface and like the other mapping objects it inherits its methods. These are:

- ❑ `CreateObjRef()`
- ❑ `Equals()`
- ❑ `GetHashCode()`
- ❑ `ToString()`
- ❑ `Finalize()`
- ❑ `MemberwiseClone()`

Now let's start to examine each proprietary method of the `DataTableMappingCollection` object.

The Add Method

VB.NET:

```
NotOverridable Overloads Public Function Add( _
    ByVal value As Object _
) As Integer

Overloads Public Function Add( _
    ByVal sourceTable As String, _
    ByVal dataSetTable As String _
) As DataTableMapping
```

C#:

```
public int Add(
    object value
);

public DataTableMapping Add(
    string sourceTable,
    string dataSetTable
);
```

This method allows adding a `DataTableMapping` object to the collection. The method comes in two versions; one accepts a `DataTableMapping` parameter, `value`, while the other creates and adds a `DataTableMapping` to the collection having the `sourceTable` and `dataSetTable` names specified in the string parameter. This example uses the first version of the method. A `DataTableMapping` object is created before passing it to the `Add()` method.

VB.NET:

```
Dim dtmAuthors As New Common.DataTableMapping("Table", "Authors")

Dim dtmcAuthors As New Common.DataTableMappingCollection()

dtmcAuthors.Add(dtmAuthors)

Console.WriteLine(dtmcAuthors("Table").DataSetTable)
```

C#:

```
using System;
using System.Data.Common;

DataTableMappingCollection dtmcAuthors = new DataTableMappingCollection();

DataTableMapping dtmAuthors = new DataTableMapping("Table","Authors");

dtmcAuthors.Add(dtmAuthors);

Console.WriteLine (dtmcAuthors["Table"].DataSetTable);
```

Using the second version of the method the code will be like this:

VB.NET:

```
Dim dtmcAuthors As New Common.DataTableMappingCollection()

dtmcAuthors.Add("Table","Authors")

Console.WriteLine(dtmcAuthors("Table").DataSetTable)
```

C#:

```
using System;
using System.Data.Common;

DataTableMappingCollection dtmcAuthors = new DataTableMappingCollection();

dtmcAuthors.Add("Table","Authors");

Console.WriteLine (dtmcAuthors["Table"].DataSetTable);
```

The AddRange Method

VB.NET:

```
Public Sub AddRange( ByVal value() _
    As DataTableMapping)
```

C#:

```
public void AddRange(DataTableMapping[]
    value);
```

This method either adds an array of `DataTableMapping` objects to the collection, if it is empty, or appends at the end of the collection if other objects have already been inserted. The `value` parameter represents just the array of mapping objects.

In the example below, is shown the use of the `AddRange()` method with a `DataTableMapping` object's creation before the method's call, directly inside the method parameters setting.

VB.NET:

```
Dim dtmcAuthors As New Common.DataTableMappingCollection()

dtmcAuthors.AddRange(New Common.DataTableMapping() {New
Common.DataTableMapping("Table", "Authors"), New
Common.DataTableMapping("NewTable", "NewAuthors")})

Console.WriteLine(dtmcAuthors("Table").DataSetTable)
Console.WriteLine(dtmcAuthors(1).DataSetTable)
```

C#:

```
using System;
using System.Data.Common;

DataTableMapping[] dtmAuthors = {new DataTableMapping("Table","Authors"), new
DataTableMapping("NewTable","NewAuthors")};

DataTableMappingCollection dtmcAuthors = new DataTableMappingCollection();

dtmcAuthors.AddRange(dtmAuthors);

Console.WriteLine (dtmcAuthors["Table"].DataSetTable);
Console.WriteLine (dtmcAuthors[1].DataSetTable);
```

The Clear Method

VB.NET:

```
NotOverridable Public Sub Clear()
```

C#:

```
public void Clear();
```

Use this method when you need to clear the collection removing every object inside it.

VB.NET:

```
Dim dtmcAuthors As New Common.DataTableMappingCollection()

dtmcAuthors.Clear()
```

C#:

```
DataTableMappingCollection dtmcAuthors = new DataTableMappingCollection();

dtmcAuthors.Clear();
```

The Contains Method

VB.NET:

```
NotOverridable Overloads Public Function Contains( _
   ByVal value As Object _
) As Boolean

NotOverridable Overloads Public Function Contains( _
   ByVal value As String _
) As Boolean
```

C#:

```
public bool Contains(object value);

public bool Contains(string value);
```

This method returns a Boolean value indicating whether an object is already present inside the collection (true) or not (false). The method comes in two versions; one requires a valid `DataTableMapping` object, and the other requires the source table name. The following example shows how to use the `Contains()` method for each of versions:

VB.NET:

```
Dim dtmcAuthors As New Common.DataTableMappingCollection()

dtmcAuthors.AddRange(New Common.DataTableMapping() {New
Common.DataTableMapping("Table", "Authors"), New
Common.DataTableMapping("NewTable", "NewAuthors")})

Console.WriteLine(dtmcAuthors.Contains("Table").ToString)
```

C#:

```
DataTableMapping[] dtmAuthors = {new DataTableMapping("Table","Authors"), new
DataTableMapping("NewTable","NewAuthors")};

DataTableMappingCollection dtmcAuthors = new DataTableMappingCollection();

dtmcAuthors.AddRange(dtmAuthors);

Console.WriteLine(dtmcAuthors.Contains(dtmAuthors[0]).ToString());
```

The output will be:

True

The CopyTo Method

VB.NET:

```
NotOverridable Public Sub CopyTo( _
    ByVal array As Array, _
    ByVal index As Integer _
)
```

C#:

```
public void CopyTo(Array array,
    int index);
```

This method copies the elements contained in the collection into an array. The first parameter, `array`, has to be the destination array, while the second parameter, `index`, represents the starting index to copy to. This method could be useful when an array parameter is required inside a method like the `AddRange()` ones. In the following example, we are copying into `dtmAuthors` starting at the beginning (index of 0):

VB.NET:

```
Dim dtmcAuthors As New Common.DataTableMappingCollection()
```

```
Dim dtmAuthors(2) As Common.DataTableMapping

dtmcAuthors.AddRange(New Common.DataTableMapping() {New
Common.DataTableMapping("Table", "Authors"), New
Common.DataTableMapping("NewTable", "NewAuthors")})

. . .
. . .

' Retrieve the array from the collection
dtmcAuthors.CopyTo(dtmAuthors, 0)

Console.WriteLine(dtmAuthors(0).ToString)
```

C#:

```
DataTableMappingCollection dtmcAuthors = new DataTableMappingCollection();

dtmcAuthors.AddRange(new DataTableMapping[] {new
DataTableMapping("Table","Authors"), new
DataTableMapping("NewTable","NewAuthors")});

DataTableMapping[] dtmAuthors = {new DataTableMapping(),new DataTableMapping()};

. . .
. . .

// Retrieve the array from the collection
dtmcAuthors.CopyTo(dtmAuthors,0);

Console.WriteLine(dtmAuthors[0].ToString());
```

The GetByDataSetTable Method

VB.NET:

```
Public Function GetByDataSetTable(ByVal dataSetTable As String _
) As DataTableMapping
```

C#:

```
public DataTableMapping GetByDataSetTable(
    string dataSetTable
);
```

You can retrieve a DataTableMapping object contained in the collection, by passing the DataSet table name to the unique parameter of this method, as in the example below:

VB.NET:

```
Dim dtmcAuthors As New Common.DataTableMappingCollection()

Dim dtmAuthors As New Common.DataTableMapping()

dtmcAuthors.AddRange(New Common.DataTableMapping() {New
```

```
Common.DataTableMapping("Table", "Authors"), New
Common.DataTableMapping("NewTable", "NewAuthors")})

dtmAuthors = dtmcAuthors.GetByDataSetTable("Authors")

Console.WriteLine(dtmAuthors.SourceTable.ToString())
```

C#:

```
DataTableMappingCollection dtmcAuthors = new DataTableMappingCollection();

dtmcAuthors.AddRange(new DataTableMapping[] {new
DataTableMapping("Table","Authors"), new
DataTableMapping("NewTable","NewAuthors")});

DataTableMapping dtmAuthors = new DataTableMapping();

dtmAuthors = dtmcAuthors.GetByDataSetTable("Authors");

Console.WriteLine(dtmAuthors.SourceTable.ToString());
```

The GetTableMappingBySchemaAction Method

VB.NET:

```
Public Shared Function GetTableMappingBySchemaAction( _
    ByVal tableMappings As DataTableMappingCollection, _
    ByVal sourceTable As String, _
    ByVal dataSetTable As String, _
    ByVal mappingAction As MissingMappingAction _
) As DataTableMapping
```

C#:

```
public static DataTableMapping GetTableMappingBySchemaAction(
    DataTableMappingCollection tableMappings,
    string sourceTable,
    string dataSetTable,
    MissingMappingAction mappingAction
);
```

This method, like the previous one, allows the retrieval of a DataTableMapping object, but here you have to specify its source and DataSet table names, the DataTableMappingCollection object that contains the required object and the action to do if the DataTableMapping object has not been found. MissingMappingAction can assume one of the following values:

MissingMappingAction values	Description
Error	If you specify this value and the DataTableMapping object you are looking for is missing in the collection, then a SystemException object will be returned.

MissingMappingAction values	Description
Ignore	If you specify this value and the `DataTableMapping` object you are looking for is missing in the collection, then a null reference will be returned. In VB.NET language it will return a `Nothing` value.
Passthrough	If you specify this value and the `DataTableMapping` object you are looking for is missing in the collection, then it will be created using the name you passed to the second and third parameter. The new object however will not added to the collection.

If you examine carefully the prototype of the method you'll see that it is a `static` method (`Shared` for VB.NET). This means, that you have to use the method without creating a `DataTableMappingCollection` object as can be seen from the following example:

VB.NET:

```
Dim dtmcAuthors As New Common.DataTableMappingCollection()

Dim dtmAuthors As New Common.DataTableMapping()

dtmcAuthors.AddRange(New Common.DataTableMapping() {New
Common.DataTableMapping("Table", "Authors"), New
Common.DataTableMapping("NewTable", "NewAuthors")})

dtmAuthors = DataTableMappingCollection.GetTableMappingBySchemaAction(dtmcAuthors,
"NewTable", "NewAuthors", MissingMappingAction.Error)

Console.WriteLine(dtmAuthors.SourceTable.ToString())
```

C#:

```
DataTableMappingCollection dtmcAuthors = new DataTableMappingCollection();

dtmcAuthors.AddRange(new DataTableMapping[] {new
DataTableMapping("Table","Authors"), new
DataTableMapping("NewTable","NewAuthors")});

DataTableMapping dtmAuthors = new DataTableMapping();

dtmAuthors =
DataTableMappingCollection.GetTableMappingBySchemaAction(dtmcAuthors,"NewTable","N
ewAuthors", MissingMappingAction.Error);

Console.WriteLine(dtmAuthors.SourceTable.ToString());
```

The IndexOf Method

VB.NET:

```
NotOverridable Overloads Public Function IndexOf( _
    ByVal value As Object _
) As Integer

NotOverridable Overloads Public Function IndexOf( _
    ByVal sourceTable As String _
) As Integer
```

C#:

```
public int IndexOf(object value);

public int IndexOf(string sourceTable);
```

When you need to retrieve the position of a `DataTableMapping` object inside the collection, you can specify either its name or itself as a parameter for this method. Usually, you'll use this method together with the `RemoveAt()` function as you'll see soon. The example shows how we retrieve the position using the objects name:

VB.NET:

```
Dim dtmcAuthors As New Common.DataTableMappingCollection()

dtmcAuthors.AddRange(New Common.DataTableMapping() {New
Common.DataTableMapping("Table", "Authors")})

Dim dtmAuthors As New Common.DataTableMapping("NewTable", "NewAuthors")

dtmcAuthors.Add(dtmAuthors)

Console.WriteLine(dtmcAuthors.IndexOf(dtmAuthors).ToString())
```

C#:

```
DataTableMappingCollection dtmcAuthors = new DataTableMappingCollection();

dtmcAuthors.AddRange(new DataTableMapping[] {new
DataTableMapping("Table","Authors"), new
DataTableMapping("NewTable","NewAuthors")});

Console.WriteLine(dtmcAuthors.IndexOf("NewTable").ToString());
```

The IndexOfDataSetTable Method

VB.NET:

```
Public Function IndexOfDataSetTable( _
    ByVal dataSetTable As String _
) As Integer
```

C#:

```
public int IndexOfDataSetTable(
    string dataSetTable
);
```

As in the previous method, the `IndexOfDataSetTable()` method retrieves the position of a `DataTableMapping` object inside the collection. The difference resides in the input parameter; here you have to provide the `DataSet` table name instead of the source table name, for example, `"NewAuthors"`:

VB.NET:

```
Dim dtmcAuthors As New Common.DataTableMappingCollection()

dtmcAuthors.AddRange(New Common.DataTableMapping() {New
Common.DataTableMapping("Table", "Authors")})

Dim dtmAuthors As New Common.DataTableMapping("NewTable", "NewAuthors")

dtmcAuthors.Add(dtmAuthors)

Console.WriteLine(dtmcAuthors.IndexOfDataSetTable("NewAuthors").ToString())
```

C#:

```
DataTableMappingCollection dtmcAuthors = new DataTableMappingCollection();

dtmcAuthors.AddRange(new DataTableMapping[] {new
DataTableMapping("Table","Authors"), new
DataTableMapping("NewTable","NewAuthors")});

Console.WriteLine(dtmcAuthors.IndexOfDataSetTable("NewAuthors").ToString());
```

The Insert Method

VB.NET:

```
NotOverridable Public Sub Insert(ByVal index As Integer, _
    ByVal value As Object _
)
```

C#:

```
public void Insert(int index,
    object value
);
```

This method adds a new `DataTableMapping` object to the collection. The difference between `Add()` method and this one, resides in the possibility to insert the new object in any collection array's index position . Recall that `Add()` appends to the last position in the collection the `DataTableMapping` object. If you choose to insert an object in the middle of the array, where this method will increment each remaining element a position automatically, as below, you are adding to position 1:

VB.NET:

```
Dim dtmcAuthors As New Common.DataTableMappingCollection()

dtmcAuthors.AddRange(New Common.DataTableMapping() {New
Common.DataTableMapping("Table", "Authors"), New
Common.DataTableMapping("NewTable", "NewAuthors")})

Dim dtmAuthors As New Common.DataTableMapping("AgainNewTable", "AgainNewAuthors")

dtmcAuthors.Insert(1, dtmAuthors)

Console.WriteLine(dtmcAuthors.IndexOfDataSetTable("NewAuthors").ToString())
```

C#:

```
DataTableMappingCollection dtmcAuthors = new DataTableMappingCollection();

dtmcAuthors.AddRange(new DataTableMapping[] {new
DataTableMapping("Table","Authors"), new
DataTableMapping("NewTable","NewAuthors")});

DataTableMapping dtmAuthors = new
DataTableMapping("AgainNewTable","AgainNewAuthors");

dtmcAuthors.Insert(1,dtmAuthors);

Console.WriteLine(dtmcAuthors.IndexOf("NewTable").ToString());
```

As expected, the output of this example, showing the new index of the `DataSetTable`, will be:

Index: 2

The Remove Method

VB.NET:

```
NotOverridable Public Sub Remove( _
    ByVal value As Object _
)
```

C#:

```
public void Remove(object value
);
```

Use this method when you need to remove a specified object from the collection.

VB.NET:

```
Dim dtmcAuthors As New Common.DataTableMappingCollection()

Dim dtmAuthors As New Common.DataTableMapping()

dtmcAuthors.AddRange(New Common.DataTableMapping() {New
Common.DataTableMapping("Table", "Authors"), New
Common.DataTableMapping("NewTable", "NewAuthors")})

dtmAuthors = dtmcAuthors.GetByDataSetTable("Authors")

dtmcAuthors.Remove(dtmAuthors)

Console.WriteLine(dtmcAuthors.Count.ToString())
```

C#:

```
DataTableMappingCollection dtmcAuthors = new DataTableMappingCollection();

dtmcAuthors.AddRange(new DataTableMapping[] {new
DataTableMapping("Table","Authors"), new
DataTableMapping("NewTable","NewAuthors")});

DataTableMapping dtmAuthors = new DataTableMapping();

dtmAuthors = dtmcAuthors.GetByDataSetTable("Authors");

dtmcAuthors.Remove(dtmAuthors);

Console.WriteLine(dtmcAuthors.Count.ToString());
```

The RemoveAt Method

VB.NET:

```
NotOverridable Overloads Public Sub RemoveAt( _
    ByVal index As Integer _
)

NotOverridable Overloads Public Sub RemoveAt( _
    ByVal sourceTable As String _
)
```

C#:

```
public void RemoveAt(int index);

public void RemoveAt(string sourceTable);
```

589

This method allows the removal of a `DataTableMapping` object from the collection specifying either its source table name or its index position. In the example below, the source table name, `"NewTable"`, is specified for removal:

VB.NET:

```
Dim dtmcAuthors As New Common.DataTableMappingCollection()

dtmcAuthors.AddRange(New Common.DataTableMapping() {New
Common.DataTableMapping("Table", "Authors"), New
Common.DataTableMapping("NewTable", "NewAuthors")})

dtmcAuthors.RemoveAt("NewTable")

Console.WriteLine(dtmcAuthors.Count.ToString())
```

C#:

```
DataTableMappingCollection dtmcAuthors = new DataTableMappingCollection();

dtmcAuthors.AddRange(new DataTableMapping[] {new
DataTableMapping("Table","Authors"), new
DataTableMapping("NewTable","NewAuthors")});

dtmcAuthors.RemoveAt(dtmcAuthors.IndexOf("NewTable"));

Console.WriteLine(dtmcAuthors.Count.ToString());
```

The DataColumnMappingCollection Object

Each column you map from a source database to a `DataSet` column is inserted inside a collection managed by the `DataTable`'s property called `ColumnMappings`. This is a `DataColumnMappingCollection` object contained in the `DataTable` that manages all the operations such as a new column, adding an array of new columns, removing one or more mapped columns adding and so on. A `DataColumnMappingCollection` object offers a very similar set of properties and methods as the `DataTableMappingCollection` that we have seen before in this chapter. Naturally they refer to columns and not to tables.

In the last part of this chapter, we will study every property and method exposed by the `DataColumnMappingCollection` object.

DataColumnMappingCollection Constructor

The `DataColumnMappingCollection` object is derived from `MarshallByRefObject` class and from the Objects class, and it implements a few interfaces that characterize its collection functionalities. They are: `IColumnMappingCollection`, `IList`, `Icollection`, and `IEnumerable`. The first is the core interface, because it allows implementation of the `DataColumnMapping` collection functionalities. The second represents the abstract base class present in each collection object. The third is an interface that defines the size of the collection and the synchronization methods. It is derived from the fourth interface that implements the enumerate functionality.

The Default Constructor

VB.NET:

```
Public Sub New()
```

C#:

```
public DataColumnMappingCollection();
```

This is the only constructor available for this object that allows the creation of an empty `DataColumnMappingCollection` variable.

VB.NET:

```
Dim dcmcAuthors As New DataColumnMappingCollection
```

C#:

```
DataColumnMappingCollection dcmcAuthors = new DataTableMappingCollection();
```

DataColumnMappingCollection Properties

The two properties exposed by this object allow the elements to count and point to a specific element in the collection. Their behavior is the same as the `DataTableMappingCollection`' properties.

The Count Property

VB.NET:

```
Public ReadOnly Property Count As Integer
```

C#:

```
public int Count {get;}
```

You can use this property to retrieve the number of `DataColumnMapping` objects contained in the collection. This is a read-only property so no settings are permitted.

VB.NET:

```
Dim dcmcAuthors As New Common.DataColumnMappingCollection()

dcmcAuthors.Add("au_id", "Author_ID")
dcmcAuthors.Add("au_fname", "Author_FirstName")
dcmcAuthors.Add("au_lname", "Author_LastName")

Console.WriteLine("Count={0}", dcmcAuthors.Count.ToString())
```

C#:

```
using System;
using System.Data.Common;

DataColumnMappingCollection dcmcAuthors = new DataColumnMappingCollection();

dcmcAuthors.Add("au_id","Author_ID");
dcmcAuthors.Add("au_fname","Author_FirstName");
dcmcAuthors.Add("au_lname","Author_LastName");

Console.WriteLine("Count={0}",dcmcAuthors.Count.ToString());
```

The output of this simple example will be:

Count=3

The Item Property

VB.NET:

```
Overloads Public Default Property Item( _
    ByVal index As Integer _
) As DataTableMapping

Overloads Public Default Property Item( _
    ByVal sourceTable As String _
) As DataTableMapping
```

C#:

```
public DataTableMapping this[int index
] {get; set;}

public DataTableMapping this[string sourceTable
] {get; set;}
```

Use this property to retrieve a `DataColumnMapping` object contained in the collection passing either a numeric index or a source column name string. You can also point to a specific element in the collection in order to change its content. Both of these methods are shown in the following example:

VB.NET:

```
Dim dcmcAuthors As New Common.DataColumnMappingCollection()

dcmcAuthors.Add("au_id", "Author_ID")
dcmcAuthors.Add("au_fname", "Author_FirstName")
dcmcAuthors.Add("au_lname", "Author_LastName")

Console.WriteLine(dcmcAuthors("au_id").DataSetColumn)
Console.WriteLine(dcmcAuthors(2).DataSetColumn)
```

C#:

```
using System;
using System.Data.Common;


DataColumnMappingCollection dcmcAuthors = new DataColumnMappingCollection();

dcmcAuthors.Add("au_id","Author_ID");
dcmcAuthors.Add("au_fname","Author_FirstName");
dcmcAuthors.Add("au_lname","Author_LastName");

Console.WriteLine(dcmcAuthors["au_id"].DataSetColumn);
Console.WriteLine(dcmcAuthors[2].DataSetColumn);
```

For this example, the output will be:

Author_ID
Author_LastName

DataColumnMappingCollection Methods

Using the DataColumnMappingCollection methods, we can manage every element contained in the collection. The operations are always the same; we can add a `DataColumnMapping` object and remove an old one, insert an object in a specific position, and remove it from a specific position.

Even this collection is derived from `IMarshallByRefObject` interface and like the other mapping objects, it inherits its methods as listed:

- ❑ `CreateObjRef()`
- ❑ `Equals()`
- ❑ `GetHashCode()`
- ❑ `ToString()`
- ❑ `Finalize()`
- ❑ `MemberwiseClone()`

Now we can start to study all the proprietary methods.

The Add Method

VB.NET:

```
NotOverridable Overloads Public Function Add( _
    ByVal value As Object _
) As Integer

Overloads Public Function Add( _
    ByVal sourceColumn As String, _
    ByVal dataSetColumn As String _
) As DataColumnMapping
```

C#:

```
public int Add(
   object value
);

public DataColumnMapping Add(
   string sourceColumn,
   string dataSetColumn
);
```

This method adds a `DataColumnMapping` object to the collection. The method comes in two versions; one accepts a `DataColumnMapping` object as a parameter, `value`, while the other creates and adds a `DataColumnMapping` object to the collection having the `sourceColumn` and `dataSetColumn` names specified in the string parameter, as can be seen below:

VB.NET:

```
Dim dcmcAuthors As New Common.DataColumnMappingCollection()

dcmcAuthors.Add("au_id", "Author_ID")
```

C#:

```
using System;
using System.Data.Common;

DataColumnMappingCollection dcmcAuthors = new DataColumnMappingCollection();

DataColumnMapping dcmAuthors = new DataColumnMapping("au_id","Author_ID");

dcmcAuthors.Add(dcmAuthors);
```

The AddRange Method

VB.NET:

```
Public Sub AddRange( _
   ByVal value() As DataColumnMapping _
)
```

C#:

```
public void AddRange(
   DataColumnMapping[] value
);
```

This method either adds an array of `DataColumnMapping` objects to the collection, if it's empty, or appends it at the end if other objects have been already inserted. The `value` parameter just represents the array of mapping objects.

VB.NET:

```
Dim dcmcAuthors As New Common.DataColumnMappingCollection()

dcmcAuthors.AddRange(New Common.DataColumnMapping() {New
Common.DataColumnMapping("au_id", "Author_ID"), New
Common.DataColumnMapping("au_fname", "Author_FirstName")})
```

C#:

```
using System;
using System.Data.Common;

DataColumnMapping[] dcmAuthors = {new DataColumnMapping("au_id","Author_ID"), new
DataColumnMapping("au_fname","Author_FirstName")};

DataColumnMappingCollection dcmcAuthors = new DataColumnMappingCollection();

dcmcAuthors.AddRange(dcmAuthors);
```

The Clear Method

VB.NET:

```
NotOverridable Public Sub Clear()
```

C#:

```
public void Clear();
```

Use this method when you need to remove all the elements from the collection.

VB.NET:

```
Dim dcmcAuthors As New Common.DataColumnMappingCollection()

dcmcAuthors.Clear()
```

C#:

```
DataColumnMappingCollection dcmcAuthors = new DataColumnMappingCollection();

dcmcAuthors.Clear();
```

The Contains Method

VB.NET:

```
NotOverridable Overloads Public Function Contains( _
    ByVal value As Object _
) As Boolean

NotOverridable Overloads Public Function Contains( _
    ByVal value As String _
) As Boolean
```

C#:

```
public bool Contains(
    object value
);

public bool Contains(
    string value
);
```

This method retrieves a Boolean value indicating if the given Object is present in the collection. The method comes in two versions; one requires a `DataColumnMapping` object as a parameter, and the other wants the source column name.

VB.NET:

```
Dim dcmcAuthors As New Common.DataColumnMappingCollection()

dcmcAuthors.AddRange(New Common.DataColumnMapping() {New
Common.DataColumnMapping("au_id", "Author_ID"), New
Common.DataColumnMapping("au_fname", "Author_FirstName")})

Console.WriteLine(dcmcAuthors.Contains("au_id").ToString())
```

C#:

```
DataColumnMapping[] dcmAuthors = {new DataColumnMapping("au_id","Author_ID"), new
DataColumnMapping("au_fname","Author_FirstName")};

DataColumnMappingCollection dcmcAuthors = new DataColumnMappingCollection();

dcmcAuthors.AddRange(dcmAuthors);

Console.WriteLine(dcmcAuthors.Contains(dcmAuthors[0]).ToString());
```

The example above shows how to use the `Contains()` method for each version. The output will be:

True

The CopyTo Method

VB.NET:

```
NotOverridable Public Sub CopyTo( _
    ByVal array As Array, _
    ByVal index As Integer _
)
```

C#:

```
public void CopyTo(
    Array array,
    int index
);
```

This method copies the elements contained in the collection into an array. The first parameter, `array`, has to be the destination array, dcmAuthor/dcmAuthorsTemp, while the second parameter, `index`, represents the starting index to copy to, 0. This method could be useful when an array parameter is required inside a method such as the `AddRange()` ones.

VB.NET:

```
Dim dcmcAuthors As New Common.DataColumnMappingCollection()

dcmcAuthors.AddRange(New Common.DataColumnMapping() {New
Common.DataColumnMapping("au_id", "Author_ID"), New
Common.DataColumnMapping("au_fname", "Author_FirstName")})

Dim dcmAuthor(2) As Common.DataColumnMapping

dcmcAuthors.CopyTo(dcmAuthor, 0)

Console.WriteLine(dcmAuthor(0).ToString())
```

C#:

```
DataColumnMapping[] dcmAuthors = {new DataColumnMapping("au_id","Author_ID"), new
DataColumnMapping("au_fname","Author_FirstName")};

DataColumnMappingCollection dcmcAuthors = new DataColumnMappingCollection();

dcmcAuthors.AddRange(dcmAuthors);

DataColumnMapping[] dcmAuthorsTemp = {new DataColumnMapping(), new
DataColumnMapping()};

dcmcAuthors.CopyTo(dcmAuthorsTemp,0);

Console.WriteLine(dcmAuthorsTemp[0].ToString());
```

The GetByDataSetColumn Method

VB.NET:

```
Public Function GetByDataSetColumn( _
    ByVal value As String _
) As DataColumnMapping
```

C#:

```
public DataColumnMapping GetByDataSetColumn(
    string value
);
```

You can retrieve a `DataColumnMapping` object contained in the collection by passing the `DataSet` column name, `"Author_ID"`, as a parameter of this method.

VB.NET:

```
Dim dcmcAuthors As New Common.DataColumnMappingCollection()

dcmcAuthors.AddRange(New Common.DataColumnMapping() {New
Common.DataColumnMapping("au_id", "Author_ID"), New
Common.DataColumnMapping("au_fname", "Author_FirstName")})

Dim dcmAuthor As New Common.DataColumnMapping()

dcmAuthor = dcmcAuthors.GetByDataSetColumn("Author_ID")

Console.WriteLine(dcmAuthor.ToString())
```

C#:

```
DataColumnMapping[] dcmAuthors = {new DataColumnMapping("au_id","Author_ID"), new
DataColumnMapping("au_fname","Author_FirstName")};

DataColumnMappingCollection dcmcAuthors = new DataColumnMappingCollection();

dcmcAuthors.AddRange(dcmAuthors);

DataColumnMapping dcmAuthorsTemp = dcmcAuthors.GetByDataSetColumn("Author_ID");

Console.WriteLine(dcmAuthorsTemp.ToString());
```

The GetColumnMappingBySchemaAction Method

VB.NET:

```
Public Shared Function GetColumnMappingBySchemaAction( _
   ByVal columnMappings As DataColumnMappingCollection, _
   ByVal sourceColumn As String, _
   ByVal mappingAction As MissingMappingAction _
) As DataColumnMapping
```

C#:

```
public static DataColumnMapping GetColumnMappingBySchemaAction(
   DataColumnMappingCollection columnMappings,
   string sourceColumn,
   MissingMappingAction mappingAction
);
```

The static method, Shared in VB.NET, provides another way to retrieve a DataColumnMapping object contained into a collection. In this method, you have to specify a DataColumnMappingCollection parameter when looking for the mapped column, the source column name, and a MissingMappingAction enum value. The latter can assume one of the following values:

MissingMappingAction values	Description
Error	If you specify this value and the `DataColumnMapping` object you are looking for is missing in the collection, then a `SystemException` object will be returned.
Ignore	If you specify this value and the `DataColumnMapping` object you are looking for is missing in the collection, then a null reference will be returned. In VB.NET language it will return a `Nothing` value.
Passthrough	If you specify this value and the `DataColumnMapping` object you are looking for is missing in the collection, then it will be created using the name you passed to the second parameter. The new object however will not added to the collection.

VB.NET:

```
Dim dcmcAuthors As New Common.DataColumnMappingCollection()

dcmcAuthors.AddRange(New Common.DataColumnMapping() {New
Common.DataColumnMapping("au_id", "Author_ID"), New
Common.DataColumnMapping("au_fname", "Author_FirstName")})

Dim dcmAuthor As New Common.DataColumnMapping()

dcmAuthor =
Common.DataColumnMappingCollection.GetColumnMappingBySchemaAction(dcmcAuthors,
"au_fname", MissingMappingAction.Error)

Console.WriteLine(dcmAuthor.ToString())
```

C#:

```
DataColumnMapping[] dcmAuthors = {new DataColumnMapping("au_id","Author_ID"), new
DataColumnMapping("au_fname","Author_FirstName")};

DataColumnMappingCollection dcmcAuthors = new DataColumnMappingCollection();

dcmcAuthors.AddRange(dcmAuthors);

DataColumnMapping dcmAuthorsTemp =
DataColumnMappingCollection.GetColumnMappingBySchemaAction(dcmcAuthors,"au_fname",
MissingMappingAction.Error);

Console.WriteLine(dcmAuthorsTemp.ToString());
```

The IndexOf Method

VB.NET:

```
NotOverridable Overloads Public Function IndexOf( _
    ByVal value As Object _
) As Integer

NotOverridable Overloads Public Function IndexOf( _
    ByVal sourceColumn As String _
) As Integer
```

C#:

```
public int IndexOf(object value
);

public int IndexOf(string sourceColumn
);
```

This method retrieves the position of a DataColumnMapping object inside the collection. You can find the object by specifying either its name, as in the following example, or the object itself as a parameter for this method. Usually, you'll use this method together with the RemoveAt() function.

VB.NET:

```
Dim dcmcAuthors As New Common.DataColumnMappingCollection()

dcmcAuthors.AddRange(New Common.DataColumnMapping() {New
Common.DataColumnMapping("au_id", "Author_ID"), New
Common.DataColumnMapping("au_fname", "Author_FirstName")})

Dim dcmAuthor As New Common.DataColumnMapping()

dcmAuthor = dcmcAuthors.GetByDataSetColumn("Author_FirstName")

Console.WriteLine(dcmcAuthors.IndexOf(dcmAuthor).ToString())
```

C#:

```
DataColumnMapping[] dcmAuthors = {new DataColumnMapping("au_id","Author_ID"), new
DataColumnMapping("au_fname","Author_FirstName")};

DataColumnMappingCollection dcmcAuthors = new DataColumnMappingCollection();

dcmcAuthors.AddRange(dcmAuthors);

Console.WriteLine(dcmcAuthors.IndexOf("au_fname").ToString());
```

The IndexOfDataSetColumn Method

VB.NET:

```
Public Function IndexOfDataSetColumn( _
    ByVal dataSetColumn As String _
) As Integer
```

C#:

```
public int IndexOfDataSetColumn(
    string dataSetColumn
);
```

The IndexOfDataSetTable() method also retrieves the position of a DataColumnMapping object inside the collection, but here you have to provide the DataSet column name instead, of the source column name. In the following example, the data column name used is "Author_ID":

VB.NET:

```
Dim dcmcAuthors As New Common.DataColumnMappingCollection()

dcmcAuthors.AddRange(New Common.DataColumnMapping() {New
Common.DataColumnMapping("au_id", "Author_ID"), New
Common.DataColumnMapping("au_fname", "Author_FirstName")})

Console.WriteLine(dcmcAuthors.IndexOfDataSetColumn("Author_ID").ToString())
```

C#:

```
DataColumnMapping[] dcmAuthors = {new DataColumnMapping("au_id","Author_ID"), new
DataColumnMapping("au_fname","Author_FirstName")};

DataColumnMappingCollection dcmcAuthors = new DataColumnMappingCollection();

dcmcAuthors.AddRange(dcmAuthors);

Console.WriteLine(dcmcAuthors.IndexOfDataSetColumn("Author_ID").ToString());
```

The output from the code above is:

Index = 0

The Insert Method

VB.NET:

```
NotOverridable Public Sub Insert( _
    ByVal index As Integer, _
    ByVal value As Object _
)
```

C#:

```
public void Insert(
    int index,
    object value
);
```

This method inserts a new `DataColumnMapping` object, `dcmAuthorLastName`, into the collection at the specified index position, 1. If you choose to insert an object in the middle of the array, this method will increment the position of each of the remaining elements.

VB.NET:

```
Dim dcmcAuthors As New Common.DataColumnMappingCollection()

dcmcAuthors.AddRange(New Common.DataColumnMapping() {New
Common.DataColumnMapping("au_id", "Author_ID"), New
Common.DataColumnMapping("au_fname", "Author_FirstName")})

Dim dcmAuthorLastName As New Common.DataColumnMapping("au_lname",
"Author_LastName")

dcmcAuthors.Insert(1, dcmAuthorLastName)

Console.WriteLine(dcmcAuthors.IndexOf("au_fname").ToString())
```

C#:

```
DataColumnMapping[] dcmAuthors = {new DataColumnMapping("au_id","Author_ID"), new
DataColumnMapping("au_fname","Author_FirstName")};

DataColumnMappingCollection dcmcAuthors = new DataColumnMappingCollection();

dcmcAuthors.AddRange(dcmAuthors);

DataColumnMapping dcmAuthorLastName = new
DataColumnMapping("au_lname","Author_LastName");

dcmcAuthors.Insert(1,dcmAuthorLastName);

Console.WriteLine(dcmcAuthors.IndexOf("au_fname").ToString());
```

The output of this example, showing the new index of the `DataSetColumn`, will be:

Index: 2

The Remove Method

VB.NET:

```
NotOverridable Public Sub Remove( _
    ByVal value As Object _
)
```

C#:
```
public void Remove(
    object value
);
```

Use this method when you need to remove a specified object from the collection.

VB.NET:
```
Dim dcmcAuthors As New Common.DataColumnMappingCollection()

dcmcAuthors.AddRange(New Common.DataColumnMapping() {New
Common.DataColumnMapping("au_id", "Author_ID"), New
Common.DataColumnMapping("au_fname", "Author_FirstName")})

dcmcAuthors.Remove(dcmcAuthors.GetByDataSetColumn("Author_FirstName"))

Console.WriteLine(dcmcAuthors.Count.ToString())
```

C#:
```
DataColumnMapping[] dcmAuthors = {new DataColumnMapping("au_id","Author_ID"), new
DataColumnMapping("au_fname","Author_FirstName")};

DataColumnMappingCollection dcmcAuthors = new DataColumnMappingCollection();

dcmcAuthors.AddRange(dcmAuthors);

dcmcAuthors.Remove(dcmcAuthors.GetByDataSetColumn("Author_FirstName"));

Console.WriteLine(dcmcAuthors.Count.ToString());
```

The RemoveAt Method

VB.NET:
```
NotOverridable Overloads Public Sub RemoveAt( _
    ByVal index As Integer _
)

NotOverridable Overloads Public Sub RemoveAt( _
    ByVal sourceColumn As String _
)
```

C#:
```
public void RemoveAt(
    int index
);

public void RemoveAt(
    string sourceColumn
);
```

With this method, you can remove a `DataColumnMapping` object from the collection by specifying either its source column name or its index position. The source column name is used to specify the object in the following example:

VB.NET:

```
Dim dcmcAuthors As New Common.DataColumnMappingCollection()

dcmcAuthors.AddRange(New Common.DataColumnMapping() {New
Common.DataColumnMapping("au_id", "Author_ID"), New
Common.DataColumnMapping("au_fname", "Author_FirstName")})

        dcmcAuthors.RemoveAt(dcmcAuthors.IndexOfDataSetColumn("Author_FirstName"))

Console.WriteLine(dcmcAuthors.Count.ToString())
```

C#:

```
DataColumnMapping[] dcmAuthors = {new DataColumnMapping("au_id","Author_ID"), new
DataColumnMapping("au_fname","Author_FirstName")};

DataColumnMappingCollection dcmcAuthors = new DataColumnMappingCollection();

dcmcAuthors.AddRange(dcmcAuthors);

dcmcAuthors.RemoveAt("au_fname");

Console.WriteLine(dcmcAuthors.Count.ToString());
```

Summary

The mapping functionality is a new entry in the ADO family and is very useful. You can use it to map from database's columns and tables to a `DataSet` object, but where it gives its best, is when you use it to map from a XML schema to the database. We have seen how to use the objects in both these contexts and then every property and method they provide. You'll find the more important examples inside the code provided with the book.

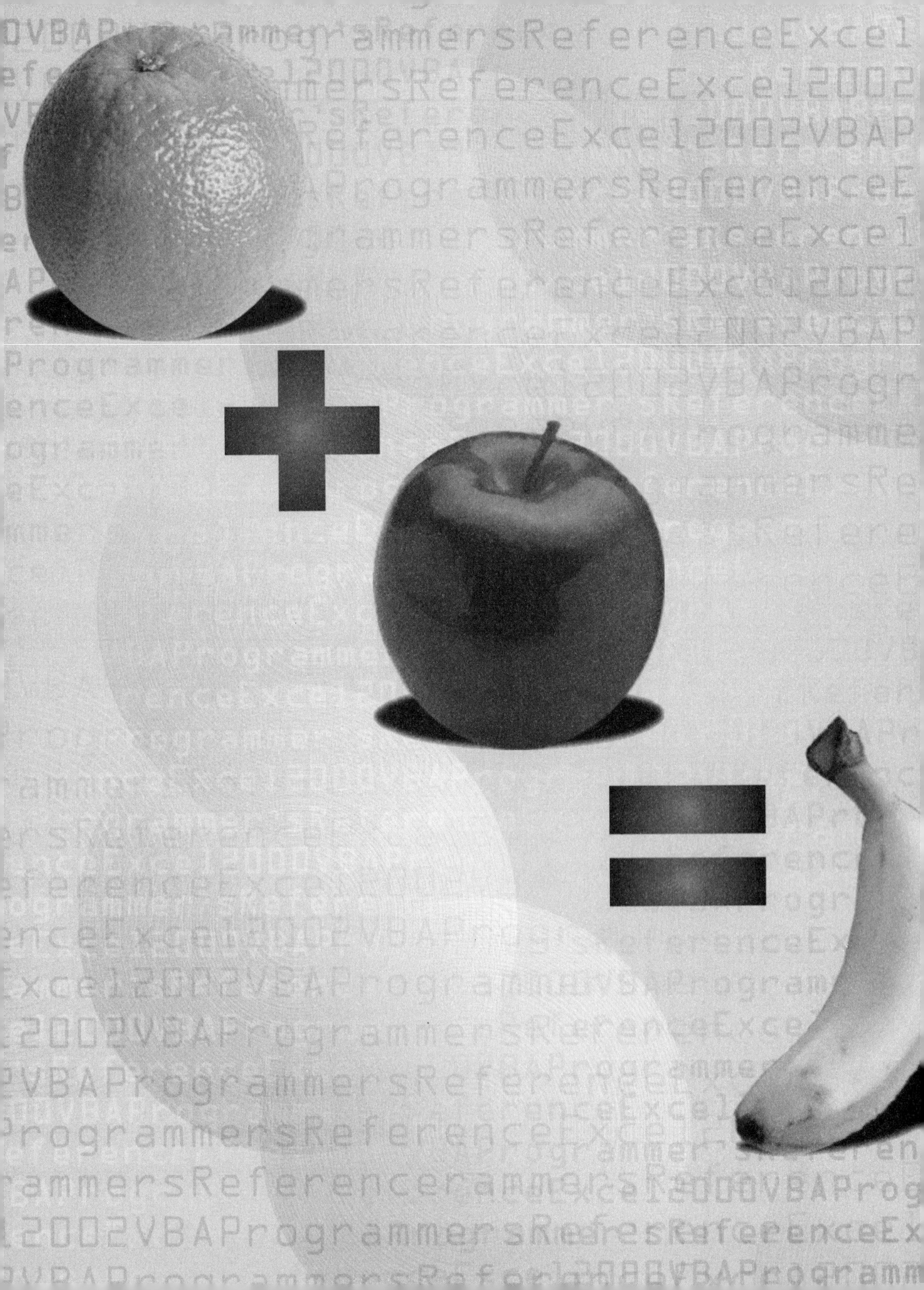

Transactions

Understanding Transactions

A transaction is a single logical unit of work involving the reading and/or writing of data. Transactions enable us to write to data located in several tables or several records with one process. Distributed transactions are transactions whose actions span multiple data stores.

For example, let's look at a cash transfer between two bank accounts. In order for the transfer to succeed, both the debit from the source account and the credit to the target account must succeed. If either action fails, the entire process must fail so we wrap these actions in a transaction. We can represent this in pseudo-code in the following way:

```
Begin Transaction
Attempt debit
If debit was successful, then
    Attempt credit
    If credit was successful, then
        Complete transaction
    Else
        Cancel transaction
    End If
Else
    Cancel transaction
End If
```

Notice that any outcome results in either a completed or a cancelled transaction. This ensures that the transaction behaves properly: it either performs all or none of the operations. This is known as **atomicity**. There are three other guidelines for well-designed transactions. The four are known as the **ACID** guidelines – ACID standing for Atomicity, Consistency, Isolation, and Durability. We will discuss these in more detail.

ACID Guidelines

❑ **Atomicity** – a transaction is either successful or it is not – it either completes all of the work or none of it (the original meaning of atom implied the smallest thing possible – something that could not be split)

❑ **Consistency** – the data involved in a transaction is in a known state when the transaction began, and is in a known state when it ends

❑ **Isolation** – a transaction should appear to itself to be the only transaction running in a data store – changes made by other transactions should not be visible to a particular transaction (sometimes called **Serializability**)

❑ **Durability** –when a transaction is complete, the system guarantees that the changes committed are posted to the data source; usually this involves the use of a transaction log, which records actions performed by a transaction and can be used to post any changes which failed (due to a system failure, for example)

There are valid programming circumstances where these guidelines are violated. For example, nested transactions, which we will discuss next, violate the Atomicity guideline, as they allow a partial transaction to be committed. There are isolation levels, discussed later, which allow other processes to read or even write to the data involved in your transaction, which clearly violates the Isolation guideline. This does not mean that the guidelines are inherently faulty or that code using nested transactions and isolation levels is inherently faulty. The guidelines *are* guidelines – its okay to break them, but have a good reason first.

Nested Transactions

There are times when you want to perform a group of actions, but allow for the possibility of deciding what to rollback, should one or more of the actions fail. For example, say we're creating an order. The transaction should create the order record and the order details records. We want to ensure that the order record is created, but if the order details records cannot be added, we want to have them logged or try again later without removing the order record.

Nested transactions provide the solution. There are two approaches to nesting transactions: hierarchical transactions and named savepoints.

In a hierarchical transaction group, one or more separate transactions are created within a single transaction. The nesting level is not limited, except by memory and data source allowances. The order transaction described above would look like this:

```
Begin Order Transaction
     Begin CreateOrder Transaction
           Create order
     Commit CreateOrder Transaction
     Begin CreateOrderDetails Transaction
           Create order details
     Commit CreateOrderDetails Transaction
Commit Order Transaction
```

A named savepoint is a point in the transaction which is labeled. You can then rollback the transaction to a given named point. The same order transaction would look like this:

```
Begin Order Transaction
      Create order
      Save 'OrderCreated'
      Create order details
Commit Order Transaction
```

To undo creation of the order details in the hierarchical transaction, we rollback the CreateOrderDetails transaction. Using the named savepoint transaction we rollback to the OrderCreated savepoint.

Concurrency and Locking

The nature of client/server applications is that there are multiple clients operating on a server. Users' actions can overlap meaning more than one user accesses the same data at the same time. This is called **concurrency**. In order to ensure the integrity of data as it is read and written, different types of locking mechanisms are used, each of which restricts access to data in different degrees:

❑ **No lock** – other processes have read and write access to the data; keep in mind this means you can be reading data that is in the process of being modified (a 'dirty read'), or data that is being removed; no guarantee is made as to the integrity and reliability of the data.

❑ **Shared lock** – other processes have read access, but not write access to the data; multiple shared locks can exist on the same data.

❑ **Update lock** – other processes have read access, but not write access to the data; only one update lock can exist on the data, but additional shared locks are allowed. This lock is used for pending updates, which require an exclusive lock. Without an Update lock, two transactions can acquire a shared lock on a row, for example, and attempt to acquire an exclusive lock to update the data; they will deadlock waiting for one another to release their shared locks.

❑ **Exclusive lock** – other processes have neither read nor write access to the data; no other locks can exist on the data.

When a process encounters a lock that it needs released, it will wait until the release. The wait time is usually determined by the database administrator, but can be also specified in a process command.

The granularity of the lock is important as well. Data sources can lock resources in many different levels of granularity (for example records, pages, and tables). Some data sources use bigger page sizes than others. This is important, because some data sources cannot perform record locks, but rather perform page locks. So if you access a single record on a page, your lock is issued on the entire page.

The Isolation Level determines how transactions interact with other transactions. Isolation Levels define locking mechanisms that prevent one or more of the following:

❑ Dirty Read – reading data which has been modified by another transaction but not committed

❑ Nonrepeatable Read – retrieving different data results when re-reading data, meaning the data has been modified

❏ Phantom Rows – retrieving different row results when re-reading data, meaning rows were added (or if the read contained criteria, rows that previously did not match the criteria were updated and now match the criteria)

There are several specific isolation levels commonly used (shown in increasing level of isolation)

❏ Read Uncommitted – no locks are placed on the data, meaning all data can be read; dirty reads, nonrepeatable reads and phantom rows can all occur (NO LOCK, READUNCOMMITTED in T-SQL)

❏ Read Committed – reads during the course of a transaction do not include pending (uncommitted) changes; no dirty reads can occur, but nonrepeatable reads and phantom rows can occur (READCOMMITTED in T-SQL)

❏ Repeatable Read – other processes do not have write access to the data during the course of a transaction, but insertions into tables to which the data belongs are allowed; no dirty reads nor nonrepeatable reads can occur, but phantom rows can occur (REPEATABLE READ in T-SQL)

❏ Serializable – other processes do not have read nor write access to the data during the course of the transaction and insertions into tables to which the data belongs are not allowed; no dirty reads, nonrepeatable reads nor phantom rows can occur (SERIALIZABLE, HOLDLOCK in T-SQL)

While data sources achieve these levels in different ways, appropriate locking mechanisms are used to guarantee the isolation level. For example, in order to prevent repeatable reads, a transaction can issue and hold locks on all rows it reads or writes for the duration of the transaction.

As isolation increases the reliability of the data increases, but the level of concurrency decreases. For example, Read Committed allows for less concurrency than Read Uncommitted, but it also does not read data which has changes pending, meaning it avoids dirty reads.

For the Isolation Level options in ADO.NET, see the `IsolationLevel` property under the `Transaction` Class section, later in this chapter.

We need to be careful when setting locking. We must be aware of the code we've written as well as the default locking mechanisms used by the data source. There are situations when our program can hold locks unnecessarily because of implied locks. Some examples:

❏ A SELECT or UPDATE statement with no WHERE clause can issue your lock on the entire table, because you have not specified which records in the table you will be accessing

❏ Accessing many rows which are stored on the same page can issue your lock on the entire page, an optimization performed by some data sources to avoid issuing many record locks (assuming the data source supports record locks)

❏ Locks are held on all the data accessed by nested transactions until the entire transaction is done, even if some of the transaction actions have been rolled back

Changes from ADO 2.6

The most obvious change regarding the implementation of transactions from ADO 2.6, is the presence of `Transaction` objects in ADO.NET. Each data provider has a `Transaction` object:

- ❑ `OleDbTransaction` – manages transactions on an OLE DB connection
- ❑ `SqlTransaction` – manages transactions on a SQL Server connection
- ❑ `OdbcTransaction` – manages transactions on an ODBC connection

These allow for greater control over transaction processing. The only interaction with the `Connection` object comes with the creation of the `Transaction` object. All other commands and properties are handled through the `Transaction` object itself.

The data providers differ in the way they handle nested transactions:

- ❑ `OleDbTransaction` objects create nested transactions by calling the `BeginTransaction` method on an existing `OleDbTransaction` object; they use hierarchical transactions
- ❑ `SqlTransacion` and `OdbcTransaction` use the `Save` method to create named savepoints (this emulates the T-SQL SAVE TRANSACTION call)
- ❑ At the time of writing, the current version of `OdbcTransaction` (Beta 1) does not support nested transactions.

The Transaction Class

The Transaction class represents a single transaction executed against a data source. In ADO.NET, there are three Transaction classes:

- ❑ `OleDbTransaction` – transactions accessing an OLE DB data source
- ❑ `SqlTransaction` – transactions accessing a SQL Server
- ❑ `OdbcTransaction` – transactions accessing an ODBC data source

Transaction Constructors

We construct a `Transaction` object by invoking the `BeginTransaction` method on the `Connection` object. Once the transaction exists, we use a command object to operate on the data, so we must assign the `Transaction` object to the `Command` object using its `Transaction` property.

```
MyTransaction = MyConnection.BeginTransaction()
MyCommand.Transaction = MyTransaction
```

Transaction Properties

The IsolationLevel Property

The `IsolationLevel` property indicates the isolation level (transaction lock) for the current transaction.

VB.NET:

```
ReadOnly Property IsolationLevel As IsolationLevel
```

C#:

```
IsolationLevel IsolationLevel {get;}
```

The `IsolationLevel` property is set using the `IsolationLevel` enumeration (from the `System.Data` namespace). The `IsolationLevel` enumeration constants describe the same Isolation Levels discussed earlier (repeated here) and include two other isolation levels, Chaos and Unspecified. The constants are:

- ❑ `Chaos` – no write access is allowed on pending changes from a transaction with a higher level of isolation (equivalent to `adXactChaos` in ADO 2.6)

- ❑ `Unspecified` – the provider is using an isolation level that cannot be determined (equivalent to `adXactUnspecified` in ADO 2.6)

- ❑ `ReadUncommitted` – no locks are placed on the data, meaning all data can be read; dirty reads, nonrepeatable reads, and phantom rows can all occur (NO LOCK, READUNCOMMITTED in T-SQL; equivalent to `adXactBrowse` or `adXactReadUncommitted` in ADO 2.6)

- ❑ `ReadCommitted` – reads during the course of a transaction do not include pending (uncommitted) changes; no dirty reads can occur, but nonrepeatable reads and phantom rows can occur (READCOMMITTED in T-SQL; equivalent to adXactCursorStability or adXactReadCommitted in ADO 2.6)

- ❑ `RepeatableRead` – other processes do not have write access to the data during the course of a transaction, but insertions into tables to which the data belongs are allowed; no dirty reads nor nonrepeatable reads can occur, but phantom rows can occur (REPEATABLE READ in T-SQL; equivalent to adXactRepeatableRead in ADO 2.6)

- ❑ `Serializable` – other processes do not have read nor write access to the data during the course of the transaction and insertions into tables to which the data belongs are not allowed; no dirty reads, nonrepeatable reads nor phantom rows can occur (SERIALIZABLE, HOLDLOCK in T-SQL; equivalent to adXactIsolated or adXactSerializable in ADO 2.6)

The `IsolationLevel` property is read-only in `Transaction` objects. We can set the `IsolationLevel` for a `Transaction` object by passing the `IsolationLevel` to the `BeginTransaction` method of the current `Connection`:

```
MyTransaction = MyConnection.BeginTransaction (IsolationLevel.RepeatableRead)
```

Nested `OleDbTransaction` objects are created using the `Begin` method. You can set the `IsolationLevel` property of the resulting nested `OleDbTransaction` by passing the `IsolationLevel`:

```
MyTransaction.Begin (IsolationLevel.RepeatableRead)
```

Transaction Methods

The Begin Method (OleDbOnly)

This method creates a nested transaction within the current `OleDbTransaction`.

Transact-SQL: BEGIN TRAN

VB.NET:
```
Overloads Public Function Begin() as OleDbTransaction
```

C#:
```
public OleDbTransaction Begin();
```

Or

VB.NET:
```
Overloads Public Function Begin(
    ByVal isolevel as IsolationLevel) as OleDbTransaction
```

C#:
```
public OleDbTransaction Begin(
    IsolationLevel isolevel);
```

Exceptions:

❑ `InvalidOperationException` - returned when the provider does not support nested transactions

The `Begin` method creates a nested transaction and returns a reference to the new `OleDbTransaction` object. It is called on an existing `OleDbTransaction` object, therefore, the new transaction is nested within the existing `OleDbTransaction` object. If no isolation level is specified, `ReadCommit` is used.

For example, let's code the orders nested transactions we discussed earlier.

VB.NET:
```
Public Function CreateOrder(ByRef MyConnection as OleDbConnection)
    Dim tranOrders as OleDbTransaction
    Dim tranOrderDetails as OleDbTransaction
    ' begin the Order transaction
    tranOrders = MyConnection.BeginTransaction()
```

```
        MyConnection.Transaction = tranOrder
        ' code to write an order to the data source goes here...
        ' begin CreateOrderDetails Transaction
        tranOrderDetails = tranOrders.Begin()
        ' code to write order details to the data source goes here...
        ' commit CreateOrderDetails Transaction
        tranOrderDetails.Commit()
        ' commit Order Transaction
        tranOrder.Commit()
    End Function
```

C#:

```
public void CreateOrder(OleDbConnection MyConnection)
{
    OleDbTransaction tranOrders;
    OleDbTransaction tranOrderDetails;
    // begin the Order transaction
    tranOrders = MyConnection.BeginTransaction();
    MyConnection.Transaction = tranOrder;
    // code to write an order to the data source goes here...
    // begin CreateOrderDetails Transaction
    tranOrderDetails = tranOrders.Begin();
    // code to write order details to the data source goes here...
    // commit CreateOrderDetails Transaction
        tranOrderDetails.Commit();
        // commit Order Transaction
        tranOrder.Commit();
    }
```

This method is pretty straightforward and includes no error checking. The example at the end of the chapter uses `Try... Catch... Finally` along with `Begin`, `Commit` and `Rollback`.

The Commit Method

The `Commit` method commits pending changes made to the database within the current transaction.

Transact-SQL: COMMIT TRAN

VB.NET:

```
NotOverridable Public Sub Commit();
```

C#:

```
public void commit();
```

Exceptions:

- ❑   `Exception` – returned when an unspecified error has occurred

- ❑   `InvalidOperationException` – returned then the transaction is not in a modified state (it has been committed or rolled back), or when the connection is no longer valid

You can only commit changes to a transaction which has been initiated and not committed or rolled back. When calling this method will rolled back any nested transactions within the current transaction that have been initiated, but not committed or rolled back.

In the example below, `MyNested1` will be committed, `MyNested2` will be rolled back, and `MyNested3` will be rolled back, because it was initiated, but not explicitly committed or rolled back.

VB.NET:

```
Imports System.Data.OleDb
Public Function TestNesting(ByRef MyConnection as OleDbConnection)
    Dim MyTran As OleDbTransaction
    Dim MyNestedTran1 As OleDbTransaction
    Dim MyNestedTran2 As OleDbTransaction
    Dim MyNestedTran3 As OleDbTransaction
    Dim MyCommand As New OleDbCommand()

    OleDbConnection1.Open()

    ' start a transaction
    MyTran = OleDbConnection1.BeginTransaction()

    ' set up the command object
    MyCommand.Transaction = MyTran
    MyCommand.Connection = OleDbConnection1

    ' start a nested transaction and commit it
    MyNestedTran1 = MyTran.Begin()
    MyCommand.Transaction = MyNestedTran1
    MyCommand.CommandText = "Insert into Log (Notes) VALUES ('nested1')"
    MyCommand.ExecuteNonQuery()
    MyNestedTran1.Commit()

    ' start a nested transaction and roll it back
    MyNestedTran2 = MyTran.Begin()
    MyCommand.Transaction = MyNestedTran2
    MyCommand.CommandText = "Insert into Log (Notes) VALUES ('nested2')"
    MyCommand.ExecuteNonQuery()
    MyNestedTran2.Commit()

    ' start a nested transaction, but do not commit or roll back
    MyNestedTran3 = MyTran.Begin()
    MyCommand.Transaction = MyNestedTran3
    MyCommand.CommandText = "Insert into Log (Notes) VALUES ('nested3')"
    MyCommand.ExecuteNonQuery()

    ' commit the parent transaction
    MyTran.Commit()
    OleDbConnection1.Close()

End Function
```

C#:

```csharp
uses System.Data.OleDb;

public void TestNesting(OleDbConnection MyConnection)
{
    OleDbTransaction MyTran;
    OleDbTransaction MyNestedTran1;
    OleDbTransaction MyNestedTran2;
    OleDbTransaction MyNestedTran3;
    OleDbCommand MyCommand = new OleDbCommand();

    OleDbConnection1.Open();

     // start a transaction
    MyTran = OleDbConnection1.BeginTransaction();

    // set up the command object
    MyCommand.Transaction = MyTran;
    MyCommand.Connection = OleDbConnection1;

    // start a nested transaction and commit it
    MyNestedTran1 = MyTran.Begin();
    MyCommand.Transaction = MyNestedTran1;
    MyCommand.CommandText = "Insert into Log (Notes) VALUES ('nested1')";
    MyCommand.ExecuteNonQuery();
    MyNestedTran1.Commit();

    // start a nested transaction and roll it back
    MyNestedTran2 = MyTran.Begin();
    MyCommand.Transaction = MyNestedTran2
    MyCommand.CommandText = "Insert into Log (Notes) VALUES ('nested2')";
    MyCommand.ExecuteNonQuery();
    MyNestedTran2.Commit();

    // start a nested transaction, but do not commit or roll back
    MyNestedTran3 = MyTran.Begin();
    MyCommand.Transaction = MyNestedTran3;
    MyCommand.CommandText = "Insert into Log (Notes) VALUES ('nested3')";
    MyCommand.ExecuteNonQuery();

    // commit the parent transaction
    MyTran.Commit();
    OleDbConnection1.Close();
}
```

The Rollback Method

This method rolls back pending changes made to the database within the current transaction.

Transact-SQL: ROLLBACK TRAN

VB.NET:

```
Not Overridable Public Sub Rollback();
```

C#:

```
public void rollback();
```

Exceptions:

- ❑ `Exception` – returned when an unspecified error has occurred

- ❑ `InvalidOperationException` – returned then the transaction is not in a modified state (it has been committed or rolled back) or when the connection is no longer valid

Initiated nested transactions will all be rolled back, regardless of whether they were committed or rolled back.

For example, in the VB code listing above (`Commit` method), let's change the last block of code to now roll back the parent transaction like this:

```
' commit the parent transaction
MyTran.Rollback()
OleDbConnection1.Close()
```

In this case, `MyNestedTran1`, `MyNestedTran2`, and `MyNestedTran3`, would all be rolled back.

The Rollback Method Using Savepoints (Sql Only)

Rolls back pending changes made to the database since a named savepoint within the current transaction.

Transact-SQL: ROLLBACK TRAN <SAVEPOINT_NAME>

VB.NET:

```
Not Overridable Public Sub Rollback(ByVal transactionName As String);
```

C#:

```
public void rollback(string transactionName);
```

Exceptions:

❑ `ArgumentException` – returned when no valid savepoint name was specified

❑ `InvalidOperationException` – returned then the transaction is not in a modified state (it has been committed or rolled back) or when the connection is no longer valid

This `Rollback` method rolls back any pending changes to a database made by the current transaction following a named savepoint. Rolling back to a named savepoint does not preclude you from continuing with further actions within the parent transaction.

In the example below, only the order creation is committed.

VB.NET:

```
Public Function CreateOrder(ByRef MyConnection as SqlConnection)
    Dim tranOrders as SqlTransaction
    ' begin the Order transaction
    tranOrders = MyConnection.BeginTransaction()
    MyConnection.Transaction = tranOrder
    ' code to write an order to the data source goes here...
    ' begin CreateOrderDetails section
    tranOrders.Save ("OrderDetails")
    ' code to write order details to the data source goes here...
    ' rollback CreateOrderDetails
    tranOrders.Rollback("OrderDetails")
    ' commit Order Transaction
    tranOrder.Commit()
End Function
```

C#:

```
public void CreateOrder(SqlConnection MyConnection)
{
    SqlTransaction tranOrders;
    // begin the Order transaction
    tranOrders = MyConnection.BeginTransaction();
    MyConnection.Transaction=tranOrder;
    // code to write an order to the data source goes here...
    // begin CreateOrderDetails section
    tranOrders.Save ("OrderDetails");
    // code to write order details to the data source goes here...
    // rollback CreateOrderDetails
    tranOrders.Rollback("OrderDetails");
    // commit Order Transaction
    tranOrder.Commit();
}
```

The Rollback Method Using Named Transactions (Sql Only)

Rolls back pending changes made to the database within a named transaction.

Transact-SQL: ROLLBACK TRAN <TRAN_NAME>

VB.NET:

```
Not Overridable Public Sub Rollback(ByVal transactionName As String);
```

C#:

```
public void rollback(string transactionName);
```

Exceptions:

❑   `ArgumentException` – returned when no name was specified

❑   `InvalidOperationException` – returned then the transaction is not in a modified state (it has been committed or rolled back), or when the connection is no longer valid

When creating a `SqlTransaction` (using the `BeginTransaction` method of the `SqlConnection` object), you have the option of using a name for the transaction. You can rollback the full transaction using this method, by specifying the transaction name.

The Save Method (Sql Only)

Creates a named savepoint in the current transaction.

Transact-SQL: SAVE TRANSACTION <SAVEPOINT_NAME>

VB.NET:

```
Public Sub Save(savepointName As String);
```

C#:

```
public void Save(string savepointName);
```

Exceptions:

❑   `Exception` – returned when an unspecified error has occurred

❑   `InvalidOperationException` – returned then the transaction is not in a modified state (it has been committed or rolled back), or when the connection is no longer valid

You can use named savepoints to rollback pending changes made to the database within the current transaction after the `Save` command was issued.

A Transaction Example

This example demonstrates the use of `BeginTransaction`, `Commit`, and `Rollback` methods. We'll be coding the banking example used in the chapter introduction.

We should use parameterized stored procedures and a significantly more robust security model, but for the purposes of this illustration, we've simplified things.

Suppose we have an `Accounts` table and each account is associated with a unique ID called `Account_ID`. We will build a method called `TransferFunds`, which accepts the source and target account Ids, as well as the transfer amount, `curAmount`. The method will attempt to debit the source account, and then credit the target account. The results will be returned to the calling code in a string.

VB.NET:

```
Imports System.Data.OleDb

Public Sub TransferFunds(lngSourceAcct As Long, lngTargetAcct As Long, & _
    curAmount As Currency, ByRef cnMaster As SqlConnection) As String

    Dim cmdTransfer as SqlCommand
    Dim tranTransfer as SqlTransaction

    ' open the connection, create the transaction and reference the command
      object
    cnMaster.Open()
    tranTransfer = cnMaster.BeginTransaction()
    cmdTransfer.Transaction = tranTransfer

    Try
        With cmdTransfer
            ' credit the target account
            .CommandText = "UPDATE Accounts (Amount) " & curAmount & " & _
                "WHERE Account_ID = " & lngTargetAcct
            .ExecuteNonQuery()
            ' debit the source account
            .CommandText = "UPDATE Accounts (Amount) " & (-1 * curAmount) & _
                " WHERE Account_ID = " & lngSourceAcct
            .ExecuteNonQuery()
            ' commit the transaction
            .Commit()
        End With
        TransferFunds = "Transferred " & curAmount & " from Account " & _
            lngSourceAcct & " to Account " & lngTargetAcct & "."
    Catch e As Exception
        cmdTransfer.RollBack()
        TransferFunds = "Transfer failed. Error (" & e.ToString & ")."
    Finally
        cnMaster.Close()
    End Try
End Sub
```

C#:

```
uses System.Data.OleDb;

public string TransferFunds(lngSourceAcct As Long, lngTargetAcct As Long, & _
    curAmount As Currency, ByRef cnMaster As SqlConnection)
{
    SqlCommand cmdTransfer;
    SqlTransaction tranTransfer;

    // open the connection, create the transaction and reference the command
object
```

620

```
cnMaster.Open();
tranTransfer = cnMaster.BeginTransaction();
cmdTransfer.Transaction = tranTransfer;

try
{
    // credit the target account
    cmdTransfer.CommandText = "UPDATE Accounts (Amount) " &
        curAmount & " WHERE Account_ID = " & lngTargetAcct;
    cmdTransfer.ExecuteNonQuery();
    // debit the source account
    cmdTransfer.CommandText = "UPDATE Accounts (Amount) " & _
        (-1 * curAmount) & " WHERE Account_ID = " & lngSourceAcct;
    cmdTransfer.ExecuteNonQuery();
    // commit the transaction
    cmdTransfer.Commit();
    TransferFunds = "Transferred " & curAmount & _
        " from Account " & lngSourceAcct & " to Account " & _
        lngTargetAcct & ".";
}
catch (Exception e)
{
    cmdTransfer.RollBack();
    TransferFunds = "Transfer failed. Error (" & e.ToString & ").."
}
finally
{
    cnMaster.Close();
}
}
```

Transaction Guidelines

In addition to the ACID guidelines, there a few other guidelines for good transaction design:

❑ Keep transactions brief – this prevents long locks and the transaction log's inability to recover free space, as it cannot close until a transaction is complete

❑ Know your isolation levels – the data you are reading and writing can be unreliable if it is in the process of being modified or deleted; be aware of the limitations you impose on concurrency when setting the IsolationLevel property

❑ Try to avoid using transactions for reads, unless you need to guarantee clean reads

Summary

The use of separate Transaction objects is new in ADO.NET. Creating a Transaction object involves invoking the BeginTransaction method on the Connection object. All subsequent interactions with the transaction are handled through the Transaction object.

Each data provider in ADO.NET (OleDb, SqlClient and Odbc) has a separate Transaction object to manage transactions.

Begin, Commit, and Rollback bind transactions. Even though you can omit Commit or Rollback as the transaction will be rolled back with the absence of an explicit instruction, you should avoid doing this as the locks placed at the data source can remain in place, limiting concurrency.

ProgrammersReferenceExcel
ersReferenceExcel2002
ReferenceExcel2002VBAP
ProgrammersReferenceE
Excel2002VBAProgramm
2002VBAProgrammersReferenceExcel
VBAProgrammersReference
ProgrammersReferenceExcel
2002VBAProgrammersReferenceEx

13

The XmlDataDocument Object

The `XmlDataDocument` object represents the fusion of ADO.NET and XML support within the . NET Framework.

XML is, of course, the **eXtensible Markup Language**: an Internet standard defined by the World Wide Web (W3C) consortium (see `http://www.w3.org/TR/REC-xml`). XML is a standard embraced and heavily promoted by Microsoft (see `http://www.microsoft.com/xml`).

An introduction to XML is a book-length subject: a good place to start is *Beginning XML* (Wrox Press, ISBN 1861003412). The W3C and Microsoft web sites mentioned in the previous paragraph are good places to start for a more advanced introduction.

`XmlDataDocument` is an intriguing object: it represents a single set of data that can be viewed as both an XML document and a relational set of tables. `XmlDataDocument` is part of ADO.NET, since it is actually contained within the ADO.NET assembly `System.Data.dll`. Yet it is a member of the `System.Xml` namespace, not `System.Data`, and is derived from the `XmlDocument` and `XmlNode` objects within the `System.Xml` namespace. These objects contain properties and methods that enable us to read, write, and manipulate XML documents. Since these parent objects are not part of ADO.NET, we will only describe the properties and methods inherited from them by `XmlDataDocument` in this chapter.

The most important property of an `XmlDataDocument` is the `DataSet` property, which is an ADO.NET `DataSet` object. The `DataSet` associated with an `XmlDataDocument` permits relational access to all its contained data as a set of tables. Any changes made to the `XmlDataDocument` are reflected in the `DataSet`, and vice versa.

To load the `DataSet` with XML data, we would build a relational mapping with the `ReadXmlSchema` method of `DataSet`. The XML data can then be loaded using `XmlDocument.LoadXml()` or `XmlDataDocument.Load()`. To load existing relational data, we would specify the `DataSet` containing the relational data as the parameter in the `DataSet` form of the `XmlDataDocument` constructor.

`XmlDataDocument` inherits all of the rich W3C Document Object Model (DOM) functionality of its parent objects. The DOM is a tree representation of an XML document, and many of its methods and properties serve to locate, navigate, and manipulate the nodes (branches and leaves) of the tree.

`XmlDataDocument` implements the XML standard `DOMDocument` interface as defined in the W3C DOM Level 1 Core (`http://www.w3.org/TR/REC-DOM-Level-1`) and Level 2 Core (`http://www.w3.org/TR/DOM-Level-2-Core`). It also implements the necessary interfaces to allow XML `XPath` queries and XSL transformations of its data.

`XmlDataDocument` is at the center of what ADO.NET is all about, marrying the rich, hierarchical, Internet-standard, self-defining functionality of XML with the object-based access to relational data in ADO.

Sample XML Files

Several of this chapter's examples use the file `bookdata.xml`, which contains some sample XML data for a collection of books. This file is very simple to create: the contents are as follows:

```
<!--sample XML for bookdata.xml -->
<bookstore>
 <book genre='computer' ISBN='1861005-466'>
 <title>Professional SQL Server 2000 XML</title>
 <price>49.99</price>
 </book>
 <book genre='computer' ISBN='1861004-990'>
 <title>Professional C#</title>
 <price>59.99</price>
 </book>
</bookstore>
```

Several examples also use the file `book.xsd`, which contains an example XML schema. This file follows the XML schema definition language, specified by the W3C in `http://www.w3.org/TR/xmlschema-1` and `http://www.w3.org/TR/xmlschema-2`. It defines the XML structure for books, as used in `bookdata.xml`.

This file is used in several of the .NET SDK samples. However, it has been slightly modified from the original for our examples. The contents of `book.xsd` are as follows:

```
<schema id="book1" targetNamespace="" xmlns="http://www.w3.org/2001/XMLSchema"
xmlns:msdata="urn:schemas-microsoft-com:xml-msdata">
 <element name="book">
  <complexType>
   <all>
    <element name="title" minOccurs="0" type="string"/>
    <element name="author">
     <complexType>
      <all>
       <element name="first-name" minOccurs="0" type="string"/>
       <element name="last-name" minOccurs="0" type="string"/>
      </all>
     </complexType>
    </element>
    <element name="price" minOccurs="0" type="string"/>
   </all>
   <attribute name="genre" type="string"/>
   <attribute name="publicationdate" type="string"/>
   <attribute name="ISBN" type="string"/>
  </complexType>
 </element>
</schema>
```

XML Namespaces

Several of the methods described in this chapter use parameters relating to the concept of **XML namespaces**. XML Namespaces are described and defined by the W3C at `http://www.w3.org/TR/REC-xml-names`.

We use XML namespaces to ensure that names in XML documents are globally unique. For example, the element name `<title>` might refer to a book title in one part of an XML document, and refer to a personal title such as Mr. or Mrs. in another element in the same XML document. Namespaces allow multiple usages such as this to be distinguished.

Let's define some terms used with XML namespaces.

A simple name with no namespace implicitly using the document's namespace is called a **local name**. This XML document fragment contains only local names such as `book` and `genre`.

```
<book genre='computer' ISBN='1861005-466'>
 <title>Professional SQL Server 2000 XML</title>
 <price>49.99</price>
 </book>
```

A namespace declaration allows a **prefix** to be defined to distinguish one use of a name from others. For example, we might define a prefix `books:` for use with names referring to books. The prefix is used with a colon separating it from the local part of the name, as in `books:title`. This full name, containing both the prefix and the local part of the name, is called a **qualified name.**

The namespace declaration uses the special XML keyword attribute `xmlns` (for XML namespace) and associates the namespace with a **namespace URI**: a Universal Resource Identifier defining a globally unique namespace. URIs look like URLs (for example, `http://www.books.org/ns/books`) and are used because they can be guaranteed to be globally unique. Note that the URI does not have to define a reachable location on the Internet. The namespace declaration looks like the following:

```
xmlns:books=http://www.books.org/ns/books
```

Once this declaration has been made, the `books:` prefix will always refer to the unique namespace URI `http://www.books.org/ns/books`.

Constructors of the XmlDataDocument

An example is shown for each of the `XmlDataDocument` constructors. Subsequent examples show code fragments that can be inserted into complete programs, usually at the point following the construction of the `XmlDataDocument` object.

XmlDataDocument () Constructor

This version of the `XmlDataDocument` constructor takes no parameters. It is typically used when the data source for your application is an existing XML text or stream.

VB.NET:

```
Imports System.Xml
Dim xdoc As XmlDataDocument = New XmlDataDocument()
```

625

C#:

```
using System.Xml;
XmlDataDocument xdoc = new XmlDataDocument();
```

Since this version of the `XmlDataDocument` constructor does not use an existing `DataSet` for initialization, the `DataSet` will initially be empty. It is the version we would probably use when reading existing XML data into the `XmlDataDocument` to be accessed as relational tables, as in the following example.

The following example program requires that the files `bookdata.xml` and `books.xsd`, discussed earlier, be present in the current directory of the running program (usually this is the same as location of `.exe` file).

The example creates an empty XML data document using the no-data-set form of the constructor. We then define a schema for the document using `ReadXmlSchema` method with the `books.xsd` file, then load data for the document (and data set) from `bookdata.xml`. We then modify the data by changing an individual field through the `Tables` property of the `DataSet`. Then we show the modified document in XML format with the `Save` method (described later in this chapter) directing the output to `Console.Out` for display.

VB.NET:

```
    Imports System
    Imports System.Data
    Imports System.Xml
Module Example
  Sub Main()
   'Create an XmlDataDocument. Insert code from other examples starting here.
   Dim doc As XmlDataDocument = New XmlDataDocument()
   'Load the schema.
   doc.DataSet.ReadXmlSchema("books.xsd")
   'Load the XML data.
   Dim reader As XmlTextReader = New XmlTextReader("bookdata.xml")
   doc.Load(reader)
   'Change the price on the first book imports the DataSet methods.
   Dim books As DataTable = doc.DataSet.Tables.Item("book")
   books.Rows.Item(0).Item("price") = "14.99"
   Console.WriteLine("Display the modified XML data...")
   doc.Save(Console.Out)
  End Sub
End Module
```

C#:

```
using System;
using System.Data;
using System.Xml;

class Example
{
public static void Main()
  {
   //Create an XmlDataDocument. Insert code from other examples starting here.
   XmlDataDocument doc = new XmlDataDocument();
   //Load the schema file.
   doc.DataSet.ReadXmlSchema("books.xsd");
   //Load the XML data.
```

```
        doc.Load("bookdata.xml");
        //Update the price on the first book using the DataSet methods.
        DataTable books = doc.DataSet.Tables["book"];
        books.Rows[0]["price"] = "14.99";
        Console.WriteLine("Display the modified XML data...");
        doc.Save(Console.Out);
    }
}
```

The `DataSet` property is read-only, so we cannot construct a document with a Null `DataSet`, assigning a filled data set later on. This is because the structure of the `XmlDataDocument` is determined by the `DataSet`. However, this is very easy to work around: simply using the `DataSet` form of the `XmlDataDocument` constructor. We'll look at this next.

XmlDataDocument (DataSet) Constructor

This version of the `XmlDataDocument` constructor takes an existing `DataSet` object as a parameter. It is typically used when the data source for an application is a set of existing relational tables.

VB.NET:

```
Imports System.Xml
Imports System.Data
Dim ds As DataSet = New DataSet () ' next would likely fill data set with a query
Dim xdoc As XmlDataDocument = New XmlDataDocument(ds)
```

C#:

```
using System.Xml;
using System.Data;
DataSet ds = new DataSet(); // next would likely fill data set with a query
XmlDataDocument xdoc = new XmlDataDocument(ds);
```

Parameters are as follows:

Parameter	Type	Description
ds	DataSet	An existing ADO.NET DataSet.

The `DataSet` version of the `XmlDataDocument` constructor is what you would use when exporting or viewing relational data as an XML document, as in this example.

The example creates a new empty dataset object, then connects to the `Northwind` sample database in SQL Server. We define a query for the `Customers` table in the sample data, selecting all the customers in France. We then execute the query by using it to define a `DataAdapter` object and calling the `Fill` command to fill the `DataSet`. Next we want to display the found data as XML. To do this, we create an `XmlDataDocument` object, passing the filled `DataSet` as a parameter to the `XmlDataDocument` constructor. Finally, we show the XML output by calling the `XmlDataDocument` `Save` method (described later in this chapter), directing the output to `Console.Out` for display:

VB.NET:

```
Imports System
Imports System.Data
Imports System.Data.SqlClient
Imports System.Xml
```

```
Module Example
Sub Main()
Dim dsNorthwind As DataSet = New DataSet()
'Create the connection string.
Dim sConnection As String
    ' if (local) does not work in following connection string, try (local)\NetSDK
    sConnection = "Data Source=(local);Integrated Security=SSPI;Initial
Catalog=Northwind"
'Create a connection object to connect to the northwind db.
Dim nwconnect As SqlConnection
nwconnect = New SqlConnection(sConnection)
'Create a command string to select all the customers in France
Dim sCommand As String = "Select * from Customers where Country='France'"
'Create an Adapter to load the DataSet.
Dim myDataAdapter As SqlDataAdapter
myDataAdapter = New SqlDataAdapter(sCommand, nwconnect)
'Fill the DataSet with the selected records.
myDataAdapter.Fill(dsNorthwind, "Customers")
'Load the XML document with the DataSet.
Dim doc As XmlDataDocument = New XmlDataDocument(dsNorthwind)
'Display the XmlDataDocument.
doc.Save(Console.Out)
End Sub
End Module
```

C#:

```
using System;
using System.Data;
using System.Data.SqlClient;
using System.Xml;

class Example
{
public static void Main()
  {
DataSet dsNorthwind = new DataSet();
//Create the connection string.
String sConnection;
   // if (local) does not work in following connection string, try (local)\\NetSDK
sConnection=
"Data Source=(local);Integrated Security=SSPI;Initial Catalog=Northwind";
//Create a connection object to connect to the northwind db.
SqlConnection nwconnect = new SqlConnection(sConnection);
//Create a command string to select customers in France
String sCommand = "Select * from Customers where Country='France'";
//Create an adapter to load the DataSet.
SqlDataAdapter myDataAdapter = new SqlDataAdapter(sCommand, nwconnect);
//Fill the DataSet with the selected records.
myDataAdapter.Fill(dsNorthwind,"Customers");
//Load the XML document with the DataSet.

XmlDataDocument doc = new XmlDataDocument(dsNorthwind);

//Display the XmlDataDocument.
doc.Save(Console.Out);
  }
}
```

Properties of XmlDataDocument

Attributes Property

Use this read-only property to get the collection of attributes, if any, for this node. This property is inherited from `XmlNode`.

VB.NET:

```
Dim doc As XmlDataDocument = New XmlDataDocument()
Dim a As XmlAttributeCollection = doc.Attributes
```

C#:

```
XmlDataDocument doc = new XmlDataDocument();
XmlAttributeCollection a = doc.Attributes;
```

`Attributes` returns an `XmlAttributeCollection` object containing a collection of the `XmlAttribute` objects for each attribute associated with this node, if the node has attributes. If the node does not have attributes (that is, it is not an element node) then `Attributes` returns a Null reference (`Nothing` in Visual Basic). We can use methods and properties defined in the `IEnumerator` interface in `System.Collection` so as to manipulate this collection, as shown in this example:

VB.NET:

```
Imports System.Collections

Dim doc As XmlDataDocument = New XmlDataDocument()
doc.Load("bookdata.xml")
Dim attrColl As XmlAttributeCollection = doc.DocumentElement.FirstChild.Attributes
Dim ienum As IEnumerator = attrColl.GetEnumerator()
Dim attr As XmlAttribute
While (ienum.MoveNext())
attr = CType(ienum.Current, XmlAttribute)
Console.WriteLine("{0} = {1}", attr.Name, attr.Value)
End While
```

C#:

```
Using System.Collections;
…
XmlDataDocument doc = new XmlDataDocument();
doc.Load("bookdata.xml");

XmlAttributeCollection attrColl = doc.DocumentElement.FirstChild.Attributes;
IEnumerator ienum = attrColl.GetEnumerator();
while (ienum.MoveNext())
{
XmlAttribute attr = (XmlAttribute)ienum.Current;
// get current member of collection
// display name & value of each attribute
Console.WriteLine("{0} = {1}", attr.Name, attr.Value);
}
```

629

Our sample code first loads the XML from the `bookdata.xml` file into our `XmlDataDocument` (see the sample XML file in the introduction of this chapter for a description of `bookdata.xml`). We then create an `XmlAttributeCollection` and assign it using the `Attributes` property of the document's root element (`DocumentElement`) `FirstChild` property. The root is the bookstore element, and the first child of the bookstore is the book, Professional SQL Server. We then get an `IEnumerator` object, so we process the collection in a loop, and call the `MoveNext` method in `IEnumerator` to move to the first member of the collection, which is the genre attribute. We create an `XmlAttribute` object to represent each individual attribute, and assign this object to be the current member of the enumerator representing the collection. Finally we print out the `Name` and `Value` properties of this attribute, and loop to find the next attribute until we are done.

This example prints out:

```
genre = computer
ISBN = 1861005-466
```

These are the attributes of the first book element. If we had specified `LastChild` instead of `FirstChild` in this example, we would have displayed the attributes of the last book instead.

BaseURI Property

Use this read-only property to obtain the base **URI** or **Universal Resource Identifier** associated with the document object. This property is inherited from `XmlDocument`.

VB.NET:

```
Dim doc As XmlDataDocument = New XmlDataDocument()
Dim s As String = doc.BaseURI
```

C#:

```
XmlDataDocument doc = New XmlDataDocument();
string s = doc.BaseURI;
```

The URI (Universal Resource Identifier) is typically a web address such as `http://localhost/mydocument.xml`. The `BaseURI` property enables us to ask, in effect, "where did this come from?" For the document itself, this shows where the document was loaded from, as in this example:

VB.NET:

```
Dim doc As XmlDataDocument = new XmlDataDocument()
'Load the schema.
doc.DataSet.ReadXmlSchema("books.xsd")
'Load the XML data.
Dim fn As String = "http://localhost/bookdata.xml"
doc.Load(fn)
Console.WriteLine(doc.BaseURI)
```

C#:

```
//Create an XmlDataDocument.
XmlDataDocument doc = new XmlDataDocument();
//Load the schema file.
doc.DataSet.ReadXmlSchema("books.xsd");
```

```
//Load the XML data.
string fn = "http://localhost/bookdata.xml";
doc.Load(fn);
// display base uri property
Console.WriteLine(doc.BaseURI);
```

The file name or web address passed to the Load method is returned as the BaseURI for the document. This example prints out:

```
http://localhost/bookdata.xml
```

This was passed to the Load method. XML documents may be assembled from multiple locations; the BaseURI property for each node reflects this information if the node (such as an entity, schema, or DTD node) came from another location.

If the document was loaded from a local file, the document's BaseURI property returns a URI name for the file such as file:///C:/tmp/localdata.xml. For an XmlDataDocument constructed using a DataSet, the BaseURI property returns an empty string. Therefore, this property is most useful when going from XML to relational tables rather than from relational tables to XML.

ChildNodes Property

Use this read-only property to get a list of the children nodes of this XML node. This property is inherited from XmlNode.

VB.NET:

```
Dim doc As XmlDataDocument = New XmlDataDocument()
Dim kids As XmlNodeList = doc.ChildNodes
```

C#:

```
XmlDataDocument doc = new XmlDataDocument();
XmlNodeList kids = doc.ChildNodes;
```

This property is an XmlNodeList object, which is an ordered list of child nodes. If there are no children, the property contains an empty node list. You can reference the list of nodes as if it were an array, using code like this example:

VB.NET:

```
Dim doc As XmlDataDocument = New XmlDataDocument(dsNorthwind)
'Display the contents of the child nodes.
If root.HasChildNodes Then
Dim i As Integer
For i = 0 To root.ChildNodes.Count - 1
Console.WriteLine(root.ChildNodes(i).InnerXml)
Next i
End If
```

C#:

```
XmlDataDocument doc = new XmlDataDocument(dsNorthwind);
XmlNode root = doc.FirstChild;
```

```
//Display the contents of the child nodes.
if (root.HasChildNodes)
{
for (int i=0; i<root.ChildNodes.Count; i++)
{
Console.WriteLine(root.ChildNodes[i].InnerXml);
}
}
```

The `HasChildNodes` property is used to first make sure child nodes exist. In the initialization of the `for` loop, the `Count` property of `ChildNodes` is used to get the total count of the children in the list. The index of the `for` loop is used as the index of the array to print out the XML of the child nodes. With the Northwind database, and a query of the customers with `CustomerID=BLONP`, the example prints out the following:

```
<CustomerID>BLONP</CustomerID><CompanyName>Blondesddsl père et fils</CompanyName>
<ContactName>Frédérique Citeaux</ContactName><ContactTitle>Manager</ContactTitle>
<Address>24, place Kléber</Address><City>Strasbourg</City>
<PostalCode>67000</PostalCode><Country>France</Country>
<Phone>88.60.15.31</Phone><Fax>88.60.15.32</Fax>
```

The XML is dumped out in a non-indented form, as `InnerXml` returns the raw text with no formatting.

DataSet Property

This read-only property is a `DataSet` object associated with the `XmlDataDocument` object, to be used for relational table-oriented access to the data contained in the `XmlDataDocument`.

VB.NET:

```
Dim doc As XmlDataDocument = New XmlDataDocument()
Dim ds As DataSet = doc.DataSet
```

C#:

```
XmlDataDocument doc = new XmlDataDocument();
DataSet ds = doc.DataSet;
```

The `DataSet` property is read-only; to assign an existing `DataSet` to an `XmlDataDocument` object, invoke the `DataSet` form of the `XmlDataDocument` constructor, described in the Constructors section of this chapter.

The `DataSet` property is typically used to directly invoke `DataSet` methods or to read or assign `DataSet` child object properties, as in these examples:

VB.NET:

```
Dim doc As XmlDataDocument = new XmlDataDocument()
'Load a relational schema.
doc.DataSet.ReadXmlSchema("books.xsd")
doc.Load("bookdata.xml")
'Change the price on the first book using the DataSet methods.
Dim books As DataTable = doc.DataSet.Tables.Item("book")
books.Rows.Item(0).Item("price") = "14.99"
```

C#:

```
XmlDataDocument doc = new XmlDataDocument();
//Load a relational schema
doc.DataSet.ReadXmlSchema("books.xsd");
doc.Load("bookdata.xml");
//Update the price on the first book using the DataSet methods.
DataTable books = doc.DataSet.Tables["book"];
books.Rows[0]["price"] = "14.99";
```

In this example, we create a new empty XmlDataDocument. We create the relational structure for it by using the ReadXmlSchema method of the DataSet (see Chapter 5 describing DataSet's methods for more information on this). We then load the data itself from an XML file with the Load method. Once the data is loaded, we can modify it using the standard ADO relation table manipulations; in this case we access the Tables property of the DataSet to get the DataTable object for the Book table, then use the Rows/Item property of the DataTable to set the value of the Price field in the table.

Since essentially all of ADO.NET's relational table manipulation objects are available via the DataSet or its properties, this property enables us to do almost any relational operation on an XmlDataDocument object, such as referring to tables via the DataSet.Tables collection, as shown above, or creating and using a DataAdapter object associated with the DataSet to update data, and so on.

DocumentElement Property

Use this read-only property to obtain the root element of the XML document. This property is inherited from XmlDocument.

VB.NET:

```
Dim doc As XmlDataDocument = new XmlDataDocument()
Dim xe As XmlElement = doc.DocumentElement
```

C#:

```
XmlDataDocument doc = new XmlDataDocument();
XmlElement xe = doc.DocumentElement;
```

We can use this method to get the root element either to edit it or to use the root element as a starting point for node insertion or other navigational operations. This example finds the first child of the root and displays its XML:

VB.NET:
```
Dim doc As XmlDataDocument = new XmlDataDocument()(dsNorthwind)
'Display the document element.
Console.WriteLine(doc.DocumentElement.FirstChild.OuterXml)
```

C#:

```
XmlDataDocument doc = new XmlDataDocument(dsNorthwind);
// Display the document element.
Console.WriteLine(doc.DocumentElement.FirstChild.OuterXml);
```

If the document has no root (that is, it is empty, or not well formed), DocumentElement returns a Null reference (null in C#, or Nothing in Visual Basic).

DocumentType Property

We would use this read-only property to get the DOCTYPE declaration for this document, if it exists. This property is inherited from XmlDocument.

VB.NET:

```
Dim doc As XmlDataDocument = new XmlDataDocument()
Dim xn As XmlNode = doc.DocumentType
```

C#:

```
XmlDataDocument doc = new XmlDataDocument();
XmlNode xn = doc.DocumentType;
```

The DOCTYPE declaration references an XML **Document Type Definition** (**DTD**), either internal or external to the XML document. There can be only one DocumentType node in the XML document. There may not be a DOCTYPE declaration, in which case DocumentType returns a Null reference (null in C#, Nothing in Visual Basic).

The XML document constructed from a DataSet does not contain a DOCTYPE declaration, as XSD schemas are now a preferred way to describe the structure of XML documents. Therefore the message "Document Type is Null" will be displayed by this example:

VB.NET:

```
Dim doc As XmlDataDocument = new XmlDataDocument(dsNorthwind)
'Check to see if document type is available
If (doc.DocumentType = Nothing) Then Console.WriteLine("Document Type is Null")
End If
```

C#:

```
XmlDataDocument doc = new XmlDataDocument(dsNorthwind);
// check to see if document type is available
if (doc.DocumentType == null) Console.WriteLine("Document Type is Null");
```

FirstChild Property

Use this read-only property to find the first child of this XML node. This property is inherited from XmlNode.

VB.NET:

```
Dim doc As XmlDataDocument = New XmlDataDocument()
Dim xn As XmlNode = doc.FirstChild
```

C#:

```
XmlDataDocument doc = new XmlDataDocument();
XmlNode xn = doc.FirstChild;
```

We often would use this property as a starting point for node insertion or other navigational operations within XmlDocuments. The first child of a document is the root node (same as DocumentElement). FirstChild is also available for every other node in the document, so it can be used in a nested fashion when navigating a document, as shown in this example with a data document based on a query of the Northwind database:

VB.NET:

```
Dim doc As XmlDataDocument = New XmlDataDocument(dsNorthwind)
'Display the document element.
Console.WriteLine(doc.FirstChild.Name)
Console.WriteLine(doc.FirstChild.FirstChild.Name)
Console.WriteLine(doc.FirstChild.FirstChild.FirstChild.Name)
```

C#:

```
XmlDataDocument doc = new XmlDataDocument(dsNorthwind);
// Display the document element.
Console.WriteLine(doc.FirstChild.Name);
Console.WriteLine(doc.FirstChild.FirstChild.Name);
Console.WriteLine(doc.FirstChild.FirstChild.FirstChild.Name);
```

This example prints out the following:

> NewDataSet
> Customers
> CustomerID

It visits, in turn, the root node of the document, the uppermost element for the first customer, and then the first child of the customer, the element corresponding to the `CustomerID` field. `NewDataSet` is the name created for the root node of an `XmlDataDocument` constructed from a `DataSet`.

If the node has no child, `FirstChild` will return a Null reference (`null` in C#, or `Nothing` in Visual Basic). We can test using the `HasChildNodes Boolean` property before referencing a child to avoid a Null reference exception.

HasChildNodes Property

We would use this read-only property to find out if an XML node has children. This property is inherited from `XmlNode`.

VB.NET:

```
Dim doc As XmlDataDocument = New XmlDataDocument()
Dim b As Boolean = doc.HasChildNodes
```

C#:

```
XmlDataDocument doc = new XmlDataDocument();
bool b = doc.HasChildNodes;
```

If a node has no child, `FirstChild`, `LastChild`, and other node location methods may return a Null reference (`null` in C#, or `Nothing` in Visual Basic). We can use the `HasChildNodes Boolean` property to test for this condition before referencing a child to avoid a Null reference exception, as shown in this example:

VB.NET:

```
Dim doc As XmlDataDocument = New XmlDataDocument(dsNorthwind)
'Display the document element first child name.
If (doc.DocumentElement.HasChildNodes) Then
Console.WriteLine(doc.DocumentElement.FirstChild.Name)
End If
```

C#:

```
XmlDataDocument doc = new XmlDataDocument(dsNorthwind);
// Display the document element first child name.
if (doc.DocumentElement.HasChildNodes) {
Console.WriteLine(doc.FirstChild.Name);
}
```

This example will print out the first-level element name returned from the query that filled the `DataSet` from the Northwind database, but only if there are child elements present.

Implementation Property

Use this read-only property to get the `XmlImplementation` object for the current document. This property is inherited from `XmlDocument`.

VB.NET:

```
Dim doc As XmlDataDocument = new XmlDataDocument()
Dim xo As XmlImplementation = doc.Implementation
```

C#:

```
XmlDataDocument doc = new XmlDataDocument();
XmlImplementation xo = doc.Implementation;
```

The `XmlImplementation` object provides the W3C `DOMImplementation` interface as defined in `http://www.w3.org/TR/DOM-Level-2-Core/core.html#ID-102161490`.

This example uses the `XmlImplementation` `CreateDocument` method to create another document with the same implementation:

VB.NET:

```
Dim doc As New XmlDocument()
doc.Load("books.xml")
Dim newdoc As XmlDocument = doc.Implementation.CreateDocument()
```

C#:

```
XmlDocument doc = new XmlDocument();
doc.Load("books.xml");
XmlDocument newdoc = doc.Implementation.CreateDocument();
```

Documents created from the same `XmlImplementation` share resources such as the `XmlNameTable`. However, to actually move data from one document to another we must use the `XmlDocument` `ImportNode` method.

InnerText Property

Use this property to read or write the concatenation of the values of this node and its children. This property is inherited from `XmlNode`.

VB.NET:

```
Dim doc As XmlDataDocument = New XmlDataDocument()
Dim itxt As String = doc.InnerText
```

C#:

```
XmlDataDocument doc = new XmlDataDocument();
XmlNodeList itxt = doc.InnerText;
```

InnerText squashes all the values of the current node and its children into one long string. Here is an example using the Northwind data:

VB.NET:

```
Dim doc As XmlDataDocument = New XmlDataDocument(dsNorthwind)
'Display the contents of the child nodes.
Console.WriteLine(doc.InnerText)
Console.WriteLine(doc.InnerXml)
```

C#:

```
XmlDataDocument doc = new XmlDataDocument(dsNorthwind);
Console.WriteLine(doc.InnerText);
Console.WriteLine(doc.InnerXml);
```

In this example we first print out the InnerText starting at the root, then the InnerXml which includes the markup. The output is as shown below, in which the difference between these two properties is apparent, as InnerText contains only the values:

```
BLONPBlondesddsl père et filsFrédérique Citeaux Manager24, place Kléber
Strasbourg67000France88.60.15.32

<NewDataSet>
<Customers>
<CustomerID>BLONP</CustomerID>
<CompanyName>Blondesddsl père et fils</CompanyName>
<ContactName>Frédérique Citeaux</ContactName>
<ContactTitle>Manager</ContactTitle>
<Address>24, place Kléber</Address>
<City>Strasbourg</City>
<PostalCode>67000</PostalCode>
<Country>France</Country>
<Phone>88.60.15.31</Phone>
<Fax>88.60.15.32</Fax>
</Customers>
</NewDataSet>
```

InnerXml Property

We would use this read/write property to get or set the XML markup for the children of the current node. This property is inherited from XmlDocument.

VB.NET:

```
Dim doc As XmlDataDocument = new XmlDataDocument()
Dim str As String = doc.InnerXml
```

C#:

```
XmlDataDocument doc = new XmlDataDocument();
String str = doc.InnerXml;
```

This property is in contrast to `OuterXml`, which returns the XML markup for both the parent (current node) and children. See the following example:

VB.NET:

```
Dim doc As New XmlDataDocument()
doc.LoadXml(("<book genre='computer' ISBN='1861005-466'>" & _
"<title>Professional SQL Server 2000 XML</title>" & _
"<price>49.99</price>" & _
"</book>"))

Dim root As XmlNode = doc.DocumentElement

'InnerXml does not include the markup of the current node.
'As a result, the attributes are not displayed.
Console.WriteLine()
Console.WriteLine("Display the InnerXml property...")
Console.WriteLine(root.InnerXml)

'OuterXml includes the markup of current node.
Console.WriteLine("Display the OuterXml property...")
Console.WriteLine(root.OuterXml)
```

C#:

```
//Create an XmlDataDocument.
XmlDataDocument doc = new XmlDataDocument();

doc.LoadXml("<book genre='computer' ISBN='1861005-466'>" +
"<title>Professional SQL Server 2000 XML</title>" +
"<price>49.99</price>" +
"</book>");

XmlNode root = doc.DocumentElement;

//InnerXml does not include the markup of the current node.
//As a result, the attributes are not displayed.
Console.WriteLine();
Console.WriteLine("Display the InnerXml property...");
Console.WriteLine(root.InnerXml);

//OuterXml includes the markup of current node.
Console.WriteLine("Display the OuterXml property...");
Console.WriteLine(root.OuterXml);
```

The output of this example is as follows:

```
Display the InnerXml property...
<title>Professional SQL Server 2000 XML</title><price>49.99</price>
Display the OuterXml property...
<book genre="computer" ISBN="1861005-466"><title>Professional SQL Server 2000
XML</title><price>49.99</price></book>
```

Note that `InnerXml` shows only the contained elements `<title>` and `<price>`, but `OuterXml` also shows the attributes of the containing `<book>` element.

You can write to `InnerXml` as well as read it; the .NET run-time will parse the XML in the string you assign and replace the children of the node with the parsed contents. For example, the following code:

```
doc.DocumentElement.InnerXml = "<A>content of A</A><B>content of B</B>"
```

replaces the child nodes of the document root with 2 child elements A & B. This can be a handy shortcut for constructing a set of elements if the XML text is readily available to you.

> Note: that before assigning **InnerXml** on a document created from a **DataSet**, we
> need to set the document **DataSet.EnforceConstraints** property to false just as
> with any other XML editing operation on a **DataSet** constructed **XmlDataDocument**.
> See Chapter 5 for more information on the **EnforceConstraints** property.

An example is shown here:

VB.NET:

```
Dim doc As XmlDataDocument() = new XmlDataDocument(dsNorthwind)
doc.DataSet.EnforceConstraints = false
doc.DocumentElement.InnerXml = "<A>content of A</A><B>content of B</B>"
```

C#:

```
XmlDataDocument doc = new XmlDataDocument(dsNorthwind);
doc.DataSet.EnforceConstraints = false;
doc.DocumentElement.InnerXml = "<A>content of A</A><B>content of B</B>";
```

Note that `InnerXml` manages XML namespace declarations when parsing the XML so that redundant namespace declarations are reduced to only one in the returned XML. While this means that the XML you get out of `InnerXml` may not be exactly the same as you put in, it keeps the XML in its simplest equivalent form at all times. This allows you to cut and paste between documents with namespace declarations while keeping the XML simple.

IsReadOnly Property

Use this read-only property to detect if the current node is read-only. This property is inherited from `XmlDocument`.

VB.NET:

```
Dim doc As XmlDataDocument = new XmlDataDocument()
Dim readonly As Boolean = doc.IsReadOnly
```

C#:

```
XmlDataDocument doc = new XmlDataDocument();
bool readonly = doc.IsReadOnly;
```

`IsReadOnly` is a `Boolean` value either True or False; use this as a simple check before attempting to modify a node:

VB.NET:

```
Dim doc As New XmlDocument()
If doc.DocumentElement.FirstChild.IsReadOnly Then
Console.WriteLine("First child is read-only")
End If
```

C#:

```
XmlDocument doc = new XmlDocument();
If (doc.DocumentElement.FirstChild.IsReadOnly) {
Console.WriteLine("First child is read-only");
}
```

Certain kinds of XML nodes, such as entity references, are always read-only.

Item Property

Use this read-only indexer property to obtain a child element by name. This property is inherited from `XmlNode`.

VB.NET:

```
Dim doc As New XmlDataDocument()
Dim elem As XmlElement = doc(name)
Dim elem As XmlElement = doc(localname, namespaceuri)
```

C#:

```
XmlDataDocument doc = new XmlDataDocument();
XmlElement elem = doc[name];
XmlElement elem = doc[localname, namespaceuri];
```

Parameters are as follows:

Parameter	Type	Description	Default
Name	String	qualified or local name of desired element	none
Localname	String	local name of desired element	none
Namespaceuri	String	namespace URI of desired element	none

We can find a child element of the current node by name using this property; it is the indexer for this class in C# so it looks like an array reference.

The name may be a simple local name ("Customer") or a fully qualified name ("prefix:name") with an optional namespace URI, in which case it takes the form of a multidimensional array reference with two indexes ([String, String] in C#). See the introduction of the chapter for a discussion of namespaces and local/qualified names.

The following example gets the first Customer child of an XML document loaded from the Northwind `DataSet`:

VB.NET

```
'Create an XmlDataDocument.
Dim doc As XmlDataDocument = New XmlDataDocument(dsNorthwind)
' get first Customer child
Dim root As XmlNode = doc.FirstChild
Console.WriteLine(root("Customer").OuterXml)
```

C#

```
// Create an XmlDataDocument.
XmlDataDocument doc = new XmlDataDocument(dsNorthwind);
// get first Customer child
XmlNode root = doc.FirstChild;
Console.WriteLine(root["Customer"].OuterXml);
```

The Northwind `DataSet` is loaded in previous lines of code; see the full example code in the `DataSet` constructor of `XmlDataDocument`. We then navigate to the root element (`NewDataSet`) of the document, then print out the XML of the first `Customer` element.

LastChild Property

Use this read-only property to find the last child of this XML node. This property is inherited from `XmlNode`.

VB.NET:

```
Dim doc As XmlDataDocument = New XmlDataDocument()
Dim xn As XmlNode = doc.LastChild
```

C#:

```
XmlDataDocument doc = new XmlDataDocument();
XmlNode xn = doc.LastChild;
```

We would often use this property as a starting point for node insertion or other navigational operations within `XmlDocuments`. The first and last child of a document are the root node (same as `DocumentElement`). `LastChild` is also available for every other node in the document, so it can be used in a nested fashion when navigating a document, as shown in this example with a data document based on a query of the Northwind database:

VB.NET:

```
Dim doc As XmlDataDocument = New XmlDataDocument(dsNorthwind)
'Display the document element.
Console.WriteLine(doc.LastChild.Name)
Console.WriteLine(doc.LastChild.LastChild.Name)
Console.WriteLine(doc.LastChild.LastChild.LastChild.Name)
```

C#:

```
XmlDataDocument doc = new XmlDataDocument(dsNorthwind);
// Display the document element.
Console.WriteLine(doc.LastChild.Name);
Console.WriteLine(doc.LastChild.LastChild.Name);
Console.WriteLine(doc.LastChild.LastChild.LastChild.Name);
```

This example prints out the following:

```
NewDataSet
Customers
Fax
```

as it visits, in turn, the root node of the document, the uppermost element for the last customer, and then the last child of the customer, the element corresponding to the Fax field. NewDataSet is the name created for the root node of an XmlDataDocument constructed from a DataSet.

If the node has no child, LastChild will return a Null reference (null in C#, or Nothing in Visual Basic). We can test using the HasChildNodes Boolean property before referencing a child to avoid a Null reference exception.

LocalName Property

We use this read-only property to find the local name of the current node. This property is inherited from XmlDocument.

VB.NET:

```
Dim doc As XmlDataDocument = new XmlDataDocument()
Dim lname As String = doc.LocalName
```

C#:

```
XmlDataDocument doc = new XmlDataDocument();
String lname = doc.LocalName;
```

This property displays the **local name** associated with this node. See the discussion of namespaces in the introduction of this chapter for a definition of this term. For the XmlDocument object itself, the local name is always #document. For the root element node within an XmlDataDocument object derived from a DataSet, the local name is NewDataSet:

VB.NET:

```
Dim doc As New XmlDocument(dsNorthwind)

// Display the local name.
Console.WriteLine(doc.LocalName)
Console.WriteLine(doc.DocumentElement.LocalName)
```

C#:

```
XmlDataDocument doc = new XmlDocument(dsNorthwind);

// Display the local name.
Console.WriteLine(doc.LocalName);
Console.WriteLine(doc.DocumentElement.LocalName);
```

The output of the example is:

```
#document
NewDataSet
```

Name Property

Use this read-only property to get the name of the current node. This property is inherited from XmlDocument.

VB.NET:

```
Dim doc As XmlDataDocument = new XmlDataDocument()
Dim lname As String = doc.Name
```

C#:

```
XmlDataDocument doc = new XmlDataDocument();
String lname = doc.Name;
```

The Name property may be queried for any node within an XML document. For an element or attribute, the name is the name of the node: "Book" for a <Book> element, for example. The name returned may be a qualified name with a prefix (see the discussion of the XML Namespaces at beginning of the chapter).

For an XmlDataDocument object no prefix is generated, and the local name is always "#document", so the qualified name is also "#document". Similarly, for the root element node of an XmlDataDocument object derived from a DataSet: again, no prefix is generated and the local name is "NewDataSet", so the qualified name is also "NewDataSet". The following example shows this particular case:

VB.NET:

```
Dim doc As New XmlDocument(dsNorthwind)
// Display the local name.
Console.WriteLine(doc.LocalName)
Console.WriteLine(doc.DocumentElement.Name)
```

C#:

```
XmlDataDocument doc = new XmlDocument(dsNorthwind);
// Display the local name.
Console.WriteLine(doc.Name);
Console.WriteLine(doc.DocumentElement.Name);
```

The output of the example is:

```
#document
NewDataSet
```

NamespaceURI Property

Use this read-only property to get the **URI (Universal Resource Identifier)** of the namespace for this node's name, if it exists. This property is inherited from XmlNode.

VB.NET:

```
Dim doc As New XmlDataDocument()
Dim uri As String = doc.NamespaceURI
```

C#:

```
XmlDataDocument doc = new XmlDataDocument();
String uri = doc.NamespaceURI;
```

See the beginning of this chapter for a discussion of namespaces and names. We can find the URI of this node's namespace by reading this property. If there is no namespace, it will return an empty string (`String.Empty`).

The following example shows how to get the URI:

VB.NET:

```
'Create an XmlDataDocument.
Dim doc As XmlDataDocument = New XmlDataDocument()
' required before editing XML data document with XML operations
doc.DataSet.EnforceConstraints = false
//Create an element with fully qualified name.
Dim newElem As XmlElement
newElem = doc.CreateElement("myns", "myname", "http://www.myuri.com/myns")
Dim uri As String = newElem.NamespaceURI
```

C#:

```
// Create an XmlDataDocument.
XmlDataDocument doc = new XmlDataDocument(dsNorthwind);
// required before editing XML data document with XML operations
doc.DataSet.EnforceConstraints = false;
//Create an element with fully qualified name.
XmlElement newElem=doc.CreateElement("myns", "myname",
"http://www.myuri.com/myns");
String uri = newElem.NamespaceURI;
```

The variable `uri` contains the namespace URI, which is `http://www.myuri.com/myns`.

NameTable Property

We use this read-only property to get the `XmlNameTable` object for the current document's implementation. This property is inherited from `XmlDocument`.

VB.NET:

```
Dim doc As XmlDataDocument = new XmlDataDocument()
Dim xnt As XmlNameTable = doc.NameTable
```

C#:

```
XmlDataDocument doc = new XmlDataDocument();
XmlNameTable xnt = doc.NameTable;
```

The `NameTable` object for an `XmlDocument` object is used to store names of elements and attributes. `Names` referenced multiple times in the document are still stored just once in the `NameTable`. For example, if the document had multiple elements with the name "#document", `NameTable` returns the same object whenever it is asked for that particular name, saving redundant usage of memory. `NameTable` is the default implementation for the abstract `XmlNameTable` class. `NameTable` provides methods such as `Get` to access strings in the `NameTable`, as shown in the following example:

VB.NET:

```
Dim doc As New XmlDocument(dsNorthwind)
Dim s As String = doc.NameTable.Get("#document")
```

C#:

```
XmlDocument doc = new XmlDocument(dsNorthwind);
String s = doc.NameTable.Get("#document")
```

The names in the name table correspond to the names obtained with LocalName and/or Name.

NextSibling Property

We use this read-only property to get the next sibling of this node in the list of children. This property is inherited from XmlNode.

VB.NET:

```
Dim doc As New XmlDataDocument()
Dim xn As XmlNode = doc.NextSibling
```

C#:

```
XmlDataDocument doc = new XmlDataDocument();
XmlNode xn = doc.NextSibling;
```

We can find the next child in a list of children with this property. The property returns a Null reference (Nothing in Visual Basic) if there is none. The following example loops through the list of children using NextSibling:

VB.NET:

```
'Create an XmlDataDocument.
Dim doc As XmlDataDocument = New XmlDataDocument(dsNorthwind)
' find first child of root element
Dim xn As XmlNode = doc.DocumentElement.FirstChild
' loop through list
Do Until xn = Nothing
xn = xn.NextSibling
Loop
```

C#:

```
// Create an XmlDataDocument.
XmlDataDocument doc = new XmlDataDocument(dsNorthwind);
// find first child of root element
XmlNode xn = doc.DocumentElement.FirstChild;
// loop through list
while (xn != null) {
xn = xn.NextSibling;
}
```

This example uses an XmlDataDocument object created from a DataSet based on the Northwind database and already filled with data as shown in the full sample shown in the previous chapter for the XmlDataDocument(DataSet) constructor.

We then create an `XmlNode` and initialize it to the first child of the document root. Then we loop through the children using `NextSibling` to find the next one. In a real program, of course, we'd have additional code in the loop to do some processing at each node, but it is easiest to see the process with an empty loop.

NodeType Property

We use this read-only property to get the `XmlNodeType` for the current node. This property is inherited from `XmlDocument`.

VB.NET:

```
Dim doc As XmlDataDocument = new XmlDataDocument()
Dim xnt As XmlNodeType = doc.NodeType
```

C#:

```
XmlDataDocument doc = new XmlDataDocument();
XmlNodeType xnt = doc.NodeType;
```

Each node in the XML DOM representation of an XML document has an associated node type. `XmlNodeType` is defined as a list of these enumerated constants, representing different XML node types:

```
Attribute
CDATA
Comment
Document
DocumentFragment
DocumentType
Element
EndElement
EndEntity
Entity
EntityReference
None
Notation
ProcessingInstruction
SignificantWhitespace
Text
Whitespace
XmlDeclaration
```

The node type of the `XmlDocument` and `XmlDataDocument` objects themselves are always `Document`, as shown here:

VB.NET:

```
Dim doc As New XmlDocument(dsNorthwind)
Console.WriteLine(doc.NodeType.ToString())
```

C#:

```
XmlDocument doc = new XmlDocument(dsNorthwind);
Console.WriteLine(doc.NodeType.ToString())
```

This code always displays the "Document". The NodeType property display for other nodes within the document will correspond to one of the listed types.

OuterXml Property

We use this read-only property to get the XML markup for the current node and its children. This property is inherited from XmlNode.

VB.NET:

```
Dim doc As XmlDataDocument = new XmlDataDocument()
Dim s As String = doc.OuterXml
```

C#:

```
XmlDataDocument doc = new XmlDataDocument();
String s = doc.OuterXml;
```

This property is in contrast to InnerXml, which gets or sets the XML markup representing only the children of the current node. See the description of InnerXml in the section "InnerXml Property, preceeding this chapter, as well as the following example:

VB.NET:

```
Dim doc As New XmlDataDocument()
doc.LoadXml(("<book genre='computer' ISBN='1861005-466'>" & _
"<title>Professional SQL Server 2000 XML</title>" & _
"<price>49.99</price>" & _
"</book>"))

Dim root As XmlNode = doc.DocumentElement

'InnerXml does not include the markup of the current node.
'As a result, the attributes are not displayed.
Console.WriteLine()
Console.WriteLine("Display the InnerXml property...")
Console.WriteLine(root.InnerXml)

'OuterXml includes the markup of current node.
Console.WriteLine("Display the OuterXml property...")
Console.WriteLine(root.OuterXml)
```

C#:

```
//Create an XmlDataDocument.
XmlDataDocument doc = new XmlDataDocument();

doc.LoadXml("<book genre='computer' ISBN='1861005-466'>" +
"<title>Professional SQL Server 2000 XML</title>" +
"<price>49.99</price>" +
"</book>");

XmlNode root = doc.DocumentElement;

//InnerXml does not include the markup of the current node.
//As a result, the attributes are not displayed.
Console.WriteLine();
Console.WriteLine("Display the InnerXml property...");
```

```
Console.WriteLine(root.InnerXml);

//OuterXml includes the markup of current node.
Console.WriteLine("Display the OuterXml property...");
Console.WriteLine(root.OuterXml);
```

The output of the example is as follows:

```
Display the InnerXml property...
<title>Professional SQL Server 2000 XML</title><price>49.99</price>
Display the OuterXml property...
<book genre="computer" ISBN="1861005-466"><title>Professional SQL Server 2000
XML</title><price>49.99</price></book>
```

Note that `OuterXml` displays the contained elements `<title>` and `<price>` as well as the attributes of the containing `<book>` element, but `InnerXml` shows only the contained elements.

OwnerDocument Property

This read-only property returns the owner document, which is always `null` (`Nothing` in Visual Basic) for `XmlDocument` and `XmlDataDocument` objects. For `XmlNode` objects this property returns the owner XML document. This property is inherited from `XmlDocument`.

ParentNode Property

We use this read-only property to get the parent node of this node. This property is inherited from `XmlNode`.

VB.NET:

```
Dim doc As New XmlDataDocument()
Dim xn As XmlNode = doc.ParentNode
```

C#:

```
XmlDataDocument doc = new XmlDataDocument();
XmlNode xn = doc.ParentNode;
```

If the node does not or cannot have a parent (such as `XmlDocument`, `XmlDocumentFragment`, and `XmlAttribute` nodes), then `ParentNode` contains a `null` reference (`Nothing` in Visual Basic). A just-created node will not have a parent until you insert it into a document.

The following example shows how the parent node complements the first/last child methods:

VB.NET:

```
Dim doc As XmlDataDocument = New XmlDataDocument(dsNorthwind)
Dim xn As XmlNode = doc.FirstChild.FirstChild
Dim pn As XmlNode = xn.ParentNode.ParentNode
If (pn = xn) Then Console.WriteLine("Same!") End If
```

C#:

```
XmlDataDocument doc = new XmlDataDocument(dsNorthwind);
XmlNode xn = doc.FirstChild.FirstChild;
XmlNode pn = xn.ParentNode.ParentNode;
if(pn == xn) { Console.WriteLine("Same!") }
```

We create an `XmlNode` that is the grandchild of the root of the document. Then we use `ParentNode` to find the grandparent of the node we just created, and test for equality.

Prefix Property

We use this read-only property to get the name prefix for this node's name, if it exists. This property is inherited from `XmlNode`.

VB.NET:

```
Dim doc As New XmlDataDocument()
Dim uri As String = doc.Prefix
```

C#:

```
XmlDataDocument doc = new XmlDataDocument();
String uri = doc.Prefix;
```

See the beginning of this chapter for a discussion of namespaces and prefixes. We can find the prefix of this node's name by reading this property; if there is no prefix, it will return an empty string (`String.Empty`).

The following example shows how to get the prefix:

VB.NET:

```
'Create an XmlDataDocument.
Dim doc As XmlDataDocument = New XmlDataDocument()
' required before editing XML data document with XML operations
doc.DataSet.EnforceConstraints = False
//Create an element with fully qualified name.
Dim newElem As XmlElement
newElem = doc.CreateElement("myns:myname", "http://www.myuri.com/myns")
Dim pfix As String = newElem.Prefix
```

C#:

```
// Create an XmlDataDocument.
XmlDataDocument doc = new XmlDataDocument(dsNorthwind);
// required before editing XML data document with XML operations
doc.DataSet.EnforceConstraints = false;
//Create an element with fully qualified name.
XmlElement newElem=doc.CreateElement("myns:myname", "http://www.myuri.com/myns");
String pfix = newElem.Prefix;
```

The variable `pfix` contains the prefix, which is "myns".

PreserveWhitespace Property

We use this read/write property to control whether to preserve whitespace during the load and save process for an XML document. This property is inherited from `XmlDocument`.

VB.NET:

```
Dim doc As XmlDataDocument = new XmlDataDocument()
Dim pw As Boolean = doc.PreserveWhitespace
```

C#:

```
XmlDataDocument doc = new XmlDataDocument();
bool pw = doc.PreserveWhitespace;
```

Whitespace characters include space, tab, carriage return, and linefeed. By default, `PreserveWhitespace` is `false`. If `PreserveWhitespace` is False, then the output XML is automatically indented when `Save` is called. When `Load` or `LoadXml` are called, any whitespace in the source document will be ignored.

If `PreserveWhitespace` is True, whitespace nodes are preserved during document load. During save, whitespace in the document is preserved in the output, if the property is set to True

This example shows how to use the `PreserveWhitespace` property to remove whitespace from an XML source file:

VB.NET:

```
'Load XML data which includes whitespace, but ignore the whitespace during load.
Dim doc As XmlDocument = new XmlDocument()
doc.PreserveWhitespace = false
doc.Load("bookdata.xml")

'Save the document as is (no whitespace).
doc.PreserveWhitespace = true
doc.Save(Console.Out)
```

C#:

```
//Load XML data which includes whitespace, but ignore whitespace during load.
XmlDocument doc = new XmlDocument();
doc.PreserveWhitespace = false;
doc.Load("bookdata.xml");

//Save the document as is (no whitespace).
doc.PreserveWhitespace = true;
doc.Save(Console.Out);
```

In the example, `PreserveWhitespace` is set to `false` before the `Load` call, so the whitespace is taken out as the document is loaded into memory. `PreserveWhitespace` is set to True before displaying the data with `Save`. This prevents any automatic indentation of the output, and since no whitespace was preserved during `Load`, the output is all jammed together without any formatting:

```
<NewDataSet><Customers><CustomerID>BLONP</CustomerID><CompanyName>Blondesddsl père
et fils</CompanyName><ContactName>Frédérique Citeaux</ContactName><ContactTitle>
 . . .
```

> **Removal of whitespace makes for more efficient document processing at the expense of readability. However, we can use the automatic indentation behavior of Save to easily produce readable XML, even when the XML is stored in the most memory-efficient manner without whitespace.**

PreviousSibling Property

We use this read-only property to get the previous sibling of this node in the list of children. This property is inherited from `XmlNode`.

VB.NET:

```
Dim doc As New XmlDataDocument()
Dim xn As XmlNode = doc.PreviousSibling
```

C#:

```
XmlDataDocument doc = new XmlDataDocument();
XmlNode xn = doc.PreviousSibling;
```

We can find the previous child in a list of children with this property. The property returns a `null` reference (`Nothing` in Visual Basic) if there is none.

The following example loops backward through the list of children using `PreviousSibling`:

VB.NET:

```
'Create an XmlDataDocument.
Dim doc As XmlDataDocument = New XmlDataDocument(dsNorthwind)
' find last child of root element
Dim xn As XmlNode = doc.DocumentElement.LastChild
' loop through list
Do Until xn = Nothing
xn = xn.PreviousSibling
Loop
```

C#:

```
// Create an XmlDataDocument.
XmlDataDocument doc = new XmlDataDocument(dsNorthwind);
// find last child of root element
XmlNode xn = doc.DocumentElement.LastChild;
// loop through list
while (xn != null) {
xn = xn.PreviousSibling;
}
```

This example uses an `XmlDataDocument` object, created from a `DataSet`, based on the Northwind database, and already filled with data, as shown in the full sample, shown in the next section, for the `XmlDataDocument(DataSet)` constructor.

We then create an `XmlNode`, and initialize it to the last child of the document root. Then we loop backward through the list of children using `PreviousSibling` to find the preceding child of the current node. In a real program of course we'd have additional code in the loop to do some processing at each node, but it is easiest to see the process with an empty loop.

Value Property

We use this read/write property to get or set the value of a node, such as an attribute value. This property is inherited from `XmlNode`.

VB.NET:

```
Dim doc As XmlDataDocument = New XmlDataDocument()
Dim s As String = doc.Value
```

C#:

```
XmlDataDocument doc = new XmlDataDocument();
String s = doc.Value;
```

These types of nodes have particular values: `Attribute`, `CDATA`, `Comment`, `ProcessingInstruction`, `Text`, `SignificantWhitespace`, `Whitespace`, and `XmlDeclaration`. The `Value` represents the contents of that node type, such as the comment for a `Comment`, the whitespace for the `Whitespace` node types, and so on.

These node types do not have values: `Document`, `DocumentFragment`, `DocumentType`, `Element`, `Entity`, `Entity Reference`, and `Notation`. The `Value` attribute returns a `null` reference (`Nothing` in Visual Basic) for these node types.

To use the `Value` property, we simple assign to or from it when we have navigated to the node we want, as shown here:

VB.NET:

```
Imports System.Collections
…
Dim doc As XmlDataDocument = New XmlDataDocument()
doc.Load("bookdata.xml")
Dim attrColl As XmlAttributeCollection = doc.DocumentElement.FirstChild.Attributes
Dim ienum As IEnumerator = attrColl.GetEnumerator()
Dim attr As XmlAttribute
While (ienum.MoveNext())
attr = CType(ienum.Current, XmlAttribute)
Console.WriteLine("{0} = {1}", attr.Name, attr.Value)
End While
```

C#:

```
Using System.Collections;
…
XmlDataDocument doc = new XmlDataDocument();
doc.Load("bookdata.xml");

XmlAttributeCollection attrColl = doc.DocumentElement.FirstChild.Attributes;
IEnumerator ienum = attrColl.GetEnumerator();
while (ienum.MoveNext())
{
XmlAttribute attr = (XmlAttribute)ienum.Current; // get current member of
collection
// display name & value of each attribute
Console.WriteLine("{0} = {1}", attr.Name, attr.Value);
}
```

The `bookdata.xml` file used in this example contains the following XML:

```
<bookstore>
<book genre='computer' ISBN='1861005-466'>
<title>Professional SQL Server 2000 XML</title>
```

```
<price>49.99</price>
</book>
<book genre='computer' ISBN='1861004-990'>
<title>Professional C#</title>
<price>59.99</price>
</book>
</bookstore>
```

Our sample code first loads the XML from the `bookdata.xml` file into our `XmlDataDocument`. We then create an `XmlAttributeCollection` and assign it using the `Attributes` property of the document's root element (`DocumentElement`) `FirstChild` property. The root is the bookstore element, and the first child of the bookstore is the book Professional SQL Server. We then get an `IEnumerator` object so we process the collection in a loop, and call the `MoveNext` method in `IEnumerator` to move to the first member of the collection, which is the genre attribute. We create an `XmlAttribute` object to represent each individual attribute, and assign this object to be the `Current` member of the enumerator representing the collection. Finally we print out the `Name` and `Value` properties of this attribute, and loop to find the next attribute until we are done.

This example prints out the following:

```
genre = computer
ISBN = 1861005-466
```

These are the attribute names and values of the first book element.

XmlResolver Property

We would use this write-only property to set the `XmlResolver` object for resolving external references in the current document. This property is inherited from `XmlDocument`.

VB.NET:

```
Dim doc As XmlDataDocument = new XmlDataDocument()
doc.XmlResolver = new XmlResolver
```

C#:

```
XmlDataDocument doc = new XmlDataDocument();
doc. XmlResolver = new XmlResolver();
```

The `XmlResolver` object will load DTDs or expand external entity references for us. This property is provided to allow us to set custom security credentials or call a custom `XmlResolver`.

However, the default implementation of `XmlResolver`, `XmlUrlResolver`, is called with default security credentials if an `XmlResolver` is not specified, so there is little need to set this property unless you have unusual security needs.

The following example shows theuse of this property with the default `XmlUrlResolver` object, but with a custom security credential specifying a specific username and password:

VB.NET:

```
    Imports System.Net ' for NetworkCredential
      ...
      'Create an XmlDataDocument.
    Dim doc As XmlDataDocument = New XmlDataDocument()
    Dim nc As NetworkCredential = New NetWorkCredential("username", "password",
"domain")

    Dim resolver As XmlUrlResolver = New XmlUrlResolver()
    resolver.Credentials = nc
    doc.XmlResolver = resolver
    'Load from file
    doc.Load("http://somehost/bookdata.xml")
```

C#:

```
using System.Net; // for NetworkCredential
   ...
   //Create an XmlDataDocument.
XmlDataDocument doc = new XmlDataDocument();
NetworkCredential nc = new NetWorkCredential("username", "password", "domain");
XmlUrlResolver resolver = new XmlUrlResolver();
resolver.Credentials = nc;
doc.XmlResolver = resolver;
doc.Load("http://somehost/bookdata.xml");
```

The `System.Net` namespace is referenced to get the `NetworkCredential` object.
The empty XML document is created. A network credential object is created specifying a specific user name, password, and domain. An XML resolver object is created using the system implementation, `XmlUrlResolver`. The `Credentials` property of this XML resolver object is set to the customer network credential just created, and then the XML document's `XmlResolver` property is set to specify this credential. Then the document is loaded from a network URL; the custom security credential will be used to access the network resource.

This example assumes that the file `bookdata.xml` is available in the root directory of the web server.

Methods of XmlDataDocument

AppendChild Method

We use this method to add a child node to the end of the current node's list of children. This method is inherited from `XmlNode`.

VB.NET:

```
Dim doc As New XmlDataDocument()
Dim n As XmlNode = doc.AppendChild(new)
```

C#:

```
XmlDataDocument doc = new XmlDataDocument();
XmlNode n = doc.AppendChild(new);
```

Parameters are as follows:

Parameter	Type	Description	Default
new	XmlNode	new child node	none

We typically call one of the node creation methods such as `CreateElement` to create the new node object, then call `AppendChild()` to actually add it to a document tree.

The following example adds a new comment node to the root element of an existing XML document:

VB.NET:

```
'Create an XmlDataDocument.
Dim doc As XmlDataDocument = New XmlDataDocument(dsNorthwind)
'required before editing XML data document with XML operations
doc.DataSet.EnforceConstraints = False

dim newComment As XmlComment = doc.CreateComment("comment appended with
AppendChild method")
'this appends the new Comment to the root element
dim currNode As XmlNode = doc.DocumentElement
currNode.AppendChild(newComment)
'Display the XmlDataDocument.
doc.Save(Console.Out)
```

C#:

```
// Create an XmlDataDocument.
XmlDataDocument doc = new XmlDataDocument(dsNorthwind);
// required before editing XML data document with XML operations
doc.DataSet.EnforceConstraints = false;
XmlComment newComment = doc.CreateComment("comment appended with AppendChild
method");
// this appends the new Comment as a child of the root element
XmlNode currNode = doc.DocumentElement;
currNode.AppendChild(newComment);
//Display the XmlDataDocument.
doc.Save(Console.Out);
```

The example uses an `XmlDataDocument` object created from a `DataSet` based on the Northwind database and already filled with data as shown in the full sample shown in the previous chapter for the `XmlDataDocument(DataSet)` constructor.

The `DataSet.EnforceConstraints` property must be set to `false` to allow XML nodes to be added to the document, based on the Northwind `DataSet`. We create the new node, in this case, a comment, with the call to the `CreateComment` method. We then create an `XmlNode` object to use for navigation and insertion; we set this node to the root element of the document by assigning it the `DocumentElement` (which is the root element), then use the `AppendChild` method to add the comment as a child of the root element (`NewDataSet`) at the end of the root's list of children.

The added child section appears in the output XML at the end, immediately preceding the close of the root `NewDataSet` element:

```
...
</Customers>
<!--comment appended with AppendChild method--/>
</NewDataSet>
```

Clone Method

We use this to duplicate an existing node. This method is inherited from `XmlNode`.

VB.NET:

```
Dim doc As New XmlDataDocument()
Dim xn As XmlNode = doc.Clone()
```

C#:

```
XmlDataDocument doc = new XmlDataDocument();
XmlNode = doc.Clone();
```

This method has no parameters. We can create a complete copy including children and attributes of a node with `Clone`, the same as `CloneNode(True)`. This example clones the entire document:

VB.NET:

```
'Create an XmlDataDocument.
Dim doc As XmlDataDocument = New XmlDataDocument(dsNorthwind)
' required before editing with XML operations
doc.DataSet.EnforceConstraints = False
'Create a copy of the XmlDataDocument.
Dim newdoc As XmlDataDocument
newdoc = CType(doc.Clone(), XmlDataDocument)
'Display the XmlDataDocument.
newdoc.Save(Console.Out)
```

C#:

```
// Create an XmlDataDocument.
XmlDataDocument doc = new XmlDataDocument(dsNorthwind);
// required before editing with XML operations
doc.DataSet.EnforcedConstraints = false;
XmlDataDocument newdoc = (XmlDataDocument) doc.Clone();
//Display the XmlDataDocument.
newdoc.Save(Console.Out);
```

The `DataSet.EnforceConstraints` property must be set to False to allow the creation of a new document based on the Northwind `DataSet`. We then make a new `XmlDataDocument` object and use clone to copy it starting at the root node.

CloneNode Method

The `CloneNode` method creates a duplicate of the current XML node or subtree.

VB.NET:

```
Dim doc As New XmlDataDocument(dataset)
Dim newdoc As XmlDataDocument = CType (doc.CloneNode(deep), XmlDataDocument)
```

C#:

```
XmlDataDocument doc = new XmlDataDocument(dataset);
XmlDataDocument newdoc = (XmlDataDocument) doc.CloneNode(deep);
```

Parameters are as follows:

Parameter	Type	Description	Default
deep	Boolean	False to clone only current node or document; True to clone entire subtree rooted at this node, including data within the DataSet	none

This method serves as a copy constructor. It returns an XmlNode which, within ADO.NET, usage would usually be cast to an XmlDataDocument in order to make a new XmlDataDocument. This example sets the deep parameter to True, cloning the entire document including all the data in the associated DataSet:

VB.NET:

```
'Create an XmlDataDocument.
Dim doc As XmlDataDocument = New XmlDataDocument(dsNorthwind)
'required before editing with XML operations
doc.DataSet.EnforceConstraints = False
'Create a copy of the XmlDataDocument.
Dim newdoc As XmlDataDocument
newdoc = CType(doc.CloneNode(True), XmlDataDocument)
'Display the XmlDataDocument.
newdoc.Save(Console.Out)
```

C#:

```
// Create an XmlDataDocument.
XmlDataDocument doc = new XmlDataDocument(dsNorthwind);
// required before editing with XML operations
doc.DataSet.EnforcedConstraints = false;
XmlDataDocument newdoc = (XmlDataDocument) doc.CloneNode(true);
//Display the XmlDataDocument.
newdoc.Save(Console.Out);
```

If the deep parameter is set to False, the DataSet schema is copied but not the data itself; that is, the DataSet is empty (no rows). This is useful if you want to copy a data document having the same schema but you wish to insert a differing set of data in it. This copying of the DataSet property is what is different about XmlDataDocument's CloneNode method, which overrides the CloneNode method inherited from the parent XmlDocument and XmlNode objects.

CloneNode can be used to copy the nodes contained within a document as well as the document node itself. The behavior depends on the XmlNodeType of the contained node.

For Attribute nodes, CloneNode always clones the given node including its children. For CData, Comment, ProcessingInstruction, SignificantWhitespace, Text, and Whitespace and XmlDeclaration nodes, CloneNode always clones the given node including its text or data content.

For `Document`, `DocumentFragment`, and `Element` nodes, `CloneNode(true)` clones the entire given node including its children. `CloneNode(false)` clones only the given node (including attributes), but not children. For `DocumentType` and `EntityReference` nodes, `CloneNode` always clones only the given node. `Entity` and `Notation` nodes cannot be cloned so no action is taken for these node types.

CreateAttribute Method

We use this method to create an XML attribute object to add to the XML document. This method is inherited from `XmlDocument`.

VB.NET:

```
Dim doc As New XmlDataDocument()
Dim elem As XmlAttribute = doc.CreateAttribute(prefix, localname, namespaceURI)
Dim elem As XmlAttribute = doc.CreateAttribute(qualifiedName, namespaceURI)
Dim elem As XmlAttribute = doc.CreateAttribute(name)
```

C#:

```
XmlDataDocument doc = new XmlDataDocument();
XmlAttribute elem = doc.CreateAttribute(prefix, localname, namespaceURI);
XmlAttribute elem = doc.CreateAttribute(qualifiedname, namespaceURI);
XmlAttribute elem = doc.CreateAttribute(name);
```

Parameters are as follows:

Parameter	Type	Description	Default
name qualifiedname localname	String	Name of attribute to create	None
Prefix	String	Name prefix	String.Empty
NamespaceURI	String	URI of namespace	String.Empty

`CreateAttribute` creates an `XmlAttribute` object, which represents an XML attribute such as the attribute "`myattribute`" in this snippet of XML:

```
<myelement myattribute="my value" />
```

We call `CreateAttribute` to create the `XmlAttribute`, then call an insert method such as `XmlElement.SetAttributeNode()` to actually add it to an element in a document object. The created `XmlAttribute` object has the context of the current XML document, meaning that all the defaults for the current document apply.

See the discussion of namespaces in the introduction of this chapter for a definition of the terms local name, qualified name, prefix, and namespace URI.

`CreateAttribute` has different overloaded forms supporting the creation of attributes with either a simple local name or a complex name using namespaces. This method call creates an attribute with a simple local name:

```
doc.CreateAttribute("myname")
```

This creates an attribute equivalent to the following XML (the value of the attribute is empty by default):

```
<myelement myname="">
```

This version of the method call creates an attribute with a prefix and namespace URI:

```
doc.CreateAttribute("myns", "myname", "http://www.myuri.com/myns")
```

This creates an attribute equivalent to the following XML :

```
<myelement myns:myname="" xmlns:myns="http://www.myuri.com/myns">
```

A qualified name consists of the prefix and the local name separated by a colon. Therefore, the following call is equivalent to the above example:

```
doc.CreateAttribute("myns:myname", "http://www.myuri.com/myns")
```

In order to use the `namespaceURI` parameter, we must reference a URI to define a recognized URI such as `http://www.w3.org/2000/xmlns/` for XML namespace ("`xmlns`"). Otherwise, we should not use this parameter or leave it empty. In particular, the .NET run-time will throw an exception if a prefix of "xmlns" is used with any value for `namespaceURI` other than "`http://www.w3.org/2000/xmlns/`".

Let's look at an example that adds a new attribute to the root element of an existing XML data document:

VB.NET:

```
'Create an XmlDataDocument.
Dim doc As XmlDataDocument = new XmlDataDocument()(dsNorthwind)

'required before editing XML data document with XML operations
doc.DataSet.EnforceConstraints = false
Dim newAttr As XmlAttribute = doc.CreateAttribute("myns",
"myname","http://www.myuri.com/myns")
newAttr.Value = "my value"

'append the new attribute to the root element
doc.DocumentElement.SetAttributeNode(attr)

'Display the XmlDataDocument.
doc.Save(Console.Out);
```

C#:

```
// Create an XmlDataDocument.
XmlDataDocument doc = new XmlDataDocument(dsNorthwind);

// required before editing XML data document with XML operations
doc.DataSet.EnforceConstraints = false;

//Create an attribute.
XmlAttribute newAttr=doc.CreateAttribute("myns", "myname",
"http://www.myuri.com/myns");
```

```
newAttr.Value = "my value";

//append the new attribute to the root element.
doc.DocumentElement.SetAttributeNode(attr);

//Display the XmlDataDocument.
doc.Save(Console.Out);
```

Let's go through this example in detail. We create a new `XmlDocument` of a `DataSet` created from a query using the Northwind sample database as shown in the complex example referenced in the section describing the `XmlDataDocument(DataSet)` constructor. This `DataSet` has been filled with data from the query.

Before any XML editing can be performed on an `XmlDataDocument`, the `EnforceConstraints` property of the `DataSet` must be set to False so that changes not reflected in the underlying relational data are allowed.

The `XmlAttribute` object is created using the `CreateAttribute` method. We're using the full 3-parameter version of the method with prefix, local name, and namespace URI. We set the value of the attribute using the `Value` property. Remember, at this point the `XmlAttribute` object has been created but it has not been inserted into the DOM tree of the `XmlDataDocument`. We now do the insertion by calling `SetAttributeNode` on the `XMLDataDocument`'s `DocumentElement` property, which is an `XmlElement` object corresponding to the root element of the document. The name of this root element defaults to "NewDataSet" for an `XmlDataDocument` newly created from a `DataSet`.

We print out the XML for the document by calling the `XmlDataDocument Save` method, specifying the console as the destination for the XML output. The attribute we added shows up in the root element (`NewDataSet`) at the start of the XML output as:

```
<NewDataSet myns:myname="my value" xmlns:myns="http://www.myuri.com/myns">
```

If we had used the simple version of `CreateAttribute` specifying only a local name we would see:

```
<NewDataSet myname="my value">
```

CreateCDataSection Method

We can use this method to create a CDATA section for the current XML document. This method is inherited from `XmlDocument`.

VB.NET:

```
Dim doc As New XmlDataDocument()
Dim cdata As XmlCDataSection = doc.CreateCDataSection(data)
```

C#:

```
XmlDataDocument doc = new XmlDataDocument();
XmlCDataSection cdata = doc.CreateCDataSection(data);
```

Parameters are as follows:

Parameter	Type	Description	Default
data	String	Character data to be contained within the CDATA section.	none

In XML, a CDATA section is used to quote or escape blocks of text that you do not want interpreted as XML. This method creates an XmlCDataSection object, which represents a CDATA section in the .NET DOM model.

We call CreateCDataSection to create the XmlCDataSection object, then call an insert method such as XmlNode.AppendChild() to actually add it to a document tree. The created XmlCDataSection object has the context of the current XML document, meaning that all the defaults for the current document apply.

The following example adds a new CDATA section to the existing XML document:

VB.NET:

```
'Create an XmlDataDocument.
Dim doc As XmlDataDocument = new XmlDataDocument()(dsNorthwind)

'required before editing XML data document with XML operations
doc.DataSet.EnforceConstraints = false
Dim newCData As XmlCDataSection =
doc.CreateCDataSection("!g@o#b$b%l%e^d&y*g<o)o+k")

'this appends the new CDataSection to the root element
Dim currNode As XmlNode = doc.DocumentElement
currNode.AppendChild(newCData)

'Display the XmlDataDocument.
doc.Save(Console.Out)
```

C#:

```
// Create an XmlDataDocument.
XmlDataDocument doc = new XmlDataDocument(dsNorthwind);

// required before editing XML data document with XML operations
doc.DataSet.EnforceConstraints = false;
XmlCDataSection newCData = doc.CreateCDataSection("!g@o#b$b%l%e^d&y*g<o)o+k");

// this appends the new CDataSection as a child of the root element
XmlNode currNode = doc.DocumentElement;
currNode.AppendChild(newCData);

//Display the XmlDataDocument.
doc.Save(Console.Out);
```

As in the previous example, the EnforceConstraints property of the DataSet must be set to false so that changes not reflected in the underlying relational data are allowed.

The CDATA section appears in the last line of the output XML immediately preceding the close of the NewDataSet element:

```
<![CDATA[!q@o#b$b%l%e^d&y*g<o)o+k]]></NewDataSet>
```

661

CreateComment Method

We use this method to create a comment section in an XML document. This method is inherited from `XmlDocument`.

VB.NET:

```
Dim doc As New XmlDataDocument()
Dim cmt As XmlComment = doc.CreateComment(data)
```

C#:

```
XmlDataDocument doc = new XmlDataDocument();
XmlComment cmt = doc.CreateComment(data);
```

Parameters are as follows:

Parameter	Type	Description	Default
data	String	Comment text	none

A comment node is parsed by the DOM and will appear in the output XML when the document is saved or displayed as XML, but it will not affect the execution or display of the XML markup. We can use it to add comments about the structure of the document or other information of use to XML developers who may view the XML markup of the document.

We call `CreateComment` to create the `XmlComment` object, then call an insert method such as `XmlNode.AppendChild()` to actually add it to a document tree. The created `XmlComment` object has the context of the current XML document, meaning that all the defaults for the current document apply.

The following example adds a new comment to the existing XML document:

VB.NET:

```
'Create an XmlDataDocument.
Dim doc As XmlDataDocument = New XmlDataDocument()(dsNorthwind)

'required before editing XML data document with XML operations
doc.DataSet.EnforceConstraints = false
Dim newComment As XmlComment = doc.CreateComment("comment added by CreateComment
method")

'this appends the new Comment to the root element
Dim currNode As XmlNode = doc.DocumentElement
currNode.AppendChild(newComment)

'Display the XmlDataDocument.
doc.Save(Console.Out)
```

C#:

```
// Create an XmlDataDocument.
XmlDataDocument doc = new XmlDataDocument(dsNorthwind);

// required before editing XML data document with XML operations
doc.DataSet.EnforceConstraints = false;
```

```
XmlComment newComment = doc.CreateComment("comment added by CreateComment
method");

// this appends the new Comment as a child of the root element
XmlNode currNode = doc.DocumentElement;
currNode.AppendChild(newComment);

//Display the XmlDataDocument.
doc.Save(Console.Out);
```

The example uses an `XmlDataDocument` object created from a `DataSet` based on the Northwind database, and already filled with data, as shown in the full sample shown for the `XmlDataDocument(DataSet)` constructor.

The `DataSet.EnforceConstraints` property must be set to False to allow XML nodes to be added to the document based on the Northwind `DataSet`. We create the `XmlComment` object `newComment` with the call to the `CreateComment` method. We then create an `XmlNode` object to use for navigation and insertion; we set this node to the root element of the document by assigning it the `DocumentElement` (which is the root element), then use the `XmlNode AppendChild` method to add the comment as a child of the root element. The root element of an `XmlDataDocument` is called `NewDataSet`.

The `Comment` section appears in the output XML immediately preceding the close of the root `NewDataSet` element:

```
...
</Customers>
<!--comment added by CreateComment method-->
</NewDataSet>
```

CreateDocumentFragment Method

We use this method to create a document fragment object using the context of this XML document. This method is inherited from `XmlDocument`.

VB.NET:

```
Dim doc As New XmlDataDocument()
Dim frag As XmlDocumentFragment = doc.CreateDocumentFragment()
```

C#:

```
XmlDataDocument doc = new XmlDataDocument();
XmlDocumentFragment frag = doc.CreateDocumentFragment();
```

There are no parameters.

A document fragment is an incomplete XML document that lacks a root element. We would use the `XmlDocumentFragment` object for tree insert operations or other operations where you want to use a lightweight object that can contain several nodes. We cannot insert an `XmlDocumentFragment` node directly into an XML document (that is, no child nodes within a document can have the type `XmlDocumentFragment`). However, the child nodes of an `XmlDocumentFragment` can be inserted as shown in this example:

VB.NET:

```
'Create an XmlDataDocument.
Dim doc As XmlDataDocument = new XmlDataDocument(dsNorthwind)

'required before editing XML data document with XML operations
doc.DataSet.EnforceConstraints = false
Dim newDocumentFragment As XmlDocumentFragment = doc.CreateDocumentFragment()

'Set the contents of the document fragment.
docFrag.InnerXml ="<item>widget</item><item>widget2</item>"

'Add the children of the document fragment to the original document.
doc.DocumentElement.AppendChild(docFrag);

'Display the XmlDataDocument.
doc.Save(Console.Out)
```

C#:

```
// Create an XmlDataDocument.
XmlDataDocument doc = new XmlDataDocument(dsNorthwind);

// required before editing XML data document with XML operations
doc.DataSet.EnforceConstraints = false;

//Create a document fragment.
XmlDocumentFragment docFrag = doc.CreateDocumentFragment();

//Set the contents of the document fragment.
docFrag.InnerXml ="<item>widget</item><item>widget2</item>";

//Add the children of the document fragment to the original document.
doc.DocumentElement.AppendChild(docFrag);

//Display the XmlDataDocument.
doc.Save(Console.Out);
```

We call `doc.DocumentElement.AppendChild` to add the nodes from the fragment as children of the root of the document object.

The nodes from the document fragment appear immediately before the close of the root `NewDataSet` element:

```
    ...
    </Customers>
    <item>widget</item>
    <item>widget2</item>
    </NewDataSet>
```

CreateDocumentType Method

We would use this method to create a `DOCTYPE` node for the XML document. This method is inherited from `XmlDocument`.

VB.NET:

```
Dim doc As New XmlDataDocument()
Dim dt As XmlDocumentType = doc.CreateDocumentType(name, publicId, systemId,
internalSubset)
```

C#:

```
XmlDataDocument doc = new XmlDataDocument();
XmlDocumentType dt = CreateDocumentType(name, publicId, systemId, internalSubset);
```

Parameters are as follows:

Parameter	Type	Description	Default
name	String	Name of the document type	None
publicId	String	The public identifier of the document type	None - may be a null reference (Nothing in Visual Basic)
systemId	String	The system identifier of the document type	None - may be a null reference (Nothing in Visual Basic)
internalSubset	String	The DTD internal subset of the document type	None - may be a null reference (Nothing in Visual Basic)

An XML document may have one DocumentType node, which represents a DOCTYPE declaration referencing an XML document type definition (DTD) either internal to the XML document or external. The DOCTYPE declaration is not required to exist, but this method can be used to create one. We have to insert the DocumentType node before the root element of the XmlDocument is inserted. Therefore, if the document already has a root element, we cannot add a DocumentType node. This precludes this method being used with an XmlDataDocument constructed from an already-existing DataSet.

We call CreateDocumentType to create the XmlDocumentType object, then call an insert method such as XmlNode.AppendChild() to actually add it to a document tree. The created XmlDocumentType object has the context of the current XML document, meaning that all the defaults for the current document apply.

The following example adds a new DocumentType to the existing XML document:

VB.NET:

```
'Create an XmlDataDocument.
Dim doc As XmlDataDocument = new XmlDataDocument()

'Create a document type node
Dim doctype As XmlDocumentType
doctype = doc.CreateDocumentType("book", Nothing, Nothing, "<!ELEMENT book ANY>")

'add it to the document.
doc.AppendChild(doctype)

'Create the root element and add it to the document.

doc.AppendChild(doc.CreateElement("book"))

'Display the XmlDataDocument.
doc.Save(Console.Out)
```

C#:

```
// Create an XmlDataDocument.
XmlDataDocument doc = new XmlDataDocument();

//Create a document type node and add it to the document.
XmlDocumentType doctype;
doctype = doc.CreateDocumentType("book", null, null, "<!ELEMENT book ANY>");
doc.AppendChild(doctype);

//Create the root element and add it to the document.
doc.AppendChild(doc.CreateElement("book"));
doc.Save(Console.Out);
```

The document type is displayed in the generated XML as:

```
...
<!DOCTYPE book[<!ELEMENT book ANY>]>
<book />
```

CreateElement Method

Creates an `XmlElement` within the context of the XML document.

VB.NET:

```
Dim doc As New XmlDataDocument()
Dim elem As XmlElement = doc.CreateElement(prefix, localname, namespaceURI)
Dim elem As XmlElement = doc.CreateElement(qualifiedName, namespaceURI)
Dim elem As XmlElement = doc.CreateElement(name)
```

C#:

```
XmlDataDocument doc = new XmlDataDocument();
XmlElement elem = doc.CreateElement(prefix, name, namespaceURI);
XmlElement elem = doc.CreateElement(name, namespaceURI);
XmlElement elem = doc.CreateElement(name);
```

Parameters are as follows:

Parameter	Type	Description	Default
name	String	Name of element to create	None
Prefix	String	Name prefix	String.Empty
NamespaceURI	String	URI of namespace	String.Empty

This method creates an XML element within the `XmlDataDocument`. The XML element must have a name (also called the local name); optionally it may have a namespace URI (Universal Resource Identifier) and/or a prefix, to place the name in a recognized XML namespace. Therefore the method call:

```
doc.CreateElement("myprefix", "myname", "myuri")
```

will create an element equivalent to the following XML text:

```
<myprefix:myname xmlns:myprefix="myuri"/>
```

A qualified name consists of the prefix and the local name separated by a colon. Therefore the following call is equivalent to the above example:

```
doc.CreateElement("myprefix:myname", "myuri")
```

If the prefix is set to "xmlns" (for XML namespace), then the namespaceURI parameter must be "http://www.w3.org/2000/xmlns/"; otherwise an exception is thrown. The namespaceURI parameter should remain empty unless the prefix is a recognized built-in prefix such as xmlns.

Although this method creates the new object in the context of the document, it does not automatically add the new object to the document tree. To add the new object, we must explicitly call one of the XML node insert methods such as AppendChild. The following example adds a new element to the existing XML document:

VB.NET:

```
'Create an XmlDataDocument.
Dim doc As XmlDataDocument = New XmlDataDocument(dsNorthwind)
'Required before editing XML data document with XML operations
doc.DataSet.EnforceConstraints = false
dim newElem As XmlElement = doc.CreateElement("myprefix", "myname", "myuri")
newElem.InnerText="hardcover"
'This appends the new element as a child of the root element
dim currNode As XmlNode = doc.DocumentElement
currNode.AppendChild(newElem)
'Display the XmlDataDocument.
doc.Save(Console.Out)
```

C#:

```
// Create an XmlDataDocument.
XmlDataDocument doc = new XmlDataDocument(dsNorthwind);
// required before editing XML data document with XML operations
doc.DataSet.EnforceConstraints = false;
XmlElement newElem=doc.CreateElement("myprefix", "myname", "myuri");
newElem.InnerText="hardcover";
// this appends the new element as a child of the root element
XmlNode currNode = doc.DocumentElement;
currNode.AppendChild(newElem);
// Display the XmlDataDocument.
doc.Save(Console.Out);
```

CreateEntityReferenceMethod

This method is not supported by XmlDataDocument. It throws a NotSupportedException if called.

CreateNavigator Method

The CreateNavigator method is a protected factory-type method that creates an XPathNavigator object used for XPath navigation and querying of the XmlDataDocument. This method is inherited from XmlNode.

VB.NET:

```
Imports System.Xml.XPath
...
Dim doc As New XmlDataDocument()
Dim nav As XPathNavigator = CType(doc, IXPathNavigable).CreateNavigator()
```

C#:

```
Using System.Xml.XPath;
...
XmlDataDocument doc = new XmlDataDocument();
XPathNavigator nav = doc.CreateNavigator();
```

There is one optional parameter, `XmlNode`:

Parameter	Type	Description	Default
node	XmlNode	The node at which the XPath navigation is to start	Root node of document

`CreateNavigator` is part of the `IXPathNavigable` interface, implemented by `XmlDataDocument`. XPath is the XML Path Language (http://www.w3.org/TR/xpath) used to query and address parts of an XML document. The `XPathNavigator` object returned by `CreateNavigator` enables programs to navigate XML documents using XPath queries, especially to support XSLT transformations (http://www.w3.org/TR/xslt) of XML documents.

This example uses an XPath navigator to iterate through the book elements in the `bookdata.xml` sample file:

VB.NET:

```
Imports System.Xml.XPath
...
Dim doc As New XmlDataDocument()
//Create an XmlDataDocument.
XmlDataDocument doc = new XmlDataDocument();
' Load the schema file.
doc.DataSet.ReadXmlSchema("books.xsd")
' Load the XML data.
doc.Load("bookdata.xml")
Console.WriteLine("Display the XML data...")
Dim nav As XPathNavigator = CType(doc, IXPathNavigable).CreateNavigator()
   ' move to the root element
nav.MoveToRoot();
Dim naviter As XPathNodeIterator = nav.Select("bookstore/book")
While naviter.MoveNext()
      Console.Write("<" + naviter.Current.Name + ">")
End While
Console.WriteLine()
```

C#:

```
Using System.Xml.XPath;
...
//Create an XmlDataDocument.
XmlDataDocument doc = new XmlDataDocument();
```

```
//Load the schema file.
doc.DataSet.ReadXmlSchema("books.xsd");
//Load the XML data.
doc.Load("bookdata.xml");
Console.WriteLine("Display the XML data...");
XPathNavigator nav = doc.CreateNavigator();
nav.MoveToRoot();
XPathNodeIterator naviter = nav.Select("bookstore/book");
while (naviter.MoveNext())
{
    Console.Write("<" + naviter.Current.Name + ">");
}
Console.WriteLine();
```

The document is created and loaded from the XML sample file. An `XpathNavigator` is created for the document using the `CreateNavigator` method. We move to the root element using the `XpathNavigator.MoveToRoot` method, then calling `XpathNavigator`'s `Select` method with an XPath query, locating the book elements in the document. We then create an `XpathNodeIterator` object to iterate through the nodes located by the `Select` method as a collection, and display the names:

```
Display the XML data...
<book><book>
```

The example output lists the element names of the two book elements.

CreateNode Method

We can use this method to create an XML node of any type, specifying node type, name, and other creation parameters. This method is inherited from `XmlDocument`.

VB.NET:

```
Dim doc As New XmlDataDocument()
Dim nod As XmlNode = doc.CreateNode(nodetype, prefix, localname, namespaceURI)
Dim nod As XmlNode = doc.CreateNode(nodetype, qualifiedname, namespaceURI)
Dim nod As XmlNode = doc.CreateNode(nodetypestr, qualifiedname, namespaceURI)
```

C#:

```
XmlDataDocument doc = new XmlDataDocument();
XmlNode nod = doc.CreateNode(nodetype, prefix, localname, namespaceURI);
XmlNode nod = doc.CreateNode(nodetype, qualifiedname, namespaceURI);
XmlNode nod = doc.CreateNode(nodetypestr, qualifiedname, namespaceURI);
```

Parameters are as follows:

Parameter	Type	Description	Default
nodetype	XmlNodeType	Enum constant representing the node type	none
nodetypestr	String	String name of node type	none

Table continued on following page

669

Parameter	Type	Description	Default
name qualifiedname localname	String	Name of node to create	None
Prefix	String	Name prefix	String.Empty
NamespaceURI	String	URI of namespace	String.Empty

This method creates an XML Node within the `XmlDataDocument`.

The XML node must have a nodetype. Node types can be specified using either a string containing the string name of the node type, or one of the `XmlNodeType` enum constants. This table shows the string and enumerated constants for the allowable node types:

String name of node type	XmlNodeType enum constant
"element"	Element
"attribute"	Attribute
"text"	Text
"cdatasection"	CDATA
"entityreference"	EntityReference
"processinginstruction"	ProcessingInstruction
"comment"	Comment
"document"	Document
"documenttype"	DocumentType
"documentfragment"	DocumentFragment

See the discussion of namespaces in the introduction of this chapter for a definition of the terms local name, qualified name, prefix, and namespace URI.

`CreateNode` has different overloaded forms supporting the creation of attributes with either a simple local name or a complex name using a prefix and namespace. This method call creates an attribute node with a simple local name:

```
doc.CreateNode(XmlNodeType.Attribute, "myname")
```

This creates an attribute equivalent to the following XML (the value of the attribute is empty by default):

```
<myelement myname="">
```

This version of the method call creates an attribute node with a prefix and namespace URI:

```
doc.CreateNode(XmlNodeType.Attribute, "myns", "myname",
"http://www.myuri.com/myns")
```

creating an attribute equivalent to the following XML:

```
<myelement myns:myname="" xmlns:myns="http://www.myuri.com/myns">
```

A qualified name consists of the prefix and the local name separated by a colon; therefore the following call is equivalent to the above example:

```
doc.CreateNode(XmlNodeType.Attribute, "myns:myname", "http://www.myuri.com/myns")
```

In order to use the `namespaceURI` parameter, we must reference a URI we have defined ourselves, or a recognized URI such as `http://www.w3.org/2000/xmlns/`, for the XML namespace ("`xmlns`"). If we do not, we should not use this parameter. In particular, the .NET run-time will throw an exception if a prefix of "`xmlns`" is used with any value for `namespaceURI` other than "`http://www.w3.org/2000/xmlns/`".

We call `CreateNode` to create the `XmlNode` object, then call an insert method such as `XmlNode.AppendChild()` to actually add it to a document tree. The created `XmlNode` object has the context of the current XML document, meaning that all the defaults for the current document apply.

The following example adds a new attribute node to the existing XML document:

VB.NET:

```
'Create an XmlDataDocument.
Dim doc As XmlDataDocument = new XmlDataDocument(dsNorthwind)

'required before editing XML data document with XML operations
doc.DataSet.EnforceConstraints = false
Dim newAttr As XmlNode
newAttr = doc.CreateNode(XmlNodeType.Attribute, "myns", "myname",
"http://www.myuri.com/myns")
newAttr.Value = "my value"

'append the new Node to the root element
doc.DocumentElement.SetAttributeNode(CType(newAttr, XmlAttribute))

'Display the XmlDataDocument.
doc.Save(Console.Out)
```

C#:

```
// Create an XmlDataDocument.
XmlDataDocument doc = new XmlDataDocument(dsNorthwind);

// required before editing XML data document with XML operations
doc.DataSet.EnforceConstraints = false;

//Create an attribute node.
XmlNode newAttr=doc.CreateNode(XmlNodeType.Attribute, "myns", "myname",
"http://www.myuri.com/myns");
newAttr.Value = "my value";
```

```
//append the new Node to the root element.
doc.DocumentElement.SetAttributeNode((XmlAttribute)newAttr);

//Display the XmlDataDocument.
doc.Save(Console.Out);
```

The example uses an `XmlDataDocument` object created from a `DataSet`, based on the Northwind database, and already filled with data, as shown in the full sample for the `XmlDataDocument(DataSet)` constructor.

The `DataSet.EnforceConstraints` property must be set to False to allow XML nodes to be added to the document, based on the Northwind `DataSet`. We create the `XmlNode` with the call to the `CreateNode` method, specifying the enumerated constant `XmlNodeType.Attribute` as the type. We could also have used the string `"attribute"` in place of the enumerated constant. We then set the value of the attribute using the `Value` property, then append the node to the root element of the document (`DocumentElement`) with the `XmlAttribute.SetAttributeNode` method.

The attribute node added shows up in the root element (`NewDataSet`) at the beginning of the XML output as:

```
<NewDataSet myns:myname="my value" xmlns:myns="http://www.myuri.com/myns">
```

CreateProcessingInstruction Method

We use this to create an XML processing instruction (such as an xml-stylesheet transformation) for the current XML document. This method is inherited from `XmlDocument`.

VB.NET:

```
Dim doc As New XmlDataDocument()
Dim cmt As XmlProcessingInstruction = doc.CreateProcessingInstruction(target,
data)
```

C#:

```
XmlDataDocument doc = new XmlDataDocument();
XmlProcessingInstruction cmt = doc.CreateProcessingInstruction(target, data);
```

Parameters are as follows:

Parameter	Type	Description	Default
target	String	The name of the processing instruction	none
data	String	The data for the processing instruction	none

This method creates an `XmlProcessingInstruction` object (representing an XML processing instruction) using the context of the current XML document. The W3C 1.0 XML Spec (`www.w3.org/TR/1998/REC-xml-19980210`) indicates that XML processing instructions are allowed only for document and element nodes; see the XML spec for information on specific processing instructions.

We call `CreateProcessingInstruction` to create the `XmlProcessingInstruction` object, then call an insert method such as `XmlNode.InsertBefore()` to actually add it to your document tree. The created `XmlProcessingInstruction` object has the context of the current XML document, meaning that all the defaults for the current document apply.

The following example adds a new processing instruction to the existing XML document:

VB.NET:

```
'Create an XmlDataDocument.
Dim doc As XmlDataDocument = new XmlDataDocument(dsNorthwind)

'required before editing XML data document with XML operations
doc.DataSet.EnforceConstraints = false
Dim dataProcInst As String = "type='text/xsl' href='book.xsl'"
Dim targProcInst As String = "xml-stylesheet"

'Add the new node to the document.
Dim newProcInst As XmlProcessingInstruction
newProcInst = doc.CreateProcessingInstruction(targProcInst, dataProcInst)

'this adds the new ProcessingInstruction before the root element
Dim root As XmlElement = doc.DocumentElement
doc.InsertBefore(newProcInst, root)

'Display the XmlDataDocument.
doc.Save(Console.Out)
```

C#:

```
// Create an XmlDataDocument.
XmlDataDocument doc = new XmlDataDocument(dsNorthwind);

// required before editing XML data document with XML operations
doc.DataSet.EnforceConstraints = false;
String dataProcInst = "type='text/xsl' href='book.xsl'";
String targProcInst = "xml-stylesheet";
XmlProcessingInstruction newProcInst =
doc.CreateProcessingInstruction(targProcInst, dataProcInst);

// this adds the new ProcessingInstruction before the root element
XmlElement root = doc.DocumentElement;
doc.InsertBefore(newProcInst, root);

//Display the XmlDataDocument.
doc.Save(Console.Out);
```

The `DataSet.EnforceConstraints` property must be set to False to allow XML nodes to be added to the document based on the Northwind `DataSet`. We create the strings to pass to the `CreateProcessingInstruction` method; in this case we are creating an instruction to use an XSL stylesheet so we need to specify "xml-stylesheet" as the target parameter. In the data parameter, we need to specify the MIME type (text/xsl) and the source URL for the XSL stylesheet: `href='book.xsl'`.

We then create the `XmlProcessingInstruction` node using the `CreateProcessingInstruction` method, then get an `XmlElement` object for the root element of the document (`DocumentElement`), and call `InsertBefore`, specifying the root element as the place to do the insertion.

The processing instruction appears at the start of the output immediately preceding the root `NewDataSet` element, as shown here:

```
<?xml-stylesheet type='text/xsl' href='book.xsl'?>
<NewDataSet>
<Customers>
```

CreateSignificantWhitespace Method

Can be used to create whitespace for formatting an XML document. This method is inherited from `XmlDocument`.

VB.NET:

```
Dim doc As New XmlDataDocument()
Dim sws As XmlSignificantWhitespace = doc.CreateSignificantWhitespace(data)
```

C#:

```
XmlDataDocument doc = new XmlDataDocument();
XmlSignificantWhitespace sws = doc.CreateSignificantWhitespace(data);
```

Parameters are as follows:

Parameter	Type	Description	Default
data	String	String of whitespace characters to be inserted	none

Normally **whitespace** (space, tab, carriage return, and linefeed characters) is ignored during the processing of XML. However, in some cases it is necessary to handle whitespace in a special way for readability of text, for example, when displaying sourcecode. This is termed **significant whitespace**, and is described in the W3C XML standard (`http://www.w3.org/TR/1998/REC-xml-19980210#sec-white-space`). Whitespace is considered significant in text in mixed content mode, where elements and text may be interspersed, and also when the `xml:space` attribute is set to `preserve`.

The DOM model provides a special `SignificantWhitespace` node type for this situation, represented in the .NET framework as an `XmlSignificantWhitespace` node. Significant whitespace nodes are created automatically when a document is loaded only if the document's `PreserveWhitespace` property is `true`. `XmlSignificantWhitespace` nodes can be created explicitly by this method. These nodes are allowed only within `Document` and `Element` nodes. We pass the specific whitespace characters to be inserted in the `data` parameter.

> Only space (' '), tab (\t), carriage return (\r) and linefeed (\n) characters may be part of the string for the **data** parameter. In Visual Basic the **ControlChars** constants may be used: **ControlChars.Space**, **ControlChars.Tab**, **ControlChars.Cr**, and **ControlChars.Lf**.

To create the node, call `CreateSignificantWhitespace` to create the
`XmlSignificantWhitespace` object, then call an insert method such as
`XmlNode.InsertAfter()` to actually add it to your document tree. The created
`XmlSignificantWhitespace` object has the context of the current XML document, meaning that all
the defaults for the current document apply.

The following example adds a new significant whitespace node to the existing XML document:

VB.NET:

```
'Create an XmlDataDocument.
Dim doc As XmlDataDocument = new XmlDataDocument(dsNorthwind)

'required before editing XML data document with XML operations
doc.DataSet.EnforceConstraints = false

'add whitespace
Dim currNode As XmlNode
currNode = doc.DocumentElement
Dim sws As XmlSignificantWhitespace =
doc.CreateSignificantWhitespace(ControlChars.Tab)
currNode.InsertAfter(sws, currNode.FirstChild)

'display the XmlDataDocument.
doc.Save(Console.Out)
```

C#:

```
// Create an XmlDataDocument.
XmlDataDocument doc = new XmlDataDocument(dsNorthwind);

// required before editing XML data document with XML operations
doc.DataSet.EnforceConstraints = false;

//add whitespace
XmlNode currNode=doc.DocumentElement;
XmlSignificantWhitespace sws=doc.CreateSignificantWhitespace("\t");
currNode.InsertAfter(sws, currNode.FirstChild);

//Display the XmlDataDocument.
doc.Save(Console.Out);
```

The `DataSet.EnforceConstraints` property must be set to False to allow XML nodes to be added
to the document based on the Northwind DataSet. Then we get an `XmlElement` object for the root
element of the document (`DocumentElement`), then create the whitespace node. The node is actually
inserted by calling `InsertAfter` specifying the root element as the place to do the insertion. Then we
display the output.

The `SignificantWhitespace` section changes the display at the end of the generated XML,
instead of:

```
</Customers>
</NewDataSet>
```

a tab now separates the elements with no line separation or indentation:

```
</Customers> </NewDataSet>
```

675

CreateTextNode Method

We use this to create a text node within the current XML document. This method is inherited from `XmlDocument`.

VB.NET:

```
Dim doc As New XmlDataDocument()
Dim txt As XmlText = doc.CreateTextNode(text)
```

C#:

```
XmlDataDocument doc = new XmlDataDocument();
XmlText txt = doc.CreateTextNode(text);
```

Parameters are as follows:

Parameter	Type	Description	Default
text	String	Text for text node	none

This method creates an `XmlText` object, which represents a `Text` node.

The W3C 1.0 XML Spec (`www.w3.org/TR/1998/REC-xml-19980210`) allows `Text` nodes only within `Element`, `Attribute`, and `EntityReference` nodes.

We call `CreateText` to create the `XmlText` object, then call an insert method such as `XmlNode.AppendChild()` to actually add it to our document tree. The created `XmlText` object has the context of the current XML document, meaning that all the defaults for the current document apply.

The following example adds new text to the existing XML document:

VB.NET:

```
'Create an XmlDataDocument.
Dim doc As XmlDataDocument = new XmlDataDocument(dsNorthwind)

'required before editing XML data document with XML operations
doc.DataSet.EnforceConstraints = false

'Create a new node and add it to the document.
'The text node is the content of the price element.
Dim elem As XmlElement = doc.CreateElement("Discounts")
Dim text As XmlText = doc.CreateTextNode("Preferred Customer Club")
doc.DocumentElement.FirstChild.AppendChild(elem)
doc.DocumentElement.FirstChild.LastChild.AppendChild(text)

'display XML document
doc.Save(Console.Out)
```

C#:

```
// Create an XmlDataDocument.
XmlDataDocument doc = new XmlDataDocument(dsNorthwind);
```

```
// required before editing XML data document with XML operations
doc.DataSet.EnforceConstraints = false;

//Create a new node and add it to the document.
//The text node is the content of the price element.
XmlElement elem = doc.CreateElement("Discounts");
XmlText text = doc.CreateTextNode("Preferred Customer Club");
doc.DocumentElement.FirstChild.AppendChild(elem);
doc.DocumentElement.FirstChild.LastChild.AppendChild(text);

//Display the XmlDataDocument.
doc.Save(Console.Out);
```

The `DataSet.EnforceConstraints` property must be set to False to allow XML nodes to be added to the document based on the Northwind `DataSet`. We then create an `XmlElement` object for new `Discounts` element, followed by the text node creation with `CreateTextNode`. We insert both nodes into the document by first appending the `Discounts` element to the first child of the root element of the document (`DocumentElement`), then we reference that node with the `LastChild` method to append the text. We then display the output.

The new element with added text section appears at the end of the Customer information in the program output:

```
<NewDataSet>
<Customers>
<CustomerID>BLONP</CustomerID>
<CompanyName>Blondesddsl père et fils</CompanyName>
<ContactName>Frédérique Citeaux</ContactName>
<ContactTitle>Marketing Manager</ContactTitle>
<Address>24, place Kléber</Address>
<City>Strasbourg</City>
<PostalCode>67000</PostalCode>
<Country>France</Country>
<Phone>88.60.15.31</Phone>
<Fax>88.60.15.32</Fax>
<Discounts>Preferred Customer Club</Discounts>
</Customers>
</NewDataSet>
```

CreateWhitespace Method

We use the CreateWhitespace method to create a whitespace node within an XML document. This method is inherited from `XmlDocument`.

VB.NET:

```
Dim doc As New XmlDataDocument()
Dim ws As XmlWhitespace = doc.CreateWhitespace(text)
```

C#:

```
XmlDataDocument doc = new XmlDataDocument();
XmlWhitespace ws = doc.CreateWhitespace(text);
```

Parameters are as follows:

Parameter	Type	Description	Default
text	String	String of whitespace characters to be inserted	none

Whitespace characters (space, tab, carriage return, and linefeed characters) are useful for formatting an XML document. XmlWhitespace nodes represent whitespace within element content, as opposed to significant whitespace, which occurs in text outside of elements in mixed content mode. See a more extended discussion of whitespace in the CreateSignificantWhitespace section, earlier in this chapter. XmlWhitespace nodes are created when the document is loaded only if the PreserveWhitespace property is true.

> Only space (' '), tab (\t), carriage return (\r), and linefeed (\n) characters may be part of the string for the **text** parameter. In Visual Basic the **ControlChars** constants may be used: **ControlChars.Space**, **ControlChars.Tab**, **ControlChars.Cr**, and **ControlChars.Lf**.

We call CreateWhitespace to create the XmlWhitespace object, then call an insert method such as XmlNode.InsertAfter() to actually add it to a document tree. The created XmlWhitespace object has the context of the current XML document, meaning that all the defaults for the current document apply.

The following example adds a new XmlWhitespace node to the existing XML document:

VB.NET:

```
'Create an XmlDataDocument.
Dim doc As XmlDataDocument = new XmlDataDocument(dsNorthwind)

'required before editing XML data document with XML operations
doc.DataSet.EnforceConstraints = false

'add whitespace
Dim currNode As XmlNode
currNode = doc.DocumentElement
Dim sws As XmlWhitespace = doc.CreateWhitespace(ControlChars.Tab)
currNode.InsertAfter(sws, currNode.FirstChild)

'display the XmlDataDocument.
doc.Save(Console.Out)
```

C#

```
// Create an XmlDataDocument.
XmlDataDocument doc = new XmlDataDocument(dsNorthwind);

// required before editing XML data document with XML operations
doc.DataSet.EnforceConstraints = false;

//add whitespace
XmlNode currNode=doc.DocumentElement;
XmlWhitespace sws=doc.CreateWhitespace("\t");
currNode.InsertAfter(sws, currNode.FirstChild);

//Display the XmlDataDocument.
doc.Save(Console.Out);
```

The `DataSet.EnforceConstraints` property must be set to False to allow XML nodes to be added to the document based on the Northwind `DataSet`. We then get an `XmlElement` object for the root element of the document (`DocumentElement`), then create the `whitespace` node. The node is actually inserted by calling `InsertAfter`, specifying the root element as the place to do the insertion. We then display the output.

The whitespace section changes the display at the end of the generated XML. Instead of:

```
</Customers>
</NewDataSet>
```

A tab now separates the elements with no line separation or indentation:

```
</Customers>  </NewDataSet>
```

CreateXmlDeclaration Method

We use this to create an XML declaration (such as `<?xml version="1.0"?>`) at the start of the document. This method is inherited from `XmlDocument`.

VB.NET:

```
Dim doc As New XmlDataDocument()
Dim elem As XmlDeclaration = doc.CreateXmlDeclaration(version, encoding,
standalone)
```

C#:

```
XmlDataDocument doc = new XmlDataDocument();
XmlDeclaration elem = doc.CreateXmlDeclaration(version, encoding, standalone);
```

Parameters are as follows:

Parameter	Type	Description	Default
Version	String	Must be "1.0"	None
encoding	String	The value of the encoding attribute	None (may be `null` or `String.Empty`)
standalone	String	Must be "yes" or "no"	None (may be `null` or `String.Empty`)

If you set the encoding parameter, it must be a string supported by the `Encoding` class such as UTF-8 or UTF-16, for Unicode characters. If you do not set it, no encoding attribute is placed in the XML document, and the default UTF-8 encoding is used. The encoding needs to match the encoding used when the document was saved.

In XML the standalone declaration indicates if the document contains external markup declarations; if so the value is "yes". You can just leave this parameter as a Null and `Save` will simply omit the standalone attribute on the XML declaration.

You call `CreateXmlDeclaration` to get the declaration object, add the node to the document with a method such as `InsertBefore`. The following example adds a new attribute to the root element of an existing XML data document:

VB.NET:

```
'Create an XmlDataDocument.
Dim doc As XmlDataDocument = new XmlDataDocument(dsNorthwind)

'required before editing XML data document with XML operations
doc.DataSet.EnforceConstraints = false

'Create an XML declaration.
Dim xmldecl As XmlDeclaration
xmldecl = doc.CreateXmlDeclaration("1.0", Nothing, Nothing)

'Add the new node to the document.
Dim root As XmlElement = doc.DocumentElement
doc.InsertBefore(xmldecl, root)

'Display the XmlDataDocument.
doc.Save(Console.Out);
```

C#:

```
// Create an XmlDataDocument.
XmlDataDocument doc = new XmlDataDocument(dsNorthwind);

// required before editing XML data document with XML operations
doc.DataSet.EnforceConstraints = false;

//Create an XML declaration.
XmlDeclaration xmldecl;
xmldecl = doc.CreateXmlDeclaration("1.0",null,null);

//Add the new node to the document.
XmlElement root = doc.DocumentElement;
doc.InsertBefore(xmldecl, root);

//Display the XmlDataDocument.
doc.Save(Console.Out);
```

The `DataSet.EnforceConstraints` property must be set to False to allow XML nodes to be added to the document based on the Northwind `DataSet`. We then create the XML declaration object and set it using the `CreateXmlDeclaration` method, specifying version 1.0, as required with default encoding, and no standalone declaration. We then get an `XmlElement` object for the root element of the document (`DocumentElement`), and insert the declaration by calling `InsertBefore` specifying the root element as the place to do the insertion. We then display the output.

The XML declaration appears at the beginning of the output XML as follows:

```
<?xml version="1.0"?>
```

GetElementByID Method

This method is not supported by `XmlDataDocument`, and throws an exception if called.

GetElementFromRow Method

Returns the `XmlElement` associated with the given `DataRow`.

VB.NET:

```
Dim doc As New XmlDataDocument(dataset)
Dim elem As XmlElement = doc.GetElementFromRow(row)
```

C#:

```
XmlDataDocument doc = new XmlDataDocument(dataset);
XmlElement elem = doc.GetElementFromRow(row);
```

Parameters are as follows:

Parameter	Type	Description	Default
row	DataRow	Row in table corresponding to desired XmlElement	none

This method is typically used when the original source of the data in the `XmlDataDocument` object is relational and the application is exporting data to XML. This example shows the retrieval of the first customer record in the Northwind sample data as an XML element.

VB.NET:

```
'Load the document with the DataSet.
Dim doc As XmlDataDocument = New XmlDataDocument(dsNorthwind)
'Create an element representing the first customer record.
Dim row As DataRow = doc.DataSet.Tables.Item(0).Rows.Item(0)
Dim elem As XmlElement = doc.GetElementFromRow(row)
Console.WriteLine(elem.OuterXml)
```

C#:

```
//Load the document with the DataSet.
XmlDataDocument doc = new XmlDataDocument(dsNorthwind);
//Create an element representing the first customer record.
DataRow row = doc.DataSet.Tables[0].Rows[0];
XmlElement elem = doc.GetElementFromRow(row);
Console.WriteLine(elem.OuterXml);
```

We create the XML data document based on the query of the Northwind sample data (see the description of the `XmlDataDocument (DataSet)` constructor at the start of the chapter). We create a `DataRow` object based on the first row in the first table of the data set. We then create an XML element object and call `GetElementFromRow` to initialize the `XmlElement` based on the `DataRow`. The output from the example (formatted for readability) is shown here:

```
<Customers>
 <CustomerID>BLONP</CustomerID>
 <CompanyName>Blondesddsl père et fils</CompanyName>
 <ContactName>Frédérique Citeaux</ContactName>
 <ContactTitle>Marketing Manager</ContactTitle>
```

```
    <Address>24, place Kléber</Address>
    <City>Strasbourg</City>
    <PostalCode>67000</PostalCode>
    <Country>France</Country>
    <Phone>88.60.15.31</Phone>
    <Fax>88.60.15.32</Fax>
</Customers>
```

This is indeed the data from the first row of the first and only table (`Customers`).

GetElementsByTagName Method

We use this method to find elements within the document matching the requested tag name. This method is inherited from `XmlDocument`.

VB.NET:

```
Dim doc As New XmlDataDocument()
Dim nodelist As XmlNodeList = doc. GetElementsByTagName(qualifiedname)
Dim nodelist As XmlNodeList = doc. GetElementsByTagName(localname, namespaceURI)
```

C#:

```
XmlDataDocument doc = new XmlDataDocument();
XmlNodeList nodelist = doc. GetElementsByTagName (qualifiedname);
XmlNodeList nodelist = doc. GetElementsByTagName (localname, namespaceURI);
```

Parameters are as follows:

Parameter	Type	Description	Default
qualifiedname localname	String	The name of the tag to match	none
namespaceURI	String	The namespace URI	optional

This search method returns an `XmlNodeList` object containing a list of the elements whose `Name` property matches the specified name. The name may be a local name or a qualified name with a prefix.

See the discussion of namespaces in the introduction of this chapter for a definition of the terms local name, qualified name, prefix, and namespace URI. An asterisk ("*") serves as a wildcard that matches all names.

The example uses `GetElementsByTagName` to find all the Northwind `CompanyName` elements in the XML data document:

VB.NET:

```
'Create an XmlDataDocument.
Dim doc As XmlDataDocument = new XmlDataDocument(dsNorthwind)

'Display all the company names.
Dim elemList As XmlNodeList = doc.GetElementsByTagName("CompanyName")
Dim i As Integer
```

```
For i = 0 To elemList.Count - 1
Console.WriteLine(elemList(i).InnerXml)
Next i
```

C#:

```
// Create an XmlDataDocument.
XmlDataDocument doc = new XmlDataDocument(dsNorthwind);

//Display all the company names.
XmlNodeList elemList = doc.GetElementsByTagName("CompanyName");
for (int i=0; i < elemList.Count; i++)
{
Console.WriteLine(elemList[i].InnerXml);
}
```

The document is created from the Northwind DataSet, filled by a query as shown in the XmlDataDocument(DataSet) constructor example in the previous chapter. We fill an XmlNodeList with the results of the GetElementsByTagName method call. The XmlNodeList Count property tells us how many nodes are in the list; we use this in a for loop to display each one. All the company names found by the query filling the Northwind DataSet are listed.

GetEnumerator Method

We use this to get an enumerator interface to navigate through the nodes as a collection. This method is inherited from XmlNode.

VB.NET:

```
Dim doc As New XmlDataDocument()
Dim ie As IEnumerator = doc.GetEnumerator()
```

C#:

```
XmlDataDocument doc = new XmlDataDocument();
Ienumerator ie = doc.GetEnumerator();
```

This method has no parameters. We can use collection-navigation members such as MoveNext and Current in the IEnumerator interface by using the object returned by GetEnumerator. In the following example, we loop through a collection using an enumerator:

VB.NET:

```
imports System.Collections
...
'Create an XmlDataDocument.
Dim doc As XmlDataDocument = New XmlDataDocument(dsNorthwind)
' get the root node
Dim root As XmlNode = doc.DocumentElement
Dim ie As IEnumerator = root.GetEnumerator()
Dim nextnode As XmlNode
While (ienum.MoveNext())
nextnode = CType(ienum.Current, XmlNode)
Console.WriteLine(nextnode.OuterXml)
Console.WriteLine()
End While
```

C#:

```
using System.Collections;
...
// Create an XmlDataDocument.
XmlDataDocument doc = new XmlDataDocument(dsNorthwind);
// get the root node
XmlNode root = doc.DocumentElement;
IEnumerator ienum = root.GetEnumerator();
XmlNode nextnode;
while (ienum.MoveNext())
{
nextnode = (XmlNode) ienum.Current;
Console.WriteLine(nextnode.OuterXml);
Console.WriteLine();
}
```

The `IEnumerator` interface requires the `System.Collections` namespace. The example uses an `XmlDataDocument` object created from a `DataSet` based on the Northwind database and already filled with data as shown in the full sample shown in the previous chapter for the `XmlDataDocument(DataSet)` constructor. We then get the root node of the document and create an enumerator based on the root; then we move through the collection with the `MoveNext` method, displaying the XML for each node as we encounter it (using `Current` to reference the current node).

GetNamespaceOfPrefix Method

We use this read-only property to get the URI (Universal Resource Identifier) of the namespace for the given prefix. This method is inherited from `XmlNode`.

VB.NET:

```
Dim doc As New XmlDataDocument()
Dim uri As String = doc.GetNamespaceOfPrefix(prefix)
```

C#:

```
XmlDataDocument doc = new XmlDataDocument();
String uri = doc.GetNamespaceOfPrefix(prefix);
```

Parameters are as follows:

Parameter	Type	Description	Default
Prefix	String	prefix for which you want to find matching namespace	None

See the beginning of this chapter for a discussion of namespaces and names. You may need the URI of the namespace for a particular prefix in order to do some later operation that requires both namespace and prefix. This method looks up the closest XML namespace (`xmlns`) declaration in the document that applies and returns that namespace URI.

The following example shows how to get the URI for a prefix:

VB.NET:

```
'Create an XmlDataDocument.
Dim doc As XmlDataDocument = New XmlDataDocument()
' required before editing XML data document with XML operations
doc.DataSet.EnforceConstraints = False
//Create an element with fully qualified name.
Dim newElem As XmlElement
newElem = doc.CreateElement("myns", "myname", "http://www.myuri.com/myns")
Dim uri As String = newElem. GetNamespaceForPrefix("myns")
```

C#:

```
// Create an XmlDataDocument.
XmlDataDocument doc = new XmlDataDocument(dsNorthwind);
// required before editing XML data document with XML operations
doc.DataSet.EnforceConstraints = false;
//Create an element with fully qualified name.
XmlElement newElem=doc.CreateElement("myns", "myname",
"http://www.myuri.com/myns");
String uri = newElem.GetNamespaceForPrefix("myns");
```

The variable `uri` contains the namespace URI, which is `http://www.myuri.com/myns`.

GetPrefixOfNamespace Method

We use this read-only property to get the name prefix for this node's name, if it exists. This method is inherited from `XmlNode`.

VB.NET:

```
Dim doc As New XmlDataDocument()
Dim uri As String = doc.GetPrefixOfNamespace(namespaceURI)
```

C#:

```
XmlDataDocument doc = new XmlDataDocument();
String uri = doc. GetPrefixOfNamespace(namespaceURI);
```

Parameters are as follows:

Parameter	Type	Description	Default
namespaceURI	String	namespace URI for which you want to find a prefix	None

See the beginning of Chapter 14 for a discussion of namespaces and prefixes. You may need the prefix of the namespace in order to do some later operation that requires both namespace and prefix. This method looks up the closest XML namespace (`xmlns`) declaration in the document that applies and returns the prefix defined there. If no prefix applies, this method returns `String.Empty`.

The following example shows how to get the prefix:

VB.NET:

```
'Create an XmlDataDocument.
Dim doc As XmlDataDocument = New XmlDataDocument()
' required before editing XML data document with XML operations
doc.DataSet.EnforceConstraints = False
//Create an element with fully qualified name.
Dim newElem As XmlElement
newElem = doc.CreateElement("myns:myname", "http://www.myuri.com/myns")
Dim pfix As String = newElem.GetPrefixOfNamespace("http://www.myuri.com/myns")
```

C#:

```
// Create an XmlDataDocument.
XmlDataDocument doc = new XmlDataDocument(dsNorthwind);
// required before editing XML data document with XML operations
doc.DataSet.EnforceConstraints = false;
//Create an element with fully qualified name.
XmlElement newElem=doc.CreateElement("myns:myname", "http://www.myuri.com/myns");
String pfix = newElem.GetPrefixOfNamespace("http://www.myuri.com/myns");
```

The variable `pfix` contains the prefix, which is "myns".

GetRowFromElement Method

The `GetRowFromElement` method returns the `DataRow` associated with the given `XmlElement`.

VB.NET:

```
Dim doc As New XmlDataDocument(dataset)
Dim row As DataRow = doc.GetRowFromElement(elem)
```

C#:

```
XmlDataDocument doc = new XmlDataDocument(dataset);
DataRow row = doc. GetRowFromElement(elem);
```

Parameters are as follows:

Parameter	Type	Description	Default
elem	XmlElement	XML element corresponding to desired row	none

This method would typically be used when the original source of the data in the `XmlDataDocument` object is XML and the application is exporting data to relational tables. This example stores book information in a set of tables and then retrieves the `DataRow` for the first book in order to change the price.

VB.NET:

```
'Create an XmlDataDocument.
Dim doc As XmlDataDocument = New XmlDataDocument()
'Load the schema.
doc.DataSet.ReadXmlSchema("books.xsd")
'Load the XML data.
doc.Load("bookdata.xml")
```

```
'Change the price on the first book.
Dim book As XmlElement
book = CType(doc.DocumentElement.FirstChild, XmlElement)
Dim row As DataRow
row = doc.GetRowFromElement(book)
row.Item("price") = "14.99"
```

C#:

```
// Create an XmlDataDocument.
XmlDataDocument doc = new XmlDataDocument();
// Load the schema file.
doc.DataSet.ReadXmlSchema("books.xsd");
// Load the XML data.
doc.Load("bookdata.xml");
//Change the price on the first book.
XmlElement root = doc.DocumentElement;
DataRow row = doc.GetRowFromElement((XmlElement)root.FirstChild);
row["price"] = "14.99";
```

ImportNode Method

We use this to import a node from another XML document. This method is inherited from `XmlDocument`.

VB.NET:

```
Dim doc As New XmlDataDocument()
Dim targetnode As XmlNode = doc.ImportNode(sourcenode, deep)
```

C#:

```
XmlDataDocument doc = new XmlDataDocument();
XmlNode targetnode = doc.ImportNode(sourcenode, deep);
```

Parameters are as follows:

Parameter	Type	Description	Default
sourcenode	XmlNode	Node in source document that you wish to import	none
deep	Boolean	True to perform a deep copy, False for shallow	none

We can use this method to copy any of the node types listed in the table overpage. This table describes how different node types are imported, including differences when the deep parameter is set to True or False.

XmlNodeType	Deep = True	Deep = False
`Attribute`	Children are recursively imported.	Children are recursively imported (deep parameter doesn't apply to attribute nodes).
`DocumentFragment`	Children are recursively imported.	An empty `XmlDocumentFragment` object is generated.
`Element` (Default attributes not copied. Defaults from target are used instead)	Children are recursively imported.	Only the specified attribute nodes of the source element are imported.
`EntityReference`	Not available for `XmlDataDocuments`	Not available for `XmlDataDocuments`.
`Cdata`, `Comment`, `DocumentType`, `ProcessingInstruction`, `Text`, `SignificantWhitespace`, `Whitespace`	Copies node and its contents.	Copies node and its contents.
`XmlDeclaration`	Copies the target and data value from the imported node.	Copies the target and data value from the imported node.
All other node types	These node types cannot be imported.	These node types cannot be imported.

The source node and document are not altered. The returned target node is a copy of the source node with the same name and node type, owned by the importing document and having no parent.

The new node also has the same attributes related to namespaces as the source (`Prefix`, `LocalName`, and `NamespaceURI`). See the discussion of namespaces in the introduction of this chapter for definitions of these terms.

We can think of this method as emulating the result we expect when a fragment of XML or HTML source is copied from one document into another.

The following example imports a customer node from a second XML document into the original XML document:

VB.NET:

```
'Create an XmlDataDocument.
Dim doc As XmlDataDocument = new XmlDataDocument()

' Load the schema file.
doc.DataSet.ReadXmlSchema("books.xsd")

'Create another XmlDocument which holds a list of books.
Dim newdoc As XmlDataDocument = new XmlDataDocument()
newdoc.Load("bookdata.xml");
```

```
'Import the last book node from newdoc into the original document.
Dim newBook As XmlNode = doc.ImportNode(newdoc.DocumentElement.LastChild, true)
doc.DocumentElement.AppendChild(newBook)
doc.Save(Console.Out);
```

C#:

```
//Create an XmlDataDocument.
XmlDataDocument doc = new XmlDataDocument();

//Load the schema file.
doc.DataSet.ReadXmlSchema("books.xsd");

//Create another XmlDocument which holds a list of books.
XmlDataDocument newdoc = new XmlDataDocument();
newdoc.Load("bookdata.xml");

//Import the last book node from newdoc into the original document.
XmlNode newBook = doc.ImportNode(newdoc.DocumentElement.LastChild, true);
doc.DocumentElement.AppendChild(newBook);
doc.Save(Console.Out);
```

In this example, we create an empty data document. We map it to tables with a schema. Following this, another document is created and loaded from the `bookdata.xml` file. We import the last child of the root element (`DocumentElement`) of the document, with the deep parameter set to True so as to recursively copy all the children nodes. We append the newly created book node to the root of the original document, and we are finished, except for displaying the output.

InsertAfter Method

Use this method to insert a new node after the specified node. This method is inherited from `XmlNode`.

VB.NET:

```
Dim doc As New XmlDataDocument()
Dim n As XmlNode = doc.InsertAfter(new, here)
```

C#:

```
XmlDataDocument doc = new XmlDataDocument();
XmlNode n = doc.InsertAfter(new, here);
```

Parameters are as follows:

Parameter	Type	Description	Default
new	XmlNode	New child node	None
here	XmlNode	Existing node that new node will follow	None

You will typically call one of the node creation methods such as `CreateElement` to create the new node object, then call `InsertAfter()` to actually add it to your document tree.

If the `here` parameter is Null, the new node is added at the start of the children list. If `here` is not a child of this node, this method throws an exception. An exception is also thrown if the `new` parameter is an ancestor of this node or has an `XmlNodeType` that is not permitted as a child of the current node.

The following example adds a new significant whitespace node to the existing XML document and inserts it after the last `Customers` element:

VB.NET:

```
'Create an XmlDataDocument.
Dim doc As XmlDataDocument = New XmlDataDocument(dsNorthwind)
'required before editing XML data document with XML operations
doc.DataSet.EnforceConstraints = False
'add whitespace
Dim currNode As XmlNode
currNode = doc.DocumentElement
Dim sws As XmlSignificantWhitespace =
doc.CreateSignificantWhitespace(ControlChars.Tab)
currNode.InsertAfter(sws, currNode.FirstChild)
'display the XmlDataDocument.
doc.Save(Console.Out)
```

C#:

```
// Create an XmlDataDocument.
XmlDataDocument doc = new XmlDataDocument(dsNorthwind);
// required before editing XML data document with XML operations
doc.DataSet.EnforceConstraints = false;
//add whitespace
XmlNode currNode=doc.DocumentElement;
XmlSignificantWhitespace sws=doc.CreateSignificantWhitespace("\t");
currNode.InsertAfter(sws, currNode.FirstChild);
//Display the XmlDataDocument.
doc.Save(Console.Out);
```

The DataSet.`EnforceConstraints` property must be set to `false` to allow XML nodes to be added to the document based on the Northwind `DataSet`. We create the whitespace node, then insert it by calling `InsertAfter` specifying the root element as the place to do the insertion. We then display the output.

The `SignificantWhitespace` section changes the display at the end of the generated XML. Instead of:

```
</Customers>
</NewDataSet>
```

A tab now separates the elements with no line separation or indentation:

```
</Customers>  </NewDataSet>
```

InsertBefore Method

We use this method to insert a new node before the specified node. This method is inherited from `XmlNode`.

VB.NET:

```
Dim doc As New XmlDataDocument()
Dim n As XmlNode = doc.InsertBefore(new, here)
```

C#:

```
XmlDataDocument doc = new XmlDataDocument();
XmlNode n = doc.InsertBefore(new, here);
```

Parameters are as follows:

Parameter	Type	Description	Default
new	XmlNode	New child node	None
here	XmlNode	Existing node that new node will precede	None

We would typically call one of the node creation methods such as CreateElement to create the new node object, then call InsertBefore() to actually add it to a document tree.

The following example adds an XML declaration node preceding the root element of an existing XML data document:

VB.NET:

```
'Create an XmlDataDocument.
Dim doc As XmlDataDocument = New XmlDataDocument(dsNorthwind)
'required before editing XML data document with XML operations
doc.DataSet.EnforceConstraints = False
'Create an XML declaration.
Dim xmldecl As XmlDeclaration
xmldecl = doc.CreateXmlDeclaration("1.0", Nothing, Nothing)

'Add the new node to the document.
Dim root As XmlElement = doc.DocumentElement
doc.InsertBefore(xmldecl, root)
'Display the XmlDataDocument.
doc.Save(Console.Out);
```

C#:

```
// Create an XmlDataDocument.
XmlDataDocument doc = new XmlDataDocument(dsNorthwind);
// required before editing XML data document with XML operations
doc.DataSet.EnforceConstraints = false;
//Create an XML declaration.
XmlDeclaration xmldecl;
xmldecl = doc.CreateXmlDeclaration("1.0",null,null);
//Add the new node to the document.
XmlElement root = doc.DocumentElement;
doc.InsertBefore(xmldecl, root);
//Display the XmlDataDocument.
doc.Save(Console.Out);
```

The DataSet.EnforceConstraints property must be set to False to allow XML nodes to be added to the document based on the Northwind DataSet. We then create the XML declaration object, find the root element of the document (DocumentElement), and insert the declaration by calling InsertBefore, specifying the root element as the node that the new node should precede.

The XML declaration appears at the beginning of the output XML as follows:

```
<?xml version="1.0"?>
<NewDataSet>
```

Load (Stream) Method

The `Load` method loads the `XmlDataDocument` from an XML data source. It is overloaded and takes several different forms depending on the form of the source; this version reads from a `Stream` object.

VB.NET:

```
Dim doc As XmlDataDocument = New XmlDataDocument()
doc.Load(stream)
```

C#:

```
XmlDataDocument doc = new XmlDataDocument();
doc.Load(stream);
```

Parameters are as follows:

Parameter	Type	Description	Default
s-tream	Stream	Stream to read XML document from. May be `FileStream`, `NetworkStream`, or any other `Stream` type	None

Streams are defined in the `System.IO` namespace, which must be included as in this example:

VB.NET:

```
Imports System.IO
...
Dim doc As XmlDataDocument = New XmlDataDocument()
'Load the schema.
doc.DataSet.ReadXmlSchema("books.xsd")
'Load the XML data.
Dim fs As FileStream = New FileStream("bookdata.xml", FileMode.OpenOrCreate,
FileAccess.Read)
' load from file stream
doc.Load(fs)
```

C#:

```
Using System.IO;
...
//Create an XmlDataDocument.
XmlDataDocument doc = new XmlDataDocument();
//Load the schema file.
doc.DataSet.ReadXmlSchema("books.xsd");
//Load the XML data.
FileStream fs = new FileStream("bookdata.xml", FileMode.OpenOrCreate,
FileAccess.Read);
doc.Load(fs);
```

A stream is a low-level object; for reading from text files it is more convenient to use the `Load(XmlTextReader)` version of load than to load from a file stream. However, a network application might require reading from a `NetworkStream` or other variation of `Stream`.

Whitespace nodes are not created unless the `XmlReader` has been set to return whitespace and the `PreserveWhitespace` property is set to True.

If the reader is in the initial state, `Load` consumes the entire contents of the reader to build the contents of the document. If the reader is positioned on a subnode, the results will vary depending on the contents of the node and the relation of the node to its siblings. `Load` will read the subnode and all its siblings up to the tag that encloses the same level as the subnode. If this results in a document with multiple root elements, `Load` will throw an exception. If this results in a document with no root elements, a root must be added before saving the document with the `Save` method.

`Load` does not validate the XML data loaded; that is, it does not make sure that the elements and attributes conform to a DTD, XDR or XSD schema for the document. It also does not resolve external entity references. If you want this kind of validation, specify an `XmlValidatingReader` as the source of the document.

Load (String) Method

The `Load` method loads the `XmlDataDocument` from an XML data source. It is overloaded and takes several different forms depending on the form of the source; this version reads from a `String` object.

VB.NET:

```
Dim doc As XmlDataDocument = New XmlDataDocument()
doc.Load(filename)
```

C#:

```
XmlDataDocument doc = new XmlDataDocument();
doc.Load(filename);
```

Parameters are as follows:

Parameter	Type	Description	Default
filename	String	Local file name or URL of file to read XML data from	none

The example shows a Web URL as the file name; a local file name could also be used:

VB.NET:

```
Create an XmlDataDocument.
Dim doc As XmlDataDocument = New XmlDataDocument()
'Load the schema.
doc.DataSet.ReadXmlSchema("books.xsd")
'Load URL for XML data.
Dim fn As String = "http://localhost/bookdata.xml"
'Load from file
doc.Load(fn)
```

C#:

```
//Create an XmlDataDocument.
XmlDataDocument doc = new XmlDataDocument();
//Load the schema file.
doc.DataSet.ReadXmlSchema("books.xsd");
// load URL for XML data.
String fn = "http://localhost/bookdata.xml";
doc.Load(fn);
```

The example assumes that the file `bookdata.xml` is available in the root directory of the web server (`\inetpub\wwwroot`).

See the remarks under `Load(Stream)` on whitespace node creation, start reading at a subnode, and schema validation: these apply to this form of `Load` as well.

Load (TextReader) Method

The Load method loads the `XmlDataDocument` from an XML data source. It is overloaded and takes several different forms depending on the form of the source; this version reads from a `TextReader` object.

VB.NET:

```
Dim doc As XmlDataDocument = New XmlDataDocument()
doc.Load(textreader)
```

C#:

```
XmlDataDocument doc = new XmlDataDocument();
doc.Load(textreader);
```

Parameters are as follows:

Parameter	Type	Description	Default
Textreader	TextReader	Text reader object set up to read a source of XML data	None

`TextReader` is defined in the `System.IO` namespace. `TextReader` is an abstract class for which `StreamReader` and `StringReader` are specific implementations. This example uses `StreamReader`:

VB.NET:

```
Imports System.IO
...
Dim doc As XmlDataDocument = New XmlDataDocument()
'Load the XML data.
Dim fn As String = "bookdata.xml"
Dim tr As StreamReader = New StreamReader(fn)
' load from file stream
doc.Load(tr)
```

C#:

```
Using System.IO;
...
//Create an XmlDataDocument.
XmlDataDocument doc = new XmlDataDocument();
//Load the schema file.
doc.DataSet.ReadXmlSchema("books.xsd");
//Load the XML data.
String fn = "bookdata.xml";
StreamReader tr = new StreamReader(fn);
doc.Load(tr);
```

A stream is a low-level object; for reading from text files it is usually more convenient to use the `Load(XmlTextReader)` version of load than to load from a stream reader.

See the remarks under `Load(Stream)` on whitespace node creation, start reading at a subnode, and schema validation; these apply to this form of `Load` as well.

Load (XmlTextReader) Method

The `Load` method loads the `XmlDataDocument` from an XML data source. It is overloaded and takes several different forms depending on the form of the source; this version reads from an `XmlTextReader` object.

VB.NET:

```
Dim doc As XmlDataDocument = New XmlDataDocument()
doc.Load(xmlreader)
```

C#:

```
XmlDataDocument doc = new XmlDataDocument();
doc.Load(xmlreader);
```

Parameters are as follows:

Parameter	Type	Description	Default
xmlreader	XmlReader	XML reader object set up to read a source of XML data	none

Since this version of the `XmlDataDocument` constructor does not use an existing `DataSet` for initialization, the `DataSet` will initially be empty. It is the version we probably use when reading existing XML data into the `XmlDataDocument` to be accessed as relational tables, as in this example:
VB.NET

```
'Create an XmlDataDocument.
Dim doc As XmlDataDocument = New XmlDataDocument()
'Load the schema.
doc.DataSet.ReadXmlSchema("books.xsd")
'Load the XML data.
Dim reader As XmlTextReader = New XmlTextReader("bookdata.xml")
doc.Load(reader)
```

```
'Change the price on the first book imports the DataSet methods.
Dim books As DataTable = doc.DataSet.Tables.Item("book")
books.Rows.Item(0).Item("price") = "14.99"
Console.WriteLine("Display the modified XML data...")
doc.Save(Console.Out)
```

C#:

```
//Create an XmlDataDocument.
XmlDataDocument doc = new XmlDataDocument();
//Load the schema file.
doc.DataSet.ReadXmlSchema("books.xsd");
XmlTextReader reader = new XmlTextReader("bookdata.xml");
//Load the XML data.
doc.Load(reader);
//Update the price on the first book using the DataSet methods.
DataTable books = doc.DataSet.Tables["book"];
books.Rows[0]["price"] = "14.99";
Console.WriteLine("Display the modified XML data...");
```

Whitespace nodes are not created unless the `XmlReader` has been set to return whitespace and the `PreserveWhitespace` property is set to True.

If the reader is in the initial state, `Load` consumes the entire contents of the reader to build the contents of the document. If the reader is positioned on a subnode, the results will vary depending on the contents of the node and the relation of the node to its siblings. `Load` will read the subnode and all its siblings up to the tag that encloses the same level as the subnode. If this results in a document with multiple root elements, `Load` will throw an exception. If this results in a document with no root elements, a root must be added before saving the document with the `Save` method.

`Load` does not do schema evaluation or resolution of entities; this can be accomplished by specifying an `XmlValidatingReader` as the source of the document.

LoadXml Method

Use this method to load the `XmlDataDocument` from a string containing the XML you want to load. This method is inherited from `XmlDocument`.

VB.NET:

```
Dim doc As XmlDataDocument = new XmlDataDocument()
doc.LoadXml(xmlstring )
```

C#:

```
XmlDataDocument doc = new XmlDataDocument();
doc.LoadXml(xmlstring);
```

Parameters are as follows:

Parameter	Type	Description	Default
Xmlstring	String	String containing the literal XML you want to load	none

In this example, we load one book as a literal XML string:

VB.NET:

```
' Create an XmlDataDocument
Dim doc As New XmlDataDocument()

' Load it
doc.LoadXml(("<book genre='computer' ISBN='1861005-466'>" & _
"<title>Professional SQL Server 2000 XML</title>" & _
"<price>49.99</price>" & _
"</book>"))

' display XML document
doc.Save(Console.Out)
```

C#:

```
//Create an XmlDataDocument.
XmlDataDocument doc = new XmlDataDocument();

// Load it
doc.LoadXml("<book genre='computer' ISBN='1861005-466'>" +
"<title>Professional SQL Server 2000 XML</title>" +
"<price>49.99</price>" +
"</book>");

// display XML document
doc.Save(Console.Out);
```

LoadXml does not do schema validation or external entity resolution; for these cases you can use the Load method and specify an XmlValidatingReader as the document source.

Normalize Method

Can be used to normalize the format of an XML document. This method is inherited from XmlNode.

VB.NET:

```
Dim doc As New XmlDataDocument()
doc.Normalize()
```

C#:

```
XmlDataDocument doc = new XmlDataDocument();
doc.Normalize();
```

Normalize returns no data (void in C#) and has no parameters.

Normalize is used to reformat an XML document to remove redundant structure. For example, it replaces adjacent XmlText nodes with a single XmlText node containing the combined text. This ensures that the document has the same node structure as it would if it were saved and reloaded. It is not something we generally use with documents based on ADO.NET data sets, as these are created in normal form in the first instance.

PrependChild Method

We use this method to add a child node to the start of the current node's list of children. This method is inherited from `XmlNode`.

VB.NET:

```
Dim doc As New XmlDataDocument()
Dim n As XmlNode = doc.PrependChild(new)
```

C#:

```
XmlDataDocument doc = new XmlDataDocument();
XmlNode n = doc.PrependChild(new);
```

Parameters are as follows:

Parameter	Type	Description	Default
new	XmlNode	New child node	none

We typically call one of the node creation methods such as `CreateElement` to create the new node object, then call `PrependChild()` to actually add it to a document tree.

An exception is thrown if the new parameter is an ancestor of this node or has an `XmlNodeType` that is not permitted as a child of the current node. If the new node is already in the document, it is removed before the prepend operation is performed.

The following example adds a new comment node to the root element of an existing XML document:

VB.NET:

```
'Create an XmlDataDocument.
Dim doc As XmlDataDocument = New XmlDataDocument(dsNorthwind)
'required before editing XML data document with XML operations
doc.DataSet.EnforceConstraints = False

Dim newComment As XmlComment = doc.CreateComment("comment added with PrependChild
method")
'this appends the new Comment to the root element
Dim currNode As XmlNode = doc.DocumentElement
currNode.PrependChild(newComment)
'Display the XmlDataDocument.
doc.Save(Console.Out)
```

C#:

```
// Create an XmlDataDocument.
XmlDataDocument doc = new XmlDataDocument(dsNorthwind);
// required before editing XML data document with XML operations
doc.DataSet.EnforceConstraints = false;
XmlComment newComment = doc.CreateComment("comment added with PrependChild
method");
// this appends the new Comment As a child of the root element
XmlNode currNode = doc.DocumentElement;
currNode.PrependChild(newComment);
//Display the XmlDataDocument.
doc.Save(Console.Out);
```

The example uses an `XmlDataDocument` object created from a `DataSet` based on the Northwind database and already filled with data as shown in the full sample in the previous chapter for the `XmlDataDocument(DataSet)` constructor.

The `DataSet.EnforceConstraints` property must be set to False to allow XML nodes to be added to the document based on the Northwind `DataSet`. We create the new node, in this case a comment, with the call to the `CreateComment` method. We then create an `XmlNode` object to use for navigation and insertion; we set this node to the root element of the document by assigning it the `DocumentElement` (which is the root element), then use the `PrependChild` method to add the comment as a child of the root element (`NewDataSet`) at the start of the root's list of children.

The added child section appears in the output XML at the start, immediately following the root `NewDataSet` element:

```
<NewDataSet>
 <!--comment added with PrependChild method--/>
 <Customers>
  ...
```

ReadNode Method

We use this method to read a node from an `XmlReader`. This method is inherited from `XmlDocument`.

VB.NET:

```
Dim doc As XmlDataDocument = new XmlDataDocument()
doc.ReadNode(xmlreader)
```

C#:

```
XmlDataDocument doc = new XmlDataDocument();
doc.ReadNode(xmlreader);
```

Parameters are as follows:

Parameter	Type	Description	Default
xmlreader	XmlReader	XmlReader object containing the data for the node you want to add	none

The return value from `ReadNode` is either a new `XmlNode` object or a Null reference (`Nothing` in Visual Basic) meaning no more nodes are available to be read (as at the end of the source file, for example). The created `XmlNode` has the same `NodeType` as the one just read.

Position the `XmlReader` object on a node or attribute. If the reader is at the start of the file, `ReadNode` advances the reader to the first node and reads it. `ReadNode` will read one node object from the reader and then position the reader on the next node. If the reader is positioned at the start of an element, `ReadNode` reads all the attributes and any children, up to and including the end-tag of the current node. The returned node object contains the subtree of all objects read. The reader is then positioned immediately following the end-tag.

We can also use ReadNode to read attributes, but be aware that ReadNode doesn't advance the reader to the next attribute. This allows code to use the MoveToNextAttribute method to check the status of each attribute read while MoveToNextAttribute returns True. ReadNode does read the attribute value, so after calling ReadNode on an attribute, ReadAttributeValue will return False.

The following example uses ReadNode to load the sample XML document into an enclosing XML document:

VB.NET:

```
'Create an XmlDataDocument
Dim doc As New XmlDataDocument()

'Load it
doc.LoadXml("<chain type='bookstore'>" & _
"<region>Western</region>" & _
"</chain>")

'Create a reader.
Dim reader As XmlTextReader = New XmlTextReader("bookdata.xml")
reader.MoveToContent() ' Move to the first element.

'Create a node representing the next element node.
Dim nextbook As XmlNode = doc.ReadNode(reader)

'Insert the new node into the document.
doc.DocumentElement.AppendChild(nextbook)

'display XML document
doc.Save(Console.Out)
```

C#:

```
//Create an XmlDataDocument.
XmlDataDocument doc = new XmlDataDocument();

// Load it
doc.LoadXml("<chain type='bookstore'>" +
"<region>Western</region>" +
"</chain>");

//Create a reader.
XmlTextReader reader = new XmlTextReader("bookdata.xml");
reader.MoveToContent(); //Move to the first element.

//Create a node representing the next element node.
XmlNode nextbook = doc.ReadNode(reader);

//Insert the new node into the document.
doc.DocumentElement.AppendChild(nextbook);

// display XML document
doc.Save(Console.Out);
```

The document object is created and then loaded with a literal string using the LoadXml method. The XML specified in the string is intended to be an outer wrapper that will be filled with content from the reader.

Next, the reader is created, reading the XML from the bookdata.xml file. The MoveToContent method positions the reader on the first element, and then the ReadNode method is called to read the first book. The node object created by our ReadNode call is then inserted as a child of the root element (DocumentElement) of the wrapper document, and that also brings in all the children of the node.

The generated XML document shows a hierarchy with a chain of stores at the top level, containing an individual bookstore and some of its books:

```xml
<chain type="bookstore">
 <region>Western</region>
 <bookstore>
 <book genre="computer" ISBN="1861005-466">
 <title>Professional SQL Server 2000 XML</title>
 <price>49.99</price>
 </book>
 <book genre="computer" ISBN="1861004-990">
 <title>Professional C#</title>
 <price>59.99</price>
 </book>
 </bookstore>
</chain>
```

RemoveAll Method

We use this method to remove all children and attributes from a node in an XML document. This method is inherited from `XmlNode`.

VB.NET:

```vbnet
Dim doc As New XmlDataDocument()
doc.RemoveAll()
```

C#:

```csharp
XmlDataDocument doc = new XmlDataDocument();
doc.RemoveAll();
```

This method returns no data (`void` in C#) and has no parameters.

The following example removes all children of the root in an existing XML document, creating an empty document.

VB.NET:

```vbnet
'Create an XmlDataDocument.
Dim doc As XmlDataDocument = New XmlDataDocument(dsNorthwind)
'required before editing XML data document with XML operations
doc.DataSet.EnforceConstraints = False

Dim root As XmlNode = doc.DocumentElement
' Remove all
root.RemoveAll()

Console.WriteLine("Display the modified XML...")
doc.Save(Console.Out)
```

C#:

```csharp
// Create an XmlDataDocument.
XmlDataDocument doc = new XmlDataDocument(dsNorthwind);
// required before editing XML data document with XML operations
doc.DataSet.EnforceConstraints = false;
```

```
XmlNode root = doc.DocumentElement;
// Remove all
root.RemoveAll();

Console.WriteLine("Display the modified XML...");
doc.Save(Console.Out);
```

The example uses an `XmlDataDocument` object created from a `DataSet` based on the Northwind database, and already filled with data, as illustrated earlier in the `XmlDataDocument(DataSet)` constructor section.

The `DataSet.EnforceConstraints` property must be set to `false` to allow XML nodes to be added to the document based on the Northwind `DataSet`. We create a node to hold the root element of the document, then use the `RemoveAll` method to remove all children from the document, creating an empty document with only a root:

```
<NewDataSet></NewDataSet>
```

RemoveChild Method

We use this method to remove an existing child node from a document. This method is inherited from `XmlNode`.

VB.NET:

```
Dim doc As New XmlDataDocument()
Dim n As XmlNode = doc.RemoveChild(child)
```

C#:

```
XmlDataDocument doc = new XmlDataDocument();
XmlNode n = doc. RemoveChild(child);
```

Parameters are as follows:

Parameter	Type	Description	Default
child	XmlNode	child node to remove	none

The `child` node is not destroyed, but is simply removed from the document tree. An argument exception is thrown if the `child` node is not actually a child of this node. The removed child `XmlNode` object is the return value of this method; we can use this to insert in a new document or do other processing with it if desired.

The following example removes the `Company Name` element in an existing XML document:

VB.NET:

```
'Create an XmlDataDocument.
Dim doc As XmlDataDocument = New XmlDataDocument(dsNorthwind)
'required before editing XML data document with XML operations
doc.DataSet.EnforceConstraints = False
```

```
Dim root As XmlNode = doc.DocumentElement
' Remove the child element.
root.RemoveChild(root("CompanyName"))

Console.WriteLine("Display the modified XML...")
doc.Save(Console.Out)
```

C#:

```
// Create an XmlDataDocument.
XmlDataDocument doc = new XmlDataDocument(dsNorthwind);
// required before editing XML data document with XML operations
doc.DataSet.EnforceConstraints = false;

XmlNode root = doc.DocumentElement;
//Remove the child element.
root.RemoveChild(root["CompanyName"]);

Console.WriteLine("Display the modified XML...");
doc.Save(Console.Out);
```

The example uses an XmlDataDocument object created from a DataSet based on the Northwind database and already filled with data as shown in the full sample shown in the previous section for the XmlDataDocument(DataSet) constructor.

The DataSet.EnforceConstraints property must be set to False to allow XML nodes to be added to the document based on the Northwind DataSet. We create a node to hold the root element of the document, to be used for locating the child to be removed. We then use the RemoveChild method to remove the current company name element, located by use of the indexer operator using the element name (root["CompanyName"]).

ReplaceChild Method

We use this method to replace a child node with the given new child. This method is inherited from XmlNode.

VB.NET:

```
Dim doc As New XmlDataDocument()
Dim n As XmlNode = doc.ReplaceChild(new,old)
```

C#:

```
XmlDataDocument doc = new XmlDataDocument();
XmlNode n = doc. ReplaceChild(new,old);
```

Parameters are as follows:

Parameter	Type	Description	Default
new	XmlNode	New child node	none
old	XmlNode	Child node to be replaced	none

We typically call one of the node creation methods such as `CreateElement` to create the new node object, then call `ReplaceChild()` to actually replace an existing child in a document tree with the new node. The old child node is the return value of this method.

If the `old` parameter is not a child of this node, this method throws an exception. An exception is also thrown if the `new` parameter is an ancestor of this node or has an `XmlNodeType` that is not permitted as a child of the current node.

The following example replaces the `Company Name` element in an existing XML document:

VB.NET:

```
'Create an XmlDataDocument.
Dim doc As XmlDataDocument = New XmlDataDocument(dsNorthwind)
'required before editing XML data document with XML operations
doc.DataSet.EnforceConstraints = False

Dim root As XmlNode = doc.DocumentElement

'Create a new element.
Dim elem As XmlElement = doc.CreateElement("CompanyName")
elem.InnerText = "Acme, Inc."

'Replace the old element.
root.ReplaceChild(elem, root("CompanyName"))

Console.WriteLine("Display the modified XML...")
doc.Save(Console.Out)
```

C#:

```
// Create an XmlDataDocument.
XmlDataDocument doc = new XmlDataDocument(dsNorthwind);
// required before editing XML data document with XML operations
doc.DataSet.EnforceConstraints = false;

XmlNode root = doc.DocumentElement;

//Create a new title element.
XmlElement elem = doc.CreateElement("CompanyName");
elem.InnerText=" Acme, Inc ";

//Replace the title element.
root.ReplaceChild(elem, root["CompanyName"]);

Console.WriteLine("Display the modified XML...");
doc.Save(Console.Out);
```

The example uses an `XmlDataDocument` object created from a `DataSet` based on the Northwind database, and already filled with data, as illustrated earlier in the `XmlDataDocument(DataSet)` constructor section.

The `DataSet.EnforceConstraints` property must be set to False to allow XML nodes to be added to the document based on the Northwind `DataSet`. We create a node to hold the root element of the document, then create a new node, in this case a company name element, with the call to the `CreateElement` method. We set the contents to the new company name. We then use the `ReplaceChild` method to replace the current company name element, located by use of the indexer operator using the element name (`root["CompanyName"]`).

Save (Stream) Method

We use the `Save` method to write the `XmlDataDocument` to a target object. It is overloaded and takes several different forms depending on the target object; this version writes to a `Stream` object. This method is inherited from `XmlDocument`.

VB.NET:

```
Dim doc As XmlDataDocument = new XmlDataDocument()
doc.Save(stream)
```

C#:

```
XmlDataDocument doc = new XmlDataDocument();
doc.Save(stream);
```

Parameters are as follows:

Parameter	Type	Description	Default
stream	Stream	Stream to write XML document to. May be `FileStream`, `NetworkStream`, or any other `Stream` type	none

This form of the `Save` method has been used with the `Console.Out` stream in most of the other examples in this and the preceding chapter. Streams can also be used with files or other forms of I/O. Streams are defined in the `System.IO` namespace, which must be included as in this example:

VB.NET:

```
Imports System.IO
...
Dim doc As XmlDataDocument = New XmlDataDocument(dsNorthwind)

'Save the XML data to a file:.
Dim fs As FileStream = New FileStream("nwind.xml", FileMode.OpenOrCreate,
FileAccess.Write)

' Save to file stream
doc.Save(fs)
```

C#:

```
Using System.IO;
...
XmlDataDocument doc = new XmlDataDocument(dsNorthwind);

//Save the XML data.
FileStream fs = new FileStream("nwind.xml", FileMode.OpenOrCreate,
FileAccess.Write);
doc.Save(fs);
```

A stream is a low-level object; for writing text files you'll probably find it easier to use the `Save(String)` version of `Save` than to save to a file stream. However, a network application might require reading from a `NetworkStream` or other variation of `Stream`.

When the document is saved, namespace attributes are generated to ensure that the complete node identity is preserved. See the discussion of namespaces in the introduction of this chapter for a definition of the terms local name, qualified name, prefix, and namespace URI. Whitespace is not preserved, unless the document's `PreserveWhitespace` property is set to True.

Save (String) Method

We use the `Save` method to save the `XmlDataDocument` to a target. This method is overloaded and takes several different forms depending on source parameter; this version writes to a file named by a `String` parameter. This method is inherited from `XmlDocument`.

VB.NET:

```
Dim doc As XmlDataDocument = new XmlDataDocument(dsNorthwind)
doc.Save(filename)
```

C#:

```
XmlDataDocument doc = new XmlDataDocument(dsNorthwind);
doc.Save(filename);
```

Parameters are as follows:

Parameter	Type	Description	Default
filename	String	Name of file to write to	none

The example simply writes the contents of the document to a file:

VB.NET:

```
Dim doc As XmlDataDocument = New XmlDataDocument(dsNorthwind)
doc.Save("nwind.xml")
```

C#:

```
XmlDataDocument doc = new XmlDataDocument(dsNorthwind);
doc.Save("nwind.xml");
```

When the document is saved, namespace attributes are generated to ensure that the complete node identity is preserved. See the discussion of namespaces in the introduction of this chapter for a definition of the terms local name, qualified name, prefix, and namespace URI. Whitespace is not preserved, unless the document's `PreserveWhitespace` property is set to True.

Save (TextWriter) Method

We use the `Save` method to save the `XmlDataDocument` to a target object. It is overloaded and takes several different forms depending on the target object; this version writes to a `TextWriter` object. This method is inherited from `XmlDocument`.

VB.NET:

```
Dim doc As XmlDataDocument = new XmlDataDocument()
doc.Save(textwriter)
```

C#:

```
XmlDataDocument doc = new XmlDataDocument();
doc.Save(textwriter);
```

Parameters are as follows:

Parameter	Type	Description	Default
textwriter	TextWriter	TextWriter object set up to read a source of XML data	none

TextWriter is defined in the System.IO namespace. It is an abstract class for which StreamWriter and StringWriter are specific implementations. This example uses StreamWriter:

VB.NET:

```
Imports System.IO
…
Dim doc As XmlDataDocument = New XmlDataDocument(dsNorthwind)

'Save the XML data.
Dim tw As StreamWriter = New StreamWriter("nwind.xml")

' Save to file stream
doc.Save(tw)
```

C#:

```
Using System.IO;
…
//Create an XmlDataDocument.
XmlDataDocument doc = new XmlDataDocument(dsNorthwind);

//Save the XML data.
StreamWriter tw = new StreamWriter("nwind.xml");
doc.Save(tw);
```

When the document is saved, namespace attributes are generated to ensure that the complete node identity is preserved. See the discussion of namespaces in the introduction of this chapter for a definition of the terms local name, qualified name, prefix, and namespace URI. Whitespace is not preserved, unless the document's PreserveWhitespace property is set to True.

Save (XmlWriter) Method

We use the Save method to save the XmlDataDocument to a target object. It is overloaded and takes several different forms depending on the target object; this version writes to an XmlWriter object. This method is inherited from XmlDocument.

VB.NET:

```
Dim doc As XmlDataDocument = new XmlDataDocument()
doc.Save(xmlwriter)
```

C#:

```
XmlDataDocument doc = new XmlDataDocument();
doc.Save(xmlwriter);
```

Parameters are as follows:

Parameter	Type	Description	Default
xmlwriter	XmlWriter	XmlWriter object set up to read a source of XML data	none

XmlWriter is an abstract class for which XmlTextWriter is a specific implementation. This example uses XmlTextWriter:

VB.NET:

```
Dim doc As XmlDataDocument = New XmlDataDocument(dsNorthwind)

'Save the XML data.
Dim xw As XmlTextWriter = New XmlTextWriter("nwind.xml", Nothing)
xw.Formatting = Formatting.Indented
doc.Save(xw)
```

C#:

```
//Create an XmlDataDocument.
XmlDataDocument doc = new XmlDataDocument(dsNorthwind);

//Save the XML data.
XmlTextWriter xw = new XmlTextWriter("nwind.xml", null)
xw.Formatting = Formatting.Indented;
doc.Save(xw);
```

By default, the output will not be formatted, but we can set the Formatting property to Indented, as shown, to make the output readable.

When the document is saved, namespace attributes are generated to ensure that the complete node identity is preserved. See the discussion of namespaces in the introduction of this chapter for a definition of the terms local name, qualified name, prefix, and namespace URI. Whitespace is not preserved, unless the document's PreserveWhitespace property is set to true.

SelectNodes Method

We use this to locate nodes within the XML document using an XPath query. This method is inherited from XmlNode.

VB.NET:

```
Dim doc As New XmlDataDocument()
Dim xnl As XmlNodeList = doc.SelectNodes(path)
  Dim xnl As XmlNodeList = doc.SelectNodes(path, nsmanager)
```

C#:

```
XmlDataDocument doc = new XmlDataDocument();
XmlNodeList xnl = doc.SelectNodes(path);
  XmlNodeList xnl = doc.SelectNodes(path, nsmanager);
```

Parameters are as follows:

Parameter	Type	Description	Default
path	String	XPath query	None
nsmanager	XmlNamespace Manager	XML namespace manager object	None

The `nsmanager` parameter specifies an optional `XmlNamespaceManager` object, which can be used to resolve namespace references for prefixes used in the `XPath` query string. This is rarely used; most commonly we use the form of this method passing the `XPath` query by itself.

We can find nodes within the document using the XML `XPath` (`http://www.w3.org/TR/xpath`) query language to locate the desired nodes.

The following example shows a simple `XPath` pattern-matching query:

VB.NET:

```
'Create an XmlDataDocument based on Northwind data set filled with Orders &
OrderDetails.
Dim doc As XmlDataDocument = New XmlDataDocument(dsNorthwind)
' search for Orders having OrderDetail children with Quantity attribute > 10
Dim xnl As XmlNodeList = doc.SelectNodes("Order/OrderDetail[@Quantity>10]")
```

C#:

```
// Create an XmlDataDocument based on filled Northwind data set.
XmlDataDocument doc = new XmlDataDocument(dsNorthwind);
// search for Orders having OrderDetail children with Quantity attribute > 10
XmlNodeList xnl = doc.SelectNodes("Order/OrderDetail[@Quantity>10]");
```

The Northwind data set is loaded in previous lines of code; see the full example code in the `DataSet` constructor of `XmlDataDocument`. We then create an `XmlNodeList` object to receive the result of the `XPath` query, which finally navigates from the `Order` element of the current location to the `OrderDetail` children of `Order` to locate nodes with `Quantity` attributes having a value greater than 10.

SelectSingleNode Method

We use this to locate the first nodes within an XML document using an `XPath` query. This method is inherited from `XmlNode`.

VB.NET:

```
Dim doc As New XmlDataDocument()
Dim xn As XmlNode = doc.SelectSingleNode(path)
  Dim xn As XmlNode = doc.SelectSingleNode(path, nsmanager)
```

C#:

```
XmlDataDocument doc = new XmlDataDocument();
XmlNode xn = doc.SelectSingleNode(path);
   XmlNode xn = doc.SelectSingleNode(path, nsmanager);
```

Parameters are as follows:

Parameter	Type	Description	Default
path	String	XPath query	None
nsmanager	XmlNamespace Manager	XML namespace manager object	None

The `nsmanager` parameter specifies an optional `XmlNamespaceManager` object which can be used to resolve namespace references for prefixes used in the `XPath` query string. This is rarely used; most commonly we use the form of this method passing the `XPath` query by itself.

You can find nodes within the document using the XML `XPath` (`http://www.w3.org/TR/xpath`) query language to locate the desired nodes.

The following example shows a simple `XPath` pattern-matching query to find the first node matching the given criteria:

VB.NET:

```
'Create an XmlDataDocument based on Northwind data set filled with Orders &
OrderDetails.
Dim doc As XmlDataDocument = New XmlDataDocument(dsNorthwind)
' search for Orders having OrderDetail children with Quantity attribute > 10
Dim xn As XmlNode = doc. SelectSingleNode("Order/OrderDetail[@Quantity>10]")
```

C#:

```
// Create an XmlDataDocument based on filled Northwind data set.
XmlDataDocument doc = new XmlDataDocument(dsNorthwind);
// search for Orders having OrderDetail children with Quantity attribute > 10
XmlNode xn = doc.SelectSingleNode("Order/OrderDetail[@Quantity>10]");
```

The Northwind data set is loaded in previous lines of code; see the full example code in the `DataSet` constructor of `XmlDataDocument`. We then create an `XmlNode` object to receive the result of the `XPath` query, which finally navigates from the `Order` element of the current location to the `OrderDetail` children of `Order` to locate the first node with a `Quantity` attribute having a value greater than 10.

Supports Method

This is a method required by the W3C DOM standard to indicate the version of XML supported. This method is inherited from `XmlNode`.

VB.NET:

```
Dim doc As New XmlDataDocument()
Dim yn As Boolean = doc.Supports(feature, version)
```

C#:

```
XmlDataDocument doc = new XmlDataDocument();
bool yn = doc.Supports(feature, version);
```

Parameters are as follows:

Parameter	Type	Description	Default
feature	String	Name of feature	None
version	String	Version of feature	None

This method is required by the W3C DOM standard but is not one you're likely to need in practical use. It allows a developer to test to make sure a particular version of the DOM is supported, which might be of use if working in systems that runs in multiple environments such as Java, but in .NET with just one environment supported there is not much point . Supports returns True for XML 1.0 and XML 2.0 and False otherwise.

The following example shows how the method might be used:

VB.NET:

```
'Create an XmlDataDocument.
Dim doc As XmlDataDocument = New XmlDataDocument()
If doc.Supports("XML", "1.0") Then Console.WriteLine("1.0 Supported") End If
If doc.Supports("XML", "2.0") Then Console.WriteLine("2.0 Supported") End If
```

C#:

```
// Create an XmlDataDocument.
XmlDataDocument doc = new XmlDataDocument();
if (doc.Supports("XML", "1.0")) { Console.WriteLine("1.0 Supported"); }
if (doc.Supports("XML", "2.0")) { Console.WriteLine("2.0 Supported"); }
```

WriteContentTo Method

We use this method to write the content of the current document, excluding the root node, to a stream or file using XmlWriter object . This method is inherited from XmlDocument.

VB.NET:

```
Dim doc As New XmlDataDocument(dataset)
Dim elem As XmlElement = doc.WriteContentTo(writer)
```

C#:

```
XmlDataDocument doc = new XmlDataDocument(dataset);
XmlElement elem = doc.WriteContentTo(writer);
```

Parameters are as follows:

Parameter	Type	Description	Default
writer	XmlWriter	XmlWriter object associated with target	none

XmlWriter is an abstract class implemented by the XmlTextWriter class, so we must actually create an XmlTextWriter object to use with this method. We specify the target stream or file when the XmlTextWriter is created, as in this example, where data is written to the nwind.xml text file:

VB.NET:

```
Dim doc As XmlDataDocument = new XmlDataDocument(dsNorthwind)

' Write the data to a file. Nothing for second parameter means use default
encoding
Dim writer As XmlTextWriter = new XmlTextWriter("nwind.xml", nothing)
writer.Formatting = Formatting.Indented
doc.WriteContentTo(writer)
writer.Close()
```

C#:

```
XmlDataDocument doc = new XmlDataDocument(dsNorthwind);

// Write data to a file. Null for second parameter means use default encoding
XmlTextWriter writer = new XmlTextWriter("nwind.xml", null);
writer.Formatting = Formatting.Indented;
doc.WriteContentTo(writer);
writer.Close();
```

Note that the XmlTextWriter Formatting property is used to control the appearance of the output XML.

WriteTo Method

This writes relational data to an XML file using the XmlWriter object.

VB.NET:

```
Dim doc As New XmlDataDocument(dataset)
Dim elem As XmlElement = doc.WriteTo(writer)
```

C#:

```
XmlDataDocument doc = new XmlDataDocument(dataset);
XmlElement elem = doc.WriteTo(writer);
```

Parameters are as follows:

Parameter	Type	Description	Default
writer	XmlWriter	XmlWriter object associated with target	none

This method writes the data contained within the `XmlDataDocument` to a text file or other target supported by an `XmlWriter` object. `XmlWriter` is an abstract class, so our example uses the system-provided implementation of `XmlWriter`, `XmlTextWriter`. The target is specified when the `XmlTextWriter` is created, as in this example, where data is written to the `nwind.xml` text file:

VB.NET:

```
Dim doc As XmlDataDocument = New XmlDataDocument(dsNorthwind)
'Write the data to a file.
Dim writer As XmlTextWriter = new XmlTextWriter("nwind.xml", nothing)
writer.Formatting = Formatting.Indented
doc.WriteTo(writer)
```

C#:

```
XmlDataDocument doc = new XmlDataDocument(dsNorthwind);
//Write data to a file.
XmlTextWriter writer = new XmlTextWriter("nwind.xml", null);
writer.Formatting = Formatting.Indented;
doc.WriteTo(writer);
```

Events of XmlDataDocument

The events associated with `XMLDataDocument` are inherited from the `XmlDocument` class, and are fired by the .NET run-time when the content of the XML document is changed by a program. Most applications would handle this kind of processing in a simpler fashion – we use these events only in a very advanced XML editing situation.

The events enable us to add our own custom response to each event processing either after the fact, as in the case of the `NodeChanged`, `NodeRemoved`, and `NodeInserted` events, or to intercept the change before the fact, as in the case of the `NodeChanging`, `NodeRemoving`, and `NodeInserting` events.

Interception of an edit before it is made enables us to write code in an event handler to perhaps do some validation such as consistency checks peculiar to a document. We can throw an exception in the event handler to prevent the change if the validation check fails. If an exception is thrown, then the XML document will remain unchanged.

The possible events are listed below (these are pre-defined by the .NET run-time). An example of an event handler and a program that uses it is then shown.

NodeChanged

This is an after-the-fact event that is fired when the `Value` property of a node in this document has been changed. It only applies to nodes that have a value, such as attributes.

NodeChanging

This before-the-fact event will fire when the `Value` property of a node is about to be changed. It also only applies to nodes that have a value.

NodeInserted

This after-the-fact event fires when one of this document's nodes has been inserted into another node.

NodeInserting

This before-the-fact event will fire when one of this document's nodes is about to be inserted into another node.

NodeRemoved

This after-the-fact event fires when one of this document's nodes has been removed from its parent node.

NodeRemoving

This before-the-fact event will fire when one of this document's nodes is about to be removed.

Event Handler Routine

To handle events, we must write a specific subroutine or function to be the event handler. We then register the event handler with the .NET runtime for the event we wish to handle.

We can give your event handler any name we wish; however, it must accept two parameters as follows:

Parameter	Type	Description	Default
src	Object	Object for which event is fired (in this case, the XmlData Document object)	none
args	XmlNodeChanged EventArgs	Contains information about node change event; see following paragraph	none

The `args` parameter is an `XmlNodeChangedEventArgs` object. This object has four properties that can be used to determine information relating to the node change event:

Property	Type	Description
Action	XmlNodeChangedAction	Object describing action associated with change eventd
NewParent	XmlNode	New parent node if node is being inserted
OldParent	XmlNode	Former parent node if node is being removed
Node	XmlNode	Node being changed, inserted, or removed

The `NewParent`, `OldParent`, and `Node` properties are all `XmlNode` objects, so we can query the `XmlNode.Name`, `XmlNode.Value`, or other node information properties to get information about the node being changed.

Event Handler Example

As an example, let's create a handler for the `XmlDataDocument NodeChanged` event. We'll first look at the event handling code itself, and then show the full program in which it is used. We will call the event handler routine `MyEventHandler`. The code for this routine in both Visual Basic and C# is shown below; see the description following the example for a discussion:

VB.NET:

```
Public Shared Sub MyEventHandler(ByVal src As Object, ByVal args As
XmlNodeChangedEventArgs)
  Console.Write("Node Changed Event: <" + args.Node.Name + "> changed")
  If Not (args.Node.Value Is Nothing) Then
    Console.WriteLine(" with value " + args.Node.Value)
  Else
    Console.WriteLine("")
  End If
End Sub
```

C#:

```
// Handle the Node Changed Event
public static void MyEventHandler(Object src, XmlNodeChangedEventArgs args)
{
    Console.Write("Node Changed Event: <" + args.Node.Name + "> changed");
    if (args.Node.Value != null)
    {
        Console.WriteLine(" with value " + args.Node.Value);
    }
    else
        Console.WriteLine("");
}
```

The handler is defined to accept both the required parameters: source object and `XmlNodeChangedEventArgs` object. We use `Console.Writeline` to display the value of the changed node, using the `Name` property of the `XmlNodeChangedEventArgs.Node` property. Then we also display the changed node's value using the `Value` property of the `XmlNodeChangedEventArgs.Node`, checking first to make sure the `Value` property is not Null.

That's all there is to it! In this handler we are merely displaying information about the event, not trying to change the action of the program. We could throw an exception if we detected an event we wanted to prevent; the type of exception is up to you (it should be one you can catch in the main program and act appropriately upon). This handler also illustrates that you don't have to use all the properties of the passed parameter or the `XmlNodeChangedEventArgs` object; they are available if you need them but if your needs are simple you can keep your event handler routine simple as well.

To invoke the handler, we need to register the event handler with the system. Here is the code that does it:

VB.NET:

```
Dim doc As XmlDataDocument = New XmlDataDocument(dsNorthwind)
AddHandler doc.NodeChanged, New XmlNodeChangedEventHandler(AddressOf
MyEventHandler)
```

C#:

```
XmlDataDocument doc = new XmlDataDocument(dsNorthwind);
//adding Event Handlers here
doc.NodeChanged += new XmlNodeChangedEventHandler(MyEventHandler);
```

We are registering our event routine as a handler for the NodeChanged event of a particular XmlDataDocument object. To do this we create a new XmlNodeChangedEventHandler object, passing the address of the handler routine as a parameter to the constructor. To register this XmlNodeChangedEventHandler for the particular event, in Visual Basic we use the AddHandler operation. In C#, we use the += operator to add it. As you might expect, this implies that more than one event handler can be registered for a particular event on an object: each handler routine will be invoked when the event fires.

Now that we've seen the event handling code itself, let's look at the entire program that uses it. This is a completely self-contained example. Let's imagine that a certain postal code used by some of our customers has changed. We will find and change these particular codes using XML operations, and our event handler will detect the change.

VB.NET:

```
Imports Microsoft.VisualBasic
Imports System
Imports System.IO
Imports System.Xml
Imports System.Xml.Xpath
Imports System.Data
Imports System.Data.SqlClient

Namespace EventSample
```

Initially, a DataSet object is created, which is initialized with the same query on the Northwind sample data used in our other samples in this chapter, though in this example, the initialization is contained within the function OpenDS():

```
Public Class EventSample
    Public Shared Function OpenDS() As DataSet
        Dim dsNorthwind As DataSet = New DataSet()
        'Create the connection string.
        Dim sConnection As String
        ' if (local) does not work in following connection string, try
(local)\NetSDK
        sConnection = "Data Source=(local);Integrated Security=SSPI;Initial
Catalog=Northwind"
        'Create a connection object to connect to the northwind db.
        Dim nwconnect As SqlConnection
        nwconnect = New SqlConnection(sConnection)
        'Create a command string to select all the customers in France
        Dim sCommand As String = "Select * from Customers where Country='France'"
        'Create an Adapter to load the DataSet.
        Dim myDataAdapter As SqlDataAdapter
        myDataAdapter = New SqlDataAdapter(sCommand, nwconnect)
        'Fill the DataSet with the selected records.
        myDataAdapter.Fill(dsNorthwind, "Customers")
        OpenDS = dsNorthwind
    End Function
    Public Shared Sub Main()
```

```
        Try
          'Load the XML from file
          Console.WriteLine()
          Console.WriteLine("Loading DS ...")
          Dim dsNorthwind As DataSet
          dsNorthwind = OpenDS()
```

At this point, we create an `XmlDataDocument` object associated with the filled data set:

```
        Dim doc As XmlDataDocument = New XmlDataDocument(dsNorthwind)
        Console.WriteLine("XmlDataDocument loaded successfully ...")
        ' this is required before using XML editing operations on the XML data
document
        doc.DataSet.EnforceConstraints = False

        'Add MyEvent Handlers here
        AddHandler doc.NodeChanged, New XmlNodeChangedEventHandler(AddressOf
MyEventHandler)

        ' Create a list of the postal codes and change their values
```

Here, we use the `SelectNodes` operation to locate the XML element nodes within the document for the postal codes:

```
        Dim myXmlNodeList As XmlNodeList =
            doc.SelectNodes("descendant::PostalCode")
        Console.WriteLine("SelectNodes found {0} nodes...", myXmlNodeList.Count)
        Dim myXmlNode As XmlNode
```

We display the number of nodes found, and change any that have the value 67000 to 67020. Note that the `if` statement which checks for the value 67000 and changes it to 67020 gives no output informing us of the change.

```
        For Each myXmlNode In myXmlNodeList
          Console.WriteLine("<" + myXmlNode.Name + "> " + myXmlNode.InnerText)
          If myXmlNode.InnerText = "67000" Then
            myXmlNode.InnerText = "67020"
          End If
        Next

      Catch e As Exception
        Console.WriteLine("Exception: {0}", e.ToString())
      End Try
    End Sub

    ' Handle the Node Changed Event
    Public Shared Sub MyEventHandler(ByVal src As Object, ByVal args As
XmlNodeChangedEventArgs)
      Console.Write("Node Changed Event: <" + args.Node.Name + "> changed")
      If Not (args.Node.Value Is Nothing) Then
        Console.WriteLine(" with value " + args.Node.Value)
      Else
        Console.WriteLine("")
      End If
    End Sub


  End Class ' EventSample
End Namespace 'EventSample
```

C#:

```
namespace EventSample
{
 using System;
 using System.Globalization;
 using System.IO;
 using System.Xml;
 using System.Xml.XPath;
 using System.Data;
 using System.Data.SqlClient;

 public class EventSample
 {
  public static DataSet OpenDS()
  {
```

Initially, a DataSet object is created, which is initialized with the same query on the Northwind sample data used in our other samples in this chapter, though in this example, the initialization is contained within the function OpenDS():

```
       DataSet dsNorthwind = new DataSet();
       //Create the connection string.
       String sConnection;
       // if (local) does not work, try (local)\\NetSDK
       sConnection=
             "Data Source=(local);Integrated Security=SSPI;Initial
Catalog=Northwind";
       //Create a connection object to connect to the northwind db.
       SqlConnection nwconnect = new SqlConnection(sConnection);
       //Create a command string to select customers in France
       String sCommand = "Select * from Customers where Country='France'";
       //Create an adapter to load the DataSet.
       SqlDataAdapter myDataAdapter = new SqlDataAdapter(sCommand, nwconnect);
       //Fill the DataSet with the selected records.
       myDataAdapter.Fill(dsNorthwind,"Customers");
       return dsNorthwind;
   }

   public static void Main()
   {
     try
     {
       // Load the DataSet from the Northwind sample
       Console.WriteLine ();
       Console.WriteLine ("Loading DS ...");
       DataSet dsNorthwind = OpenDS();
```

At this point, we create an XmlDataDocument object associated with the filled data set:

```
       XmlDataDocument doc = new XmlDataDocument(dsNorthwind);
       Console.WriteLine ("XmlDataDocument loaded successfully ...");
       // this is required before using XML editing operations on the XML data
document
       doc.DataSet.EnforceConstraints = false;
       //adding Event Handlers here
       doc.NodeChanged += new XmlNodeChangedEventHandler(MyEventHandler);
```

Here, we use the `SelectNodes` operation to locate the XML element nodes within the document for the postal codes:

```
// Create a list of the postal codes and change their values
XmlNodeList myXmlNodeList = doc.SelectNodes("descendant::PostalCode");

Console.WriteLine("SelectNodes found {0} nodes...", myXmlNodeList.Count);
```

We display the number of nodes found, and change any that have the value 67000 to 67020. Note that the `if` statement which checks for the value 67000 and changes it to 67020 gives no output informing us of the change.

```
foreach (XmlNode myXmlNode in myXmlNodeList)
    {
            Console.WriteLine("<" + myXmlNode.Name + "> " + myXmlNode.InnerText);
            if (myXmlNode.InnerText == "67000")
            {
                    myXmlNode.InnerText = "67020";
            }
    }

  }
  catch (Exception e)
    {
            Console.WriteLine ("Exception: {0}", e.ToString());
    }
 }

// Handle the Node Changed Event
 public static void MyEventHandler(Object src, XmlNodeChangedEventArgs args)
 {
     Console.Write("Node Changed Event: <" + args.Node.Name + "> changed");
     if (args.Node.Value != null)
     {
             Console.WriteLine(" with value " + args.Node.Value);
     }
     else
             Console.WriteLine("");
 }

} // End class EventSample
} // End namespace EventSample
```

The output of this example is as follows:

```
Loading DS ...
XmlDataDocument loaded successfully ...
SelectNodes found 11 nodes...
<PostalCode> 67000
Node Changed Event: <#text> changed with value 67020
<PostalCode> 13008
<PostalCode> 44000
<PostalCode> 59000
<PostalCode> 44000
<PostalCode> 78000
<PostalCode> 31000
<PostalCode> 75012
<PostalCode> 75016
<PostalCode> 69004
<PostalCode> 51100
```

The `SelectNodes` operation found eleven postal code nodes. We can see that the `Node` event handler intercepted the changed node event and displayed information showing that the change happened, even though the main program logic fails to indicate that a change was made.

This shows one use of the XML document change events; it can be a quick way to add code to ensure that a particular operation or check is performed on all operations that affect a particular XML document without having to find all the places in our code where nodes are changed. This can be very handy.

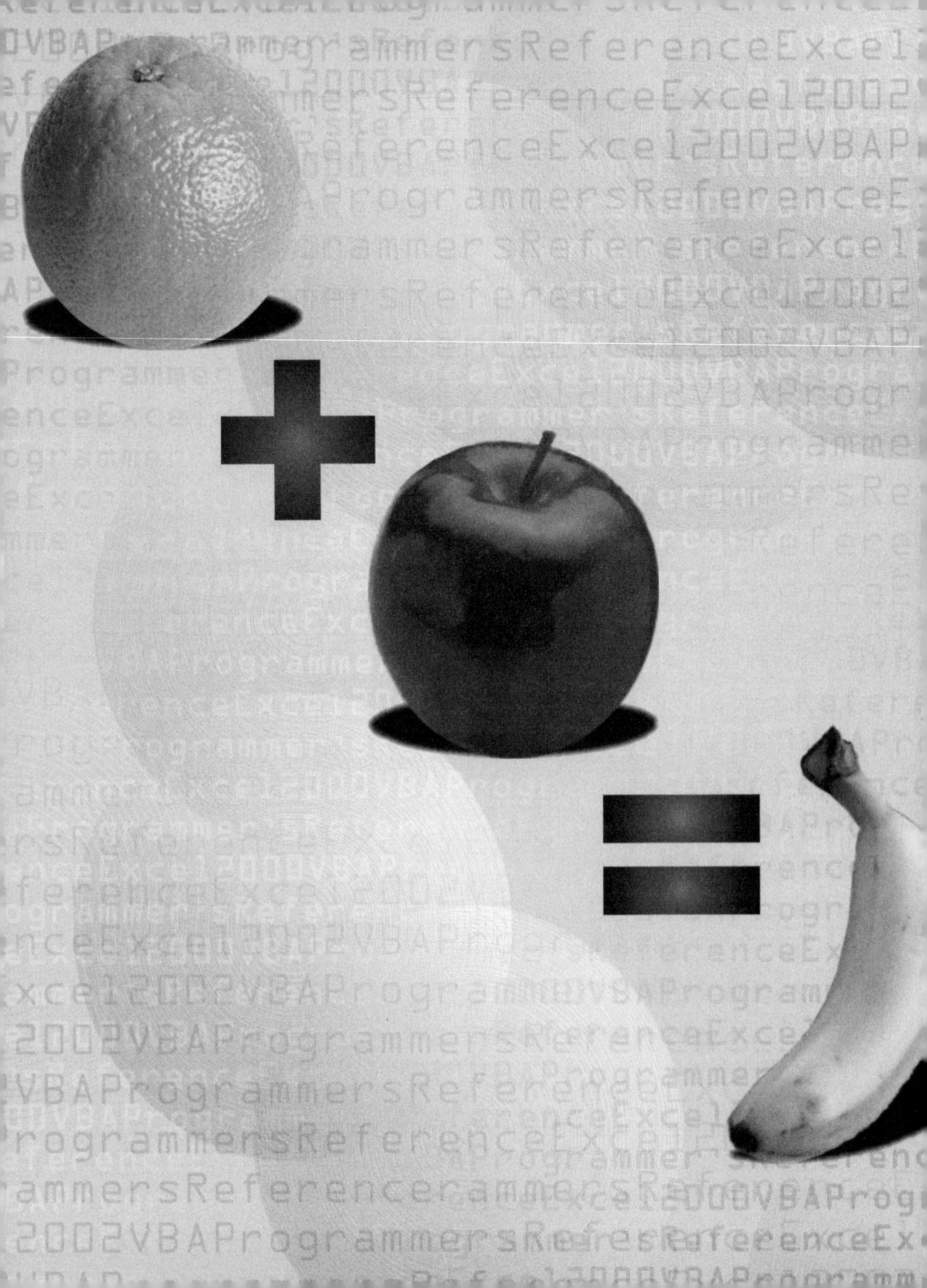

14

Exceptions and Error Handling

Every good programmer knows that an essential element of good programming is error handling. When working with data from any type of data source, this is especially true: even if the code is error free, exceptional circumstances will arise. Network outages, crashed servers, and user error are just a few of the issues programmers deal with when working with data. These exceptional circumstances and how to handle them is the subject of this chapter. These exceptions are bound to happen, therefore, a well designed and developed application will always take into account exceptional situations and plan to handle them.

Handling Exceptions

The goal of most programmers when dealing with exceptions is to have the application continue seamlessly, as if the error was anticipated. Usually, we want to either continue without the user being aware of the error, or to inform the user that the error has occurred so that they can fix it and try again. To do this, we need to determine when an error has occurred, and perform operations in response to it. In the .NET framework, this is achieved using **Exception objects**.

This section focuses on the general information regarding handling exceptions in the .NET framework. If you are already familiar with this error-handling framework, then you may want to skip ahead to the next section.

First, some language used in this framework. In .NET, when an error occurs, an exception, in other words an exception object, is **thrown**. A given method is said to **throw** an exception when it encounters an error. In order to handle these exceptions, a programmer must **catch** them. As a developer, you must not only plan to handle exceptions, but also plan to throw them. The .Net framework base classes contain many functions that throw exceptions to indicate error conditions. This framework of communicating error information is extremely powerful and allows for creating more robust and stable applications.

In order to better understand how to catch an exception, it is helpful to understand how to throw an exception. We create a new instance of the exception we would like to throw, set any properties on the exception and then throw it. The example below provides an example of throwing a `DataException`.

VB.NET:

```
Dim de As New DataException("Could not connect to database")
Throw de
```

C#:

```
DataException de = new DataException("Could not connect to database");
throw de;
```

While it is unlikely that you would throw a `DataException`, this example shows how easy it is to throw an exception. If this code existed in an application with no exception handling, the exception would bubble up and cause a runtime error.

In order to catch exceptions that are thrown, we use code like that shown below.

VB.NET:

```
Try
'some code that could cause an error

Catch e as Exception
        'handle exception here
End Try
```

C#:

```
Try {
        //some code that could throw an exception
  }
catch(Exception e)
  {
        //handle exception here
  }
```

We place code that could cause an error in a `try` block. We then place error handling code in the `catch` block. If no error occurs in the `try` block, then the code in the `catch` block is not executed – execution resumes after the `try catch` block ends (with `End Try` in VB, or `}` in C#). If an error occurs however, an exception is thrown and execution moves to the catch block. This scheme makes sense: try to perform these actions, and if any of the code used throws an exception then catch it and deal with it.

It is useful to know that something has gone wrong, but it is much more useful to be able to catch specific exceptions. For example, when accessing a file, it might be useful to know if the disk is missing, as opposed to having a corrupt file, or when dealing with data, it would be helpful to know that a constraint was violated, or if a null value was entered. The response that the program takes in these different circumstances is likely to be significantly different.

In addition, if we decide not to handle errors, the .Net framework will handle them for us, by causing the equivalent of a runtime error and ending our program. When an exception is thrown, it is passed up the method call stack until an exception handler is found and catches the exception. If the exception bubbles to the top of the stack, the application will fail.

Handling and reacting to errors is made easier when information about the errors is available and when the programmer can distinguish between varying causes of error. In this way, we can provide intelligent handling facilities by handling given exceptions in different ways. In .NET, we can catch a specific error based on its type and deal with that specific error – VB developers no longer need to deal with error numbers and long `CASE` statements.

VB.NET:

```
Try
        'code that might cause multiple types of exception

Catch ce as ConstraintException
        'handle specific constraint exception

Catch nne as NoNullsAllowedException
        'handle the "no nulls" specific exception

Catch de as DataException
        'handle any previosly unhandled data exceptions
End Try
```

C#:

```
Try
{
        //code that might cause multiple types of exception
}
catch (ConstraintException ce)
{
        //handle the specific constraint exception
}

catch (NoNullAllowedException nne)
{
        //handle the specific "no nulls" exception
}

catch(DataException e)
{
        //handle any previously unhandled data exceptions
}
```

As in the first example, code that might cause an error is placed in a try block. In this example however, several catch blocks are present. If an error occurs in the try block, then the catch statements are evaluated in order to find a handler for the exception. The first catch statement that can handle the exception (in other words the catch statement that handles exceptions of the same type as the exception being thrown, or one of its superclasses) will. For example, if we placed the DataException catch statement first in the list, then the other catch statements would become useless, because all DataExceptions (or subclasses) will be caught by the first statement. In fact, the compiler will complain about putting the catch statements in this order because it creates unreachable code.

So far, we can catch an exception when it is thrown, and respond to different types of exceptions in different ways by including several catch blocks. Additional information about the exception is passed as the properties and methods of the Exception object, which ultimately derives from System.Exception, passed to the catch block. The sections that follow provide reference information about the different types of exception related to data access, the information that we can mine from them and how that information is useful.

Finally, we have the finally statement. After we are done testing for and potentially handling exceptions, there may be code that needs to run to finish up the process; that's where the finally statement comes into play. Any code in the finally block gets executed regardless of whether there was an error – whether the code in the `try` block executes without error or there are errors that get handled, this code will run. This is a perfect place to perform operations, such as cleaning up database connections, closing streams, and releasing variables, as these are actions that need to happen whether our code succeeds or fails. For example, when working with database connections, rather than closing the connection in the try block, we close it in the finally block so that, regardless of whether an exception occurs after opening the connection, the connection will get closed:

```
C#
Try {
        //some code that could cause an error
}
catch(Exception e)
{
        //handle exception here
}
finally
{
        //close database connections e.g.
}

VB
Try
    'some code that could cause an error
Catch e as Exception
    'handle exception here
Finally
    'close database connections e.g.
End Try
```

Exceptions

The classes in this section represent the exceptions thrown when working with data in .NET. All exception classes inherit most of their properties and methods from the `Object` and `Exception` classes. The following section outlines those common methods and properties and how to use them.

Following this is information about each specific exception class, how they are caused and how to deal with them.

Exception Constructor

The following four constructors are found throughout the `Exception` classes in the `System.Data` namespaces. Not every class exposes all four constructors. These constructors are used to create new instances of an exception in order to throw it. While, as a developer, you will most likely not call the data exceptions directly, it is helpful to know how these exceptions are created, as it is similar to how all exceptions are created. Detailed information follows the table explaining the effect of using each:

Function	Syntax
DataException	DataException()
	DataException(string)
	DataException(SerializationInfo, StreamingContext)
	DataException(string, Exception)

Creating an exception with no parameters in the constructor builds an exception object with a default message regarding the error. To specify the error message, the constructor can be called passing a string parameter that represents the error message. For example, a `DataException`, created without specifying the message provides the default message "System Error".

A constructor exists with two parameters where the first is an instance of the `SerializationInfo` class and the second an instance of the `StreamingContext` class to provide for deserializing a `DataException` object. This constructor is used by the runtime to build an `exception` object from the serialized data. Finally, a constructor is available which allows for passing in the message string as well as an inner exception. This inner exception can be referenced via a property on the exception object to get more information regarding the actual cause of the error.

Exception Methods

All of the exceptions in the `System.Data` namespaces derive ultimately from the `Exception` class (and `Object`, of course, as all other classes), and therefore, expose the methods found in that class. This section covers the methods that all exceptions in this section expose.

The GetBaseException Method

`GetBaseException` returns the original exception that was thrown. It also points to the exceptions referenced by the `InnerException` property. When an exception is thrown, the programmer writing the code may wish to handle that exception by wrapping it in another more appropriate exception which is then thrown up to the calling code. For example, if we write a business object that wraps up the data access methods, we may wish to handle data exceptions by wrapping them in our own, custom defined exceptions. In order to allow a consumer of our classes to fully understand the error, however, we'd want to pass on the information in the original exception so that the consumer can examine that in their own code. This might look something like this:

VB.NET:

```
Try
        'code that throws a SqlException
Catch SqlExcept as SqlException

'Throw a new custom exception passing in the SqlException we are catching
        Throw new CustomException("Unable to load object state", SqlExcept)
        End Try
```

C#:

```
Try{
            //code that throws a SqlException
}
Catch(SqlException SqlExcept)
{
            //throw a new custom exception passing in the SqlException we are
catching
            throw new CustomException("Unable to load object state", SqlExcept);
}
```

Now the consumer of my class can catch my exception and then examine it to find the base, or first, exception thrown. The exception I have passed into the constructor of my `CustomException` class sets that object's `InnerException` property, which will be included in the search for the base exception.

The consumer code follows:

VB.NET:

```
Try
        'loads the object by passing in an ID
        Dim bo as new BusinessObject(5)
Catch ce as CustomException
        System.Console.WriteLine(ce.GetBaseException().ToString())
End Try
```

C#:

```
Try{
        //loads the object by passing an ID
        BusinessObject bo= new BusinessObject(5);
}
Catch(CustomException ce)
{
        System.Console.WriteLine(ce.GetBaseException().ToString());
}
```

The GetHashCode Method

Gets a hash code which can be used in a hash table or in hashing algorithms. In reality, if you want to use your object in this way, you would override this method, and provide a hashing mechanism for your object. The method defined in `Object` only guarantees that the same instance of an object will always return the same `Hash`.

The GetObjectData Method

This method is part of the serialization process. The `SerializationInfo` object is filled with the serializable data from the `DataException` object. This method is called by the framework when the object needs to be serialized. All of the data about the exception that can be serialized is placed into the `SerializationInfo` object and then persisted. The following `Exception` constructor creates the object upon deserialization using the opposite process:

```
ClassName(SerializationInfo, StreamingContext)
```

The GetType Method

The `GetType` method, inherited from the `Object` class, gets the `Type` object for the `Exception` class. This type object allows for determining the specific type of the exception. If for instance, you find that you need to capture a more generic exception, such as the `DataException`, you can use the `GetType` method to find out the specific type of the exception. This can be helpful for logging errors or other situations where you might need to know the exact type of the exception.

The ToString Method

The Exception classes override ToString so that it gives the name of the exception, the error messages from the thrown exception as well as the inner exception, and if possible the stack trace. This can be particularly useful when creating error logs for debugging purposes. For example, the following code throws a DataException which has an Exception as its inner exception. The resulting output shows that the message from both is displayed followed by the information about where the exception was thrown.

VB.NET:

```
Try
    Dim e As New Exception("Inner Exception Message")

        'Create a new DataException passing in e, our exception
        Dim de As New DataException("Bad Data", e)
    Throw de

Catch de As DataException

    Console.WriteLine(de.ToString())

End Try
```

C#:

```
try {
    Exception e = new Exception("Inner Exception Message");

//Create a new DataException setting the inner exception to e, our exception
    DataException de = new DataException("Bad Data",e);
    throw de;
    }
catch(DataException de)
    {
        Console.WriteLine(de.ToString());
    }
```

The output would look like this:

```
System.Data.DataException: Bad Data ---> System.Exception: Inner Exception Message
at ADOProgRefExceptionsInC.Class1.Main(String[] args) in c:\documents and
settings\administrator\my documents\visual studio
projects\adoprogrefexceptionsinc\class1.cs:line 27
```

Exception Properties

The following properties are exposed by all exceptions in the System.Data namespaces and allow the consumer of these objects to extract information regarding the exception and its cause.

The HelpLink Property

The HelpLink Property gets or sets a URN or URL to a file that acts as the help file for this exception. This property allows us to provide a link, or directly pull up the help information associated with the exception to provide the user with a means to determine the cause of the error, and hopefully a way to avoid it in the future.

The InnerException Property

Gets a reference to an exception that is the inner or source exception for this exception. Earlier, the GetBaseException method was discussed as being able to get the first exception which started the error stack. The InnerException property allows the developer to define the inner exception upon creation of the exception object using the specific constructor. After this has been done, InnerException can be used to access that inner exception and get more information about the cause of the error. Modifying the sample from our ToString method example, we can work directly with the inner exception that we passed into the constructor. Here we show the modified catch block and the resulting output:

VB.NET:

```
Catch de As DataException

    Console.WriteLine(de.InnerException.Message)
```

C#:

```
catch(DataException de)
{
        Console.WriteLine(de.InnerException.Message);
}
```

The output would look like this:

```
Inner Exception Message
```

In this case, since we are not explicitly catching the first exception and then including it in our exception, the message is the main property we will have access to. If we caught the first exception, and then included it in another exception to be thrown; when we caught the second exception we would be able to access stack trace information, target site, and other useful properties.

The Message Property

The Message Property gets the message associated with the exception. The message is set when the DataException is constructed. If no message is explicitly set, then a default message is created. The message property provides the quickest and most easily digestible reason for an error and is, therefore, a very important property.

We could use the message property in the following way:

VB.NET:

```
Try
      'code that causes an exception
Catch de as DataException
      System.Windows.Forms.MessageBox.Show(de.Message)
End Try
```

C#:

```
Try{
          //code that causes an exception
}
Catch(DataException de)
{
      System.Windows.Forms.MessageBox.Show(de.Message);
}
```

The Source Property

The Source Property gets or sets a string containing the name of the application or the object that causes the error. For example, if we have a business object named `ADOProgRef.BusinessObject`, and an exception is thrown in that object, we would set the source property to a string value representing that object name – "ADOProgRef.BusinessObject". If the name is not set by the developer, however, the name of the assembly where the exception originated, is returned.

The StackTrace Property

The `StackTrace` property returns a string value listing every method call between the current `try catch` block and the method in which the exception was originally thrown. This stack trace can be used to follow the flow of the error to determine where the error occurred and how the error flowed up into the calling procedure. This information can be useful in bug fixing and finding the root of the error.

Sample output from a stack trace could look like this:

```
System.Data.ConstraintException: Column 'OrderID' is constrained to be unique.
Value '10248' is already present.at System.Data.DataTable.SetNewRecord (DataRow
row, Int32 proposedRecord, DataRowAction action)
   at System.Data.DataRow.SetNewRecord(Int32 record)
   at System.Data.DataRow.EndEdit()
   at CADOExceptions.Class1.Constraint(DataSet ds) in c:\documents and
settings\administrator\my documents\visual studio
projects\cadoexceptions\class1.cs:line 125
```

This trace shows that the error was caught by the method `Constraint(DataSet ds)`, at the bottom of the trace, but the error originally occured in `SetNewRecord()`, at the top of the trace. The `StackTrace` property uses the `System.Environment.StackTrace` property to provide the information about the call stack. The `System.Environment` class allows access to a great deal of information about the current environment, the call stack information being just one useful item that pertains here. Keep in mind, that the stack trace begins when an exception is thrown, not before.

The TargetSite Property

The `TargetSite` property attempts to return the method that threw the exception. If the stack trace is not `null`, then the method will be returned. If the stack trace is `null`, then there is no record of the methods, and therefore, this property will be `null` as well. This could happen if a developer clears the `System.Environment.StackTrace` property using its remove method after the exception has been thrown. This method will return the method that appears at the top of the stack trace if it is found.

The System.Data.DataException Class

The `DataException` is the base class for many of the exceptions in the `System.Data` namespace. As such, it is an important class to understand. A lot of the methods and properties possessed by the exceptions described in this chapter derive from this class. In addition, this class of exception is thrown in several situations to denote a general data related error:

Thrown By	Cause
DataTableCollection. Item Property	The exception is thrown when a table with the given name does not exist.
DataRelation.CheckStateForProperty Method	This method checks to see if the `DataRelation` is a valid object. The exception is thrown when the child and parent data columns are not in the same dataset, if there is a type mismatch in any of the related columns, or if the parent column and child column is the same column.
DataTable.PrimaryKey Property	The exception is thrown if the column(s) is already a foreign key.
DataTable.Clear Method	The exception is thrown if there are any relations or constraints on the table that would be violated by removing all of the data from the table. For example, a foreign key relationship would be violated if parent table data were removed causing data in the related child table to be orphaned.

In the following example, an attempt is made to create a data relation using the same data column, causing a `DataException`.

VB.NET:

```
  Try
    Dim dr As New DataRelation("InvalidRelation",
ds.Tables.Item("customers").Columns("customerid"),
ds.Tables.Item("customers").Columns("customerid"))

  Catch de As DataException

    PrintError(de)

  End Try
```

C#:

```
try
{
    DataRelation dr = new DataRelation("InvalidRelation",
    ds.Tables["customers"].Columns["customerid"],
    ds.Tables["customers"].Columns["customerid"]);
}
    catch(DataException de)
{
    PrintError(de);
}
```

The System.Data.ConstraintException Class

The ConstraintException is thrown when editing data structures with constraints defined. The exception will be thrown if any constraint is violated:

Thrown By	Cause
DataSet.Merge Method	When merging into a dataset the exception is thrown if the constraints in the dataset cannot be maintained while adding the data from the source object
DataRowCollection.Add Method	When a new row is added to the collection and it does not meet the constraints the exception is thrown
DataRow.ItemArray Property	Adding a new row via an array throws an exception when the values in the array do not fit the constraints
DataRow.EndEdit Method	If the edit operation violated a constraint then the exception is thrown
DataTable.LoadDataRow Method	If a value in the new row violates an existing constraint

In the following example, a unique constraint is created on the orderid column, and then added to the orders table. A unique constraint constricts a column such that no duplicate values can exist. In the try block we attempt to set the second row to 10248, which is the value for this column in the first row. A constraint exception is thrown and caught.

VB.NET:

```
        'create a unique constraint on the orderid column and add to the constraints
    collection
        Dim uc As New UniqueConstraint(ds.Tables.Item("orders").Columns("orderid"))
        ds.Tables.Item("orders").Constraints.Add(uc)

        Try
            ds.Tables.Item("orders").Rows(1).BeginEdit()
            ds.Tables.Item("orders").Rows(1)("orderid") = 10248
            ds.Tables.Item("orders").Rows(1).EndEdit()

            Dim i As Integer
            For i = 0 To 2
```

```
Console.WriteLine(ds.Tables.Item("orders").Rows(i)("orderid").ToString())

    Next

    Catch ce As ConstraintException
        PrintError(ce)
    End Try
```

C#:

```
UniqueConstraint uc = new
UniqueConstraint(ds.Tables["orders"].Columns["orderid"]);
ds.Tables["orders"].Constraints.Add(uc);

try
{
    ds.Tables["orders"].Rows[1].BeginEdit();
    ds.Tables["orders"].Rows[1]["orderid"] = 10248;
    ds.Tables["orders"].Rows[1].EndEdit();
    for(int i =0;i<2;i++)
    {
    Console.WriteLine(ds.Tables["orders"].Rows[i]["orderid"].ToString());
    }

}
catch(ConstraintException ce)
{
    PrintError(ce);

}
```

The System.Data.DBConcurrencyException Class

The DbConcurrencyException is thrown when an error occurs while trying to update information in the database. If the number of rows affected by the update operation is zero then the DataAdapter throws this exception. For example, if data is brought into a DataSet and modified, while another user deletes the row(s) modified, when the DataAdapter attempts to update the data source, a DBConcurrency exception will be thrown as zero rows will be affected:

Thrown By	Cause
DataAdapter.Update Method	Thrown when the update affects no rows in the database

In the following example, after filling a dataset, we attempt to execute a delete command to remove one of the rows:

VB.NET:

```
cnn.Open()
Dim cmdDel As New SqlCommand("delete customers where customerid='PARIS'", cnn)
Try
   cmdDel.ExecuteNonQuery()
Catch se As SqlException
   Console.WriteLine(se.ToString())
```

```
End Try

cnn.Close()
```

We then try to update the row in the `dataset` that we just deleted:

```
Try

    Dim dcary(1) As DataColumn
    Dim dc As DataColumn
    dc = ds.Tables.Item("customers").Columns("customerid")
    dcary(0) = dc
    ds.Tables.Item("customers").PrimaryKey = dcary

    dc = ds.Tables.Item("orders").Columns("orderid")
    ds.Tables.Item("orders").PrimaryKey = dcary

    dc = ds.Tables.Item("orderdetails").Columns("orderdetailid")
    ds.Tables.Item("orderdetails").PrimaryKey = dcary

    Dim dr As DataRow
    dr = ds.Tables.Item("customers").Rows.Find("PARIS")
    dr.BeginEdit()
    dr("contactname") = "Wrox Press"
    dr.EndEdit()

    Dim uc As New SqlCommand("update customers set contactname = 'Wrox Press' where
customerid = 'PARIS'", sda.SelectCommand.Connection)
    sda.UpdateCommand() = uc

    sda.Update(ds, "customers")

Catch dce As DBConcurrencyException

    PrintError(dce)

End Try
```

C#:

```
cnn.Open();
SqlCommand cmdDel = new SqlCommand("delete customers where
customerid='PARIS'",cnn);
try
{
    cmdDel.ExecuteNonQuery();
}
catch(SqlException se)
{
    Console.WriteLine(se.ToString());
}
cnn.Close();
try
```

```
{
      //create a simple update command for the data adapter to modify the
      //row we are editing
      sda.UpdateCommand = new SqlCommand("update customers set contactname = 'Wrox
Press' where customerid = 'PARIS'",sda.SelectCommand.Connection);

      //try to update the data set using the data adapter
      sda.Update(ds, "customers");
}

//catch the concurrency exception when it occurs
catch(DBConcurrencyException dce)
{
      //print out the error information to the console
      PrintError(dce);

}
```

We should receive the following output:

Error Source:
  System.Data

Error Message:
  Concurrency violation: the UpdateCommand affected 0 records.

Target Site:
  Int32 Update(System.Data.DataRow[], System.Data.Common.DataTableMapping)

Stack Trace:
  at System.Data.Common.DbDataAdapter.Update(DataRow[] dataRows, DataTableMappi
ng tableMapping)
  at System.Data.Common.DbDataAdapter.Update(DataSet dataSet, String srcTable)
  at CADOExceptions.Class1.Concurrency(DataSet ds, SqlDataAdapter sda) in C:\Do
cuments and Settings\Administrator\My Documents\Visual Studio Projects\CADOExcep
tions\Class1.cs:line 175

The Syste.Data.DeletedRowInaccessibleException Class

The DeletedRowInaccessibleException is thrown when an action is attempted on a DataRow that has been deleted. The deleted status is determined by the DataRowState property of the DataRow. Once a row has been marked as deleted, by calling the Delete method of the DataRow object, any operations on that row results in a DeletedRowInaccessibleException.

This exception is important, because the DataRow may have been deleted outside the current procedure. Checking the DataRowState of a DataRow before acting on it will help to avoid this exception.

Thrown By	Cause
DataRow.BeginEdit Method	Thrown when the method is called because a deleted row cannot be edited
DataRow.Delete Method	Thrown when trying to delete a row that has been marked as deleted
DataRow.ItemArray Method	Thrown when attempting to get all of the values in a DataRow when it has already been marked as deleted
DataRow.Item Property	Thrown when an attempt is made to access an item in the DataRow after the row has been marked as deleted

In the following example, the first row of the data table is deleted, and then an attempt is made to begin editing this row. The DeletedRowInaccessibleException is thrown and caught.

VB.NET:

```
ds.Tables.Item("customers").Rows(0).Delete()
Try

   ds.Tables.Item("customers").Rows(0).BeginEdit()

Catch drie As DeletedRowInaccessibleException

   PrintError(drie)
End Try
```

C#:

```
ds.Tables ["customers"].Rows[0].Delete();
try
{
ds.Tables["customers"].Rows[0].BeginEdit();
}
catch(DeletedRowInaccessibleException drie)
{
     PrintError(drie);
}
```

The System.Data.DuplicateNameException Class

The DuplicateNameException is thrown when adding or renaming an item in a collection where an item with that same name already exists:

Thrown By	Cause
DataRelationCollection.Add Method	Thrown when a DataRelation with the same name already exists in the collection
DataTableCollection.Add Method	Thrown when a DataTable with the same name already exists in the collection

Table continued on following page

Thrown By	Cause
`DataTable.TableName` Property	Thrown when the `DataTable` is in a `DataSet` that already has a `DataTable` with the same name
`DataRelationCollection.AddCore` Method	Thrown when a `DataRelation` with the same name already exists in the collection
`DataColumnCollection.Add` Method	Thrown when a `DataColumn` with the same name already exists in the collection
`ConstraintCollection.Add` Method	Thrown when a `Constraint` with the same name already exists in the collection
`DataColumn.ColumnName` Property	Thrown when a `DataColumn` in the collection has the same name as the assigned string
`Constraint.ConstraintName` Property	Thrown when a `Constraint` in the collection has the same name as the assigned string
`DataRelation.RelationName` Property	Thrown when a `DataRelation` in the collection has the same name as the assigned string

In the following example, the `orders` table is renamed to "customers", but the `customers` table already exists in the dataset, so the `DuplicateNameException` is thrown. If the table is successfully renamed, it will now need to be referenced, or indexed, by the new name. Attempting to access the table by its old name will result in an `ArrayIndexOutofBoundsException`.

VB.NET:

```
Try
   ds.Tables.Item("orders").TableName = "customers"

Catch dne As DuplicateNameException

   PrintError(dne)
End Try
```

C#:

```
try
{
    ds.Tables["orders"].TableName="customers";
}
catch(DuplicateNameException dne)
{
    PrintError(dne);
}
```

The System.Data.EvaluateException Class

Within a `DataTable` object a `DataColumn` can be a calculated value. These columns use an expression to define the calculation. These expressions may be calculations using other columns in the table, such as multiplying a unit price times a quantity to get the total cost for a line item, or an aggregate function such as a sum of total prices to get the total order cost. The `EvaluateException` is thrown when an error occurs in the evaluation of one of these columns:

Thrown By	Cause
DataColumnCollection.Add Method	Thrown when adding a new column to the collection if there is an error in attempting to evaluate the expression (calculation) for the column

In the example, a new `DataColumn` is created as an integer type. Next the expression for the `DataColumn` is set to be "unitprice * qty". An attempt is made to add this column to the `customers` table in the `DataSet`, but an exception is thrown, because there is no column named "UnitPrice" or "Qty".

VB.NET:

```
Dim dc As New DataColumn("TotalPrice", Type.GetType("System.Int32"), "UnitPrice *
Quantity")
Try

    'will throw an error because there is no UnitPrice column in the orders table
    ds.Tables.Item("orders").Columns.Add(dc)
    Console.WriteLine(ds.Tables.Item("orders").Rows(0)("TotalPrice").ToString())

Catch ee As EvaluateException

    PrintError(ee)
End Try
```

C#:

```
DataColumn dc = new DataColumn("TotalPrice", Type.GetType("System.Int32"),
"UnitPrice * Quantity");
try
{
//will throw an error because there is neither a UnitPrice nor Qty column in the
orders table
    ds.Tables["orders"].Columns.Add(dc);
}
catch(EvaluateException ee)
{
    PrintError(ee);
}
```

The System.Data.InRowChangingEventException Class

The `InRowChangingEventException` is thrown when trying to perform an edit action on a `DataRow` from within that `DataRow`'s `RowChanging` event handler:

Thrown By	Cause
DataRow.BeginEdit Method	Thrown when the method is called inside an event handler for the row's RowChanging event
DataRow.CancelEdit Method	Thrown when the method is called inside an event handler for the row's RowChanging event
DataRow.EndEdit Method	Thrown when the method is called inside an event handler for the row's RowChanging event

In the following example, an event handler is assigned to the RowChanging event of the customers datatable, and then an attempt is made to edit the first row of this table. In the event handler, an attempt is made to edit the row upon which the original edit is taking place, thus causing an InRowChangingEventException.

VB.NET:

```
Dim WithEvents dt As DataTable

dt = ds.Tables.Item("customers")

'start changing a row to trigger the row changing event
ds.Tables.Item("customers").Rows(0)("contactname") = "Wrox Press"

    'private event handler for the the row changing event--used in conjunction with the
    'above method to show the errors when working in this event handler
Private Sub RowChange_Handler(ByVal sender As Object, ByVal rcea As
DataRowChangeEventArgs) Handles dt.RowChanging

Try
  Console.WriteLine("Row Changing . . . ")
  rcea.Row.BeginEdit()

Catch irce As InRowChangingEventException

  PrintError(irce)


End Try
End Sub
```

C#:

```
ds.Tables ["customers"].RowChanging+= new
DataRowChangeEventHandler(this.RowChange_Handler);
ds.Tables["customers"].Rows[0]["contactname"] = "Wrox Press";
...
...
//private event handler for the row changing event in
//above method to show the errors when working in this event handler
private void RowChange_Handler(Object sender,DataRowChangeEventArgs rcea)
{
try{
    rcea.Row.BeginEdit();
}
catch (InRowChangingEventException irce)
{
    PrintError(irce);
}
}
```

The System.Data.InvalidConstraintException Class

The `InvalidConstraintException` is thrown when dealing with relations between data tables. When creating relations or foreign key constraints, this exception is thrown when the relation cannot be completed because of existing constraints:

Thrown By	Cause
`DataRelationCollection.Add` Method	Thrown when the `DataRelation` being added violates a constraint on one of the `DataTables`
`ForeignKeyConstraint` Method	Thrown when the data columns included in the constraint have different data types or if the `DataTables` being constrained are not in the same `DataSet`
`DataRowCollection.Clear` Method	Thrown when there are foreign key constraints on the columns in the `DataRow`, because the constraints link each of the `DataTable` objects and force a related item to exist in the related table
`DataRow.SetParentRow` Method	Thrown when the `DataRow` object is not in the child `DataTable` as defined in the `DataRelation`
`DataRow.GetParentRow` Method	Thrown when the `DataRow` object does not belong to the child `DataTable` as defined in the `DataRelation`
`DataRow.GetParentRows` Method	Thrown when the `DataRow` object does not belong to the child `DataTable` as defined in the `DataRelation`
`DataRelation` Method	Thrown when creating a `DataRelation` and either the joining data columns are not of the same type, data columns from multiple data tables are passed in as one side of the relation, or the tables being joined are not in the same dataset

In the following example, a `DataRelation` is created joining the customers and orders tables on their respective ID columns. Unfortunately, these columns are of different data types, and so the `InvalidConstraintException` is thrown.

VB.NET:

```
'create a unique constraint on the orderid column and add to the constraints
collection
Dim uc As New UniqueConstraint(ds.Tables.Item("orders").Columns("orderid"))
ds.Tables.Item("orders").Constraints.Add(uc)

Try
  ds.Tables.Item("orders").Rows(1).BeginEdit()
  ds.Tables.Item("orders").Rows(1)("orderid") = 10248
  ds.Tables.Item("orders").Rows(1).EndEdit()

  Dim i As Integer
```

```
    For i = 0 To 2
        Console.WriteLine(ds.Tables.Item("orders").Rows(i)("orderid").ToString())
    Next

Catch ce As ConstraintException
    PrintError(ce)
End Try
```

C#:

```
try
{
DataRelation dr = new  DataRelation("CustomerRelation",
    ds.Tables["customers"].Columns["customerid"],
    ds.Tables["orders"].Columns["orderid"]);
}
catch(InvalidConstraintException ice)
{
    PrintError(ice);
}
```

The System.Data.InvalidExpressionException Class

In the `DataSet` object, we can identify `DataColumn` objects that have a calculated value. For example, a column could provide the `UnitCost * Qty` to give the total cost. An expression column can also give a summary calculation, such as `Count(Qty)`. These calculations are much like the calculations available in T-SQL.

The `InvalidExpressionException` is the base class for the `SyntaxErrorException` and the `EvaluateException`. Each of these classes represents a more specific exception and is defined elsewhere in this chapter. This relationship is similar to the relationship between the `DataException` and most of the other exceptions defined in this chapter. What this means is that the developer has the options to catch the specific exception, `EvaluateException` or `SyntaxException`, or the more generic `InvalidExpressionException`. If we just want to know that the expression set for the column is invalid, we would use the `InvalidExpressionException`. If we want to provide the user with more detailed information, perhaps so they can fix some input, however, then we would use the more specific exceptions:

Thrown By	Cause
`DataColumnCollection.Add` Method	Thrown when adding a `DataColumn` to the collection when the `Expression` property is already set to a value which is not valid for the collection
`DataColumn.Expression` Property	Thrown when the expression is set to a value that is not valid for the `DataTable` (therefore referencing column names that do not exist in the table)

In the following example, a new `DataColumn` is created and its expression property is set to "UnitPrice * Quantity". When an attempt is made to add this column to the `customers` table, however, an exception is thrown because there is no `UnitPrice` or `Quantity` column in the `customers` table. This may look familiar, as it is the same issue that caused us to have to catch the `EvaluateException`. `EvaluateException` derives from the `InvalidExrpessionException` class so it makes sense to trap a more specific error with our more general exception class.

VB.NET:

```
      Dim dc As New DataColumn("totalprice", Type.GetType("System.Int32"))
   dc.Expression = "UnitPrice * Quantity"

   Try

      ds.Tables.Item("customers").Columns.Add(dc)

   Catch iee As InvalidExpressionException

      PrintError(iee)
   End Try
```

C#:

```
   DataColumn dc = new DataColumn("totalprice",Type.GetType("System.Int32"));
   dc.Expression = "UnitPrice * Quantity";

   try
   {
      ds.Tables["customers"].Columns.Add(dc);
   }
   catch(InvalidExpressionException iee)
   {
      PrintError(iee);
   }
```

The System.Data.MissingPrimaryKeyException Class

The `MissingPrimaryKeyException` is thrown when an attempt is made to search a `DataRowCollection` that does not have a primary key. The primary key is required to allow this search and to uniquely identify the row.

Thrown By	Cause
DataRow.Contains Method	Thrown when the DataTable being searched does not have a primary key.
DataRow.Find Method	Thrown when the DataTable being searched does not have a primary key.

In the following example an attempt is made to see if the `DataRowCollection` contains an item with the primary key of 5. However since we have not created a primary key on this `DataTable`, the `MissingPrimaryKeyException` is thrown.

VB.NET:

```
   Dim blnExists As Boolean

   'try to search for a value in the data table
   Try
      blnExists = ds.Tables.Item("orderdetails").Rows.Contains(5)

   Catch mpke As MissingPrimaryKeyException
      PrintError(mpke)

   End Try
```

C#:

```
try
{
    Boolean RowExists = ds.Tables["orderdetails"].Rows.Contains(5);
}
catch(MissingPrimaryKeyException mpke)
{
    PrintError(mpke);
}
```

The System.Data.NoNullAllowedException Class

The `NoNullAllowedException` is thrown when an attempt is made to enter a null value into a `DataColumn` that has had its `AllowDBNull` property set to `False`:

Thrown By	Cause
`DataRowCollection.Add` Method	Thrown when a new row is added to the collection with a null value in the column marked as not allowing `Null` values
`DataRow.EndEdit` Method	Thrown when a null value has been placed in a column marked as not allowing null values and the `EndEdit` method is called signaling that the edits are complete
`DataRow.ItemArray` Property	Thrown when the array contains a null value for a column with its `AllowDBNull` property set to `False`
`DataTable.LoadDataRow` Method	Thrown when a null object exists in the array and the corresponding `DataColumn` has its `AllowDBNull` property set to `False`

In the following example, the `AllowDBNull` property of the `customerid` field is set to false. Then an attempt is made to add a new row with an array of empty, or `null`, objects. This causes and exception, because by not specifying a value for the objects, we default to `null`, which is not allowed in the `customerid` column.

VB.NET:

```
'indicate that we do not want to allow null values in the customerid column
ds.Tables.Item("customers").Columns("customerid").AllowDBNull = False

Try

    Dim obj(1) As Object
    obj(0) = 11
    ds.Tables.Item("customers").Rows.Add(obj)

Catch nnae As NoNullAllowedException

    PrintError(nnae)

End Try
```

C#:

```csharp
try
{
    ds.Tables["customers"].Columns["customerid"].AllowDBNull = false;
    ds.Tables["customers"].Rows.Add(new object[11]);
}
catch(NoNullAllowedException nnae)
{
    PrintError(nnae);
}
```

The System.Data.ReadOnlyException Class

The `ReadOnlyException` is thrown when an attempt is made to edit a read-only column in a `DataTable`. The read-only status is determined by the Boolean `ReadOnly` property of the `DataColumn` object. This exception only gets thrown when the `DataRow` being edited is already in the `DataTable` object:

Thrown By	Cause
`DataRow.EndEdit` Method	Thrown when ending an editing session, the `DataRow` being edited is contained in a DataTable and the `ReadOnly` property of the `DataColumn` is set to True
`DataRow.ItemArray` Property	Thrown when a value in the array of objects corresponds to a `DataColumn` in the `DataTable` that is marked as `ReadOnly`

In the following example, we set the `customerid` column to be read only and then attempt to write a new value into the field.

VB.NET:

```vbnet
ds.Tables.Item("customers").Columns("customerid").ReadOnly = True

Try

  ds.Tables.Item("customers").Rows(0)("customerid") = "nCust"

Catch roe As ReadOnlyException

  PrintError(roe)

End Try
```

C#:

```csharp
ds.Tables["customers"].Columns["customerid"].ReadOnly = true;

try
{
    ds.Tables["customers"].Rows[0]["customerid"] = "nCust";
}
catch(ReadOnlyException roe)
{
    PrintError(roe);
}
```

The System.Data.RowNotInTableException Class

The RowNotInTableException is thrown when an action is taken on a DataRow that is not a member of a DataTable. If a DataRow is not in a DataTable then trying to edit the row or to refer to its DataRelations will result in this error. This exception keeps the program from acting on a DataRow as if it were part of a DataSet and DataTable when it is a stand-alone object:

Thrown By	Cause
DataRow.AcceptChanges Method	When trying to accept the changes to a DataRow, it must be contained in a DataTable object.
DataRow.GetChildRows Method	Thrown when attempting to access the child rows, based on a DataRelation object, when the DataRow is not a member of a DataTable. A DataRelation defines the relationship between two DataTable objects so a DataRow not in a DataTable cannot legally get access to related rows.
DataRow.GetParentRow Method	Thrown when attempting to get the individual DataRow that acts as the parent row to the current row based on the DataRelation specified in the parameters.
DataRow.GetParentRows Method	Like the GetChildRows method, trying to get the parent row of a DataRow that is not in a DataTable throws this exception, because a DataRelation is defined between DataTables.
DataRow.RejectChanges Method	The RejectChanges methods implicitly calls the CancelEdit method, which will throw this exception if the DataRow is not in a DataTable.
DataRow.SetParentRow Method	Thrown when attempting to set the parent row of a DataRow using a DataRelation.

In the following example, a new DataRow is created from the DataTable, which creates a row with the schema of the table but does not insert it into the table. Then an attempt is made to edit the row but because the row is not in a table the RowNotInTableException is thrown.

VB.NET:

```
Dim dr As DataRow
dr = ds.Tables.Item("customers").NewRow()

Try

    dr.BeginEdit()
    dr("customerid") = "WROX"
    dr.EndEdit()
    dr.AcceptChanges()

Catch rnite As RowNotInTableException

    PrintError(rnite)

End Try
```

C#:

```
DataRow dr = ds.Tables["customers"].NewRow();

try
{
    dr.BeginEdit();
    dr["customerid"]="WROX";
    dr.EndEdit();
    dr.AcceptChanges();
}
catch(RowNotInTableException rnite)
{
    PrintError(rnite);
}
```

The System.Data.StrongTypingException Class

The StrongTypingException is thrown when working with a strongly typed DataSet. If code accesses a DBNull value from the strongly typed dataset this exception is thrown. The strongly typed dataset is a class wrapping a dataset that causes all fields to be treated as their defined type. The benefit of this framework is that you have much more control over your data consistency and have greater ability and flexibility when working with your dataset. The strongly typed dataset also allows for accessing members in a much more familiar syntax, much like accessing properties on objects. For example, a DataSet could be generated from a customers table in a database, thus allowing you to treat it as a customers object, accessing data as you would properties as shown below:

```
Customers.FirstName
```

The StrongTypingException will be thrown any time a null value is encountered in a strongly typed dataset.

In the following example, we attempt to access a data field which is null. If you examine the source code for this chapter, you'll be able to see that the properties for the strongly typed dataset check for null values and throw this exception if they are found. See the files strongtyped.cs and strongtyped.vb. As an example, here is the Region property from our strongly typed dataset as defined in VB.NET. Notice how an InvalidCastException is caught and a new StrongTypingException is then thrown passing the InvalidCastException as the inner exception.

VB.NET:

```
Dim cnnTyped As New
SqlConnection("server=(local);database=northwind;uid=sa;pwd=;")
Dim daTyped As New SqlDataAdapter()
Dim cmdTyped As New SqlCommand()

'define data access parameters
cmdTyped.Connection = cnnTyped
cmdTyped.CommandText = "select * from customers"
daTyped.SelectCommand = cmdTyped

'create new instance of our strongly typed dataset
Dim wroxDS As New vbstronglytyped.Wrox.NewDataSet()
```

```vb
'fill the strongly typed dataset
daTyped.Fill(wroxDS, "customers")

'create a new customer typed datatable
Dim tblCustomer As vbstronglytyped.WROX.NewDataSet.customersDataTable

'try to access the region column which contains a null value
Try
  'get a reference to our customer table
  tblCustomer = wroxDS.customers

  Dim strRegion As String

  'attempt to access the null value in the region property
  strRegion = tblCustomer(0)._Region

  'write the region out to the console
  Console.WriteLine(strRegion)

Catch strongEx As StrongTypingException
  PrintError(strongEx)
End Try
```

C#:

```csharp
SqlConnection cnnTyped = new
SqlConnection("server=(local);database=northwind;uid=sa;pwd=;");
SqlDataAdapter daTyped = new SqlDataAdapter();
SqlCommand cmdTyped = new SqlCommand();

//define data access parameters
cmdTyped.Connection = cnnTyped;
cmdTyped.CommandText = "select * from customers";
daTyped.SelectCommand = cmdTyped;

//create new instance of our strongly typed dataset
WROX.NewDataSet wroxDS = new WROX.NewDataSet();

//fill the strongly typed dataset
daTyped.Fill(wroxDS, "customers");

//create a new customer typed datatable
WROX.NewDataSet.customersDataTable tblCustomer;

//try to access the region column which contains a null value
try
{
    //get a reference to our customer table
    tblCustomer = wroxDS.customers;

    string strRegion;

    //attempt to access the null value in the region property
    strRegion = tblCustomer[0].Region;
```

```
        //write the region out to the console
Public Property _Region() As String
  Get
    Try
Return CType(Me(Me.tablecustomers._RegionColumn), String)
    Catch e As InvalidCastException
Throw New StrongTypingException("Cannot get value because it is DBNull.", e)
    End Try
  End Get
  Set(ByVal Value As String)
    Me(Me.tablecustomers._RegionColumn) = value
  End Set
End Property
      Console.WriteLine(strRegion);
}
catch(StrongTypingException strongEx)
{
      PrintError(strongEx);
}
```

The System.Data.SyntaxErrorException Class

The `SyntaxErrorException` is thrown when an expression is defined for a `DataColumn` and the syntax of the expression is invalid. This exception derives from the more generic `InvalidExpressionException` and provides more specific information indicating that the exception is caused by the syntax of the expression:

Thrown By	Cause
`DataColumnCollection.Add` Method	Thrown when adding a `DataColumn` to the collection with the `Expression` property set when the expression contains a syntax error
`DataColumn.Expression` Property	Thrown when the expression is set to a value that is not syntactically correct

In the following example, a new `DataColumn` is created and its `Expression` property is set to `"unitprice */ quantity"`. When this expression is evaluated it causes a `SyntaxErrorException` because the `"*/"` syntax is incorrect.

VB.NET:

```
    Try

  ds.Tables.Item("orderdetails").Columns.Add(New DataColumn("TotalPrice",
Type.GetType("System.Int32")))
  ds.Tables.Item("orderdetails").Columns("TotalPrice").Expression = "unitprice */
quantity"

'Console.WriteLine(ds.tables.Item("orderdetails").rows(0)("TotalPrice").ToString()
)

Catch se As SyntaxErrorException

  PrintError(se)

End Try
```

C#:

```
try
{
ds.Tables["orderdetails"].Columns.Add
   (new DataColumn("TotalPrice",Type.GetType("System.Int32")));
ds.Tables["orderdetails"].Columns["TotalPrice"].Expression =
   "unitprice */ quantity";
}
catch(SyntaxErrorException se)
{
   PrintError(se);
}
```

The System.Data.TypedDataSetGeneratorException Class

The `TypedDataSetGeneratorException` is thrown when creating a typed dataset and a naming conflict occurs. This means that an item within the dataset has an invalid name or that the name conflicts with another item in the given namespace. This class is intended to be used as a base class to be subclassed by a developer wanting to create their own process for defining strongly-typed datasets. The developer would also subclass the `TypedDataSetGenerator` class in order to create a strongly typed dataset. It is from within this class that the `TypedDataSetGeneratorException` would be thrown. For example, if two tables have the same name, or multiple columns in the same table have the same name, this exception can be thrown:

Thrown By	Cause
`TypedDataSetGenerator.Generate` Method	Thrown when attempting to generate a typed `DataSet` from an existing `DataSet` and a naming conflict occurs

In this example, we show a sample method that could be part of a custom `TypedDataSetGenerator`, which adds a given table to the database schema. We check to ensure that we don't already have a table with the same name as the one we are adding. If we do, then we throw the `TypedDataSetGeneratorException`.

VB.NET:

```
Private sub AddTable(byval Name as string)
     If me.Tables.Contains(Name) Then
          Throw new TypedDataSetGeneratorException("A Tabled named " & Name & "
already exists in the dataset.")

End Sub
```

C#:

```
private void AddTable(string Name)
{
     if(this.Tables.Contains(Name))
     {
          throw new TypedDataSetGeneratorException("A Table named " + Name + "
already exists in the dataset.");
     }
}
```

The System.Data.VersionNotFoundException Class

`DataRows` can handle different versions of the data: current, default, proposed, and original. The available versions change as the rows are edited to reflect the state of the data. This version property can be used determine the editing state of the `DataRow` and can be used to search for a specific version of the data. The `DataRowVersion` property allows read-only access to this version information:

Thrown By	Cause
`DataRow.GetChildRows` Method	Thrown when attempting to access a version of the `ChildRows` of a `DataRow` using a `DataRelation` if the version does not exist
`DataRow.GetParentRows` Method	Thrown when attempting to access the parent rows of a particular version of the `DataRow` as defined in a `DataRelation` if the requested version does not exist
`DataRow.GetParentRow` Method	Thrown when attempting to access the parent row of the current row using a `DataRelation` if the requested version does not exist.
`DataRow.Item` Property	Thrown when attempting to access a specific version of an item in a `DataRow` if the requested version does not exist.

In the example, an attempt is made to set a string to the value of the `orderid` field's proposed value. As no editing has begun, this version of the `orderid` column does not exist for this row, so we get a `VersionNotFoundException`.

VB.NET:

```
Try
  Dim result As String

  result = ds.Tables.Item("orders").Rows(0)("orderid",
DataRowVersion.Proposed).ToString()

Catch vnfe As VersionNotFoundException

  PrintError(vnfe)
End Try
```

C#:

```
try
{
  string result = ds.Tables["orders"].Rows[0]["orderid",
    DataRowVersion.Proposed].ToString();
}
catch(VersionNotFoundException vnfe)
{
    PrintError(vnfe);
}
```

Managed Provider Errors

In addition to the exceptions covered up to this point, there are three other exception classes that serve a special role. The SqlException, OdbcException, and OleDBException classes serve to collect and provide access to the errors that are generated outside of the .NET managed environment. For the SqlException, this means a collection of SqlError objects representing errors generated by SQL Server. The OleDbException holds error information from the given OLE Database provider, and the OdbcException contains information regarding errors generated by ODBC providers.

The System.Data.SqlClient.SqlException Class

The SqlException acts as the general exception for the SQL Server managed provider. Errors generated by SQL Server are passed up in the code via the SqlException to be captured and handled. The SqlException encapsulates the errors generated and provides a means to access the specifics of the errors raised:

Thrown By	Cause
SqlConnection.Close Method	Thrown to indicate the errors originally encountered when the connection was opened
SqlConnection.Open Method	Thrown to indicate an error opening the connection
SqlCommand.ExecuteNonQuery, SqlCommand.ExecuteReader, SqlCommand.ExecuteResultSet, SqlCommand.ExecuteScalar, SqlCommand.ExecuteXmlReader Methods	Thrown when the command being processed by SQL Server is in error, or causes an error in the DBMS

SQLException Properties

These properties are in addition to the shared properties defined earlier in the chapter. With the exception of the Errors property the properties of the SqlException represent the first error in the collection:

Property	Description
Class	Returns and integer representing the severity level of the error as returned by the SQL Server adapter. This severity level indicates the "class" of error as follows: 1-10 = general input errors 11-17 = correctable user errors 17-25 = Hardware or software errors
Errors	Returns the SQLErrorCollection object that provides access to the collection of errors generated by the SQL Adapter.
LineNumber	Returns an integer representing the line number in the T-SQL statement which caused the error.

Property	Description
Number	Returns an integer corresponding to the error number in the SQL Server Sysmessages table.
Procedure	Returns a string representing the stored procedure name where the error occurred.
Server	The name of the SQL Server where the error occurred.
Source	Returns the source of the error as set at the time of throwing the exception. For the SqlException this is "Sql Server Managed Provider".
State	Gets the number modifying the error message to provide additional information.

The System.Data.SqlClient.SqlErrorCollection Class

The SqlErrorCollection is the collection class that holds the SqlError objects. SqlException acts as a wrapper class for the SqlErrorCollection class, allowing access using the familiar exception framework.

The SqlErrorCollection is not an exception and therefore, is not thrown. When an instance of SQLException is thrown, the SqlErrorCollection is accessed using the Errors property of the SqlException.

Methods of the System.Data.SqlClient.SqlErrorCollection Class

Method Signature	Description
CopyTo(Array, Int)	Copies the items in the error collection to the array starting at the given index

Properties of the System.Data.SqlClient.SqlErrorCollection Class

Property Name	Description
Count	Returns an integer representing the number of errors in the collection.
IsReadOnly	Returns a Boolean value indicating whether the collection is read-only. In the case of the SqlErrorCollection this property is always true, as it is not possible to add errors to the collection manually.
IsSynchronized	Returns a Boolean value indicating whether the collection is synchronized with the data source. This value is always false for the SqlErrorCollection class.
Item	Gets the Error object representing the error at the specified index in the collection.
SyncRoot	Gets an object to be used to synchronize the access to the collection. When attempting to perform a thread safe operation on the collection, this object can be used to provide that synchronous access.

The System.Data.SqlClient.SqlError Class

The `SqlError` class represents a single error generated from SQL Server. We can use this class to get specific information about a generated error including detailed information about where the error occurred.

The `SqlError` is not an exception and is therefore, not thrown.

Methods of the System.Data.SqlClient.SqlError Class

Method Signature	Description
ToString()	Overrides the `ToString` method from the Object class to return "SqlError:" plus the error message

Properties of the System.Data.SqlClient.SqlError Class

Property Name	Description
Class	Returns the severity level of the error as returned by the SQL Server adapter to indicate the type of error.
LineNumber	Returns an integer representing the line number in the T-SQL statement which caused the error.
Message	A string property that allows us to get or set the message related to the error.
Number	Returns and integer corresponding to the error number in the SQL Server Sysmessages table.
Procedure	Returns a string representing the stored procedure name where the error occurred.
Server	The name of the SQL server where the error occurred.
Source	Returns the source of the error, which is the managed provider. For this collection this will be "Sql Server Managed Provider".
State	Gets the number modifying the error message to provide additional information.

In the following example, a `SqlCommand` is created and setup to execute a stored procedure named `NonExistentProc`. As you might have guessed from the name, this stored procedure does not exist in the database. Therefore, when the command is executed a `SqlException` is thrown and caught. Using a `foreach` loop, the `SqlErrors` in the `SqlErrorCollection` are enumerated and written out to the console.

VB.NET:

```
Console.WriteLine(vbTab & vbTab & vbTab & "SqlExeption:" & vbCrLf & vbCrLf)
Dim cnnConnection As New
SqlConnection("server=(local);database=northwind;uid=sa;pwd=;")
Dim errorcommand As New SqlCommand("NonexistentProc", cnnConnection)
errorcommand.CommandType = CommandType.StoredProcedure
errorcommand.Parameters.Add(New SqlParameter("@inval", SqlDbType.Int))
errorcommand.Parameters("@inval").Value = 5
```

```vb
1Try
  cnnConnection.Open()
  errorcommand.ExecuteNonQuery()

Catch sqe As SqlException

  Console.WriteLine("Error processing stored procedure:" & vbCrLf)

  Dim se As SqlError
  For Each se In sqe.Errors
    Console.WriteLine(se.Message)
    Console.WriteLine("Server:" + vbTab + se.Server.ToString())
    Console.WriteLine("Error number:" + vbTab + se.Number.ToString())
    Console.WriteLine("Severity:" & vbTab + se.Class.ToString())
    Console.WriteLine("Stored proc:" & vbTab + se.Procedure.ToString())
    Console.WriteLine("T-SQL Line number:" & vbTab + se.LineNumber.ToString())
    Console.WriteLine("Source:" & vbTab + se.Source.ToString())
    Console.WriteLine("State:" & vbTab + se.State.ToString())

  Next
End Try
```

C#

```csharp
SqlCommand errorcommand = new SqlCommand("NonexistentProc",cnn);
errorcommand.CommandType = CommandType.StoredProcedure;
errorcommand.Parameters.Add(new SqlParameter("@inval",SqlDbType.Int));
errorcommand.Parameters["@inval"].Value = 5;

try
{
    cnn.Open();
    errorcommand.ExecuteNonQuery();
}
catch(SqlException sqe)
{
    Console.WriteLine("Error processing stored procedure:\n");
    foreach(System.Data.SqlClient.SqlError se in sqe.Errors)
    {
        Console.WriteLine(se.Message);
        Console.WriteLine("Server:\t" + se.Server.ToString());
        Console.WriteLine("Error number:\t" +
    se.Number.ToString());
        Console.WriteLine("Severity:\t" + se.Class.ToString());
        Console.WriteLine("Stored proc:\t" +
    se.Procedure.ToString());
        Console.WriteLine("T-SQL Line number:\t" +
    se.LineNumber.ToString());
        Console.WriteLine("Source:\t" + se.Source.ToString());
        Console.WriteLine("State:\t" + se.State.ToString());
    }
}
```

The output for this would be as follows:

Error processing stored procedure:

Could not find stored procedure 'NonexistentProc'.
Server: VSTUDIO
Error number: 2812
Severity: 16
Stored proc:
T-SQL Line number: 0
Source: SQL Server Managed Provider
State: 62

The System.Data.OleDb.OleDbException Class

The OleDbException acts as the general exception for OLE database connections. Errors generated by the database are passed up in the code via the OleDbException to be captured and handled. The OleDbException encapsulates the errors generated and provides a means to access the specifics of the errors raised:

Thrown By	Cause
OleDbConnection.Open Method	Thrown when there are errors connecting to the database using the ADO provider
OleDbConnection.Close Method	Thrown to indicate that there were errors upon opening the connection
OleDbCommand.ExecuteNonQuery, OleDbCommand.ExecuteReader, OleDbCommand.ExecuteScalar Methods	Thrown when an error occurs while processing the command

Methods of the System.Data.OleDb.OleDbException Class

The OleDbException class does not provide any new exceptions, but it does provide one overridden method.

Method	Description
ToString	Overridden to provide the fully qualified name of the exception and if possible the error message, stack trace and name of the inner exception

Properties of the System.Data.OleDb.OleDbException Class

Property	Description
ErrorCode	Gets the HRESULT or Windows error code for the error generated by the provider.
Errors	Gets an OleDbErrorsCollection object which allows for iterating over the various errors involved in causing this exception.
Message	Gets a description of the error. While this is similar to the Message property on most of the other exceptions, the message in this case represents the error thrown by the provider rather than a message created by the exception.
Source	Returns the name of the object where the errors originated.

The System.Data.OleDb.OleDbErrorCollection Class

The OleDbErrorCollection is the collection class that holds the OleDbError objects. OleDbException acts as a wrapper class for the OleDbErrorCollection class, allowing access using the familiar exception framework.

As the OleDbErrorCollection is not an exception class it is not thrown, but is accessed from the OleDbException class.

Methods of the System.Data.OleDb.OleDbErrorCollection Class

There are no methods defined for the OleDBErrorCollection other than those originally defined in the Object class.

Properties of the System.Data.OleDb.OleDbErrorCollection Class

Property	Description
Count	Gets an integer representing the number of errors in the collection
Item	Gets the error at the specified index

The System.Data.OleDb.OleDbError Class

The OleDbError class represents a single error generated from an OLE database connection. We can use this class to get specific information about a generated error including detailed information about where the error occurred.

As the OleDbError is not an exception, it is not thrown directly, but is accessed from the OleDbException via the OleDbErrorsCollection object.

Methods of the System.Data.OleDb.OleDbError Class

There are no methods defined for the OleDBErrorCollection other than those originally defined in the Object class.

Properties of the System.Data.OleDb.OleDbError Class

Property	Description
Message	Returns a string value that describes the error
NativeError	Returns a string that provides the specific information for the error from the database
Source	Gets the name of the object that generated the error
SQLState	Provides the ANSI SQL standard error code, which is a five-character code, which identifies the error in a standards based framework

VB.NET:

```
Dim cnnCustomers As New OleDbConnection("provider=Microsoft.Jet.OLEDB.4.0;data
source=c:\grocertogo.mdb;")
Dim daCustomers As New OleDbDataAdapter("select * from table1", cnnCustomers)
Dim dsCustomers As New DataSet("customers")

Try

    daCustomers.Fill(dsCustomers)

Catch oe As OleDbException

    Dim oleError As OleDbError
    For Each oleError In oe.Errors

        Console.WriteLine("OleDbError:")
        Console.WriteLine(vbTab & "Error Message: " + oleError.Message)
        Console.WriteLine(vbTab & "Native Error: " + oleError.NativeError.ToString())
        Console.WriteLine(vbTab & "Source: " + oleError.Source.ToString())
        Console.WriteLine(vbTab & "State: " + oleError.SQLState.ToString())
    Next
End Try
```

C#:

```
    OleDbConnection cnnCustomers = new
OleDbConnection("provider=Microsoft.Jet.Oledb.4.0;data
source=c:\\grocertogo.mdb;");
    OleDbDataAdapter daCustomers = new OleDbDataAdapter("select * from
table1",cnnCustomers);
    DataSet dsCustomers = new DataSet("customers");

    try
    {
daCustomers.Fill(dsCustomers);
    }
```

```
        catch(OleDbException oe)
        {
    foreach(OleDbError oleError in oe.Errors)
    {
        Console.WriteLine("OleDbError:");
        Console.WriteLine("\tError Message: " + oleError.Message);
        Console.WriteLine("\tNative Error: " + oleError.NativeError.ToString());
        Console.WriteLine("\tSource: " + oleError.Source.ToString());
        Console.WriteLine("\tState: " + oleError.SQLState.ToString());
    }
        }
```

The output from this would be as follows:

```
OleDbError:
    Error Message: The Microsoft Jet database engine cannot find the input table or query 'table1'. Make
sure it exists and that its name is spelled correctly.
    Native Error: -524420377
    Source: Microsoft JET Database Engine
    State: 3078
```

The System.Data.OdbcException Class

The OdbcException class is the mechanism by which errors generated by the various ODBC data providers are communicated to the .Net framework. It acts as a general exception encompassing any errors that get thrown specific to the data provider.

Methods of the System.Data.OdbcException Class

The OdbcException class does not define any new methods and only exposes those provided by the base classes from which it inherits.

Properties of the System.Data.OdbcException Class

Errors	Returns an OdbcErrorCollection object which acts as a container for the errors generated.
Message	Returns a string value that describes the first error in the errors collection
Source	Allows for getting or setting the source that generated the error

The System.Data.Odbc.OdbcErrorCollection Class

The OdbcErrorCollection class provides a container for the OdbcError objects returned from the provider. This class implements the ICollection interface and therefore provides all of the common collection behaviors.

As the `OdbcErrorCollection` is not an exception itself, it is not thrown. Instead, it is accessed from the `OdbcException` class as a means to get information about the specific errors thrown.

Methods of the System.Data.Odbc.OdbcErrorCollection Class

The `OdbcErrorCollection` class does not define any new methods and only exposes those provided by the base classes from which it inherits.

Properties of the System.Data.Odbc.OdbcErrorCollection Class

Property Name	Description
Count	Returns an integer representing the number of errors in the collection.
Item	Returns the `OdbcError` object at the given index in the collection. This property acts as the indexer in C# allowing for indexed, array-like, access.

The System.Data.Odbc.OdbcError Class

The `OdbcError` class represents an individual error from the `Odbc` data provider. This object is the base object in understanding errors from ODBC data sources as it provides the most detailed information about the given error.

As the `OdbcError` class is not an exception, it is not thrown. Instead, it is accessed from the `OdbcException` class via the errors property.

Methods of the System.Data.Odbc.OdbcError Class

Method Signature	Description
ToString()	Overrides the `ToString` method from the `Object` class to return the complete error message

Properties of the System.Data.Odbc.OdbcError Class

Property	Description
Message	Returns a string value that describes the error
NativeError	Returns a string that provides the specific information for the error from the ODBC data provider
Source	Gets the name of the ODBC driver that generated the error
State	Provides the ANSI SQL standard error code which is a five-character code which identifies the error in a standards based framework

VB.NET:

```
Dim cnnPubs As New OdbcConnection("DSN=pubs")
Dim cmdPubs As New OdbcCommand("SELECT sum(authorid) FROM authors", cnnPubs)

Try

   cnnPubs.Open()
   Dim AuthorCount As Integer
   AuthorCount = CInt(cmdPubs.ExecuteScalar())
   cnnPubs.Close()

Catch odbcex As OdbcException

   Dim odbcErr As OdbcError
   For Each odbcErr In odbcex.Errors

     Console.WriteLine("OdbcError:")
     Console.WriteLine(vbTab & "Error Message: " + odbcErr.Message)
     Console.WriteLine(vbTab & "Native Error: " + odbcErr.NativeError.ToString())
     Console.WriteLine(vbTab & "Source: " + odbcErr.Source.ToString())
     Console.WriteLine(vbTab & "State: " + odbcErr.SQLState.ToString())
   Next
End Try
```

C#:

```
     OdbcConnection cnnPubs = new OdbcConnection("DSN=pubs");
     OdbcCommand cmdPubs = new OdbcCommand("SELECT sum(authorid) FROM
authors",cnnPubs);

     try
     {
cnnPubs.Open();
int AuthorCount = (int)cmdPubs.ExecuteScalar();
cnnPubs.Close();
     }
     catch(OdbcException odbcex)
     {
foreach(OdbcError odbcErr in odbcex.Errors)
{
     Console.WriteLine("OdbcError:");
     Console.WriteLine("\tError Message: " + odbcErr.Message);
     Console.WriteLine("\tNative Error: " + odbcErr.NativeError.ToString());
     Console.WriteLine("\tSource: " + odbcErr.Source.ToString());
     Console.WriteLine("\tState: " + odbcErr.SQLState.ToString());
}
     }
```

The output from this would be as follows:

```
OdbcError:
   Error Message: [Microsoft][ODBC SQL Server Driver][SQL Server]Invalid object name 'authors'.
   Native Error: 208
   Source: SQLSRV32.DLL
   State: 42S02
```

Summary

While it would be nice if every program we ever wrote behaved exactly as we planned, and that all users would interact with our programs as we want them to, this is not reality. The reality is that exceptional circumstances will arise and any well-developed application must be designed to handle these situations.

We have covered the exceptions that are part of the System.Data namespace. These exceptions allow for handling errors when accessing data, manipulating data on the client, and updating data. They provide the framework for ensuring data integrity and stable applications.

In this chapter, we have looked at:

❑ Throwing exceptions

❑ Catching and handling exceptions

❑ The specific data related exceptions and when they are thrown

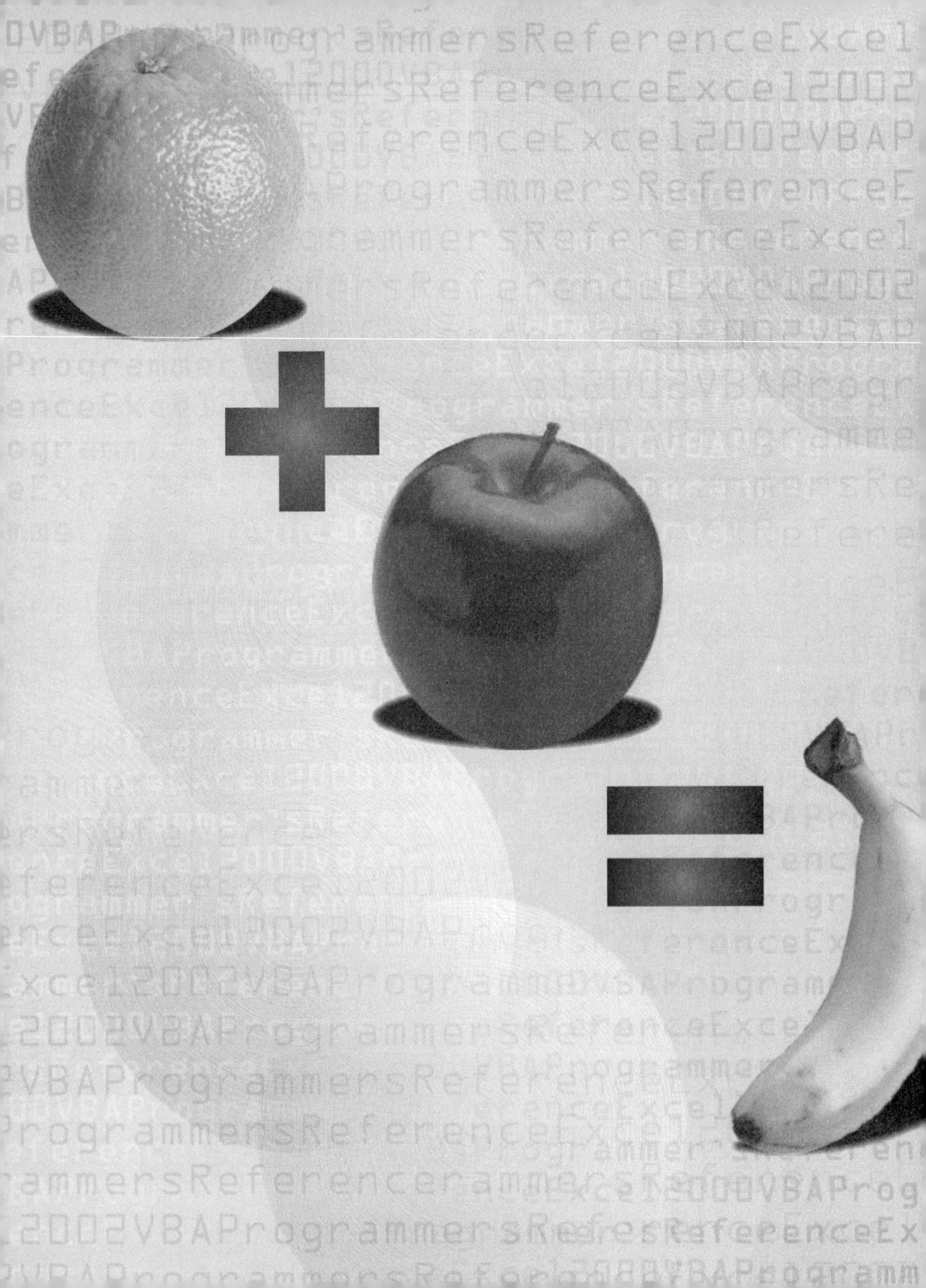

15

Permissions

Security In .NET

Developing solutions with previous versions of ADO limited us to relying on permissions established either by the operating system or the data source, such as Microsoft SQL Server. The alternative was to implement our own security modules. With the advent of .NET, ADO has inherited a set of permissions classes that implement .NET security.

As we go through the new security functionality, however, keep the following in mind:

> **Regardless of permissions granted by the CLR, all processes are restricted by the underlying OS security. Similarly, regardless of the permissions to the data source granted by the CLR, all processes are restricted by the data source security.**

There are three levels of security implemented by the .NET framework:

- ❑ Identity Permissions – permissions based on the identity of the assembly (or application); used to establish allowable permissions for the assembly

- ❑ Code Access Permissions – permissions to resources implemented in code modules and assemblies; restricts the allowable permission set and defines permissions requirements for other code modules

- ❑ Role-Based Permissions – permissions based on role(s) to which a user belongs; involve the credentials of the user or account the process is running under, and do not generally come into play in ADO.NET security classes directly

All permissions objects in ADO.NET are code access permission objects.

Evidence and the Security Policy

Security in .NET begins with the evaluation of the assembly. The CLR gathers information about the origin of the assembly, which is collectively called **evidence** and can include: the publisher's digital signature, the originating web site, and the originating URL.

Each machine has a security policy set up by the administrator. The security policy outlines allowable permissions based on various evidence parameters. For example, there may be a security policy in place, which requires that all assemblies from XYZ Company (digital signature) downloaded from their FTP site (originating url: ftp://ftp.xyz.com) are allowed permissions to all local databases. Without additional policies in place, any other combinations of evidence (for example code downloaded from ftp://ftp.xyz.com belonging to ABC company, or code downloaded from ftp://ftp.abc.com belonging to XYZ company) would have no allowable permissions on the local machine.

Using the evidence and the security policy, the CLR can then determine the allowed permission set for the assembly.

Code Access Permissions: Requests, Demands and Overrides

Once the allowable permission set is determined, code access permissions begin to be enforced as the CLR determines the final set of granted permissions for the assembly.

Code access permissions accomplish two objectives:

❑ Define security for the assembly in the form of **Requests** handled at grant time

❑ Enforce security on its callers in the form of **Demands** and **Overrides** handled at compile time, load time, or run time

Requests, Demands, and Overrides are known as Security Actions and are specified in the SecurityAction Enumeration, which are discussed in more detail in the PermissionAttribute section.

Requests

As stated previously, requests are handled at grant time. Once the allowed permission set is determined, the CLR determines the granted permission set using the following three permission requests:

❑ RequestMinimum – describes the minimum set of permissions the assembly needs to run

❑ RequestOptional – describes the optional set of permissions the assembly would like to have, but are not required for its execution

❑ RequestRefuse – describes the set of permissions the assembly does not want to have

These requests are not required, and if they are not specified, the assembly is granted the full allowable permission set.

> **Regardless of permissions requested within the assembly, no permissions will be granted which lie outside the scope of the assembly's allowed permission set as determined by the CLR.**

If the minimum requested permissions do not fall within the scope of the allowed set, the assembly is refused permission to run, and a PolicyException is thrown. Otherwise, the CLR uses the following formula to determine the final set of granted permissions:

> **Granted = Minimum + (Optional«Allowed) – Refuse**

The formula reads as follows: the granted permission set is determined by adding the minimum permission set to any optional permissions which exist in the allowed permission set, and subtracting the refused permission set.

Now the assembly is executed, carrying its granted permission set. While identity permissions and code access permissions (in the form of requests) shaped the granted permission set, code access permissions (in the form of demands and overrides) can also request specific permissions involving other assemblies linked in a process. All assemblies involved in the process are collectively known as a **call stack**.

Call stacks

As stated in the previous section, a call stack is composed of all assemblies involved in a process. Each module has certain permissions, and a module in the call stack can request a certain level of permissions from the other modules in the stack.

For example, let's look at the diagram of a call stack below where Method D calls Method B, which in turns calls Method F. These three assemblies are members of the call stack:

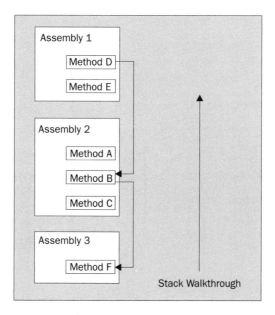

When a method issues a `Demand`, the stack walkthrough begins at that method and works its way backward as shown.

Demands and Overrides

The specific permission requirements you can ask based on members in the call stack are:

- ❑ LinkDemand (enforced at compile time) – demands a permission from the immediate caller in the stack

- ❑ InheritanceDemand (enforced at load time) – demands a permission from any inheriting classes

- ❑ Demand (enforced at load time) – demands specific permissions be satisfied by all members in the stack

- ❑ Assert (enforced at run time) – requests specific permissions be granted regardless of the granted permissions of members higher in the call stack

- ❑ Deny (enforced at run time) – requests specific permissions be granted regardless of the granted permissions of members higher in the call stack

The interaction of Assert, Demand, and Deny is important. A Demand begins a walkthrough of the stack, which continues until all callers in the stack satisfy the permission. If it encounters an Assert, the walkthrough stops if the required permission is equal to or is a subset of the asserted permission. Otherwise, the demanded permission is not yet satisfied and the walkthrough continues. Using the figure below, we will go through an example of a walkthrough of a stack:

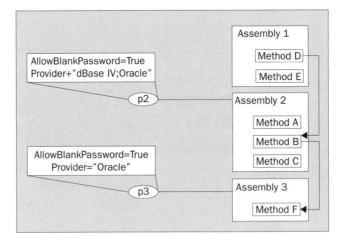

As can be seen, Assembly 2 is granted permission p2, which specifies that AllowBlankPassword=True and Provider="dBase IV;Oracle". Assembly 3 is granted permission p3, which specifies that AllowBlankPassword=True and Provider="Oracle".

Lets assume Method B issues an Assert for permission p2 and that Method F issues a Demand for permission p3. The walkthrough would first go to Assembly 3, since p3 satisfies p2, the walkthrough stops and the Demand is successful. Even though Assembly 1 has no granted permissions, the Assert from Assembly 2 satisfies the Demand as it asserts its permission regardless of the permissions of callers higher in the call stack.

If Method B instead issued a `Deny` for permission 2, however, then the Assert walkthrough would fail. This is because p2 and p3 have a common element (`AllowBlankPassword=True`), and thus guaranteeing that no members in the call stack can satisfy the entire permission p2.

Why use `Demands` and `Overrides`? One reason is that the CLR can enforce permissions along the call stack, which helps prevent misuse of secure code as we can see in the following figure:

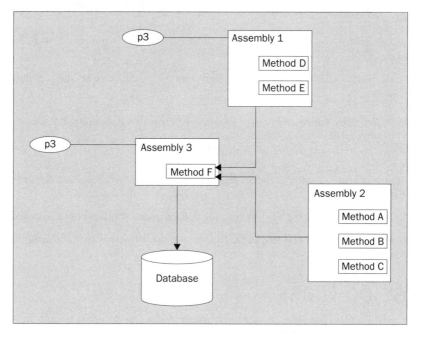

Method F has been granted permission p3, which includes access to secure areas of a local database. As such, both Assembly 1 and Assembly 2 can call Method F and gain the same level of access. The problem arises when Assembly 2 contains malicious code designed to damage the data. Method F however, can issue a `Demand` for permission p3. By enforcing permissions along the call stack, the CLR prevents unauthorized access by throwing an exception when the `Demand` fails for Assembly 2.

It's at the location of the security action (such as `Assert`, `Demand`, `Deny`), that the CLR performs the requested security check. This is important, because it also defines the scope of the permission: `Overrides` placed at the assembly level cover the entire assembly, `Overrides` placed at the module level cover the module only, and, finally, `Overrides` placed at the member level cover the member only (for a detailed discussion of code placement see the Code Placement of Security Actions section.)

This is one of the huge benefits of the .NET security model in that security implementations can be fine tuned to the specific needs of the code.

ADO.NET security

Each resource group in .NET has a `Permission` and `PermissionAttribute` class pair to manage its permissions. For example, the `FileIOPermission` and `FileIOPermissionAttribute` class pair manages read/write/append access to files and directories. ADO.NET has the following class pairs:

- ❑ `OleDbPermission` / `OleDbPermissionAttribute`– manages access to data sources using OLEDB

- ❑ `OdbcPermission` / `OdbcPermissionAttribute`– manages access to data sources using ODBC

- ❑ `SqlClientPermission` / `SqlClientPermissionAttribute` – manages access to SQL data sources

Note you can still use OLEDB and ODBC to access Microsoft SQL Servers, but this is not recommended.

ADO.NET permissions cover the following accesses:

- ❑ `AllowBlankPassword` – specifies whether the code can access a data source using a blank password

- ❑ `Unrestricted` – specifies whether the code is granted full access to a data source

- ❑ `Provider` (OleDb only) – specifies the providers allowed (Odbc and SqlClient are providers themselves, so this property is unnecessary)

Permission Class

The `Permission` class provides security verification for access to a data source. In ADO.NET, there are three `Permission` objects:

- ❑ `OleDbPermission` – secures access to an OLE DB data source

- ❑ `SqlClientPermisson` – secures access to a SQL Server

- ❑ `OdbcPermission` – secures access to an ODBC data source

Construction

There are five ways to construct a new `Permission` object. You can use one of the four overloaded class constructors, or you can use the `CreatePermission` method of the `PermissionAttribute` object (for the syntax in creating a new `Permission` object from a `PermissionAttribute` object, see the `CreatePermission` method under `PermissionAttribute` Methods).

The following syntax is that for the `OleDbPermission` class, but the other provider `Permission` classes follow the same syntax, with the noted exceptions.

To start with, here is the syntax to create the `Permission` object using no parameters:

VB.NET:

```
Public Sub New()
```

C#:

```
public OleDbPermission();
```

Next, specified `PermissionStates` are used to create the `Permission` object. The `PermissionState` Enum indicates whether the `Permission` object is created with all access (`PermisisonState = Unrestriced`) or no access (`PermisisonState = None`).

VB.NET:

```
Public Sub New(
    ByVal state As PermissionState)
```

C#:

```
public OleDbPermission(
    PermissionState state);
```

The Permission object can be created using a specified connection string and `AllowBlankPassword` property (OleDb and SqlClient Only):

VB.NET:

```
Public Sub New(
    ByVal connectionstringproperties As Hashtable,
    ByVal allowblankpassword As Boolean)
```

C#:

```
public OleDbPermission (
    Hashtable connectionstringproperties,
    bool allowblankpassword);
```

Finally, create the object using specified `PermissionState` and `AllowBlankPassword` properties (OleDb and SqlClient Only):

VB.NET:

```
Public Sub New(
    ByVal state As PermissionState,
    ByVal allowblankpassword As Boolean)
```

C#:

```
public OleDbPermission(
    PermissionState state,
    bool allowblankpassword);
```

Properties

AllowBlankPassword Property

Specifies whether a blank password is allowed.

Source: `DBDataPermission`

VB.NET:
```
Public Property AllowBlankPassword As Boolean
```

C#:
```
public bool AllowBlankPassword {get; set;}
```

The `AllowBlankPassword` property specifies whether calling code can use a blank password when accessing a data source. The default setting is `False`. It is a good idea to leave this setting and create passwords at the data source.

This can be a common tripping point for Microsoft Access based applications because, by default, Microsoft Access creates a blank admin password.

Provider Property (OleDb only)

Gets or sets the delimited list of supported providers.

VB.NET:
```
Public Property Provider As String
```

C#:
```
public string Provider {get; set;}
```

The `Provider` property will be ignored unless the `Unrestricted` property is set to `False` (to see how the `Unrestricted` property is set for a `Permission` object, see the `IsUnrestricted` method).

The `Provider` property is semicolon delimited, not comma delimited, so the `Permission` object parses the `Provider` string using semicolons as delimiters. In the example below, is an XML string of the corresponding `SecurityElement` object. Note the providers are sorted, but only when persisted to an XML object (for a complete discussion of XML and `SecurityElement` objects based on a `Permission` object, see the `ToXML/FromXML` Methods).

Using VB.NET:

```
Dim MyPermission as System.Data.OleDb.OleDbPermission
Dim MyPermissionAttribute as System.Data.OleDb.OleDbPermissionAttribute = New _
    System.Data.OleDb.OleDbPermissionAttribute

    With MyPermissionAttribute
        .AllowBlankPassword = True
        .Unrestricted = False
        '' set three providers, but only separate two using a semicolon
        .Provider = "Visual Foxpro; Microsoft.Jet.4.0, dBase IV"
    End with

    MyPermission = MyPermissionAttribute.CreatePermission
    Console.Write(MyPermission.Provider)
    Console.Write(ControlChars.Cr + MyPermission.ToXML.ToString)
```

The command window would contain the following, showing how the providers have been sorted:

```
Visual FoxPro; Microsoft.Jet.4.0, dBase IV
<IPermission class="System.Data.OleDb.OleDbPermission, System.Data, Version=1.0.2411.0,
        Culture=neutral, PublicKeyToken=b77a5c561934e089"
        version="1"
        AllowBlankPassword="True">
    <keyword name="provider">
        <value value=" Microsoft.Jet.4.0, dBase IV"/>
        <value value="Visual FoxPro"/>
    </keyword>
</IPermission>
```

Methods

Assert, Deny and PermitOnly Methods

These methods represent `Demand` and `Override` security actions.

As discussed earlier, it's at the location of the `Assert`, `Deny`, and `PermitOnly` commands that the CLR performs the requested security check. This also defines the scope of the permission. For a detailed discussion of code placement, see the Code Placement of Security Actions section.

Assert

When invoked on a `Permission` object, requests that the code be granted the current `Permission`, regardless of permissions granted to calls higher in the call stack.

VB.NET:

```
Not Overridable Public Sub Assert()
```

C#:

```
public void Assert();
```

Exceptions:

❑ `SecurityException` – returned when the calling code does not have permission to assert

As `Assert` is very powerful, it needs to be used carefully. Remember, administrators can install security policies to deny assertions, so your modules would not work at all in those cases.

In the example below, only the `AddNew` method is protected, because the `Assert` command is placed in the method code block.

VB.NET:

```
Imports System.Data.Odbc
Imports System.Security
Public Class DBManager
     Public Sub New()
            ''constructor code…
     End Sub
     Public Sub AddNew()
            Dim OdbcPerm As New OdbcPermission()
            OdbcPerm.AllowBlankPassword=True
            OdbcPerm.Assert()
            ''code…
     End Sub
     Public Sub GetDetails()
            ''code…
     End Sub
End Class
```

C#:

```
using System.Data.Odbc;
using System.Security;
public class DBManager {
     public DBManager(){
            //constructor code…
     }
     public void AddNew() {
            OdbcPerrmission OdbcPerm = new OdbcPermission();
            OdbcPerm.AllowBlankPassword=True;
            OdbcPerm.Assert();
            //code…
     }
     public void GetExisting() {
            //code…
     }
}
```

Deny

When invoked on a `Permission` object, requests that the code be denied the current `Permission`, regardless of permissions granted to calls higher in the call stack.

VB.NET:

```
Not Overridable Public Sub Deny()
```

C#:

```
public void Deny();
```

`Deny` is used to restrict permissions granted to your code by the CLR. Just because your code has been granted certain permissions, does not mean you want to grant all of these permissions to any calling code. You can deny certain permissions by using the `Deny` method on a `Permission` object.

You can call `Deny` on only one `Permission` object at a time with subsequent calls replacing any existing calls. In the example below, only `MyPermission1` is denied, even though both permissions have been issued `Deny` commands.

In VB.NET:

```
Dim MyPermission1 as OleDbPermission = New OleDbPermisson
Dim MyPermission2 as OleDbPermission = New OleDbPermisson

    MyPermission1.AllowBlankPassword=True
    MyPermission2.Provider="Oracle"
    MyPermission1.Deny
    MyPermission2.Deny
```

If you want both `AllowBlankPassword=True` and `Provider="Oracle"` to be denied, create one `Permission` object, set those properties within it and then issue a `Deny`:

```
Dim MyPermission1 as OleDbPermission = New OleDbPermisson

    MyPermission1.AllowBlankPassword=True
    MyPermission1.Provider="Oracle"
    MyPermisssion1.Deny
```

PermitOnly

When invoked on a `Permission` object, requests that the code be granted the current `Permission` only, regardless of permissions granted to calls higher in the call stack.

VB.NET:

```
Not Overridable Public Sub PermitOnly()
```

C#:

```
public void PermitOnly();
```

The `PermitOnly` method works as an inverted `Deny`, in that it refuses all permissions except the current `Permicison`.

775

Demand Method

When invoked on a `Permission` object, requests that all calls higher in the call stack satisfy the current `Permission`.

VB.NET:
```
Not Overridable Public Sub Demand()
```

C#:
```
public void Demand();
```

Exceptions:

❑ `SecurityException` – returned when a caller higher in the call stack does not satisfy the `Permission`

If the stack walkthrough finds a module that does not have the required `Permission`, or a module, which has invoked a `Deny` on a part of the required `Permission`, then a `SecurityException` is thrown.

Intersect and Union Methods

Two `Permission` objects can be combined with a `Union` or `Intersect` method to get a `Permission` object with their additive or common functionalities, respectively.

Union Method

The `Union` method returns an `IPermission` interface to a `Permission` object, which represents the sum of two `Permission` objects.

VB.NET:
```
Overrides Public Sub Union (ByVal target As IPermission) As IPermission
```

C#:
```
public override IPermission Union (IPermission target);
```

Intersect Method

The `Intersect` method returns an `IPermission` interface to a `Permission` object, which represents the common properties of two `Permission` objects.

VB.NET:
```
Overrides Public Sub Intersect (ByVal target As IPermission) As IPermission
```

C#:
```
public override IPermission Intersect (IPermission target);
```

A `Permission` object will always be the result of a `Union` as the method is cumulative and requires non-null objects. You may get null objects (`Nothing` in VB.NET) as the result of an `Intersect`, because the method is exclusive, demands that pass both original permissions will pass the intersection. It is important that you test the resulting `Permission` object before using it. This is shown in the following example in the `If ...Else` block:

```
Dim MyPer1 as System.Data.OdbcPermission = New System.Data.OdbcPermission
Dim MyPer2 as System.Data.OdbcPermission = New System.Data.OdbcPermission
Dim MyPer3 as System.Data.OdbcPermission = New System.Data.OdbcPermission

    MyPer1.AllowBlankPassword = True
    MyPer2.AllowBlankPassword = False
    MyPer3 = MyPer1.Intersect(MyPer2)

    If MyPer3 Is Nothing then
        Console.Write("Nothing")
    Else
        Console.Write(MyPer3.AllowBlankPassword)
    End if
```

As we have seen, the following attribute properties are dealt with in ADO.NET permissions: `Unrestricted` (Boolean), `AllowBlankPassword` (Boolean) and `Provider` (delimited string). The `Provider` property is only for `OleDbPermission` objects. The `Union` and `Intersect` methods do not always behave as we would expect them to, however, as we can see in the following sections.

Provider Property Unions and Intersects

In a union, the `Provider` property contains (as it should) all of the providers from both objects, including duplicates:

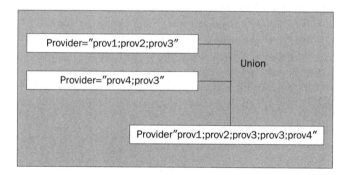

In an intersect, the `Provider` property should contain all of the common providers from both objects. In the example above, the intersect should contain prov3 only. It actually contains all of the providers from both objects, however, excluding duplicates:

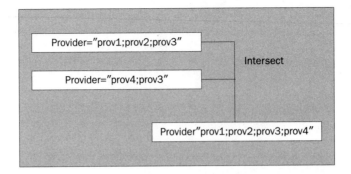

If one of the provider strings is empty, the intersect generates a null (`Nothing`) object:

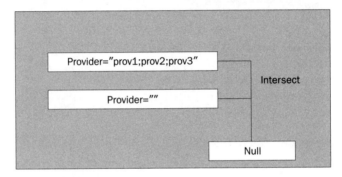

Unrestricted Unions and Intersects

As discussed earlier, the `Unrestricted` property is set in the `PermissionAttribute`. To obtain the `Unrestricted` property value of a `Permission` object, the `IsUnrestricted` method needs to be used, which will be discussed later in the chapter.

In a union, the `Unrestricted` property is set to the following values, based on the two `Permission` objects:

❑ `True/True` or `False/False` - If both `Unrestricted` properties are the same, then the `Unrestricted` property in the union is set to that value. This is the same for an intersect.

❑ `True/False` - If the `Unrestricted` properties are different then the `Unrestricted` property of the union is set to `True`.

When the values for the two `Permission` objects are different, the result for the `Unrestricted` property in an intersect is the opposite of that for a union. In this case, the `Unrestricted` property for the intersect is set to `False` instead of `True`, as previously.

AllowBlankPassword Unions and Intersects

In a union, the `AllowBlankPassword` property is set to the following values, based on the two `Permission` objects:

❑ True/True or False/False - If both `AllowBlankPassword` properties are `True` or `False`, then the `AllowBlankPassword` property for the union is set to this value

❑ True/False - If the `AllowBlankPassword` properties are different, the value for the union is set to `False`

You'll notice the true-false combination produces different results for `Unrestricted` and `AllowBlankPassword` properties.

In an intersect, the `AllowBlankPassword` property is set the same way as with the union, based on the two `Permission` objects. If the resulting `AllowBlankPassword` property is false and the resulting `Unrestricted` property is false, the intersect generates a null (`Nothing`) `Permission` object.

IsSubsetOf

Specifies whether the current `Permission` object is a subset of, or has the same properties as, a given `Permission` object.

VB.NET:

```
Overrides Public Sub IsSubsetOf (ByVal target As IPermission) As Boolean
```

C#:

```
public override bool IsSubsetOf (IPermission target);
```

The target `Permission` object is of type `IPermission`, but must be of the same type as the current `Permission` object. (For example, you can compare two `SqlClientPermission` objects, but not a `SqlClientPermisison` object and an `OleDbPermission` object).

`AllowBlankPassword` is not analyzed; the `IsSubsetOf` returns values for all combinations of `Unrestricted` and `Provider` independent of any `AllowBlankPassword` settings.

The `Unrestricted` properties are evaluated first, and dictate `IsSubsetOf` in the following manner:

❑ True/True - If both `Unrestricted` properties are `True`, then the two `Permission` objects are subsets of one another, regardless of the `AllowBlankPassword` and `Provider` properties.

❑ True/False - If the `Unrestricted` properties are different, the rule applied is that the object with the `False` value is a subset of the object with the `True` value.

❑ False/False – If both `Unrestricted` properties are `False`, then it is the `Provider` property result that dictates the `IsSubsetOf` result.

The IsSubsetOf method does not evaluate individual providers listed in the Provider property. Provider properties dictate IsSubsetOf in the following manner:

❑   An empty string is a subset of an empty string

❑   A non-empty string is a subset of an empty string

❑   A non-empty string is not a subset of a non-empty string

IsUnrestricted

Specifies whether the current Permission object allows unrestricted access to its resources.

VB.NET:

```
Not Overridable Public Function IsUnrestriced() As Boolean
```

C#:

```
public bool IsUnrestricted();
```

You can only set the Unrestricted property in the PermissionAttribute class; IsUnrestricted returns the value of the Unrestricted property. By default, the Unrestricted property is False. If you want to allow unrestricted access to the data source, create a PermissionAttribute object, set its Unrestricted property to True, and use its CreatePermission method to create the Permission object, as shown in the VB.NET example below:

```
Dim MyPermission As System.Data.SqlClientPermission
Dim MyPermissionAtrtibute as System.Data.SqlClientPermissionAttyribute = New _
        System.Data.SqlClientPermissionAttrubute
    MyPermissionAttribute.Unrestricted = True
    MyPermission = MyPermissionAttribute.CreatePermission
```

FromXML, ToXML

A Permission object can be persisted to an XML object (ToXML) and restored from an XML object (FromXML).

ToXML

VB.NET:

```
Overrides Public Function ToXml() As SecurityElement
```

C#:

```
public override SecurityElement ToXml();
```

FromXML

VB.NET:

```
Overrides Public Sub FromXml(ByVal securityelement As SecurityElement)
```

C#:

```
public override void FromXml(SecurityElement securityelement);
```

The XML object used in both functions is a `SecurityElement`. This object carries an XML schema, which defines XML elements of security related objects. If you want to access the XML string, remember that the `ToXML` function does not return a string, but rather a `SecurityElement` object. This object can then be converted to a string, using `ToString` as in the VB.NET example that follows:

```
Dim MyPermission as System.Data.OleDb.Permission
Dim MyPermissionAttribute as System.Data.OleDb.PermissionAttribute = New _
    System.Data.OleDb.PermissionAttribute

    With MyPermissionAttribute
        .AllowBlankPassword = True
        .Unrestricted = False
        .Provider = "Microsoft.Jet.4.0;Visual Foxpro"
    End with

    MyPermission = MyPermissionAttribute.CreatePermission
    Console.Write(MyPermission.ToXML.ToString)
```

The output in the command window would contain the following:

```
<IPermission class="System.Data.OleDb.OleDbPermission, System.Data, Version=1.0.2411.0,
Culture=neutral, PublicKeyToken=b77a5c561934e089"
        version="1"
        AllowBlankPassword="True">
  <keyword name="provider">
    <value value="Microsoft.Jet.4.0"/>
    <value value="Visual FoxPro"/>
  </keyword>
</IPermission>
```

Notice that the `Provider` has been parsed into keyword values and sorted. If you separate the provider list using commas, it will be treated as a single provider name:

```
Dim MyPermission as System.Data.OleDb.Permission
Dim MyPermissionAttribute as System.Data.OleDb.PermissionAttribute = New
System.Data.OleDb.PermissionAttribute

With MyPermissionAttribute
    .AllowBlankPassword = True
    .Unrestricted = False
```

```
        .Provider = "Microsoft.Jet.4.0,Visual Foxpro"
End with
MyPermission = MyPermissionAttribute.CreatePermission
Console.Write(MyPermission.ToXML.ToString)
```

Giving the following output as a result:

```
<IPermission class="System.Data.OleDb.OleDbPermission, System.Data, Version=1.0.2411.0,
Culture=neutral, PublicKeyToken=b77a5c561934e089"
        version="1"
        AllowBlankPassword="True">
  <keyword name="provider">
    <value value="Microsoft.Jet.4.0,Visual FoxPro"/>
  </keyword>
</IPermission>
```

PermissionAttribute Class

The `PermissionAttribute` class represents an action related to a `Permission` object.

Note the declarations used in this section are those of an `OleDbPermissionAttribute` class, but the other data provider `PermissionAttribute` classes follow the same syntax.

VB.NET:

```
Not Inheritable Public Class OleDbPermissionAttribute
        Inherits DBDataPermissionAttribute
```

C#:

```
public sealed class OleDbPermissionAttribute : DBDataPermissionAttribute
```

Construction

VB.NET:

```
Public Sub New(ByVal action As SecurityAction)
```

C#:

```
public OleDbPermissionAttribute(Security action);
```

The PermissionAttribute constructor creates a new instance of the PermissionAttribute class. Each permission attribute is associated with a specific action, which is specified with the SecurityAction enumeration. The SecurityAction enumeration constants are:

❑ RequestMinimum – describes the minimum set of permissions the assembly needs to run; evaluated at grant time

❑ RequestOptional – describes the optional set of permissions the assembly would like to have, but are not required for its execution; evaluated at grant time

❑ RequestRefuse – describes the set of permissions the assembly does not want to have; evaluated at grant time

❑ LinkDemand – demands a permission from the immediate caller in the stack; enforced at compile time

❑ InheritanceDemand – demands a permission from any inheriting classes; enforced at load time

❑ Demand – demands specific permissions be satisfied by all members in the stack; enforced at load time

❑ Assert – requests specific permissions be granted regardless of granted permissions of members higher in the call stack; enforced at run time

❑ Deny – requests specific permissions be granted regardless of granted permissions of members higher in the call stack; enforced at run time

Properties

Action Property

Gets or sets a security action.

VB.NET:

```
Public Property Action As SecurityAction
```

C#:

```
public securityaction Action {get; set;}
```

The Action property specifies the security action associated with the PermissionAttribute. The action is set using the SecurityAction Enum (see the PermissionAttribute constructor for a discussion of the SecurityAction Enum constants).

AllowBlankPassword Property

This property performs the same function in the Permission object.

Provider Property (OleDb only)

This property performs the same function in the `Permission` object.

Unrestricted Property

Specifies whether the current `PermissionAttribute` object allows unrestricted access to its resources.

VB.NET:

```
Public Property Unrestriced As Boolean
```

C#:

```
public bool Unrestricted {get; set;}
```

The `Unrestricted` property is used to grant/deny complete access to resources linked by the `PermissionAttribute` object. More often than not, you will not use this property. If you need unrestricted access to a database, use the database administrator credentials during creation of the `Connection` object instead.

Methods

CreatePermission Method

Creates a `Permission` object configured using the current `PermissionAttribute` object properties.

VB.NET:

```
Overrides Public Function CreatePermission () As IPermission
```

C#:

```
public override IPermission CreatePermission();
```

The `CreatePermission` method creates an instance of a `Permission` object, which inherits the specifications laid out in the current `PermissionAttribute`. This is the preferred way of creating `Permission` objects. You can set the `Unrestriced` property only in a `PermissionAttribute`.

Code Placement of Security Actions

Declarative Security Syntax

Declarative syntax implements security by defining attributes which are placed in the code metadata. The attribute describes both the `SecurityAction` and any other properties of the `Permission`. The placement of the attribute defines the scope of the permission, as demonstrated in the code below. `Requests`, `Demands`, and `Overrides` can use Declarative syntax, which is also shown in the following examples.

This first code example shows the creation of an unprotected assembly (in VB.NET):

```
Imports System.Security.Permissions
Improts System.Data.Oledb
Namespace MyNamespace
     Public class MyClass
            Public Function MyMethod_1()
                    'code...
            End Function
            Public Function MyMethod_2()
                    'code...
            End Function
     End Class
     Public class MyOtherClass
            Public Function MyOtherMethod()
                    'code...
            End Function
     End Class
End Namespace
```

In order to protect the assembly, the highlighted line can be used:

```
Imports System.Security.Permissions
Improts System.Data.Oledb
<Assembly: OleDbPermission(SecurityAction.RequestOptional, Unrestricted:=True)>
Namespace MyNamespace
     Public Class MyClass
            Public Function MyMethod_1()
                    'code...
            End Function
            Public Function MyMethod_2()
                    'code...
            End Function
     End Class
     Public Class MyOtherClass
            Public Function MyOtherMethod()
                    'code...
            End Function
     End Class
End Namespace
```

If you want to protect the class instead, you could insert the following code into your example:

```
Imports System.Security.Permissions
Improts System.Data.Oledb
Namespace MyNamespace
     <OleDbPermission(SecurityAction.Demand, Provider:="Oracle" > Public class
MyClass
            Public Function MyMethod_1()
                    ''code...
            End Function
            Public Function MyMethod_2()
                    ''code...
```

```
        End Function
    End Class
    Public class MyOtherClass
        Public Function MyOtherMethod()
            'code...
        End Function
    End Class
End Namespace
```

Finally, should you wish to only protect the method, the code addition could be made as follows:

```
Imports System.Security.Permissions
Improts System.Data.Oledb
Namespace MyNamespace
    Public Class MyClass
        Public Function <OleDbPermission(SecurityAction.Deny,
AllowBlankPassword=True> MyMethod()
            'code...
        End Function
        Public Function MyMethod_2()
            'code...
        End Function
    End Class
    Public Class MyOtherClass
        Public Function MyOtherMethod()
            'code...
        End Function
    End Class
End Namespace
```

Imperative Security Syntax

Imperative syntax implements security by creating new `Permission` objects in code. Again, the placement of the attribute defines the scope of the permission, as demonstrated in the VB.NET code below. Unlike Declarative syntax, only `Demands` and `Overrides` can use Imperative syntax.

To begin with, we look at an unprotected class:

```
Imports System.Security.Permissions
Improts System.Data.Oledb
Namespace MyNamespace
    Public Class MyClass
        Public Function MyMethod_1()
            'code...
        End Function
        Public Function MyMethod_2()
            'code...
        End Function
    End Class
    Public Class MyOtherClass
        Public Function MyOtherMethod()
            'code...
        End Function
    End Class
End Namespace
```

Once again, by making a code addition, we protect the class:

```
Imports System.Security.Permissions
Improts System.Data.Oledb
Namespace MyNamespace
      Public Class MyClass
            Dim MyPermission As OleDbPermission = New OleDbPermission
            MyPermission.AllowBlankPassword = True
            MyPermission.Demand
            Public Function MyMethod_1()
                  'code...
            End Function
            Public Function MyMethod_2()
                  'code...
            End Function
      End Class
      Public class MyOtherClass
            Public Function MyOtherMethod()
                  'code...
            End Function
      End Class
End Namespace
```

Finally, we can protect the method by inserting the code as follows:

```
Imports System.Security.Permissions
Improts System.Data.Oledb
Namespace MyNamespace
      Public Class MyClass
            Public Function MyMethod_1()
                  Dim MyPermission As OleDbPermission = New OleDbPermission
                  MyPermission.AllowBlankPassword = True
                  MyPermission.Demand
                  'code...
            End Function
            Public Function MyMethod_2()
                  'code...
            End Function
      End Class
      Public class MyOtherClass
            Public Function MyOtherMethod()
                  'code...
            End Function
      End Class
End Namespace
```

Syntax Usage

As previously stated, `Requests` can only be performed by Declarative syntax and not Imperative. They are used to inform the CLR security system of any permissions your applications needs or doesn't need. `Demands` and `Overrides`, on the other hand, can be implemented using both types of syntax. You would usually use imperative syntax over declarative when you want to make checks at run time, for example passing a user-provided `Provider` property. Finally, you can use Declarative syntax when you want to protect the entire assembly

Summary

ADO.NET introduced several significant security functionalities, which are inherited from the .NET framework. ADO.NET uses code access permissions to

- ❑ Specify assembly permissions requirements at load time
- ❑ Request specific permissions requirements of calls higher in the call stack

Each data provider in ADO.NET (OleDb, SqlClient and Odbc) has a class pair to manage permissions. The following three permissions are enforced using ADO.NET:

- ❑ `AllowBlankPassword` – specifies whether the code can access a data source using a blank password
- ❑ `Unrestricted` – specifies whether the code is granted full access to a data source
- ❑ `Provider` (OleDb only) – specifies the providers allowed (Odbc and SqlClient are providers themselves, so this property is unnecessary)

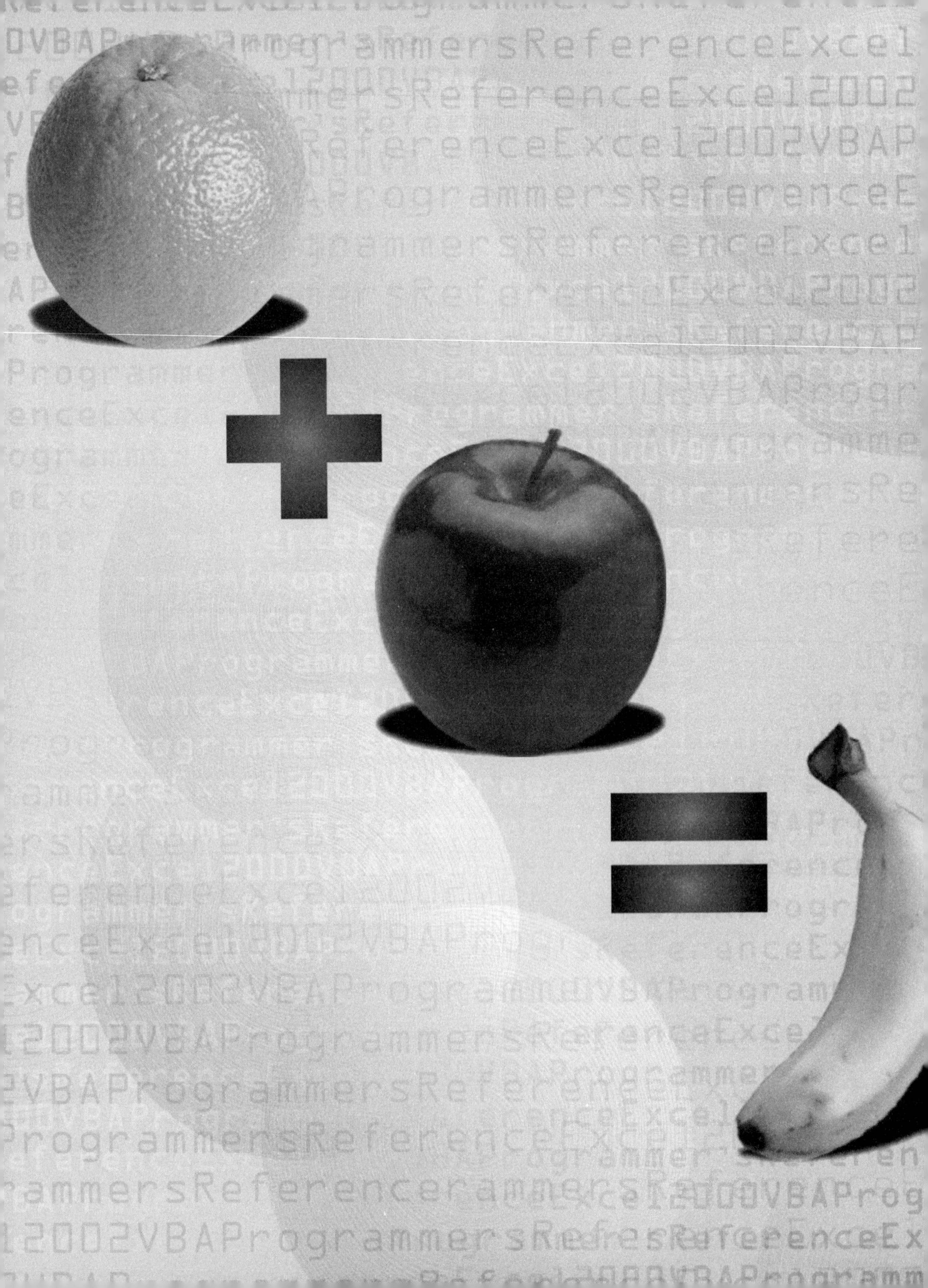

16

COM Interoperability

What is **COM Interoperability** (**Interop**)? Why is it important? These are some of the basic questions that might come to mind when **Interop** is mentioned. And if you are developing a data access layer, another question pops into mind. How does this affect our components when we have ADO.NET to take care of all the needs as far as data access is concerned? In this chapter, we will arrive at some answers to these questions, and gain an understanding of how to use Interop in our applications.

Interop enables the interoperation of managed code with unmanaged code, and vice versa.

> **The code that runs under the** Common Language Runtime (CLR) **is managed code, and the code that runs outside CLR is unmanaged code. For example, all the components (assemblies) that are created using the .NET framework are managed code, and all the components that are developed with Win32 API are unmanaged code.**

The.NET framework introduces a completely new model for application development and deployment. We no longer have to think about the choice of programming language because every language generates the same metadata in **Microsoft Intermediate Language** (**MSIL**) format. At the end of the day it does not matter how the metadata was generated, it will all be **Just In Time** (**JIT**) compiled to same native (for example x86) code.

If we closely study all the evolutionary changes that every developer will have to take into consideration, it may not be very incorrect to say that we will have to unlearn all the old concepts and start from square one. Does this mean that all the old applications and components that you have been using for quite some time on the server side or middle tier will stop working in .NET framework, or cannot be used in the .NET enabled applications? Absolutely not. Our efforts and investment in the old and tested components will not be wasted at all. This is where **Interop** comes into play.

COM Interop allows us to utilize existing COM (Component Object Model) components in our .NET applications without needing to modify the COM components in any way. As .NET gains acceptance we will hear a lot about **Interop** in the .NET framework. This chapter will first give a brief overview of **Interop** and then demonstrate the ways in which it can be used to access classic ADO components, and exploit facilities not yet developed for ADO.NET to leverage your .NET data access components.

Interop enables managed code to call unmanaged code transparently, and for unmanaged code to call managed code. In practice, this means that we do not need to rewrite unmanaged components to operate with .NET applications, and that we can develop managed components to work with unmanaged components. All we need to do, is make use of some utilities and tools provided with the .NET SDK to integrate existing applications with managed applications. We will look at these tools and utilities later in the chapter.

In an ideal world, we would probably want to covert all existing unmanaged code to managed code. In many cases this would be impractical, given certain design constraints, however, and – more importantly – the time framework in which to roll out the new application. Sometimes it is not possible to convert the unmanaged code to managed code at all: for example, if the source code is not available. Also, there may be a particular type of operation that we wish to implement: for instance, utilizing a recordset with a server side cursor, which cannot be achieved with ADO.NET. In both these types of situations, **Interop** comes to the rescue by enabling the use of classic ADO technology. Also, there are some other technologies, complementing ADO, such as **Microsoft ActiveX Data Objects Extensions for Data Definition Language and Security** (ADOX), **Jet Engine and Replication Objects** (JRO) and **ADO for Multi-Dimensional Data** (ADOMD) that are not supported by ADO.NET. Interop is the only way to integrate these technologies into a managed application. Therefore, **Interop** is going to play a very important role when migrating existing applications to .NET.

This chapter will not discuss how to use ADO, ADOX, JRO, and ADOMD data access technologies. If you wish to learn more about them, please consult Professional ADO 2.5 Programming (Wrox Press, ISBN 1-861002-75-0) and ADO 2.6 Programmer's Reference (Wrox Press, ISBN 1-861004-63-X).

Garbage Collection

All the managed objects are garbage collected, meaning that when a particular object is not required anymore, and there is no one holding any reference to it, the garbage collector (GC) releases memory associated with it from the managed memory heap. We are however, talking about **Interop** with unmanaged code. We know that there is no GC for code running outside the CLR. So what happens to the managed components that are used by the unmanaged components? What releases the references for unmanaged COM components when they are used inside the managed code?

The .NET framework performs the following operations for the interoperation of managed and unmanaged code:

- When a managed object is marshaled out of CLR to the unmanaged code, a COM Callable Wrapper (**CCW**) is created

- When an unmanaged object is referenced in the managed code, a Runtime Callable Wrapper (**RCW**) is created

These wrapper objects act as the conduits between managed and unmanaged execution engines. These objects act as the proxies that marshal the calls between the managed and unmanaged objects.

When a COM client calls into a managed object, the runtime creates a new managed object and a CCW for that object. The object's lifetime is managed by this CCW. When the COM client calls `AddRef` on this managed object, the CCW holds the reference count for it. Therefore, to the COM client, this managed object appears exactly like a regular COM component. When the `Release` method is called on the object, CCW decrements the reference count on it. When there are no outstanding references to this managed object (in other words the reference count drops down to zero), the CCW releases the managed object in the CLR. In the next cycle of garbage collection, this released managed object gets removed from the managed heap. The COM clients using the managed objects should follow the classic COM rules for reference counting, and should make a `Release` call for every `AddRef` call. If the unmanaged code forgets to release the managed code, the CCW will keep on holding to the object, and the garbage collector will never collect it.

When the managed code creates an instance of unmanaged COM components, the CLR creates the RCW for this component and maintains the reference count for it. Every time a new object of this component is created, the reference count is incremented on this RCW. When all of the referenced object are no longer needed, the RCW releases the reference to the COM object and during next garbage collection cycle this wrapper (RCW) gets collected.

Error Handling

Before we dig deep into the use of **Interop** for data access components, there is one important aspect that we should look at. It is the way error handling mechanism works in **Interop**. In the existing COM components, the error conditions are communicated to the caller via HRESULT codes. If the call succeeds, the components return S_OK, otherwise an error code (E_FAIL, or some custom code) is returned to the caller.

The managed code takes a different approach. The errors are reported by means of exceptions. If a component wants to report a failure condition to the caller, it throws an exception. This exception can be one of the .NET framework provided exception classes (for example, InvalidCastException, InvalidOperationException, and so on) or it can be a user-defined exception (a class derived from System.Exception class). When a COM component returns an error, the **Interop** layer converts it to one of the framework-defined classes and stores the HRESULT code into HResult property of the System.Exception class object. When a managed code throws an exception, the **Interop** layer converts it to an HRESULT value.

Therefore, if our managed code is calling method of unmanaged code, then we should guard our implementation by providing exception handlers for the errors that will be returned. On the other side of spectrum, if we are implementing a managed code that will be used by unmanaged code, we should store the HRESULT code in the HResult property of the exception class before throwing the exception to the caller.

Tools For Interop

Managed code, running in CLR, is not capable, by itself, of crossing the CLR boundary to make calls into unmanaged components. The managed code has no knowledge of the data types defined by the unmanaged code. The .NET framework is all about data types, so it needs some mechanism to refer to the data types defined in unmanaged code. The COM components define their types in the type library, which could be present in a separate file (.TLB file) or embedded as a resource in the DLL or EXE file. The .NET component's meta-data is contained in the assembly file. The .NET framework provides the tools to convert between CLR and COM data type information.

TLBIMP (Type Library Importer)

This is a command line tool that can be used to convert the co classes and interfaces information, contained in a COM component's type library, into the .NET metadata information. The following example shows the simplest use of this tool to convert the ADO type library, embedded in MSADO15.DLL, to the .NET metadata, defining the corresponding CRL types:

```
C:\>tlbimp msado15.dll /out:ClassicADO.dll
```

The first argument is the name of the file that contains the COM type library. This file can be a DLL, EXE, OLB, OCX or TLB file. The second argument is optional parameter that can be used to fine-tune the output from the tool. In this case, I have used the /out parameter, which specifies the name of the output file (ClassicADO.dll in this case). The detailed explanation of each optional parameter is out of scope of this book. We can call this tool with a /? option to see all the options supported, and a brief explanation of each one of them. The following screen short shows the list of options generated by the /? Parameter:

For detailed explanation of these optional parameters, refer to the .NET Framework Tools section in the .NET Framework SDK Documentation.

The tool converts the entire type library into the .NET metadata assembly. It cannot be used for partial conversion of the type library. Once we have created the assembly describing the metadata, we can discard the source type library file. The **Interop** operation does not depend on the source file anymore. The MANIFEST created in the assembly saves the GUID of the co class as `GuidAttribute`. The CLR creates the instance of COM object using this information from the registry.

We can create the unmanaged objects in your managed applications simply by calling new operator. There is no `CoCreateInstance` and no `QueryInterface` call. The RCW takes care of all these steps behind the scene. It calls the `CoCreateInstance` method by using the GUID stored in the manifest of the metadata assembly generated for the COM object.

TLBEXP (Type Library Exporter)

This command line tool is the counterpart of the TLBIMP tool. It converts the metadata contained in a managed assembly into a type library. The following example shows the use of this tool:

```
C:\>tlbexp myassembly.dll /out:unmancode.dll
```

Like TLBIMP, this tool also supports a few optional parameters. The above example uses the /out parameter to specify the name of the output file. The detailed explanation of each optional parameter is out of scope of this book. We can call this tool with the /? option to see all the options supported and a brief explanation of each one of them. The following screen short shows the list of options generated by the /? Parameter:

For detailed explanations of these optional parameters, refer to the *.NET Framework Tools* section in the *.NET Framework SDK Documentation*.

Visual Studio.NET

We can directly add references to an already registered COM component's type library using Visual Studio 7.0. It will generate the assembly containing the metadata information corresponding to the types contained in the type library. It is like using TLBIMP tool where the IDE defines the optional parameter.

We can add reference to the type library by selecting COM tab on the **Add Reference** dialog box. This will bring up the list of all type libraries registered on the system. Select the one that you want to add the reference to. These two steps will create the assembly and add the reference to the project. The following screen shots show the addition of reference for ADO 2.7 type library in a project:

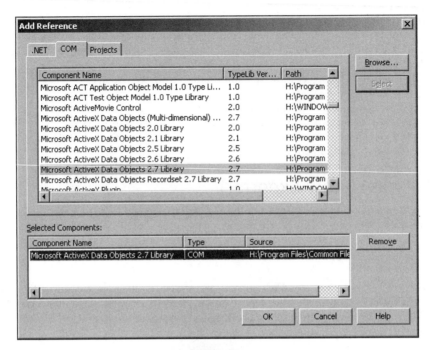

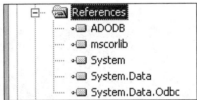

The type library has been added with the namespace ADODB.

TypeLibConverter Class

This class, defined in `System.Runtime.InteropServices` namespace, provides a programmatic way of creating the metadata information from a COM type library. This class has two methods, `ConvertTypeLibToAssembly` and `ConvertAssemblyToTypeLib` that do the conversion of types. We will not be discussing these methods in this book. For more details, refer to this class in .NET Framework Documentation.

After the assembly has been created using one of the above tools, we need to refer to this assembly when compiling the source code. Depending on the programming language used, we can refer to the namespace of this assembly as shown below:

VB.NET:

```
Imports ClassicADO
```

C#:

```
using ClassicADO;
```

If you are using Visual Studio 7.0, then you don't have to do any manual steps to add reference to the assembly containing the metadata information. For command line compilation of the code, use the /r option to add the reference to the DLL.

VB.NET:

```
vbc /r:ClassicADO.dll Foo.vb
```

C#:

```
csc /r:ClassicADO.dll Foo.cs
```

ADO in Managed Applications

In the last few years, ADO technology has come a long way. A lot of hard work and investment has been poured into developing robust, scalable, and reliable components that use this data access technology. The .NET data access class, `OleDbDataAdapter`, takes this into account and provides the `Fill` method, which takes an ADO `Recordset` object as its input parameter and populates the `DataSet` object with the supplied data. For more details, refer to the `Fill` method of the `OleDbDataAdapter` class in the `DataAdapter` chapter.

This is one approach that we can use to employ ADO `Recordset` objects in our managed application. We can use the `TlbImp` tool to import the type library from existing COM objects, that have methods and properties returning the `Recordset` objects.

Consider a case of a typical COM component, for example, `Shop.dll`, which has a method returning a `Recordset` of inventory records. First, we would use `TlbImp` to import the type library into a .NET assembly:

```
C:\>tlbimp /out:ShopObjects.dll Shop.dll
```

This imports the type library to `ShopObjects.dll`. Next, add reference to this managed assembly into a managed application:

```
vbc /r:ShopObjects.dll /r:ClassicADO.dll ShopApplication.vb
```

```
csc /r:ShopObjects.dll /r:ClassicADO.dll ShopApplication.cs
```

Then in our managed assembly, create this unmanaged component as a regular CLR object using the new operator.

Creating .NET Metadata For ADO

The first step for using classic ADO objects in our managed application is to establish a reference to the metadata file, describing all the interfaces exposed by it. By default, the ADO library file, `msado15.dll`, is present in the following folder:

```
<System Drive>\Program Files\Common Files\System\Ado
```

We would use the TLBIMP tool to generate the .NET compatible assembly that we will refer to from managed code:

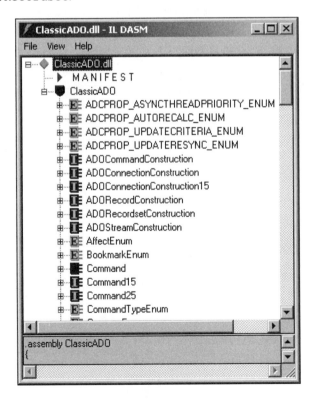

In the above example, we have called TLBIMP from root directory, while the msado15.dll file is located in that folder. The reason we are able to do is, because we have specified the folder location of ADO files in the path variable of the system environment. Otherwise, it would be necessary that the TLBIMP tool be invoked from the same folder as the source file. Although the source file is not in the root folder, the output will be created in the root folder (C:/) and then copied to any folder from where we want to refer this metadata assembly. All the examples in the subsequent sections in this chapter invoke the TLBIMP tool from the root folder using the same approach of setting system environment's path variable.

This operation will generate a .NET assembly ClassicADO.dll containing the metadata for the ADO library with the namespace ClassicADO. We can provide a fully qualified name for all the ADO objects scoped within this namespace such as ClassicADO.Connection, ClassicADO.Command, and ClassicADO.Recordset:

Reference to the ADO Assembly

To compile the ADO assembly generated by the TLBIMP tool into the managed code, we would add a reference as follows:

VB.NET:

```
vbc /t:library /r:ClassicADO.dll /out:EmployeeDB.dll EmployeeDB.vb
```

C#:

```
csc /t:library /r:ClassicADO.dll /out:EmployeeDB.dll EmployeeDB.cs
```

Using a Recordset to Populate a DataSet

The following example shows the use of ADO objects in a managed assembly. This example requires use of server side cursor support, which is not provided by ADO.NET. It opens an ADO Connection by providing a connection string and then calls the Execute method to get the Recordset object. It then uses this Recordset object to populate the DataSet using the Fill method of the OleDbDataAdapter class. This approach can also be used to get a Recordset with a server side cursor and pass it to the unmanaged code.

VB.NET:

```
Dim strQuery As String = "SELECT * FROM Employees WHERE EmployeeID = 1"
Dim strConn As String = "Provider=SQLOLEDB; Data Source = SYNCMONK" & _
                "; Initial Catalog = Northwind; User ID = sa; Pwd ="

' Create a new instance ADO Connection object
Dim dbConn As New Connection ()
dbConn.CursorLocation = CursorLocationEnum.adUseClient

' Open the connection with specified connection string.
dbConn.Open (strConn, "", "", (int)ConnectModeEnum.adModeUnknown)

' Execute SQL query to get the emploee record.
Object recsAffected = Null
Dim rs Recordset = dbConn.Execute (strQuery, recsAffected,
                    CType (CommandTypeEnum.adCmdText, Integer))

Dim dtSet As New DataSet ()
Dim dtAdapter As New OleDbDataAdapter ()
dtAdapter.Fill (dtSet, rs, "Employee")
rs.Close ()
```

C#:

```
string strQuery = "SELECT * FROM Employees WHERE EmployeeID = 1";
string strConn = "Provider=SQLOLEDB; Data Source = Northwind";
strConn += "; Initial Catalog = Northwind";
strConn += "; User ID = sa; Pwd = ;";

// Create a new instance ADO Connection object
Connection dbConn = new Connection ();
dbConn.CursorLocation = CursorLocationEnum.adUseServer;
// Open the connection with specified connection string.
dbConn.Open (strConn, "", "", (int)ConnectModeEnum.adModeUnknown);

// Execute SQL query to get the employee record.
object recsAffected = null;
_Recordset rs = dbConn.Execute (strQuery, out recsAffected,
                    (int)CommandTypeEnum.adCmdText);
```

```
DataSet dtSet = new DataSet ();
OleDbDataAdapter dtAdapter = new OleDbDataAdapter ();
dtAdapter.Fill (dtSet, rs, "Employee");
rs.Close ();
```

Note that the second parameter to the `Execute` method call on the ADO `Connection` has been passed as a `System.Object` and not as a `VARIANT`. The reason is that `VARIANT` is an unmanaged data type and **Interop** marshals this as a `System.Object`.

> Whenever we are not clear about what data types to use for the unmanaged method parameters, it is a good idea to use the *ILDASM* tool and take a look at the IL Code generated for the method. IL Code generated by the TLBIMP can provide complete information about the type of parameters that need to be passed into a method call, and what kind of output it will return. The IL code acts like documentation for the imported unmanaged objects.

ADOX In Managed Applications

ADO.NET provides a framework for manipulating existing data sources. Like classic ADO, it does not provide direct support for creating new data source objects, such as physical data files, maintaining users, and groups and working with the permission objects. ADO provides the **Microsoft ActiveX Data Objects Extension for Data Definition Language and Security (ADOX)** model, an extension library, to accomplish these tasks. But in ADO.NET, there is no direct or indirect support for these tasks. This means that we must rely on **Interop** to make calls into the ADOX library and perform these operations. Although ADO.NET provides managed providers for SQL Server (version 7.0 and higher), OLE DB providers, and native ODBC drivers, the use of ADOX through **Interop** is still limited by the ADOX features supported by the particular OLE DB provider. Of the OLE DB providers currently available, Microsoft Jet has complete support for ADOX. The OLE DB providers for SQL Server, Oracle, DB2, and others, provide a very limited implementation of ADOX.

Creating .NET Metadata For ADOX

The first step for using ADOX in a managed app is to establish a reference to the metadata file describing all the interfaces exposed by it. The ADOX library file name is `msadox.dll`, which is present in the following folder on your machine.

```
<System Drive>\Program Files\Common Files\System\Ado
```

Use the TlbImp tool to generate the .NET compatible assembly that we will refer to from managed code:

This operation will generate a .NET assembly `ADOX.dll` containing the metadata for the ADOX library with the ADOX namespace. We can provide fully qualified names for all the ADOX model objects scoped within this namespace, such as `ADOX.Catlog` and `ADOX.Table`:

Reference to the ADOX Assembly

We will need to add reference to the ADOX assembly, generated by the TLBIMP tool, to compile it with our managed code. The following example adds a reference to `ADOX.dll` to generate a managed component `EmployeeDB.dll`.

VB.NET:

```
vbc /t:library /r:ADOX.dll /out:EmployeeDB.dll EmployeeDB.vb
```

C#:

```
csc /t:library /r:ADOX.dll /out:EmployeeDB.dll EmployeeDB.cs
```

Creating a Microsoft Access Database File

The Catalog object in ADOX can be used to create a new Access database by calling the `Create` method.

The following code shows the use of the ADOX metadata assembly in a managed assembly to create a new database. First, it creates a new instance of the `Catalog` object simply by calling `New` operator. It instantiates a `Catalog` object, and then the `Create` method is called on it with a connection string. The connection string specifies that Jet4.0 OLE DB provider will be used to create the new Microsoft Access Database file:

VB.NET:

```
Option Explicit On
Option Strict On
Imports System
Imports ADOX

Namespace ADOX_Interop
 Public Class ADOX_EmployeeDB

 Public Function CreateEmployeeDB () As Boolean

    Try
        Dim strConn As String = "Provider=Microsoft.JET.OLEDB.4.0;" & _
                          "Data Source = C:\\EmployeeDB.mdb"
        ' Create instance of Catalog object.
        Dim dbCatalog As New Catalog ()
        ' Call Create method to create mdb file.
        dbCatalog.Create (strConn)
    Catch ex As System.Exception
        Console.WriteLine (ex.Message)
        Return False
    End Try
    Return True
  End Function
 End Class
End Namespace
```

C#:

```
using System;
using ADOX;

namespace ADOX_Interop
{
  public class ADOX_EmployeeDB
  {
    public ADOX_EmployeeDB (){}
    public void CreateEmployeeDB ()
    {
      try
      {
        string strConn="Provider=Microsoft.JET.OLEDB.4.0;";
          strConn += "Data Source = C:\\EmployeeDB.mdb";
        // Create instance of Catalog object.
        Catalog dbCatalog = new Catalog ();
        //Call Create method to create mdb file.
          dbCatalog.Create (strConn);
      }
      catch (System.Exception ex)
      {
          Console.WriteLine (ex.Message);
          Return false;
      }
      return true;
    }
  }
}
```

Creating Tables in an Access Database

The Catalog object in ADOX exposes Tables object. The Tables object exposes the Columns, Index, Keys, and Properties collections. We can use these objects to append a new table to the database.

The following code sample shows how we can use a Catalog object to create a Microsoft Access 2000 database .mdb file. First, the Catalog object is created to which the table will be added. Then a new instance of the Table object is created. This is the object to which all the data columns will be added. Then new data columns are appended to the Columns collection of the Table. The Column object exposes properties like Name, Attributes, DefinedSize, NumericScale, Precision, and Type. For the sake of brevity, in this example only three properties have been specified for each column, name, data type and the size. After adding the columns to the collection, the table is appended to Tables collection of the catalog by calling Append method. Finally, a primary key index is added to the Indexes collection of the table. The Index object exposes properties like Name, Unique, PrimaryKey, and so on, that can be used to control its action.

VB.NET:

```
Dim strConn As String = "Provider=Microsoft.JET.OLEDB.4.0;" & _
                   "Data Source = C:\\EmployeeDB.mdb"
' Create instance of Catalog object
Dim dbCatalog As New Catalog ()
dbCatalog.Create (strConn)

' Create instance of Table object
Dim dtTable As New Table ()
With dtTable
     .Name = "Address"
     .Columns.Append ("AddressID", ADOX.DataTypeEnum.adInteger, 4)
     .Columns.Append ("Street", ADOX.DataTypeEnum.adVarWChar, 128)
     .Columns.Append ("City", ADOX.DataTypeEnum.adVarWChar, 128)
     .Columns.Append ("State", ADOX.DataTypeEnum.adVarWChar, 128)
     .Columns.Append ("Zip", ADOX.DataTypeEnum.adVarWChar, 128)
     .Columns.Append ("Country", ADOX.DataTypeEnum.adVarWChar, 128)
End With

' Append the table to catalog.
dbCatalog.Tables.Append (CType(dtTable, Object))

' Create the primary key column with unique values.
Dim primKeyIdx As New Index ()
With primKeyIdx
     .Name = "UniqueAddrID"
     .Unique = True
     .PrimaryKey = True
     .Columns.Append ("AddressID", ADOX.DataTypeEnum.adInteger, 4)
End With
' Append the primary index to table.
dtTable.Indexes.Append (CType (primKeyIdx, Object), Nothing)
```

C#:

```
string strConn = "Provider=Microsoft.JET.OLEDB.4.0;" +
               "Data Source = J:\\NetProjects\\EmployeeDB.mdb";
// Create instance of Catalog object.
Catalog dbCatalog = new Catalog ();
dbCatalog.Create (strConn);

// Create instance of Table object.
Table dtTable = new Table ();
```

```
dtTable.Name = "Address";
dtTable.Columns.Append ("AddressID", ADOX.DataTypeEnum.adInteger, 4);
dtTable.Columns.Append ("Street", ADOX.DataTypeEnum.adVarWChar, 128);
dtTable.Columns.Append ("City", ADOX.DataTypeEnum.adVarWChar, 128);
dtTable.Columns.Append ("State", ADOX.DataTypeEnum.adVarWChar, 128);
dtTable.Columns.Append ("Zip", ADOX.DataTypeEnum.adVarWChar, 128);
dtTable.Columns.Append ("Country", ADOX.DataTypeEnum.adVarWChar, 128);

// Append the table to catalog.
dbCatalog.Tables.Append ((object)dtTable);

// Create the primary key column with unique values.
Index primKeyIdx = new Index ();
primKeyIdx.Name = "UniqueAddrID";
primKeyIdx.Unique = true;
primKeyIdx.PrimaryKey = true;
primKeyIdx.Columns.Append ("AddressID", ADOX.DataTypeEnum.adInteger, 4);

// Append the index to table.
dtTable.Indexes.Append ((object)primKeyIdx, null);
```

We can use ADOX objects through **Interop** to improve the functionality of the managed applications. Before using any of the ADOX features it is important to read the documentation for that particular OLE DB managed provider to check what support is available and what is not. For example, using the OLE DB managed provider for SQL Server, we cannot create a new table in the database as we would have using the `Create` method of the `Catalog` object in classic ADO.

The following example shows how to use ADO and ADOX objects to create a new data table in a SQL Server database.

VB.NET:

```
Dim strConn As String = "Provider=SQLOLEDB;" & _
 "Data Source = DOTNET; Database = FashionHouse;" & _
 "User ID = foo; Pwd = ;"
' Create instance of Catalog object.
Dim dbCatalog As New Catalog ()
' Create ADO Connection object
Dim dbConn As New Connection ()
dbConn.Open (strConn)
dbCatalog.ActiveConnection = CType (dbConn, Object)

' Create instance of Table object.
Dim dtTable As New Table ()
With dtTable
    .Name = "Categories"
    .Columns.Append ("CategoryID", ADOX.DataTypeEnum.adInteger, 4)
    .Columns.Append ("Name", ADOX.DataTypeEnum.adVarWChar, 64)
    .Columns.Append ("Descr", ADOX.DataTypeEnum.adVarWChar, 128)
End With

' Append the table to catalog.
dbCatalog.Tables.Append (CType(dtTable, Object))
```

JRO In Managed Applications

ADO.NET does not provide direct support for features such as compacting a database, database replication, replica synchronization, setting passwords, and encryption on databases, and so on. These features are available in the classic ADO model through **Jet and Replication Objects** (JRO). An application can provide all these features by using Interop to access JRO objects.

Creating .NET Metadata For JRO

To establish a reference to the metadata file, describing all the interfaces exposed by the JRO library, we would use the TlbImp tool on `msjro.dll` to create a .NET enabled assembly. This library file resides, by default, in the following folder on your machine:

```
<System Drive>\Program Files\Common Files\System\Ado
```

This operation will generate a .NET assembly `JRO.dll` containing the metadata for the JRO library with JRO namespace. We can provide a fully qualified name for all the JRO model objects scoped within this namespace, such as `JRO.Replica` and `JRO.Filter`:

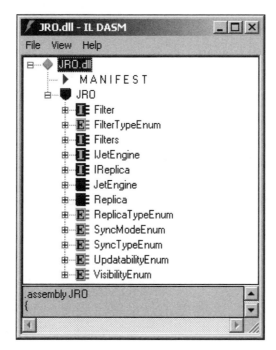

Reference to the JRO Assembly

To compile the JRO assembly generated by the TLBIMP tool into the managed code, we would add a reference, as follows:

VB.NET:

```
vbc /t:library /r:JRO.dll /out:EmployeeDB.dll EmployeeDB.vb
```

C#:

```
csc /t:library /r:JRO.dll /out:EmployeeDB.dll EmployeeDB.cs
```

Replicating an Access Database

The following example shows how a JRO Replica object can be used to create a full replication of a Microsoft Access database.

VB.NET:

```
Dim strConn As String = "Provider=Microsoft.JET.OLEDB.4.0;" & _
                    "Data Source = C:\\EmployeeDB.mdb"
Dim strRep As String = "J:\\ EmployeeDB_Rep.mdb"
'Create an instance of Replica object
Dim dbRep As New Replica ()
dbRep.MakeReplicable ("J:\\NetProjects\\EmployeeDB.mdb", True)

' Call CreateReplica method to create replica of Employee database
dbRep.CreateReplica (strRep, "Replica of Employee Database", _
                    ReplicaTypeEnum.jrRepTypeFull)
```

C#:

```
string strRep = "C:\\EmployeeDB_Rep.mdb";
// Create an instance of Replica object
Replica dbRep = new Replica ();
dbRep.MakeReplicable ("C:\\EmployeeDB.mdb", true);
// Call CreateReplica method to create replica of Employee database
dbRep.CreateReplica (strRep, "Replica of Employee Database",
                    ReplicaTypeEnum.jrRepTypeFull,
                VisibilityEnum.jrRepVisibilityGlobal, -1,
                UpdatabilityEnum.jrRepUpdFull);
```

Please note that all parameters for the CreateReplica method (ReplicaType, Visibility, Priority and Updatability) must be specified in C#, whereas in VB they are optional. Does this mean that the managed code generated for VB is different than that generated for C#? Before I answer this question, lets look at the method signature generated by TLBIMP tool:

```
.method public hidebysig newslot virtual
    instance void  CreateReplica(
            [in] string  marshal( bstr) replicaName,
                [in] string  marshal( bstr) description,
                [in][opt] valuetype JRO.ReplicaTypeEnum ReplicaType,
                [in][opt] valuetype JRO.VisibilityEnum Visibility,
                [in][opt] int32 Priority,
                [in][opt] valuetype JRO.UpdatabilityEnum updatability
            ) runtime managed internalcall
{
  .custom instance void
  [mscorlib]System.Runtime.InteropServices.DispIdAttribute::.ctor(int32)
      = ( 01 00 0E 00 02 60 00 00 )                  // .....`..
  .param [3] = int32(0x00000002)
  .param [4] = int32(0x00000001)
  .param [5] = int32(0xFFFFFFFF)
  .param [6] = int32(0x00000000)
  .override JRO.IReplica::CreateReplica
}
```

Pay attention to the last four parameters of the `CreateReplica` method. There are two attributes associated with each one of these. The first is `[in]` indicating that it is an `INPUT` parameter, and the second is `[opt]` indicating that it is an `OPTIONAL` parameter.

Visual Basic allows the missing parameters in the methods. In case of VB, the framework replaces the missing parameters with `Type.Missing` object that indicates that if there are any default values specified for these parameters, use those values. The C# language specifications do not allow the use of missing parameters. You will have to specify the values for these optional parameters either explicitly or provide the `Type.Missing` objects for these values.

> The `Type.Missing` class is defined in the `System.Reflection` namespace.

ADOMD In Managed Applications

.NET provides no support for manipulating **On Line Analytical Processing** (OLAP) server data. Classic ADO provided this support through the companion ADOMD library. Once again, through **Interop**, we can incorporate ADOMD features into our managed applications.

Creating .NET Metadata For ADOMD

To establish a reference to the metadata file, describing all the interfaces exposed by ADO library, use TlbImp tool on `msado.dll` to create a .NET enabled assembly. This file resides, by default, in the following folder on your machine:

```
<System Drive>\Program Files\Common Files\System\Ado
```

```
C:\>tlbimp /out:ADOMD.dll msadomd.dll
TlbImp - Type Library to .NET Assembly Converter Version 1.0.2914.16
Copyright (C) Microsoft Corp. 2001.  All rights reserved.

Type library imported to C:\ADOMD.dll

C:\>
```

This operation will generate a .NET assembly – `ADOMD.dll` – containing the metadata for the ADOMD library with ADOMD namespace. We can provide fully qualified names for all the ADOMD objects scoped within this namespace, such as `ADOMD.Catalog` and `ADOMD.CubeDef`. These fully qualified names will be essential if you are using ADOX objects along with ADOMD objects, because there is name collision in two namespaces: for example, both the namespaces contain the `Catalog` object:

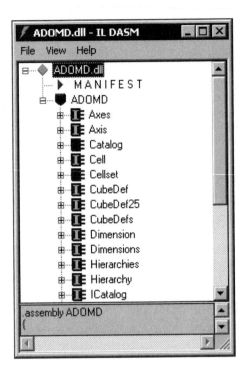

Reference to ADOMD Assembly

To compile the ADOMD assembly generated by the TlbImp tool into the managed code, add a reference as follows:

VB.NET:

```
vbc /t:library /r:ADOMD.dll /out:EmployeeDB.dll EmployeeDB.vb
```

C#:

```
csc /t:library /r:ADOMD.dll /out:EmployeeDB.dll EmployeeDB.cs
```

Enumerating Cubes In The Catalog

The following example shows how ADOMD objects `Catalog`, `CubeDefs`, and `CubeDef` can be used along with an ADO `Connection` object to find all the cubes defined in the `FoodMart` data source provided with SQL Analytical Server 2000.

The code follows the following steps:

1. It creates a new instance of ADO connection by specifying the connection string. Notice that there is no `Initial Catalog` in the connection string. This is due to the fact that there is only one catalog per OLAP server.

2. The connection is opened with the server.

3. A new instance of `Catalog` object is created and the opened connection is set as its `ActiveConnection` property.

4. The `CubeDefs` property provides the collection of `CubeDef` objects in the database.

5. Each object in the `CubeDefs` collection is accessed to printout its name.

VB.NET:

```
Dim strConn As String = _
    "Provider=msolap; Data Source = localhost; " & _
    "Initial Catalog = FoodMart 2000; User ID=sa; Pwd="
Dim dbConn As New ClassicADO.Connection ()
dbConn.Open (strConn)
Dim dtCatalog As New ADOMD.Catalog ()
dtCatalog.ActiveConnection = CType (dbConn, Object)

Dim cubes As ADOMD.CubeDefs = dtCatalog.CubeDefs
Dim cube As ADOMD.CubeDef
For Each cube in cubes
    Console.WriteLine (cube.Name)
Next
```

C#:

```
string strConn = "Provider=msolap; Data Source = SULTAN;" +
    "Initial Catalog = FoodMart 2000; User ID =; Pwd=";
ClassicADO.Connection dbConn = new ClassicADO.Connection ();
dbConn.Open (strConn, "", "", (int)ConnectModeEnum.adModeUnknown);
ADOMD.Catalog dtCatalog = new ADOMD.Catalog ();
dtCatalog.ActiveConnection = (object)dbConn;

CubeDefs cubes = dtCatalog.CubeDefs;
Console.WriteLine ("Number of Cubes = {0}", cubes.Count.ToString ());
foreach (ADOMD.CubeDef cube in cubes)
{
    Console.WriteLine (cube.Name);
}
```

The output of the above example is as follows:

```
Number Of Cubes = 3
Sales
Warehouse
Warehouse and Sales
```

The above example can be extended to access the `Dimension`, `Hierarchy`, `Level`, and `Member` objects contained in the various `CubeDef` objects. The following C# code can be added to the above example to print out the information from Time dimension of `Warehouse CubeDef`:

```
ADOMD.CubeDef warehouse = cubes["Warehouse"];
ADOMD.Dimension timeDim = warehouse.Dimensions["Time"];
foreach (ADOMD.Level lvl in timeDim.Hierarchies[0].Levels)
{
    Console.WriteLine (lvl.Caption);
    foreach (ADOMD.Member mem in lvl.Members)
    {
        Console.WriteLine ("\t" + mem.Caption + "\t" + mem.UniqueName);
    }
}
```

The following screen shot shows the output of the above code.

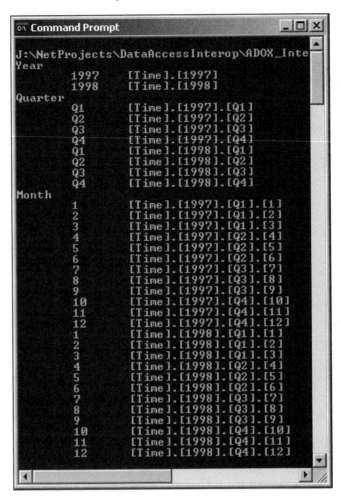

Summary

In this chapter, we have seen how to use **Interop** to incorporate the features from our existing unmanaged components and other classic ADO objects. This is a very powerful mechanism provided by the .NET framework to ease the migration path from unmanaged components to managed assemblies.

There are some features that mandate the use of **Interop** on the existing platform. The most important of these are the transaction services. The MTS and COM+ infrastructure is COM based. Therefore, if we want to create a managed component that should be able to participate in the transactions, we will have to implement it in such a way that it can be registered as a COM component. The .NET components can be registered as native COM objects using the **REGASM** tool. Then the component can be installed in the COM+ explorer. Now the .NET component can participate in the transactions by using **Interop** capabilities. Calls have to cross the CLR boundary, therefore, performance will suffer. Therefore, **Interop** should only be used where there is no other .NET option available.

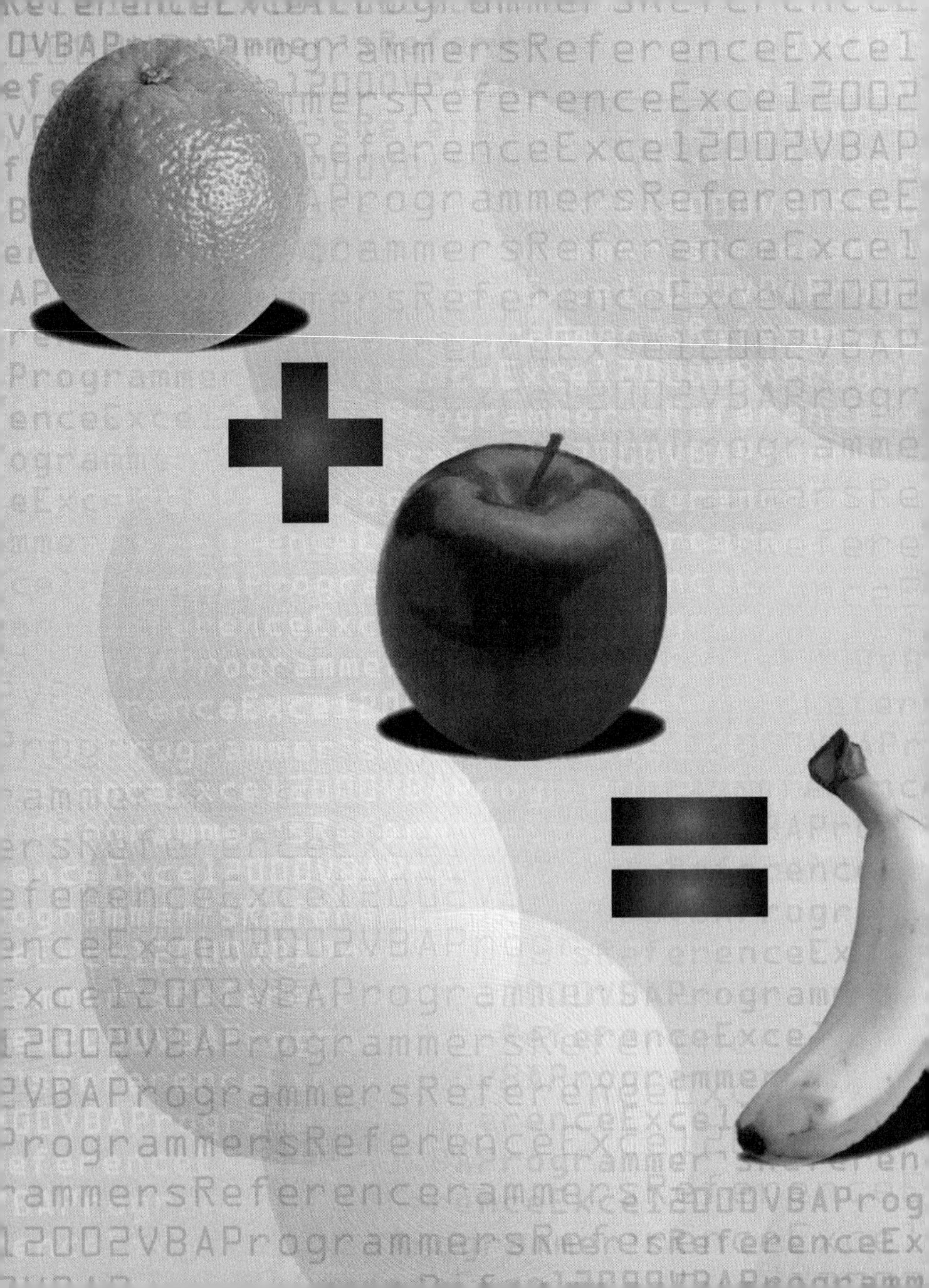

Examples

This section provides a few examples of how to work with the key ADO.NET objects. It will also provide a reminder of how to perform common operations.

Specifically, we provide examples that show ways to perform the following operations:

- ❑ Retrieving a DataSet
- ❑ Setting a DataRelation
- ❑ Filtering a DataSet using a DataView
- ❑ Adding Keys and Constraints
- ❑ Using the DataReader
- ❑ Updating Data using the DataSet object
- ❑ Merging two DataSets
- ❑ Merging a DataTable into a DataSet
- ❑ Merging DataRow objects into a DataSet
- ❑ Checking each change before updating
- ❑ Identifying DataTable changes
- ❑ Identifying DataSet changes
- ❑ Updating explicit rows and columns
- ❑ Adding and deleting rows

Retrieving a DataSet

The DataSet object is populated by the Fill method of a DataAdapter object. The DataAdapter object is the bridge between the data source and the DataSet – it interacts directly with the other managed provider objects such as Command and Connection. The DataSet object interacts with managed provider objects only through the DataAdapter.

In this example, the ListCountriesInDataSet function opens a connection to the SQL Server Northwind database and populates a DataSet with data from the Countries table. The FillComboBoxFromDataSet uses ListCountriesInDataSet to obtain the DataSet, and binds the DataTable within it to the combo box cboCountries.

```
Const SQL_CONNECTION = "Data Source=SQL1;Initial Catalog=Northwind;" & _
    "User ID=sa;"
Const SQL_COUNTRIES = "SELECT DISTINCT Suppliers.Country FROM Suppliers"

    Private Sub FillComboBoxFromDataSet()

        ' Purpose:  Populate the combo box with countries list, from a DataSet

        Dim dsCountries As DataSet          ' Form-level DataSet object

        ' Load list of countries into the combo box, from the DataSet
        dsCountries = ListCountriesInDataSet()

        ' Bind the combo box, cboCountries, to the DataSet
        cboCountries.DataSource = dsCountries.Tables("Countries")
        cboCountries.DisplayMember = "Country"

    End Sub

    Public Function ListCountriesInDataSet() As System.Data.DataSet

        ' Purpose:  Return the Supplier Countries, in a DataSet

        Dim sqlConn As SqlConnection
        Dim sqlCmd As SqlCommand
        Dim sqlAdapt As SqlDataAdapter

        ' New Dataset, named "ListOfCountries"
        Dim rowDataSet As New DataSet("ListOfCountries")

        Try
            ' Create a new connection object
            sqlConn = New SqlConnection(SQL_CONNECTION)

            ' Create a new command object
            sqlCmd = New SqlCommand(SQL_COUNTRIES, sqlConn)

            ' Open the connection
            sqlConn.Open()

            ' Open a DataAdapter object, using the command object
            sqlAdapt = New SqlDataAdapter(sqlCmd)

            ' Execute the command and retrieve the records in the DataSet
            ' The DataTable is named "Countries"
            sqlAdapt.Fill(rowDataSet, "Countries")

        Catch e As SqlException
            MsgBox("Error " & e.Number & ": " & e.Message & " [" & _
                e.Source & "]")
        Finally
            sqlConn.Close() ' The connection is not needed anymore
        End Try

        Return (rowDataSet)

    End Function
```

In the `ListCountriesInDataSet` function, both the `DataSet` and the `DataTable` are named. The name of the `DataSet` is set to "ListOfCountries" by providing a parameter in the constructor. The `DataTable` name is set to "Countries" in the line where the `SqlAdapter` object's `Fill()` method is called:

814

```
sqlAdapt.Fill(rowDataSet, "Countries")
```

In the `FillComboBoxFromDataSet` function, the combo box is populated by binding it to a specific `DataTable` in the `DataSet`. In this case, we are binding the combo box to the `Countries` `DataTable`. This `DataSet` only contains one `DataTable` so we did not need to reference it by name, although doing so produces clearer code. It is also a good safeguard for the future, when the `ListCountriesInDataSet` function could be modified to hold more than one `DataTable`.

Setting a DataRelation

The `DataRelation` object represents a link between two related tables. It is similar in concept to a SQL `INNER JOIN`, which relates two tables that share at least one common key. The `DataRelation` object defines a parent-child relationship, so that by accessing the parent, you automatically get access to the children. Much in the same way that a primary key – foreign key join allows you to execute queries that return a one-to-many set of records.

Let's look at an example to illustrate this. The `Suppliers` table in the `Northwind` database lists several suppliers located in different countries around the world. The `Products` table contains a listing of available products. The two tables are related by the `SupplierID`, which is the primary key of the `Suppliers` table and a foreign key of the `Products` table. One supplier provides several products: a classic one-to-many relationship.

Let's say that you are a purchaser in France who wants a listing of all the products that you can buy from French suppliers. You could find this information by executing a query to return all products from suppliers in France. The SQL statement looks something like this:

```
SELECT Suppliers.SupplierID, Suppliers.CompanyName,
Products.ProductName, Products.UnitPrice, Products.UnitsInStock
FROM Suppliers INNER JOIN Products ON Suppliers.SupplierID = Products.SupplierID
WHERE Suppliers.Country = 'France'
```

Here is the resultset that gets returned by running this statement in SQL Query Analyzer:

ID	CompanyName	ProductName	UnitPrice	UnitsInStock
18	Aux joyeux ecclésiastiques	Côte de Blaye	263.5000	17
18	Aux joyeux ecclésiastiques	Chartreuse verte	18.0000	69
27	Escargots Nouveaux	Escargots de Bourgogne	13.2500	62
28	Gai pâturage	Raclette Courdavault	55.0000	79
28	Gai pâturage	Camembert Pierrot	34.0000	19

Using a `DataRelation` instead has several advantages:

- ❑ We can relate data from different data sources
- ❑ We can work with the relationship while the data is open – using a SQL `JOIN` returns the data as a single table with repeated values
- ❑ We can avoid complex SQL strings – the only SQL required is a simple SELECT statement for each table
- ❑ We can export the dataset to XML or another database yet maintain the relationships in the original data

The code listing below shows how to retrieve both tables in a single `DataSet`, and then define a `DataRelation` object to represent their relationship:

```
Const SQL_CONNECTION = "Data Source=SQL1;Initial Catalog=Northwind;" & _
    "User ID=sa;"
Const SQL_SUPPLIERS = "SELECT * FROM Suppliers"
Const SQL_PRODUCTS = "SELECT * FROM Products"

Public Function ListSuppliersAndProducts() As DataSet

    ' Purpose:  Return list of Suppliers AND Products
    ' in a DataSet object, with multiple resultsets

    Dim sqlConn As SqlConnection
    Dim sqlCmdSuppliers As SqlCommand
    Dim sqlCmdProducts As SqlCommand
    Dim sqlAdaptSuppliers As SqlDataAdapter
    Dim sqlAdaptProducts As SqlDataAdapter
    Dim rowDataSet As New DataSet()

        Try
        ' Create a new connection object
        sqlConn = New SqlConnection(SQL_CONNECTION)

        ' Assign one command object per table
        sqlCmdProducts = New SqlCommand(SQL_PRODUCTS, sqlConn)
        sqlCmdSuppliers = New SqlCommand(SQL_SUPPLIERS, sqlConn)

        ' Open the connection
        sqlConn.Open()

        ' Open DataAdapter objects, using the command objects
        sqlAdaptSuppliers = New SqlDataAdapter(sqlCmdSuppliers)
        sqlAdaptProducts = New SqlDataAdapter(sqlCmdProducts)

        ' Populate the DataSet from the DataAdapters
        sqlAdaptSuppliers.Fill(rowDataSet, "Suppliers")
        sqlAdaptProducts.Fill(rowDataSet, "Products")

        ' Define a DataRelation between Suppliers and Products, on SupplierID
        Dim relSuppliersToProducts As New DataRelation( _
            "SuppliersToProducts", _
```

```
              rowDataSet.Tables("Suppliers").Columns("SupplierID"), _
              rowDataSet.Tables("Products").Columns("SupplierID"))

          rowDataSet.Relations.Add(relSuppliersToProducts)

      Catch e As SqlException
          MsgBox("Error " & e.Number & ": " & e.Message & " [" & e.Source & "]")
      Finally
          sqlConn.Close()
      End Try

      Return (rowDataSet)

  End Function
```

This code listing sets up the `DataRelation`, but does not actually do anything with it. The following code – to be attached to a button – uses the above function to return a `DataSet` containing both of the tables and the relationship. It then sets this `DataSet` as the `DataSource` for `DataGrid1`. This allows the user to explore the suppliers and products.

```
  Private Sub btnListProductByCountry_Click(ByVal sender As System.Object, _
      ByVal e As System.EventArgs) Handles btnListProductByCountry.Click

          ' Purpose: Populate the DataGrid with Suppliers and Products, by Country

          Dim rowProduct As DataRow

          dsSuppliersProducts = ListSuppliersAndProducts()

          DataGrid1.DataSource = dsSuppliersProducts

  End Sub
```

The `DataGrid` continues to show the full `DataSet`, not just the data for suppliers based in France. However, we can filter a `DataSet` without re-querying the database using a `DataView`. This will allow us to display only the products that come from suppliers in the chosen country.

Filtering a DataSet Using a DataView

The `DataView` object provides facilities for filtering and sorting a `DataSet`. Let's extend the above application by adding a button called `btnDataView` that filters suppliers by the country that is currently selected in the combo box. Here is the code listing for the button:

```
  Private Sub btnDataView_Click(ByVal sender As System.Object, _
      ByVal e As System.EventArgs) Handles btnDataView.Click

          ' Purpose: Populate the DataGrid with Suppliers using a DataView
          ' by (selected) Country

          Dim dsSuppliers As DataSet
          Dim dsDataView As DataView
```

```
        Dim strCountry As String

        ' Use the combobox created in the "retrieving a dataset" example
        strCountry = cboCountries.Text.ToString

        ' Use the function given above that returns all Suppliers, Products
        ' and their relationship
        dsSuppliers = ListSuppliersAndProducts()

        ' Construct a DataView, filtered by the selected country
        dsDataView = New DataView(dsSuppliers.Tables("Suppliers"))
        dsDataView.RowFilter = "Country Like '" & strCountry & "*'"

        ' Sort DataView, by Supplier CompanyName ASC
        ' Note, this will add a sort arrow to the datagrid for this field
        dsDataView.Sort = "CompanyName ASC"

        ' Populate DataGrid with the DataView
        DataGrid1.DataSource = dsDataView

    End Sub
```

This example uses the `ListSuppliersAndProducts` function, presented above, to return a `DataSet` containing the `suppliers` table, the `products` table, and the relationship between them. It then uses a `DataView` to filter and sort the data.

Adding Keys and Constraints

In this example we load a `DataSet` with data from an OleDb source and then place constraints on the table and add a primary key to the table.

Using C#, we could perform this in the following way:

```
OleDbConnection cnn = new _
    OleDbConnection("Provider=Microsoft.Jet.Oledb.4.0;data " +
    "source=c:\data\northwind.mdb;");
OleDbDataAdapter da = new OleDbDataAdapter("select * from products",cnn);
DataSet ds = new DataSet();

da.Fill(ds, "Products");

//add a Unique Constraint to the "OrderID" column of the first data table
UniqueConstraint uc = new UniqueConstraint(ds.Tables[0].Columns["ProductID"]);
ds.Tables[0].Constraints.Add(uc);

//set the primary key column of the first data table by passing in an array
//of data columns
ds.Tables[0].PrimaryKey=new DataColumn[]{ds.Tables[0].Columns["ProductID"]};

//make sure the dataset enforces the constraint we set on it
ds.EnforceConstraints = true;
```

and using VB.NET:

```
Dim cnn As New OleDbConnection("Provider=Microsoft.Jet.Oledb.4.0;" & _
    "data source=c:\data\northwind.mdb;")
Dim da As New OleDbDataAdapter("select * from products", cnn)
Dim ds As New DataSet()

da.Fill(ds, "Products")

'add a Unique Constraint to the "OrderID" column of the first data table
Dim uc As New UniqueConstraint(ds.Tables.Item(0).Columns.Item("ProductID"))
ds.Tables.Item(0).Constraints.Add(uc)

'set the primary key column of the first data table by passing in an array
'of data columns
ds.Tables.Item(0).PrimaryKey = New DataColumn() _
    {ds.Tables.Item(0).Columns.Item("ProductID")}

'make sure the dataset enforces the constraint we set on it
ds.EnforceConstraints = True
```

If we now use this dataset as the `DataSource` for a `DataGrid`, for example, attempts to violate the constraint will be caught automatically. Also when merging datasets, a primary key must be defined in order to differentiate between new records and modifications to existing records.

Using the DataReader

The above examples demonstrate that the `DataSet` object provides powerful ways for querying and manipulating data. However, it also is fairly resource (and code) intensive. For simple operations the `DataReader` will often produce code that is shorter and runs faster. This example uses the `DataReader` instead of a `DataSet` to populate the countries combo box.

Using C#, we could perform this in the following way:

```
SqlConnection cnn = new SqlConnection
    ("Data Source=localhost;Initial Catalog=Northwind;User ID=sa;");
SqlCommand cmd = new SqlCommand & _
    ("SELECT DISTINCT Suppliers.Country FROM Suppliers ", cnn);
SqlDataReader dr;

// open the connection
cnn.Open();

//execute the command to return a DataReader
dr = cmd.ExecuteReader();

//while there are still values in the data reader, add them to the list

while(dr.Read())
{
    //we read a string because we know to expect a string and
    //not another value type
```

```
                cboCountries.Items.Add(dr.GetString(0));
    }


    //close our datareader when we are done with it
    cnn.Close();
```

In VB.Net:

```
Dim cnn As New SqlConnection _
    ("Data Source=localhost;Initial Catalog=Northwind;User ID=sa;")
Dim cmd As New SqlCommand _
    ("SELECT DISTINCT Suppliers.Country FROM Suppliers", cnn)
Dim dr As SqlDataReader

' open the connection
cnn.Open()
' execute the command to return a DataReader
dr = cmd.ExecuteReader()

' while there are still values in the data reader, add them to the list
While dr.read()
    ' we read a string because we know to expect a string and
    ' not another value type
    cboCountries.Items.Add(dr.GetString(0))
End While
cnn.Close()
```

Updating Data Using the DataSet Object

This example obtains the DataSet object from the DataGrid, where the data will have been modified. It constructs a new Connection and Adapter to write the changes back to the database. DataSet changes are written back to the original data source via the DataAdapter object, which provides an Update method for this purpose. Here's the code listing:

```
Const SQL_CONNECTION = "Data Source=SQL1;Initial Catalog=Northwind;User ID=sa;"
Const SQL_SUPPLIERS = "SELECT * FROM Suppliers"
Const SQL_PRODUCTS = "SELECT * FROM Products"

Private Sub btnUpdate_Click(ByVal sender As System.Object, _
    ByVal e As System.EventArgs) Handles btnUpdate.Click

    ' Purpose: Update changes to the Product DataSet
    Dim dsProductsAndSuppliers As DataSet

    dsProductsAndSuppliers = DataGrid1.DataSource

    ' Synchronize the updates to the original data source
    Dim sqlConn As New SqlConnection(SQL_CONNECTION)
    Dim sqlProductsCmd As New SqlCommand(SQL_PRODUCTS, sqlConn)
    Dim sqlSuppliersCmd As New SqlCommand(SQL_SUPPLIERS, sqlConn)
    Dim sqlProductsAdapter As New SqlDataAdapter()
    Dim sqlSuppliersAdapter As New SqlDataAdapter()
```

```
' Set the SelectCommand property, so that the UpdateCommand will be
' generated automatically
sqlProductsAdapter.SelectCommand = sqlProductsCmd
sqlSuppliersAdapter.SelectCommand = sqlSuppliersCmd

' Use SqlCommandBuilder to automatically generate an UpdateCommand
Dim proCB As SqlCommandBuilder = New SqlCommandBuilder(sqlProductsAdapter)
Dim supCB As SqlCommandBuilder = New _
    SqlCommandBuilder(sqlSuppliersAdapter)

' Update the data source with the changes
sqlProductsAdapter.Update(dsProductsAndSuppliers, "Products")
sqlSuppliersAdapter.Update(dsProductsAndSuppliers, "Suppliers")

End Sub
```

The above code goes through the following stages:

1. The `DataSource` of `DataGrid1` is assigned to the `DataSet` object `dsProductsAndSuppliers`

2. We construct a new `Connection` object called `sqlConn`

3. We construct two `Command` objects, one for each of the two tables in the `DataSet`. We assign a `Select` statement and `sqlConn` to them

4. We construct two `Adapter` objects, one for each table in the `DataSet`

5. Each `Adapter` has its `SelectCommand` property set to the relevant `SqlCommand` object constructed above

6. `SqlCommandBuilder` uses the `SelectCommand` assigned to each `Adapter` to generate corresponding `Update`, `Insert`, and `Delete` commands automatically.

7. For each `Adapter` we call the `Update` method, providing the `DataSet` and the table name to extract from the `DataSet` as parameters (note that the table's name in the DataSet, given here, could be different to the table name in the database, given in the SqlCommand constructer). The `Adapter` writes the changes back to the database.

The `SqlCommandBuilder` demonstrated in step 6 is able to automatically generate `Update`, `Insert`, and `Delete` for a `DataAdapter` commands provided that:

❑ A `Select` command has been provided

❑ The table has a primary key

❑ The `Select` command does not involve `JOINS` of several tables

Merging Data: DataSet, DataTable, and arrays of DataRow Objects

The DataSet object provides methods for merging other DataSets, DataTables, and DataRows into an existing DataSet. These examples demonstrate ways to use this facility.

Merging Two DataSets

In the following example, DataGrid1 contains a DataSet representing the Customers table in the Northwind database. A new customer exists in the file c:\data\xmldata.xml. We wish to merge data from the XML file with the DataSet. Note that the VB code would be identical regardless of how many new customers appeared in the XML file.

The XML file could look like this:

```xml
<?xml version="1.0" standalone="yes" ?>
<NewDataSet>
  <Customers>
    <CustomerID>PERRW</CustomerID>
    <CompanyName>Will's Wines</CompanyName>
    <ContactName>William Perrin</ContactName>
    <ContactTitle>Sales Representative</ContactTitle>
    <Address>West Str. 52</Address>
    <City>London</City>
    <PostalCode>WX12 3YZ</PostalCode>
    <Country>UK</Country>
    <Phone>0123 456 789</Phone>
    <Fax>0123 456 780</Fax>
  </Customers>
</NewDataSet>
```

We can quickly merge the data in the XML file with the DataGrid. This example obtains a dataset of the grid's DataSource, reads the XML file into a second DataSet, merges the new data into the original data, and then writes the result back to the DataGrid:

```vb
Private Sub btnMerge_Click _
  ByVal sender As System.Object, ByVal e As System.EventArgs) _
  Handles btnMerge.Click

  Dim dsOrg As DataSet = DataGrid1.DataSource
  Dim dsToMerge As DataSet = New DataSet()

  ' Read new data
  dsToMerge.ReadXml("c:\data\xmldata.xml", XmlReadMode.Auto)

  ' Perform the merge
  dsOrg.Merge(dsToMerge)

  DataGrid1.DataSource = dsOrg
End Sub
```

The same method can be used to perform updates as well as inserts: the XML file simply needs to use an existing value for its primary key (in this case `CustomerID`) and the primary key must be defined in the `DataTable`.

Of course both the main `DataSet` and the `Dataset` to be merged can come from any source.

Merging datasets can result in the introduction of `DataSet` errors. The following method `WXShowPerTableErrors` (written out in C#), traverses all of the errors in a table and writes their details to the console:

```
static void WXShowPerTableErrors(DataTable table)
{
    if (table.HasErrors)
    {
        int index = 1;

        Console.WriteLine("Table with Error(s): {0}",
                          table.TableName);
        foreach (DataRow row in table.GetErrors())
        {
            Console.WriteLine("Row in error {0}", index);
            index++;
            foreach(DataColumn column in table.Columns)
            {
                Console.WriteLine("Column in Error: {0}, Error: {1}",
                    column.ColumnName,
                    row.GetColumnError(column));
            }

            row.ClearErrors();
        }
    }

    else
    {
        Console.WriteLine("Table without Error(s): {0}",
            table.TableName);
    }
}
```

Method `WXShowThatDataSetMerge` demonstrates two `DataSet` objects being retrieved from separate files (persisted XML) and merged. It then writes the result back to one of the original XML files:

```
static void WXShowThatDataSetMerge(string strFileNameOrg,
                                   string strFileNameToMerge)
{
    DataSet dsOrg = new DataSet();
    DataSet dsToMerge = new DataSet();

    dsOrg.ReadXml(strFileNameOrg, XmlReadMode.Auto);
    dsToMerge.ReadXml(strFileNameToMerge, XmlReadMode.Auto);
    dsOrg.Merge(dsToMerge); // DataSet overload
    foreach (DataTable table in dsOrg.Tables)
```

```
    {
        WXShowPerTableErrors(table);
    }

    dsOrg.AcceptChanges();
    dsOrg.WriteXml(strFileNameOrg, XmlWriteMode.WriteSchema);
}
```

If errors occur in the table then the call to WXShowPerTableErrors will write details of them to the console.

Merging a DataTable into a DataSet

Method WXShowThatDataTableMerge demonstrates a DataTable (provided as a parameter) being merged with a DataSet (obtained from an XML file):

```
static void WXShowThatDataTableMerge(string strFileNameOrg,
                                     DataTable dataTableToMerge)
{
    DataSet dsOrg = new DataSet();
    DataTable affectedTable;

    dsOrg.ReadXml(strFileNameOrg, XmlReadMode.Auto);
    dsOrg.Merge(dataTableToMerge); // DataTable overload
    affectedTable = dsOrg.Tables[dataTableToMerge.TableName];
    Debug.Assert(affectedTable != null,
                "Corresponding table should be found in original DataSet");
    WXShowPerTableErrors(affectedTable);
}
```

Merging DataRow Objects into a DataSet

Method WXShowThatDataRowMerge demonstrates a DataRow array being merged with a DataSet:

```
static void WXShowThatDataRowMerge(string strFileNameOrg,
                                   DataRow [] dataRowsToMerge)
{
    DataSet dsOrg = new DataSet();
    DataTable affectedTable;
    // Hint: using System.Collections
    SortedList tableList = new SortedList();

    dsOrg.ReadXml(strFileNameOrg, XmlReadMode.Auto);
    dsOrg.Merge(dataRowsToMerge); // DataRow overload
    foreach (DataRow row in dataRowsToMerge)
    {
        // Ensure we only examine each table once by storing
        // processed table names in a sorted list
        if (!tableList.ContainsKey(row.Table.TableName))
        {
            //          key                  data (null since none)
            tableList.Add(row.Table.TableName, null);
```

```
                    affectedTable = dsOrg.Tables[row.Table.TableName];
                    Debug.Assert(affectedTable != null,
                        "Corresponding table should be found in original DataSet");
                    WXShowPerTableErrors(affectedTable);
                }
        }
    }
```

Controlling DataSet and DataTable Changes

ADO.NET possesses many features for controlling data change. The following examples illustrate some ways in which these features can be used.

Checking Each Change Before Updating

The following example saves changes to the `Customers` table, in the `DataSource` of `DataGrid1`, back to the database. It confirms each change with the user, and only updates those rows that the user confirms should be updated:

```
Private Sub btnUpdateCustomers_Click(ByVal sender As System.Object, _
    ByVal e As System.EventArgs) Handles btnUpdateCustomers.Click
    Dim con As SqlConnection = New SqlConnection(SQL_CONNECTION)
    Dim cmd As SqlCommand = New SqlCommand("select * from customers", con)
    Dim ad As SqlDataAdapter = New SqlDataAdapter(cmd)

    Dim ds As DataSet = New DataSet()
    Dim dt As DataTable = New DataTable()

    ' Obtain DataSet from DataGrid1
    ds = DataGrid1.DataSource

    ' If something in the DataSet has changed...

    ' Extract the changes to the customers table
    dt = ds.Tables("customers").GetChanges()

    ' Only attempt updates if the customers table did change
    ' if it did not, dt will be Nothing
    If Not dt Is Nothing Then
        Dim dRow As DataRow
        ' Check whether to save changes row-by-row
        For Each dRow In dt.Rows
            ' Ask whether to save change to current row.
            ' DataRowVersion.Original specified to prevent error
            ' if row is being deleted.
            If MsgBox("Do you wish to save the change to """ & _
                dRow("CompanyName", DataRowVersion.Original) & """?", _
                MsgBoxStyle.YesNo, "Save Changes?") <> MsgBoxResult.Yes Then
                ' Reject changes to the current row
                dRow.RejectChanges()
            End If
        Next
```

```
            'Automatically generate Update, Insert etc. commands
            Dim proCB As SqlCommandBuilder = New SqlCommandBuilder(ad)

            con.Open()
            ad.Update(dt)
            con.Close()
        End If
    End Sub
```

Note that if the user rejects a change, the DataGrid will continue to display the changed values because it is not bound to the DataTable. Adding the line ds.merge(dt, False, MissingSchemaAction.Ignore) after the For Each loop will cause the rejected changes to be merged back in to the DataGrid.

Identifying DataTable Changes

The above example shows a practical application of the GetChanges method of a DataTable. By providing an additional parameter we can return only a particular type of change. The possible uses are:

❑ GetChanges(DataRowState.Modified)

❑ GetChanges(DataRowState.Added)

❑ GetChanges(DataRowState.Deleted)

❑ GetChanges(DataRowState.Unchanged)

All are self explanatory except GetChanges(DataRowState.Unchanged), which returns all rows that *haven't* changed.

The method WXShowChanges demonstrates the contents of a DataTable generated using the GetChanges method of an object of type DataTable. In order to view the actual data that is stored in the DataTable containing the changes, the individual rows of the DataTable should be traversed. In turn the columns of each DataRow should be traversed.

Different ways to call the method WXShowChanges to display DataTable changes are as follows (where table is an object of type DataTable):

```
WXShowChanges("All changes for DataSet", tableRow.GetChanges());
WXShowChanges("Only modified rows for DataSet",
    table.GetChanges(DataRowState.Modified));
WXShowChanges("Only added rows for DataSet",
    table.GetChanges(DataRowState.Added));
WXShowChanges("Only deleted rows for DataSet",
    table.GetChanges(DataRowState.Deleted));
```

The method WXShowChanges accepts a string acting as a description and a DataTable containing the changed rows as parameters. The code – in C# – reads as follows:

```
static void WXShowChanges(string strWhatIsUp,
                          DataTable dataTableChanges)
{
    if (null == dataTableChanges)
```

```
        {
            Console.WriteLine("No changes for DataTable: {0}",
                                strWhatIsUp);
            return;
        }

        int index = 1;

        Console.WriteLine("Changes for DataTable ({0}): {1}",
                            dataTableChanges.TableName,
                            strWhatIsUp);
        foreach(DataRow row in dataTableChanges.Rows)
        {
            Console.WriteLine("Row containing changes {0}", index);
            index++;
            foreach (DataColumn column in dataTableChanges.Columns)
            {
                Console.WriteLine(row[column]);
            }
        }
    }
```

Identifying DataSet Changes

We can overload the WXShowChanges method to take a DataSet as its second parameter instead of a DataTable.

There are several ways to call WXShowChanges to display DataSet changes, as follows (where ds is an object of type DataSet):

```
WXShowChanges("All changes for DataSet", ds.GetChanges());
WXShowChanges("Only modified rows for DataSet",
    ds.GetChanges(DataRowState.Modified));
WXShowChanges("Only added rows for DataSet",
    ds.GetChanges(DataRowState.Added));
WXShowChanges("Only deleted rows for DataSet",
    ds.GetChanges(DataRowState.Deleted));
```

WXShowChanges overloaded to accept a DataSet as the second parameter is defined as follows:

```
static void WXShowChanges(string strWhatIsUp,
                            DataSet dataSetChanges)
{
    if (null == dataSetChanges)
    {
        Console.WriteLine("No changes for DataSet: {0}",
                            strWhatIsUp);
        return ;
    }

    Console.WriteLine("Changes for DataSet ({0}): {1}",
                        dataSetChanges.DataSetName,
                        strWhatIsUp);
```

```
        foreach(DataTable table in dataSetChanges.Tables)
        {
            // Show changes for each table in DataSet
            // using the "table" overload of WXShowChanges
            WXShowChanges("Changed table in DataSet", table);
        }
    }
```

Explicit Row and Column Updates

So far we have looked at retrieving data, and using filters and relationships, merging data, and writing back to the data source. We have also used `DataGrid` to allow users to edit the data. At times however we will want to perform edits programmatically. These examples demonstrate ways in which we can do that.

Data Notes

The data used in each example of explicit row and column updates was generated using the `Northwind` database and the following `FOR XML RAW` query:

```
SELECT ShipperID, CompanyName, Phone
FROM SHIPPERS
FOR XML RAW, XMLDATA
```

The `XMLDATA` portion of the query generates a schema for the generated XML. The `FOR XML RAW` creates an XML document where each row returned by the query is contained in an XML element named `row`. When this XML document is associated with a `DataSet`, the `DataSet` contains a table (class type, `DataTable`) named `row`.

Example Updating Explicit Row and Column

The `WXDataSetUpdate` method demonstrates updating a `DataSet` by setting a specific column within a specific row. An example of this is as follows where `colCompanyName` is a variable of type `DataColumn` and `rows` is a collection of `DataRow` objects:

```
rows[0][colCompanyName] = "More Most Fasterest Delivery";
```

Highlights of the `WXDataSetUpdate` method include:

- ❑ Using a Yes/No `MessageBox` in order to ask the user if they would like to accept their changes (`DataSet` method `AcceptChanges`) or reject their changes (`DataSet` method `RejectChanges`).

- ❑ Using the `DataTable` class's `Select` method to find a specific row or rows that match a given criteria (for example, for rows that match criteria, `ShipperID='2'`).

The `WXDataSetUpdate` method is implemented as follows:

```
// Loads DataSet from file (persisted XML), modifies dataset and
// re-persists file.
//
```

```
// Make sure to use: System, System.Data, System.Diagnostics;
//
// XML initially generated using FOR XML RAW against Northwind
//     SELECT * FROM SHIPPERS FOR XML RAW, XMLDATA
//
// XML persisted to file in the following form
// <?xml version="1.0" standalone="yes"?>
// <Schema1>
//     <xsd:schema> ... </xsd:schema>
//     <row ShipperID="1" CompanyName="company name here"
//          Phone="(xxx) xxx-xxxx" />
//     ...
// </Schema1>
static void WXDataSetUpdate(string strFileName)
{
    DataSet ds = new DataSet(); // persisted XML loaded to Dataset ds
    DataTable tableRow; // Table named 'row' found in xml
    DataColumn colCompanyName, //
        colPhone;
    DataRow [] rows; // results of DataSet.Select returned here

    // Load DataSet with persisted XML (XML stored in file)
    ds.ReadXml(strFileName, XmlReadMode.Auto);
    // FOR XML RAW produces a set of rows named "row" so table is called "row"
    tableRow = ds.Tables["row"];

    /// In order to increase the performance of data change
    /// methods, BeginLoadData, turns off notifications,
    /// index maintenance, and constraints enforcement.
    /// In database terms compare this to bulk load or not adding
    /// a table's indexes until after all the data is added.
    tableRow.BeginLoadData();

    colPhone = tableRow.Columns["Phone"];

    // search for all rows with ShipperID='2'
    rows = tableRow.Select("ShipperID='2'");
    rows[0][colPhone] = "(800) 555 1234";

    colCompanyName = tableRow.Columns["CompanyName"];

    // Search for all rows with CompanyName='Federal Shipping'
    rows = tableRow.Select("CompanyName='Federal Shipping'");

    rows[0][colCompanyName] = "More Most Fasterest Delivery";

    tableRow.EndLoadData();

    DialogResult diagResult;

    diagResult =
        MessageBox.Show("Accept Changes (yes) or Reject Changes (no)?",
                        "Ch-Ch-Changes",
                        MessageBoxButtons.YesNo);
```

```
        if (DialogResult.Yes == diagResult)
        {
            ds.AcceptChanges();
            ds.WriteXml(strFileName, XmlWriteMode.WriteSchema);
        }

        else // if (DialogResult.No == diagResult)
        {
            ds.RejectChanges();
        }
    }
```

Adding and Deleting Rows

The WXDataSetAddNewAndDelete method demonstrates adding rows to a DataTable and ultimately a DataSet. The DataTable object's NewRow method is used to generate the DataRow, and once the row has been set up the DataTable object's Rows collection is used to add the new row to the collection.

Deleting a row is achieved by finding a particular row using the DataTable object's Select method (find a row matching ShipperID='1'). Once the row is found (a DataRow object) it can be deleted using the DataRow object's Delete method.

When all modifications are completed the changes are accepted using the DataSet object's AcceptChanges method and the DataSet is then persisted to a file using DataSet object's WriteXml method.

The WXDataSetAddNewAndDelete method is implemented as follows:

```
static void WXDataSetAddNewAndDelete(string strFileName)
{
    DataSet ds = new DataSet(); // persisted XML loaded to Dataset ds
    DataTable tableRow; // Table named 'row' found in xml
    DataRow [] rows; // results of DataSet.Select returned here
    DataRow row;
    long lMaxShipperID = 0;

    // Load DataSet with persisted XML (XML stored in file)
    ds.ReadXml(strFileName, XmlReadMode.Auto);

    // FOR XML RAW produces a set of rows named "row" hence table "rows"
    tableRow = ds.Tables["row"];

    tableRow.BeginLoadData();
    // This means rows[0] will contain the MAX(ShipperID)
    rows = tableRow.Select("ShipperID>0", "ShipperID DESC");
    lMaxShipperID = Convert.ToInt32(rows[0]["ShipperID"].ToString());
    row = tableRow.NewRow();
    // If we were persisting back to Northwind.Shippers this would
    // be dangerous because ShipperID is an IDENTITY column
    row["ShipperID"] = ++lMaxShipperID;
    row["CompanyName"] = "Zoom, Zoom Delivery";
```

```
        row["Phone"] = "(800) 555-4321";
        tableRow.Rows.Add(row);

        rows = tableRow.Select("ShipperID='1'");
        row = rows[0];
        row.Delete();

        tableRow.EndLoadData();
        ds.AcceptChanges();
        ds.WriteXml(strFileName, XmlWriteMode.WriteSchema);
}
```

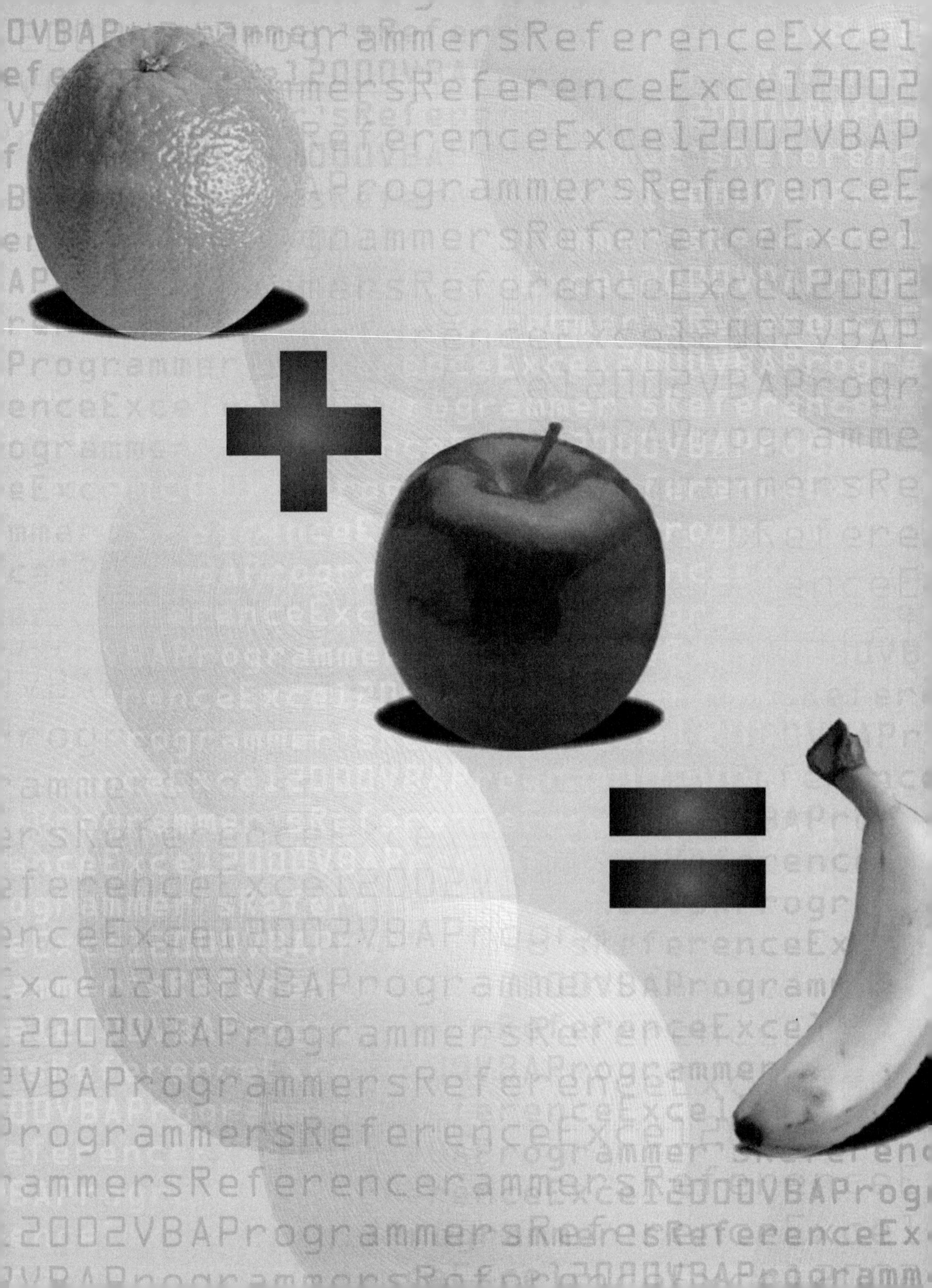

Miscellaneous Class Reference

The .NET Class Library is vast, and there was no possibility of discussing all of the classes in just the ADO.NET namespaces in this book (that is, classes contained in the `system.data`, `system.data.common`, `system.data.oledb`, and `system.data.sqlclient namespaces`). We've endeavored to discuss the key classes in the body of this book: the DataSet class, the Connection class, the Command class, the DataAdapter class, and so on. There are a multitude of more obscure classes that are contained in these namespaces however, which are no less essential in their own particular ways.

In this appendix, we provide details of all the classes in the ADO.Net namespaces that haven't been discussed elsewhere in the book. We give a brief explanation of each class, and document each method and property. We provide information about parameters, return types, and brief explanations of what they do.

System.Data Class Reference

The Constraint Object

See Chapter 9.

The ConstraintCollection Object

See Chapter 9.

The ConstraintException Object

Violating a constraint, represented by a `Constraint` object, fires a `ConstraintException`.

The ConstraintException constructor is overloaded, and may be initialized in three ways:

❑ With default field values.

❑ With a specified string variable, which will be displayed when the exception is thrown.

❑ Specifying serialization information, and the source and destination of the serialization stream. These parameters are necessary if the object is to be serialized.

Public Properties of the ConstraintException Object

Name	Parameters	Return Type	Notes
HelpLink		String	See Exception Class
InnerException		Exception	See Exception Class
Message		String	See Exception Class
Source		String	See Exception Class
StackTrace		String	See Exception Class
TargetSite		MethodBase	See Exception Class

Public Methods of the ConstraintException Object

Name	Parameters	Return Type	Notes
Equals	(Object:Obj) (Object:ObjA Object:ObjB)	Boolean	See Object Class
GetBaseException		Exception	Gets the original exception that was thrown
GetHashCode		Int32	See Object Class
GetObjectData	(SerializationInfo:Info StreamingContext:Context)	Void	See Exception Class
GetType		Type	See Object Class
ToString		String	See Exception Class

Protected Properties of the ConstraintException Object

Name	Parameters	Return Type	Notes
HResult			See Exception Class

Protected Methods of the ConstraintException Object

Name	Parameters	Return Type	Notes
Finalize			See Object Class
MemberwiseClone			See Object Class

DataColumn

See Chapter 8.

DataColumnChangeEventArgs

The `DataColumnChangeEventArgs` object provides the arguments for the `ColumnChanging` event.

Public Properties of the DataColumnChangeEventArgs Object

Name	Parameters	Return Type	Notes
Column		DataColumn	Provides the name of the column that contains a value that has changed
ProposedValue		Object	Specifies the new value
Row		DataRow	Specifies the row of the changed value

Public Methods of the DataColumnChangeEventArgs Object

Name	Parameters	Return Type	Notes
Equals	(Object:Obj) (Object:ObjA Object:ObjB)	Boolean	See Object class
GetHashCode		Int32	See Object class
GetType		Type	See Object class
ToString		String	See Object class

Protected Methods of the DataColumnChangeEventArgs Object

Name	Parameters	Return Type	Notes
Finalize			See Object class.
MemberwiseClone			See Object class.

The DataColumnCollection Object

See Chapter 8.

The DataException Object

A `DataException` object is created to represent any exception that is thrown by any of the ADO.NET components. It inherits from the base `System.Exception` class, and in turn it is the base class of the more specific exception classes:

❑ `ConstraintException`

❑ `DeletedRowInaccessibleException`

❑ `DuplicateNameException`

- ❑ InRowChangingEventException
- ❑ InvalidConstraintException
- ❑ InvalidExpressionException
- ❑ MissingPrimaryKeyException
- ❑ NoNullAllowedException
- ❑ ReadOnlyException
- ❑ RowNotInTableException
- ❑ StrongTypingException
- ❑ TypedDataSetGeneratorException
- ❑ VersionNotFoundException

Public Properties of the DataException Object

Name	Parameters	Return Type	Notes
HelpLink		String	See Exception Class
InnerException		Exception	See Exception Class
Message		String	See Exception Class
Source		String	See Exception Class
StackTrace		String	See Exception Class
TargetSite		Methodbase	See Exception Class

Public Methods of the DataException Object

Name	Parameters	Return Type	Notes
Equals	(Object:Obj) (Object:ObjA (Object:ObjB)	Boolean	See Object Class
GetBaseException		Exception	See Exception Class
GetHashCode		Int32	See Object Class
GetObjectData	(SerializationInfo:Info StreamingContext:Context)	Void	See Exception Class
GetType		Type	See Object Class
ToString		String	See Exception Class

Protected Properties of the DataException Object

Name	Parameters	Return Type	Notes
HResult			See Exception Class

Protected Methods of the DataException Object

Name	Parameters	Return Type	Notes
Finalize			See Object Class
MemberwiseClone			See Object Class

The DataRelation Class

See Chapter 9.

The DataRelationCollection Class

See Chapter 9.

The DataRow Class

See Chapter 8.

The DataRowChangeEventArgs Class

The DataRowChangeEventArgs object specifies arguments for the following events:

❑ RowChanged

❑ RowChanging

❑ OnRowDeleting

❑ OnRowDeleted

Public Properties of the DataRowChangeEventArgs Object

Name	Parameters	Return Type	Notes
Action		DataRowAction	Specifies the action that might have occurred on a DataRow
Row		DataRow	Specifies the row on which an action has been performed

Public Methods of the DataRowChangeEventArgs Object

Name	Parameters	Return Type	Notes
Equals	(Object:Obj) (Object:ObjA Object:ObjB)	Boolean	See Object Class
GetHashCode		Int32	See Object Class
GetType		Type	See Object Class
ToString		String	See Object Class

rotected Methods of the DataRowChangeEventArgs Object

Name	Parameters	Return Type	Notes
Finalize			Specifies the action that might have occurred on a DataRow
MemberwiseClone			Specifies the row on which an action has been performed

The DataRowCollection Class

See Chapter 8.

The DataRowView Class

The DataRowView represents a particular view of a DataRow object.

Public Properties of the DataRowView Class

Name	Parameters	Return Type	Notes
DataView		DataView	Specifies the DataView object with which a particular row is associated.
IsEdit		Boolean	This read-only property specifies whether it is possible to edit a particular row or not.
IsNew		Boolean	This read-only property specifies whether a particular DataRowView instance is new.
Item	(Int32:Index) (String:Property)	Object	This overloaded property specifies the value of a particular column. In C#, this is used as the indexer for this class.
Row		DataRow	This property provides the particular DataRow object which is to be viewed.
RowVersion		DataRowVersion	This specifies the version description of the particular DataRow.

Public Methods of the DataRowView Class

Name	Parameters	Return Type	Notes
BeginEdit		Void	This initiates an edit
CancelEdit		Void	This cancels an edit.
CreateChildView	(DataRelation:Relation) (String:RelationName)	DataView	This overloaded method returns a `DataView` for a child `DataTable`
Delete		Void	This simply deletes a particular row
EndEdit		Void	This ends an edit
Equals	(Object:Other)	Boolean	See `Object` Class
GetHashCode		Int32	This overridden method returns the hash code for a particular DataRow object
GetType		Type	See `Object` Class
ToString		String	See `Object` Class

Protected Methods of the DataRowView Class

Name	Parameters	Return Type	Notes
Finalize			See `Object` Class
MemberwiseClone			See `Object` Class

The DataSet Class

See Chapter 5.

The DataSysDescriptionAttribute Class

An `DataSysDescriptionAttribute` object specifies a description for a particular property, event, or extender.

Public Properties of the DataSysDescriptionAttribute Class

Name	Parameters	Return Type	Notes
Description		String	This overridden property provides us with an appropriate description
TypeId		Object	The TypeID property is used to ensure that, when this is implemented in a derived class, a unique identifier is associated with the attribute

Public Methods of the DataSysDescriptionAttribute Class

Name	Parameters	Return Type	Notes
Equals	(Object:Obj) (Object:ObjA Object:ObjB)	Boolean	See Object Class
GetHashCode		Int32	This overridden method provides a hash code for a particular instance of the class
GetType		Type	See Object Class
IsDefaultAttribute		Boolean	This method indicates whether the value of a particular instance of this class has default values
Match		Boolean	This method indicates whether a particular instance of this class is equal to a particular object
ToString		String	See Object Class

Protected Properties of the DataSysDescriptionAttribute Class

Name	Parameters	Return Type	Notes
DescriptionValue			Specifies the description as a string

Protected Methods of the DataSysDescriptionAttribute Class

Name	Parameters	Return Type	Notes
Finalize			See Object Class
MemberwiseClone			See Object Class

The DataTable Class

See Chapter 8.

The DataTableCollection Class

This contains a set of `DataTables` for the `DataSet` object.

Public Properties of the DataTableCollection Class

Name	Parameters	Return Type	Notes
Count		Int32	Specifies the number of particulars in the collection
IsReadOnly		Boolean	This indicates whether or not a particular `InternalDataCollectionBase` object is read-only
IsSynchronized		Boolean	This indicates whether the `InternalDataCollectionBase` is synchonized
Item	(Int32:Index) (String:Name)	DataTable	This overloaded property retrieves a specific `DataTable` object from the collection
SyncRoot		Object	Retrieves an object that may be used to synchronize the collection.

Public Methods of the DataTableCollection Class

Name	Parameters	Return Type	Notes
Add	(String:Name) (DataTable:Table)	DataTable Void	This overloaded method simply adds a table to the collection.
AddRange	(DataTable[ ]:Tables)	Void	Copies the elements of a `DataTable` array to the end of the collection.
CanRemove	(DataTable:Table)	Boolean	Specifies whether a particular table can be removed from a collection.
Clear		Void	Removes all tables from the collection.
Contains	(String:Name)	Boolean	This checks whether a particular table resides in the collection.
CopyTo	(Array:Ar Int32:Index)	Void	See `InternalDataCollectionBase` Class.

Table continued on following page

Name	Parameters	Return Type	Notes
Equals	(Object:Obj) (Object:ObjA Object:ObjB)	Boolean	See Object Class.
GetEnumerator		Ienumerator	See InternalDataCollectionBase Class. Gets an IEnumerator for the collection.
GetHashCode		Int32	See Object Class.
GetType		Type	See Object Class.
IndexOf	(String:TableName) (DataTable:Table)	Int32	This overloaded method gets the index of a particular table.
Remove	(DataTable:Table) (String:Name)	Void	This overloaded method removes a particular table from a collection.
RemoveAt	(Int32:Index)	Void	This method removes a table at a particular index from a collection.
ToString		String	See Object Class.

Public Events of the DataTableCollection Class

Name	Parameters	Return Type	Notes
CollectionChanged			This is generated when a collection has changed in any way
CollectionChanging			This is generated when a collection is in the process of changing in any way

Protected Properties of the DataTableCollection Class

Name	Parameters	Return Type	Notes
List		ArrayList	This overidden property gets the tables in a particular collection, returning them as an ArrayList object.

Protected Methods of the DataTableCollection Class

Name	Parameters	Return Type	Notes
Finalize			See Object Class.
MemberwiseClone			See Object Class.
OnCollectionChanged			This method generates the OnCollectionChanged event.
OnCollectionChanging			This method generated the OnCollectionChanging event.

The DataView Class

See Chapter 10.

The DataViewManager Class

See Chapter 10.

The DataViewSetting Class

See Chapter 10.

The DataViewSettingCollection Class

See Chapter 10.

The DBConcurrencyException Class

If an update operation is undertaken when using the DataAdapter and no rows are affected, then the DBConcurrencyException is generated.

Public Properties of the DBConcurrencyException Class

Name	Parameters	Return Type	Notes
HelpLink		String	See Exception Class
InnerException		Exception	See Exception Class
Message		String	See Exception Class
Row		DataRow	See Exception Class
Source		String	See Exception Class
StackTrace		String	See Exception Class
TargetSite		MethodBase	See Exception Class

Public Methods of the DBConcurrencyException Class

Name	Parameters	Return Type	Notes
Equals	(Object:Obj) (Object:ObjA Object:ObjB)	Boolean	See Object Class
GetBaseException		Exception	See Exception Class
GetHashCode		Int32	See Object Class
GetObjectData	(SerializationInfo:Info StreamingContext:Context)	Void	See Exception Class
GetType		Type	See Object Class
ToString		String	See Exception Class

Protected Properties of the DBConcurrencyException Class

Name	Parameters	Return Type	Notes
HResult			See Exception Class

Protected Methods of the DBConcurrencyException Class

Name	Parameters	Return Type	Notes
Finalize			See Object Class
MemberwiseClone			See Object Class

The DeletedRowInaccessibleException Class

When any action is attempted on a DataRow that has been deleted or doesn't exist, a DeletedRowInaccessibleException object is thrown.

Public Properties of the DeletedRowInaccessibleException Class

Name	Parameters	Return Type	Notes
HelpLink		String	See Object Class
InnerException		Exception	See Exception Class
Message		String	See Object Class
Source		DataRow	See Exception Class
StackTrace		String	See Object Class
TargetSite		String	See Exception Class

Public Methods of the DeletedRowInaccessibleException Class

Name	Parameters	Return Type	Notes
Equals	(Object:Obj) (Object:ObjA Object:ObjB)	Boolean	See Object Class
GetBaseException		Exception	See Exception Class
GetHashCode		Int32	See Object Class
GetObjectData	(SerializationInfo:Info StreamingContext:Context)	Void	See Exception Class
GetType		Type	See Object Class
ToString		String	See Exception Class

Protected Properties of the DeletedRowInaccessibleException Class

Name	Parameters	Return Type	Notes
HResult			See Exception Class

Protected Methods of the DeletedRowInaccessibleException Class

Name	Parameters	Return Type	Notes
Finalize			See Object Class
MemberwiseClone			See Object Class

The DuplicateNameException Class

When using an Add operation on any DataSet associated object, there is always a possibility that we will encounter duplicate names for a particular database element – a table, column, row, constraint, or relation . If this happens, a DuplicateNameException object is thrown.

Public Properties of the DuplicateNameException Class

Name	Parameters	Return Type	Notes
HelpLink		String	See Object Class
InnerException		Exception	See Exception Class
Message		String	See Object Class
Source		DataRow	See Exception Class
StackTrace		String	See Object Class
TargetSite		String	See Exception Class

Public Methods of the DuplicateNameException Class

Name	Parameters	Return Type	Notes
Equals	(Object:Obj) (Object:ObjA Object:ObjB)	Boolean	See Object Class
GetBaseException		Exception	See Exception Class
GetHashCode		Int32	See Object Class
GetObjectData	(SerializationInfo:Info StreamingContext:Context)	Void	See Exception Class
GetType		Type	See Object Class
ToString		String	See Exception Class

Protected Properties of the DuplicateNameException Class

Name	Parameters	Return Type	Notes
HResult			See Exception Class

Protected Methods of the DuplicateNameException Class

Name	Parameters	Return Type	Notes
Finalize			See Object Class
MemberwiseClone			See Object Class

The EvaluateException Class

If the Expression property of a DataColumn cannot be evaluated, an EvaluateException is thrown.

Public Properties of the EvaluateException Class

Name	Parameters	Return Type	Notes
HelpLink		String	See Object Class
InnerException		Exception	See Exception Class
Message		String	See Object Class
Source		DataRow	See Exception Class
StackTrace		String	See Object Class
TargetSite		String	See Exception Class

Public Methods of the EvaluateException Class

Name	Parameters	Return Type	Notes
Equals	(Object:Obj) (Object:ObjA Object:ObjB)	Boolean	See Object Class
GetBaseException		Exception	See Exception Class
GetHashCode		Int32	See Object Class
GetObjectData	(SerializationInfo:Info StreamingContext:Context)	Void	See Exception Class
GetType		Type	See Object Class
ToString		String	See Exception Class

Protected Properties of the EvaluateException Class

Name	Parameters	Return Type	Notes
HResult			See Exception Class

Protected Methods of the EvaluateException Class

Name	Parameters	Return Type	Notes
Finalize			See Object Class
MemberwiseClone			See Object Class

The FillErrorEventArgs Class

The FillErrorEventArgs simply specifies arguments for the DataAdapter object's FillError event.

Public Properties of the FillErrorEventArgs Class

Name	Parameters	Return Type	Notes
Continue		Boolean	This gets or sets a value that indicates whether a fill operation should be continued
DataTable		DataTable	Gets the particular DataTable which was being updated when the FillError event was fired
Errors		Exception	Gets particular errors

Name	Parameters	Return Type	Notes
Values		Object()	Gets the values for the row which was being updated when the error occurred

Public Methods of the FillErrorEventArgs Class

Name	Parameters	Return Type	Notes
Equals	(Object:Obj) (Object:ObjA Object:ObjB)	Boolean	See Object Class
GetHashCode		Int32	See Object Class
GetType		Type	See Object Class
ToString		String	See Object Class

Protected Methods of the FillErrorEventArgs Class

Name	Parameters	Return Type	Notes
Finalize			See Object Class
MemberwiseClone			See Object Class

The ForeignKeyConstraint Class

A ForeignKeyConstraint object represents a constraint on a particular column or columns within particular tables. By representing a relationship between a primary key and a foreign key, it restricts changes that may be made to values within specified columns.

Public Properties of the ForeignKeyConstraint Class

Name	Parameters	Return Type	Notes
AcceptRejectRule		AcceptRejectRule	When changes are made to a DataRow or DataTable, they are not finalized until AcceptChanges is called. The AcceptRejectRule property indicates the types of changes that should be made to the appropriate related columns. Values may be: None: the default. Cascade: values are also changed appropriately in related columns.

Name	Parameters	Return Type	Notes
Columns		DataColumn[ ]	Gets the child columns of a particular constraint.
ConstraintName		String	See `Constraint` class.
DeleteRule		Rule	When elements are deleted in a particular table, the `DeleteRule` property determines what will happen to values contained in related columns in child tables. Values may be: `Cascade`: the default. Values are also deleted in related columns. `None`: no changes, but an exception is thrown. `SetNull`: related values are set to null. `SetDefault`: related values are set to a specified default. `Default`: related values are set to the default values for a particular column.
RelatedColumns		DataColumn[ ]	Specifies the parent columns of a particular constraint.
RelatedTable		DataTable	Gets the parent table of a particular constraint.
Table		DataTable	This overridden property gets the child table of a particular constraint.

Name	Parameters	Return Type	Notes
UpdateRule		Rule	When elements are updated in a particular table, the DeleteRule property determines what will happen to values contained in related columns in child tables. Values may be: Cascade: the default. Values are also updated in related columns. None: no changes, but an exception is thrown. SetNull: related values are set to null. SetDefault: related values are set to a specified default. Default: related values are set to the default values for a particular column.

Public Methods of the ForeignKeyConstraint Class

Name	Parameters	Return Type	Notes
Equals	(Object:Obj) (Object:ObjA Object:ObjB)	Boolean	See Object Class
GetHashCode		Int32	See Object Class
GetType		Type	See Object Class
ToString		String	See Object Class

Protected Methods of the ForeignKeyConstraint Class

Name	Parameters	Return Type	Notes
Finalize			See Object Class
MemberwiseClone			See Object Class

The InRowChangingEventException Class

Represents the exception that is thrown when calling the EndEdit method within the RowChanging event.

When the EndEdit method is called within the RowChanging event, the InRowChangingEventException object is thrown.

Public Properties of the InRowChangingEventException Class

Name	Parameters	Return Type	Notes
HelpLink		String	See Exception Class
InnerException		Exception	See Exception Class
Message		String	See Exception Class
Source		DataRow	See Exception Class
StackTrace		String	See Exception Class
TargetSite		String	See Exception Class

Public Methods of the InRowChangingEventException Class

Name	Parameters	Return Type	Notes
Equals	(Object:Obj) (Object:ObjA Object:ObjB)	Boolean	See Object Class
GetBaseException		Exception	See Exception Class
GetHashCode		Int32	See Object Class
GetObjectData	(SerializationInfo:Info StreamingContext:Context)	Void	See Exception Class
GetType		Type	See Object Class
ToString		String	See Exception Class

Protected Properties of the InRowChangingEventException Class

Name	Parameters	Return Type	Notes
HResult			See Exception Class

Protected Methods of the InRowChangingEventException Class

Name	Parameters	Return Type	Notes
Finalize			See Object Class
MemberwiseClone			See Object Class

The InternalDataCollectionBase Class

The InternalDataCollectionBase is the base class of specific Collection objects.

Public Properties of the InternalDataCollectionBase Class

Name	Parameters	Return Type	Notes
Count		Int32	Specifies the number ofparticulars in the collection
IsReadOnly		Boolean	This indicates whether or not a particular InternalDataCollectionBase object is read-only
IsSynchronized		Boolean	This indicates whether the InternalDataCollectionBase is synchonized
SyncRoot		Object	Retrieves an object that may be used to synchronize the collection

Public Methods of the InternalDataCollectionBase Class

Name	Parameters	Return Type	Notes
CopyTo	(Array:Ar Int32:Index)	Void	This method copies elements from a particular InternalDataCollectionBase to a one-dimensional array, from a specified InternalDataCollectionBase index
Equals	(Object:Obj) (Object:ObjA Object:ObjB)	Boolean	See Object Class.
GetEnumerator		IEnumerator	Gets an IEnumerator for a particular collection
GetHashCode		Int32	See Object Class
GetType		Type	See Object Clas
ToString		String	See Object Class

Protected Properties of the InternalDataCollectionBase Class

Name	Parameters	Return Type	Notes
List			Lists all the items in a collection

Protected Methods of the InternalDataCollectionBase Class

Name	Parameters	Return Type	Notes
Finalize			See Object Class
MemberwiseClone			See Object Class

The InvalidConstraintException Class

When an error is made when trying to create or access a particular relation, an InvalidConstraintException is thrown.

Public Properties of the InvalidConstraintException Class

Name	Parameters	Return Type	Notes
HelpLink		String	See Exception Class
InnerException		Exception	See Exception Class
Message		String	See Exception Class
Source		DataRow	See Exception Class
StackTrace		String	See Exception Class
TargetSite		String	See Exception Class

Public Methods of the InvalidConstraintException Class

Name	Parameters	Return Type	Notes
Equals	(Object:Obj) (Object:ObjA Object:ObjB)	Boolean	See Object Class
GetBaseException		Exception	See Exception Class
GetHashCode		Int32	See Object Class
GetObjectData	(SerializationInfo:Info StreamingContext:Context)	Void	See Exception Class
GetType		Type	See Object Class
ToString		String	See Exception Class

Protected Properties of the InvalidConstraintException Class

Name	Parameters	Return Type	Notes
HResult			See Exception Class

Protected Methods of the InvalidConstraintException Class

Name	Parameters	Return Type	Notes
Finalize			See Object Class
MemberwiseClone			See Object Class

The InvalidExpressionException Class

When attempting to add a `DataColumn` to a `DataColumnCollection`, if the `DataColumn` contains an invalid `Expression`, an `InvalidExpressionException` will be thrown.

Public Properties of the InvalidExpressionException Class

Name	Parameters	Return Type	Notes
HelpLink		String	See Exception Class
InnerException		Exception	See Exception Class
Message		String	See Exception Class
Source		DataRow	See Exception Class
StackTrace		String	See Exception Class
TargetSite		String	See Exception Class

Public Methods InvalidExpressionException Class

Name	Parameters	Return Type	Notes
Equals	(Object:Obj) (Object:ObjA Object:ObjB)	Boolean	See Object Class
GetBaseException		Exception	See Exception Class
GetHashCode		Int32	See Object Class
GetObjectData	(SerializationInfo:Info StreamingContext:Context)	Void	See Exception Class
GetType		Type	See Object Class
ToString		String	See Exception Class

Protected Properties InvalidExpressionException Class

Name	Parameters	Return Type	Notes
HResult			See Exception Class

Protected Methods InvalidExpressionException Class

Name	Parameters	Return Type	Notes
Finalize			See Object Class
MemberwiseClone			See Object Class

The MergeFailedEventArgs Class

When a target and a source `DataRow` happen to share the same primary key values, a `MergeFailedEventArgs` object is generated. This only occurs when the `EnforceConstraints` property of a `DataSet` object is set to true.

Public Properties of the MergeFailedEventArgs Class

Name	Parameters	Return Type	Notes
Conflict		String	Provides details about the type of merge conflict encountered
Table		DataTable	Provides the name of the relevant `DataTable`

Public Methods of the MergeFailedEventArgs Class

Name	Parameters	Return Type	Notes
Equals	(Object:Obj) (Object:ObjA Object:ObjB)	Boolean	See `Object` Class
GetHashCode		Int32	See `Object` Class
GetType		Type	See `Object` Class
ToString		String	See `Object` Class

Protected Methods of the MergeFailedEventArgs Class

Name	Parameters	Return Type	Notes
Finalize			See `Object` Class
MemberwiseClone			See `Object` Class

The MissingPrimaryKeyException Class

When we try to access a row in a particular table that has no primary key, a `MissingPrimaryKeyException` is thrown.

Public Properties of the MissingPrimaryKeyException Class

Name	Parameters	Return Type	Notes
HelpLink		String	See `Exception` Class
InnerException		Exception	See `Exception` Class
Message		String	See `Exception` Class
Source		DataRow	See `Exception` Class
StackTrace		String	See `Exception` Class
TargetSite		String	See `Exception` Class

Public Methods of the MissingPrimaryKeyException Class

Name	Parameters	Return Type	Notes
Equals	(Object:Obj) (Object:ObjA Object:ObjB)	Boolean	See Object Class
GetBaseException		Exception	See Exception Class
GetHashCode		Int32	See Object Class
GetObjectData	(SerializationInfo:Info StreamingContext:Context)	Void	See Exception Class
GetType		Type	See Object Class
ToString		String	See Exception Class

Protected Properties of the MissingPrimaryKeyException Class

Name	Parameters	Return Type	Notes
HResult			See Exception Class

Protected Methods of the MissingPrimaryKeyException Class

Name	Parameters	Return Type	Notes
Finalize			See Object Class
MemberwiseClone			See Object Class

The NoNullAllowedException Class

If we try to insert a null value into a column where AllowDBNull is set to false, a NoNullAllowedException object is generated.

Public Properties of the NoNullAllowedException Class

Name	Parameters	Return Type	Notes
HelpLink		String	See Exception Class
InnerException		Exception	See Exception Class
Message		String	See Exception Class
Source		DataRow	See Exception Class
StackTrace		String	See Exception Class
TargetSite		String	See Exception Class

Public Methods of the NoNullAllowedException Class

Name	Parameters	Return Type	Notes
Equals	(Object:Obj) (Object:ObjA Object:ObjB)	Boolean	See Object Class
GetBaseException		Exception	See Exception Class
GetHashCode		Int32	See Object Class
GetObjectData	(SerializationInfo:Info StreamingContext:Context)	Void	See Exception Class
GetType		Type	See Object Class
ToString		String	See Exception Class

Protected Properties of the NoNullAllowedException Class

Name	Parameters	Return Type	Notes
HResult			See Exception Class

Protected Methods of the NoNullAllowedException Class

Name	Parameters	Return Type	Notes
Finalize			See Object Class
MemberwiseClone			See Object Class

The PropertyCollection Class

The `PropertyCollection` object simply represents a set of properties that may be added to a `DataSet`, `DataTable`, or `DataColumn` object.

We would use this object to add customized properties to any `DataSet`, `DataTable`, or `DataColumn` object (these can be accessed via the `ExtendedProperties` property of the relevant object).

Public Properties of the PropertyCollection Class

Name	Parameters	Return Type	Notes
Count		Int32	Provides the total number of key-and-value pairs contained in a particular PropertyCollection object
IsFixedSize		Boolean	See Hashtable Class
IsReadOnly		Boolean	See Hashtable Class
IsSynchronized		Boolean	See Hashtable Class
Item	(Object:Key)	Object	See Hashtable Class
Keys		ICollection	See Hashtable Class

Name	Parameters	Return Type	Notes
SyncRoot		Object	See Hashtable Class
Values		ICollection	See Hashtable Class

Public Methods of the PropertyCollection Class

Name	Parameters	Return Type	Notes
Add	(Object:Key Object:Value)	Void	See Hashtable Class
Clear		Void	See Hashtable Class
Clone		Object	See Hashtable Class
Contains	(Object:Key)	Boolean	See Hashtable Class
ContainsKey	(Object:Key)	Boolean	See Hashtable Class
ContainsValue	(Object:Value)	Boolean	See Hashtable Class
CopyTo	(Array:Array Int32:ArrayIndex)	Void	See Hashtable Class
Equals	(Object:Obj) (Object:ObjA Object:ObjB)	Boolean	See Object Class
GetEnumerator		Idictionary Enumerator	See Hashtable Class
GetHashCode		Int32	See Object Class
GetObjectData	(SerializationInfo :Info StreamingContext: Context)	Void	See Hashtable Class
GetType		Type	See Object Class
OnDeserialization	(Object:Sender)	Void	See Hashtable Class
Remove	(Object:Key)	Void	See Hashtable Class
ToString		String	See Object Class

Protected Properties of the PropertyCollection Class

Name	Parameters	Return Type	Notes
comparer			See Hashtable Class
hcp			See Hashtable Class

Protected Methods of the PropertyCollection Class

Name	Parameters	Return Type	Notes
Finalize			See Object Class.
GetHash			See Hashtable Class.
KeyEquals			See Hashtable Class.
MemberwiseClone			See Object Class.

The ReadOnlyException Class

If we were to try to change the value of a read-only column, a ReadOnlyException object would be thrown.

Public Properties of the ReadOnlyException Class

Name	Parameters	Return Type	Notes
HelpLink		String	See Exception Class
InnerException		Exception	See Exception Class
Message		String	See Exception Class
Source		DataRow	See Exception Class
StackTrace		String	See Exception Class
TargetSite		String	See Exception Class

Public Methods of the ReadOnlyException Class

Name	Parameters	Return Type	Notes
Equals	(Object:Obj) (Object:ObjA Object:ObjB)	Boolean	See Object Class
GetBaseException		Exception	See Exception Class
GetHashCode		Int32	See Object Class
GetObjectData	(SerializationInfo:Info StreamingContext:Context)	Void	See Exception Class
GetType		Type	See Object Class
ToString		String	See Exception Class

Protected Properties of the ReadOnlyException Class

Name	Parameters	Return Type	Notes
HResult			See Exception Class

Protected Methods of the ReadOnlyException Class

Name	Parameters	Return Type	Notes
Finalize			See Object Class
MemberwiseClone			See Object Class

The RowNotInTableException Class

Represents the exception that is thrown when trying to perform an operation on a DataRow that is not in a DataTable.

Public Properties of the RowNotInTableException Class

Name	Parameters	Return Type	Notes
HelpLink		String	See Exception Class
InnerException		Exception	See Exception Class
Message		String	See Exception Class
Source		DataRow	See Exception Class
StackTrace		String	See Exception Class
TargetSite		String	See Exception Class

Public Methods of the RowNotInTableException Class

Name	Parameters	Return Type	Notes
Equals	(Object:Obj) (Object:ObjA Object:ObjB)	Boolean	See Object Class
GetBaseException		Exception	See Exception Class
GetHashCode		Int32	See Object Class
GetObjectData	(SerializationInfo:Info StreamingContext:Context)	Void	See Exception Class
GetType		Type	See Object Class
ToString		String	See Exception Class

Protected Properties of the RowNotInTableException Class

Name	Parameters	Return Type	Notes
HResult			See Exception Class

Protected Methods of the RowNotInTableException Class

Name	Parameters	Return Type	Notes
Finalize			See Object Class
MemberwiseClone			See Object Class

The StateChangeEventArgs Class

This object simply specifies the arguments for the StateChange event of a Connection object (the StateChange event occurs when the state of a connection changes in any way).

Public Properties of the StateChangeEventArgs Class

Name	Parameters	Return Type	Notes
CurrentState		ConnectionState	This read-only property specifies the *new* state of a connection
OriginalState		ConnectionState	This read-only property specifies the previous state of a connection

Public Methods of the StateChangeEventArgs Class

Name	Parameters	Return Type	Notes
Equals	(Object:Obj) (Object:ObjA Object:ObjB)	Boolean	See Object Class
GetHashCode		Int32	See Object Class
GetType		Type	See Object Class
ToString		String	See Object Class

Protected Methods of the StateChangeEventArgs Class

Name	Parameters	Return Type	Notes
Finalize			See Object Class
MemberwiseClone			See Object Class

The StrongTypingException Class

When we try to access a DBNull value in a strongly-typed DataSet object, a StrongTypingException object will be generated.

Public Properties of the StrongTypingException Class

Name	Parameters	Return Type	Notes
HelpLink		String	See Exception Class
InnerException		Exception	See Exception Class
Message		String	See Exception Class
Source		DataRow	See Exception Class
StackTrace		String	See Exception Class
TargetSite		String	See Exception Class

Public Methods of the StrongTypingException Class

Name	Parameters	Return Type	Notes
Equals	(Object:Obj) (Object:ObjA Object:ObjB)	Boolean	See Object Class
GetBaseException		Exception	See Exception Class
GetHashCode		Int32	See Object Class
GetObjectData	(SerializationInfo:Info StreamingContext:Context)	Void	See Exception Class
GetType		Type	See Object Class
ToString		String	See Exception Class

Protected Properties of the StrongTypingException Class

Name	Parameters	Return Type	Notes
HResult			See Exception Class

Protected Methods of the StrongTypingException Class

Name	Parameters	Return Type	Notes
Finalize			See Object Class
MemberwiseClone			See Object Class

The SyntaxErrorException Class

When a syntax error is detected in the `Expression` property of a `DataColumn` object, a `SyntaxErrorException` is thrown.

Public Properties of the SyntaxErrorException Class

Name	Parameters	Return Type	Notes
HelpLink		String	See Exception Class
InnerException		Exception	See Exception Class
Message		String	See Exception Class
Source		DataRow	See Exception Class
StackTrace		String	See Exception Class
TargetSite		String	See Exception Class

Public Methods of the SyntaxErrorException Class

Name	Parameters	Return Type	Notes
Equals	(Object:Obj) (Object:ObjA Object:ObjB)	Boolean	See Object Class
GetBaseException		Exception	See Exception Class
GetHashCode		Int32	See Object Class
GetObjectData	(SerializationInfo:Info StreamingContext:Context)	Void	See Exception Class
GetType		Type	See Object Class
ToString		String	See Exception Clas

Protected Properties of the SyntaxErrorException Class

Name	Parameters	Return Type	Notes
HResult			See Exception Class

Protected Methods of the SyntaxErrorException Class

Name	Parameters	Return Type	Notes
Finalize			See Object Class
MemberwiseClone			See Object Class

The TypedDataSetGenerator Class

The `TypedDataSetGenerator` is used to create a strongly typed `DataSet`.

Public Shared Methods of the TypedDataSetGenerator Class

Name	Parameters	Return Type	Notes
Generate	(DataSet:DataSet CodeNamespace:CodeNamespace IcodeGenerator:CodeGen)	Void	Generates a strongly-typed `DataSet`
GenerateIdName	(String:Name IcodeGenerator:CodeGen)	String	Transforms a string in a valid typed `DataSet` name

Public Methods of the TypedDataSetGenerator Class

Name	Parameters	Return Type	Notes
Equals	(Object:Obj) (Object:ObjA Object:ObjB)	Boolean	See `Object` Class
GetHashCode		Int32	See `Object` Class
GetType		Type	See `Object` Class
ToString		String	See `Object` Class

Protected Methods of the TypedDataSetGenerator Class

Name	Parameters	Return Type	Notes
Finalize			See `Object` Class
MemberwiseClone			See `Object` Class

The TypedDataSetGeneratorException Class

If a name conflict occurs when we are attempting to create a strongly-typed `DataSet`, a `TypedDataSetGeneratorException` object is generated.

Public Properties of the TypedDataSetGeneratorException Class

Name	Parameters	Return Type	Notes
ErrorList		ArrayList	Provides a dynamic list of generated errors
HelpLink		String	See `Exception` Class
InnerException		Exception	See `Exception` Class
Message		String	See `Exception` Class
Source		DataRow	See `Exception` Class
StackTrace		String	See `Exception` Class
TargetSite		String	See `Exception` Class

Public Methods of the TypedDataSetGeneratorException Class

Name	Parameters	Return Type	Notes
Equals	(Object:Obj) (Object:ObjA Object:ObjB)	Boolean	See Object Class
GetBaseException		Exception	See Exception Class
GetHashCode		Int32	See Object Class
GetObjectData	(SerializationInfo:Info StreamingContext:Context)	Void	See Exception Class
GetType		Type	See Object Class
ToString		String	See Exception Class

Protected Properties of the TypedDataSetGeneratorException Class

Name	Parameters	Return Type	Notes
HResult			See Exception Class

Protected Methods of the TypedDataSetGeneratorException Class

Name	Parameters	Return Type	Notes
Finalize			See Object Class
MemberwiseClone			See Object Class

The UniqueConstraint Class

The UniqueConstraint class is used to ensure that all values within a column are unique.

Public Properties of the UniqueConstraint Class

Name	Parameters	Return Type	Notes
Columns		DataColumn[ ]	Gets the array of columns to which this constraint is applied
ConstraintName		String	See Constraint Class.
IsPrimaryKey		Boolean	Specifies a value which indicates whether the constraint is on a primary key
Table		DataTable	This overridden property specifies the table to which this constraint belongs

Public Methods of the UniqueConstraint Class

Name	Parameters	Return Type	Notes
Equals	(Object:Obj) (Object:ObjA Object:ObjB)	Boolean	See Object Class
GetHashCode		Int32	See Object Class
GetType		Type	See Object Class
ToString		String	See Constraint Class

Protected Methods of the UniqueConstraint Class

Name	Parameters	Return Type	Notes
Finalize			See Object Class
MemberwiseClone			See Object Class

The VersionNotFoundException Class

If we were to try to return a DataRow that has been deleted, a VersionNotFoundException object is generated.

Public Properties of the VersionNotFoundException Class

Name	Parameters	Return Type	Notes
HelpLink		String	See Exception Class
InnerException		Exception	See Exception Class
Message		String	See Exception Class
Source		DataRow	See Exception Class
StackTrace		String	See Exception Class
TargetSite		String	See Exception Class

Public Methods of the VersionNotFoundException Class

Name	Parameters	Return Type	Notes
Equals	(Object:Obj) (Object:ObjA Object:ObjB)	Boolean	See Object Class
GetBaseException		Exception	See Exception Class
GetHashCode		Int32	See Object Class
GetObjectData	(SerializationInfo:Info StreamingContext:Context)	Void	See Exception Class

Name	Parameters	Return Type	Notes
GetType ToString		Type String	See Object Class See Exception Class

Protected Properties of the VersionNotFoundException Class

Name	Parameters	Return Type	Notes
HResult			See Exception Class

Protected Methods of the VersionNotFoundException Class

Name	Parameters	Return Type	Notes
Finalize			See Object Class
MemberwiseClone			See Object Class

System.Data.Common Class Reference

The DataAdapter Class

See Chapter 7.

The DataColumnMapping Class

See Chapter 11.

The DataColumnMappingCollection Class

See Chapter 11.

The DataTableMapping Class

See Chapter 11.

The DataTableMappingCollection Class

See Chapter 11.

The DbDataAdapter Class

See Chapter 7.

The DBDataPermission Class

This class enables a .NET application to control the access granted to particular users to data providers.

Public Properties of the DBDataPermission Class

Name	Parameters	Return Type	Notes
AllowBlankPassword		Boolean	This simply specifies whether a blank password may be used to access a particular data source

Public Methods of the DBDataPermission Class

Name	Parameters	Return Type	Notes
Assert		Void	Grants permissions to calling code to access the data source specified by a particular permission object (even when callers higher in the call stack have been revoked permissions).
Copy		Ipermission	This overridden method creates a copy of a particular permission object.
Demand		Void	Indicates whether callers higher in the call stack to the current caller have been granted particular permissions by the permission object.
DemandImmediate		Void	Indicates whether the immediate caller of the code that accesses this method has been granted particular permissions by the permission object.
Deny		Void	Prevents callers who are higher in the call stack from accessing a particular resource.
Equals	(Object:Obj) (Object:ObjA Object:ObjB)	Boolean	See Object Class.
FromXml	(SecurityElement: SecurityElement)	Void	This overridden method uses an XML specification to reconstruct a particular security object.
GetHashCode		Int32	See Object Class.
GetType		Type	See Object Class.

Name	Parameters	Return Type	Notes
Intersect	(IPermission: Target)	IPermission	This overridden method will return a permission object that represents the set of permissions from two other permission objects (the intersection) that must be passed to access a particular resource.
IsSubsetOf	(IPermission: Target)	Boolean	This overridden method indicates whether the permission object is a subset of a specific other permission object.
IsUnrestricted		Boolean	This indicates whether a particular permission can be unrestricted.
PermitOnly		Void	This ensures that only those resources that are specified by a particular permission object can be accessed by the calling code. String.
ToString		String	This overridden method returns a string representing the permission object.
ToXml		SecurityElement	This overridden method returns an XML representation of the permission object.
Union	(IPermission:Target)	IPermission	This overridden method returns a new permission object that represents the permissions of both the current permission object and another specified permission object.

Protected Fields of the DBDataPermission Class

Name	Parameters	Return Type	Notes
connectionStringRestrictions			A collection of security specifications associated with particular connection strings. Hashtable

Protected Methods of the DBDataPermission Class

Name	Parameters	Return Type	Notes
Finalize			See Object Class
MemberwiseClone			See Object Class

The DBDataPermissionAttribute Class

See Chapter 15.

The RowUpdatedEventArgs Class

Public Properties of the RowUpdatedEventArgs Class

Name	Parameters	Return Type	Notes
Command		IdbCommand	Specifies the IDbCommand which is called when Update is called
Errors		Exception	Specifies any errors that might have been generated when a Command is executed
RecordsAffected		Int32	Specifies the number of records which were affected by the command
Row		DataRow	Specifies the DataRow that was sent to Update
StatementType		StatementType	Specifies the type of SQL statement that was used (SELECT, INSERT, UPDATE, or DELETE)
Status		UpdateStatus	Specifies the UpdateStatus of the Command
TableMapping		DataTableMapping	Specifies the DataTableMapping object that was sent to Update

Public Methods of the RowUpdatedEventArgs Class

Name	Parameters	Return Type	Notes
Equals	(Object:Obj) (Object:ObjA Object:ObjB)	Boolean	See Object Class
GetHashCode		Int32	See Object Class
GetType		Type	See Object Clas
ToString		String	See Object Class

Protected Methods of the RowUpdatedEventArgs Class

Name	Parameters	Return Type	Notes
Finalize			See Object Clas
MemberwiseClone			See Object Class

The RowUpdatingEventArgs Class

Public Properties of the RowUpdatingEventArgs Class

Name	Parameters	Return Type	Notes
Command		IdbCommand	Specifies the IDbCommand which is called when Update is called
Errors		Exception	Specifies any errors that might have been generated when a Command is executed
Row		DataRow	Specifies the DataRow which was sent to Update
StatementType		StatementType	Specifies the type of SQL statement that was used (SELECT, INSERT, UPDATE, or DELETE)
Status		UpdateStatus	Specifies the UpdateStatus of the Command
TableMapping		DataTableMapping	Specifies the DataTableMapping object that was sent to Update

Public Methods of the RowUpdatingEventArgs Class

Name	Parameters	Return Type	Notes
Equals	(Object:Obj) (Object:ObjA Object:ObjB)	Boolean	See Object Class
GetHashCode		Int32	See Object Class

Name	Parameters	Return Type	Notes
GetType		Type	See Object Class
ToString		String	See Object Class

Protected Methods of the RowUpdatingEventArgs Class

Name	Parameters	Return Type	Notes
Finalize			See Object Class
MemberwiseClone			See Object Class

System.Data.OleDb and System.Data.SqlClient Class Reference

OleDbCommand / SqlCommand

See Chapter 4.

The OleDbCommandBuilder / SqlCommandBuilder Class

Provides a means of automatically generating single-table commands for update, delete and insert operations provided a Select command has been provided.

Public Properties of the OleDbCommandBuilder / SqlCommandBuilder Class

Name	Parameters	Return Type	Notes
Container		Icontainer	See Component Class
DataAdapter		OleDbDataAdapter / SqlDataAdapter	Specifies the OleDbDataAdapter for which SQL statements will be created
QuotePrefix		String	Specifies the prefix used in the names of particular types of database objects
QuoteSuffix		String	Specifies the suffix used in the names of particular types of database objects
Site		ISite	See Component Class

Public Methods of the OleDbCommandBuilder / SqlCommandBuilder Class

Name	Parameters	Return Type	Notes
CreateObjRef	(Type:RequestedType)	ObjRef	Provides a reference to a particular object
Dispose		Void	This overridden method frees resources that have been used by the object
Equals	(Object:Obj) (Object:ObjA Object:ObjB)	Boolean	See Object Class

Name	Parameters	Return Type	Notes
GetDeleteCommand		OleDbCommand / SqlCommand	Returns the SQL command required to delete particular rows from the database.
GetHashCode		Int32	See Object Class.

Name	Parameters	Return Type	Notes
GetInsertCommand		OleDbCommand / SqlCommand	Returns the SQL command required to insert new rows into the database.
GetLifetimeService		Object	See MarshalByRefObject Class.
GetType		Type	See Object Class.
GetUpdateCommand		OleDbCommand / SqlCommand	Returns the SQL command required to update rows in the database.
InitializeLifetimeService		Object	See MarshalByRefObject Class.
RefreshSchema		Void	This simply refreshes the database schema.
ToString		String	See Object Class.

Public Events of the OleDbCommandBuilder / SqlCommandBuilder Class

Name	Parameters	Return Type	Notes
Disposed			See Component Class

Protected Properties of the OleDbCommandBuilder / SqlCommandBuilder Class

Name	Parameters	Return Type	Notes
DesignMode			See Component Class
Events			See Component Class

Protected Methods of the OleDbCommandBuilder / SqlCommandBuilder Clas

Name	Parameters	Return Type	Notes
Finalize			See Object Class
GetService			See Component Class
MemberwiseClone			See Object Class.

OleDbConnection / SqlConnection

See Chapter 3.

OleDbDataAdapter / SqlDataAdapter

See Chapter 7.

OleDbDataReader / SqlDataReader

See Chapter 6.

OleDbError Class / SqlError

See Chapter 14.

OleDbErrorCollection / SqlErrorCollection

See Chapter 14.

OleDbException / SqlException

See Chapter 14.

The OleDbInfoMessageEventArgs / SqlInfoMessageEventArgs Class

Public Properties of the OleDbInfoMessageEventArgs / SqlInfoMessageEventArgs Class

Name	Parameters	Return Type	Notes
ErrorCode		Int32	Specifies the HRESULT in accordance with the ANSI SQL standard for the database.
Errors		OleDbErrorCollection / SqlErrorCollection	Gets the collection of errors that might have been returned from a data source.
Message		String	Gets the actual error text that might have been sent by the data source.
Source		String	Specifies the name of the object that might have generated a particular error.

874

Public Methods of the OleDbInfoMessageEventArgs / SqlInfoMessageEventArgs Class

Name	Parameters	Return Type	Notes
Equals	(Object:Obj) (Object:ObjA Object:ObjB)	Boolean	See `Object` Class.
GetHashCode		Int32	See `Object` Class.
GetType		Type	See `Object` Class.
ToString		String	This overridden method returns a string representing an `InfoMessage` event (of the connection object).

Protected Methods of the OleDbInfoMessageEventArgs / SqlInfoMessageEventArgs Class

Name	Parameters	Return Type	Notes
Finalize			See `Object` Class
MemberwiseClone			See `Object` Class

The OleDbParameter / SqlParameter Class

Public Properties of the OleDbParameter / SqlParameter Class

Name	Parameters	Return Type	Notes
DbType		DbType	Specifies the native data type of a data source.
Direction		ParameterDirection	Specifies whether a parameter is: Input only (`Input`): the default. Output only (`Output`). Bidirectional (`InputOutput`). `ReturnValue`: the parameter represents a returned value from a function or stored procedure.
IsNullable		Boolean	Indicates whether the parameter accepts null values.
OleDbType		OleDbType	Specifies the `OleDbType` of the parameter (`OleDbParameter` only).
Offset		Int32	Specifies the offset of the Value property (default 0). (`SqlParameter` only).

Table continued on following page

875

Name	Parameters	Return Type	Notes
ParameterName		String	Specifies the name of the OleDbParameter.
Precision		Byte	Specifies the maximum number of numerals that may be used for the Value property.
Scale		Byte	Specifies the number of decimal places for the Value property.
Size		Int32	Specifies the maximum size, in bytes, of the data within a column.
SourceColumn		String	Specifies a particular column which is mapped to the DataSet for loading or returning the Value.
SourceVersion		DataRowVersion	Specifies the DataRowVersion to be used when loading Value.
SqlDbType		SqlDbType	Specifies the native data type of a data source (SqlParameter only).
Value		Object	Specifies the value of the parameter.

Public Methods of the OleDbParameter / SqlParameter Class

Name	Parameters	Return Type	Notes
CreateObjRef		ObjRef	See MarshalByRefObject Class
Equals	(Object:Obj) (Object:ObjA Object:ObjB)	Boolean	See Object Class
GetHashCode		Int32	See Object Class
GetLifetimeService		Object	See MarshalByRefObject Class
GetType		Type	See Object Class
InitializeLifetimeService		Object	See MarshalByRefObject Class
ToString		String	This overridden method returns a string representing the ParameterName

Protected Methods of the OleDbParameter / SqlParameter Class

Name	Parameters	Return Type	Notes
Finalize			See `Object` Class
MemberwiseClone			See `Object` Class

The OleDbParameterCollection / SqlParameterCollection Class

Public Properties of the OleDbParameterCollection / SqlParameterCollection Class

Name	Parameters	Return Type	Notes
Count		Int32	Specifies the number of `OleDbParameter` objects in the collection
Item	(Int32: Index) (String: ParameterName)	OleDbParameter SqlParameter	This overloaded property retrieves a specific `OleDbParameter` or `SqlParameter` object from the collection

Public Methods of the OleDbParameterCollection / SqlParameterCollection Class

Name	Parameters	Return Type	Notes
Add	(OleDbParameter / SqlParameter: Value) (String: Name Object: Value) (String: Name OleDbType / SqlType: DbType) (String: Name OleDbType / SqlType: DbType Int32: Size) (String: Name OleDbType / SqlType: DbType Int32: Size String: SourceColumn) (String: Name Object: Value)	OleDbParameter / SqlParameter	This overloaded method adds an `OleDbParameter` to an `OleDbCommand`

Name	Parameters	Return Type	Notes
Clear		Void	This removes all objects from the OleDbParameterCollection
Contains	(String: Value) (Object: Value)	Boolean	This overloaded method indicates whether a particular OleDbParameter exists in the collection
CopyTo	(Array: Array Int32: Index)	Void	This copies errors from the collection to an array.
CreateObjRef	(Type: RequestedType)	ObjRef	See MarshalByRefObject Class
Equals	(Object:Obj) (Object:ObjA Object:ObjB)	Boolean	See Object Class
GetEnumerator		IEnumerator	
GetHashCode		Int32	See Object Class
GetLifetimeService		Object	See MarshalByRefObject Class
GetType		Type	See Object Class
IndexOf	(String: Parameter Name) (Object: Parameter)	Int32	This overloaded method returns the location of a particular OleDbParameter object within a collection.
InitializeLifetimeService		Object	See MarshalByRefObject Class.
Insert	(Int32: Index Object: Value)	Void	This inserts an OleDbParameter object in the collection at a specified index
Remove	(Object: Value)	Void	This removes a particular OleDbParameter object from the collection
RemoveAt	(String: Value) (Int32: Index)	Void	This overloaded method removes a particular OleDbParameter object from the collection
ToString		String	See Object Class

Protected Methods of the OleDbParameterCollection / SqlParameterCollection Class

Name	Parameters	Return Type	Notes
Finalize			See Object Class
MemberwiseClone			See Object Class

OleDbPermission / SqlPermission

See Chapter 15.

OleDbPermissionAttribute / SqlPermissionAttribute

See Chapter 15.

The OleDbRowUpdatedEventArgs / SqlRowUpdatedEventArgs Class

Public Properties of the OleDbRowUpdatedEventArgs / SqlRowUpdatedEventArgs Class

Name	Parameters	Return Type	Notes
Command		OleDbCommand / SqlCommand / IdbCommand	Specifies a particular OleDbCommand to execute when performing the Update
Errors		Exception	See RowUpdatedEventArgs Class
RecordsAffected		Int32	See RowUpdatedEventArgs Class
Row		DataRow	See RowUpdatedEventArgs Class
StatementType		StatementType	See RowUpdatedEventArgs Class
Status		UpdateStatus	See RowUpdatedEventArgs Class
TableMapping		DataTableMapping	See RowUpdatedEventArgs Class

Public Methods of the OleDbRowUpdatedEventArgs / SqlRowUpdatedEventArgs Class

Name	Parameters	Return Type	Notes
Equals	(Object:Obj) (Object:ObjA Object:ObjB)	Boolean	See Object Class
GetHashCode		Int32	See Object Class
GetType		Type	See Object Class
ToString		String	See Object Class

Protected Methods of the OleDbRowUpdatedEventArgs / SqlRowUpdatedEventArgs Class

Name	Parameters	Return Type	Notes
Finalize			See Object Class
MemberwiseClone			See Object Class

The OleDbRowUpdatingEventArgs / SqlRowUpdatingEventArgs Class

Public Properties of the OleDbRowUpdatingEventArgs / SqlRowUpdatingEventArgs Class

Name	Parameters	Return Type	Notes
Command		OleDbCommand / SqlCommand / IDbCommand	Specifies a particular OleDbCommand to execute when performing the Update
Errors		Exception	See RowUpdatedEventArgs Class
Row		DataRow	See RowUpdatedEventArgs Class
StatementType		StatementType	See RowUpdatedEventArgs Class
Status		UpdateStatus	See RowUpdatedEventArgs Class
TableMapping		DataTAbleMapping	See RowUpdatedEventArgs Class

Public Methods of the OleDbRowUpdatingEventArgs / SqlRowUpdatingEventArgs Class

Name	Parameters	Return Type	Notes
Equals	(Object:Obj) (Object:ObjA Object:ObjB)	Boolean	See Object Class
GetHashCode		Int32	See Object Class
GetType		Type	See Object Class
ToString		String	See Object Class

Protected Methods of the OleDbRowUpdatingEventArgs / SqlRowUpdatingEventArgs Class

Name	Parameters	Return Type	Notes
Finalize			See Object Class
MemberwiseClone			See Object Class

OleDbTransaction / SqlTransaction

See Chapter 12

Miscelaneous Other Classes

The foregoing classes inherit numerous methods and properties that aren't contained in the `System.Data` namespaces. A lot of classes inherit from many of these, so to avoid inordinate amounts of repetition concise explanations of these properties and methods are given, under the appropriate classes and namespaces, in the following sections.

System

The Object Class

Public Shared Methods of the Object Class

Name	Notes
Equals	Equals is an overloaded method that is used to determine whether two Object instances of any kind are the same instance
ReferenceEquals	This determines whether specified Object instances are one and the same

Public Methods of the Object Class

Name	Notes
Equals	Equals is an overloaded method that is used to determine whether two Object instances of any kind are the same instance
GetHashCode	This overridden method returns the hash code for a particular object
GetType	Returns the type of a particular instance of an object
ToString	Returns a string representation of the object

Protected Methods of the Object Class

Name	Notes
Finalize	This overridden method enables an object to release resources before management of the object is handed over to garbage collection. In C# and C++, the destructor syntax is used to implement Finalize.
MemberwiseClone	This creates a shallow copy of an object (a shallow copy being one that doesn't also copy any other objects that might be referenced by this object).

The Attribute Class

Public Shared Methods of the Attribute Class

Name	Notes
GetCustomAttribute	Overloaded. Retrieves a custom attribute of a specified type applied to a specified member of a class.
GetCustomAttributes	Overloaded. Retrieves an array of the custom attributes of a specified type applied to a specified member of a class.
IsDefined	Overloaded. Determines whether any custom attributes of a specified type are applied to a specified member of a class.

Public Properties of the Attribute Class

Name	Notes
TypeId	When implemented in a derived class, gets a unique identifier for this **Attribute**

Public Methods of the Attribute Class

Name	Notes
Equals	See Object Class
GetHashCode	Overridden. Returns the hash code for this instance.
GetType	See Object Class.
IsDefaultAttribute	When overridden in a derived class, returns an indication whether the value of this instance is the default value for the derived class.
Match	When overridden in a derived class, returns a value indicating whether this instance equals a specified object.
ToString	See Object Class.

Protected Methods of the Attribute Class

Name	Notes
Finalize	See Object Class
MemberwiseClone	See Object Class

The Exception Class

Public Properties of the Exception Class

Name	Notes
HelpLink	An exception has a help file associated with it. This property gives the link to the appropriate help file.
InnerException	References an inner exception (in other words, another exception object thrown by another object which might have been called).
Message	Specifies the error message.
Source	Specifies the object or the application that has caused the error.
StackTrace	This specifies the stack trace. The stack trace provides us with the place in the appropriate code which has caused the error.
TargetSite	Specifies the method that has thrown a particular exception.

Public Methods of the Exception Class

Name	Notes
Equals	See Object Class
GetBaseException	This gets the original exception that is thrown
GetHashCode	See Object Class
GetObjectData	Provides the SerializationInfo object with information about the exception
GetType	See Object Class
ToString	This overridden method supplies the fully qualified name of this exception and also, if the information is available, an error message, the name of the inner exception, and the stack trace

Protected Properties of the Exception Class

Name	Notes
HResult	This provides a HRESULT for a particular exception: a value associated with a particular exception

Protected Methods

Name	Notes
Finalize	See Object Class
MemberwiseClone	See Object Class

The MarshalByRefObject Class

Public Methods of the MarshalByRefObject Class

Name	Notes
CreateObjRef	The CreateObjectRef method returns a reference to an object of a given type. This is primarily used for remoting objects across component boundaries.
Equals	See Object Class.
GetHashCode	See Object Class.
GetLifetimeService	The GetLifetimeService method returns the lifetime service object managing the lifetime policy of the current transaction.
GetType	See Object Class.
InitializeLifetimeService	Creates a new lifetime service object.
ToString	See Object Class.

Protected Methods of the MarshalByRefObject Class

Name	Notes
Finalize	See Object Class.
MemberwiseClone	See Object Class.

System.ComponentModel

The Component Class

Public Properties of the Component Class

Name	Notes
Container	This returns the IContainer in which the Component is contained.
Site	Specifies the ISite associated with a particular Component. The ISite enables communication with, and binds a component with, a container.

Public Methods of the Component Class

Name	Notes
CreateObjRef	See MarshalByRefObject Class.
Dispose	This overloaded method frees up the resources that might be used by a Component.
Equals	See Object Class.
GetHashCode	See Object Class.
GetLifetimeService	See MarshalByRefObject Class.
GetType InitializeLifetimeService	See Object Class. See MarshalByRefObject Class.
ToString	See Object Class.

Public Events of the Component Class

Name	Notes
Disposed	When we need to perform some operation when a component is disposed, we need to specify the method that will handle the disposed event

Protected Properties of the Component Class

Name	Notes
DesignMode	Indicates whether a component is in design mode. If a component is in design mode, then it may be utilized by the .NET design-time functionality that enables the control and display of an object in a visual design interface.
Events	Provides a list of event handlers that are attached to a Component.

Protected Methods of the Component Class

Name	Notes
Dispose	This overloaded method frees up the resources that might be used by a Component
Finalize	See Object Class
GetService	Returns an object which represents a service that is provided by component
MemberwiseClone	See Object Class

The MarshalByValueComponent Class

Public Properties of the MarshalByValueComponent Class

Name	Notes
Container	Returns the container of a component.
DesignMode	Indicates whether a component is in design mode. If a component is in design mode, then it may be utilized by the .NET design-time functionality that enables the control and display of an object in a visual design interface.
Site	Specifies the ISite associated with a particular Component. The ISite enables communication with, and binds components with, a container.

Public Methods of the MarshalByValueComponent Class

Name	Notes
Dispose	This overloaded method frees up the resources that are used by a MarshalByValueComponent object
Equals	See Object Class
GetHashCode	See Object Class
GetService	Indicates the object that is providing a service, via the IserviceProvider interface
GetType	See Object Class
ToString	See Object Class

Public Events of the MarshalByValueComponent Class

Name	Notes
Disposed	See Component Class

Protected Properties of the MarshalByValueComponent Class

Name	Notes
Events	Provides a list of event handlers that are attached to a Component

Protected Methods of the MarshalByValueComponent Class

Name	Notes
Dispose	This overloaded method frees up the resources that might be used by a MarshalByValueComponent object
Finalize	See Object Class
MemberwiseClone	See Object Class

The DescriptionAttribute Class

Public Properties of the DescriptionAttribute Class

Name	Notes
Description	Gets the description stored in this attribute.
TypeId	See Attribute class. When implemented in a derived class, gets a unique identifier for this **Attribute**.

Public Methods of the DescriptionAttribute Class

Name	Notes
Equals	See Object Class
GetHashCode	This returns a hash code for a particular instance of this class
GetType	See Object Class
IsDefaultAttribute	This method indicates whether the value of a particular instance of this class has default values
Match	This method indicates whether a particular instance of this class is equal to a particular object
ToString	See Object Class

Protected Properties of the DescriptionAttribute Class

Name	Notes
DescriptionValue	Specifies a description (as a string)

Protected Methods of the DescriptionAttribute Class

Name	Notes
Finalize	See Object Class
MemberwiseClone	See Object Class

System.Collections

The Hashtable Class

Public Methods of the Hashtable Class

Name	Notes
Synchronized	Returns a synchronized (thread-safe) wrapper for the `Hashtable`

Public Properties of the Hashtable Class

Name	Notes
Count	Specifies the number of key-and-value pairs in a `Hashtable`
IsFixedSize	Indicates whether the size of a Hashtable is limited
IsReadOnly	Indicates whether a Hashtable is read-only
IsSynchronized	Indicates whether access to a Hashtable is synchronized
Item	Specifies a value of a specific key
Keys	Returns an `ICollection` which contains the hashtable keys
SyncRoot	The `SyncRoot` object manages synchronized access to a `Hashtable` object
Values	Returns an `ICollection` which contains the values in the `Hashtable`

Public Methods of the Hashtable Class

Name	Notes
Add	This adds an entry with a particular key and value into a `Hashtable`
Clear	This clears all entries from a `Hashtable`
Clone	This creates a shallow copy of an object (a shallow copy being one that doesn't also copy any other objects that might be referenced by this object)
Contains	This indicates whether a particular key is contained in a Hashtable
ContainsKey	This indicates whether a particular key is contained in a Hashtable
ContainsValue	This indicates whether a particular value is present in a Hashtable
CopyTo	This copies all the Hashtable entries to a one dimensional array at a particular index
Equals	See `Object` Class
GetEnumerator	Provides an enumerator that will iterate through a Hashtable
GetHashCode	See `Object` Class
GetObjectData	If it is necessary to serialize a hashtable, the `GetObjectData` method will provide the necessary data and implement the `ISerializable` interface (which enables the object to manage its own serialization)

Name	Notes
GetType	See Object Class.
OnDeserialization	When deserialization has completed, this method will implement the Iserializable interface and cause the deserialization event to be raised.
Remove	Removes an entry with a particular key from the hashtable.
ToString	See Object Class.

Protected Properties of the Hashtable Class

Name	Notes
comparer	Specifies the comparer to use for a Hashtable
hcp	Specifies an object that can dispense hash codes

Protected Methods of the Hashtable Class

Name	Notes
Finalize	See Object Class
GetHash	Returns the hash code for the specified key
KeyEquals	Compares a specific Object with a specific key in a Hashtable
MemberwiseClone	See Object Class

System.Security

The CodeAccessPermission Class

Public Methods of the CodeAccessPermission Class

Name	Notes
RevertAll	This removes all previous overrides on the current frame (in the stack).
RevertAssert	This removes all previous asserts on the current frame (in the stack).
RevertDeny	This removes any previous Deny on the current frame (in the stack).
RevertPermitOnly	This removes any previous PermitOnly on the current frame (in the stack).

Public Methods of the CodeAccessPermission Class

Name	Notes
Assert	Grants permissions to calling code to access the data source specified by a particular permission object (even when callers higher in the call stack have been revoked permissions).
Copy	This overridden method creates a copy of a particular permission object.
Demand	Indicates whether callers higher in the call stack to the current caller have been granted particular permissions by the permission object.
Deny	Prevents callers who are higher in the call stack from accessing a particular resource.
Equals	See Object Class.
FromXml	This overridden method uses an XML specification to reconstruct a particular security object.
GetHashCode	See Object Class.
GetType	See Object Class.
Intersect	This overridden method will return a permission object which represents the set of permissions from two other permission objects (the intersection) that must be passed to access a particular resource.
IsSubsetOf	This overridden method indicates whether a particular permission object is a subset of a specific other permission object.
PermitOnly	This ensures that only those resources that are specified by a particular permission object can be accessed by the calling code.
ToString	This overridden method returns a string representing the permission object.
ToXml	This overridden method returns an XML representation of the permission object.
Union	This overridden method returns a new permission object that represents the permissions of both the current permission object and another specified permission object.

Protected Methods of the CodeAccessPermission Class

Name	Notes
Finalize	See Object Class.
MemberwiseClone	See Object Class.

System.Security.Permissions

The SecurityAttribute Class

Public Properties of the SecurityAttribute Class

Name	Notes
Action	Specifies a particular security action:
	Assert: Grants permissions to calling code to access the data source specified by a particular permission object (even when callers higher in the call stack have been revoked permissions)
	Demand: Indicates whether callers higher in the call stack to the current caller have been granted particular permissions by the permission object
	Deny: Prevents callers who are higher in the call stack from accessing a particular resource
	InheritanceDemand: Derived classes must have had particular permissions granted
	LinkDemand: Immediate calling code must have had particular permissions granted
	PermitOnly: This ensures that only those resources that are specified by a particular permission object can be accessed by the calling code
	RequestMinimum: This grants the minimum necessary permissions for calling code to have access
	RequestOptional: This grants extra, non-necessary, permissions
	RequestRefuse: Denies permissions to calling code
TypeId	Returns a unique identifier for an attribute
Unrestricted	Allows unrestricted permissions to a resource

Public Methods of the SecurityAttribute Class

Name	Notes
CreatePermission	This creates a permission object
Equals	See Object Class
GetHashCode	Returns a hash code for a particular instance of this class
GetType	See Object Class
IsDefaultAttribute	This method indicates whether the value of a particular instance of this class has default values
Match	This method indicates whether a particular instance of this class is equal to a particular object
ToString	See Object Class.

Protected Methods of the SecurityAttribute Class

Name	Notes
Finalize	See Object Class.
MemberwiseClone	See Object Class.

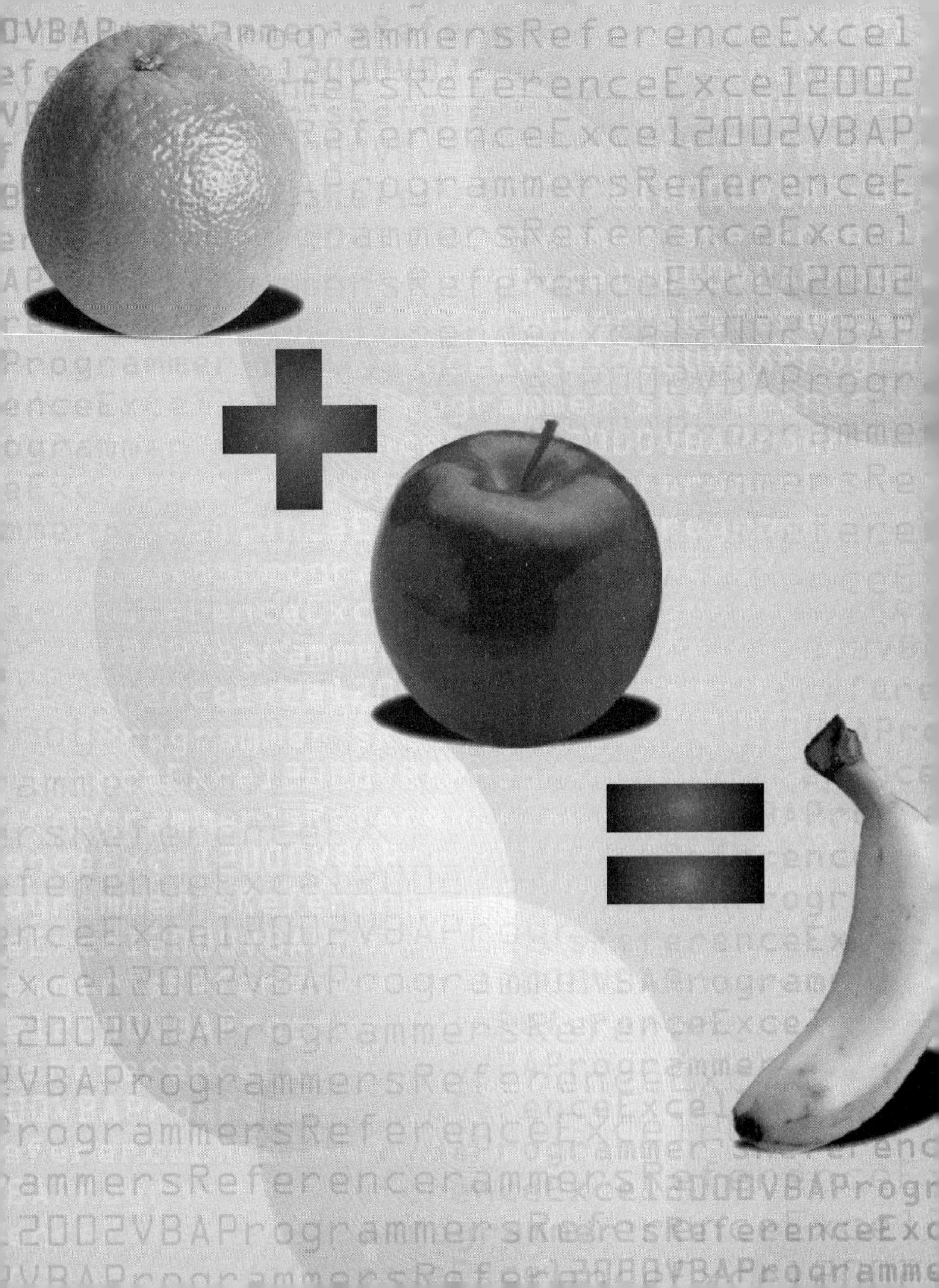

ADO.NET Class Diagrams

System.Data

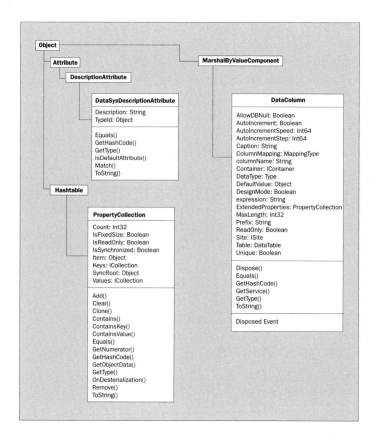

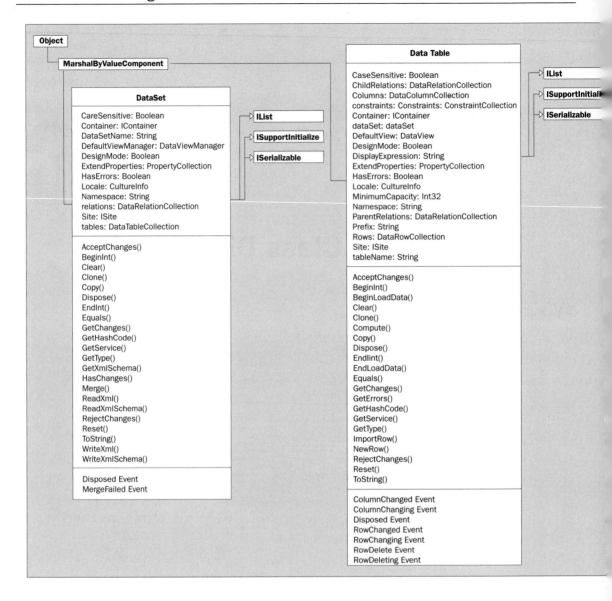

Object

MarshalByValueComponent

DataSet

CareSensitive: Boolean
Container: IContainer
DataSetName: String
DefaultViewManager: DataViewManager
DesignMode: Boolean
ExtendProperties: PropertyCollection
HasErrors: Boolean
Locale: CultureInfo
Namespace: String
relations: DataRelationCollection
Site: ISite
tables: DataTableCollection

AcceptChanges()
BeginInt()
Clear()
Clone()
Copy()
Dispose()
EndInt()
Equals()
GetChanges()
GetHashCode()
GetService()
GetType()
GetXmlSchema()
HasChanges()
Merge()
ReadXml()
ReadXmlSchema()
RejectChanges()
Reset()
ToString()
WriteXml()
WriteXmlSchema()

Disposed Event
MergeFailed Event

IList

ISupportInitialize

ISerializable

Data Table

CaseSensitive: Boolean
ChildRelations: DataRelationCollection
Columns: DataColumnCollection
constraints: Constraints: ConstraintCollection
Container: IContainer
dataSet: dataSet
DefaultView: DataView
DesignMode: Boolean
DisplayExpression: String
ExtendProperties: PropertyCollection
HasErrors: Boolean
Locale: CultureInfo
MinimumCapacity: Int32
Namespace: String
ParentRelations: DataRelationCollection
Prefix: String
Rows: DataRowCollection
Site: ISite
tableName: String

AcceptChanges()
BeginInt()
BeginLoadData()
Clear()
Clone()
Compute()
Copy()
Dispose()
EndIint()
EndLoadData()
Equals()
GetChanges()
GetErrors()
GetHashCode()
GetService()
GetType()
ImportRow()
NewRow()
RejectChanges()
Reset()
ToString()

ColumnChanged Event
ColumnChanging Event
Disposed Event
RowChanged Event
RowChanging Event
RowDelete Event
RowDeleting Event

IList

ISupportInitiali

ISerializable

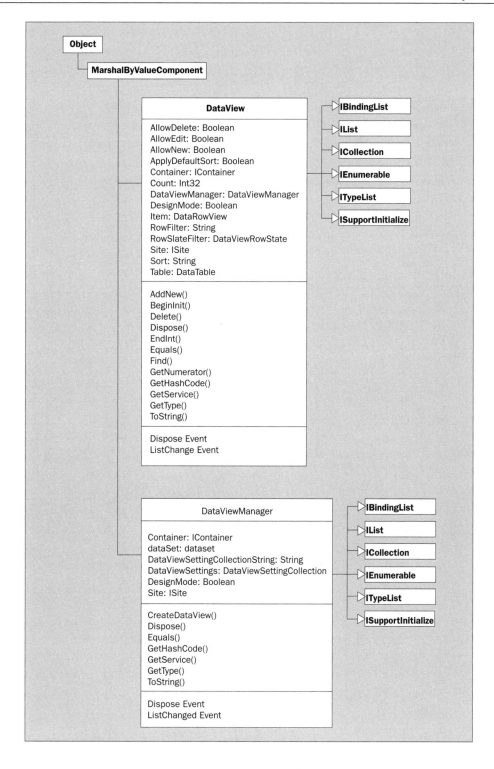

Object

MarshalByValueComponent

DataView

AllowDelete: Boolean
AllowEdit: Boolean
AllowNew: Boolean
ApplyDefaultSort: Boolean
Container: IContainer
Count: Int32
DataViewManager: DataViewManager
DesignMode: Boolean
Item: DataRowView
RowFilter: String
RowSlateFilter: DataViewRowState
Site: ISite
Sort: String
Table: DataTable

AddNew()
BeginInit()
Delete()
Dispose()
EndInt()
Equals()
Find()
GetNumerator()
GetHashCode()
GetService()
GetType()
ToString()

Dispose Event
ListChange Event

IBindingList
IList
ICollection
IEnumerable
ITypeList
ISupportInitialize

DataViewManager

Container: IContainer
dataSet: dataset
DataViewSettingCollectionString: String
DataViewSettings: DataViewSettingCollection
DesignMode: Boolean
Site: ISite

CreateDataView()
Dispose()
Equals()
GetHashCode()
GetService()
GetType()
ToString()

Dispose Event
ListChanged Event

IBindingList
IList
ICollection
IEnumerable
ITypeList
ISupportInitialize

897

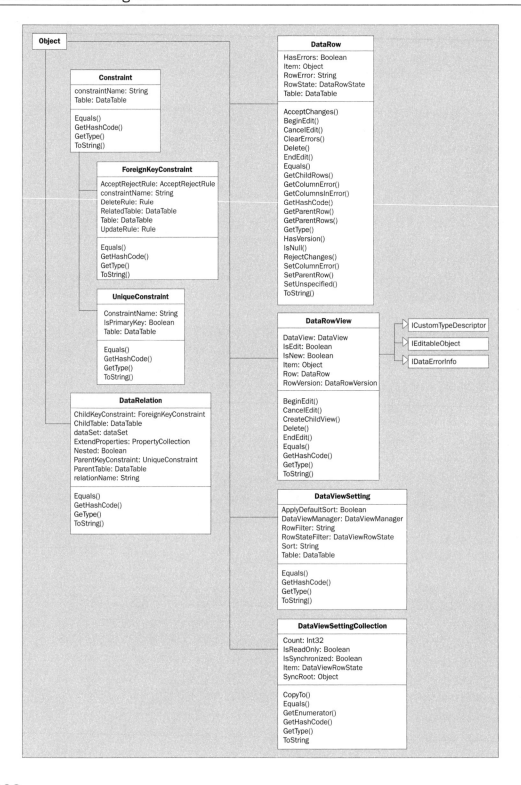

Object

Constraint

constraintName: String
Table: DataTable

Equals()
GetHashCode()
GetType()
ToString()

ForeignKeyConstraint

AcceptRejectRule: AcceptRejectRule
constraintName: String
DeleteRule: Rule
RelatedTable: DataTable
Table: DataTable
UpdateRule: Rule

Equals()
GetHashCode()
GetType()
ToString()

UniqueConstraint

ConstraintName: String
IsPrimaryKey: Boolean
Table: DataTable

Equals()
GetHashCode()
GetType()
ToString()

DataRelation

ChildKeyConstraint: ForeignKeyConstraint
ChildTable: DataTable
dataSet: dataSet
ExtendProperties: PropertyCollection
Nested: Boolean
ParentKeyConstraint: UniqueConstraint
ParentTable: DataTable
relationName: String

Equals()
GetHashCode()
GeType()
ToString()

DataRow

HasErrors: Boolean
Item: Object
RowError: String
RowState: DataRowState
Table: DataTable

AcceptChanges()
BeginEdit()
CancelEdit()
ClearErrors()
Delete()
EndEdit()
Equals()
GetChildRows()
GetColumnError()
GetColumnsInError()
GetHashCode()
GetParentRow()
GetParentRows()
GetType()
HasVersion()
IsNull()
RejectChanges()
SetColumnError()
SetParentRow()
SetUnspecified()
ToString()

DataRowView

DataView: DataView
IsEdit: Boolean
IsNew: Boolean
Item: Object
Row: DataRow
RowVersion: DataRowVersion

BeginEdit()
CancelEdit()
CreateChildView()
Delete()
EndEdit()
Equals()
GetHashCode()
GetType()
ToString()

ICustomTypeDescriptor

IEditableObject

IDataErrorInfo

DataViewSetting

ApplyDefaultSort: Boolean
DataViewManager: DataViewManager
RowFilter: String
RowStateFilter: DataViewRowState
Sort: String
Table: DataTable

Equals()
GetHashCode()
GetType()
ToString()

DataViewSettingCollection

Count: Int32
IsReadOnly: Boolean
IsSynchronized: Boolean
Item: DataViewRowState
SyncRoot: Object

CopyTo()
Equals()
GetEnumerator()
GetHashCode()
GetType()
ToString

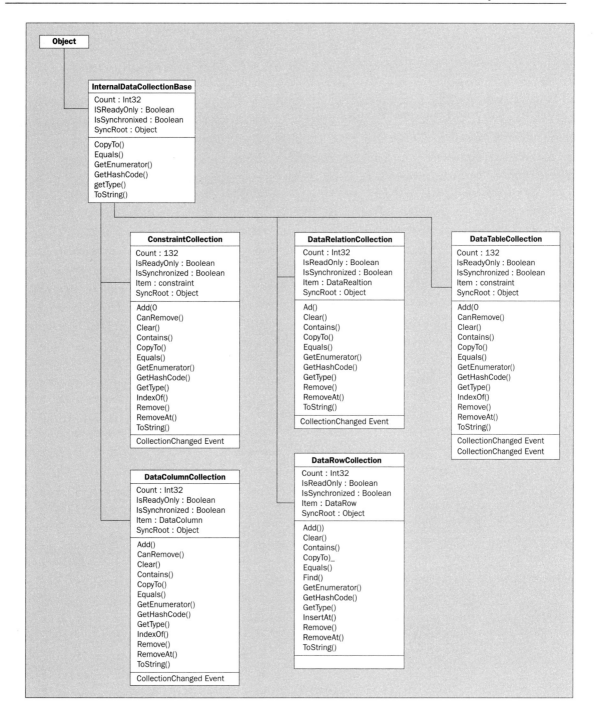

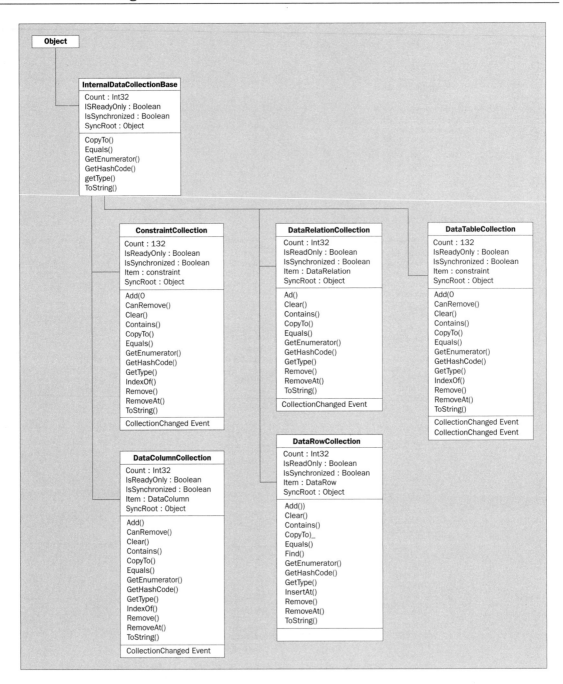

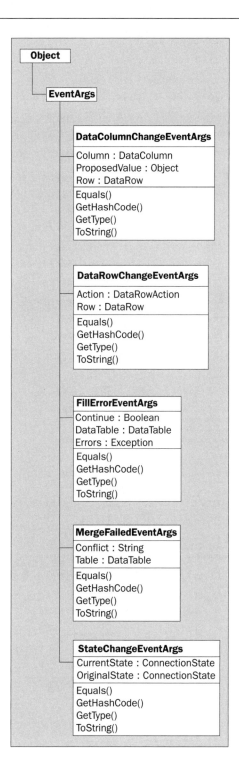

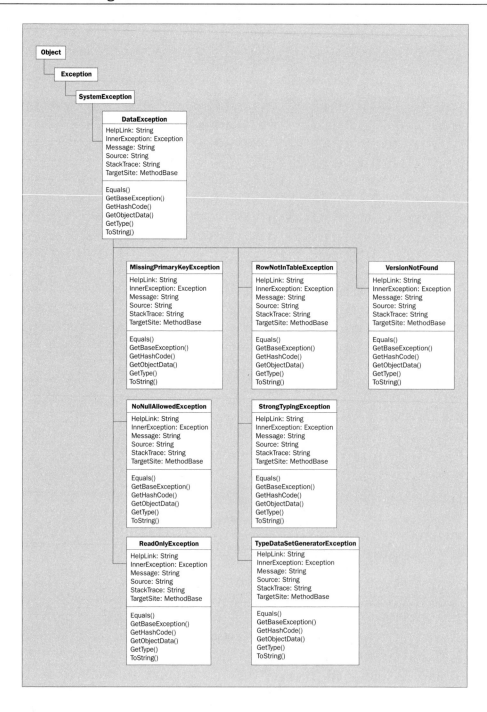

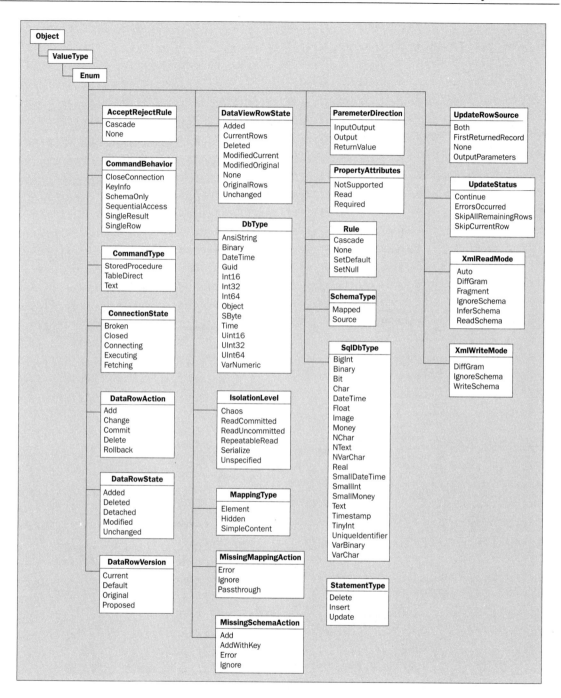

Object

ValueType

Enum

AcceptRejectRule
Cascade
None

CommandBehavior
CloseConnection
KeyInfo
SchemaOnly
SequentialAccess
SingleResult
SingleRow

CommandType
StoredProcedure
TableDirect
Text

ConnectionState
Broken
Closed
Connecting
Executing
Fetching

DataRowAction
Add
Change
Commit
Delete
Rollback

DataRowState
Added
Deleted
Detached
Modified
Unchanged

DataRowVersion
Current
Default
Original
Proposed

DataViewRowState
Added
CurrentRows
Deleted
ModifiedCurrent
ModifiedOriginal
None
OriginalRows
Unchanged

DbType
AnsiString
Binary
DateTime
Guid
Int16
Int32
Int64
Object
SByte
Time
UInt16
UInt32
UInt64
VarNumeric

IsolationLevel
Chaos
ReadCommitted
ReadUncommitted
RepeatableRead
Serialize
Unspecified

MappingType
Element
Hidden
SimpleContent

MissingMappingAction
Error
Ignore
Passthrough

MissingSchemaAction
Add
AddWithKey
Error
Ignore

ParemeterDirection
InputOutput
Output
ReturnValue

PropertyAttributes
NotSupported
Read
Required

Rule
Cascade
None
SetDefault
SetNull

SchemaType
Mapped
Source

SqlDbType
BigInt
Binary
Bit
Char
DateTime
Float
Image
Money
NChar
NText
NVarChar
Real
SmallDateTime
SmallInt
SmallMoney
Text
Timestamp
TinyInt
UniqueIdentifier
VarBinary
VarChar

StatementType
Delete
Insert
Update

UpdateRowSource
Both
FirstReturnedRecord
None
OutputParameters

UpdateStatus
Continue
ErrorsOccurred
SkipAllRemainingRows
SkipCurrentRow

XmlReadMode
Auto
DiffGram
Fragment
IgnoreSchema
InferSchema
ReadSchema

XmlWriteMode
DiffGram
IgnoreSchema
WriteSchema

903

System.Data.Common

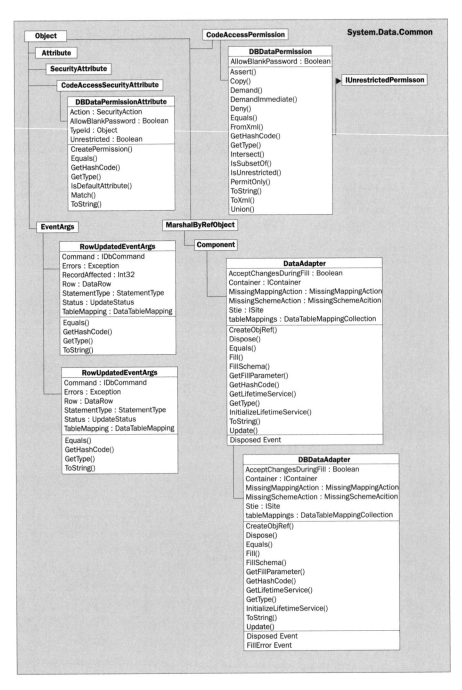

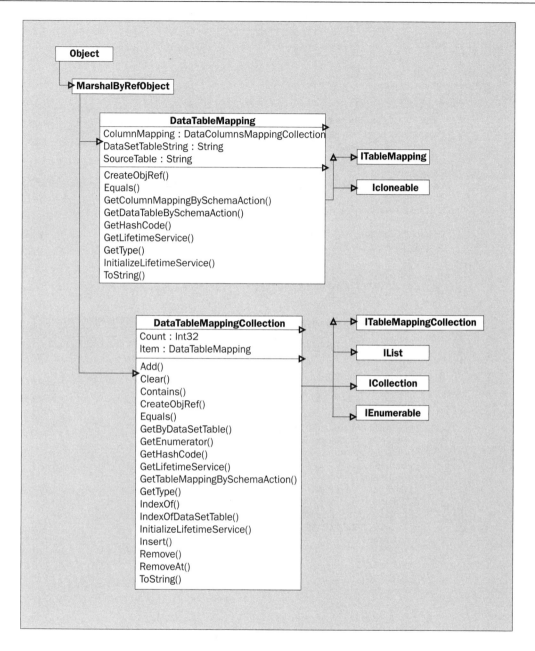

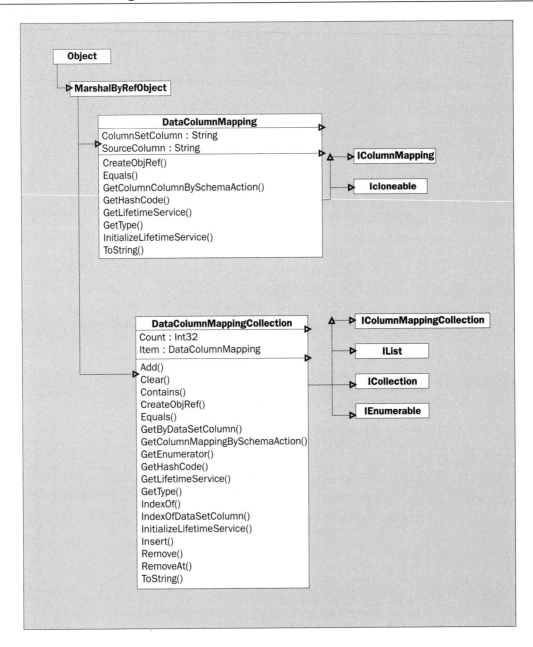

System.Data.OleDb

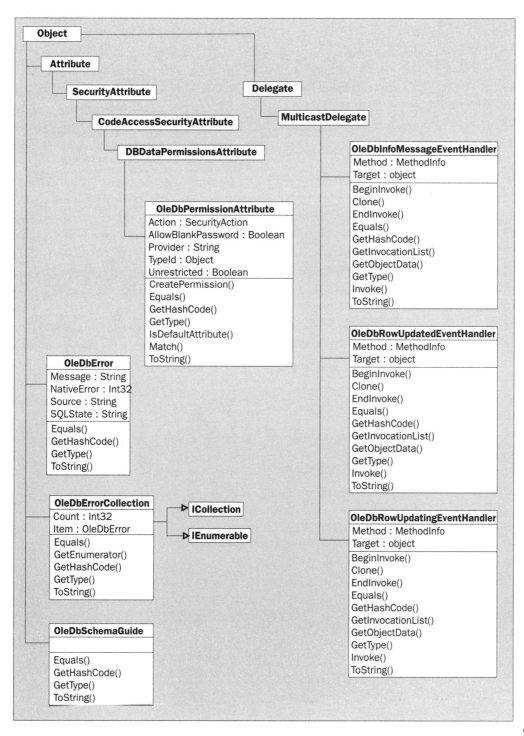

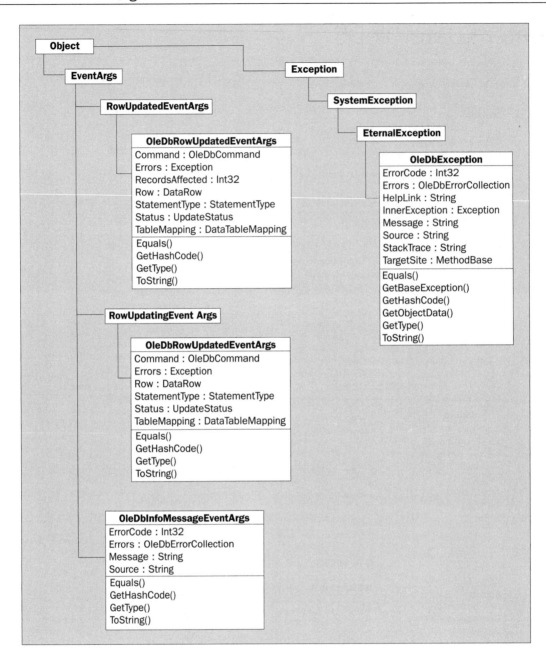

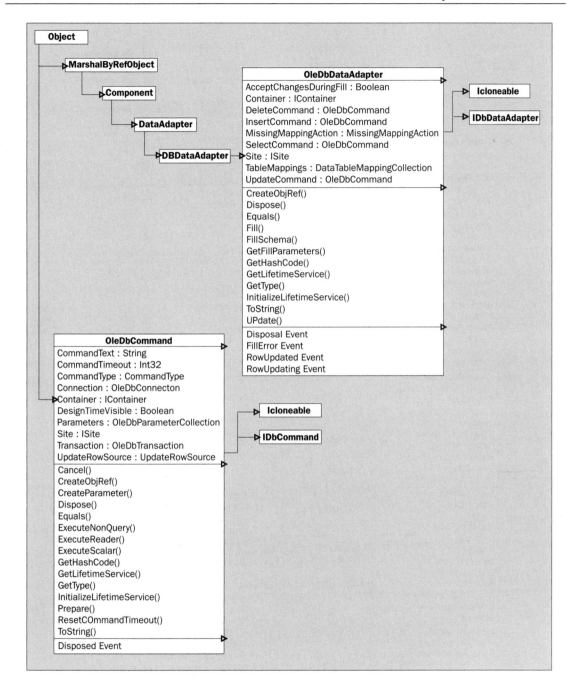

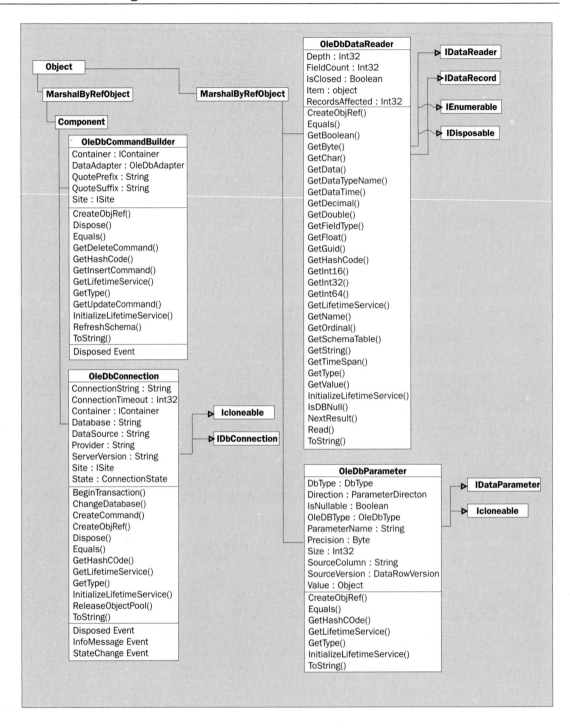

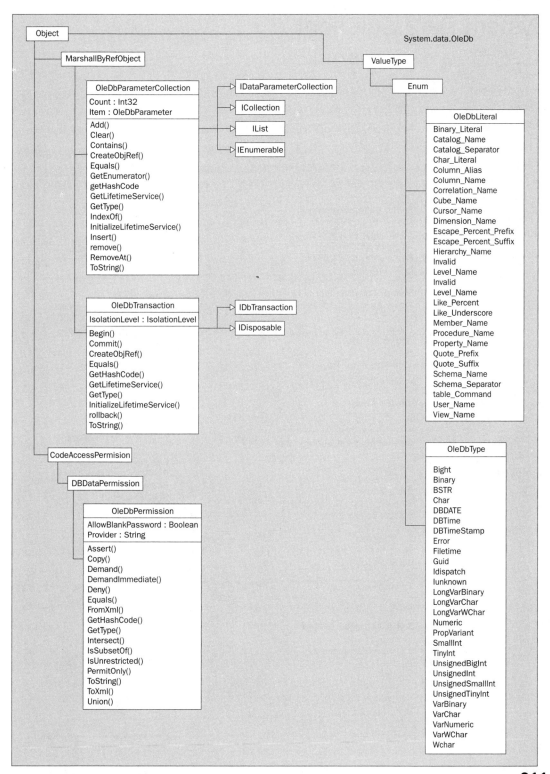

System.data.OleDb

Object

MarshallByRefObject

OleDbParameterCollection

Count : Int32
Item : OleDbParameter

Add()
Clear()
Contains()
CreateObjRef()
Equals()
GetEnumerator()
getHashCode
GetLifetimeService()
GetType()
IndexOf()
InitializeLifetimeService()
Insert()
remove()
RemoveAt()
ToString()

IDataParameterCollection

ICollection

IList

IEnumerable

ValueType

Enum

OleDbLiteral

Binary_Literal
Catalog_Name
Catalog_Separator
Char_Literal
Column_Alias
Column_Name
Correlation_Name
Cube_Name
Cursor_Name
Dimension_Name
Escape_Percent_Prefix
Escape_Percent_Suffix
Hierarchy_Name
Invalid
Level_Name
Invalid
Level_Name
Like_Percent
Like_Underscore
Member_Name
Procedure_Name
Property_Name
Quote_Prefix
Quote_Suffix
Schema_Name
Schema_Separator
table_Command
User_Name
View_Name

OleDbTransaction

IsolationLevel : IsolationLevel

Begin()
Commit()
CreateObjRef()
Equals()
GetHashCode()
GetLifetimeService()
GetType()
InitializeLifetimeService()
rollback()
ToString()

IDbTransaction

IDisposable

CodeAccessPermision

DBDataPermission

OleDbPermission

AllowBlankPassword : Boolean
Provider : String

Assert()
Copy()
Demand()
DemandImmediate()
Deny()
Equals()
FromXml()
GetHashCode()
GetType()
Intersect()
IsSubsetOf()
IsUnrestricted()
PermitOnly()
ToString()
ToXml()
Union()

OleDbType

Bight
Binary
BSTR
Char
DBDATE
DBTime
DBTimeStamp
Error
Filetime
Guid
Idispatch
Iunknown
LongVarBinary
LongVarChar
LongVarWChar
Numeric
PropVariant
SmallInt
TinyInt
UnsignedBigInt
UnsignedInt
UnsignedSmallInt
UnsignedTinyInt
VarBinary
VarChar
VarNumeric
VarWChar
Wchar

System.Data.SqlClient

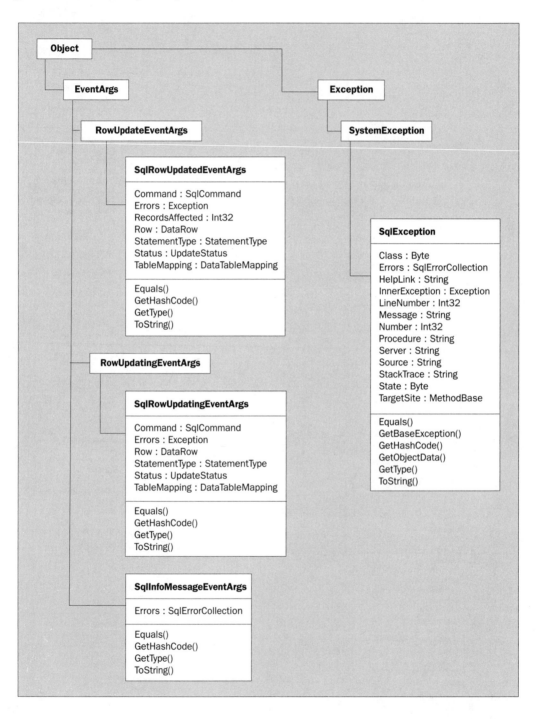

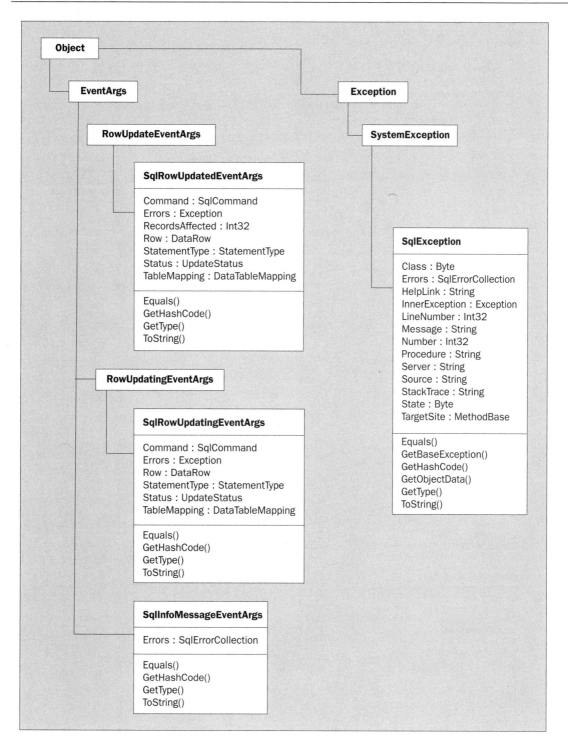

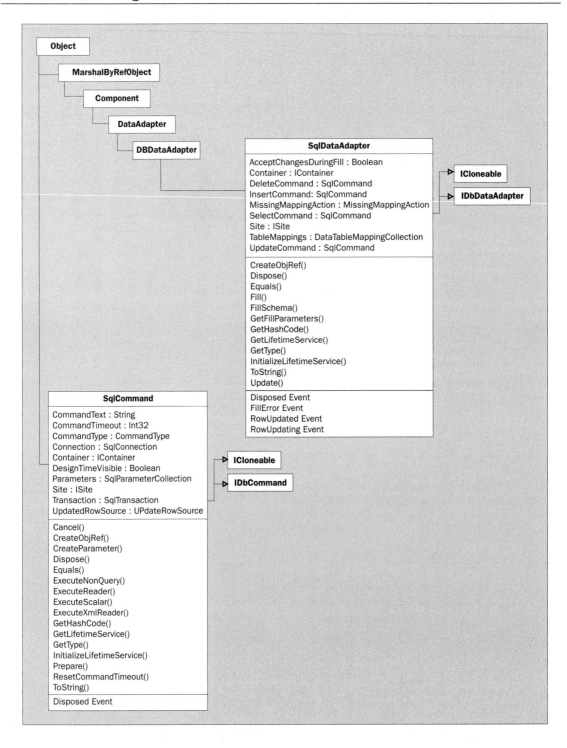

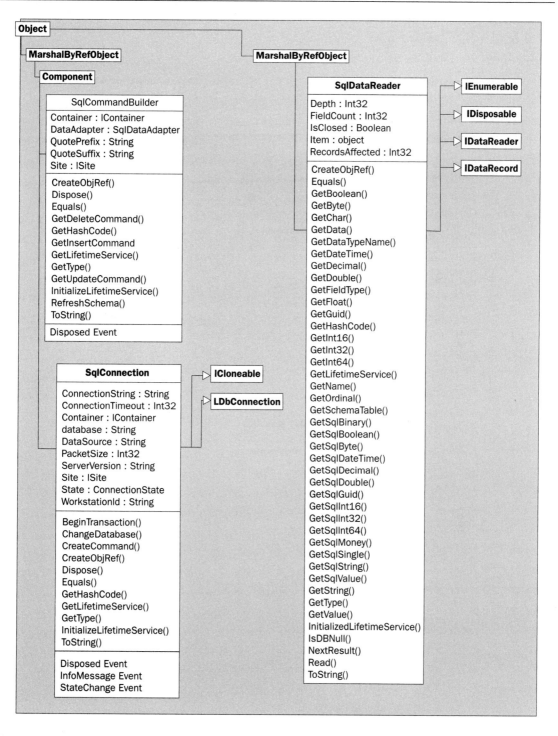

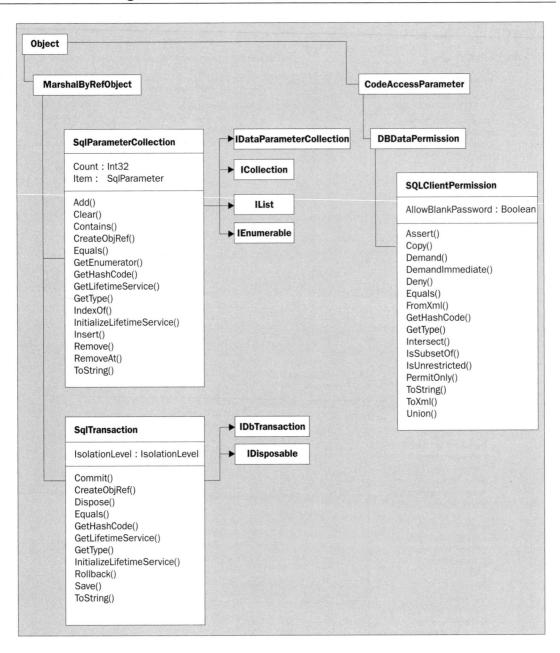

System.Data.odbc

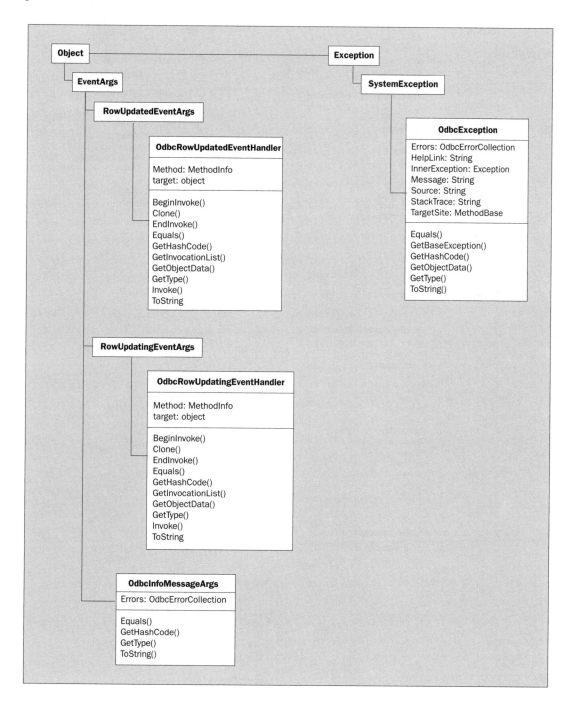

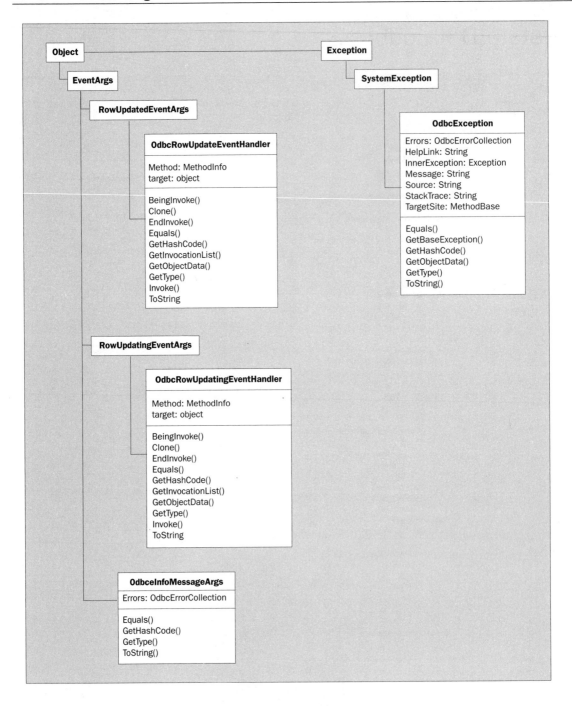

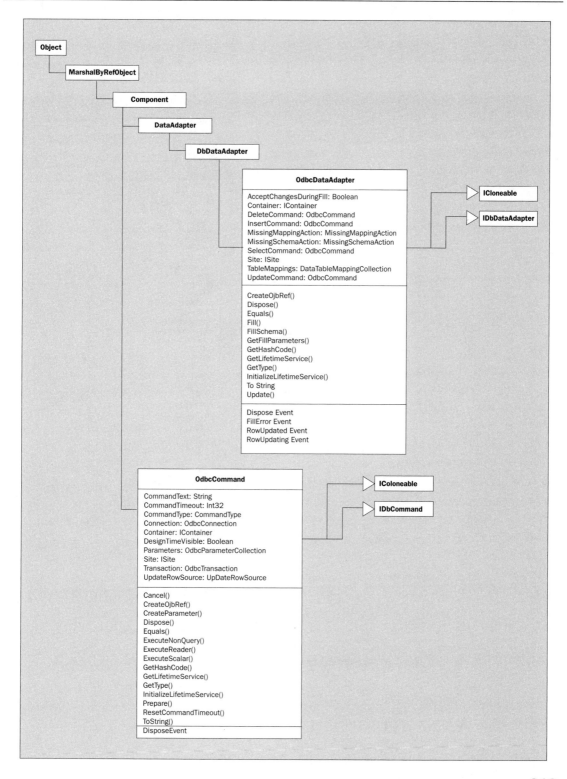

Object

MarshalByRefObject

Component

DataAdapter

DbDataAdapter

OdbcDataAdapter

AcceptChangesDuringFill: Boolean
Container: IContainer
DeleteCommand: OdbcCommand
InsertCommand: OdbcCommand
MissingMappingAction: MissingMappingAction
MissingSchemaAction: MissingSchemaAction
SelectCommand: OdbcCommand
Site: ISite
TableMappings: DataTableMappingCollection
UpdateCommand: OdbcCommand

CreateOjbRef()
Dispose()
Equals()
Fill()
FillSchema()
GetFillParameters()
GetHashCode()
GetLifetimeService()
GetType()
InitializeLifetimeService()
To String
Update()

Dispose Event
FillError Event
RowUpdated Event
RowUpdating Event

ICloneable

IDbDataAdapter

OdbcCommand

CommandText: String
CommandTimeout: Int32
CommandType: CommandType
Connection: OdbcConnection
Container: IContainer
DesignTimeVisible: Boolean
Parameters: OdbcParameterCollection
Site: ISite
Transaction: OdbcTransaction
UpdateRowSource: UpDateRowSource

Cancel()
CreateOjbRef()
CreateParameter()
Dispose()
Equals()
ExecuteNonQuery()
ExecuteReader()
ExecuteScalar()
GetHashCode()
GetLifetimeService()
GetType()
InitializeLifetimeService()
Prepare()
ResetCommandTimeout()
ToString()
DisposeEvent

IColoneable

IDbCommand

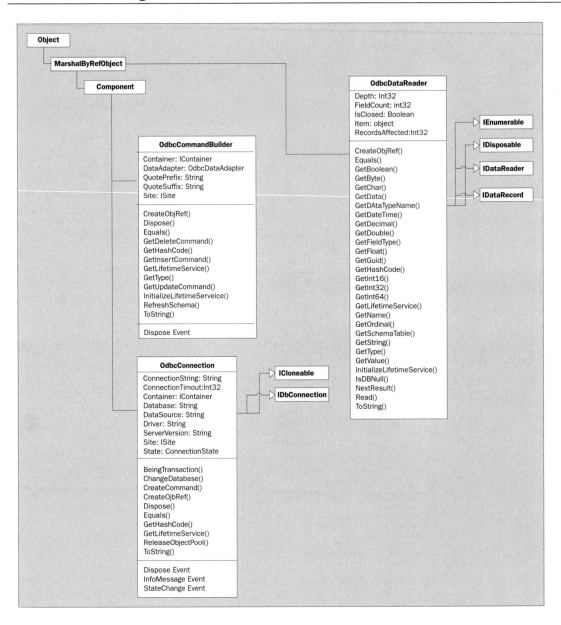

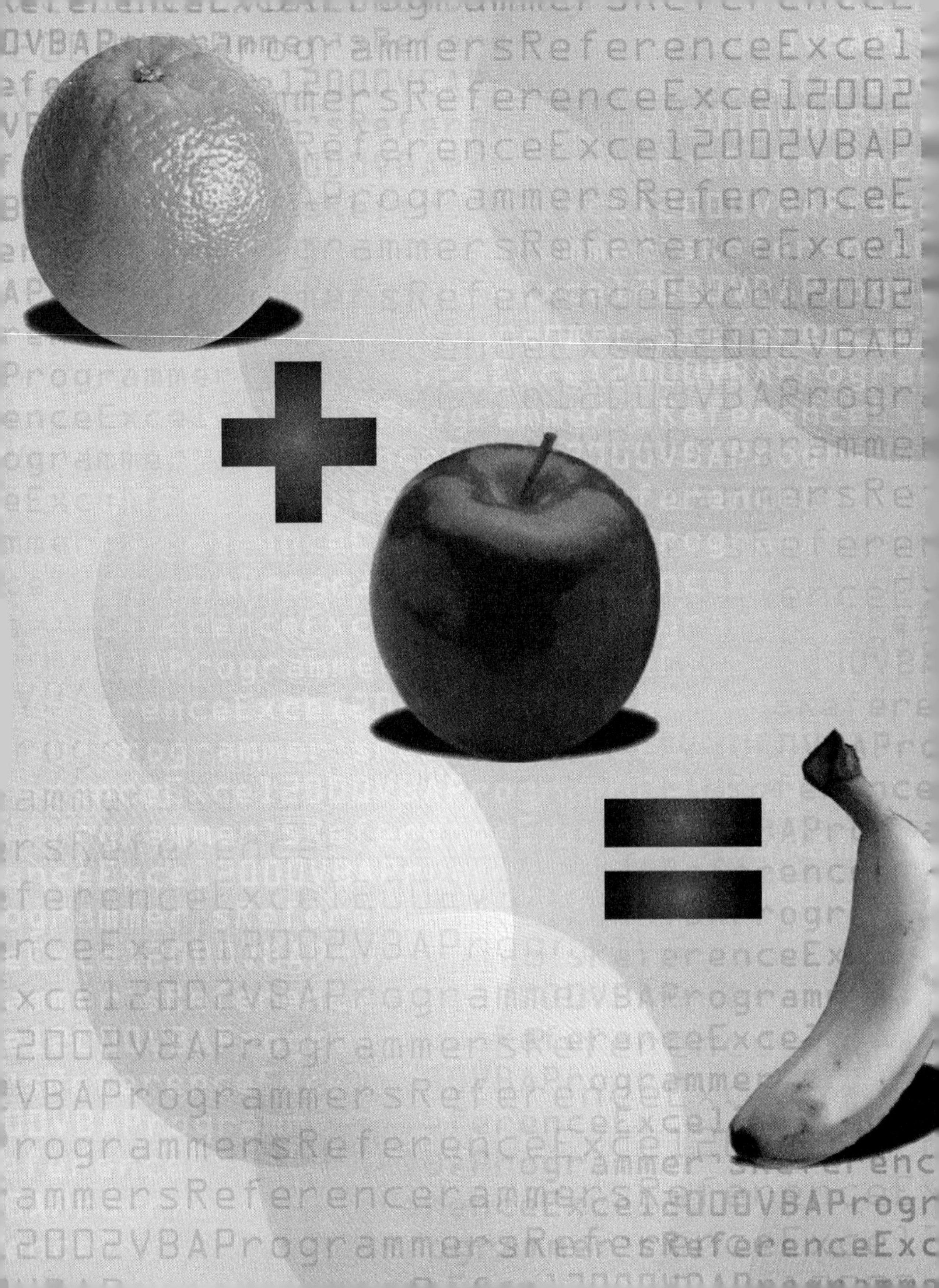

Support, Errata, and p2p.wrox.com

One of the most irritating things about any programming book is when you find that the bit of code that you've just spent an hour typing simply doesn't work. You check it a hundred times to see if you've set it up correctly, and then you notice the spelling mistake in the variable name on the book page. Of course, you can blame the authors for not taking enough care and testing the code, the editors for not doing their job properly, or the proofreaders for not being eagle-eyed enough, but this doesn't get around the fact that mistakes do happen.

We try hard to ensure that no mistakes sneak out into the real world, but we can't promise that this book is 100% error free. What we can do is offer the next best thing by providing you with immediate support and feedback from experts who have worked on the book, and who try to ensure that future editions eliminate these gremlins. We are also committed to supporting you not just while you read the book, but once you start developing applications as well – through our online forums you can put your questions to the authors, reviewers, and fellow industry professionals.

In this appendix we'll look at how to:

- ❑ Enroll in the peer to peer forums at http://p2p.wrox.com
- ❑ Post and check for errata on our main site, http://www.wrox.com
- ❑ e-Mail a query, or feedback on our books in general, to our technical support team

Between all three support procedures, you should get an answer to your problem in no time.

The Online Forums at p2p.wrox.com

We provide **programmer to programmer™ support** on mailing lists, forums, and newsgroups, all in addition to our one-to-one e-mail system, which we'll look at in a minute. You can be confident that your query is not just being examined by a support professional, but by the many Wrox authors and other industry experts present on our mailing lists.

How to Enroll for Support

Just follow this four-step system:

1. Go to p2p.wrox.com in your favorite browser:

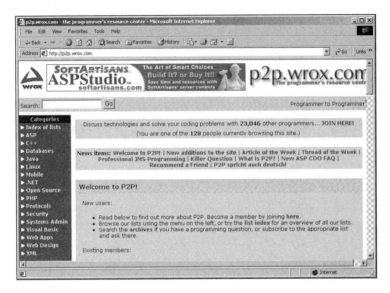

2. Click on the .NET entry in the left-hand column. You'll be presented with the lists that are currently available:

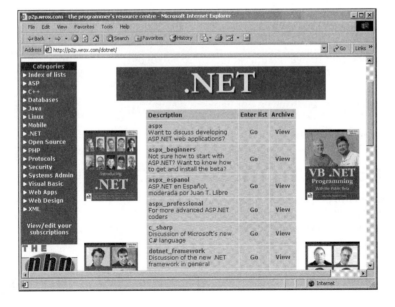

3. Choose to access the list you're interested in by clicking on its entry in the Description column.

4. If you are not a member of the list, you can choose to either view the list without joining it, or create an account in the list, by hitting the respective buttons.

5. If you choose to join, you'll be presented with a form in which you'll need to fill in your e-mail address, name, and a password (of at least 4 digits). Choose how you would like to receive the messages from the list and then hit Subscribe.

6. Congratulations. You're now a member of the mailing list.

Why This System Offers the Best Support

You can choose to join the mailing lists, or you can receive them as a daily digest. If you don't have the time or facility to receive the mailing list, then you can search our online archives.

As these lists are moderated, you can be confident of finding good, accurate information quickly. Mails can be edited or moved by the moderator into the correct place, making this a most efficient resource. Junk and spam mail are deleted, and your own e-mail address is protected by the unique Lyris system from web-bots that can automatically hoover up newsgroup mailing list addresses. Any queries about joining or leaving lists, or any query about the list should be sent to listsupport@wrox.com.

Checking the Errata Online at www.wrox.com

The following section will take you step by step through the process of posting errata to our web site to get that help. The sections that follow, therefore, are:

- ❏ Finding a list of existing errata on the web site
- ❏ Adding your own errata to the existing list
- ❏ What happens to your errata once you've posted it (why doesn't it appear immediately)?

There is also a section covering how to e-mail a question for technical support. This comprises:

- ❏ What your e-mail should include
- ❏ What happens to your e-mail once we've received it

Finding an Erratum on the Web Site

Before you send in a query, you might be able to save time by finding the answer to your problem on our web site – http://www.wrox.com:

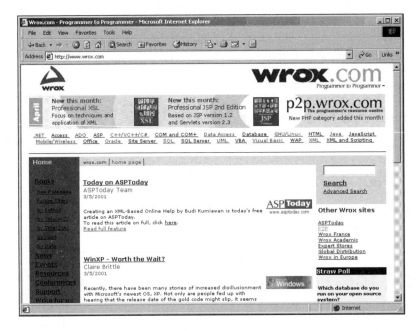

1. Each book we publish has its own page and its own errata sheet. You can get to any book's page by clicking on the subject list below the banner at the top of the page – so for this book click on .NET or ASP.

2. This will list the books available in that subject area. Click on Professional ASP.NET, and then the Book Errata link.

3. This will take you to the errata page for the book. We update these pages daily to ensure that you have the latest information on bugs and errors. You can get more details on a specific listing by clicking on the link for that error, or you can list all the errata in more detail by clicking on the view all errata link.

Add an Erratum: e-Mail Support

If the errata page doesn't solve your problem, then you should contact our customer support team. You can point out an error to put up on the web site, or directly query a problem in the book page with an expert who knows the book in detail. Either click on the submit errata link on the book support page, or send an e-mail to support@wrox.com.

A typical e-mail should include the following things:

❑ The **name**, **last four digits of the ISBN**, and **page number** of the problem in the Subject field.

❑ Your **name**, **contact info** and the **problem** in the body of the message.

We won't send you junk mail. We need the details to save your time and ours. When you send an e-mail, it will go through the following chain of support.

Customer Support

Your message is delivered to one of our customer support staff, who are the first people to read it. They have files on most frequently asked questions, and will answer anything general immediately. They answer general questions about the book and the web site.

Editorial

Deeper queries are forwarded to the technical editor responsible for that book. They have experience with the programming language or particular product, and are able to answer detailed technical questions on the subject. Once an issue has been resolved, the editor can post any errata to the web site.

The Authors

Finally, in the unlikely event that the editor can't answer your problem, he or she will forward the request to the author. We try to protect the author from any distractions from writing. However, we are quite happy to forward specific requests to them. Most Wrox authors help with the support on their books. They'll mail the customer and the editor with their response, and again all readers should benefit.

What We Can't Answer

Obviously with an ever-growing range of books and an ever-changing technology base, there is an increasing volume of data requiring support. While we endeavor to answer all questions about the book, we can't answer bugs in your own programs that you've adapted from our code. But do tell us if you're especially pleased with the routine you developed with our help.

How to Tell Us Exactly What You Think

We understand that errors can destroy the enjoyment of a book and can cause many wasted and frustrated hours, so we seek to minimize the distress that they can cause.

You might just wish to tell us how much you liked or loathed the book in question. Or you might have ideas about how this whole process could be improved. In that case you should e-mail feedback@wrox.com. You'll always find a sympathetic ear, no matter what the problem is. Above all you should remember that we do care about what you have to say and we will do our utmost to act upon it.

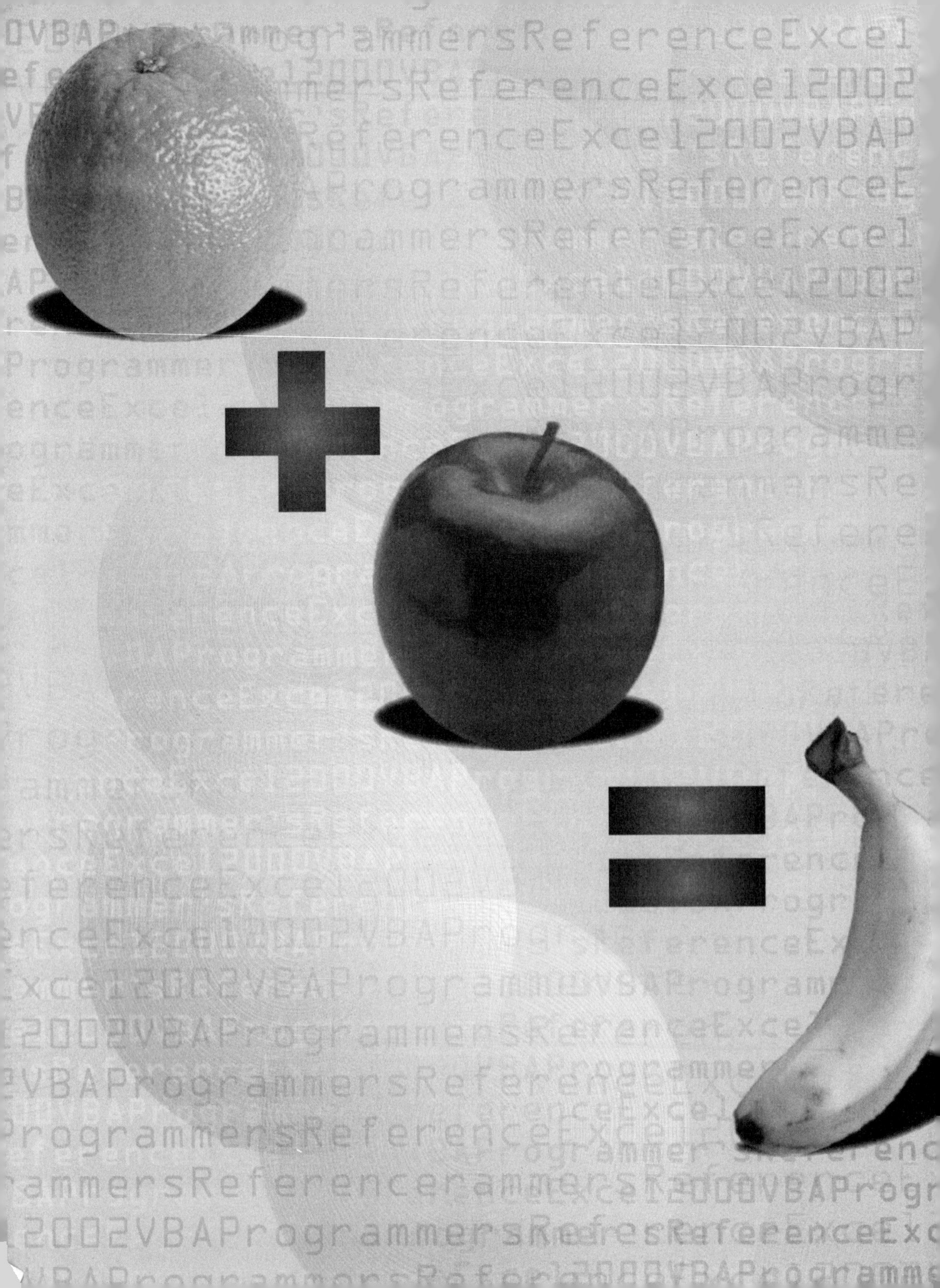

Index

A Guide to the Index

The index is arranged hierarchically, in alphabetical order, with symbols preceding the letter A. Most second-level entries and many third-level entries also occur as first-level entries. This is to ensure that users will find the information they require however they choose to search for it.

G

H

ProgrammersReferenceExcel
2002VBAProgrammersReferenceExce